THE ELGAR COMPANION TO PUBLIC CHOICE

To Willie, Frank, and their Mother – WFS
To José, Giulia, Teresa, and Isabella – LR

The Elgar Companion to Public Choice

Edited by

William F. Shughart II

Frederick A.P. Barnard Distinguished Professor of Economics, holder of the Robert M. Hearin Chair in Business Administration, University of Mississippi, USA

and

Laura Razzolini

Associate Professor of Economics, University of Mississippi, USA

Edward Elgar
Cheltenham, UK • Northampton, MA, USA

Published by
Edward Elgar Publishing Limited
Glensanda House
Montpellier Parade
Cheltenham
Glos GL50 1UA
UK

Edward Elgar Publishing, Inc.
136 West Street
Suite 202
Northampton
Massachusetts 01060
USA

A catalogue record for this book
is available from the British Library

Library of Congress Cataloguing in Publication Data

The Elgar companion to public choice / edited by William F. Shughart II, Laura
Razzolini.
    Includes bibliographical references and index.
    1. Social choice.   I. Shughart, William F. II. Razzolini, Laura. 1960–
HB846.8.E44   2001
302'.13—dc21

                                                    00–042970

ISBN 1 85278 540 3 (cased)

Typeset by Manton Typesetters, Louth, Lincolnshire, UK.
Printed and bound in Great Britain by MPG Books Ltd, Bodmin, Cornwall.

Contents

Figures

Tables

Editors

William F. Shughart II   Frederick A.P. Barnard Distinguished Professor of Economics and holder of the Robert M. Hearin Chair in Business Administration, School of Business Administration, University of Mississippi, USA.

Laura Razzolini   Associate Professor of Economics, School of Business Administration, University of Mississippi, USA.

Contributors

Gary M. Anderson Professor of Economics, California State University, Northridge, California, USA.

Lisa R. Anderson Assistant Professor of Economics, Department of Economics, College of William and Mary, Williamsburg, Virginia, USA.

Omar Azfar Research Associate, IRIS Center, Department of Economics, University of Maryland, College Park, Maryland, USA.

Bruce L. Benson DeVoe Moore Distinguished Research Professor, Department of Economics, Florida State University, Tallahassee, Florida, USA.

Geoffrey Brennan Professor of Economics in the Social and Political Theory Program, Research School of Social Sciences, Australian National University, Canberra, Australia.

Michael J.G. Cain Assistant Professor of Political Science, St Mary's College of Maryland, St Mary's City, Maryland, USA.

Kelly H. Chang Assistant Professor, Department of Political Science and Robert M. La Follette Institute of Public Affairs, University of Wisconsin, Madison, Wisconsin, USA.

Jeff R. Clark Scott L. Probasco, Jr Chair of Free Enterprise and Professor of Economics, University of Tennessee, Chattanooga, Tennessee, USA.

Roger D. Congleton Professor of Economics and General Director, Center for Study of Public Choice, George Mason University, Fairfax, Virginia, USA.

W. Mark Crain Professor of Economics and Research Associate, James M. Buchanan Center for Political Economy, George Mason University, Fairfax, Virginia, USA.

Audrey B. Davidson Associate Professor of Economics, College of Business and Public Administration, University of Louisville, Louisville, Kentucky, USA.

Louis De Alessi   Professor Emeritus of Economics, University of Miami, Coral Gables, Florida, USA.

Robert B. Ekelund, Jr   Edward L. and Catherine H. Lowder Eminent Scholar, Department of Economics, Auburn University, Auburn, Alabama, USA.

Rui J.P. de Figueiredo, Jr   Assistant Professor, Haas School of Business and Department of Political Science, University of California, Berkeley, California, USA.

Kevin B. Grier   Professor of Economics, University of Oklahoma, Norman, Oklahoma, USA.

Alan Hamlin   Professor of Economics, Department of Economics, University of Southampton, Highfield, Southampton, UK.

Randall G. Holcombe   DeVoe Moore Professor, Department of Economics, Florida State University, Tallahassee, Florida, USA.

Dwight R. Lee   Professor of Economics and holder of the Bernard B. and Eugenia A. Ramsay Chair of Private Enterprise, Department of Economics, University of Georgia, Athens, Georgia, USA.

Fred S. McChesney   Class of 1967/James B. Haddad Professor of Law, and Professor, Kellogg Graduate School of Management, Northwestern University, Evanston, Illinois, USA.

Robert E. McCormick   Professor of Economics, Clemson University, Clemson, South Carolina, USA.

William C. Mitchell   Professor Emeritus of Political Science, University of Oregon, Eugene, Oregon, USA.

Michael C. Munger   Professor of Political Science and Director, Micro-Incentives Research Center, Duke University, Durham, North Carolina, USA.

William A. Niskanen   Chairman, The Cato Institute, Washington, DC, USA.

Charles K. Rowley   Duncan Black Professor of Economics, James M. Buchanan Center for Political Economy, George Mason University, and The Locke Institute, Fairfax, Virginia, USA.

Paul H. Rubin Professor of Economics and Law, Emory University, Atlanta, Georgia, USA.

Tim R. Sass Associate Professor of Economics, Department of Economics, Florida State University, Tallahassee, Florida, USA.

Gerald W. Scully Professor of Management, University of Texas at Dallas, Richardson, Texas, USA.

Robert D. Tollison Professor of Economics and holder of the Robert M. Hearin Chair in Business Administration, School of Business Administration, University of Mississippi, USA.

Mark Toma Associate Professor of Economics, University of Kentucky, Lexington, Kentucky, USA.

Gordon Tullock Professor of Law, George Mason Law School, Arlington, Virginia, USA.

Chad S. Turner Department of Economics, Clemson University, Clemson, South Carolina, USA.

Richard E. Wagner Holbart L. Harris Professor of Economics, George Mason University, Fairfax, Virginia, USA.

Barry R. Weingast Ward C. Krebs Family Professor of Political Science, Stanford University, and Senior Fellow, Hoover Institution, Stanford, California, USA.

Bruce Yandle Alumni Distinguished Professor of Economics, Clemson University, Clemson, South Carolina, USA.

Preface

A man who writes a book, thinks himself wiser or wittier than the rest of mankind; he supposes that he can instruct or amuse them, and the publick to whom he appeals, must, after all, be the judges of his pretensions. (Samuel Johnson)

This volume, which has been more than two years in the making and represents the collaborative effort of more than thirty scholars, is intended to encapsulate the field of public choice as it stands at the close of the twentieth century. While we are certainly not the first to attempt to do so, owing to the explosive growth of the literature over the past several decades, it has become nearly impossible to survey the theory and evidence of public choice comprehensively. Multiple perspectives by multiple authorities help to fill in the unavoidable gaps and to add the nuance necessary for a deeper understanding of what has been accomplished thus far and what questions remain unanswered.

This does not mean that we have not tried to be exhaustive. Far from it. Contributions to the *Companion* were solicited with an eye toward providing its readers with a thoroughgoing rehearsal of public choice principles. Undoubtedly, however, some topics have been overlooked and some of the relevant literature left uncited. For that we apologize. But we think that those who spend time with this volume will come away with a fuller appreciation of the power of the public choice model to illuminate the behaviour of *Homo politicus*. It is our hope that students of public choice and scholars actively contributing to the field will find the *Companion* to be a valuable reference tool and will learn as much from reading as we did from writing and editing.

Many debts were accumulated in preparing this volume for publication. We are grateful to Edward Elgar for his confidence in our abilities to carry this project through to conclusion, for the free hand given to our decisions about topical coverage and authorship, and for his patient willingness to await delivery of a manuscript acceptable to us. Once that point was at last reached, his staff supervised the production process with a high level of professional competency.

While each of the contributors to the volume deserves our thanks as well – they did most of the work, after all – a number of them merit special recognition. Lisa Anderson and Randall Holcombe came to the rescue when, at nearly the last minute, prior commitments with other contributors fell through. Mark Crain and Robert Tollison not only wrote their own chapters, but provided extremely useful comments and suggestions on several others as well.

Melissa Yeoh did yeoman's work tracking down obscure bibliographic details and corroborating classical allusions; we here thank her for her able research assistance. If not for Michael Reksulak's proofreading skills, there would have been many more errors in the final product. A timely and much appreciated summer grant from the Robert M. Hearin Support Foundation afforded the senior editor the opportunity to devote his full attention to finishing the project. While we are both grateful for all the help we received along the way, the two of us accept full responsibility for any remaining defects. We lay down our red pens, turn off our computers, and submit to the judgment of the market.

William F. Shughart II
Laura Razzolini

Introduction: Public choice at the millennium

*William F. Shughart II and Laura Razzolini**

Thirty-five years ago, Dennis Mueller was able to survey the field of public choice within the space of an article-length contribution to the *Journal of Economic Literature*. Fifteen years later, *Public Choice II*, the second edition of the book expanding on that initial literature review, ran to nearly 500 pages of densely packed text and cited approximately 900 scholarly works. At the dawn of the twenty-first century, attempting to do the field justice within the covers of a single volume has become a daunting challenge.[1]

That is because the ideas and methods elaborated by Duncan Black, Anthony Downs, Kenneth Arrow, James Buchanan, Gordon Tullock, William Riker and Mancur Olson have permeated virtually every recognized area of specialization within the disciplines of economics, political science and, to a lesser extent, sociology. Not unlike the successful inroads made by neoclassical economics itself into research on the family, crime and punishment, and the law, public choice has transformed the study of *Homo politicus*. If the theories of social science are to be judged by their applications, by their ability to help explain observed human behavior within a particular set of institutional constraints (and even to help illuminate the design of the institutions that impose those constraints), then public choice has perhaps been the most successful theoretical innovation to have appeared in the past half-century or so. By Kuhnian (Kuhn 1970) standards, public choice truly has been revolutionary.

The established paradigm challenged by public choice is customarily referred to as the public-interest theory of democratic government. That theory presumes unselfish benevolence on the part of the government actors to whom ordinary citizens delegate decision-making authority. Be they elected representatives or full-time government employees, these actors are portrayed in the older way of thinking as public 'servants' motivated only by a desire to maximize society's welfare. Moreover, the public-interest model presumes that the social preferences to which government actors faithfully respond can be ascertained readily through the workings of the democratic process. Once the 'will of the people' is thus determined, the public sector's decision makers can move quickly to supply public goods in desired quantities, to intervene remedially in the economy when markets fail to produce Pareto-efficient allocations of goods or of productive resources, and to redistribute incomes more fairly.

Public choice is frequently defined as the application of economics to the study of politics. That definition highlights the subject's interdisciplinary character, places it squarely within the positive tradition of economic science that demands models, refutable predictions, and empirical tests, but, what is more important, it emphasizes the methodological individualism of economic analysis that public choice brings to the study of problems formerly the exclusive province of political scientists and sociologists.

Economics treats the individual actor as the fundamental unit of analysis. In ordinary markets, that individual actor is a person who, as a consumer, strives to maximize his own sense of wellbeing, given the constraints imposed by a limited budget and the prices of available goods, who, as a worker, strives to maximize his income, given his native talents, the skills he has acquired, and his tastes for work and leisure, and who, as a business owner, strives to maximize his profits, given the constraints imposed by technology, by the costs of inputs and the tastes and preferences of buyers. No matter what role he plays, however, the individual actor is assumed to be guided largely by self-interest.

While for model-building purposes 'self-interest' is frequently construed narrowly to mean wealth maximization, the rational actor model is in fact much more general. Economists assume that individuals pursue the maximization of utility, of which money wealth is only one component, thereby allowing for the fact that human action is guided by a variety of goals and objectives, including solicitude for the welfare of others. Choices are made by rational economic actors with reference to judgments about which of the available alternatives provides the greatest sense of personal satisfaction, and satisfaction can be derived not only from actions that increase the decision maker's own happiness, but from those that enhance the wellbeing of family, friends, neighbors, and society at large.

Two implications follow immediately from transferring this rational actor model of economic theory from the realm of ordinary markets to the realm of politics. First, actors in the public sector can be portrayed as having motivations similar to those attributed to actors in the private sector. Self-interest and not the public interest becomes the most important behavioral stimulus. Elected officials strive for re-election. Appointed officials strive to secure larger agency budgets and to advance their careers. Voters strive to make themselves personally better off. Realism displaces wishful thinking; human behavior is seen as consistent, the behavioral system is closed (Buchanan 1972). Public choice does not deny the possibility of public-interest motivations, but it insists that that model be stated in testable form.

Second, by adopting the methodological individualism of economic theory, public choice rejects the construction of monolithic decision-making units, such as 'society', the 'people', or the 'community'. Only individuals make choices. The problem then becomes how to model the process by which the various preferences of rationally self-interested individual actors get aggregated when decisions must be made collectively.

One of public choice's key insights is that political outcomes differ from market outcomes, not because the behavioral motivations of individuals are different in the two settings, but because the institutional frameworks within which rational actors pursue their self-interests differ. Private choices take place within the context of a system of well-defined and -enforced property rights that generate price and profit signals to which individuals have powerful incentives to respond; public choices take place within the context of ill-defined property rights that force decisions to be made without the benefit of explicit price and profit signals. Private choices are unilateral; public choices are multilateral. Private choices entail consequences that are in large measure borne by the decision maker himself; the benefits and costs of public choices must be shared with others. Individuals participate in private transactions voluntarily; if they find themselves in the minority, their participation in public transactions may be coerced. Private exchanges are positive sum; exchanges mediated by the public sector may be zero sum or negative sum. Competitive market conditions provide buyers and sellers with alternatives to which they readily can turn; monopoly in the public sector provides limited options among which the costs of switching tend to be high.

Within the institutional framework of markets, profit-seeking firms have strong incentives to use productive resources efficiently and to serve their customers well. Prices are kept in line with costs, factor payments reflect marginal productivities (the distribution of income mirrors contributions to value), and the sum of consumer and producer surplus is made as large as possible. To be sure, market institutions may sometimes fail to achieve Pareto efficiency. When property rights are not well defined, there may be social benefits or costs associated with private market activities which individual decision makers do not take into account but which affect third parties positively or negatively. In the presence of transaction costs that prevent bargaining to internalize such externalities (Coase 1960), some goods (education, for example) may be undersupplied by private markets and some 'bads' (pollution) may be oversupplied. Common pool resources will tend to be overutilized and some public goods may not be supplied at all if left to the private sector. Private sellers may have informational advantages over buyers or possess market power that allows them to elevate their prices and profits at consumers' expense.

While such potential market failures provide scope for remedial government intervention, the application of public choice principles to the policy responses prescribed by orthodox social welfare theory (Pigou 1920; Samuelson 1954) warns that the public sector itself may likewise fail to achieve Pareto-efficient results. The information available to government decision makers about the costs and benefits of corrective action is necessarily incomplete and biased toward the alternatives preferred by those individuals and groups having the greatest stakes in the policy options and the most means to reward or punish policy choices. Coupled with rational ignorance on the part of the mass of voter-taxpayers, the rationally self-interested behavior ascribed to policy makers by the public choice model provides no assurance that public goods will be supplied in ideal quantities or that other perceived sources of market failure will be rectified cost-effectively. The imbalance between the social costs and benefits of intervention and the personal costs and benefits confronting those having the authority to intervene may well lead to the adoption of policies that, while privately beneficial to the policy makers themselves and to the special interests on which they rely for political support, reduce society's welfare overall. Pork barrel, a public sector that expands continuously in size and scope, and a mix of policy interventions that interferes with rather than enhances the workings of private markets are the predictable outcomes of political processes analysed from a public choice perspective.

If public choice processes cannot be relied upon always to produce Pareto-efficient results, then decisions about the constraints imposed on those processes become of first-order importance. The second key insight of the public choice model is that political institutions matter. Institutions determine which activities will be undertaken by the public sector and which will be undertaken by the private sector. Moreover, for those activities that are shifted to the public sector, institutions establish the decision rules that will determine outcomes. Can action be taken by a plurality, a simple majority, or will the agreement of a more inclusive set of voters be required? In short, if actors in the public sector have the same behavioral motives as actors in the private sector, what 'rules of the game' will be chosen to govern the political process, that is, to help align private interests with the public interest?

These themes are elaborated in a variety of contexts by the contributors to this volume, and we shall summarize many of the insights offered by the public choice model in our précis below. Before doing so, however, it is useful to address some broader questions. We begin by considering three concerns broached by the critics of public choice. The next section explores the morality of public choice. Subsequent sections deal with ongoing debates about the efficiency of political markets and the value of public choice prescriptions for institutional reform. Finally, we delve into the timing of the public choice revolution: why did public choice emerge in the 1950s and 1960s rather than earlier or later?

Is public choice immoral?

To paraphrase William Mitchell's apt analogy (see Chapter 1 of this volume), if orthodox welfare economics can be thought of as a pathology of markets, public choice is a pathology of politics. Scholars working in the tradition of Pigou seem to find market failures demanding remedial action on every street corner; scholars working in the public choice tradition seem to find the seeds of government failure in every public program and policy. Indeed, 'one of the most important contributions public choice has made to our understanding of how political systems work has been to demonstrate the serious shortcomings of the simple majority rule' (Mueller 1997, p. 137).

One need look no further than the work of two of the founders of modern public choice, Duncan Black and Anthony Downs, to see the source of the uneasiness created in some minds when forced to confront what in James Buchanan's (1979) artful phrase is 'politics without romance'. Studying collective decision making by committees, Black (1948a, b) deduced what has since been known as the median voter theorem.[2] If voters' preferred outcomes can be arrayed along a single dimension (for example, left–right), preferences are 'single-peaked' (have unique maxima), and decisions are made by simple majority rule, then the preferences of the voter at the median of the preference array will be decisive. Any proposal to the left or the right of the median will be defeated in a majority-rule election by one which is closer to the median voter's preferred outcome. Because extreme proposals lose to centrist proposals under the assumptions of the median-voter theorem, candidates and political parties will move toward the center and, as a result, their platforms and campaign promises will tend to differ only slightly. Reversing 1964 presidential hopeful Barry Goldwater's catchphrase, majority-rule elections will present voters with an echo, not a choice.

Anthony Downs (1957) added a second reason why voters might find participatory democracy to be instrumentally unrewarding under simple majority rule. Modeling the decision to vote in a rational choice context, Downs concluded that the costs of voting (registering, going to the polls, marking ballots) will almost always exceed the associated benefits. That is because the probability of an individual's vote being decisive (determining an election's outcome) is vanishingly small. If there are N voters and two choices (candidates) on the ballot, one person's vote will be decisive only if the votes of the other $N - 1$ voters are evenly split. And as N becomes large, that probability quickly approaches zero. Hence, if voters are narrowly rational, evaluating the act of voting purely in benefit–cost terms, they will not vote. The 'paradox of voting' to which Downs's analysis gave rise asks not why voter turnout rates are so low in democratic elections, at least in the recent American experience, but rather why millions of voters participate in an activity that fails a benefit–cost test.

The two implications produced by the work of Black and Downs, namely that the options presented to voters will not be very sharp and that the act of voting is narrowly irrational, lie at the heart of concerns that public choice endangers the democratic process by subverting the values on which its operation depends. If popular support declines, the public sector's ability to act for the public good will be compromised. Government will lose its legitimacy. These concerns are reinforced by subsequent theoretical contributions that demonstrate the impossibility of a social choice mechanism having desirable democratic properties (Arrow [1951] 1963), attribute parochial motives to government bureaucracies (Niskanen 1971), see regulatory agencies as being vulnerable to 'capture' by the firms they are responsible for regulating (Stigler 1971; Peltzman 1976), and portray politicians not just as beholden to special interests, but as active brokers of wealth transfers among them (McCormick and Tollison 1981).

As one critic puts it, the 'tragedy of public choice' is that

> cynical descriptive conclusions about behavior in government threaten to under-
> mine the norm prescribing public spirit. The cynicism of journalists – and even
> the writings of professors – can decrease public spirit simply by describing what
> they claim to be its absence. Cynics are therefore in the business of making
> prophecies that threaten to become self-fulfilling. If the norm of public spirit dies,
> our society would look bleaker and our lives as individuals would be more impov-
> erished. (Kelman 1987, pp. 93–4)

But public choice no more denies the existence of 'public spirit' than economics denies the existence of altruism. Specialists in neither field have ever argued that self-interest is the *only* motivator of human action. Rather, the shared assumption of economics and public choice is that self-interest is the *most important* of the many and varied forces that animate the behavior of complex individuals. The basis of this assumption is not unrelieved cynicism about the human condition, but rather confidence in the results of repeated empirical testing showing that models based on self-interest do a better job of explaining observed behavior than models based on alternative behavioral assumptions. And, to reiterate, self-interest is a broad concept.

Although public choice, like economics, has significant normative content, the value of the assumption of self-interest lies not in its realism, which can be debated endlessly, but in its contribution to the explanatory powers of the positive theories grounded in it. To be sure, there might be something called 'public spirit' that motivates individuals in the realm of civic life, but how can it be measured and what are its testable implications? An even more important question is, can those implications be refuted? Variations in voter turnout rates over time might depend on the ebb and flow of public spirit. The same data might also be explained by changes in the underlying benefits and costs of voting facing a rationally self-interested citizenry. While the latter hypothesis can be (and has been) tested by public choice scholars, admittedly with only mixed success, the former is essentially little more than an *ex post* rationalization with no predictive power. We might attribute increases in voter turnout to a rise in public spirit, but it is not clear that we have done anything more than state a tautology. Resort to 'public spirit' is the same as attributing bull markets to Keynesian 'animal spirits' or Greenspanian 'irrational exuberance'. Still, people *do* vote. A sharper distinction between voting as an investment in electoral outcomes and voting as a consumption activity might help resolve the paradox.

An increase in the supply of volunteers willing to fight a 'popular' war might likewise be evidence of public spirit. Enlistment might also be a calculated decision based on the expectation that volunteers get better military assignments than draftees or that failure to participate invites social stigmatization that will adversely affect the slacker's post-war income-earning abilities. In times of crisis or national emergency, selfish and selfless motives doubtless influence every person's decision-making calculus to varying degrees.[3]

The public choice model does not rule out the possibility of public spirit, because it cannot be ruled out. The methodology of public choice places self-interest at center stage, at the same time recognizing that the motivations of human beings are much richer than can be accommodated by the simplified rational actor model. Individuals do make donations to charitable causes, but only a model built on self-interest can explain why charitable giving tends to be higher the more favorable is its tax treatment (Clotfelter 1980). Individuals do register to vote and go to the polls, but only a model built on self-interest can explain why voter registration rates tend to be lower the greater is the registered voter's vulnerability to being called for jury duty (Knack 1993).[4]

The positive insights into political processes contributed by public choice scholars are neither moral nor immoral; they simply describe how those processes work. Knowing the outcomes produced by particular political institutions is especially valuable when the perspective shifts 'away from the analysis of policy choice by existing agents within *existing* rules, and towards the examination of alternative sets of rules' (Brennan and Buchanan 1988, p. 187; emphasis in original). Because the public choice perspective sees policy outcomes as depending, not on the behavioral motivations of the policy makers themselves but on the constraints imposed on their policy choices by the institutional 'rules of the game', policy failures can be corrected only by changing the constraints. If all agents are self-interested, it will do no good to replace one set of them with another. Appeals to policy makers' senses of propriety or public spirit will fall on deaf ears. 'Better' people will not make 'better' government, and no amount of preaching can transform basic human nature into something nobler. Meaningful reform requires changing the institutional rules in ways that more closely align policy makers' self-interest with the public's interest.

Hence, the morality of public choice is found in its ability to illuminate the behavior of living, breathing political actors operating under the rules at hand and, in so doing, to suggest ways in which the rules might be changed to improve observed outcomes. Dispelling blind faith in the institutions of governance may be distressful for some, but the hardnosed analysis of political processes brought to bear by public choice offers prescriptions for improvement that cannot be deduced from any other known model. Far from undermining confidence in the workings of democratic government, by pointing the path to substantive reform, public choice can help strengthen it.

Are political markets efficient?

While acknowledging the value of the rational actor model as an engine of positive analysis, some critics of public choice have nevertheless argued that democratic political markets produce outcomes that are every bit as efficient as the outcomes produced by ordinary markets. The most eloquent of these critics, Donald Wittman (1989, 1995), contends that public choice has failed to appreciate the power of competition between interest groups and between political entrepreneurs to squeeze out inefficiencies from political exchanges and, hence, to generate a set of political institutions and a mix of public policies that ensure the realization of all potential gains from political trade. In the best Chicago-school tradition, Wittman maintains that what is, is efficient. Were it not, that is, were it possible to increase the efficiency of a particular government program or policy in the Paretian sense, thereby making at least one person better off without making anyone else worse off, the welfare- (wealth-) enhancing change would already have been implemented because it is in somebody's self-interest to have done so. Government failure is therefore only a 'myth', or at least political failures are no more severe in the public sector than market failures are in the private sector.

Wittman reaches this conclusion by distancing himself from the operating principles of public choice. In Wittman's world, voters are well informed about the impacts of government programs and policies on their personal welfare, political markets are robustly competitive, and transaction costs in these markets are not excessively high. Under such assumptions, incumbent politicians and policy makers must select efficient methods for achieving desired ends or lose their offices to rivals who will do so. This means not only that the particular policy tool chosen (taxes versus regulation, for instance) must obey Paretian principles, but that the decision to intervene in the first place must satisfy the same efficiency criteria: government will only undertake those activities in which it has a comparative advantage.[5] If political market conditions allow for intervention into private markets, however, government will intervene in the most efficient way possible.

Consider one of Wittman's many examples. Economists since the time of Pigou (1920) have extolled the efficacy of pollution taxes as ways of forcing firms to curtail their discharges of environmentally harmful toxic wastes. Yet apparently less-efficient command-and-control regulation mandating the adoption of specific pollution abatement technologies has long been the policy tool of choice for internalizing the externality. Wittman (1995, pp. 118–21) emphasizes that the relative efficiency of pollution taxes depends critically on regulators having precise and detailed information about the marginal benefits and costs of pollution abatement. If such information is available, then taxes can be set optimally and that policy tool is indeed more efficient (generates smaller deadweight costs) than regulation. But if information is imperfect (as it is likely to be), regulation is superior to taxes under certain circumstances.[6]

The controversial conclusion reached by Wittman in this situation and many others is not that tradeoffs must be made in choosing appropriate policy tools, but that democratic processes can generally be relied on to select the most efficient of the available options. Comparing command-and-control regulation with more market-friendly approaches to externality, Gary Becker (1976a, p. 247) stated the case in the strongest possible terms by suggesting 'that the traditional emphasis on the waste caused by industrial regulation be reversed: regulations that survive the keen competition for votes tend to be relatively efficient ways to redistribute resources'. Disputing the received wisdom of neoclassical economic theory that cash transfers are always preferred to in-kind transfers as ways of redistributing wealth, Becker (p. 247) writes that 'if quotas are used instead of cash, the dead weight loss from cash must *exceed* that from quotas; otherwise, the number of votes would not be maximized, and could be increased by replacing the quotas by cash' (emphasis in original). The prescriptions of theory notwithstanding, 'economists are no more able to discover better ways to redistribute than they are able to discover better ways to produce the products of business' (p. 248).

In short, a vigorously competitive political marketplace populated by vote-maximizing politicians and reasonably well-informed voters tends to minimize the excess burdens of taxes and the deadweight costs of regulations (Becker 1983, 1985). This is not to say that government waste does not occur or, in fact, that the waste is not considerable. The key implication of the preceding analysis is rather that alternative means of achieving desired policy objectives carry higher deadweight costs per dollar redistributed than do existing means.

Although pressure groups play roles in Wittman's analysis, they do so primarily as conduits of information to the politicians who make policy choices and to the voters who elect them. Majoritarian interests dominate special interests. Congress regularly rejects stringent gun-control legislation and regularly votes to increase veterans' benefits not because of intense lobbying by the National Rifle Association and the American Legion, but because those actions reflect majority opinion as evidenced by the results of voter referenda in California (Wittman 1995, pp. 83–4).

The proof of the pudding is in the tasting. While Wittman's analysis clearly would be undermined by evidence that voters are ignorant (Boudreaux 1996b; Rowley 1997) or that political markets are less than perfectly competitive because barriers to entry are high (Lott 1997), the scientific value of the efficiency postulate will ultimately depend on its empirical content. Is it superior to competing models in predicting which policy tool will be chosen in particular circumstances? Are existing policies in fact efficient? Conducting such tests will not be easy, given that one must consider the welfare costs of alternative government policies to all affected groups. A comparison of the efficiency of sugar tariffs relative to the payment of cash subsidies to sugar growers, for example, requires evaluating not only the deadweight costs of the two policies in the market for cane sugar but the impact of trade protection versus subvention on input markets as well as on the markets for substitute sweeteners (for example, beet sugar and high fructose corn syrup).

One important limitation of the efficiency postulate is its failure to incorporate the costs of rent seeking into the welfare analytics of political-market outcomes. Only the deadweight costs of alternative policies enter into the determination of efficiency. If, on the other hand, some or all of the value of the wealth transfers brokered by government is converted into social costs (Tullock 1967b), then existing institutions and policies may no longer be superior to the available alternatives. This criticism is especially telling in light of the incentives of the current beneficiaries of wealth transfers to defend their rents against attempts to expropriate them. Rent defending may produce a bias in favor of the status quo, even when the status quo is inefficient.[7]

The efficiency postulate advanced by Becker and Wittman raises a challenge to the public choice perspective that has not yet been resolved – and is not likely to be without considerable additional work. But as a positive proposition, it deserves its day in court.

Is constitutional political economy valuable?

One of the path-breaking contributions of *The Calculus of Consent* (Buchanan and Tullock 1962) was to focus attention on the document – the constitution – that creates the institutions and establishes the rules under which the political process subsequently plays out. If voters are not well informed, if incumbency confers substantial benefits on the politicians currently in office, and if special interests dominate political processes at the expense of majoritarian interests, then the constitution imposes the only operative check on 'in-period' politics.

The importance of constitutional constraints was recognized by James Madison in *The Federalist* No. 51, where he staunchly defended the federal principle as the most effective guardian of minority interests and the chief counterweight to potential government abuse:

> But what is government itself, but the greatest of all reflections of human nature? If men were angels, no government would be necessary. If angels were to govern men, neither external nor internal controls on government would be necessary. In framing a government which is to be administered by men over men, the great difficulty lies in this: you must first enable the government to control the governed; and in the next place oblige it to control itself. A dependence on the people is, no doubt, the primary control on the government; but experience has taught mankind the necessity of auxiliary precautions. (p. 356)

The general question raised by the constitutional perspective is, what set of rules would rational individuals collectively agree to in order to ensure that they will all be better off after the government is formed than they are in some pre-constitutional 'state of nature'? To motivate their analysis, Buchanan and Tullock (1962, pp. 63–91) assumed that individuals were uncertain about whether they would be in the majority or the minority in any future (post-constitutional) collective decision. Constitutional design, in other words, takes place behind what John Rawls (1971) later called a 'veil of ignorance'. Moreover, to ensure that everyone would in fact be made better off, Buchanan and Tullock assumed further that acceptance of the constitution requires unanimous consent so that any one person may veto a provision that threatens to lower his own welfare (Wicksell [1896] 1967).

Constitutional choice in this model requires an analysis of two types of costs involved in making any collective decision. The first of these are *decision-making costs*, the direct and indirect (opportunity) costs of gathering information, negotiating, and reaching agreement on a common course of action. The magnitude of these costs depends on the fraction of the voting population whose consent is required for a particular option to be selected. If one may choose for all (dictatorship), these costs will be zero. Decision-making costs rise as the required majority rises and they reach a maximum with a rule of unanimity that allows one to block action agreed to by all but one.

The second category of costs is *external costs*, which measure the reduction in wealth or welfare that members of the minority can expect to endure as a result of actions taken by the majority. These costs will be at a maximum with dictatorship, since a dictator is likely to place little weight on the costs his decisions impose on others. External costs then fall as the required majority rises, reaching zero with a rule of unanimity under which decisions are blocked unless everyone is made better off either in fact or through the payment of the compensation necessary to secure consensus. Only Pareto-superior proposals pass.

The optimal majority minimizes the sum of decision-making costs and external costs. At this optimum, the expected marginal gain from reducing the external costs of collective action just balances the expected marginal decision-making cost of increasing the required majority. Several important implications follow immediately from this analysis. First, there is no particular reason why the cost minimum should occur just to the right of 50 per cent (simple majority rule): 'at best, majority rule should be viewed as one among many practical expedients made necessary by the costs of securing wide-spread agreement on political issues when individual and group interests diverge' (Buchanan and Tullock 1962, p. 96). Second, nothing in the theory requires that the same voting rule be used for all collective decisions. Other things being equal, more inclusive voting rules are optimal when external costs are high relative to decision-making costs and less-inclusive rules are optimal when the configuration of costs runs in the opposite direction. Third, 'it is rational to *have a constitution*' (p. 81; emphasis in original). That document's purpose is to define the range of decisions that will be governed by collective choice processes and to specify the particular decision-making rule to be used in each case. Generally speaking, while the 'analysis suggests that the individual will choose to shift *more* activities to the public sector the more inclusive is the decision-making rule' that will govern those activities (pp. 82–3; emphasis in original), the key point is that these decisions are interdependent.

This last implication is crucial if a constitution is to have substantive effect: 'if a single rule is to be chosen for all collective decisions, no constitution in the normal sense will exist' (p. 81). The external costs of some decisions are so great that they should not be made without the agreement of a qualified majority approaching unanimity. A constitutional proscription is equivalent to imposing such a collective decision-making rule. For example, the introductory phrase of the First Amendment to the US Constitution, 'Congress shall make no law', recognizes that the freedoms of religion, speech, press, and peaceable assembly are so essential to individual liberty that it would be foolhardy to allow proposals to abridge them to be subject to ordinary democratic processes. *Any* collective action is ruled out unless it first secures the broad consensus necessary to amend the Constitution's language.

A constitution, in other words, imposes constraints, thereby setting the 'rules of the game'. It specifies the powers delegated to government (that is, those activities to be governed by ordinary democratic processes). It may go further to enumerate activities subject to more inclusive voting rules, including procedures for amending the constitution, or to prohibit certain actions altogether.[8] But in any case, the constitution must bind. If anything and everything is subject to the whims of the majority, there is no constitution in any meaningful sense.

The erosion of constitutional protections and the consequent expansion in the size and scope of the federal government that began during the American Civil War and was accelerated by the Great Depression (Higgs 1987; Couch and Shughart 1998) is testimony to the importance of binding constraints and of the dangers of failing to respect them. Even the most ardent of the federalist supporters of a strong central government, Alexander Hamilton, would be stunned by the extent to which national authority intrudes at the end of the twentieth century:

> Allowing the utmost latitude to the love of power which any reasonable man can acquire, I confess I am at a loss to discover what temptation the persons entrusted with the administration of the general government could ever feel to divest the States of the authorities of that description. The regulation of the mere domestic police of a State appears to me to hold out slender allurements to ambition. Commerce, finance, negotiation, and war seem to comprehend all the objects which have charms for that passion; and all the powers necessary to those objects ought, in the first instance, to be lodged in the national repository. The administration of private justice between the citizens of the same State, the supervision of agriculture and of other concerns of similar nature, all those things, in short, which are proper to be provided for by local legislation, can never be desirable cares of a general jurisdiction. (*The Federalist* No. 17, pp. 167–8)

Federal legislation funding 100 000 police or subsidizing the price of milk may have been inconceivable to the Founding Fathers, but represents business as usual for today's members of Congress.

Constitutional public choice supplies a way of thinking about rule design and emphasizes the importance of the role institutional rules play in determining the outcomes produced by political markets. As such, it has a strong normative flavor. How, in other words, *should* political institutions be designed? The constitutional perspective does have positive implications as well, though. Developers write 'constitutions' for condominiums and other collective homeownership arrangements, presumably with an eye toward maximizing the return on their investments (the aggregate value of the development's housing units). Among other things, these constitutions contain provisions allocating voting rights to homeowners with respect to decisions setting the monthly fees charged for maintaining the development's grounds, building exteriors and other 'public goods', such as swimming pools and tennis courts. These voting rights become operative after a pre-specified number of housing units have been sold and governance authority is transferred from the developer to the homeowners' association. Studies by Barzel and Sass (1990) and Sass (1992) suggest that developers are inclined to write constitutions incorporating modes of representation and voting rules that balance the decision-making costs and external costs of collective action. For instance, the more heterogeneous is the association's membership (the greater the variance of housing unit values), the more inclusive the voting rule tends to be.

Hence, the Buchanan–Tullock model seems to be broadly consistent with the provisions of extant constitutions. Such empirical findings have obvious practical implications for the constitutional transitions under way in many corners of the globe.

In that vein, it is important to think about how constitution makers might be expected actually to behave. Will new constitutions be written and existing constitutions amended behind a veil of ignorance where self-interest is muted, or will constitutional change be influenced by the same forces that tend to dominate ordinary political processes? Much of the available evidence seems to support the latter conclusion. In his pioneering analysis of the US Constitution, Charles Beard ([1913] 1986) argued that the Founding Fathers, whose own personal wealth was based largely on land and slaves, wrote a document designed to protect the interests of their fellow aristocrats at the expense of the propertyless masses. More recently, Anderson et al. (1988a) suggest that the constitutional provision banning the importation of slaves after 1808 and imposing an import duty not to exceed $10 per head until then (Article I, section 9) fostered an internal market in slaves that benefited the slave owners in the upper South who dominated the Constitutional Convention. Systematic analyses of votes taken during the 1787 'constitutional moment' in Philadelphia point to self-interest as a driving force in the writing of the US Constitution (McGuire 1988; McGuire and Ohsfeldt 1986).

On the other hand, David Friedman contends (not to our knowledge published) that, because everyone would realize that the aggregate welfare cost of enshrining personal advantages in the constitution would exceed the value of the benefits thereby gained, the delegates to a constitutional convention would have incentives to overcome the temptations of self-interest. Similarly, Holcombe (1992) concludes that when the writers of the constitution of the Confederate States of America had the opportunity to revisit the US Constitution after about 70 years of experience with it, almost all of the changes made were designed to limit the ability of the central government to undertake policies to benefit special interests. The analyses of both Friedman and Holcombe suggest that a general constitutional convention in which the entire document is subject to revision would be less likely to be subverted by special interests than piecemeal reform. In the end, the value of constitutional political economy as a positive theory depends on which of the two foregoing hypotheses is closer to the truth, that is, whether self-interest or public interest will rule constitution writing in practice.

Why did the public choice revolution begin when it did?

Although the intellectual roots of public choice can be traced back to the mathematical analyses of alternative voting rules by Jean-Charles de Borda (1781) and the Marquis de Condorcet (1785), the latter of whom ultimately paid the heavy price demanded by Dr Guillotine's sublime invention, leaving aside the related work of a century later by Charles Dodgson ('Lewis Carroll'), modern public choice began in the 1940s with Duncan Black, continued into the 1950s with important contributions by Anthony Downs, and finally took off in the mid-1960s with the publication of *The Calculus of Consent* (Buchanan and Tullock 1962), *The Theory of Political Coalitions* (Riker 1962), and *The Logic of Collective Action* (Olson 1965). Why then? Why not earlier or later?

Scholars are not immune to the influence of events occurring around them (Stigler 1960), and so it is no mystery why, for example, John Maynard Keynes wrote *The General Theory of Employment, Interest and Money* when he did (1936). Confusing effect with cause, tight money, high tariffs and futile attempts to prop up prices and wages had precipitated global economic free-fall. Production collapsed, unemployment reached historically high levels, and desperate millions turned to government for succor. A theory suggesting that the public sector could prime the economic pump by using fiscal policy tools to stimulate aggregate demand seemed to be just what the doctor ordered.

When we ask why public choice arrived on the scene when it did, the answer is less apparent. We know from James Buchanan's (1992, pp. 5–6) own account the profound influence a chance encounter in the stacks of the University of Chicago's Harper Library with Knut Wicksell's 1896 dissertation, *Finanztheoretische Untersuchungen*,[9] had on the formative thinking of one of the field's founding fathers. Marginal personal income tax rates were certainly at prohibitive levels on the eve of the dramatic cuts announced by President Kennedy nearly contemporaneously with the appearance of *The Calculus*, and perhaps a heavy tax burden spurred interest in theories of Leviathan. But the publication of that path-breaking book antedated the massive expansion of the welfare state fulfilling Lyndon Johnson's vision of the 'Great Society' and bringing Keynesian prescriptions to full flower.

The 1960s were not a propitious time for serious scholarship of any kind, let alone a research program launched in a small Virginia town that gave the impression of being 'conservative'. But positive science will out. Within a quarter-century or so, public choice had colonized most of its sister disciplines and changed the terms of the policy debate. While we may not be able to explain why the public choice revolution began when it did, its ultimate impact is undeniable.

The Companion's anatomy

The contributions to the volume are organized under five main headings. William Mitchell opens Part I with a wide-ranging essay that compares and contrasts the operating assumptions and methods of analysis that distinguish the 'Chicago-school' approach to political economy from the public choice logic of the 'Virginia school'. Mitchell places these two schools of thought in historical context and then carefully teases out the points of agreement and disagreement between them, delving into monetarism and rational expectationism along the way. Sharing as they do the assumption that all actors are rational, the differences between Chicagoans and Virginians are not always sharp – indeed, as Mitchell observes, some scholars have their feet in both camps – but fundamentally contradictory conclusions about the efficiency properties of political markets ultimately divide the two groups.

Chapter 2, by Louis De Alessi, brings the modern theory of property rights to bear in discussing the relative strengths and weaknesses of market solutions and government solutions to problems of public goods, externalities, and common pool resources. Ill-defined property rights are in fact the underlying basis of all such market 'failures'. The relevant question then becomes, can government agents allocate resources more efficiently than private agents? Answers to that question turn not on a comparison of imperfect markets with some unattainable ideal (the 'nirvana fallacy'), but on a hardnosed evaluation of the incentives of the relevant actors to recognize potential gains from trade and on the magnitude of the costs of transacting that may impede efforts to take advantage of them. The comparative weakness of property rights in the public sector – the inability of individual agents to personally appropriate gains – suggests that government intervention will rarely improve matters and that, while competition in political markets is better than no competition, these markets will frequently fail to produce efficient results. Markets may not always be perfect, but nor is government. De Alessi's comparative analysis of the imperfect alternatives leads to the conclusion, however, that the public sector's role should be a limited one.

In Chapter 3, Omar Azfar summarizes the seminal contributions of the late Mancur Olson. In *The Logic of Collective Action*, Olson (1965) questioned the then-common characterization of interest groups as monolithic actors and advanced a theory (sometimes called the 'law of the few') suggesting that group size and cohesiveness are the underpinnings of effective political lobbying. Coupled with a byproduct theory that stressed the value of selective incentives in overcoming rational actors' propensities to free ride, Olson did much to advance our understanding of interest-group dynamics. Dissenting from an overly narrow view of rationality, Azfar recapitulates the rich theory of *The Logic* and explores some of its many applications, including labor unions, global environmental treaties, international alliances, and the impact of interest groups on economic growth.

Part I closes with an essay by Michael Cain on the contributions of Kenneth Arrow, Amartya Sen and other modern social choice theorists (Chapter 4). Taking a methodological approach decidedly distinct from Virginia-school public choice, which begins and ends with the individual as the unit of analysis, these theorists ask whether it is possible to construct a measure of the aggregate welfare of a group of individuals that both respects the values and preferences of the individuals who comprise the group and satisfies a minimal set of desirable normative criteria, such as non-dictatorship. While the short answer at this point seems to be no, in addition to fundamental contributions to theories of voting and institutional design, social choice theory has yielded insights having broader implications for economics, political science and philosophy.

Part II takes up the constitutional framework that imposes structure on the political process. Geoffrey Brennan and Alan Hamlin begin, in Chapter 5, by revisiting *The Calculus of Consent* (Buchanan and Tullock 1962), the work that triggered renewed interest in constitutional political economy, and then go on to provide an overview of the more recent contributions to this still relatively new area of study. In Chapter 6, Gordon Tullock contributes an essay discussing monarchies and dictatorships, focusing especially on the difficulties autocrats have in holding on to power and of transferring power to successors. Chapter 7, by Tim Sass, closes Part II with a discussion of a fundamental issue in constitutional design, namely the extent to which individuals will participate directly in political decisions. Taking *The Calculus* as a starting point, he compares the three principal variants of democratic political processes, direct democracy, parliamentary democracy and representative democracy, and summarizes the empirical evidence on the divergent outcomes produced by these alternative constitutional frameworks. Institutions indeed 'matter'.

Following an introductory essay by Mark Crain that highlights the role of institutions in imparting stability to political transactions (Chapter 8), the remaining contributors to Part III look closely at the collective choice machinery characteristic of modern representative democracies. In Chapter 9, Michael Munger surveys theories of voting, comparing the outcomes produced by simple majority rule with alternatives such as the Borda count, shows how majority rule outcomes can be manipulated by strategic voting, and discusses the advantages and disadvantages of systems of proportional representation. The diverse structures and operating rules of US state legislatures are explored by Robert McCormick and Chad Turner in Chapter 10. They then offer new empirical evidence on the determinants of legislator compensation, evidence that supports an efficiency wage theory of politics.

In particular, rates of economic growth seem to be higher in states where legislators are paid more. Chapters 11 and 12 turn our attention to bureaucracy. William Niskanen's summary of his own path-breaking contributions to the theory of government bureaus, criticisms of that theory, and evolving thinking on the matter, is followed by a wide-ranging survey of recent rational choice theories of bureaucracy, co-authored by Kelly Chang, Rui de Figueiredo, Jr and Barry Weingast, that situate these organizations in a multiple-principal, multiple-agent context. In Chapter 13, Gary Anderson next focuses on the small but growing literature that brings public choice principles to bear in explaining the behavioral motives of the 'independent' judiciary. If *all* actors are rationally self-interested, judges cannot be treated differently. Anderson summarizes the theory and evidence that lends support to a rational choice perspective on the 'third branch' of government. Political parties and campaign finance are the subject of Kevin Grier's essay in Chapter 14. Following that, Paul Rubin contributes a piece that explores the impact of political ideology on public choice processes (Chapter 15). Part III ends, in Chapter 16, with an essay by Gary Anderson, William Shughart and Robert Tollison summarizing James Buchanan's (1965a) theory of clubs and the numerous empirical implications thereof.

A variety of public choice perspectives on government and the economy is contained in Part IV. Chapter 17, by Robert Ekelund, Jr and Robert Tollison, reviews the theory and evidence of interest-group influence on democratic political processes. Politicians serve as passive brokers of interest-group demands for wealth transfers in that model, but as Fred McChesney shows in the next essay (Chapter 18), they can also actively seek rents for themselves by threatening to expropriate wealth, but forebearing from doing so, in exchange for various kinds of political support. Randall Holcombe looks at the contributions of public choice to orthodox theories of public finance in Chapter 19. In Chapter 20, Richard Wagner examines the links between politics and the macro economy (discussing the theory and evidence on the existence of a 'political business cycle'), Mark Toma places monetary policy in public choice perspective (Chapter 21), and Roger Congleton contributes new empirical evidence showing that spare public choice models do a surprisingly good job of explaining the growth of government in the post-Second World War period (Chapter 22). An essay by Dwight Lee and Jeff R. Clark (Chapter 23) closes Part IV by advancing the provocative hypothesis that there exists an optimal level of trust in government; beyond that optimum, the citizenry's faith in governmental processes is subject to exploitation by those having selfish interests in a larger public sector.

The public choice revolution is documented under the volume's final main heading. Lisa Anderson describes in Chapter 24 how public choice theories, especially those related to the problem of eliciting truthful revelation of preferences for public goods, have provided fertile ground for the emerging discipline of experimental economics. Chapter 25, by Robert Ekelund, Jr and Audrey Davidson, puts the power of public choice reasoning to illuminate economic history to successful test. Bruce Benson next (Chapter 26) contributes a detailed survey of the insights gained through the cross-fertilization taking place between public choice and law and economics and, in Chapter 27, Bruce Yandle discusses the inroads made by public choice into the field of environmental economics. The next two chapters, by Gerald Scully (Chapter 28) and Randall Holcombe (Chapter 29), summarize the contributions of public choice to the new thinking on economic development. The emphasis placed by public choice on institutions has borne fruit in a greater appreciation for the role played by 'market-friendly' public policies in explaining why some nations are rich and others poor. The volume ends, in Chapter 30, with Charles Rowley's essay summarizing much that has gone before and placing the international economy in public choice perspective.

Unanswered questions
The foregoing overview of the main themes struck in this volume indicates, we trust, that the contributions of public choice to the literature of economics and political science have been both wide and deep. This does not mean, however, that all of the important questions raised by the scholars who have sought to apply the rational actor model to politics have been answered or, for that matter, even asked. While public choice thinking has gained wide acceptance in many areas of study (no one any longer takes seriously the idea that traditional economic regulation of price and entry is in the 'public interest', for example), it has been stubbornly resisted in others – antitrust policy being exhibit A (McChesney and Shughart 1995). There is much yet to be done.

The act of voting, that most basic institution of representative democracy, has defied explanation on narrow self-interest grounds. Some inklings of a resolution of the 'paradox' posed by Anthony Downs's (1957) analysis of the vote motive have been advanced in work showing that larger electoral majorities translate into more active lawmaking (Crain et al. 1988b)[10] and in investigations of voting as a low-cost way of expressing policy preferences (Brennan and Lomasky 1993), but a fully satisfying rational choice model of an essentially irrational activity has thus far remained elusive. Nor have public choice scholars provided an answer to the related question of why much of the wealth redistributed by government flows to groups that tend not to vote at all.

By identifying who wins and who loses when government intervenes to regulate prices and conditions of entry into an industry, public choice (interest-group) models have shed considerable light on the origins of regulation.

But as the twentieth century comes to a close, the regulatory state is in broad retreat. The commercial airline, motor carrier, banking, and telecommunications industries, among others, have been deregulated, state-owned enterprises have been privatized and, most noteworthy of all, the centrally planned economies of Eastern Europe have collapsed. Not only were these events wholly unanticipated, existing models are of little help in understanding how entrenched interests came to be displaced. More generally, the supply of political entrepreneurship necessary to effect changes in the status quo is still an unopened 'black box'.

A menu of some of the ongoing research questions still facing public choice scholars might take the following form:

- Is voting expressive or instrumental?
- How do interest groups form?
- How efficient is democracy?
- Are the benefits of voting rules more inclusive than simple majority greater than their costs?
- Is constitutional choice different from ordinary choice?
- Why not cash transfers?
- Why are so many government benefits channeled to non-voters?
- Are direct democracies (for example, Switzerland) less protectionist than representative democracies?
- How do the outcomes produced by proportional representation systems compare with geographically based, single-member districts?
- Why does government grow? Or decline?
- What are the effects of fiscal and monetary rules, such as balanced budget requirements or limits on the rate of money growth? Are such rules time-consistent?
- What changes in the political equilibrium trigger privatization and deregulation?
- Why is the 'third way' ('market socialism') so popular?
- Is secession a viable exit option?
- How do political institutions impact economic growth?
- Is money a means of entry into politics or a barrier to entry?
- Why did Bill Clinton 'end welfare as we know it'?
- Why did Richard Nixon go to China?
- Is democracy the 'end of history'?
- How encompassing is a dictator's interest?

Public choice is still young, and so it would be demanding too much to expect answers to every question asked of it. Readers of this volume will see, however, that the rich and varied testable (and tested) implications the public choice model has already yielded supply grounds for thinking that the un-answered questions will eventually be answered.

Notes

* We benefited from comments and suggestions by Robert Tollison and Hilary Shughart.
1. The collected works of James Buchanan alone fill a 20-volume set in the process of being published by the Liberty Fund. See Buchanan (1999).
2. Black's seminal contributions are reprinted in Black ([1958] 1987). See Chapter 9 of this volume for a formal statement of the median-voter theorem. The work of Harold Hotelling (1929) was an important precursor to Black.
3. The rise of public spirit during national crises provides unique opportunities for the public sector to expand. See Higgs (1987), who documents the growth of government during wars and depressions and suggests that it is not beneath government to manufacture crisis mentalities (for example, the 'War on Poverty') in order to take advantage of the citizenry's greater willingness to cede powers to the public sector.
4. Knack (1993) finds that aversion to jury duty depresses voter registration rates by more than seven percentage points. Based on survey data suggesting that barely half the popula-tion professes any knowledge of how juries are chosen, that just 42 percent of respondents believe that jury panels are selected from voter registration lists, and that registration rates are not disproportionately lower for self-employed individuals who face relatively high opportunity costs of jury service, Oliver and Wolfinger (1999) conclude that fear of being called to serve on juries accounts for less than a one percentage point drop in voter registration rates.
5. 'To say that democratic political markets tend toward efficiency does not imply that political markets are superior to economic markets; rather it implies that democratic governments will allocate to economic markets those tasks in which the economic market is most efficient' (Wittman 1995, p. 193).
6. The particular circumstances are that 'government has less information about the marginal benefit curve than the marginal cost curve or when the marginal benefit curve is more elastic than the marginal cost curve' (Wittman 1995, p. 120). To avoid confusion, note that Wittman defines the marginal benefits of pollution from the point of view of the polluter (denominated in profits) and marginal costs of pollution from the point of view of society.
7. Although change is clearly possible – the past several decades have witnessed a wave of deregulation and privatization in the First World and the collapse of communism in the Third – the impediments to reform are nevertheless formidable. See McChesney (1999).
8. Alexander Hamilton (*The Federalist* No. 84, p. 535) clearly foresaw the 'unintended' consequences of proposals advanced by supporters of the Bill of Rights to enumerate proscribed activities: it might supply an excuse for arguing that powers not specifically forbidden to government have in fact been granted. As he put it,

> bills of rights, in the sense and to the extent in which they are contended for, are not only unnecessary in the proposed Constitution, but would even be dangerous. They would contain various exceptions to powers not granted; and, on this very account, would afford a colorable pretext to claim more than were granted. For why declare that things shall not be done which there is no power to do? Why, for instance, should it be said that the liberty of the press shall not be restrained, when no power is given by which restrictions may be imposed? I shall not contend that such a provision would confer a regulating power; but it is evident that it would furnish, to men disposed to usurp, a plausible pretence for claiming that power. They might urge with a semblance of reason, that the Constitution ought not to be charged with the absurdity of providing against the abuse of an authority which was not given, and that the provision against restraining the liberty of the press afforded a clear implication, that a power to prescribe proper regulations concerning it was intended to be vested in the national government.

9. Translated by Buchanan under the title 'A new principle of just taxation'. Listed in the references to this volume as Wicksell ([1896] 1967).

10. A recent paper in the spirit of Crain et al. (1988b) by Shachar and Nalebuff (1999) combines notions of electoral 'closeness' with a 'follow-the-leader' model that assumes voters respond to the efforts of party leaders to 'get out the vote' when races are expected to be tight. Using state-level data, Shachar and Nalebuff report evidence suggesting that a one percent increase in the predicted closeness of presidential elections raises voter turnout rates by 0.34 percent. Hence, taking account of the incentives of political elites (leaders of political parties in Shachar and Nalebuff; leaders of interest groups in Crain et al.) to internalize the benefits and costs facing rank-and-file voters may yet help restore empirical credibility to the rational voter model.

PART I

METHODOLOGY

1 The old and new public choice: Chicago versus Virginia

William C. Mitchell

1 Introduction

In the pages that follow I attempt to sort out the distinctive contributions of two schools of thought concerning the use of economics in analysing politics: one is the now well-known Virginian version and the other, perhaps less well-known set of theories associated with the Economics Department at the University of Chicago.

Although the University of Chicago's Economics Department has been a leader with high status since the 1920s and has always had a keen interest in politics and economic policies, it never founded public choice. In fact, when certain members of the Economics Department at the University of Virginia first began formulating notions of public choice, it was regarded and sometimes known as 'Chicago East'. The connection had to do with their shared 'conservatism'.

The seeds of public choice were sown at Charlottesville but they were uprooted in a distasteful way and transplanted at Blacksburg only to be transplanted again at George Mason University in Fairfax, Virginia. During that time public choice was widely regarded as a Virginian product. Chicago's entry into the field was far more gradual and not really distinctive until the appearance in the 1980s of the landmark studies of Gary Becker (1983, 1985) on interest groups and Sam Peltzman (1980) on the growth of government. George Stigler's research into regulation came much earlier under the rubric of 'political economy', but it never really formed the basis of what we now call 'public choice' nor was it within the purview of social choice.

The Chicago contribution to the study of politics developed piecemeal but ended up with an extraordinary perspective that sets it directly at odds with that of Virginia. We now have a better view of both schools of thought because of the publication of Donald Wittman's *The Myth of Democratic Failure: Why Political Institutions are Efficient* (1995). Of course, it may be that Becker and his colleagues do not accept all of Wittman's arguments, a matter no Chicagoan has as yet addressed. Then, too, Wittman does not explicitly identify himself with Chicago; in fact, he makes startlingly few references to Chicagoans. The book is really an assault on Virginian empirical research, or lack thereof, and the logic of its arguments.

My own treatment of Chicagoan ideas is derived chiefly from the work the school's members have done rather than from Wittman's case against public choice. While Wittman attacks Virginians it must be remembered that he is also an economist and his arguments are written in the language of economics. Thus, he may be a poor ally for those political scientists who like his conclusions but do not understand his logic. He has not abandoned the axioms of economics or criticized it for being more concerned with efficiency than equity. Wittman has been important for me because he has put together a case that gets at the basics of Virginian public choice. We owe him a great debt.

A further caveat: delineating 'schools' of thought is not an easy task. Just what constitutes a school and who may or may not be its members is almost always debatable. I use the word in a casual rather than a rigorous way to signify or designate some commonly held beliefs and, to a lesser extent, values.

Not everyone who studied or was a faculty member at Chicago accepts all of the tenets or methods we loosely associate with Chicagoan ideas about reality; the same is true of Virginia. Nevertheless, most economists are prepared to accept the contention that there is something distinctive about both Virginia and Chicago as centers interested in the study of politics. Complicating matters is the fact that some students of public choice have their feet in both camps; I have in mind Robert Tollison, in particular. While he is a true-blue Virginian, in substance, he has always regarded himself as a methodological follower of Stigler. In my own case, I have for more than thirty years identified myself as a Virginian; at the same time, I also taught from the pages of Stigler, Peltzman, Becker, et al. I saw not inconsistency, only complementarity. The Chicagoans provided me with empirical data about economic policies while the Virginians offered explanations for why good politics rarely produces good policies. Now, of course, we know that all is not complementary and that the analytical fissure is deep and, perhaps, widening. Most Virginians believe that politics is rarely efficient while Chicagoans, apparently, believe that political institutions routinely achieve efficient results. The contending arguments are both powerful and subtle. We shall have to make some judgments.

2   Virginian public choice: the revolution at Charlottesville, Blacksburg, and Fairfax

That a revolutionary theory of politics should have arisen and developed in three quite small towns in Virginia must seem odd to scholars who identify serious thought with the cloistered halls of the Ivy League. But it did. Furthermore, much of the revolution took place in one of the nation's most tradition-bound universities, blossomed at a backwater, mostly technical institution and matured in the shadows of none other than the home of real politics, Washington, DC. The State of Virginia, with its glorious role in the American Revolution and the founding of a nation was also, of course, to lead in the southern effort to dissolve that Union. Less than a century later a small group of scholars at the University of Virginia were to change the face of economics and political science. I merely note these coincidences, but do not attempt to explain them.

2.1 Some basic tenets

The revolution consisted of the unrelenting application of basic economic axioms – rationality and self-interest – to the phenomenon of politics. Various economists, including Knut Wicksell, Vilfredo Pareto, Gaetano Mosca, and Joseph Schumpeter, had made casual use of these assumptions in their respective analyses but the task was never quite accomplished until Kenneth Arrow, Duncan Black, James Buchanan and some of his colleagues showed the way in more precise and useful contributions during the late 1940s and early 1950s.

The interactions that constitute politics, especially in democracies, may be termed or described as involving 'collective' as opposed to 'individual' choice, with the chief difference being the means of aggregating the choices. In ordinary markets, individuals make choices without reference to others and the results or outcomes are simply totaled up, whereas in democracies individual voters cast individual ballots (secretly) and the collective decision is made according to some rule, usually simple majority. Thus, a basic and fundamental difference is to be noted: in politics, a less than unanimous choice is imposed on the losers by the winning plurality or majority. Accordingly, a citizen may vote for something, but if she is not on the winning side will not get what she voted for, while another voter may vote against some proposal or candidate and if on the losing side gets what is not wanted. Obviously, these results are at sharp variance with market experiences and outcomes. This basic insight was to provide the foundations of modern Virginian public choice. More precisely, this insight led Virginian public choice to be viewed as a pathology of politics or democracy. No matter how scientific or objective-sounding public choice may be there is always a theme of inefficiency lurking in the background. Just as welfare economics is a pathology of markets, so public choice is its equivalent in politics.

This view is based primarily on budgetary or fiscal and monetary issues and their resolution. The principal finding has been that in politics there is no invisible hand leading to socially beneficial outcomes. The reason is quite simple: unlike markets where costs and benefits are by and large internalized by the decision maker, in politics they are separated or divorced so that the one who benefits is not the one who pays or vice versa. Thus, majorities may and do exploit minorities, and intense minorities may exploit indifferent majorities. This now commonplace view was, prior to *The Calculus of Consent* (Buchanan and Tullock 1962), an uncommon insight.

As noted above, Virginians are much concerned with the operating rules and constitutional rules that provide the normative setting for political institutions. This research agenda has waxed and waned over the decades, having begun with the publication of *The Calculus of Consent* in 1962, hastened by the launching of the academic journal *Public Choice* in 1968, and complemented by the appearance of a second journal, *Constitutional Political Economy*, in 1990. Properly designed constitutional provisions can improve the political process by providing for more frequent and substantial efficiency gains as well as more equitable outcomes. The tone and, indeed, explicit references in this regard are to *The Federalist*, whose status as political philosophy has undoubtedly been elevated by Buchanan and other Virginians.

The beginning of political wisdom is, however, not *The Federalist* but Thomas Hobbes's *Leviathan* in which the most dire of initial circumstances, namely the Hobbesian jungle, is so designed as to explain and justify the origins of the state, in this case, a dictatorial one. While Buchanan rejects Hobbes's form of the state, he accepts the Hobbesian portrayal of its origin. It would have been easier had he begun with John Locke's description but, then, Buchanan has never taken the easy route in anything.

In following the lead of Buchanan and Tullock, Virginians are neither anarchists nor defenders of Leviathan. They seek to promote exchanges – both private and public – mutually arrived at and accepted. Individual liberties and preference orderings are of primary importance in informing and powering their analytical engines. They seek not weak or impotent governments but ones having sufficient authority to carry out Adam Smith's limited governmental agenda. And, as Buchanan has often stated, he is more interested in finding acceptable political structures and processes than in pushing predetermined, specific outcomes. But, it must be said that most of our preferences among processes or institutions are based on the outcomes that are expected to follow from them. In any case, constitutions are regarded as public goods that should command widespread support. When they do not, discord and revolution become distinct possibilities.

In this analytical scheme, property rights and political liberties are fundamental elements of the constitutional order. What has happened to each during the past two centuries has been a crucial concern for Virginians, most of whom believe that they have eroded to an alarming degree. While Virginians are not in agreement about the causes, they do focus on certain events and developments, including accumulating forces favoring income redistribution, wars and other crises, interacting to produce larger budgets, inflation, and an expanded public sector that has also become more intrusive both in our private and market lives, all in the interests of producing a less uncertain economy and a more caring or nurturing Nanny State. Virginians have been particularly good at elaborating on economic changes, but have been less convincing on the so-called 'social issues'. Chicagoans have been more successful in that regard.

The outstanding exception is the now classic *Best of the New World of Economics* (McKenzie and Tullock 1989), in which all sorts of non-market behavior are explored. Another exception is the work of Tollison and Wagner on *Smoking and the State* (1988) and an edited volume by Tollison, also on smoking, *Clearing the Air* (1988). Other work with a Virginian slant includes analyses by Rasmussen and Benson (1994) on drug policy and North and Miller in their oft-reprinted *Economics of Public Issues* (1971), a volume that has added more social issues with each revision. There is a unifying theme in all these treatments and it is a libertarian one suggesting that the state or political process has not handled any of these divisive matters very well; what makes for good politics is bad economics. How the polity might be reformed so that there would be greater incentives to produce good economics is not clear. Simply abdicating political responsibility makes sense in some areas, such as marijuana, but not in many others where externalities are not only prevalent but severe and private transaction costs among individuals prohibitive.

Both economic issues and social problems enter the Virginian constitutional analysis, but the former do seem more prominent. In any event, the hope is to design constitutional provisions that will more likely convert private interests into social good. Unlike a competitive market this end is not as easily achieved or sustained. An unbounded Leviathan (monopoly) must be contained by 'parchment' and a supportive social and civic political culture. Unfortunately, Virginians have been more insightful on the former than the latter necessity.

Buchanan and Tullock (1962) as well as Hayek (1960) have argued that we need a constitution in the same way we need business contracts (that is, protections based on the assumption that the worst can occur or, in Hayek's words, so that 'bad men can do the least harm'). While Buchanan and Tullock recognize the existence of social norms and that such norms sanctified by time are among our best protections in regulating both daily life and long-run political relationships, neither has been particularly informative on these 'sociological' factors. Instead they have emphasized the importance of parchment or rationally designed rules of order (that is, devising political incentives and constraints thereon that will, in the long run, be effective and efficient). Paradoxically, we should, then, base our constitutions on a lack of trust.

Accordingly, simple majority is questioned as an effective decision-making rule in all situations. As we have learned, majority rule can generate some undesirable collective choices, especially in its encouragement of pork barrel and rent seeking by small, cohesive special-interest groups. Then, too, elected governments are the prisoners of the short term, a constraint making it more difficult to conduct efficient political market transactions. This particular point was made with considerable skill by Buchanan and Lee (1982) in their adaptation of the Laffer curve. An efficient polity is one that will make use of a variety of decision rules, ranging from the decisive choice of one individual to unanimous consent and that, indeed, is what most democracies do. When the costs of decision making are outweighed by the externalities, we adopt super-majority rules; when the reverse holds, we choose plurality.

Virginians tend to support constitutional reforms that are extensions of the reasoning underlying the US Constitution (that is, they choose to constrain government rather than to expand its powers). Thus, many support a balanced budget amendment. Many also advocate a limit to federal expenditures, taxes, or both, by relating them to changes in the national income. Some support provisions to restrict the growth in the money supply, while nearly all are agreed that various federal spending programs should be transferred to state and local governments. Some support abolishing the income tax while others prefer a flat tax and, perhaps, a few might vote for a national sales tax. For both political and economic reasons many favor term limits for members of Congress as well as for state legislators. A presidential line-item veto surely gains the support of some Virginians. Some practical success has been achieved with regard to these proposals, but perhaps the most important result has been a favorable shift in public opinion during the past 15 or so years. The Keynesian vision is no longer the dominant one in political economy or everyday politics.

2.2 Elections, voters, and inefficiency

There is nary a Virginian nor a political scientist who has not embraced the notion that voters are poorly motivated and rationally ignorant. The personal costs of gathering information and the nature of political choices are such that the expected benefit of voting is so low that citizens typically stay away from the polls – and do so in increasing numbers. This view is not condemnatory; in fact, the voter is 'celebrated' for being sensible in making her cold-blooded cost–benefit calculations as well as correctly assessing the probability of determining an electoral outcome. We might remind ourselves that one of the most popular of post-Second World War presidents, Ronald Reagan, was elected by massive electoral college majorities but won only 28 percent of the eligible voting population. And, many voters liked him personally rather more than his policies.

The basic situation of the voter has been further described and analysed by social choice theorists who concentrate on the formal rules of elections. It is safe to say that the plight of the voter has been shown to involve all sorts of 'impossibility' theorems with no stable, efficient outcome under simple majority voting being the principal one. It is not that a majority cannot be found, but that there are too many possible majorities; thus the problem of cycling. Most Virginians have not been surprised by the results of these highly mathematical investigations, arguing instead that the theories have overlooked or misunderstood important aspects of the democratic process; there are myriad institutional ways to promote stability (see, for example, Chapter 8 of this volume). Buchanan (1954) and Tullock (1967a) independently set forth such critiques long ago.

The political process is seen by Virginians as a complex web of relationships among voters, politicians, interest groups, and bureaucrats, each of whom pursues self-interest or that of some group in rationally adaptive ways. We now know a good deal about these interactions and likely outcomes under different rules or institutions. Some are more efficient or less inefficient than others. Virginians have been particularly interested in the median-voter theorem and how officials can manipulate budgetary options so as to ensure supra-large revenues (see Romer and Rosenthal 1978a, b). They have also contributed to the debate over the normative properties of majority rule by, for example, comparing the outcomes produced by the Condorcet and Borda counts. Approval voting has won some adherents among Virginians, as have point voting and voting by veto. Tideman and Tullock (1976) made a major contribution to the previously mordant analysis of the supply of public goods, namely the demand-revealing process. Perhaps a major reason for the current lack of interest in these analyses stems from the brute fact that the optimal matching of supply and demand for public goods is nearly impossible in any practical sense. All of the ingenious schemes so far developed have either some practical or theoretical difficulty owing to the intractable nature of collective choice and its accompanying free-rider problem.

2.3   Rent seeking

As an analytical problem, rent seeking has been a staple of Virginian public choice since at least 1967 when Tullock (1967b) published his famous paper on the subject. Actually, 'rent seeking' (but not the term) first appeared in Chapter 19 of *The Calculus of Consent* (Buchanan and Tullock 1962) where many of the essential characteristics were identified, including its origins, processes, and negative outcomes. Since Tullock's 1967 and 1971 papers, the field has burgeoned into a major industry not only among Virginians but public choice scholars more generally. Several edited volumes have appeared along with original full-length studies and countless articles in the pages of *Public Choice*. And, Tullock continues to express himself on the matter.

The basic approach to interest groups and rent seeking is quite simple even if its ramifications have become increasingly technical and even esoteric. As with most social science, few propositions are ever finally or definitively tested and resolved. When Virginian notions on rent seeking became conventional learning, Chicago's Gary Becker (1983, 1985) raised a fundamental challenge that has yet to be answered effectively.

According to Virginians, rent seeking begins when individuals or groups discover that at the margin it is more profitable to spend the next dollar on political action than on productive activity in the market. Apparently, this discovery in America occurred during the last quarter of the nineteenth century. However, Ekelund and Tollison (1981, 1997a, b) treated Mercantilism as a rent-seeking society. Regardless of its precise origins, rent seeking has imposed enormous costs in the form of social welfare losses, up to 12–13 percent of the GNP according to some estimates (see Mueller 1989, ch. 13). Although the costs of government-sponsored monopoly appear to be substantial, it is paradoxical that whether viewed against expected returns or the assets of the rent seeker, the amounts spent on rent seeking are very low; in short, there is underdissipation of available rents. But not everyone agrees with Tullock about the latter estimate or his explanation for it. Perhaps one possibility is that eliciting contributions from rent seekers has the same problem encountered in financing any public good, namely free riding. The individual contributor must surely view any contribution as pure cost with little likelihood of a significant payoff. That is exactly what Olson (1965) maintained.

Virginians do take rent seeking seriously and worry not only about its overall social, economic, and political costs but also its distributional effects. Some groups are more effective than others. We still know relatively little about the winners and losers – and perhaps even less about the evolution of winners into losers and vice versa. It seems apparent that farmers, who have been among the most effectual American rent seekers, now enjoy much less success in protecting their previous gains. Likewise, the National Rifle Association has taken some serious blows during the past decade. Perhaps the newest Virginian work has switched from seeing private interests as the primary seekers of rents to viewing governments and their bureaucracies and politicians as organizers of political extortion. That is, the rent-seeking model also accommodates officials threatening to take wealth away from or punish groups who will not voluntarily do their bidding (see McChesney 1987 and 1997, Mitchell and Munger 1991, and Chapter 18 of this volume). While historians have long documented stories of such activities on the part of big city bosses and their machines, they never really provided rigorous theories thereof; such explanations are now available (Rose-Ackerman 1978).

On a more general level, the rent-seeking process has been modeled best by McCormick and Tollison (1981) as a transfer institution centered on legislatures, with each interest group being potentially both a demander and supplier of rents. In each role they face competition from other groups. Legislators perform the task of arranging deals by pairing those who want something the most with those who are least capable of resisting demands. All this is summarized in the graphic form of a supply and demand curve with the former depicted as a kind of reverse demand curve. Each group acts on the principle that it is not worth spending more than a dollar to gain a dollar and each calculates that it is not worth spending an additional dollar to avoid having to pay another dollar. This simple economic notion is then applied in a non-simple, imaginative way to explain rent seeking and the role of politicians as brokers who match potential traders. Chicagoans might well share this view of rent seeking as an unproductive activity since it is no more than redistribution of existing wealth, not its creation.

Viewed in redistributive terms, the model suggests that some groups do better than others because they are more efficient in obtaining information and making use of it. This in turn suggests that small groups – usually but not exclusively industrial – will have a competitive advantage over larger and more diffuse groups of consumers or taxpayers, excepting, of course, large industrial users of some resource supplied by another rent seeker. As Olson showed much earlier, small groups can handle free riders more cost-effectively than large groups. Such groups usually have been organized earlier than, say, consumers and, therefore, do not confront start-up costs.

Another neat feature of the model is the effort on the part of Tollison and others to confront the role of actual political institutions within which the trading occurs. Most of this research published in book form (Crain and Tollison 1990) deals with legislative voting, districting, committees, regulators, campaign expenditures, and constitutional constraints in such empirical detail that it defies convenient summary. While not all of the papers collected there are directly concerned with rent seeking, the volume does provide a rich and typically Virginian empirical context in which to see the model at work. It also suggests, rather strongly, that the polity is not an efficient machine. That polity is in need of reform and the best reform for rent seeking is to eliminate or, at least, to reduce the role of politics in life and in particular to dismantle the political institutions that create and sustain rents. The problem, of course, is how to employ the very institutions that provide rent-seeking incentives to reduce or eliminate them. That is the question.

Posed in this abstract manner there is no way out of the dilemma; the facts, however, indicate that a robust reform movement has begun the world over with the demise of totalitarianism and the decentralization of democracies, the privatization movement, the deregulation of once powerful industries, and the break-up of large-scale industries. And, now, under a Democratic president we are witnessing the reduction of welfare programs and the military–industrial complex.

2.4   Bureaucracy and regulation

Clearly, Gordon Tullock (1965) is chiefly responsible for bringing a rational choice perspective to the study of bureaucracy. However, it was William Niskanen (1971) who supplied the first formal treatment, an analysis he was later to amend, but the original book is still regarded as the classic exposition of Virginian views.

Both Tullock and Niskanen treated the bureau and the bureaucrat in purely economic terms, meaning that property rights, transaction costs, and organizational incentives have enormous roles to play in explaining their decision-making process and in accounting for the well-known inefficiencies of most public-sector bureaucracies. Unlike political scientists, Niskanen chose to focus on the size of the bureau's budget and the cost-effectiveness with which it operates. His benchmark was the firm operating in both competitive and monopoly markets, something that would never have occurred to a political scientist, or even to many economists.

Niskanen began with a narrow but powerful assumption: that bureaucrats wish to maximize the sizes of their budgets. And, they were able to achieve that objective because they had an asymmetrical relationship with the sponsoring body – the legislature – a relationship that can best be described as a 'bilateral monopoly', meaning the bureau had a distinct informational advantage. Critics, both in public choice and political science, were later to criticize this assumption and not without good theoretical reason and empirical evidence. In more refined models, the bureau maximized its budget but did so only to the extent that the additional costs beyond the point of efficiency were equaled by the sum total of the consumer surplus that might be ascribed to that budget request. In short, marginal cost exceeded marginal benefit, but since the added costs were diffused broadly and anonymously among the millions of taxpayers while the benefits were concentrated among the bureau and its clientele, a highly inefficient budget could easily pass political muster. Because the incentives and constraints perpetuating bureaucratic inefficiencies are the norm rather than the exception, total governmental budgets are grossly outsized, leading to increased taxation, deficit financing, or both. Of lesser concern to Tullock and, especially, Niskanen were the traditional concerns of political science – political control and citizen relationships with bureaucrats.

It should be noted that the Niskanen model paved the way for the Chicago theory of interest groups and rent seeking in that Niskanen made use of the consumer surplus notion which, in turn, anticipated Becker's theory that expected social welfare losses are an important element in shaping expenditure and taxing policies as well as regulatory choices. Of course, Tullock had never argued that social welfare costs were unimportant; he actually said that the rent-seeking costs had to be added to the social welfare losses. Becker argued, contrary to Harberger (1954), that these latter losses were not insignificant in the choice of policies and, in turn, that losses were a function of the locations and slopes of the demand and supply functions for the bureaucratically supplied good.

2.5 Micro politics and macroeconomics

Virginian public choice was formed largely during the 1960s and 1970s, a period marked by high rates of inflation. This fact of history had a great impact on theories of how and why governments behave in their fiscal and monetary policy making. Now that inflation has receded markedly, it is a good time to assess the earlier public choice contributions.

Much of the early work on social choice, but also public choice, was based on a demand theory of politics, namely the role of voters and elections in the political process. Hence, the concern over median voters, majority voting and impossibility theorems. It was not long, however, before Buchanan and others began to shift their attention away from Downsian formulations to emphasize the role of public suppliers of goods and services, their official positions, incentives, and so on. In brief, suppliers have some distinct advantages over the electorate and they make use of them. Politicians and bureaucrats can and do take advantage of the voters in this view and are facilitated in pursuing their parochial interests by the formal institutional arrangements that they know far better than do rationally ignorant voters.

Within this biased set of democratic institutions, the fiscal choices for society are made or enacted. Virginians have studied, in detail, the supply of governmental output or the size and composition of public expenditures; the choice of monetary policy tools and budget deficits; tax bases and tax rates; and variations thereof, over time.

While there is far too much theory and data to summarize succinctly, one can convey the flavor of the analysis and outline a version of politics that does not garner the approval of many political scientists. For Virginians, the budget is the central document of politics and it is not a pretty one. In the first place, the budget is usually viewed as inefficient (that is, consumes far too large a portion of the nation's resources). The argument involves many considerations with an emphasis on fiscal illusion, majority voting rules, and an evolving ideology among the citizenry and intellectuals that has undermined the traditional fiscal constraints observed throughout the nineteenth century. Buchanan and Wagner (1977) laid out the rationales underlying these arguments and especially the changes in beliefs and values. The role of majority rule had been explored earlier by Buchanan and Tullock (1962).

Collective choice is basically choice without the benefit of explicit price signals to guide voters and politicians. A price links costs and benefits in a way that forces the buyer and seller to be better informed and to weigh the requisite tradeoffs carefully. Necessarily, we all become more responsible. Since the political process tends to break these links, we are encouraged to be less prudent and base our public decisions on so-called 'needs' or 'priorities'. Then, too, politicians, bureaucrats and voters usually prefer to pay for other people's 'needs' as well as their own using still other people's money. All these factors contribute to larger budgets.

Political suppliers operate in an institutional setting that differs from markets. They do not possess property rights in their offices; they cannot claim residual profits from sensible decisions; they must trade with other suppliers without the aid of a common currency; and they are elected to fixed terms of office. Because of these constraints they do not ask how much citizens value public services, so as to tax them accordingly, but how many voters value them enough to vote for the program or politician. For the politician and all other political actors, the important fact is not the total of benefits as compared with costs, but their distribution among voters.

Recognizing this situation, the politician opts to oversupply at least some items in the budget. She or he also prefers to supply those goods that are most visible, readily available, and can be justified by simple, appealing claims to justice and equity or fairness. At the same time, politicians prefer to tap revenue sources that spread the burden as much as possible, to conceal costs through the use of indirect taxes, and practice deficit financing whenever possible, which is often. According to Niskanen, this is all rather 'peculiar' economics, but sensible politics. Another element of sensible politics but questionable economics is found in the politician's penchant for ignoring sunk costs; for the politician and many voters the appropriate response to inefficient operations is to continue rather than terminate losses. Throwing good money after bad, as has been the case with nationalized industries in Britain and countless civil and military projects in the United States, is an imperative principle among politicians.

Other imperatives in the Virginian analysis include the effects of logrolling which may, at least in blackboard exercises, produce productive exchange, but in reality is more likely to expand budgets and breed cynicism among citizens. The response of legislators to competing demands for public funds is not to end or reduce them but to find ways to distribute more money among more groups. 'You support my constituents and I'll support yours' is the refrain, although rarely in such explicit terms. Majority rule and an unlimited budget are responsible for these outcomes. The same thing is true on the revenue side of the budget as manifested in the existence of relatively high income tax rates accompanied by an incredible array of exemptions or loopholes easily exploited by tax accountants and lawyers. Since the 1986 federal income tax 'reform', Congress has been auctioning off hundreds of scarce privileges for still higher electoral contributions.

Presumably citizens could end dissembling, exaggerations, obfuscation, and suppressed information about our collective lives but such an outcome is unlikely for a couple of good reasons: first, citizens are themselves the primary demanders of publicly provided services. Second, they may with the best of intentions desire an efficient government but are faced with extraordinarily high monitoring costs. It is costly to monitor business people, but those costs are nowhere near those encountered in the polity. For one thing, the nature of many public goods is such that one needs a PhD in economics to determine or even estimate the costs and benefits from governmental programs. Then, too, the voter has but one vote and needs to persuade countless others to support his endeavor, something less necessary in the private market. The game of politics does indeed produce winners and losers, one more manifestation of the coercive nature of political life.

In the Virginian polity, voters and taxpayers play favored roles but are constrained by the rules of the electoral game and the power of politicians and bureaucrats. Despite this bias, voters do influence the other participants and do so through both political and non-political ways. This set of relationships is especially marked in the making of macroeconomic policy, where a kind of tragedy of the commons is enacted. Or, one might characterize the resultant situation as a battle with Leviathan.

Virginians share the Austrian view that macroeconomics is really microeconomics shaped by micro politics. The great variables of Keynesian analysis, consumption, savings, investment, and government spending, are not real, but contrived aggregates. Neither policy makers nor citizens live in abstract models; instead, they deal with their own wages, salaries, prices, and so forth, and attempt to advance their own interests in both the market and polity. Politicians, as we have seen, are remarkably sensitive to these concerns and especially to their vote implications. Policies are chosen by politicians, not for their macro responses, but for their micro-distributive benefits and costs.

The beautiful thing about Keynesian analysis and its policy prescriptions is that they seemingly only produce winners, particularly during recessions and depressions. Politicians have no hard choices to make in spending more, taxing less and deferring debts to unborn voters. Policies that would enhance production have little political appeal since they might improve the profits of producers and investors. Then, too, the Keynesian apparatus is built upon assumptions that encourage economists to believe they understand the economy better than they in fact do, and that the data upon which policy rests are accurate and timely. Computers and formal mechanical models are themselves the products of fallible minds that cannot undo the past or predict the future with any reasonable accuracy.

Buchanan and Wagner (1977) and Brennan and Buchanan (1980) laid out the classic Virginian analysis and prognosis of macroeconomic policy. Keynes, they maintain, never addressed the role of politics in the making of macro policy and, therefore, never understood how, in the long run, his prescriptions would not materialize and that other unintended, socially costly results would be produced. He never understood that democracies have policy biases and among them are susceptibility to fiscal illusions created by politicians and accepted by the citizenry, and the shortsightedness of all political actors. Markets place a certain constraint on people who value the present more than the future; this constraint is largely absent in the polity.

In the nineteenth century, Buchanan and Wagner contend, a norm of balanced budgets or more generally 'fiscal responsibility' held sway; just why they never really explained. In any event, after Keynes wrote his great book economists were able to argue, persuasively, that public debt was no longer immoral, but actually wise policy to be manipulated at will. But unlike Stigler, Virginians include ideas as causal factors in explanations of policy choices. Clearly, they believe that ideas have consequences.

In turning traditional public finance on its head, Brennan and Buchanan set forth some truly revolutionary ideas about public finance and macro policy based on the ideas described in the previous section of this chapter. Adopting the analytical stance of Hobbes, they view government as a monolithic entity seeking to maximize its revenues. With this starting point they then set forth a collection of policies such a government, with monopoly powers, might enact. Many of them are startlingly similar to what liberal governments have been doing for decades. The question, then, is how will rational, informed citizens respond in order to protect themselves?

Basically, they will opt for constitutional changes to restrain the government. Given the inflationary times in which they wrote, Buchanan and his co-authors stressed measures to promote that objective, including constitutional provisions requiring a balanced budget, with any surpluses to be used for reducing the accumulated public debt. Likewise, the constitution would contain an amendment requiring the Federal Reserve Board to increase the money supply at the same rate as the growth in the national economy. They also supported Hayek's advocacy of privatizing the money supply; in other words, eliminating the government's monopoly over that important function. They even advocated constitutional protections of tax loopholes (that is, encouraging taxpayers to make use of exemptions and exclusions to reduce their tax loads). Traditional public finance recommends exactly the opposite. By ignoring the standard excess burden argument Virginians rationalize limitations on the growth of government revenues.

Mixed in with this analysis are various explanations of the growth of government, the major one being that citizen perceptions of public benefits and costs tend to be skewed in such a way that they tend to overestimate the benefits and underestimate the costs. The modern Virginian view contrasts sharply with that of Downs (1957) and Galbraith (1958), both of whom argued that voters systematically underestimate benefits (especially of public goods) and, because of the immediacy of taxes, overestimate costs. No empirical evidence seems able to resolve this dilemma about citizen perceptions. Perhaps the wisest position is one that enables us to understand that an individual citizen may do both depending on the spending and revenue choices at hand. Thus, government may spend too much on some projects and too little on others. Certainly it is the case that every citizen sees too much spent on at least one program and too little on some other, more favored activity.

3 Chicago and the new political economy

In the 40-plus years public choice has been around, only one serious intellectual challenge has arisen to offer powerful counterinterpretations grounded within the basic framework of economic reasoning and that, of course, is the newly recognized Chicago school. What makes this challenge interesting, in addition to the substantive differences, is the fact that its conclusions seem at such variance with what most economists regard as the classical Chicago view of politics and public policy. That view, formed by Frank Knight, Henry Simons, and Jacob Viner, was critical of politics and viewed interference in the market as inefficient and morally suspect. Later, Milton Friedman and George Stigler were to establish a more rigorous basis on which to challenge public policy, but in so doing they probably annoyed their predecessors with their scientific pretensions and insistence on rigorous statistical inquiry. Abstract theory was not enough.

But now we have what seems to be a complete rejection of previous Chicagoan pro-market proclivities and at least a begrudging acceptance of a greater role for government in society and the economy. We are told, for example, that voters are not so uninformed as generally thought in Virginian analyses, that interest groups are not all bad, and, in general, that the Virginian program is both analytically suspect and its empirical foundations are, at best, questionable. In my remaining pages I want to state their case. It is powerful and not easily summarized. The format is similar to the one used in describing Virginian public choice.

3.1 Some basic tenets

Modern Chicagoans are justly renowned for their imaginative and rigorous scholarly contributions to economics proper, contributions based on positive analysis and quantitative testing of predictions derived from a singular adherence to price theory. The latter is held to be applicable to most if not all of human behavior. While the progenitors would surely have doubts about the scope of economics, Gary Becker and his generation have little doubt and much enthusiasm for extending the boundaries of traditional economics. That enthusiasm is based on the notion that humans are both self-interested and rational in all spheres of life, not just the marketplace. Thus, Becker and his students have explored such traditional sociological phenomena as racial discrimination, immigration, criminal activity, law enforcement, family matters including sex, marriage and divorce, family size and relationships, addictive behavior, religion and churches, fads, and health issues. In the process, Becker et al. have broadened the meaning of 'self-interest' and clarified the use of the term 'preferences'. They have also taught us about the allocation of time and its importance as a constraint on choice. People are viewed throughout as forward looking and, importantly, consistent through time.

In all these forays, Chicagoans are committed to the idea that individuals and groups achieve some sort of efficient results, with efficiency being defined in essentially Paretian terms such that no one can be made better off without someone else being made worse off. This idea, combined with an evolutionary notion of institutional selection suggests, rather strongly, that whatever outcome prevails must be the most efficient, otherwise it would be displaced by a superior one; the fact that it is not suggests that the costs of change outweigh the potential benefits.

One cannot overestimate the importance of this conclusion, especially in contrast with the analytic *modus operandi* of Virginians and their interpretations of politics. James Buchanan has been fond of saying that individuals are not bifurcated, with one part of their brains dealing with markets in rational, self-interested ways and doing the opposite in non-market situations. Chicagoans go one step further and conclude that politics also has Paretian or efficiency propensities, something Virginians find hard to believe.

The very political institutions that Virginians find inefficient in the sense of the outcomes produced are, according to Becker, Peltzman, Posner, and Wittman, quite efficient. There may be a way out of this dilemma and that is to say that Virginians view collective choice, *per se*, as imposing constraints that do not facilitate Pareto outcomes. These constraints form the basis of such books as Olson's *Logic of Collective Action* and this author's essay on *The Anatomy of Public Failure* (Mitchell 1978). To be sure, some institutional redesign would facilitate more rational choices but they are only rarely adopted, for a variety of reasons. The Chicago view is that the institutions of collective choice are themselves the most efficient available. So, Virginians believe that all the actors in politics pursue their own self-interests and they do so through the use of rational courses of action in inefficient institutional settings. I am tempted to say that the Chicagoans are more logical in their application of the basic economic axioms to the analysis of the political rules of the game. Buchanan and Tullock's *Calculus of Consent* attempted to show how economics could be applied to the choice of constitutional rules or provisions, but in an important sense they failed to show why less-efficient institutions or rules are, in fact, chosen. It would seem that Virginians are in these matters somewhat idealistic while the Chicagoans appear more practical. Virginians like to contrast political choices and outcomes with what might be obtained in private settings and especially markets, whereas Chicagoans compare one political rule with another and one political outcome with another. Given the supremacy of the market in traditional Chicago economics, this new approach seems revolutionary.

3.2   Elections, voters, and efficiency

The Chicago view of elections and voting seems, at least superficially, to be the standard economic view shared by all public choice analysts, namely that voting behavior is shaped by a cost–benefit calculus on the part of individual citizens faced with a peculiar set of institutional constraints. Elections are episodic events in which social choices are made by aggregating individual votes according to some decision rule such as simple majority. Except for unanimity, all such rules produce winners and losers, although not always in zero-sum terms. Stigler, true to neoclassical price theory, reminded us that margins count and that losers do not often lose everything and winners do not win everything. And, so, the winning coalitions are seldom permanent nor are they made up of the same interest groups and voters over the long run.

Chicago economists have not produced studies of voting equivalent to, say, *The American Voter* (Campbell et al. 1960) or *Voting* (Berelson et al. 1954). In fact, there are but a handful of major studies, mostly by Peltzman (1980, 1984, 1985, 1990), but see Matsusaka (1992). These studies, especially those of Peltzman, are impressive indeed and stand in sharp contrast with those of political scientists not only in terms of the types of data employed but more importantly in terms of the basic question asked. That question is, how efficient are elections? And the answer is very much at odds with those of most political scientists and Virginian economists. In short, Peltzman concludes that voters do make good use of the information available to them in selecting among competing politicians and parties. Using macroeconomic data for the period from 1950 to 1988, as well as election results in presidential, senatorial and gubernatorial races, he concluded that the voters appeared quite rational; voters rewarded those office holders who presided during periods when national income was increasing and inflation was decreasing. Voters also were more long- than short-run oriented, a conclusion that contradicts many political business-cycle studies. Voters, we are also told, are more interested in permanent than in transitory gains. In short, voters are seen as more than able to acquire and process information; could this be the influence of Lucasian rational expectations? Voters, it seems, are more efficacious in electoral settings than one might deduce from Virginian analyses. Still, it should be emphasized that Virginians do not fault the voters; rather it is the unfortunate nature of the institutional constraints that puts voters in a terrible bind. Chicagoans agree about the constraints but not about the abilities of voters to overcome them.

I would be remiss if I did not consider the role that ideology or beliefs and ideals play in the minds of voters (see also Chapter 15). Stigler and Becker (1977) have argued that such factors as tastes and, more broadly, ideals and ideas are not necessary in explaining consumer and voter behavior. This exclusion surely facilitates the construction of formal models, but possibly at a high cost. Chicagoans contend that the economic theory of choice must not rely on 'tastes' because there is no theory to explain how tastes are formed or to predict their effects. All a student of choice requires is data about prices and income and changes therein.

This conclusion is surely more applicable to the market than to the polity, where monetary phenomena are less pervasive. It is ironic that Becker, who has done much to expand the application of economics beyond the market-place, has done so using the narrowest of economic assumptions. Perhaps that is why so many social scientists are unenamored of his efforts. To be sure, Virginians have no theory of the origins of or changes in political tastes but they, like Max Weber, view ideas and ideals and symbols of prime importance in the polity. Only recently has a serious effort been made to incorporate these elements into formal theories of political behavior (see Hinich and Munger 1994; Kuran 1995).

3.3   Rent seeking

Perhaps the best-known Chicago-style economics, at least among political scientists, is Stigler's theory of government regulation, first published in 1971, and later amplified and modified by Peltzman (1976) and others. The theory is remarkably simple and straightforward; hence its appeal to many liberal political scientists; it also confirmed some of their liberal ideology.

The theory claims that business interests can improve their positions by organizing pressure groups that, in turn, influence the regulators who write or shape the regulations that will govern them. Thus, the idea has become known as the 'capture theory' of regulation and it had a good deal to be said for it during the post-New Deal era. The theory may be described as a demand theory of rent seeking in so far as it explains why special interests become politically active. And that also constitutes a limitation of the theory since it assumes that regulation is imposed upon those who will be regulated, a not unreasonable assumption to make during the heyday of the New Deal and the Fair Deal. However, businesses and other interests may also perceive gains to be made by originating a demand for regulation and not simply waiting while other hostile interests impose their rules from the outside. Regulation may also be viewed as a public good for would-be cartels whose members cannot regulate their own competition. Hire the government to do the necessary controlling of entry, prices, and so on.

Stigler agreed with Olson (1965) and Schattschneider (1935, 1960, 1969) that business interests have some distinct advantages over consumers in the regulation game, namely their smaller size, the fact that they are already organized and, therefore, incur lower start-up costs, while the benefits they can anticipate are concentrated and the costs diffused among millions of customers and taxpayers. Stigler's analysis has not been negated, but made into a special case by his younger colleagues Becker (1983, 1985) and, especially, Peltzman (1976). The latter also provided a more abstract and presumably more generalized model which includes the voting public as a major influence on regulatory decisions. Since voters do not directly influence or participate in bureaucratic decisions, Peltzman had to construct a model not of voters but of the bureaucratic chiefs who anticipate how voters might respond to regulations. No doubt cabinet secretaries attempt to read the public's 'mind', but just how – and how successfully – is not very clear. In any case, Stigler's theory remains quite narrow for it is concerned solely with explaining why some interests will want to decide who the regulators will be and what sort of regulations they will enact. Peltzman explains why they may not succeed, making his theory a more general and, in a sense, more realistic explanation.

We have learned during the past 20 years that both Stigler and Olson were partly in error when their theories failed to predict or account for the obvious fact that many environmental and consumer groups not only formed but become powerful actors in the polity. Each has managed to shape public policies detrimental to business and labor groups. Although each has helped to enact positive laws their more important achievement may be preventing more favorable laws for industry and labor from being enacted. One might reasonably contend that this sort of achievement is at the heart of the American democratic process – the ability of interest groups to modify and soften the demands of contending interests. Likewise, we can note that in the 'give and take' of the political process, no group is permanently excluded.

The long-lived Stigler contribution has been eclipsed during more recent years by Becker's (1983, 1985) challenging foray into the rent-seeking literature. Oddly enough, Becker's work has provided political scientists who like government with powerful models to justify that position. But, like Virginians, Becker argues that a major, if not the chief, function of government and politics is to redistribute income.

Interest groups enter the political arena to affect the taxes they pay and the subsidies they may receive, with competition among them determining the outcomes. Like David Truman (1951), Becker contends that under balanced budgets the efficiency of each group is an important determinant of the outcome; so, too, are the social costs and benefits of public policies, a consideration not often found in Virginian analyses. Becker's treatment of efficiency is but a formalized version of Truman's powerful analysis of the cohesion of each group; that is, he attempts to explain the factors that affect cohesion and free riding among members. The more efficient a group is at controlling free riding, the more successful it will be in competition with other groups.

In Becker's analysis we discover that public policies rarely favor one group to the exclusion of others; there are inevitable compromises and no one is permanently a winner or a loser. We also learn that governments can and do enact policies that promote Paretian outcomes and reduce deadweight costs, another departure from the Virginian view. In short, Becker's position sustains the market-failure arguments while also making room for the political-failure school. He would seem to have a more complex analysis than Wittman, who finds little to support in the government-failure school.

3.4   Bureaucracy and regulation

In distinguishing interests, rent seeking, and regulation we create some artificiality of analysis. Thus, much of what Chicago has to say about rents and bureaucrats is commingled with what we have just discussed in the previous section. In any event, perhaps the major Chicago contribution to bureaucracy has come under the label of regulation. Here, I have in mind the work of Peltzman (1976), who generalized the Stigler model and in the process said the idea of outright capture of bureaucratic agents is too simple; regulators must respond to the demands of consumers as well as to those of the regulated. Regulation increases prices and therefore profits, which naturally appeals to the industry. But consumers who face the welfare losses that regulation creates may become discontented and angry enough to vote against incumbents held responsible for higher prices. The major political problem for regulators is to design 'efficient' regulation. This problem was addressed by Peltzman (ibid.), who argued that efficient regulation requires that prices be raised only to the point where votes gained per dollar of price increase exactly offset votes lost among consumers. The diagrammatics of this vote-maximization model as applied to regulation are presented in Figure 1.1.

By increasing price the regulators gain support from suppliers, who obtain higher profits, but lose support from consumers, who must pay the higher prices. The curves labeled M_1, M_2, and M_3 depict 'isovote' curves, or sets of prices and profits that yield equal numbers of votes. Curves that are higher or

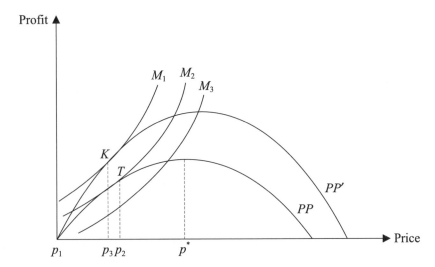

Figure 1.1   Vote maximization and government choices

to the left denote larger numbers of votes (M_1 represents more votes than M_2, and so on). Each isovote curve has a positive slope, so that to hold political support constant votes lost through a price increase must be made up through increases in profits. The precise slopes of the curves reflect this tradeoff, with the convexity reflecting diminishing returns: voters are less and less willing to accept price increases, so that a larger increment of profit (and hence more gains to the regulator) is required to offset a given price increase. The potential profit curve, PP, depicts the combinations of price and profit that are feasible given demand and costs of suppliers. Peltzman's conclusion is that combination T is chosen by a vote-maximizing regulator, with observed price p_2, which is between the monopoly (that is, profit-maximizing) price, p^*, and the competitive (zero-profit) price, p_1. A shift in the potential profit curve to PP' should lead regulators to select combination K, associated with lower price p_3, a Pareto-superior move since consumers pay lower prices, the industry obtains higher profits, and the regulators gain more support from each group than would be obtained at T.

   Despite the attractions of the Chicago theory, there remain some sticky problems. The theory cannot predict precisely which industries will be regulated. The theory does predict, though, that regulators will focus their attention on industries that are either perfectly competitive or approximate the performance of pure monopoly. This is because movements away from p_1 or p^* on PP produce the largest vote increments. More seriously, the theory does not explain deregulation save for the tautology that the industry is now, for some reason, better off without regulation. As an empirical matter, of course, some industries with large memberships have secured regulation while others have not. Truckers and farmers have for long periods done very well by the government, while utilities and other service industries have not. The theory can be applied to a variety of other economic regulatory policies (for example, Dougan 1984 gives a rigorous application to the expected incidence of tariffs), but in general its chief predictions are either tautological or are not borne out empirically.

The theory asserts a strangely passive pattern of behavior by regulatory agencies in the face of significant opportunities to do better. Long-term 'capture' may develop into a bilateral power struggle where agency officials abuse their powers and privileges. Ambitious political actors may be expected to seize upon any such abuse for their own electoral purposes. Further, if one industry's rents become too costly (for example, steel makers winning significant trade barriers on imported steel), both consumers and downstream manufacturers who use such products are prompted to seek market substitutes and voice political opposition. We should not underestimate the power of one organized interest to oppose the success of another.

All in all, the Chicago theory explains a portion of what we commonly observe about the behavior and choices of the regulated and the regulators, along with various consequences for markets and the political world. It is out of this Chicago context, both intellectual and collegial, that Gary Becker was to advance his own work. And it is this same school of thought that provides inspiration for the work of certain Virginians; we refer to the remarkable Stiglerian influence on the work of Robert Tollison and his co-workers (see, for example, Chapters 17 and 25 of this volume).

3.5   Micro politics and macroeconomics

With the demise of inflationary concerns we are apt to forget that Chicago has produced two influential macroeconomic theories – the monetarism associated mostly with Milton Friedman and rational expectations, a theory devised, in substantial part, by Robert Lucas (1972). Both theories bear an unmistakable Chicago lineage, but both do so in quite different ways. I begin with the older monetary theory revolution launched in Hyde Park.

Unlike their chief antagonists, the Keynesians, monetarists have actually developed something in the nature of a political theory of inflation. While these political elements have not been formalized, they are set forth with considerable clarity and some rigor by such well-known monetarists as Friedman, Karl Brunner, Alan Meltzer, and Michael Parkin. These analysts not only lay the blame for inflation and unemployment on governmental policy but, unlike Keynesians, explain why governments adopt the 'wrong' monetary and fiscal policies, or having chosen the 'right' policies, do so in the wrong proportions or at the wrong times. Their explanations are complementary to and, indeed, have much in common with those of public choice. Having read little public choice, some monetarists appear to have reinvented the wheel even after the car has been popularized. In any event, some of them place little reliance on the existing literature of public choice and concentrate, instead, on the erratic records of the world's monetary authorities and the technical difficulties of data gathering, interpretation, and implementation of monetary policy.

Monetarists maintain that inflation is a monetary phenomenon to be discussed in the context of the well-known Fisher equation, $MV = PT$. What distinguishes modern versions of the equation is a concern over difficult questions having to do with the changing quantities of money and the output of goods and services. Since the quantity of money is largely a political responsibility and the output of goods a private one, the analyst must account for both political and private decisions. Indeed, even the latter decisions are profoundly affected by both macro and micro policies. Modern monetary theorists, therefore, examine why governments are led inexorably to expand the supply of money while adopting micro policies that discourage production. Both strategies are rooted in electoral necessities.

Inflation is seen as the major product of government efforts to cope with electoral imperatives and politicians' own incentives to be re-elected. According to this analysis, politicians learn that they are entrepreneurs competing in a volatile market for votes and influence. As such, they offer policy proposals that range from explicit redistribution to vague and vacuous patriotism. They soon learn that redistributive policies are apt to garner more support than providing public goods and that among these policies are proposals to expand the benefits of increasing numbers of beneficiaries who, typically, are better organized, better informed, and more influential than the anonymous taxpayers who provide the resources. Policy costs and benefits are asymmetrically distributed as is the information available about those costs and benefits. Politicians quickly adapt themselves to these constraints and, thereby, lend their own support to those demands that, on average, expand benefits of the most visible kind. These same politicians also learn that as the expenditures of government rapidly exceed revenues, inflationary possibilities are enhanced. And while inflation is often regarded as a public bad, it is a private good for some citizens – and most politicians – for it can be readily and easily employed to finance the inevitable deficits resulting from so-called 'functional finance'. The monetizing of the debt is an ingenious political solution to outstanding problems of providing both guns and butter. Monetizing the debt, however, solves neither the resource-allocation problem nor the Phillips dilemma.

Although the Federal Reserve Board can technically control the supply of money to a reasonable approximation over the medium term, this is no simple matter to be resolved by fiat. The incentives of most public officials and many important citizens are such that policies appealing to them are also policies that tend to increase the supply of money while decreasing the incentives and means for controlling that supply. Accordingly, governments, once they are entrapped by the Phillips dilemma of increasing inflationary expectations, find it virtually impossible to resist pressures to engage in a stop–go set of actions that lead to increasing both the money supply and public expenditures while attempting to reduce the costs of unemployment. Having increased the potential for inflation they tend to overreact, at least at higher levels of inflation, and install politically popular but ineffectual policies designed to reduce inflationary pressures but which seldom reduce the long-run level of either unemployment or inflation. So the political bias is for still more money and inflation. Complicating this perverse process is a perceptual problem induced by the realization that the benefits of diminished inflation are a public good to be shared by the many in the long run while the costs are immediate, dramatic and, as in the case of increased unemployment, concentrated among the few.

Then, too, the effects of a business downturn are broader than those experienced just by the unemployed themselves. Profits, inventories, and overtime work fall, only to create greater apprehension. As noted above, many modern monetarists spend almost as much time explaining the political sources of inefficient micro policies as on the inefficient macro policies explaining the overall supply of money. Monetarists complain about the new protectionism designed to shelter virtually every powerful interest. Such measures restrict the flow of free trade, reduce the mobility of resources and competition, raise prices, reduce consumption, and ultimately reduce the incentives to be productive (that is, the right-hand side of Fisher's identity, PT). These negative-sum games in which politicians enact measures that take from some citizens in order to give to others lead to a smaller GDP than would otherwise be achieved.

In this general analysis of inflation we detect the roots of public choice. But, unlike many public choice analysts, monetarists are not at all reluctant to prescribe alternative policies or to advocate fundamental reform of political institutions.

Although many monetarists despair of the possibilities of reversing inflationary tendencies, some, including Friedman, will not admit of defeat. How else can we account for his prolific and essentially optimistic efforts to educate the citizenry and officialdom on changing our emphasis from fiscal to monetary policy and from one kind of the latter to another? Friedman, in particular, never tires of pointing out the follies of expanding the role of government, the logrolling tendencies of legislatures that increase expenditures, the perverse results of public regulations, and so on. In all this, Friedman is profoundly aware not only of the importance of discouraging but of the necessity of restraining governments from greater spending and taxing; in this critique he accepts Hayek's belief that it is the size of government and not that of the deficit that is critical in the long run. Government is inherently inefficient, yet powerful enough to endanger the liberties of the citizenry it presumably exists to serve. Thus, Friedman and other monetarists wish to see the growth of government reduced, the use and value of money stabilized, the free market revitalized. Government's major responsibility is not to ensure full employment but to facilitate free exchange.

For monetarists the best way to accomplish their monetary ends is to corral the shortsighted, discretionary, and destabilizing powers of the monetary authorities by the adoption of some rule enabling tighter control of the money supply. This approach gets at the most immediate and visible of money problems. A return to a gold standard, privatizing the money supply, and enacting a fixed rule for monetary growth are among the best-known major proposals. It will also be useful to give the president an item veto and index taxation and incomes for the protection of all those adversely affected by inflation. But most important of all feasible reforms is the addition of a constitutional amendment that would get at the problem pointed to above, namely the expanding state.

Friedman would like to see an amendment that would limit federal government spending as a fraction of the national income and require balanced budgets. The pursuit of balanced budgets to the exclusion of the size of those budgets is, in Friedman's view, rather shortsighted. Such a requirement does not prevent government from growing, though it may induce some greater attention to efficiency. In 1978 Friedman stated that, 'I would far rather have total federal spending at $200 billion with a deficit of $100 billion than a balanced budget at $500 billion' (Friedman 1978, p. 12). Still, Friedman regards tax limitation laws, not as cure-alls, but as stopgaps until public opinion changes. As is to be expected, he has been guardedly optimistic about that possibility.

Now, however, we read that budget reforms are losing steam as the campaign for a constitutional convention to write a balanced budget amendment falls short of the necessary state endorsements. Only two more states are required, but they are apt to be difficult ones and still other states may withdraw their earlier support. Ironically, Ronald Reagan's (and Paul Volcker's) considerable success in taming inflation also reduced the demand for a budgetary amendment to the constitution. If the inflationary tendencies of governments can be harnessed by ordinary policies, why enact rigid constitutional reforms not all of whose consequences may be known?

While the more purely monetary reforms offered by monetarists are their most obvious and compelling policy recommendations, they are not the only ones. Most monetarists are firm believers in the efficiency of free exchange and free markets. They believe that inflation would not be so serious a problem if such exchanges were permitted to once more prevail and flower. It follows that Friedman and his colleagues are strong advocates of any market reforms that will strengthen competition and facilitate resource mobility. Labor markets are considered especially obnoxious in this regard. Curtailing the power of unions in both the market and the polity is high on the agenda of reforms. Unions bear a special responsibility for the enactment of full-employment policies and the perversities that goal has introduced into our political and economic lives. The political business cycle to be considered below may well be an inadvertent intellectual product of a powerful labor movement.

Monetarists believe, correctly, that the enactment of the necessary anti-inflation policies and constitutional reforms is a demanding and time-consuming task. Few such reforms are apt to prove popular among voters, politicians, and bureaucrats. Acceptance of temporary but higher unemployment, reduced government expenditures, reduction of credit, and controls over the discretion of officials cannot have much appeal. And this is the source of the monetarist dilemma: they advocate that which few want. In a democracy, that may be fatal.

Because of its totally unexpected yet rigorous line of reasoning, the rational expectations school or 'New Classical Economics' is in some ways the most fascinating Chicago theory. Simple-minded theorists can easily gener-ate simple-minded policies and develop logical constitutional implications from their premises. Since rational expectations is a highly sophisticated, and to some degree counterintuitive theory, any layman who thinks he under-stands or is able to predict the next stage of the argument is usually wrong. And that perplexity makes our task somewhat more difficult and ultimately disappointing because the New Classical Economics is precisely that; unlike Virginia it is without a political theory of inflation.

According to rational expectations theory, all 'macro problems' such as inflation and large-scale, persistent unemployment are in need of drastic redefinition, and what may then remain is subject to an entirely different sort of analysis. In Chicago's new classical analysis, information is assumed to be the linchpin of everything. Economic agents in both their market and political activities act on the basis of the very best information (past and future) available, but what is available is rarely ever complete or costless. So we have the partially blind leading the blind in both the economy and polity! In spite of this ubiquitous blindness, economic agents do act rationally and rapidly; they may learn in discontinuous rather than adaptive ways, but they learn well. No matter what occurs, Peltzman-voters and Lucas-agents are assumed to respond appropriately given the circumstances.

If exogenous events occur that are relevant, the agent amends his behavior in the proper ways. One such exogenous shock is a change in government policy. Investors, consumers, and workers all react to counter whatever governments intend to do. The countercyclical policies of Keynesians are, therefore, doomed to failure. Since everyone internalizes the changing expected values in their decisions, whatever government attempts is effectively neutralized and little is gained; indeed, something is lost because of wasted efforts on the part of the government.

But now the unexpected! If the government were to alter course in some dramatic and unexpected way, that would be the equivalent of a random shock and such a shock could make things worse if the government were to carry out the policy initiative. So, pessimism to end all pessimism, the rational expectations analysts inform us that government should continue its previous policies, unless they were random, so that its actions will be predictable. A government cannot reduce unemployment or inflation by changes in policy to offset shocks but it can make things worse by adding instability from government policies to whatever instabilities arise from the private sector.

What is of greatest concern to us is not the intricate general equilibrium theory of rational expectations and its employment in macroeconomics, but the views of government and politics held by that school. No member of the school, excepting, perhaps, Robert Barro (1973), has made any systematic contribution to the study of public choice. Although I find many of the views of the New Classicists reasonable, their conception of politics is as primitive as that of many Keynesians. Indeed, the basic ideas of equilibrium, expectations, learning, risk, and uncertainty seem to have been applied almost exclusively to the market and not extended to the choices and strategies of voters and the government. We never learn why governments tax and spend as they do. But what would such an extension entail?

In so far as political science has a theory of politicians it might best be summarized as one of adaptive expectations or, in the language of the field's practitioners, as an 'incremental' theory. Voters and politicians learn and act as though the immediate past is likely to continue without major alteration. In budgetary studies, where this theory is most often applied, it is concluded that most changes are highly predictable. Although incrementalism has held sway for quite some time, it has been modified on theoretical – and challenged on empirical – grounds as inapplicable to new allocations. And 'exogenous shocks', a term rarely if ever used in political science, suggests another phenomenon that incrementalism ignores. In any case, stability of democratic policy and budgetary expectations is usually assumed by political scientists. This is also said to be true of changes in administrations or democratic governments more generally. Things do not change very often or by very much.

Standard public choice and many electoral studies in political science display a distinct tendency to model voters, especially, as uninformed, past rather than future oriented, and subject to all sorts of fiscal and other illusions. The reduction of these costs is considered to be too high. Politicians, bureaucrats, and interest groups, on the other hand, having more direct interests in being more substantially informed, may also be less than perfectly informed, but they do have distinct advantages over the voters. Originally formulated by Downs (1957), 'rational ignorance' is now an unquestioned theorem of public choice and even some American government textbooks.

Obviously, if the rational expectationists extend their logic to that of the public sector then it also follows that the voters, politicians, interest groups, and bureaucrats are themselves rational in their political expectations. They will all make the best of whatever circumstances they confront. They will, like their market counterparts, make errors but not systematic, persistent ones. Still, the rational expectationist might well contend that there is more risk or less certainty in the polity and that would account for a greater incidence of inefficient policy choices and organizational behavior in the public sector. Faced with many more random shocks, correct anticipations and learning become less certain and ever more costly. Virginian public choice seems to view the relationship between government and citizen as one of imbalance, inequality, and admitting of manipulation. The citizen is at a distinct disadvantage in confrontations with the government. Most rational expectations analysis, however, assumes otherwise.

Although the Chicago school's New Classicists have advice for governments, they do not have a realistic model of actual government choice and behavior. They tend to view government as independent of the electorate. Oddly, then, in one important sense they are very Keynesian! More important, and unlike Keynesians, they arrive at the paradoxical conclusion that government is impotent. The reason is obvious: whereas Keynesians assume an omnicompetent government that can 'manipulate' the electorate and the economy, the New Classicists match an omniscient government against omniscient citizens and economic agents, with the latter able both to anticipate and correct for any policy change. If this state of affairs were indeed true, the principle would surely be one of the most important and devastating of all 'impossibility' theorems. Among other things, in most of its versions it would do away with the political business cycle. Informed rational individuals and organizations are simply unable to control their collective destinies.

The more supply-oriented Virginian analysts question all this. They maintain that the government not only has an effect but powerful effects on the market and society and that owing to the workings of the political process these effects are usually inefficient, inequitable, or both. And worse, monopolistic government has powerful incentives and the resources to successfully manipulate the citizenry. Both bureaucrat and politician have the superior informational resources necessary, as well as the ultimate power of state authority and coercion.

With the possible exception of Robert E. Hall, the New Classicists have not been in the forefront of popular policy debate and have not appeared as energetic sponsors of constitutional amendments; they have opted instead to pursue their mathematical truths. Of course, normative and strategic implications do emerge, sometimes directly from the pens of these theorists. Rational expectations as well as supply-side arguments were incorporated in the Reagan administration's so-called 'rosy scenario', in which inflation and unemployment were forecast to fall simultaneously.

At this stage it seems that the best we can elicit from the approach are certain precautions with respect to policy making, cautions that sound conservative even when they are not derived from explicitly conservative premises. In any event, these theorists appear to favor policies that are less activist, less discretionary, more stable, and based on a respect for consumers rather than governmental sovereignty and omnicompetence. Because we know so little about the so-called 'macro events', we should be extremely cautious about efforts to control them. When one knows so little, being less ambitious and less confident seems in order. Like many Austrians and public choice theorists, rational expectations analysts envisage pervasive policy perversity or at least the high probability of unintended consequences.

Since we know so little about aggregate policies and their micro effects, the rational expectationists advocate greater stability in whatever policies are adopted. Frequent policy changes with the hope of finding dramatic solutions will not do. While this may sound like a policy of despair, it really is not. Rational citizens may not make systematic errors but why confront them with opportunities to tax their already burdened cognitive skills? Frequent policy changes will do that and will have certain known but undesirable consequences. Some citizens will profit more than others, and they may be selected on random grounds. If policies are revised frequently, citizens will spend more time anticipating policy changes than in productive efforts. And perhaps they will also attempt to gain important information earlier and by illegal means. In any event, when policy-making changes create so much uncertainty and conflict, distrust between citizens and governments is apt to increase. One has the feeling, if not the evidence, that stability is so critical that any rule, so long as it is stable, is preferable to changing rules and policies, even if some are more efficient than existing practices. Is this 'second-best' doctrine?

Much of this overall line of reasoning is based on the fundamental assumption or belief that the private market economy is a stable and marvelously efficient institution. The market clears, and when and where it does not is a result of government interference. Unlike Keynesians, rational expectationists have a certain non-rational faith in both the allocative and distributive workings of general equilibrium. Just why the political system has become so pervasive becomes a bit of a problem; if the private economy has worked so well, how can we explain the greater reliance on the political process? Perhaps that is due to the informational disparities and inequities that some economic agents feel should and can be rectified by government. After all, the rational expectationists do not claim that all involuntary unemployment and persistent general rises in price levels are simply definitional and statistical quirks. Or do they? No, they do not. We are told that sticky labor contracts are problematic, as are the errors of some people mistaking movements in money prices for relative price changes.

4   A brief conclusion

While there is much to be said for both Virginia and Chicago it is also clear that profound schisms exist at both theoretical and empirical levels. The two schools differ on such important matters as the role of institutions in political matters, explanations of political choice on the part of voters and politicians, the role of information in the polity and, of course, the overall efficiency of the political system. I doubt that these differences will ever be fully resolved by empirical tests because testing in the social sciences tends to be shaped by analytical and ideological presuppositions and preferences.

Finally, I find it interesting that after more than 40 years of public choice the American Political Science Association has finally given formal recognition to the field by awarding one of its premier book awards to Donald Wittman for his *Myth of Democratic Failure*, a book that systematically attempts to destroy the Virginia school. While most political scientists will not or cannot read the book, its message is one likely to win their approval. Why? Because despite the language of economics, the book gives comfort to the predominantly liberal commitments of political science by declaring that political institutions are, indeed, efficient. They may not be just or equitable, but that can be taken care of by 'the people'. How odd that Stigler, Becker, Posner, and Peltzman might become heroes among political scientists.

2 Property rights: private and political institutions

*Louis De Alessi**

1 Introduction

Economic theory postulates that individuals seek a multitude of goals in a world of unrelieved scarcity. Because individuals must compete with each other for the right to use the resources available, the fundamental economic problem within any society is to evolve a set of rules for controlling competition, that is, for organizing cooperation.

These rules, which are embedded in a society's formal and informal institutions, sanction the range of permissible behavior by specifying the rights that individuals may hold to the use of scarce resources, including their own persons. The resulting system of property rights constrains the choices available to individuals acting on their own behalf or as agents for others, determining how the benefits and harms flowing from a decision are allocated between the individual making it and other members of society (Alchian 1965b).

The central insight of economics, first clearly articulated by Adam Smith ([1776] 1976), is that individuals respond predictably to opportunities for gain. Because the property rights embedded in different institutions confront decision makers with different costs and rewards, offering different opportunities for gain, they affect choices systematically and predictably (De Alessi 1980; Eggertsson 1990; Rutherford 1994; Furubotn and Richter 1997).

Given scarcity, individuals can increase their welfare through specialization and exchange. Specialization in production steers rights to the use of inputs to those activities in which they are more productive, while specialization in consumption steers rights to the use of outputs to those individuals who value them more; exchange provides individuals with the opportunity to specialize in these activities. The archetypal control mechanisms are the market and government.

The market is an institution for organizing cooperation (including redistribution) through voluntary action. Here, prices guide the allocation of property rights by providing individuals both with information and incentives in pursuing their own goals. How well the market process works depends on the extent to which property rights are fully allocated, privately held and voluntarily transferable, conditions that affect and are affected by transaction costs.

Constraints imposed by the system of property rights and transaction costs provide opportunities for other arrangements, including government.

The government is an institution for organizing cooperation (including redistribution) through coercion. Here, government employees make decisions and enforce them through the power of the state. How well this process works depends on the institutions and the success in structuring incentives, acquiring and processing information, and disseminating and enforcing directives. There are costs associated with these activities, too. Moreover, much information regarding individual circumstances of time and place cannot be known and much of what is known is lost in the process of aggregation (Hayek 1945), facilitating rent seeking and related activities.

The distinction between market and government solutions is not planning, but who does it. In a market system, individuals make their own plans, implement them through voluntary exchanges, and bear the economic consequences. In central planning, government employees make the plans and implement them through coercion but do not bear the value consequences.

A caveat is in order. Economics provides a powerful set of tools for examining the evolution and economic consequences of alternative institutions and even why and how certain norms of moral behavior arise, evolve, and interact with formal institutions (Sethi and Somanathan 1996; Benson 1997b). Economics, however, does not provide criteria for deciding which institutions are preferable or even which are more efficient on economic grounds. The choice of benchmark, like any other choice, rests on normative (ethical) values. Thus, there are no objective criteria of desirability or economic efficiency (De Alessi 1983, 1997; Buchanan 1988).

The present chapter examines the nature and economic consequences of market institutions, which rely on private rights, and government institutions, which rely on political rights.

2   Institutions and choice

The basic economic choices are when, how, what, and how much to produce, who receives it, who bears the risk, and who decides. The solutions include setting priorities and ensuring that they are mutually consistent, making relevant information available to those who decide, transmitting decisions, structuring incentives, monitoring performance, providing for innovation, adjusting to change, and accomplishing all these and related activities in a world of uncertainty.

The consequences believed to stem from alternative institutions are affected by the behavioral hypotheses made. Accordingly, it is useful to review those driving economic analysis.

2.1   Behavioral hypotheses

The working postulates of economics are few. Those regarding preferences assert that each individual seeks many goals which are substitutable at the margin, that as an individual achieves more of a goal the relative value attached to further increments falls,[1] and that, for each individual, at least some goals are unfulfilled. These propositions apply to all individuals, regardless of their economic role and the society in which they live.

Goals are difficult to observe and, sometimes, to distinguish from means. After all, the same event may be viewed by some as a goal and by others as a mean. Economists sidestep the ends–means conundrum by focusing on the demand and supply functions of the commodities that individuals use as inputs to pursue their own goals.

Moreover, individuals do not have identical preferences and constraints. Because individuals have incentive to advance the goals that they prefer, the decisions taken by a collection of individuals, such as a family, a business firm, or a government bureau, can be analysed more accurately as the outcome of a decision process (and the institutions governing the process matter) in which members of the group pursue their personal interests. These interests, of course, include the chooser's view of what is best for other individuals and for the group as a whole.

The postulates regarding production assert that inputs are substitutable, that increasing all inputs in the same proportion eventually results in output increasing at a decreasing rate, and that, at the margin, the productivity of any input eventually decreases. Thus, additional units of output eventually can be obtained only at higher cost: supply curves are positively sloped. These postulates apply to all production; in particular, they apply to production within households, firms, and government.

Economic theory yields two major implications. First, individuals respond to a shift in the rate at which they are able to substitute one commodity for another (the structure of relative prices) by consuming more of those commodities that have become relatively cheaper. Thus, the lower the opportunity cost (whatever the chooser has to forgo) of any commodity (whatever the chooser views as a source of satisfaction), the more the chooser will consume: all demand curves are negatively sloped. Second, individuals respond to an increase in the opportunities available to them (an increase in income) by consuming more of all commodities (the usual caveats about inferior goods apply). The ability of individuals to satisfy their wants is then determined by the resources they hold, their productivity, and the system of property rights.

To analyse choices, it is necessary to establish how property rights affect constraints and, thus, the structure of prices, including incomes (Alchian 1967).

2.2   Institutions and property rights

The formal and informal institutions of a society develop spontaneously as well as by design. Whatever their origin, they establish how individuals may behave, given a range of permissible alternatives; that is, they establish how individuals are permitted to benefit and harm themselves and others (Alchian 1965b). Formal institutions perform this function by specifying the legal rights that individuals may hold to the use of resources (including their own persons), to the stream of services the resources yield, and to the transferability of these rights to others. For example, the rules may allow a firm to harm a competitor by producing a better product but not by lowering prices, staying open on Sundays or torching the competitor's plant.

Custom is also a powerful determinant of acceptable behavior, affecting and being affected by formal institutions. In a system based on voluntary exchange, repeated transactions provide the incentive to observe contracts and, more generally, to invest in reputation. Indeed, Benson (1997b, p. 271) argues that, 'as private property rights and their supporting institutions evolve, incentives are created for individuals to behave cooperatively, ethically, and altruistically. On the other hand, institutions designed to produce involuntary transfers of wealth, and therefore, undermine the security of private property rights, also undermine the incentive to behave morally'. Formal laws are more likely to be observed if they are sanctioned by custom (V. Smith 1998) and groups, such as ethnic minorities, bound by norms that proscribe the breach of contract, often prosper in societies with weak legal systems (Landa 1994).

The system of property rights constrains the choices available, including the sorts of contracts that individuals may negotiate. These constraints, acting through actual or imputed prices, establish the structure of incentives, including the expectations that individuals may form in their dealings with others; that is, they determine how the harms and benefits flowing from a decision are allocated between the decision maker and other members of society.

The rules of the game (property rights) reward those individuals who have a comparative advantage in playing the game according to those rules. All societal arrangements, including anarchy, capitalism, and communism, derive their distinguishing characteristics from the structures of their property rights.

2.3   Property rights and choice

The key characteristics of property rights are their exclusivity and transferability. For example, rights may be exclusive and voluntarily transferable (private), neither exclusive nor voluntarily transferable (common with open access), or exclusive but not voluntarily transferable (usufruct). The property rights pertaining to specific resources typically are partitioned and combined in complex bundles that reflect the controlling institutional and contractual arrangements.

The evolution of economic institutions in open markets reflects the costs and benefits to consumers and producers of defining and enforcing various kinds of property rights (North 1990; Ostrom 1990). In coercive systems, other considerations often dominate. A review of the limiting types suggests the range of options available.

Private rights   In every society, the rights to the use of at least some resources are private, that is, exclusive and voluntarily transferable. The owner of the right has the exclusive authority to decide how the resource is used given a set of permissible alternatives; these usually exclude the right to affect the physical attributes of resources owned by others. The owner also has exclusive authority to receive the income generated by the resource and to transfer the right to others at any mutually agreed price. Because owners bear the economic (value) consequences of their decisions, they have incentive to take them into account. In the limit, there are no uncompensated external effects.

The authority to transfer rights implies the opportunity to establish a market for them. Rules that limit transferability by controlling prices and other conditions of exchange reduce the bundle of private property rights and, consequently, the value consequences that the chooser bears.

In an open market, prices are determined by demand and supply conditions that reflect expectations regarding future events. Thus, the value consequences of future events are capitalized into current transfer prices and reflected in owners' wealth. Intermediaries cast dollar votes on behalf of future generations and bear the value consequences of their decisions.

Private property means that individuals have the right to transact with others on any mutually agreeable terms within the institutional boundaries. Private owners can choose to use the rights themselves, rent or lease them to others, or give them away, and can contract with others to form organizations such as single proprietorships, partnerships, corporations, cooperatives, and charitable foundations.

Common (communal) rights   'Common' property covers a confusing array of alternatives, from open access enforced by the state to private ownership shared by several individuals. These arrangements have drastically different outcomes, and it is important to keep them straight.

Under open access, anyone in the group (a country, the world) has the right to use the resource and capture its fruits on a first-come, first-served basis. Because private property rights in such resources can be established only through extraction (catching the fish, harvesting the timber), there is little incentive to conserve. Relative to private ownership, resources are harvested earlier and more intensively and receive little, if any, investment. The tragedy of the commons can result.

Under private ownership shared by several individuals, access and use of the resource is restricted to members of the group and controlled by strict rules. There are incentives to conserve.

Open access can occur voluntarily when the value of a resource at the margin is sufficiently low relative to the costs of organizing group or individual ownership. An increase in the value of a resource or a decline in the cost of controlling it supplies incentives to establish group or individual ownership (Demsetz 1967). For example, early settlers in New England held some land in private and other in various communal arrangements (Field 1985); as land became more valuable, most of the commons shifted to individual ownership.[2] In the American West, the development of barbed wire lowered the costs of enforcing exclusivity and encouraged a change from open range to individual ownership (Anderson and Hill 1975). Voluntary communal arrangements are used throughout the world, often next to individual ownership, to manage forests, fisheries, and other resources (Ostrom 1990; M. De Alessi 1998).

Open access and communal ownership also arise from state coercion, often the result of rent-seeking activities. For example, in the United States antitrust laws have been used to nullify some voluntary communal arrangements and enforce open access (Johnson and Libecap 1982), while eminent domain has been used to convert private land to parks with either open or controlled use.

Usufruct rights   Usufruct rights may be voluntary, such as renting or leasing. These contracts, which facilitate the flow of resources to higher-valued uses, are limited by the possibility of opportunistic behavior. For example, a bank may lease computers but will own the vault, which is firm-specific.

Usufruct rights may also be coercive. Rights that are exclusive but not legally transferable cannot flow to their more productive uses and the individuals who hold them are unable to capitalize the future consequences of their decisions into current transfer prices; output is smaller and investments are fewer and shorter-lived. For example, Mexican farmers allotted land under the *ejido* program cannot legally sell it or lease it and can lose it if they do not work it for two consecutive years. Relative to private owners, they invest less in irrigation and other activities, use more labor, and are less likely to grow crops with long gestation periods (De Vany 1977).

Political rights   Rights to the use, income, and transferability of some resources may be held or regulated by the state. Then, state employees have the authority, following sanctioned political procedures, to decide how a right, such as the right to exclude certain groups, may be used.

The economic implications of government ownership and regulation are examined in a subsequent section. For the present, note that these arrangements attenuate the link between the welfare of decision makers and the economic consequences of their choices.

Partitioning and bundling of rights   The rights to the use of many resources are partitioned: some private, some usufruct, some communal, and some political. For example, a farmer may hold private rights to a parcel of land, a cattleman may have leased the right to graze cattle on it, a neighbor may own the right (easement) to cross it, everyone in the community may hold the right to dump noise and smoke on it, and the state may own the right to run utilities under it and to regulate the height of structures built on it.

Under private ownership, voluntary partitioning of rights provides flexibility in their use, facilitating their combination into convenient bundles and easing their flow to higher-valued uses.

Law   Systems of property rights typically include provisions for changing the rules and settling disputes. Conflicts can arise when individuals disagree about the partitioning of rights they intended in a contract or when the choices made by owners of some rights impinge on the rights of others. Enforcement of the rules, including resolution of conflicts, can take place through governmental (police and courts) or non-governmental channels (private security and arbitration).

In common law jurisdictions, statute and common law often compete in addressing conflicts. Unlike statute law, common law allows people to contract around it. This option buttresses a system of private property rights by reducing opportunities for rent seeking, facilitating adaptation to local circumstances and affording protection often displaced by statutes (Yandle 1997; Brubaker 1998).

2.4   Transaction costs

Transaction costs, defined as the costs of acquiring and processing information and of negotiating, writing, and policing contracts, affect and are affected by the system of property rights.

Transaction costs affect the choice of institutions, including the extent to which the system relies on private property rights. Of course, institutions may also be chosen because they benefit politically powerful groups, because their consequences are not well understood, because they are believed to advance certain normative values, or by a conjunction of these and other interests – a conjunction that seems to explain the persistent appeal of central planning.

Given the institutions, transaction costs then affect the choice of contracts used to organize economic activity. For example, transaction costs explain why some activities are integrated within a firm and others are contracted out (Alchian and Demsetz 1972; Joskow 1988).

The system of property rights, in turn, affects transaction costs. Institutions inhibiting the transfer of private rights raise transaction costs and reduce exchange. State ownership limits the opportunity and the incentive of government employees to trade rights among themselves and with outsiders, while government regulation limits private rights and raises transaction costs by setting side conditions on market exchanges.

3   The private (market) solution

The market is a low-cost institution for organizing cooperation in production and consumption through the voluntary exchange of rights to the use of resources. How well the market works depends on the structure of transaction costs and the reliance on private property rights.

3.1   Markets

Market institutions provide individuals, who are familiar with their own particular circumstances of time and place, with the opportunity to exchange rights to the use of resources and, through signals transmitted by prices, with the information and incentive to allocate these rights to their highest-valued uses. Thus, the market is a powerful mechanism for channeling competition toward cooperation in economic activities, fostering specialization in production and consumption; the amount of output produced is larger and its characteristics and distribution are determined by demand and supply.

Prices are simply the rates at which bundles of property rights are exchanged for each other; they exist in every economic system. In a political system, the nominal (money) price of a commodity frequently is a small fraction of the bundle of resource rights given up, which may include maintaining an information network, waiting in line, bribing clerks and officials, and so on. In a market system, prices reflect the rate at which individuals can actually exchange one bundle of rights for another. Because the opportunity cost of a choice can be observed more cheaply, market prices are more effective in providing information and incentives. Thus, constraints on prices, such as ceilings or floors, typically inhibit the solution of the underlying problem.

In a market system, individuals are rewarded according to the value of their contributions to the welfare of others as the latter see it. That is, the welfare of individuals is tied to their success in producing the kinds of commodities that others desire and in adjusting their own consumption in light of the wants of others. Unlike the political arena, where individuals formally have one vote and cannot easily express the intensity of their preferences, the market allows individuals to concentrate their dollar votes in pursuit of those goals they value most.

In an open market with large numbers of buyers and sellers, individuals considering an exchange are price takers: sellers are unable to negotiate a price above the going market price and buyers are unable to negotiate a price below it. Under these conditions, the only decision to be made is whether or not to trade (and, if so, how much) at the going rate.

Private rights tie the welfare of individuals to the value consequences of their choices. Thus, they provide decision makers with the incentive to take these consequences into account by cooperating with others and specializing in those production and consumption activities in which they have a comparative advantage, by exchanging commodities with other individuals so that each party ends up with a preferred consumption basket, and by discovering new opportunities for gain, including technological and institutional innovations. Institutional limits on private rights, including those imposed by government ownership and regulation, weaken the tie between the welfare of individuals and the value consequences of their decisions, reducing their incentive to cooperate with others and encouraging rent seeking.

Transaction costs reduce the flow of information and the gains from trade. Thus, they also weaken the tie between the welfare of individuals and the value consequences of their decisions.

3.2 *Cooperation in production*
Cooperation in production lets individuals specialize in those activities in which they have a comparative advantage, including working with other individuals within a firm.

Individuals have incentive to allocate their private property rights to those uses yielding the highest increase in value; all parties to the trade are better off as a result and the value of output is greater. For example, workers have incentive to seek the highest compensation, including job-related non-pecuniary income, and thus gravitate to those activities in which they are more productive. Similarly, employers have incentive to pay higher wages to more productive employees and to choose an input–output configuration that maximizes profits.

Indeed, private property rights tend to flow toward the same uses regardless of their initial assignment (Coase 1960).[3] The rationale is straightforward: whoever attaches the highest value to a resource right keeps it, if he or she already owns it, or acquires it, if owned by someone else. The lower are transaction costs, the greater is the extent to which this process is carried out.

To survive and prosper, entrepreneurs in a market system seek opportunities for profit by introducing new products or by increasing the quality or lowering the production cost of existing products.[4] If they are successful, they attract competitors, profits are squeezed out, and survivors earn the competitive rate of return. Competition forces price (the value that consumers attach to a unit of output) toward marginal cost (the value of the goods that the inputs could have produced in their next best use) and all mutually beneficial trade is exhausted.

Entrepreneurs also capture gains by devising contracts that lower transaction costs. For example, owners of resource rights have incentive to work together as a team when their joint output is greater than the sum of the outputs they could have produced separately. If performance is costly to monitor, however, each member of the team has incentive to shirk, enjoying the full benefits of their own reduced effort while bearing only a share of the corresponding loss in output. Firms and other contracts evolve to solve the shirking-information problem of joint production (Alchian and Demsetz 1972).

The particular form of business organization depends on how the controlling institutions and the nature of the industry affect the costs and benefits of alternative contractual arrangements. Solutions include single proprietorships, partnerships, corporations, and non-profits as well as cooperatives and other employee-owned forms of organization (for example, Butler and Ribstein 1995; Hansman 1996).

If team size can be large and monitoring costs are relatively low, then large-scale production may evolve with employer–employee contracts. For example, the modern corporation with transferable shares, limited liability, and indefinite life evolved to lower the cost of raising large sums of capital when investment in a firm's specific assets is substantial and long-lived (De Alessi and Fishe 1987). Transferability lowers costs to current and prospective shareholders of revising their portfolios, allowing shares to flow to those individuals who have a comparative advantage in their use; specialization in ownership concentrates benefits from monitoring and efforts to replace ineffective management. Shareholders who believe that a firm is badly managed can form a coalition to replace the managers or unilaterally sell their shares, making it easier for others to acquire control and replace management. Limited liability lowers transaction costs by reducing the demand for information about current and prospective shareholders on the part of creditors and other shareholders. Indefinite life reduces transaction costs by relaxing the constraints on the frequency and timing of liquidating a firm's specific assets.

Within the corporation, shareholders own the assets specific to the firm, bear the value consequences of exogenous events and decisions made within the firm, and hold ultimate control over managers. Bondholders own the assets that are not specific to the firm (or, at least, not subject to moral hazard) and monitor the firm's compliance with the loan agreements. Managers, acting as agents for stockholders, specialize in day-to-day monitoring and decision making within the firm. Other resource owners contract to provide use of their rights. The success of the coalition then depends on its success in choosing managers and other key personnel, adopting contracts that provide suitable incentives, and taking advantage of unexpected events (Alchian 1984).

Under open-market conditions, competition from other firms as well as from current and prospective members of the team, such as managers and potential shareholders, inhibits shirking and induces managers to seek to maximize owners' wealth. Competitive forces thus foster lower production costs and prices, higher quality, and innovation. A market system rewards producers for their success in reducing scarcity and satisfying consumer wants.

3.3 *Cooperation in consumption*

Exchange, with or without production, allows individuals to obtain and consume a preferred combination of commodities, making others better off while fulfilling more of their own goals.

A necessary condition for exchange is that, at the margin, individuals attach different relative values to commodities. Differences in these marginal rates of substitution may occur because of differences in tastes or in the endowment of resources, which arise from differences in natural skills, investment in human capital and control over other assets. As a prerequisite for trade, however, why these personal rates of substitution differ is irrelevant; what matters is that they are different, thereby creating an opportunity for mutual gain. Exchange allows individuals to specialize in consumption, fulfilling more of those goals that they view as relatively more valuable.

Although differences in the subjective rates of substitution are necessary for trade, they are not sufficient. The extent of trade, including whether it takes place at all, also depends on the constraints imposed by transaction costs and the system of property rights.

4 Limitations of the private (market) solution

The market process is a powerful mechanism for the dissemination and utilization of knowledge, providing individuals with the incentive to search for and, through voluntary exchange, take advantage of opportunities to improve their welfare by cooperating with others. In the limit, the market solution is Pareto efficient: it is impossible to make someone better off without making someone else worse off. Real-world institutional and cost constraints, however, can yield consequences that deviate from Pareto criteria of efficiency and other value-laden constructs.

4.1   Institutional constraints

Even market-oriented institutions frequently embody constraints that inhibit market processes. Some constraints arise unintentionally from limited knowledge, including limited understanding of the economic consequences of alternative institutions. Others arise because better alternatives are too costly. Still others are imposed to modify market outcomes and reallocate wealth. Indeed, consequences resulting from constraints on market processes often are blamed on the market and used to justify rent-seeking arrangements. Once established, institutions are difficult to change.

Formal and informal institutional constraints on private ownership are pervasive. For example, some rights may be inalienable (individuals may not sell themselves into slavery) while others may be constrained by such variables as age (minors may not have the right to buy cigarettes), health (only cancer patients may have the right to buy marijuana), time (grocery stores may not open on Sunday), location (a liquor store may not locate close to another one), special qualifications (only licensed doctors of medicine may prescribe some drugs), custom (some foods may be taboo), type of activity (a bank may not sell insurance), and other considerations such as sex and race.

4.2   Transaction costs

Transaction costs inhibit the definition, assignment, enforcement, and exchange of private property rights. Thus, some rights may not be fully defined (some eventualities may not be worth covering), assigned (most migratory fish and birds are owned in common), enforced (not all trespassers are detected, tried, and convicted) or exchanged (a good no longer wanted may be put in the dustbin). Rights still flow to higher-valued uses, but the uses often differ from – and are lesser valued than – those that would have been chosen if transaction costs had been lower.

4.3   General problems

Institutional constraints and transaction costs, jointly and separately, weaken the relationship between the welfare of individuals and the economic consequences of their choices. This divergence may yield results that some view as undesirable, such as external effects, production of too few 'public' goods, and welfare losses from monopoly. Moreover, some individuals fault outcomes that would also be generated by an ideal market system, such as catering to tastes they dislike (rock concerts instead of operas) and an unequal distribution of income.

Externalities   In a neoclassical world of zero transaction costs, the way in which private rights to the use of resources are employed does not depend upon their initial assignment – keeping in mind that wealth effects generally can be disregarded (Coase 1960). Whoever attaches the highest value to a resource right either keeps it, thereby forgoing compensation from selling it, or acquires it, thereby paying compensation. Regardless of the initial assignment, both parties must take into account the opportunity cost of the right. Because individuals bear the full value consequences of their decisions, they have incentive to take them fully into account; there are no external effects.

Coase's fundamental insight was to recognize the reciprocal nature of the problem. Using the example of damage to crops by straying cattle, he argued that 'it is true that there would be no crop damage without the cattle. It is equally true that there would be no crop damage without the crops. ... [I]t is therefore desirable that both parties should take the harmful effect (the nuisance) into account in deciding on their course of action' (p. 13). As Coase then noted, 'it is one of the beauties of a smoothly operating pricing system that ... the fall in the value of production due to the harmful effect would be a cost for both parties' (ibid.).

Conventional wisdom, buttressed by Pigou's (1920) classic work on welfare, holds that state action is necessary to attenuate externalities, with taxes used to reduce harmful effects and subsidies to encourage beneficial ones. This approach, however, ignores the reciprocal nature of the problem: 'Without the tax, there may be too much smoke and too few people in the vicinity of the factory; but with the tax there may be too little smoke and too many people. ... There is no reason to suppose that one of these results is necessarily preferable' (Coase 1960, p. 42).

Under open-market conditions, individuals have incentive to develop contractual and institutional arrangements for reducing external effects. For example, shopping malls internalize harms and benefits arising from adjacent independent stores. Indeed, if these complexes affect the value of surrounding land, the developers have incentive to purchase it and then sell it with suitable covenants, thereby inducing all parties to take the relevant costs into account (Demsetz 1964). In an open market, firms that spill harms can lose reputation and wealth as concerned consumers switch to more responsive producers (Yandle 1998).

If an externality exists, the next consideration is whether it is relevant. On Pareto criteria, an externality is relevant if 'the activity may be modified in such a way that the externally affected party, *A*, can be made better off without the acting party, *B*, being made worse off' (Buchanan and Stubblebine 1962, p. 374). Because a Pareto equilibrium may exist even though one party is imposing marginal external harm on the other, without additional information the observation of external effects is insufficient to establish the desirability of a change in existing arrangements: 'The internal benefits from carrying out the activity, net of costs, may be greater than the external damage that is imposed on other parties' (ibid., p. 381). Not every externality is worth internalizing.

Still, some externalities may be sufficiently great (for example, substantial air pollution) that collective action is desirable. Possible solutions include the development of new property relations, such as pollution rights, that provide scope for government action.

The problem of externalities often is overstated not only by those who use them to advance their special interests but also by those who do not understand how markets work. Moreover, many situations thought to give rise to external effects may not do so (Boudreaux 1996a).

The small-numbers case   In the small-numbers case, say two parties, there is no single price as would exist in an open market with large numbers of buyers and sellers. Instead, there is a set of prices ranging between the two personal price ratios that limit the gains from trade. Because both buyer and seller have incentive to engage in strategic behavior, one or both may stake out positions that reduce or even prevent mutually beneficial trade. The possibility of strategic behavior is enhanced in the case of repeat transactions, when one or both parties may seek to establish reputations as hard bargainers in order to strike better deals in the future.

Strategic behavior, however, need not inhibit the allocation of rights even if it inhibits exchange (ibid.).[5] As long as the parties bargain with each other, the buy and sell offers establish the opportunities forgone and, therefore, the costs of the choice. Thus, resources flow to their higher-valued uses whether or not they change hands. There are no external effects.

The large-numbers case   The large-numbers case is said to arise when many individuals wish to purchase a right from – or sell a right to – one or more individuals, and the cost of creating a market for the exchange, say by organizing the many, is too great.

The initial consideration is whether an externality exists. For example, let the developer of a large tract of land build a smoke-spewing factory and then sell the adjoining land to homeowners. The harm occasioned by the smoke is reflected in lower land prices and is taken into account by all parties to the exchange. The developer bears the full cost of the harm and the homeowners are fully compensated. Thus, even though the smoke from the factory harms the property of many, there is no externality. Developments are common techniques for internalizing many external effects and handling the provision of public or collective goods (Foldvary 1994).

If an externality exists, whether it is relevant has to be established empirically. Such a determination is fundamentally intractable because values (including costs) are subjective – that is, they cannot be measured objectively by an outside observer – and must be aggregated across the groups of individuals affected. In the absence of some market arrangement, an outside observer could not determine which group attaches a higher value to the right: the consumers of the product of a polluting factory or those harmed by the pollution. The solution of relevant externalities arguably lies in developing institutions that lower transaction costs.

Samuelsonian public goods   Transaction costs also give rise to Samuelsonian public goods, defined as goods (or services) for which the amount consumed by one individual does not detract from anyone else's consumption and from which exclusion is not possible at low cost (Samuelson 1954). Examples are radio and television signals: one more person tuning in a program does not reduce the quality of the signal available to others and anyone with a receiver can listen to or watch programs broadcast in the clear.

Because a public good can be consumed concurrently by many consumers, its market demand is obtained by adding individual demand curves vertically (rather than horizontally) and output is determined by the interaction of demand and supply. Individuals, however, often conceal their preferences (Kuran 1995) and consumers of public goods have special incentive to misrepresent their willingness to pay and free ride. Accordingly, higher transaction costs, such as the cost of excluding non-payers, lower the profitability of private production and output may be smaller than people are actually willing to pay for.

In many cases, of course, the cost of excluding non-payers is low enough that the price–output combination can be chosen under market or quasi-market conditions. Individuals have incentive to develop technical and contractual innovations that induce consumers to reveal their preferences and thus allow producers to be compensated for producing the 'right' amount. Examples are satellite and cable television, which control access and can charge for individual programs.

Monopoly   A monopolist is a seller who faces a negatively sloped demand curve for its product. In an open market, monopoly may arise from the non-reproducible characteristics of a commodity, such as a singer's voice or a retailer's location; information costs, including the costs of finding alternatives and determining quality; catering to the tastes of a small group of consumers; collusion, which typically is short-lived without government sanction; and economies of scale, which describe the lower per-unit cost of producing a larger planned volume of output.

If economies of scale are substantial relative to demand, then only a relatively small number of firms survive. The result can be an industry populated by a few large, seemingly powerful firms – the common concept of monopoly. Limiting cases are so-called 'natural monopolies' with only one firm; the list used to include electric power, gas, railroads, telephone, sewage, and water supply.

One criticism of monopoly is that it misallocates resources. Because a monopolist charges a price above marginal cost,[6] not all mutually beneficial trade is exhausted; using the purely competitive solution as a benchmark, a monopolist produces too little and charges too much.

This argument, however, is flawed. In an open market, price and marginal cost differ only if transaction costs inhibit buyers and seller from striking a bargain. If the parties could form and enforce a contract whereby consumers paid the maximum that each was willing to pay for each additional unit, then, in equilibrium, price would equal cost at the margin and output would equal the purely competitive solution. In practice, many firms do engage in price discrimination, moving closer to the competitive output. Moreover, in some circumstances firms can compete for the right to serve the whole market, again yielding the purely competitive solution (Demsetz 1968).

The other major criticism of monopoly is that its owners capture monopoly profits at the expense of consumers. This criticism also is flawed; in an open market, monopoly increases the welfare of consumers. First, monopoly does not assure profits. Indeed, in open markets under equilibrium conditions price is equal to average cost; there are no monopoly profits, and commodities are provided at prices below those that would prevail if maximum firm size were set by law. Second, many supposed barriers to entry, such as large outlays on advertising campaigns or on capital equipment, simply neglect the costs of creating and maintaining a good reputation, bearing the risk of innovation, and building a scale of operations appropriate to consumers' demand (Demsetz 1982). Third, profits play a major role in guiding the allocation of resources. They encourage innovation and entrepreneurship, both crucial in promoting economic growth. Fourth, monopolies due to product differentiation arise from catering to the wants of specific groups of customers. Thus, they increase users' welfare and product variety, which is itself an economic good. Fifth, monopoly profits historically are short-lived in the absence of government sanction. Finally, there is no ethically neutral judgment on how the gains from trade, which depend on the system of property rights and the choices of those trading, ought to be distributed.

Much of the concern with private monopoly in open markets is overstated, with the solutions often creating more difficulties than the problems they were intended to solve. For example, in the United States annual welfare losses from all monopolies have been estimated at less than 1 percent of gross national product (Harberger 1954) while government programs to control the allocation of resources and the distribution of income have been estimated to reduce GNP by at least 25 percent (Brozen 1990).

The distribution of income   The market system has been criticized for generating an unequal distribution of income. Although the judgment that one
distribution of income is preferable to another is an ethical issue, economic
theory can be used to examine differences in the nature and distribution of
income associated with alternative economic systems.

In a market system, the distribution of income reflects the initial allocation
of resources and the contributions made to the welfare of others through
specialization in production and consumption. Because the market links welfare to productivity, output is higher than under alternative arrangements.
Moreover, government policies intended to reduce income inequalities can
easily be counterproductive by reducing the opportunities for gain and the
incentive to pursue them. Empirically, once in-kind transfers are taken into
account, income in market systems is substantially higher and more equally
distributed than in centrally directed economies.

Interestingly, the modern record of economic growth in open economies
suggests that income equality first falls and then rises (Fields 1980). This
result presumably reflects the initial gains reaped by successful entrepreneurs
followed by an increased demand for labor and broader-based investments in
human capital.

5   The political (government) solution

Although the movement from anarchy to some form of government is predictable, the processes whereby particular forms of political control arise and
grow are not well understood. Explanations include lowering transaction
costs; remedying limitations of the market; a taste for using the political
process;[7] lack of knowledge of the consequences; and wealth redistribution
(to seek rents or modify behavior).

The actual or fancied reasons for political solutions affect behavior only to
the extent that they are reflected in effective constraints. A comprehensive
examination of the full range of political institutions is beyond the scope of
this section, which is limited to examining the consequences of the political
property rights supposedly established to lower transaction costs and alleviate limitations of the market process.

5.1   Contracting out

One option for correcting a market limitation, such as too little output of
some public good, is to contract out for private production and distribution. If
the process is competitive, private contractors will have incentive to minimize the cost of producing the output specified. Central planners, however,
choose the product specifications, quantity, and price. Inevitably, political
and other considerations promoted by the agency's cost–reward structure
dominate decisions. Moreover, in some cases the cost of ensuring that output

meets specifications may be high enough to encourage integration of production within government.

5.2   Regulation

The demand and supply of regulation are driven by considerations other than alleviating market limitations (McChesney 1997). The evidence suggests that regulation typically is established and operated for the benefit of the industries and occupations being regulated and of the regulatory agencies. Entrepreneurs have incentive to demand state support to restrict entry, enforce collusion, and pursue other wealth-increasing activities. Correspondingly, politicians and other government employees have incentive to favor organized pressure groups, extort tribute, and expand their activities. Evidence from a variety of industries indicates that regulation results in higher prices, lower output and greater wealth for the firm's owners (De Alessi 1995).

Although those to be regulated may be successful in capturing the regulatory mechanism, it does not follow that they reap the full monopoly rents. Among other reasons, transfer of control from the market to the political arena admits other rent seekers to the decision-making process, and these will exact their own payoffs. As a result, regulated firms typically are subject to a profit constraint, attenuating owners' property rights and increasing managers' discretionary authority.

Not all regulation may be intended to benefit those to be regulated. Even in these cases, however, at best it is evidence of a desire to regulate rather than of effective regulation. Regulators' budgets and wisdom are limited and their incentive to regulate effectively is deflected by the cost–reward structure built into the regulatory institution. Regulating an industry in the 'public interest' allows considerable scope for interpretation, and those with private interests at stake have incentive to press their own version.

The taxicab industry, which in some cities is regulated by independent commissions and in others by government bureaus, offers an example of how institutions affect regulatory activity (Eckert 1973). Commissioners typically are appointed by the executive; their salaries and terms of office are set by statute that can only be changed by the legislature and apply equally to all members of a commission. Bureau heads typically are career civil servants whose terms of office are open-ended and whose salary is responsive to individual performance, increasing through promotion, size of staff, budget, and case load administered. Because the compensation of individual commissioners is less dependent upon their own activities and those of their agencies, they have less incentive than government bureau heads to regulate actively. The evidence suggests that they are more likely to establish work-easing market practices, including single monopolies and simpler tariff structures (ibid.).

Scholars once believed that at least antitrust did more good than harm. Recent evidence, however, suggests that antitrust activity in the United States and elsewhere has been dominated by bureaucratic and political considerations rather than by economic measures of monopoly power and has been directed at practices that enhance rather than impede competition (McChesney and Shughart 1995). In particular, antitrust has been used to deter entry, stifle innovation, and raise prices.

5.3 Production

As noted earlier, some commodities are produced within government to deter opportunistic behavior by private contractors. For example, terms such as 'in the public interest', which frequently appear in legislation, are not specific enough to define the relevant rights and duties; a contract containing such terms would be difficult to enforce. The higher is the cost of seeing that the output produced by outside contractors meets specifications, the greater is contractors' opportunity to shirk. As these costs rise relative to the cost of monitoring inputs when production is integrated vertically, there is incentive to produce within government (De Alessi 1982). For example, governments typically buy office supplies but produce foreign policy internally.

Political firms and private firms, however, embody different incentive structures. A crucial distinction is that ownership shares in political firms are not transferable. This constraint blocks the flow of rights to those who have a comparative advantage in their use and rules out specialization in ownership, raising the cost of forming coalitions and dissipating the gains from improving a firm's performance. Taxpayers who are dissatisfied with the behavior of their political firms or do not wish to bear risk in their operation cannot simply sell their shares; they must move to a community with a preferred portfolio of political firms or try to change the firms' behavior through the political process – both costly activities. Moreover, the lack of transferable shares rules out the capitalization of future consequences into current transfer prices, reducing the information available to judge performance and guide the allocation of resources as well as inhibiting the incentive to monitor by reducing the gains from improved management.

Lack of transferable shares implies that managers of political firms have greater opportunity for discretionary behavior than do managers of comparable private firms. They have incentive to give less weight to the value consequences of their decisions and more weight to political considerations, including pressure from their customers and other special-interest groups. Private enterprises are subject to the discipline of the market and must respond to market signals to survive. Managers of political firms are less constrained by market considerations, finding it easier to obtain subsidies and mask utility-maximizing behavior under the guise of fulfilling other social goals. Indeed, political firms, especially those endowed with politically powerful clients, can survive and prosper in the presence of gross mismanagement.

The pecuniary and non-pecuniary benefits accruing to managers of political firms, including longevity in office, typically bear little relation, if any, to their effectiveness in solving alleged limitations of the market process. Relative to comparable private firms, for example, municipal electric firms charge prices that favor business customers relative to residential customers and voters relative to non-voters, relate prices less closely to demand and supply conditions, change prices less frequently (and require larger changes in underlying market data before responding), have greater production capacities, spend more on plant construction, have higher operating costs, are slower to adopt cost-reducing innovations, offer a smaller variety of output, are less successful in satisfying consumer wants, and maintain managers in office longer (De Alessi 1980).

Political firms also may be expected to generate external harms. In the United States, for example, municipal sewage systems have been major polluters. Indeed, given the incentive structure, which typically shields them from liability, political firms are more likely to generate harm than comparable private firms.

5.4   *Taxes and subsidies*
Taxes and subsidies, often masked, are frequently justified on the ground that they correct market limitations. Although in some cases that may well be the intention, in practice their main function is wealth redistribution.

6   Special limitations of political solutions
Transaction costs and institutional constraints, which vastly reduce the information and incentives provided by market prices, impose special restrictions on political solutions.

6.1   *Aggregating individual information*
A great deal of information is local, linked to individuals' personal circumstances of time and place. Indeed, information such as the 'art' inherent to many activities is simply impossible to convey; it can only be learned through experience. Because much of the information that is time and place specific either cannot be known or is lost in the process of aggregation, central planners – who must deal with aggregate data – make decisions based on incomplete and inaccurate knowledge (Hayek 1945).

Similarly, central directives necessarily apply to broad aggregates and fail to deal with individual circumstances of time and place. For example, federal regulators have incentive to establish water quality standards that apply nationwide. But even if a rule makes sense in one watershed, it may not in another. Political solutions are inherently procrustean.

6.2 Measuring values

Another facet of the information problem is that the benefits and costs of a choice depend on the preferences and constraints specific to the chooser, and reflect the alternatives and the consequences that the chooser selected for consideration (Buchanan 1969). Thus, values are wholly subjective and continually revised in response to new knowledge.

Market prices at best (under equilibrium conditions in the absence of side provisions and corner solutions) reveal the value that an individual attaches to an additional unit of a commodity. They do not reveal the value that the individual attaches to the inframarginal units; that is, prices do not measure the gains from trade. Because prices measure value at the margin, they are ideally suited to guide the allocation of rights from lower- to higher-valued uses. Precisely for that reason, however, they are not very useful for measuring total values.

If a market exists, central planners at best know the expected higher-valued use of a right only after a trade is consummated. They have no objective knowledge of the values that each actual or potential trader attached to the right and to the next best opportunities; of the existence of side conditions, which often are implicit; of possible variations during the bargaining process in the values and alternatives considered by the parties; and of strategic behavior on the part of the parties (Boudreaux and Meiners 1998). Central planners have no reliable source of information about values.

6.3 Structuring incentives

For reasons already discussed, political constraints do not provide central planners given the task of alleviating market limitations with the incentive to do so. Indeed, those who set the constraints have incentive to structure them in a way that facilitates their own rent-seeking activities. Because central planners do not bear the economic consequences of their decisions, they have incentive to take them into account only in so far as they generate bribes, reverberate through the political process, or affect their personal utility directly.

The extension of economic theory to public choices and massive evidence indicate that government officials adopt and implement policies designed to increase their own welfare, say by staying in office longer and increasing their power and wealth (McChesney 1997). And such behavior seems independent of the ideology of the political party in power (Meltzer 1991).

6.4   *Inhibiting rent seeking*

Special-interest groups have incentive to claim that a market limitation is causing them harm and seek the power of the state to achieve goals that they want but are unable or unwilling to obtain otherwise. At the same time, government employees (including politicians running for office) have incentive to supply, and to stimulate the demand for, their services (McChesney 1997).

For example, suppose that a group would like a particular wetland preserved for migrating ducks. Market solutions would be for the group to lease or buy the wetland; political solutions would be to lobby the government to lease or buy the wetland at taxpayers' expense or pass a law requiring incumbent owners to preserve the wetland. Which option the group chooses depends in part upon the system of property rights, including the propensity of the legislatures and courts to reassign (take) private rights without compensation.

Changes in the rules that make taking either easier or more difficult have broad implications for political solutions. For example, a rule that allows taking without full compensation reduces the incentive to conserve threatened property and increases the incentive to make it less attractive to those who might take it. In the long run, such a rule is counterproductive and divisive.

6.5   *Establishing reciprocity of costs*

Taxing the owners of a smoke-emitting factory an amount equal to the harm caused (assuming it could be measured) would induce them to take the harm into account and reduce the emission of smoke. Unless the nearby residents were taxed an amount equal to the costs incurred by the factory's owners (the amount of the tax plus the additional costs of reducing emissions), however, they would lack the incentive to take these costs into account and either move out of the area or take other precautions that would reduce the harm, even if their costs of doing so were lower than those incurred by the factory's owners.

Political solutions seldom provide such reciprocity, which is inherent to market solutions. For instance, the market for pollution rights is expected to reduce the quantity of resources used to achieve a given level of pollution abatement by inducing lower-cost producers to specialize in the task. The level of abatement, however, is set in the political arena and the costs of abatement are borne by the owners of polluting firms and their customers. The costs are not reciprocal.

6.6   *Promoting innovation and adjustment to change*

Once established, government controls are difficult to change. Among other reasons, government employees lack the incentive and vested interests can mount powerful opposition.

The comparison of alternative institutional arrangements usually focuses on the respective static equilibrium conditions expected to prevail. Such comparisons, however, ignore much relevant information and may be grossly misleading (De Alessi 1997).

Individuals make choices in a world of uncertainty occasioned by new knowledge, new institutional constraints, population dynamics, the vagaries of nature, and other phenomena. When anticipations change, some individuals modify their choices and thereby help nudge the economic system toward a new equilibrium. Long before that equilibrium is reached, however, new changes in anticipations generate a shift toward a new equilibrium. And so it goes. Based on an initial set of anticipations, equilibrium conditions, whether static or dynamic, are seldom attained. As a result, the process for adjusting to unanticipated change matters.

An economic system based on private property rights transmits information quickly and cheaply while simultaneously providing individuals with the incentive to adjust to change quickly and accurately. It also establishes the incentive to discover new and more productive ways of using resources, encouraging the introduction of new commodities, new production techniques, and new contractual arrangements that lower transaction costs and facilitate the internalization of external effects (Kirzner 1997). Neglecting the process of discovery and adjustment associated with alternative institutions biases the comparison in favor of bureaucratic solutions.

6.7 Inhibiting external and unintended effects

Government employees, like private managers, make decisions that have external effects, including some that are unintended and undesired. Government employees, however, have less incentive to develop new institutional and contractual arrangements to internalize these effects. They do have the incentive to blame allegedly undesirable events on the market and seek to extend government control, thereby increasing their agencies' budgets and their own welfare.

6.8 Establishing a benchmark

Suppose that all the problems just discussed are solved somehow and that government decision makers have to choose among alternatives which, as usual, entail different distributions of income. Unless the losers are fully compensated (as they see it), the choice necessarily entails a value judgment. There simply is no set of criteria that provides a value-free benchmark for aggregating individual gains and losses and for deciding whether the losses suffered by some are greater or smaller than the gains enjoyed by others.

Current institutional constraints yield policies reflecting the criteria and interests of those with a comparative advantage in the use of political power.

Not surprisingly, the special-interest groups dominating the decision process exhibit little concern for the protection of individual liberty and private property rights.

7   Political solutions to market limitations
Even when political solutions represent a genuine attempt to alleviate limitations of the market, the restrictions just discussed inhibit success.

7.1   Externalities
The problem of externalities raises the full range of government-specific problems. Because central planners typically seek to deal with externalities through government controls rather than market or quasi-market institutions, the remedies rarely are effective and typically raise more problems than they solve. Indeed, central plans generate substantial externalities of their own.

7.2   Samuelsonian public goods
The market limitation arises from the cost of excluding non-payers. Thus, consumers have incentive to mask their demand curves and to understate the values that they attach to public goods; output is smaller than if transaction costs were zero.

Central planners, however, also lack information about consumers' demand curves. Planners have incentive to use public funds to produce public goods (including essentially private goods with a public component) to win support from special-interest groups; concurrently, consumers have incentive to overstate the value they attach to a public good and form coalitions to obtain a subsidy from taxpayers. Subsidies deny useful demand information and result in greater quantity demanded. Output is larger than the market outcome under zero transaction costs, which is not an obvious improvement, and resources are diverted from other uses.

7.3   Monopoly
When significant monopoly power exists, political regulation to promote competition may seem useful. The typical outcome of such regulation, however, is to insulate monopolies from competition and to extend their lives beyond the short span they would have experienced otherwise or to hobble successful firms for the benefit of competitors.

The opportunity to earn rents provides private and political organizations with the incentive to use the power of the state to monopolize a segment of the market. In the United States, state regulation of an industry typically evolved with the active support of those to be regulated, who correctly viewed regulation as a low-cost device – much of the cost being borne by taxpayers – for excluding competitors and enforcing cartel arrangements. Licensing of most activities typically serves a similar purpose. In the same vein, the evidence suggests that antitrust activity in the United States and elsewhere is dominated by bureaucratic and political considerations rather than by economic measures of monopoly power and is directed at practices that enhance rather than impede competition (McChesney and Shughart 1995).

Government-owned monopolies as an alternative to private monopolies raise all the usual problems. Moreover, they are longer-lived, finding it easier to use the power of the state to exclude competitors and to obtain subsidies.

The regulation and management of business enterprises by government employees introduce flaws of their own when judged by the same standards applied to market processes. Indeed, few monopolies with significant market power survive and prosper in the absence of political sanction.

7.4 The distribution of income

Distributive issues entail ethical judgments that are outside the scope of economics. Empirically, however, income in centrally directed economies is lower and its distribution is more unequal than in market economies. Political redistribution typically reflects rent seeking by various special-interest groups and often harms the groups it purports to benefit. Certainly, it results in a smaller output, a larger bureaucracy, and a structure of incentives that encourages rent seeking and yields a broad range of external effects.

8 Conclusions

In any working market system, institutional constraints on private property rights and substantial transaction costs yield some consequences that seem undesirable when compared to the theoretical solutions of an ideal construct. Such limitations suggest the possibility of an improvement through political action and typically provide a cover for special-interest groups (both private and public) to use the power of the state to advance their own welfare. The result is political control of market processes to redistribute wealth.

The appropriate comparison, however, is not between actual and ideal systems. It is between real-world alternatives: between market and political processes as they actually work.

Political solutions also have limitations. In addition to institutional constraints and transaction costs, they are limited by rent seeking and the lack of a benchmark for comparing alternatives as well as by the inability to measure values, aggregate individual data, provide suitable incentives to government employees, and encourage innovation and adjustment to change. Welfare arguments for government intervention typically provide the rhetoric used by special-interest groups to advance their own goals.

Government solutions convert all decisions into political decisions. Incentives shift from the pursuit of cooperative activities that result in mutual gain to the pursuit of rent-seeking activities that result in the redistribution of wealth. The evidence is overwhelming that moving decisions from the market to the political arena (that is, from voluntary to coercive orders) yields a smaller aggregate output, encourages corruption, breeds dissent, and, most important, reduces the ability of individuals to pursue their own goals.

A strong case can be made for adopting simple rules to solve a society's increasingly complex economic problems (Epstein 1995). The cornerstone of such a system is private property rights, including self-ownership, with the implied reliance on voluntary exchange and open markets. This approach ties the welfare of individuals to their success in cooperating with others in solving a society's economic problems in a world of change and uncertainty, recognizing that much relevant information is known only to the individuals affected and is time and place specific.

The argument for limited government within a system of private property rights goes deeper than simple material considerations. Fundamentally, it rests on the ethical and moral values of voluntary choices by free individuals.

Notes

* This chapter draws on previous work by the author (De Alessi 1980, 1982, 1988, 1998a, and 1998b).
1. Each individual maximizes a single-valued, convex, twice-differentiable utility function.
2. Colonies that held all resources in common quickly vanished or privatized (Wright 1949).
3. The allocation of resources is affected only through the net effect (small in size and unpredictable in sign) on demand and supply functions of changes in the distribution of wealth.
4. A wealth-maximizing firm produces an output where marginal cost (the cost of producing an additional unit of output) is increasing and just equal to marginal revenue (the revenue from the sale of the additional unit of output).
5. There is no empirical evidence that strategic bargaining has a significant impact on exchange. This is not surprising, considering that bilateral monopoly is not a dominant market structure and that the number of trades observed in the market is large by any reasonable standard.
6. In equilibrium, firms produce where marginal revenue (MR) equals marginal cost (MC). In the limiting case of many firms selling an identical product, each firm faces a horizontal demand curve and price (P) equals MR; if $MR = MC$, then $P = MC$. Because a monopolist faces a negatively sloped demand curve, the MR curve is also negatively sloped and lies everywhere below it; thus, $P > MR$. If $MC = MR$, then $P > MC$; consumers and producers look at different values.
7. Although this hypothesis may explain some events, preference for political solutions presumably reflects the belief that they yield a preferred set of outcomes.

3 The logic of collective action

*Omar Azfar**

1 Introduction

Before Mancur Olson wrote *The Logic of Collective Action* (1965), it was widely assumed by sociologists and economists that group action and individual action are analytically similar. The central point of *The Logic* is that this is a non-trivial and often false assumption. Olson argued that individual rationality does not imply collective rationality, and that this is especially true of large groups. A collective action problem arises when a group of individuals desires a public good – such as clean air, protective tariffs, law and order, or defense – and no one individual has the means of providing it. The provision of the good thus requires aggregating the contributions of several individuals. The central problem is that each individual would like to contribute a suboptimal amount because the benefits of his expenditure will be shared by all. Olson argues that, while small groups can sometimes organize collective action by informal arrangements and peer pressure, large groups typically need formal institutions and selective incentives to organize and act collectively.[1]

There is today perhaps a greater appreciation than ever before of the importance of collective action. Not only do traditionally analysed public goods and externalities, such as infrastructure and atmospheric pollution, continue to be important, we now appreciate more deeply that there are public goods underlying all market activities. Good governance, which is essentially a public good, is now considered the key to a successful market economy.[2] (In a typically eloquent moment, Mancur Olson coined the phrase 'market-augmenting government' to drive this point home.[3]) Whether a country has good governance or not depends in part on whether it has designed institutions of government to resolve collective action problems. The answer to what is perhaps the most important question in economics, 'Why do some countries remain poor while others prosper?', may lie in the successes and failures of attempts to resolve collective action problems (Olson 1996; Azfar 1998).

We do not have a complete understanding of how to design institutions that best combat collective action problems, but we are beginning to develop such an understanding. Team production and gain sharing have been studied extensively in the context of the theory of the firm, and we can apply much of what we have learnt from those studies to collective action problems. We can look at public-good provision or government in general through the same lenses. For instance, community participation and user fees, which reduce the observability and incentive problems, respectively, in public-good provision, have led to improved outcomes. Larger questions, such as the design of political systems, can be and are being analysed by economists with rigor and precision.

But this raises a serious question. Most economists now agree that the assumptions of narrow rationality are often false,[4] although they are useful metaphors for much of what we study in economics. However, whether individual rationality is a useful assumption for models of collective action remains an open question. We are often driven by instincts other than narrow self-interest, and these instincts can often be harnessed to produce collective action. Humankind has throughout its history relied on cooperation (within the family, clan, or tribe) for survival. It is quite possible that we have evolved extra-rational emotions in order to facilitate collective action, at least in small-group settings. The broader point, that deviations from individual rationality can facilitate cooperation in small groups, was not lost on Olson and is discussed in chapter II of *The Logic* to underscore the importance of group size to the achievement of collective goals. If the methodology of economics can analyse behavior driven by factors other than narrow self-interest, perhaps we can buy a little realism at the cost of a little parsimony. If we find that group behavior is best analysed under these assumptions, this may be a choice worth making.

This chapter reviews the basic arguments of *The Logic* and the many developments along Olsonian lines in the past 30 years. I begin in Section 2 with the statement of the central theses of *The Logic*, and go on to discuss whether they remain valid if interactions within groups are repeated, and whether collective rationality could have evolved naturally. More specifically, I briefly summarize *The Logic* in Section 2.1. In Section 2.2, I discuss why groups do not always act in their collective self-interest and why this is especially true for large groups. I argue in Section 2.3 that richer members in heterogeneous groups will contribute proportionally more than poorer members, an idea known as 'the exploitation of the large by the small'. I discuss these propositions under the traditional rational actor assumptions in a static neoclassical model, where we can often show that private contributions decline and actual public-good supply deviates more from the social optimum as group size increases.

In Section 2.4, I shall discuss how, at least in small groups, repeated-interaction models that allow for retaliation and peer pressure in response to deviant behavior suggest the possibility of cooperation. Could we have evolved so that we acquired the extra-rational tendencies that elicit cooperation? I discuss the possibility of the evolution of collective rationality in Section 2.5.

In Section 2.6, I shall suggest how collective action problems can be resolved by selective incentives. The possibility of resolving collective action problems with the appropriate institutions begs the question of how these institutions emerge. Olson's theory of the emergence of these institutions, in the form of stable government and democracy, and Donald Wittman's (1995) eloquent arguments for the efficiency of democratic systems, are discussed in Section 2.7.

Section 3 turns attention to applications. In Section 3.1, I discuss whether collective action can be organized to counter global environmental degradation. In Section 3.2, I discuss Elinor Ostrom's (1990) arguments for why decentralization and the encouragement of local community-based solutions to common property resource problems are likely to be more effective than central government intervention. In Section 3.3, I review Olson's *The Rise and Decline of Nations* (1982). Finally, in Section 3.4, I shall argue that the vast differences in economic growth and prosperity across countries can be explained in large part by differential success in resolving collective action problems. A conclusion follows.

2   Individual rationality and collective action

2.1   A summary of Olson's Logic of Collective Action
The central thesis of *The Logic* is that the then-commonly held presumption that large groups would act in their collective interest is false. That we no longer operate on the basis of this presumption is in part due to the success of *The Logic* and subsequent work that has profoundly influenced the thinking of social scientists. Olson begins with the statement of this thesis:

> It is often taken for granted, at least where economic objectives are involved, that groups of individuals with common interests usually attempt to further those common interests. Groups of individuals with common interests are expected to act on behalf of their common interests much as single individuals are often expected to act on behalf of their personal interests. ... The view that groups act to serve their interests presumably is based upon the assumption that the individuals in groups act out of self-interest. ... But it is *not* in fact true that the idea that groups will act in their self-interest follows logically from the premise of rational and self-interested behavior. It does *not* follow, because ... *rational self-interested individuals will not act to achieve their common or group interests.* (Olson 1965, pp. 1–2; emphasis in original)

Olson develops these arguments both formally and informally using the now familiar logic that, if each member of a group of size N acts only to maximize his own utility, then contributions will stop at a suboptimal level. That stopping point will be where the group's marginal utility product of contributions exceeds marginal cost by a factor of N (that is, $MU_G = N \times MC_G$).

This logic provides one basis for the argument that small groups can organize collective action more effectively than large groups. But Olson also offers extra-rational reasons, drawn from the theory of organization and a discussion of 'social pressure', for why cooperation may be more effectively achieved in small groups (chs I and II of *The Logic*). Indeed, Olson's stronger conjecture that a collective good may not be provided at all in large groups may depend both on the group size and social pressure arguments. This conclusion follows because, on the one hand, 'the larger the number of members in the group, the greater the organization costs, and thus the higher the hurdle that must be jumped before any of the collective good at all can be obtained' (ibid., p. 48). On the other hand, however, 'in general, social pressure and social incentive operate only in groups of smaller size, in the groups so small that members can have face-to-face contact with one another' (p. 62).

Large 'latent' groups thus cannot be mobilized in the absence of selective incentives, which both reward members who contribute and cooperate, and punish members who do not. Access to a union shop, differential access to support in resolving grievances, and subscriptions to professional journals are examples of positive inducements that can be used to mobilize large groups (ibid., p. 51). Groups can also use negative inducements, such as peer pressure and threats of ostracism. Governments can selectively punish citizens who do not pay their taxes, for instance, and thus the citizens of a country can be thought of as members of a large, effectively mobilized group.

Within heterogeneous groups, larger or richer members will contribute more than smaller, poorer members – an idea termed 'the exploitation of the large by the small'.[5] This is because 'once the smaller member has the amount of the collective good he gets free from the larger member, he has more than he would have purchased himself, and has no incentive to obtain any of the collective good at his own expense' (ibid., p. 35). Olson and Zeckhauser (1966) apply this idea to the analysis of defense spending in NATO (North Atlantic Treaty Organization) and find that larger countries do in fact contribute disproportionate shares of the costs.

In a detailed and persuasive account of labor unions, Olson (1965, pp. 66–97) demonstrates that such organizations have used selective incentives whenever and wherever they have been effective. Attempts at organizing without selective incentives have been short-lived and ineffective because, even when it is in the workers' collective interest to strike and maintain a well-funded union, it is seldom in any worker's individual interest to participate in a work stoppage or to pay dues. Indeed, voluntary membership and refusal to work in union shops is rare: workers in unionized firms usually prefer to be represented by unions – they overwhelmingly back 'measures that will force them to support a union' (ibid., p. 86). Following this logic, Olson reasons eloquently that arguments about compulsory union membership in terms of 'rights' are therefore misleading and unhelpful. ... There is no less infringement of 'rights' through taxation for the support of a police force or a judicial system than there is in a union shop. Of course, law and order are requisites of all organized economic activity; the police force and the judicial system are therefore presumably more vital to a country than labor unions. But this only puts the argument on the proper grounds: do the results of the unions' activities justify the power that society has given them? The debate on the 'right-to-work' laws should center, not around the 'rights' involved, but on whether or not a country would be better off if its unions were stronger or weaker. (ibid., pp. 88–9)

Olson discusses the necessary infringements of 'rights' for the provision of law and order in the remainder of the chapter on unions. The detailed study of the political basis and economic effects of the provision of law and order and other institutions that underlie economic activity is a theme to which he would return in later life (see Section 2.7 below).

Olson (pp. 98–110) next criticizes orthodox and Marxist theories of state and class, which assume that classes would mobilize to act in their interest if they only knew what these interests were, and points out that individual rationality does not imply that the members of a particular social class would act in their class interest. Working-class apathy is thus not due to false consciousness but to the collective action problem of mobilizing members of the class to act in unison.

Olson next turns to an analysis of theories of pressure groups and questions the value of the 'pluralism' these groups may provide. Olson's insight is that the interests of most citizens would not be adequately represented in such pluralistic arrangements because groups that can mobilize more effectively as a result of their smaller size or access to selective incentives would have disproportionate influence in the policy-making arena. In an intriguing application of this 'law of the few' to food pricing, van Bastelaer (1998) shows that countries with a smaller proportion of farmers provide more rather than less protection to agriculture. The idea that economic stagnation can result from the accumulation of pressure groups is extensively developed by Olson (1982) in a later book, *The Rise and Decline of Nations* (see Section 3.3).

In *The Logic*'s final chapter, 'The "by-product" and "special interest" theories', Olson (1965, pp. 132–67) argues that organizations that can provide ancillary goods of value to their members can use the provision of these goods as selective incentives to elicit dues and other forms of support which allow them to mobilize political influence and to provide other group benefits that cannot be selectively targeted. In the language of public goods, if a group provides its members with non-rival but excludable public goods it can use the provision of these goods as selective incentives to mobilize the resources needed to provide non-excludable public goods. For example, if membership in a professional association provides access to technical publications, accreditation, insurance, and support in lawsuits, then these selective incentives can be used to gather membership dues, which are then used to finance the supply of non-excludable benefits such as political lobbying.

One of the great strengths of *The Logic* is the breadth and depth of discussion of real-world examples that support its basic hypothesis. The theory of public goods predates Olson's *Logic* (Samuelson's seminal contribution was published in 1954), and thus his insight about the private undersupply of public goods is not novel. But the breadth of applications outside economics to theories of pressure groups and class struggles greatly influenced later analyses in political science. The analysis of extra-rational and organizational factors that reinforced the predictions of orthodox economic theory served to answer the frequent criticism that economists rely on an unrealistic model of human behavior that makes unrealistic predictions. And the analysis of trade unions and farm lobbies persuasively demonstrates the empirical relevance of the central hypothesis of *The Logic* that large groups can only organize collective action if they have access to selective incentives.

2.2   Group size and collective action: the static case
The central point of *The Logic of Collective Action* is that individual rationality does not imply collective rationality, and goods that it would be collectively rational to produce would not be produced by a set of unorganized individuals. Rational individuals would contribute less than the optimal amount to public goods. Furthermore, as the number of individuals who benefit from the supply of a public good increases, each individual's share of the gains from his contribution to the public good declines. Thus, it is likely that as group size increases, the gap between what is collectively rational and what individual rationality can deliver will grow.

Let us consider the prototypical public good, national defense. If we assume that there are diminishing returns to national defense, then we can derive the following result. As the population increases and if everyone's contributions remained the same, the total level of provision would also increase. But this would reduce the marginal utility of defense expenditure and rational individuals would therefore want to reduce their contributions. Hence, individual contributions would fall until the total amount of the public good had declined to the point where the marginal utility of each person's contribution equaled that associated with other goods. In the absence of an income effect, this would mean that total contributions would not rise. However, if national defense were a normal good,[6] each individual being richer for sharing his defense burdens would contribute more than he would in the absence of the income effect, and the total amount of defense expenditures would rise. But if the share of non-rival public goods in total expenditure is small, then the income effect would also be small and total public-good supply would be nearly independent of group size; per-person contributions would decline approximately hyperbolically (that is, by $1/N$).

It is important to remember that these results are for ungoverned groups that have not designed institutions to achieve effective collective action. National defense is, for the reasons mentioned above, seldom supplied on a voluntary basis, but rather is financed out of general taxation which citizens are obliged to pay. It is possible that in this instance the actual per-capita expenditure on national defense would rise with the population of the country. This is especially true for large and small countries in military alliances, but we are getting ahead of our story.

Now let us suppose that there is another type of public good, say clean streets, that is essentially non-excludable in the sense that it would be too costly to charge people for the benefits of street cleanliness. If the town financed street cleaning out of voluntary contributions, street cleaning would be undersupplied. Suppose that the town merged with another town of equal size, the citizens of one town never venture into the other, and the two towns continue to pay for street cleaning by voluntary contributions. What would happen to the cleanliness of the streets? Each citizen's contribution would be divided between money spent on cleaning his town's streets and money spent on cleaning those of the other town. If contributions remained the same, the effectiveness of each dollar a citizen contributed to street cleaning, in cleaning his own town, would decline. Thus each citizen would contribute less. To be precise, contributions would fall until the marginal utility product of street cleanliness doubled. Since the optimal level of cleanliness is the same for merged and separate jurisdictions, we can see the outcomes are more suboptimal if jurisdictions are merged.

These two examples differ because national defense is a pure public good and a greater expenditure on defense improves everyone's welfare, thus merging jurisdictions would improve welfare. However, in the case of cleaner streets, the goods are consumed at the local level and so the reductions in expenditures reduce welfare. The reasons for the per-capita reductions are different in the two cases. In the case of defense, total expenditures rise, which reduces the marginal utility of extra spending, whereas in the case of street cleaning only half the contribution is being spent on a service the citizen finds useful. But in each case there is a similar wedge between social and private marginal utility, namely $MU_S = N \times MU_P$, as N people benefit from the public good.

Broadly speaking, this wedge often implies that the results of individually rational behavior deviate more from collectively rational behavior as group size rises. We discussed why this would be the case for street cleaning in the example above, but the result is not unambiguous in the case of national defense because of the income effect, which may increase total contributions to the public good. But these income effects are unlikely to be large, and analyses of standard utility functions generally show that an increase in group size does lead to a more than proportional variation from the social optimum. These analyses have typically been done in terms of quantities rather than utility, which seems like a better measure of inefficiency (Sandler 1992). Repeating these analyses in terms of utility seems like a worthwhile and feasible research project.

Sandler (ibid., pp. 49–54) contains an excellent review of these ideas. John Chamberlain (1974) and Martin McGuire (1974) contemporaneously provided analyses showing that total public-good supply could rise with group size, contradicting Olson's implicit conjecture in *The Logic*.[7] The idea that decentralized provision will be inefficient in the presence of externalities (and public goods, which are like positive externalities) predates Olson and is analysed by Pigou (1920) and Samuelson (1954). Nicholson (1995, pp. 813–24), Varian (1995, pp. 415–32) and Mas-Colell et al. (1995, pp. 359–64) each contain modern textbook analyses of the public-good problem.

2.3   Heterogeneity and voluntary contributions: 'the exploitation of the large by the small'

In this section I review the effect of heterogeneity in income on voluntary contributions. The main result is that richer and larger group members contribute proportionally more of their income to public goods, an idea known as 'the exploitation of the large by the small'.

Andreoni (1988a) provides an elegant analysis of the voluntary-contribution public-good problem that extends the results to heterogeneous populations.[8] He shows that as the size of the group increases, only the richest members will contribute and total contributions will converge to a finite amount. This amount would be the total amount contributed in an economy that had a homogeneous population with incomes equal to those of the richest people in the heterogeneous population.[9] The argument can be extended to show that any redistribution of income in the economy will not increase total contributions unless it raises the upper bound of the income distribution.[10]

Olson and Zeckhauser (1966) showed in a seminal paper on the NATO alliance that an equilibrium in public-good supply between rich and poor countries involved proportionally greater contributions from richer countries. In this analysis a country (that is, a collective) is used as a unit of analysis and the investigation concentrates on interactions between them. But this is fair because countries have designed institutions of elections and taxation so that their citizens can decide collectively how much each will contribute. By choosing a higher tax and level of defense spending, each citizen of the

United States has his contribution matched by far more citizens than does a citizen of Luxembourg. Thus, it may be rational to vote for higher expenditures. The argument can be extended to technological progress on which the US government spends more per capita than the developed-country average and the theory suggests that a unified political structure in Europe will lead to increased defense and research and development (R&D) spending.

There are, of course, substantial country-specific returns to both military and R&D expenditure,[11] and so the evidence from these two programs does not provide convincing support for the theory of voluntary contributions to public goods in heterogeneous populations, but it is broadly suggestive that the predictions of the theory appear to hold. In contrast, Andreoni (1988a) shows that many poor people contribute to charities and the pattern of charitable giving is very different from the predictions of the model.[12] Thus while many empirical regularities are consistent with rational choice models of public-good problems, there are important exceptions which suggest that human behavior is richer and more complex than the theory admits. This is the question to which we now turn.

2.4 Repetition and reputation: theory and evidence on dynamic public-good games

Collective action problems have been likened to the familiar prisoner's dilemma. The prisoner's dilemma is a problem where two prisoners who can be proved guilty of a small crime are isolated, and each is promised leniency if he confesses to a larger crime and the other prisoner does not. Each prisoner is also threatened credibly that, if the other prisoner confesses, he will be punished more severely if he does not confess. Thus, it is in the interest of each prisoner to confess to the crime, no matter what the other prisoner does. Even though the prisoners would both be better off if neither confessed, they both confess in Nash equilibrium.[13] Public-good provision games are similar in structure, because it is not in the interest of any citizen to contribute the socially optimal amount, even though everybody would be better off if he did. Thus, in equilibrium a suboptimal amount of the good is supplied.[14]

As noted by Ostrom (1990, p. 39) and Olson (1992, pp. x–xi), the prisoner's dilemma is an unrepresentative situation for most collective action problems because the parties are coerced into not communicating. In the absence of this coercion, agents might be capable of solving their dilemma. Indeed, the experimental evidence suggests that communication improves the likelihood of cooperation in public-good games. But there is another related sense in which the single-play ('one-shot') prisoner's dilemma is artificial, which is that many real-world interactions are repeated. The effectiveness of the prisoner's dilemma which is actually used by law enforcement agencies suffers from such repetition. Prisoners fear retribution, directed not only at themselves but their families. Their families are often evacuated by the witness protection agency, but of course lead less than normal lives, which makes potential confessors reluctant.

The theoretical literature in which repeated prisoner's dilemmas have been extensively analysed (Fudenberg and Tirole 1992, pp. 110–12 and 145–206) shows the possibility of rational cooperation in indefinitely repeated games.[15] If at each interaction there is a chance that the game will go on for more rounds, agents can devise punishment strategies so that it is never in the interest of any agent to defect. Robert Axelrod (1984) showed in a famous series of experiments that a favorite punishment strategy was 'tit for tat': agents punished confession by confession in the next period, but were forgiving in response to resumed cooperation on the other player's part. If players play 'tit for tat', the Nash equilibrium is to cooperate and, indeed, most players cooperated in Axelrod's experiments. Thus, the results about the possibility of cooperation in repeated games are not facetious theoretical constructs.

The theoretical results depend on indefinite repetition; if at the beginning of any round the players know that there will not be a next round, it would be rational to confess on that round. But this makes it rational to defect in the penultimate period, and so on, and the cooperative equilibrium unravels by backward induction. However, the theoretical story is not logically complete because it does not specify what players are supposed to believe when they observe deviations from rational play. Rational players, of course, know that the only rational strategy is to defect in the first round, so it is unclear what they are supposed to think if they observe cooperation (this problem is known as forward induction). It appears that this deviation from a consistent logical story is empirically relevant. A reasonable response to cooperation in a real-world situation is to expect cooperation in the next period. Indeed, experimental results show that cooperation is often observed in early periods even for finitely repeated games (Selten and Stoecker 1986). These results are often demonstrated for repeated prisoner's dilemmas and 'the centipede', a game with a similar structure to a repeated prisoner's dilemma (Kreps 1990).

Kagel and Roth (1995, pp. 26–35 and 111–95) review the experimental literature on public-good provision.[16] Marwell and Ames (1979) conducted a public-good experiment and found that there were significant voluntary contributions, contradicting the free-riding hypothesis. Curiously, later experiments that allowed repetition (Kim and Walker 1984; Isaac et al. 1985) showed declining contributions over time, contradicting the hypothesis that repetition may improve cooperation. Andreoni (1988b) tried to separate learning effects from reputation and cooperation effects by conducting separate comparable experiments with stable and changing partners. He observed more contributions with changing partners, again contradicting the Axelrod-type 'evolution of cooperation' results. It is fair to say that the experimental results on free riding are mixed – subjects free ride more at some times than others – but there are some systematic differences: subjects who benefit more from their own contributions do contribute more, contributions decline in larger groups, and preplay communication does improve outcomes. Thus, while observed behavior departs from theoretical predictions in the sense that we observe contributions when we should not,[17] the experimental results do support Olson's insight that cooperation is less likely in large groups.

The prediction that larger deviations from collective rationality are likely in large-group settings remains valid for repeated public-good games. With two agents, if contributions can fall by mistake, the most efficient punishment strategy for eliciting cooperation is for the 'injured party' to punish by not contributing in the next period and for the 'defector' to contribute more. With three or more agents, if only outcomes are observable, then this may not be feasible because the injured parties do not know who defected. As the number of agents rises it may become more and more difficult to maintain a cooperative equilibrium in a repeated public-good game. In the limit, as the number of agents becomes large and there are aggregate shocks, any agent's defection may not be observable at all and cooperation would break down.

In a realistic setting, as group size rises, so does the likelihood that there is an agent who actually prefers the non-cooperative equilibrium – a room-mate with messy tastes, a hunter with a taste for rabbits in 'the stag hunt',[18] or a person who genuinely believes that it is not worthwhile to protect the environment. If such an individual exists, a 'revenge' strategy of withholding cooperation would not be effective and would destroy the cooperative equilibrium. Thus, as the membership of a society increases it becomes increasingly unlikely that collective action problems can be resolved without institutions of governance, and it is increasingly unlikely that unanimity will be a viable rule for making political decisions.

Thus, heterogeneity may reduce the effectiveness of collective action. However, heterogeneity can itself be reduced by information based on careful study and research. Research on the costs of environmental problems and the effectiveness of remedies can reduce the uncertainty about the usefulness of these remedies, for example. Following careful research, it may be more difficult for a nation to continue to believe (or pretend to believe) that environmental protection is not worthwhile and this increases the capacity of a non-coercive supranational organization to organize collective action. Section 3.1 reviews recent supranational initiatives for controlling atmospheric pollution, which often have a significant research component. Attempts at combating corruption in the former Soviet Union have a similarly important research component.

The use of selective incentives can expand the possibilities for cooperation. A law that requires people to have catalytic converters in their cars, even if they earnestly believe the societal costs of thus protecting the environment are too high, may effectively protect the environment. The tool of punishing deviations from the cooperative equilibrium by non-cooperation is too blunt an instrument to be effective in large groups, but sanctions that selectively target defecting individuals may still produce collective action.

2.5   The evolution of individual and collective rationality: revenge is sweet
One justification for rationality is evolution, but a systematic evolutionary analysis does not lead to clear-cut predictions about non-cooperation in finitely repeated games. Evolution, after all, requires mutations, and if there is even a small chance that some individuals have mutated to a cooperative state it may make sense for even a rational player to cooperate in an early round, especially after observing cooperation. Furthermore, humankind probably evolved in surroundings where repeated games did not have a definite end. We may therefore have evolved to play them as if they were indefinitely repeated.[19]

At a deeper level, perhaps evolution in social animals can result in pheno-types that cooperate in group settings and punish those that do not (Pinker 1997, p. 402).[20] The old adage about revenge is telling: things are sweet in the literal sense when they are toothsome and therefore adaptive; and, so the adage claims, is revenge.[21] As Adam Smith argues in *The Theory of Moral Sentiments*, when a man 'injures or insults us',

> the glaring impropriety of this conduct, the gross insolence and injustice which it seems to involve in it, often shock and exasperate us more than all the mischief we have suffered. To bring him back to a more just sense of what is due to other people, to make him sensible of what he owes us, and of the wrong that he has done to us, is frequently the principal end proposed in our revenge. (Smith [1759] 1976, p. 96)

It can be argued that within a group it would be adaptive for an individual to learn to defect from the cooperative equilibrium in an unobservable way, but then so may it be adaptive to learn to detect this mutation (Pinker 1997, pp. 403–4; Trivers 1971). Technologies for defection would be followed by technologies for detection and most of the population may not be able to defect without detection most of the time. I remember once being told that if I wanted to tell a lie, I should do so on the telephone, as I would get caught if I tried to lie face to face. Perhaps that is why even in this age of information technology, the smile and handshake are still so often used, frequently at considerable cost, for sealing important agreements.

Thus, deviations from rationality, like a propensity for revenge that in turn induces cooperation, may imply that group norms can help overcome collec-tive action problems. But this may be true more for small than for large groups.[22] We evolved, perhaps, so that we could cooperate and elicit cooperation in small groups, and we use handshakes and friendships to achieve cooperation, which are more feasible in small than in large groups. The insight of *The Logic* about the greater likelihood of collective action in small groups may therefore be more true in models with a perhaps more realistic, quasi-rational view of human nature.

There are several reasons to expect a greater likelihood of collective action in small groups. In a static, voluntary-contribution, public-good game, the results of individual rationality often deviate more from collective rationality as group size rises. In repeated games, cooperative equilibria are easier to sustain in smaller groups. And deviations from rationality, which may have evolved to increase humankind's chances of survival, may support cooperation in small groups more effectively than they support cooperation in large groups.

2.6   Overcoming collective action problems by selective incentives

As Olson (1965, pp. 66–98) pointed out and elaborated in the chapter on trade unions in *The Logic*; even large groups can organize collective action if they can create institutional structures that provide selective incentives to their members for cooperating. A labor union (or other group) can create selective incentives if it can provide some goods that are excludable, and punish non-cooperators by withholding these goods.[23] Trade unions do provide access to insurance and differentially provide support to their members in resolving grievances, both of which induce workers to join unions and not work during strikes.

Even if another organization emerges that provides these same goods, once the union's organizational structure is in place, it may find it in its members' interests to continue to bargain collectively. If it chose not to, the union could stop collective bargaining and thereby punish the other organization. This is more plausible than the union choosing to punish any one member by refusing to engage in collective bargaining. There may well be some members who prefer not to be party to collective bargaining agreements and thus the collective bargaining equilibrium would break down if collective benefits were withheld whenever anyone defected. However, it is unlikely that the median voter in a large labor organization would prefer the outcome of a decentralized bargaining process to the outcome of collective bargaining. Thus, a large labor organization cannot credibly withhold support while any one worker might. Once an institutional structure is in place, even if it is meant for merriment and diversion, it may (indeed perhaps must) be used to organize collective action.

Opportunities for such selective incentives abound. Exclusion can often be used as a selective incentive, and many results from the economic theory of clubs show that the threat of such exclusion can result in collectively efficient outcomes.[24] Even on a global scale, the costs of a country being excluded from the World Trade Organization, or from the gains from trade more generally, are so large that selective incentives may well be feasible for creating international cooperation for, say, environmental problems. At a local level there are additional possibilities for censure which can be used to elicit cooperation. But there is no guarantee that they will be. One problem of institutional design is to choose from the feasible set of sanctions and censures those which provide selective incentives for collective action.

We can think of the problem of institutional design as an attempt to solve the repeated prisoner's dilemma, public-good problem. We know from the *folk theorem* that in a repeated game both cooperation and non-cooperation can be maintained as equilibrium outcomes (Fudenberg and Tirole 1992). If individuals believe non-cooperation will not be punished, do not cooperate, and do not punish non-cooperation, then this pattern of behavior forms an equilibrium. Alternatively, if individuals punish, believe they will be punished, and punish others for not punishing when punishment is called for, this too forms a (cooperative) equilibrium. Thus, there are both cooperative and non-cooperative equilibria in this repeated game and good institutional design is necessary to coordinate behavior on the cooperative equilibrium.

While the idea of punishment for not punishing may seem far-fetched, there is historical evidence of such patterns of behavior (Greif 1997). Elster's (1989) claim that these patterns of punishment cannot be used to elicit cooperation, because there would be a reluctance to punish non-punishers, therefore appears to be an overstatement. However, Elster's intuition is useful as it suggests that arranging voluntary collective action in such a setting is difficult, which is why a clear statement of the rules of the game and the expected patterns of punishments are so important.

Communication facilitates understanding of the rules and incentives and this may result in mutually beneficial collective action. Without communication and a clear statement of rules, players would inadvertently take actions that triggered punishments. Inappropriate punishments are inefficient and can destroy cooperation. It is telling that communication is disallowed in the prisoner's dilemma, that experimental results suggest that cooperation rises with communication, and that, more than two centuries ago, Adam Smith ([1776] 1976, p. 208) had pointed out that businessmen could not even meet for merriment and diversion without conspiring to raise prices.

In summary, the results suggest that it is possible to design institutions that elicit cooperation in repeated public-good games, provided that the game is repeated often enough and preferences are homogeneous. In this case, the threat of playing non-cooperatively for long enough in the future can induce players to cooperate. If the population is heterogeneous, it may still be

possible to elicit cooperation when actions are observable, punishment strategies are clearly articulated, and selective incentives such as fines or trade
sanctions can be used to target defectors.

2.7 The emergence of the institutions of government and democracy

We are left with the question of how collective action problems will be solved
for large groups, in particular at the level of the nation-state. Wittman (1995)
argues that democratic institutions can effectively resolve collective action
problems. But how do democracies emerge?

In 'Dictatorship, democracy, and development' (1993) and *Power and
Prosperity* (2000), Olson lays out a theory of the emergence of stable dictatorships and democracies from anarchic beginnings. In an anarchic world of
roving bandits, robber barons would arrive in settlements and strip people of
their belongings and more. Because of this endemic expropriation, people
would have little incentive to produce. The leader of such a group of maraud-
ers may prefer a situation where he rules a defensible fiefdom[25] and
expropriates only to the extent consistent with revenue maximization (at the
top of this ancient Laffer curve). The population may prefer to be ruled by
such a sedentary bandit, because they get to keep more of their produce and
enjoy the benefits of social peace, and this may have contributed to the
stability of such societies.

Sometimes accidents of history produce situations where the ruler needs
the support of others, and he must bargain away promises of participation in
future governance. With luck, these situations can result in the emergence of
democracy. The reforms of Clisthenes in classical Athens, as well as Magna
Carta, the Glorious Revolution and the eventual emergence of modern British
democracy, all followed from an autocrat needing to garner support which
was not forthcoming without these promises (Herodotus [c. 450 BCE] 1987,
Bk 5, ch. 66–73; Olson 1993). But surely there were other events in history
where support was similarly needed and democracy did not emerge. Perhaps
the emergence of democracy and good governance is a matter of chance, a
point we shall return to later.

Olson argues that the emergence of democracy, which necessarily includes
rights and protections and the rule of law if there is to be any credibility to the
ruler's promises of obeying democratic decisions, also provides rights to private property, and these in turn may result in economic development. More
directly, if an autocrat can be driven to provide promises of devolving political
authority, he can perhaps also be driven to guaranteeing those economic freedoms
that allow others to prosper. Indeed, democracies both today and throughout
history have been associated with economic development and prosperity. Ancient
Greece and Rome developed rapidly, as did the northern Italian city-states, The
Netherlands in the seventeenth century and Britain after the Glorious Revolu-

tion (De Long and Shleifer 1993). All of today's developed economies are democracies, a fact that was even more striking a few years ago when almost all underdeveloped economies were not democracies.

But the fact that democracies must of necessity give some rights to the people is only one of their virtues. As Donald Wittman (1995) eloquently argues, democratic institutions may be efficient at producing the rule of law and public goods because they generally produce competition among candidates, and competition leads to efficient outcomes in the political arena much as it does in more ordinary markets. Once democracy has emerged, an institution exists for the solution of collective action problems, and Wittman argues that once such an institution exists, perhaps collective action problems can in large part be solved – or at least reduced to cost-effective minima.

An obvious collective action problem with democracy is that it is almost never in any individual's narrow self-interest to bother to vote as his vote is unlikely to be pivotal. But here again a slightly richer theory of human nature could resolve this puzzle. Hardin (1982, pp. 108–12) argues that sometimes collective action problems may be resolved because people occasionally have the extra-rational desire to participate in their own history. A striking visualization of this point is a picture of South Africa's first post-apartheid election with the lines of voters weaving around a field, few of whom could have reasonably thought the African National Congress could lose the election.

The reader may object that there is a bit of *deus ex machina* in providing remedies like democracies – remedies that would not work if behavior were entirely selfish – for collective action problems which are best articulated in terms of such narrow rationality. But if a reasonable theory that seems to have empirical support – such as that people want to participate in their history and in decision making in their societies – can suggest remedies to collective action problems, perhaps social science should acknowledge this. Human behavior is probably selfish in the sense that people will not voluntarily install platinum catalytic converters in their cars to reduce emissions, but deviates from narrow rationality in the sense that many of them will vote at elections to choose among alternative remedies for this problem. Perhaps our analysis should reflect this.

3   Applications

3.1   The global environment

Perhaps the most visible collective action problem in today's world is the prevention of environmental degradation. The potential costs of environmental degradation are large. Although existing science has not attained consensus, the loss of biodiversity could reduce the potential for finding effective cures for lethal diseases; deforestation releases carbon dioxide (CO_2) into the atmosphere, and this may cause global warming with the disastrous potential of raising the sea level; chlorofluorocarbons (CFCs) can deplete the ozone layer; and sulfur and nitrogen oxides can cause acid rain which may ruin the world's forests. But the costs of environmental degradation often spill across international boundaries, and nations are jealous of their sovereignty and unwilling to create supranational bodies with coercive power over themselves. Thus, the challenge is to design institutions that can elicit cooperation in protecting the environment without creating a world government.[26]

This problem is not insurmountable and there has been limited success in slowing or halting environmental degradation in some spheres. While institutions are necessary for even limited success and entirely voluntary restraint does not seem to have worked, the institutional remedies can stop well short of world government. The key is that non-coercive incentives such as trade sanctions can sometimes be effective in eliciting cooperation. However, selective incentives must be paired with a clear statement of rules combined with careful research demonstrating the harmfulness of the relevant form of environmental degradation and the effectiveness of the proposed remedies.

In the case of reducing CFCs to protect the ozone layer, the process started with a concerted effort to study the problem in the Vienna Convention of 1985. Research pointed to the seriousness and urgency of the problem and the Montreal Convention was adopted in 1987. It came into force in 1989 and mandated gradual reductions of CFC emissions and these mandated reductions were accelerated in 1990.

As I argued in Section 2.4, careful research that illuminates both the seriousness of the problem and the effectiveness of remedies is important in eliciting supranational cooperation.[27] Incentives like trade sanctions, while effective, hurt both parties. Without careful research some countries may genuinely believe that the proposed remedies are not cost-effective and resist being bullied into adopting them. Sanctions against uncooperative governments would be inefficient and may even threaten the world trading system.

Can the success of the Montreal Convention in reducing CFC emissions be repeated for other problems? The answer seems to be that, with luck, it can. As Sandler (1997, pp. 113–14) argues, American leadership may have been important in the success of the convention. With leadership, if the problem and its costs can be clearly articulated, nations do have means of providing selective incentives to other nations by agreeing or disagreeing to trade with them. Indeed, the costs of sanctions are quite high and therefore cooperation can probably be effectively induced.

There has been some success at reducing sulfurous emissions and less at reducing nitrogen oxides and CO_2. Sandler argues that reducing sulfurous emissions has been easier because the costs are borne more by the home country and the number of affected producers within a country is more concentrated. The details of the problem might matter and some environmental problems may be solved while others may not. But to reiterate my earlier point, if the costs of environmental degradation and the effectiveness of the proposed remedies can be clearly articulated, then it is possible that collective action problems will be resolved and environmental degradation will be controlled.

3.2   Local public goods, common property resources and decentralization

Elinor Ostrom (1990) argues that common perceptions of the logic of collective action are too pessimistic for small- and medium-sized groups, which can organize themselves for the preservation and efficient use of common property resources and public goods, and have sometimes done so. These local solutions are often more efficient than solutions that would be proposed by central governments, because of local knowledge about the nature of the problem, which might elicit different solutions, and because local organizations can be monitored more effectively than a central government. Ostrom (ibid., pp. 20 and 25) contends that central governments need to acknowledge the legitimacy of rules made by local governments and non-governmental organizations, and confine themselves to providing the rule of law in the form of courts for interpretation and mechanisms for enforcement.[28] Many of the arrangements Ostrom describes are self-governed and enforced by the group itself, but these groups do seem to have formal structures, and explicit incentives and fines are used, rather than informal arrangements and peer pressure, to elicit cooperation.

The theory of public goods suggests that the goods will be underprovided by the market and should therefore be provided by the public sector. This conclusion, however, ignores the collective action problem in designing and monitoring the public sector, and public-good delivery in developing countries suffers from chronic non-performance. An explicit analysis of the informational problems faced by consumers and government officials suggests that joint public–private production, user fees, and community involvement would lead to better outcomes (Isham and Kähkönen 1997). Joint production provides valuable oversight of public officials involved in public-good delivery, and user fees can effectively demonstrate that the public good is in fact being provided. These results, which follow from economic analysis, were applied to the delivery of water and sanitation in India and Sri Lanka, and produced significant improvements in outcomes (Isham and Kähkönen 1998).

Taken together, the twin insights of *The Logic*, namely that cooperation is possible in small groups and that collective action can effectively be organized by the use of selective incentives, suggest that allowing small- and intermediate-sized groups to create selective incentives, and providing support for their enforcement, can lead to effective solutions for local public-good and common property resource problems.

3.3   *The rise and decline of nations*

In *The Rise and Decline of Nations*, Olson (1982) argues that small groups and groups that can arrange selective incentives for their members can effectively create political pressure through collective action, while large unorganized groups cannot.[29] Thus, there is no guarantee that democracies will reflect some utility-maximizing will of the people. The insight is an advance on Aristotle's *Politics*, which points out that elections lead to aristocracy, the rule of the gifted few, rather than democracy, the rule of the many. Olson's contribution was to observe that it would be the few who are gifted at organizing themselves around selective incentives, rather than the few gifted at ruling well, who would get elected. The point is perhaps unfairly taken to be a criticism of 'democracy' (in ours, not Aristotle's sense), but perhaps applies even more strongly to autocracies (Lanyi and Lee 1999). Autocrats also need organized interests to support them in power, and democracy, albeit imperfectly, provides a channel for the wishes of the many to be reflected in collective decisions.

Olson conjectured further that stable societies build up many such pressure groups over time and this eventually leads to stagnation. The theory has been criticized on the grounds that in many countries pressure groups, such as labor unions, were actually encompassing in the sense that they represented a large percentage of the population, and thus would advance national rather than parochial interests. Mokyr (2000) extends Olson's arguments to inertia in technological innovation. There have been some attempts to test Olson's hypothesis (Choi 1983; Murrell 1983; Vedder and Gallaway 1986), and the results generally seem to support the theory.

The question of how to design political institutions to avoid capture by special interests is fascinating and important but difficult. Nevertheless, we do have some idea about the answer. For example, many people would agree that campaign finance reform would help reduce the political power of special interests. However, it may not be in the interest of the incumbent members of the US Congress to enact campaign finance reform, and attempts at such reform may therefore flounder. Thus, the question of why good institutions would be adopted even if we could design them is a relevant one, and one that needs answering along with the question about how to design efficient institutions.

3.4   *Governance and growth*

At least since Adam Smith, economists have known about the prosperity-promoting effects of good governance, free trade and the provision of public goods such as the rule of law, infrastructure and a stable currency. These prescriptions remain relevant in modern analyses, and the empirical and theoretical study of modern economic growth highlights the importance of all these variables (World Bank 1994; Sachs and Warner 1995, 1997; Knack and Keefer 1995; also see Chapters 24 and 25 of this volume).

In a sense, good governance and the provision of growth-enhancing public goods are the result of solving collective action problems. There are often mercantilist interests within countries that would rather have protection than free trade, but protectionism is seldom in the interest of the population in general. Following Olson's arguments in *The Logic* and *The Rise and Decline of Nations*, these well-organized interests can prevail, and it is an important challenge for the design of political institutions to devise means of solving collective action problems at the national level. Similarly, inflations are perhaps caused by fiscal deficits resulting from expenditures on various groups that are financed by easy money policies (Mankiw 1992, pp. 154–63; Sargent 1983). The provision of infrastructure, the rule of law, and national defense for safeguarding private property is a classic case of public goods that can only be efficiently supplied if collective action problems are solved.

Why do some countries remain poor while others prosper? Traditional economic theory typically predicts convergence in incomes across countries but we see no such broad patterns of convergence. The answer, perhaps, is that many poor countries fail to resolve the collective action problems that need to be solved to allow free trade and provide the legal, monetary and physical infrastructure for successful market economies. Indeed, if we restrict our attention to countries that avoid high rates of inflation, and score above average on trade openness, education, property rights and the rule of law, we see a clear pattern of poor countries catching up with rich ones (Figure 3.1). The white diamonds represent countries that did well on all four variables. We can see that *all* countries that do well on all four variables are members of a convergence club; Malaysia growing at 4.4 per cent is the slowest-growing low-income country in that club, growing twice as fast as the advanced industrial economies. Three of the four countries that are doing well economically, despite doing badly on one or more of the variables, are guilty of relatively minor infractions, and alternative ways of parsing the data predict that they should be converging too (Azfar 1998).

Why, if satisfying these requirements is all that stands between poverty and prosperity, do all nations not adopt good policies? One possible answer is that collective action problems need to be solved for good policies to be enacted, and whether or not collective action succeeds is in some measure a matter of chance. Big bills can be left on the sidewalk if it takes collective action to pick them up.[30]

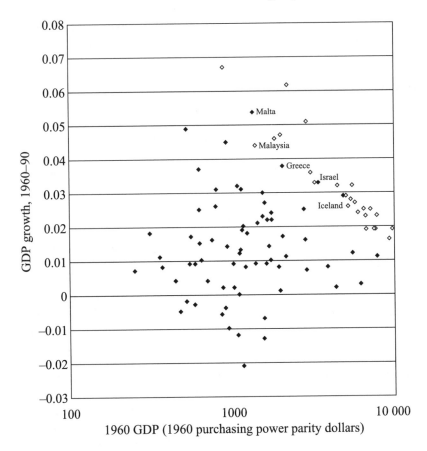

Figure 3.1   Governance and growth

Designing good governance is a difficult problem. A government needs to be well informed, investigative and powerful enough to protect its citizens from private predation. Yet it must credibly commit to desisting from public predation. The tasks required of a good government to create the legal infrastructure for many markets including the market for capital are complex and non-trivial. Governments are often barely adequate at the relatively routine task of collecting garbage, so why do we trust them with the complex ones of drafting, interpreting and enforcing laws? The answer is that we entrust them with these tasks because we must. There may simply be no realistic way, other than coercion, of resolving many collective action problems. Given the complexity of these tasks, it is no real surprise that many governments fail at them and that as a consequence many economies languish. The challenging but urgent task is to design governments that can overcome these problems, for there may be no real substitute to good government in creating prosperous economies.

4   Conclusion

The central thesis of *The Logic* is that collective action is easier to achieve in small than in large groups. I have discussed how this conjecture was reinforced rather than refuted by the consideration of repetition and evolution. The problem has a wide application, from environmental concerns to the great variation in the wealth of nations. It is thus an urgent and important question to understand why collective action succeeds at some times and in some places, but fails in others.

Details of the collective action problem matter in the design of solutions: this implies that there is a broad scope and great need for further research. Is it true that if workers form an organization for purposes other than collective bargaining, it will eventually be used for collective bargaining? Can interest-group capture of governments, as documented in *The Rise and Decline of Nations*, be stemmed by campaign finance reform? Are the costs in terms of reduced pluralism worth it? The formalization and careful study of these ideas and others is necessary for them to be accepted by the economics profession, and perhaps other social sciences.

Serious and careful research is particularly valuable in the study of collective action problems. Research can help reduce uncertainty about the value of resolving collective action problems and the effectiveness of the proposed remedies. This may make it possible to garner political support for effective remedies. Collective action problems provide not only a rich and fascinating field of study, but one in which the results of good research can have a significant impact on the world.

Thirty-five years after its writing, the arguments of *The Logic* are as relevant as they ever were. Indeed, *The Logic*'s breadth of relevance has expanded to the study of the wealth and poverty of nations and perhaps even a theory of history.

Notes

*   In memory of Mancur Olson. I am very grateful to Chris Clague, Anthony Lanyi, Patrick Meagher, Anand Swamy, and the editors for comments and suggestions.
1.   These selective incentives can either be coercive, like fines for non-cooperation, or positive, like access to a union shop.
2.   See Chapters 24 and 25 of this volume.
3.   Olson had begun to organize a conference on this topic, which was held after his passing by the IRIS Center of the University of Maryland.
4.   By narrow rationality I mean rational self-interested behavior not driven by altruism, anger, or other 'non-economic' motives. It is of course not irrational to be altruistic in

either the colloquial or economic sense. Indeed, the famous neoclassical argument for Ricardian equivalence relies on altruism (Barro 1974), and 'reciprocal altruism' is fully consistent with models of rational choice. But economists typically assume that individuals are not altruistic unilaterally or that they are driven systematically by outward-looking goals. Rather than try to invent a new phrase for the usual set of assumptions, I refer to them as rationality.

5. This conjecture has been formalized by Andreoni (1988a) and others. See Section 2.3 below.

6. The demand for a normal good rises with income. The income effect is the increase (or decrease) in the demand for a good resulting from a change in real income brought about by a change in relative prices.

7. Olson (1965) never quite says that the absolute amount of a public good will fall as the number of participants rises, but does (for example, on p. 44) state that there may be no cooperation at all in large groups, which may be thus interpreted.

8. Many results in Andreoni (1988a) follow from Bergstrom et al. (1986).

9. The intuition behind this result is that individuals contribute to the public good until their marginal utility from consuming more of the collective good equals their marginal utility from other private goods. Thus the richest individuals contribute until each of them has an amount x left to spend on private goods, and individuals earning less than x contribute nothing at all. The first-order condition that determines x is $U'(x) = U'(P)$, where P is the total amount of public good supplied when every individual with an income $y > x$ contributes $y - x$. Andreoni (1988a) assumes that people are drawn from a bounded continuous income distribution. This result may not hold if people were drawn from an unbounded distribution where the highest incomes in the sample would continue to grow as the population increased and would not converge to an upper limit.

10. Andreoni (1988a) almost makes this qualification in his footnote 16. He also extends the results to heterogeneous preferences. Warr (1983) had shown the invariance of public-good supply to income distribution prior to Andreoni.

11. Actually, Andreoni's (1988a) theoretical model suggests that smaller countries would contribute nothing in the absence of nation-specific benefits. Once we admit nation-specific effects, the theory predicts that smaller nations would invest in defense and R&D too, as we observe. Empirical results on defense and R&D spending may therefore be quite close to theoretical predictions.

12. Andreoni's (1988a) result is, however, consistent with notions of 'reciprocal altruism' if poor people tend to see themselves benefiting from the charity of others in future periods.

13. A Nash equilibrium is a set of actions by the players of a game (in this case the prisoners) such that no player has an incentive to deviate from his chosen action. In this case because each prisoner is punished more severely if he does not confess, the only Nash equilibrium is for each prisoner to confess.

14. See Hardin (1982, especially ch. 2) for an elaborate analysis along these lines.

15. These results depend on players expecting to play several future rounds and not discounting them heavily. One problem with the theoretical results about cooperation in repeated games is that almost any outcome can often be sustained as an equilibrium in repeated games, including non-cooperation.

16. Also see Chapter 22 of this volume.

17. Actually, since these games are often repeated, the theoretical predictions are not unambiguous.

18. The original reference is Rousseau ([1761] 1964); Hardin (1982, pp. 167–9) contains an analysis. A stag hunt is a game in which a group of hunters is hunting a stag, but there are also hares in the forest. A hunter can defect from a stag hunt and catch a hare if he sees one, but the whole group would eat better if they stuck to their posts. The problem is to provide incentives so that everyone cooperates.

19. Pinker (1997) provides eloquent arguments for why our cognitive skills reflect our early evolutionary requirements (pp. 299–362) and how emotions may have evolved and may be adaptive (pp. 363–424). People do make systematic mistakes, but at artificial tasks that do not closely resemble tasks humans needed to do for most of their history. He insightfully

quips that to say we have evolved badly because we do badly at these tasks is like saying we have evolved badly because our hands are not designed to get out of handcuffs.

20. Pinker's argument is adapted from Trivers (1971) who suggests the possibility of the evolution of cooperation.
21. Hardin (1982, p. 172) makes a similar point in terms of fair play rather than revenge.
22. Olson's (1965, pp. 53–65) chapter on group size in *The Logic* provides many such arguments.
23. Olson's (1965, pp. 132– 67) chapter on 'by-product' and 'special interest' theories is also relevant to this argument.
24. The economic theory of clubs analyses goods that are non-rival over some non-congested range, but excludable. See Sandler and Tschirhart (1980, 1997) and Cornes and Sandler (1986) for reviews. Club goods are the subject of Chapter 15 of this volume.
25. Almost all ancient civilizations, including Mesopotamia, Egypt, the Indus Valley and the Chinese civilization, emerged in river valleys where the productive areas were demarcated by the extent of irrigation, which made expropriation easy for the rulers, and were surrounded by deserts or mountain ranges which rendered them isolated and defensible (Carniero 1970).
26. These problems are addressed in Sandler (1997, pp. 84–129).
27. Of course scientists and social scientists whose grants and livelihoods depend on the results of research may have vested interests in certain research outcomes. This may cloud their judgments, which in turn may detract from the credibility and persuasiveness of the research, and its ultimate impact on policy.
28. I would add the condition 'unless they conflict with federal law and the basic principles of justice'. Local communities and non-governmental organizations can sometimes decide to do rather vicious things, and the protection of individuals from these acts is a legitimate role for the central government. An exit option will discipline the behavior of local communities, however (Tiebout 1956; Hirschman 1970).
29. This point was first made in *The Logic* (Olson 1965, pp. 127–8).
30. See Olson (1996) for a detailed argument.

4   Social choice theory

Michael J.G. Cain

1   Introduction

Social choice theory is concerned with the aggregation of individual preferences or values into collective preferences or values. The theory's general perspective on individual values and social choices has obvious relevance to economics, political science and philosophy. Social choice research also has important implications for theories of voting, public goods problems, constitutional design, welfare theory, normative and descriptive ethics, distributive justice and rights theory. Owing to its interdisciplinary focus, social choice theory has helped re-establish neglected intellectual linkages between economics, political science and philosophy, and helped reinvigorate interest in longstanding debates on the nature of the 'good' society, the origins of government authority and the legitimacy of democratic processes (Rowley 1993). This chapter discusses these issues by exploring two foundational questions relevant to welfare economics, philosophy and political theory.

The first question posed in this chapter asks whether – and how – a stylized social planner might use information about what individuals want to develop a rational perspective on what the society wants. I summarize the answers provided by utilitarians, welfare economists and social choice theorists. The second question addressed in this chapter focuses on mechanisms of social choice. In particular, what are the properties of that traditional hallmark of democracy, simple majority rule? Is it fair? Will it lead to the rational selection of a coherent set of social policies? I supply several answers to these questions by reviewing some of the most important findings in the social choice theories of voting. Although the implications of these findings have not yet been fully fleshed out by social choice theorists, the significance of the findings for political theory is indisputable.

2   From philosophy to economics: early perspectives on social choice

Although modern social choice research originated in welfare economics, precursors can be found in the literature of political science and philosophy.[1] The origins of social choice research on voting can be traced to the ideas of Jean-Charles de Borda (1781) and the philosopher and mathematician, the Marquis de Condorcet ([1785] 1994). Philosophers have always had an interest in what is now called social choice theory, debating the nature of the 'just' society and exploring overarching concepts of public welfare. Modern social choice theory, not surprisingly, has inherited many of the same methodological stumbling blocks found in philosophy and, for that reason, social choice research continues to have a distinctly normative flavor. Before discussing the main applications and findings in social choice theory, I introduce two traditional themes in the philosophical and economic approaches to social choice.

Contractarian philosophers, such as Thomas Hobbes, John Locke and Jean-Jacques Rousseau, were among the first modern theorists explicitly to try to connect individual desires and choices with social and political outcomes. The contractarians were mainly interested in answering questions about why rational individuals, endowed with natural rights and liberties, would voluntarily give up these rights and liberties to join a civil society and form a government. In *The Social Contract*, Rousseau ([1762] 1973, p. 53) describes the problem as follows:

> Find a form of association that defends and protects the person and goods of each associate with all the common force and by means of which each one, uniting with all, nevertheless obeys only himself and remains as free as before.

Although Rousseau was concerned primarily with describing the conditions that legitimized political associations, he was also concerned with explaining why citizens would rationally prefer or want such associations.

Rousseau and his fellow philosophers argued that individuals possess natural rights and liberties independent of any established government. The contractarians then went on to consider how citizens might make themselves better off by ceding authority to a government that protected their liberties and guaranteed their civil rights. This approach to problems of social choice is of course distinct from the classical utilitarian approach. Utilitarian philosophers, such as David Hume, Adam Smith, Jeremy Bentham and John Stuart Mill, also investigated the relations between individual values and collective outcomes. But rather than focus on natural rights and liberties, the utilitarians were concerned with how individuals might coordinate their actions to promote the social good, where 'good' is understood to be defined in terms of pleasure and freedom from pain. According to these philosophers, the best governments and best policies are those that produce the greatest happiness for the greatest number.[2]

This claim, that the best policies are those that produce the greatest happiness, implies that indicators of individual happiness can be aggregated for the purpose of making (scientific) judgments about the welfare of society as a whole. The possibility of such an aggregation and the elements thereof has occupied much of the attention of social choice researchers during the past century. The initial contribution to this question, as we shall see, was made by Kenneth Arrow. Arrow's ([1951] 1963) famous result, called the 'general possibility theorem', proves that no such aggregation is possible. This meant that a social planner's policy decisions could not be guided by an objective measure of social welfare based exclusively on individual tastes and preferences.

This result ended a long line of debate in welfare economics, which began with Abraham Bergson (1938) and continued in work by Paul Samuelson (1947), about whether a social welfare function could be specified, which, on the one hand, takes individual tastes as given and admissible, but, on the other hand, permits neither cardinal utility information nor interpersonal utility comparisons to affect a social ranking of alternative states. Arrow demonstrated that these conditions could not be satisfied simultaneously. Subsequent investigations into Arrow's theorem showed that it was one of a much larger class of impossibility results besetting many other types of collective choice rules and social choice functions.

Arrow's *Social Choice and Individual Values* ([1951] 1963) ushered in a distinctly new phase of social choice research. Although important tensions remain between the social welfare and contractarian strands of the social choice literature, much progress has been made by analysing the link between individual rationality and social outcomes within the context of abstract, axiomatic systems. This change in methods has been enormously fruitful. Besides a journal devoted exclusively to research in social choice, over 500 scholarly articles exploring social choice topics were published between 1950 and 1980 (Arrow [1986] 1995, p. 51). Since that time, at least another 200 articles have appeared in major social science journals.[3] Because of the depth, breadth and sheer volume of the social choice literature and because social choice research encompasses many different areas in economics, political science and philosophy, no attempt will be made here to summarize the findings.[4] Instead, this chapter reviews some of the more influential contributions of social choice theory to economics and political science.

3 The domain of social choice

Much current research in social choice theory can be viewed as a continuation of longstanding debates in philosophy and ethical theory. However, the methodology employed nowadays requires students of social choice to be familiar with formal axiomatic systems. The formal nature of modern social choice research makes this literature, like other formal literatures, susceptible to conflicting interpretation. Some confusion has arisen regarding the importance, applicability and implications of social choice theory to different areas of economics, political science and philosophy (Seabright 1989; Kolm 1996).

Part of the confusion can be traced to a failure on the part of social choice theorists to distinguish among essentially different practical problems in distinctly separate fields of study (Sen 1977). Arrow's ([1951] 1963, pp. 2–3) original interpretation of his own work, for example, suggested that he was concerned with passing from 'a pattern of known tastes to a pattern of social decision-making' according to a natural set of rules. Arrow was primarily interested in collective decision making, a theory of constitutions. Yet his key impossibility result was clearly about social welfare. Perhaps yielding to pointed criticisms by I.M.D. Little (1952), he readily admitted in the second edition of his book that 'a rule for social decision-making is not the same as a welfare judgment' (Arrow [1951] 1963, p. 106). Thus, at its very origins, confusion about the meaning of mathematical models and results has produced controversy about the importance and applicability of social choice theory.

Before discussing some of the important implications of social choice research, it will be useful to address some key divisions in the research domain as well as the applications of that research to different subject areas. These distinctions are important since differences in the interpretation of formal results influence the validity of the claims made for the findings in a particular subject area. When applied to democratic voting procedures, for example, Arrow's results have proven to be tremendously robust; they are more problematic when applied to constitutional decision making, but perhaps not quite as much so as once believed (Hammond 1976; Arrow 1977; d'Aspremont and Gevers 1977; Roberts 1980a).

Social choice theory has heavily influenced the research agenda in four areas of study: the measurement of society's welfare, problems in democratic decision making, issues of institutional design and constitutional decision making. These areas of study are not mutually exclusive and there has been fruitful cross-fertilization between them.

Social welfare measurement A mainstay of social choice theory, social welfare measurement falls within the domain of welfare economics. Within this domain, researchers in social choice have focused on the possibility of aggregating information about individual wellbeing into coherent measures of the wellbeing of society as a whole. For social state x to be judged better than some alternative y, for example, information about the value of social states x and y is needed and a rule for comparing them must be devised. Suppose that state x is characterized by high income and war, while y entails lower income and peace. How can the preferences of individuals over these two states be used to determine society's preferences? Will everyone's preferences be weighted equally? Will the intensities of those preferences be taken into account? Social welfare theories investigate the types of information necessary to evaluate alternative social states and the criteria to be applied in making such evaluations. The measurement of social welfare traditionally has been accomplished by means of a social welfare function. A social welfare function can be thought of as a mathematical rule that ranks states of society relative to one another, enabling one to compare the various alternatives and draw conclusions about which of them is (or are) best based on what individuals prefer.

Problems in democratic decision making Social choice researchers have also contributed to the large literature exploring the properties of alternative voting rules, but often doing so in isolation from social welfare considerations. While the theory of preference aggregation has been treated as distinctly different from the aggregation of votes, the two are in fact closely related. Consider simple majority rule, a particularly familiar democratic decision-making procedure. Mr Gates, Mr Rockefeller and Mr Indigent all have a piece of the pie, although Mr Gates's and Mr Rockefeller's pieces are considerably larger. Mr Gates and Mr Rockefeller want to improve 'society's' welfare by redistributing part of Mr Indigent's piece of the pie to themselves. Repeat the exercise whenever improvements in social welfare are necessary. Obviously, democratic voting rules might not always do as adequate approximations of social welfare; they may produce a 'tyranny of the majority'.

Simple majority rule may be a fair or reasonable collective choice procedure, but, as we can see, it need not produce the best or optimal welfare result. This is especially likely when wealth redistribution is on the agenda and outcomes are consequently zero sum. For this reason social choice researchers have also investigated the properties of alternative voting rules, studying their costs and the normative properties of the outcomes they produce under different environments of choice. This research has been especially important to comparative studies of social choice processes. Other contributors to the social choice literature have been concerned with the stability properties of different voting rules. Social choice researchers have identified many different variables that can influence voting outcomes, including the configurations of voters' preferences, the number of alternatives at issue, their order of consideration, strategic versus non-strategic behavior and so on. These results are surveyed in more detail below.

Problems in institutional design Research in institutional design draws on findings from diverse fields, including welfare economics, voting theory and game theory, to better understand the results produced by democratic decision-making processes. This research highlights the conclusion that outcomes turn on the interdependencies between the institutional framework within which collective choices will be made and the rules governing the decision-making process within that institutional framework.

Social choice perspectives on institutional design consider whether a perceived (public or private) problem should be decided by a collective or democratic decision-making procedure or instead left to the realm of individual action. Should the chicken industry be asked to pay for cleaning up

Chesapeake Bay, given that it is the main source of water pollution? Should it be forced to compensate the oyster industry and the citizens of Maryland, Virginia and Delaware, each of whom is faced with different pollution-related costs? How should this problem be resolved, by the polity, by the legislature or by the courts? What institution *is empowered* to decide this issue? What institution *should be empowered*?

Even if we could easily settle on an institution for deciding this issue, another question of institutional design arises, namely what rule should be used by the institution to reach a collective decision? Let $K = K(C)$ be the minimum number of voters required to be decisive on some issue, where C is the choice rule that will govern the voters' decisions. A problem of institutional design is that different choices or outcomes may emerge depending on the size of $K(C)$. If $K(C) = 1$, for example, then perhaps the chicken industry can be a dictator and decide the outcome for all. If $K(C) = N$, where N is the total number of individuals in society, a rule of unanimity applies and everyone affected by the decision should be consulted first. It is of course possible to consider a variety of other plurality or majority decision rules where $1 \leq K(C) \leq N$.

Each of the possible alternative voting rules entails a different configuration of costs and benefits. As $K(C)$ increases, the costs of making collective decisions rise but the potential welfare losses imposed on the members of the losing coalition fall (Buchanan and Tullock 1962). Research in social choice theory supplies answers to questions of institutional design by studying the different properties associated with different decision rules and demonstrating their implications for individual welfare and individual rights. An important result is that the protection of these rights sometimes requires that decisions not be made collectively at all.

Issues in constitutional decision making Social choice researchers have also investigated and defended various procedures for deciding foundational claims about liberties, rights, or welfare involving competing normative values. On the one hand, there are social contractarians who posit the existence of certain rights that, founded on conceptions of justice, even the welfare of the society cannot be allowed to override. On the other hand, there are theorists who urge general acceptance for the priority of a utilitarian standard over other standards of justice and rightness. Research in constitutional decision making focuses on explicating higher-order criteria for determining the proper emphasis accorded to competing principles of justice (Harsanyi 1977; Rawls 1971; Nozick 1975; Dworkin 1978).

Other issues in constitutional decision making can be treated more formally. Some of these issues involve axiomatic derivations of different constitutional or social principles of justice. Distributional principles of justice, such as utilitarianism, the maximin principle, the leximin principle, and so on, have been studied extensively to determine their underlying normative structures, their informational assumptions and their implications for welfare economics.

This last domain of social choice research highlights an important contribution the methodology of the field has made to social science and philosophy. Because of the general axiomatic approach favored by social choice researchers, the theory permits conceptual examination and analytic comparisons of different normative theories of society. It also permits researchers objectively to evaluate the extent to which the conclusions drawn from those theories depend upon underlying assumptions or variables. For example, results in social choice theory are known to be influenced by assumptions about the properties of social states and individual rationality, the method of preference aggregation, the consistency and informational conditions imposed on those preferences, and the permissible degree of interpersonal comparability. As we shall see in the next section, many of these factors have critical significance for understanding social choice behaviors.

4 Early analytic explorations in welfare economics
Modern welfare economics had its origins at a time when many economists saw their role as serving in an advisory capacity to a benevolent government seeking to maximize the welfare of the society. It was generally assumed that the welfare of the society depended on the policies government pursued and naturally these policies needed to be evaluated in terms of the welfare outcomes they generated for individuals in the society. The questions welfare economics posed about social welfare were therefore similar to questions posed about social utility by the utilitarians: what are the components of individual welfare and under what conditions will society's welfare be maximized?

Utilitarians and modern welfare economists have provided answers to both questions, consideration of which leads to a better understanding of the birth of modern social choice theory. According to the utilitarian doctrine, individuals maximize their happiness or, more simply, their utility, where utility is understood to be pleasure and freedom from pain. Yet the utilitarians did not interpret the maximization of individual utility narrowly, as many economists and public choice theorists have done (Mueller 1989). Self-interest is undoubtedly an important motive in determining choice, but other motives, such as sympathy, were also believed to be important elements in rational choice behaviors.[5] The utilitarians therefore thought that individuals should choose actions that maximize the utilities of *all those affected by their decisions*. This meant that rational individual action is (and should be) directed at the maximization of individual happiness or utility, but that rational social policy should strive to maximize the sum of everyone's happiness or utility.

Whatever the merits of this approach for social choice, several arguments against classical utilitarianism emerged from economic theory (Sugden 1993). The social planner's objective of maximizing the sum of individual utilities presupposes that a meaningful person-specific, cardinal measure of pleasure exists. This presupposition was attacked on two separate grounds. First, human satisfactions are not found in natural cardinal units. It may be difficult to compare apples with oranges, but comparing and then summing the units of happiness a person derives from qualitatively different satisfactions is even more problematic. There are not only different intensities of pleasure or happiness, but also different qualities associated with it across different dimensions. When I compare the pleasure of sitting on the beach sipping a daiquiri with the pleasure from viewing a Jackson Pollock painting, it does not seem plausible that I am comparing different *quantities* of the same thing.

However, even granting that cardinal utilities are meaningful, utilitarianism also presupposed that such quantities could be summed across different individuals to construct a measure of the overall welfare of society. Such an exercise involves making interpersonal comparisons of utility. An example of such a comparison is the claim that, say, it is better to be person A in state x than person B in state y. Welfare economists have argued against making interpersonal utility comparisons, and in a celebrated attack, Robbins (1935) argued that such judgments could not be made in a scientific manner. According to him, 'Introspection does not enable A to measure what is going on in B's mind, nor B to measure what is going on in A's' (p. 140). No doubt there are serious problems posed by the measurability and comparability assumptions presupposed in utilitarian theory. There is an important difference, however, between not admitting any interpersonal comparisons when drawing conclusions about social welfare and admitting full unit comparability when making such judgments. As we shall see, this is a crucial distinction in early welfare economics and it has received extensive critical attention in recent social choice research.

Economists came to reject Jeremy Bentham's view that individual utility is objectively measurable on a cardinal scale and began instead to develop a theory of individual rationality that relies only on ordinal utility information. The rejection of cardinal measures of utility and the acceptance of ordinal rankings led to the emergence of an important social welfare criterion, which has come to be known as *Pareto optimality*. In particular, a social policy is considered to be Pareto optimal if there is no alternative policy that could have made everybody at least as well off and one person strictly better off. This purely ordinal conception of social welfare has come to play a central role in economic theories of social welfare.

Given the assumption of ordinal individual preferences and the Pareto condition on social choices, Abraham Bergson (1948) developed a distinctive framework for social welfare analysis that tried to avoid the difficulties associated with classical utilitarianism. He assumed that social states represent complete descriptions of the amount of each type of commodity held by each individual, the amounts of each productive resource invested in each type of productive activity, the structure of rights in society, and so on. If X denotes the set of all possible social states, that is, $X = \{x, y, z\}$, Bergson defined a real-valued function, W, which assigns a 'social welfare' value, $W(x)$, to any x in X based on 'all the variables that might be considered as affecting welfare' (Bergson 1948, p. 417). Within this framework a central question concerned how to go about aggregating the welfare of individuals into a measure of social welfare. In other words, Bergson's framework naturally led to a question of the following form: since there are many possible social welfare functions, is there any systematic way of choosing among them?

4.1 Individual rationality and social choice functions

Kenneth Arrow's 'general possibility theorem' can be understood as an attempt to answer this question. Arrow defined a social welfare function as a choice rule that specifies an aggregate ordering R over individual orderings, R_i. In other words, a social welfare function (SWF) is a choice rule, f, which is restricted to the set of individual orderings of all possible social states, such that the social ordering is a function of the individual orderings, R_i.

Definition 4.1 (SWF) $R = f(R_1, R_2, \ldots, R_n)$.

In addition to assuming that there are at least three social states and two individuals in the society, Arrow assumed that all individuals in the society are rational.

Arrow's interpretation of individual rationality is crucial for understanding his answer to the question posed above, so we need to discuss his concept of rationality carefully. Individual rationality is based on preference rankings over alternative social states, where social states are understood as Bergsonian 'complete descriptions' of the allocation of commodities, labor and productive resources as well as the amounts and types of public activity (Arrow 1950). Given these states, individual preferences over them could reflect selfish, altruistic or even moral valuations. Arrow assumed that moral values would probably influence the preference orderings of most individuals. However that may be, though, the social planner must be guided exclusively by individuals' preferences.

The Arrowian framework assumes that individuals order social states using a binary preference relation. Formally this means that if X is the set of alternative social states and $x, y, z \in S \subseteq X$, then R has the following properties:

Definition 4.2   (Reflexivity) $\forall x, xRx$.
Definition 4.3   (Transitivity) $\forall x \forall y \forall z, \{[xRy \ \& \ yRz] \rightarrow xRz\}$.
Definition 4.4   (Connectedness) $\forall x \forall y, [xRy \ \text{or} \ yRx]$.

When these properties are satisfied for a subset S of X, we say that S is weakly ordered (and that R is an ordering). If a subset S of X is ordered for an individual i or a social planner, then there exists a choice function $C(S, R)$ for that individual.[6]

Theorem 4.1   If R is an ordering defined over a finite set X, then a choice function $C(S, R)$ is defined over X (Sen [1970] 1984, p. 14).

Although Theorem 4.1 is not a necessary condition for rationality to hold, it is a sufficient condition and frequently assumed to be so in social choice theory and utility theory. As we shall see, there are weaker conditions that produce orderings that do not violate the transitivity requirement.

Theorem 4.1 implies the existence of a best element.

Definition 4.5   (Best Element) $\exists x \forall y, \{(x \in S) \ \& \ (y \in S) \rightarrow xRy\}$.

A best element of a set is a version of maximizing rationality, while the existence of a choice function is in some ways a condition of rational choice – whether that function refers to individual (R_i) or social (R) preference.

4.2   The impossibility of a social welfare function

In addition to the assumptions about individual rationality described above, Arrow's framework assumed that a social welfare function satisfies several other conditions. These conditions, which can be thought of as rules for constructing the social welfare function, are as follows: *Unrestricted Domain* for preferences, a *Non-dictatorship condition*, a *Pareto rule* and the requirement of the *Independence of Irrelevant Alternatives*. Each condition is stated below and its implications for constructing a social welfare function are described.

Condition U   (Unrestricted Domain) The domain of f includes all possible individual n-tuples of individual orderings over X.

According to Arrow, individual preferences should be defined on any possible ordering of social states, not merely orderings within the feasible set.[7] Why is this important? An individual who is ill, for example, can meaningfully be said to prefer being in a state in which medicine is available for his condition, even if he could not afford such medicine. Such infeasible states should be considered in a person's ranking of alternative social states. More-over, Arrow believed that individuals should be permitted to have preferences on (or to express preferences on) matters that may be deemed taboo. Arrow's framework is therefore committed to a very liberal understanding of individual preferences and this understanding is captured by Condition *U*.

Condition non-D   (Non-dictatorship) There is no individual *i* whose strict preference xP_iy over [*x*, *y*] invariably determines the social preference (*xPy*).

Social outcomes, according to Arrow, should not be restricted to those within a set of preferences that someone deems feasible or reasonable. Arrow also required that any social welfare function not be based on the preference of a single individual. This ruled out the possibility of a single person or dictator determining what is good for the society in the aggregation process.

Condition P   ([Weak] Pareto) For any *x*, *y* in *X*, if everyone strictly prefers *x* to *y*, that is, $\forall i \; xP_iy$, then *xPy*.

In addition to these requirements, Arrow also assumed that the preferences of the social planner should reflect changes in what everyone might strictly prefer. This condition, referred to as weak Pareto optimality, can be interpreted as a monotonicity requirement on the social welfare function. In other words, a change that is advantageous for each individual must be a change that is good for the society. (Alternatively we may impose a stronger condition that if at least one individual is made better off by a change, and no one is made worse off, the change should be made.)

Condition I   (Independence of Irrelevant Alternatives) Let R and R' be social welfare functions where $R = f(\{R_i\}_{i=1,...,N})$ and $R' = f(\{R'_i\}_{i=1,...,N})$. If $\forall_i, \forall x \forall y \in S \; xR_iy \leftrightarrow xR'_iy$, then *C*(*S*, *R*) and *C*(*S*, *R'*) are the same.

This final condition on the structure of a social welfare function is perhaps the most controversial one. First, Condition *I* is violated when, in a social choice involving *x* and *y*, the individual rankings of another 'irrelevant alternative' *z* become salient in the choice of *x* or *y*. Second, this condition is also violated whenever anything other than individual orderings of *x* and *y* are considered. This is significant in so far as it rules out social choices being determined by the intensities of individuals' preferences.

Given these four rather weak conditions on constructing a social welfare function, Arrow's general possibility theorem is rather surprising. Building on the so-called 'paradox of voting' identified earlier by the Marquis de

Condorcet ([1785] 1994), Arrow proved that no social welfare function could satisfy all the conditions simultaneously.[8]

Theorem 4.2   No social welfare function satisfies Conditions *U*, *P*, *I* and non-*D*.

In other words, Conditions *U*, *P* and *I* imply Condition *D* (Dictatorship). This result is an obviously important and unsettling problem for both economics and political science. Viewed from the former perspective, Theorem 4.2 appeared to imply that an unbiased, scientific basis for social welfare judgments, similar in spirit to traditional utilitarianism, was logically impossible. After some initial skepticism,[9] pessimism seemed to prevail among welfare economists regarding any attempt objectively to construct a social welfare function having even minimally desirable properties. In a limited sense, later social choice research verified this interpretation of Arrow's result, although grounds for optimism have been found recently.

Arrow's result was even more devastating for political science, however. Liberal interpretations of democracy appeared especially vulnerable to Arrow's theorem (Riker 1982). According to liberal democratic theory, laws are legitimized by the 'general will' – the abstract concept derived by aggregating the preferences of all citizens. Social choice research, especially when applied to collective choice mechanisms, has severely undermined this position on democracy, demanding fundamental changes in thinking. This implication of Arrow is explored later in this chapter.

5   Escaping Arrow's result

Kenneth Arrow's proof of Theorem 4.2 marked the birth of modern social choice theory. As we shall see, the basic result has proven remarkably robust to various modifications in his axiomatic framework. Since that time, a considerable amount of research has been devoted to exploring various means of avoiding the impossibility result he deduced (Sen [1970] 1984; 1977).

Before discussing different strategies researchers have employed to avoid the uncomfortable consequences of Theorem 4.2, we need to ask just how reasonable the conditions imposed by Arrow on his SWF are.[10] When interpreted as an exercise in collective decision making, his restrictions are remarkably weak. In other words, Arrow advanced the set of four conditions believing they were *necessary*, but not necessarily *sufficient*, for acceptable collective decision making. Hence, even if it is possible to get around Arrow's result, we may nevertheless be left with a rather unpalatable method for deciding social issues. This is precisely what social choice researchers have discovered in democratic theory.

When interpreted as an exercise in aggregating individual welfares to measure social welfare, however, the conditions Arrow imposed on constructing a social welfare function are in some ways very restrictive. Arrow's conditions, as later results in social choice theory have shown, exclude all non-welfare characteristics of social states – things such as conceptions of freedom, autonomy and justice – as well as any information allowing one to compare individual welfares in different states (Roberts 1980a; Sen 1982, 1987). This eschewal of non-utility information and the exclusion of any type of interpersonal comparisons of utility can be viewed as overly restrictive when attempting to evaluate social welfare in different social states. Arrow's impossibility theorem can be interpreted, therefore, as precipitated by the highly restrictive informational conditions imposed in the theory. Once these conditions are relaxed, many possibilities become available to the social planner.

There has been an enormous research effort in social choice theory devoted to avoiding Arrow's result, most of it unsuccessful. Rather than focus on the failures, let us consider some of the more successful attempts to avoid Theorem 4.2. How can Arrow's result be avoided? Because the result is established deductively, the only way of doing so is to modify one or more of the assumptions used to derive it. Social choice researchers rarely modify the non-dictatorship condition. Moreover, except in discussions of liberalism, the Pareto condition is rarely weakened, perhaps because of the monotonicity property it entails.[11] That left researchers with only three things to work with – Conditions U and I and the rationality assumption. It is the last assumption we consider first.

5.1 Modifying social rationality

A social welfare function is a special type of aggregation rule that requires all social preferences to be orderings. The requirement of an ordering on R, though perhaps reasonable, is not necessary for the existence of a choice function, which we noted earlier imposes an important constraint on choice behavior. It is possible to weaken the social rationality requirement by demanding something less than full transitivity among social states, such as quasi-transitivity. Quasi-transitivity, although not necessary, is a sufficient condition for avoiding intransitive social outcomes while allowing a choice function to be derived.[12]

Definition 4.6 (Quasi-Transitivity) $\forall x \forall y \forall z, \{[xPy \ \& \ yPz] \rightarrow xPz\}$.

When a social welfare function is restricted to the class of quasi-ordered alternative social states, we have what Sen calls a *social decision function*. The distinction between a social welfare function and a social decision function is important, because it avoids Arrow's impossibility result. If we assume that a social decision function is defined on a finite set X, Sen ([1970] 1984, Theorem 4*1, p. 52) shows that it is possible to satisfy Arrow's four conditions.

Theorem 4.3   There is a social decision function that satisfies Conditions U, P, I and non-D.

Despite the apparent importance of Theorem 4.3, Sen has argued that when viewed from either an economic or political perspective, there is still no cause for jubilation.

From an economic perspective, relaxing the transitivity condition may not produce an entirely satisfactory ranking of social states. Suppose that all individuals prefer social state x to social state y and that they prefer y to z, but suppose also that the planner is indifferent between x and z. Over all three alternatives, social state x is the unique best, with no alternative being better. Yet when the planner compares x and z, either one could be chosen. This makes the choice of social states – and ultimately the rationality properties a social welfare or social decision function must satisfy – dependent on the order in which the alternatives are compared.[13]

The importance of Theorem 4.3 becomes even more questionable when viewed as a problem in voting, however. Allen Gibbard (1969) shows in an unpublished work[14] that the class of social decision functions generating a quasi-transitive R is restricted to 'oligarchies'. (An oligarchy is a subset of two or more decision makers who, if the members of the group agree, can impose a choice, or if the members of the group do not agree, each group member has veto power.) Formally, if anyone in the oligarchical group xP_iy, society must regard xRy and, moreover, if everyone in the oligarchical group xP_iy, then society must regard xPy. It therefore appears that weakening the ordering requirement that Arrow imposed on social choice functions does not take us very far from de facto dictatorship. So although a social decision function can satisfy Arrow's conditions, it does this in a very marginal way, making the result unappealing from both economic and political perspectives.[15]

5.2   Modifying individual rationality

Among other things, Condition I rules out any differences in the intensities of preferences an individual may have for different social states. Most forms of utilitarianism are also ruled out by this assumption. If we allow individuals to express the intensities of their preferences over social states, does this enrichment of the informational base allow us to escape Arrow's result? More generally, what kinds of information must be admitted into Arrow's framework to escape the implications of Theorem 4.2?

The traditional social welfare framework assumes that individual utilities defined over states are ordinal and interpersonally non-comparable. To include the possibility of cardinal utility information, consider the difference between a social welfare function and a social welfare function*al*. Social welfare functionals are similar to social welfare functions except that they permit cardinal utility information. A social welfare functional (SWFL) is a rule that specifies one and only one social ordering given a set of individual welfare functions for each individual. When Arrow's conditions *U*, *P* and *I* are suitably modified to conditions *U**, *P** and *I** so that they apply to a SWFL involving cardinal non-comparability, nothing is gained. Arrow's result stands in this new framework.

Theorem 4.4   No social welfare functional satisfies conditions *U**, *P**, *I** and *non-D*.

Theorem 4.4 shows that the social planner would gain nothing from admitting cardinal utility information (Sen [1970] 1984, p. 129). But what if the non-comparability assumption is denied? Here the situation changes dramatically.

Allowing the social planner to make even weak interpersonal utility comparisons opens up a rich set of possibility results. Interpersonal comparability, without cardinal utility information, permits judgments about alternative social states – in the spirit, for example, of Rawls's (1971) maximin principle – to be made. Dropping the non-comparability condition along with the ordinality requirement brings many other rules under consideration. Generally speaking, varying the measurability and comparability assumptions implicit in social choice research weakens Arrow's impossibility result.[16]

Theorem 4.5   When increasing degrees of precision in the measurement of utility are combined with increasing degrees of comparability permitted between individuals over their evaluation of states, a social planner can make increasingly strong welfare judgments.

Table 4.1 summarizes some of the possibility theorems deducible when the informational basis used to construct a social welfare function or social welfare functional is changed.

5.3   Conclusions on social choice and welfare economics
Kenneth Arrow proved that a social welfare function cannot be constructed based on ordinal, non-comparable individual utilities. It is, however, possible to escape this result by weakening the transitivity requirement on social choices, though the value of such social choices may not be satisfactory to

Table 4.1   Possibility theorems

Comparability assumptions*	Measurability assumptions	
	Ordinal	Cardinal
Non-comparability	Impossibility (Arrow [1951] 1963)	Impossibility (Sen 1970)
Level comparability	Possibility (Hammond 1976; Strasnick 1976)	
Unit comparability		Possibility (d'Aspremont and Gevers 1977)
Full comparability		Possibility (Deschamps and Gevers 1978)

Note: *For a description of these measurability assumptions, see Roberts (1980a, p. 423).

many democratic theorists. Admitting cardinal utility information into the Arrow framework accomplishes nothing. The key lies elsewhere.

To escape Arrow's result, comparisons of individual utility must be made. Once this is done it is possible to make claims concerning the welfare of the society based on the welfare of individuals and, contrary to the understanding of most economists, it is possible to make reasonably *strong* claims about the welfare of the society based on the welfare of individuals. But the moral of more recent research in social choice theory is that such judgments cannot be made within the narrow confines of traditional welfare economics. To make such judgments economists need to consider and compare different kinds of information about welfare and the distribution of welfare in society (Sen 1987).

6   Philosophical problems of rationality in social choice

Arrow argued that individuals should be permitted to order social states on the basis of any information or criteria they deem important or useful. This suggests, somewhat misleadingly, that both utility and non-utility information would influence a social planner's perspective when making a judgment about the welfare of society. This is not the case, however. From the perspective of the social planner, the informational base is much more restrictive.[17]

Definition 4.7   (Welfarism) Social welfare is a function of personal utility levels, so that any two social states must be ranked exclusively on the basis of personal utilities in the respective states.

Traditional frameworks for welfare economics imply welfarism, which means that non-welfare characteristics have no role in the social choice (Sen 1979; Roberts 1980a). This is clearly a very restrictive condition when deciding among social states from a social planner's perspective. But what about the perspective of an individual? Is welfarism implied by orthodox axiomatic utility frameworks? Or do axiomatic utility frameworks admit a range of welfare and non-welfare values?

6.1 Neutrality and utility theory

Many utility theorists, including Arrow himself, have argued that utility theory does not necessarily imply welfarism. These theories of preference make no behavioral assumptions about the kinds of values agents seek to maximize. Neither the axioms of the theory nor the definitions of outcomes demand that rational individuals choose actions only in their own self-interest. Agents can have a preference for any type of outcome, and individual preferences can thus reflect almost any type of valuations of those outcomes. Peter Ordeshook (1986, p. 52) makes this point very succinctly: 'Utility functions are simply abstract representations, and the a's, o's, x's, and y's that express them await interpretation.'

Axiomatic conceptions of utility theory therefore await some behavioral interpretation a theorist finds appropriate. In fact, because there appears to be no unique interpretation of axiomatic utility theory, an individual's utility function, $U^i(x)$, is relatively neutral with respect to many different behavioral responses to information in outcomes.

> *Definition 4.8* (Representational Neutrality) $U^i(x)$ represents any values or motives that influence preferences and choice.

This means that an indefinite number of behavioral interpretations of rationality may be consistent with the axioms of the theory. For example, if it is assumed that moral, altruistic or egalitarian attitudes influence an individual's preference ordering of outcomes, and if a utility function is defined on such a preference order, then information about social values must be included in the mathematical representation of preference. Therefore, whenever social or moral values influence decision making, we can still say that the best alternative is the one that maximizes a decision maker's expected utility – however an individual may behaviorally understand that alternative.

6.2 An objection to consequentialist rationality

There are many well-known empirical arguments against utility theory as a descriptive theory of rationality (for example, Tversky and Kahneman 1986). These arguments have called into question the reasonableness of the axioms

of transitivity and independence. This section reviews two normative arguments, distinct from these empirical arguments, which may cast doubt on the
reasonableness of axiomatic utility theory as a neutral framework for explaining choice behaviors. The first argument is based on the importance of different
kinds of non-welfare values in rational decision making. The existence of
non-welfare values suggests that utility theory cannot neutrally represent the
informational basis of human preferences in an axiomatic framework.

Critics of classical utilitarianism argue that values like freedom, autonomy
and justice often influence reasonable decision makers. Because these values
are not reducible to instrumental valuations for some clearly definable good,
early critics of utilitarianism maintained that moral judgments based on these
values refer to abstract properties of objects which can be known only by
moral reasoning or moral intuition. Many contemporary critics of utility
theory have taken a similar position with regard to modern decision theory.
Critics like Amartya Sen, Bernard Williams and John Rawls have argued that
values such as freedom, integrity, commitment, or fairness often influence
rational decision makers. Because these values appear to be directed less at
welfare gains or losses, and more at the promotion of abstract normative
goals, they may not fit neatly into any axiomatic representation of rationality.

Why this is so can be illustrated by looking at both the normative and
behavioral properties of some particular non-welfare values. Personal integrity, for example, has frequently been cited as a non-welfare value that often
influences individual choices (Williams 1973; Taylor 1985). The value of
integrity has more to do with the character of a person's choices – and the
relation of those choices to what an agent values personally (over the long
term) – than what outcomes are produced by their choices. Can this value be
modeled using an axiomatic framework? It can if we claim that an agent's
preferences are responding not only to what is produced by choice behavior,
but also to the side-effects of choice itself, such as the agent's character. In
other words, to include the value of integrity in decision making, utility
theorists need to assume that the integrity associated with different alternatives is already included in the state description of any outcome, along with
what is caused by the choice of an alternative. Once that is done, it is indeed
possible to represent the value of integrity using $U^i(x)$.

But philosophers may argue that this seriously misrepresents the value of
integrity. Integrity is best understood as a criterion for evaluating the relation
of choices to the character of the agent, rather than something that is produced in behavior to fulfill an agent's preferences or desires. For this reason,
we do not say that an individual's choice is motivated by his desire to
produce personal integrity, nor do we say that his choice produced integrity;
rather, a person's choice is an indicator of his integrity. In other words, the
basis for making such a judgment is found in observing the behavior of an

agent – what he says, what he does, and how he does it. When modeling choice behavior, integrity should not be included in the state descriptions of the outcomes, because to do so would suggest that agents respond to the incentive of integrity and make decisions as if this incentive mattered in their rational calculations. Of course, there is nothing that prevents the utility theorist from doing so, to preserve the instrumental character of all rational decisions. Moral philosophers would rightly object that this redescription of decision making misrepresents the moral value of integrity.

But there is another reason why non-welfare values do not fit nicely into axiomatic frameworks. Although values like personal integrity or commitment to others frequently are balanced against other motivations or interests, they sometimes have the property of taking priority in an agent's moral code. Whenever this occurs, and choice behavior is modeled, we often find that preferences are best described as lexical (Frohlich and Oppenheimer 1992; Lissowski and Swistak 1995).[18] Lexically ordered preferences cannot be represented by continuous real-valued utility functions (Shubik 1987; Varian 1995). To the extent that non-welfare values exhibit lexical properties, and to the extent that people make judgments on the basis of such values, they may be considered as counterexamples to the neutrality of axiomatic utility theory.

These problems illustrate, however, a more general difficulty with claims regarding the normative neutrality of axiomatic frameworks for rationality. If rationality is indeed motivated by both welfare and non-welfare values, and if these values are not equivalent to one another, normative differences in the informational basis for making judgments and choices may arise. For example, it seems reasonable to say that a person A enjoys greater welfare in state x than in state y and that x is therefore preferred to y. But a judgment, preference, or choice based on the total amount of welfare in states x and y is arguably distinct from an evaluation of states based on whether A enjoys the requisite kind of fairness or rights in them. It is certainly arguable that both kinds of judgments are based on similar informational properties in the two states.

Because the informational basis of judgments concerning the values of freedom, integrity, commitment, or fairness may be distinct from the informational basis of judgments concerning welfare values, critics claim that these values cannot be combined into a single index for different sets of value judgments. This suggests that welfare and non-welfare information may not be fully comparable in any single axiomatic framework. Critics, in asserting that welfare values are not fully comparable to non-welfare values, are not advancing a behavioral claim. Rather they are asserting that the comparison of different states (and ultimately moral judgments themselves) cannot be accomplished by appeal to some neutral informational properties of states which include both welfare and non-welfare values. This means that utility theorists need to demonstrate how the theory can depict any value in a general normative theory of value. If no such demonstration is forthcoming, utility representations of individual rationality may be objectionable to the extent that neutral comparisons of values are not possible within that framework (Sidgwick [1901] 1962; Taylor 1985; Williams 1973).

7   The centrality of social choice for political science

The significance of social choice theory for modern political science cannot be overestimated. Although political scientists did not initially understand the relevance of Arrow's theorem (Riker 1961), social choice theory later revolutionized political science in many ways: some directly as a result of the findings in the field and others indirectly as a result of the approach of the theory. This section focuses on three theorems in social choice theory and considers the implications of these results for democratic politics. Before discussing the importance of these theorems, however, it is worth pausing to mention the indirect influence social choice has had on the development of methodology in political science.

While change has occurred rather slowly, social choice research in political science has contributed toward establishing the centrality of deductive reasoning in political theory. Prior to 1951, when *Social Choice and Individual Values* was first published, the discipline of political science was based primarily on historical, philosophical and humanist foundations (Farr and Seidelman 1993). There were virtually no structured methods of observation, and little in the way of careful scientific methodology in the discipline. Social choice research fundamentally altered this state of affairs. The extent of the change is all the more remarkable when one considers that, as late as 1957, there were no articles in the *American Political Science Review* that relied on formal reasoning. By 1994, almost half of all the articles in that journal used a formal methodology in their research (Frohlich and Oppenheimer 2000).

Although social choice theory has influenced methodological assumptions throughout political science, its direct influence is also difficult to overestimate. The impact of social choice research has been most striking in the area of democratic theory. Social choice research in democratic theory has led to fundamental changes in the way we understand and investigate democratic institutions and the functioning of democratic processes. Two simple examples show how influential this research has been. One example deals with coalitional power, while the other example deals with voting rules.

Most interpretations of the role of individuals in democracy stress the importance of citizen participation in politics (Barber 1984; Mansbridge 1983). If a group has greater numbers of citizens participating in democratic decisions, this should translate into greater legislative voice and greater power, other things equal. But social choice theory shows that things are not that simple. Even if we disregard problems in collective action (Olson 1965), political power and legislative voice do not always increase with the numbers of legislators or votes in a coalition. Although students of democratic theory might naturally assume that groups are always better off with more representation than less, social choice research shows this is not always true. In some cases a constituency would profit from a loss of legislative voice, other things equal. To illustrate this, assume that a legislature with 100 members is divided into three voting blocks: 49 rural representatives (**R**), 23 urban representatives (**U**) and 28 suburban representatives (**S**), voting on a bill that would provide agricultural subsidies **A**, food stamps **F**, or both **AF**. The preferences of these representatives are described in Table 4.2.[19]

Table 4.2   Preferences for three constituencies

Rural citizens **R**	Urban citizens **U**	Suburban citizens **S**
49 seats	23 seats	28 seats
A	**F**	∅
AF	**AF**	**A**
∅	∅	**F**
F	**A**	**AF**

It is clear from Table 4.2 that a majority favors neither single-issue measure. However, since rural and urban legislators prefer **AF** – both subsidies and food stamps – to no bill at all, we would expect them to trade votes and pass **AF** without amendment. Suppose that the suburban citizens lose four or more seats, distributed equally to the rural and urban coalitions. Maybe they lose all of their seats to these coalitions. Because that makes the rural coalition a majority, **A** alone passes. Since suburban citizens prefer **A** to **AF**, they have profited from a loss of representation. This problem is perfectly general and it can occur under different voting processes (Schwartz 1995). Yet this example is similar to a large body of social choice research on voting, voting power and coalitional formation. Representation, voting power and coalitional strength are not linearly related to increases in the number of representatives, the number of voters or the size of a political coalition. In democracy the situation is more complex. This suggests that small changes in the rules of a democratic institution, or small changes in the coalitional structure of a legislature, will sometimes lead to large and unexpected changes in politics or policy.

Another result developed from research in social choice is equally surprising. The act of voting, whether by citizens or legislators, is fundamental to the functioning of a democracy. Unlike consumers in a market, where different allocations of income can result in unequal amounts of welfare, voting appears (at least in theory) to treat all citizens equally: citizens are allotted just one vote and no one more than one. Given this equality among citizens, it might be conjectured that democratic voting procedures are a fair and reasonable way of making social decisions. But social choice theory shows us that there are problems with this conjecture.

To understand why majority rule is sometimes neither fair nor reasonable, consider a very simple democratic society. Suppose that three voters (A, B, C) are deciding among one of three policies (x, y, z) and that each voter has preferences on these policies defined according to Table 4.3. Assume that this society uses simple majority rule applied to successive pairs of alternative policies. Although each person has a transitive preference ordering, the social ordering produced by majority rule is intransitive. Given these preferences, according to majority rule x is preferred to y and y is preferred to z. Unfortunately, however, z is preferred to x and so the social ordering – xPyPzPx – is intransitive. The individuals in the society have well-ordered preferences, but the voting procedure leads to an intransitive outcome or voting cycle. This problem in majority-rule voting is known as Condorcet's paradox of voting.

Table 4.3   Preferences for three voters resulting in a majority-rule cycle

Voter A	Voter B	Voter C
x	y	z
y	z	x
z	x	y

8   The political consequences of voting cycles

Social choice theory has investigated the problems posed by intransitive outcomes in majority-rule decisions and the consequences of voting cycles for democracy. The existence of voting cycles, as we shall see, poses serious problems for democratic theory, especially if voting is interpreted as expressing the will of the people. Consider the first problem. Whenever voting cycles exist in a democracy, there can be multiple majorities capable of winning. Unless it is shown that one procedure for voting is fairer than all other voting procedures, majorities who lose may have a legitimate claim about the justness of the vote – especially if they can show that they would have won under a different voting procedure or different agendas.

Another problem with cycles concerns the meaning of voting as a social decision process. Whenever a voting cycle exists, there is no unique majority-rule winner. A unique majority-rule winner is defined as a Condorcet winner.

Definition 4.9 (Condorcet Winner) A social alternative that beats or ties all other alternatives in paired comparisons is called a Condorcet winner.

The failure of a voting rule to choose a Condorcet winner can be interpreted as a failure of the social choice mechanism. If there is no Condorcet winner, voting cannot be interpreted as a reasonable device for expressing what the people want.

What does the society want when voting cycles are present? Using the earlier set of preferences (see Table 4.3), Table 4.4 shows how any alternative can win depending on the ordering of the pairings. The alternative chosen by the group may simply reflect how the alternatives were paired and which agenda was used to structure the vote process. Whenever cycles are present, whoever controls the agenda may control the outcome of a majority-rule contest. If competing political groups know this, we might expect groups to vie for control of the agenda. Policy disputes can therefore be expected to evolve into disputes about agenda setting and ultimately into disputes about who controls an agenda or democratic institution.

Table 4.4   Three different winners in a majority-rule contest

Stage	Agenda 1	Agenda 2	Agenda 3
First stage	x versus y: x wins	z versus x: z wins	y versus z: y wins
Second stage	x versus z: z wins	z versus y: y wins	y versus x: x wins
Social choice	z is chosen	y is chosen	x is chosen

Although cycles can lead to multiple majorities, how important are voting cycles, practically speaking? We know that cycles do not occur across every set of issues; after all, a society or group of voters could be strongly in favor of some alternative by such a large margin that it is impossible to construct a voting cycle. How often can we expect voting cycles to occur in a democracy when using majority rule to decide social policies? To help understand the likelihood of cycles in a democracy, consider the previous example once again. How many ways can a person order three alternatives? Table 4.5 shows that there are 13 possible orderings of three alternatives, six of these being strong orderings. If we consider only strong orderings, then any person may adopt any one of the six preference profiles. Assuming three people in the

Table 4.5   *Possible preference profiles for an individual voter (three alternatives)*

1	2	3	4	5	6	7	8	9	10	11	12	13
x	x	y	y	z	z	xy	xz	yz	x	y	z	
y	z	x	z	x	y							xyz
z	y	z	x	y	x	z	y	x	yz	xz	xy	

society, this yields $6^3 = 216$ possible preference profiles for the society over three alternatives. Among these possible preference profiles, 12 generate a voting cycle, so the probability of a cycle in a three-person society is approximately 6 percent (0.056).

There is nothing inevitable about voting cycles in democracy and, given our analysis of the problem, they do not appear very likely. We might therefore conclude that voting cycles pose only a slight problem to the functioning of democracy or to the reasonableness of democratic choices using majority rule. Unfortunately, research in social choice does not support this conclusion. The analysis provided above assumes a small number of voters and issues. The problem of cycling becomes more obvious and more prevalent as the number of issues or the number of voters increases. When no special restrictions are placed on the types of preference orderings individuals may have, the probability of a cycle is large, approaching one as the number of alternatives rises.[20] For this reason alone, we would expect voting cycles to occur frequently in democratic politics.

More practical considerations lead to a similar conclusion about the frequency of voting cycles in democratic politics. It can be easily shown that solving zero-sum (or constant-sum) redistributional problems using majority rule leads to cycling, since no sharing scheme is a Condorcet winner. This suggests that any policy issue having a redistributional component can easily lead to voting cycles. As Robert Dahl (1961) and others have argued, redistributional problems are central to many policy disputes and an integral part of democratic politics. Yet it is not only the prevalence of redistributional issues in democracy that leads to the conclusion that cycles are apt to be prevalent. Simple allocational problems involving the provision of public goods can be redefined by a legislature so that they too have a redistributional component. This means that even the most commonplace political issues facing a committee or legislature, those involving the provision of public goods, can result in cycling (Tullock 1959). Majority-rule voting cycles therefore appear to be endemic to democracy.

8.1 Rationality in democratic voting procedures

Social choice theory illustrates that cycles are apt to plague most democracies and that the possibility for agenda control in policy disputes is therefore high. No doubt the problem of voting cycles is a serious one for democracies, but Black ([1958] 1987) has shown that if each individual has a best alternative and his preferences are restricted to being 'single-peaked', then intransitive social choices can be avoided, even when using majority rule. The condition of single-peakedness is a type of partial agreement in a society both in terms of some outcome (everyone agrees that some alternative is not the worst when comparing three alternatives) and in terms of the 'dimension' of the choice space. In other words the general problem for the society is that it must choose a position on an issue. When a group or society has such preferences then the following theorem is true.[21]

Theorem 4.6 If x_{med} is a median position for a group of voters, then the number of votes for x_{med} is greater than or equal to the number of votes for any other alternative z in that group.

This result, known as the *median-voter theorem*, requires that preferences be defined over one issue (or dimension). Theorem 4.6 states that a median policy or candidate cannot lose in a majority-rule contest in a single dimension. People who have single-peaked preferences can therefore reach consensus using simple majority rule. This means that voting cycles are no longer a problem, since there is a Condorcet winner.[22]

The practical importance of this result for majority rule and democratic theory is limited by the very nature of the political process, however. Political decisions often involve more than one issue. Consider the ordinary and common democratic problem of deciding on a public budget. Budget decisions frequently involve allocating resources over several different projects. Theorem 4.6 does not hold over more than one political issue (or dimension), and so it is not applicable to even this common situation. Even more important than this are the complications of politics and policy. Political issues and problems usually do not come wrapped neatly in a single package. Rather they involve multiple perspectives over multiple dimensions.[23] Political issues and problems are difficult precisely because citizens or legislators do not agree politically on some feature of a problem that needs to be decided (regardless of how it should be decided). The undecidability of multidimensional issues is indeed a serious limitation with Theorem 4.6 when applied to politics.

William Riker shows that the foregoing problem is much worse. It is not simply a matter of political issues being complicated or multidimensional. Rather we can expect single-issue problems to become multidimensional issues when someone can benefit from repackaging. This occurs because forcing voters to consider a second dimension can sometimes block one-dimensional agreements. Riker's (1965) analysis of the Seventeenth Amendment to the US Constitution, which provided for the direct election of senators, illustrates this problem. Originally the Constitution's framers decided that a state's two US senators would be chosen by pluralities in their respective state legislatures. Owing to populist political pressure, the direct election of senators was part of the conventional wisdom in Washington by the late 1890s, and there appeared to be strong agreement in Congress on this. As Riker shows, however, clever parliamentary tactics by Chauncey DePew upset agreement on the proposed constitutional amendment by linking it with other issues (such as racism and party loyalty).

Theorem 4.6, the median-voter theorem, should not inspire confidence among democratic theorists regarding the stability of democracy. Most political disputes involve multiple issues that cannot always be disentangled. Agreement may not even be possible on the dimensions of a problem that need to be decided. Yet even when politicians are lucky enough to agree to resolve a single-issue dispute, this can easily be upset by the interests of only a few. To be sure, increasing the number of dimensions to a political issue would not necessarily be a problem if an analogous result, similar to Theorem 4.6, existed for multiple dimensions. Unfortunately, social choice research shows that this is not so. Adding more dimensions to a political issue dramatically increases the problem of cycling for majority-rule decision-making processes. This means that without special social or institutional structures to prevent voting cycles, multiple majorities over multiple issue spaces can be expected to emerge (Plott 1976).

8.2   Alternative voting schemes

If majority-rule voting systems imply potential irrationalities in social choices, then perhaps there are other voting systems that do not have this feature. The problem of voting cycles in majority rule led social choice researchers to investigate systems of voting that avoided intransitive social outcomes.

Voting rules, like aggregation exercises in welfare economics, use different kinds of information to make collective choices. Majoritarian methods of voting, such as plurality rule, majority rule, and extensions thereof, only use information about the best alternative to decide among social outcomes. Positional voting methods, such as approval voting and the Borda count, use information about the entire ordering of alternatives to select winners democratically. Utilitarian methods not only use information about orders but also information about intensities of voters' preferences. Because each method uses different kinds of information and sometimes aggregates this information differently, each method can lead to different social choices. This occurs even when preference profiles are identical.

How then do we decide among different voting procedures? Social choice theory, in an effort to avoid the problem of cycling, has discovered a very troubling fact about democratic voting procedures: every voting procedure, in each of the three families of voting described above, violates some criterion of consistency or fairness (Riker 1982). These criteria, when taken together, *are reasonable and minimal criteria* that we might demand of a voting system. Since no voting system satisfies all of these conditions, all voting systems are imperfect in one sense or another. Here we can see Arrow's theorem casting a long shadow over democratic voting procedures and politics. No method of voting that simultaneously satisfies several elementary conditions of fairness can also produce social choices that always satisfy elementary conditions of reasonableness. The search for a more reasonable voting system appears to lead to a new problem about the conditions one should demand of a voting system. Arrow's theorem tells us there must be some tradeoff between conditions of fairness and consistency.

8.3   Agenda setters, strategic voting, and vote trading

The search for more acceptable voting rules for deciding democratic policies does not take us very far. We are left with the problem of irrationalities in majority rule. We already know that the probability of voting cycles in democratic institutions using majority rule is likely to be high. Multiple majorities therefore appear endemic to democracy and agenda control or agenda manipulation appears to be a natural consequence. Before concluding this discussion of social choice theory, however, it is important to consider one final alternative that could influence our interpretation of these results.

The previous discussions of intransitivities in social outcomes assumed a static understanding of political processes. Democracy is a much more dynamic process with changing demands on citizens and legislators and with changing responses to these demands. If we assume a more dynamic interpretation of democratic politics, does the problem of intransitivities and cycling among policy alternatives continue or does it diminish?

Several important theorems in social choice theory not only show that cycling remains, but that it can also lead to instability and unpredictability in the democratic policy process. One result concerns the importance of an agenda setter in democratic politics while the other concerns the reactions of legislators themselves to such an authority. Consider the first result. Assuming that equilibria in n-dimensions are unlikely (similar to Plott's median in all directions), McKelvey (1976b) proved the following theorem for 'convex' preferences when a Condorcet winner does not exist.

Theorem 4.7   For all *n*-dimensional majority-rule decision procedures, social preferences can cycle over the entire outcome space using a finite amendment agenda procedure.[24]

This theorem is significant because it shows that a person who sets an agenda (and who has knowledge of the preferences of different voters) can literally choose any policy outcome and then formulate a specific agenda to reach that outcome using majority rule. Theorem 4.7 therefore appears to justify the worst fears of democratic theorists. Voting cycles not only lead to multiple majorities, voting cycles also can be systematically exploited by agenda setters in virtually any policy environment. Democratic policy outcomes, according to Theorem 4.7, may simply reflect the will (and cleverness) of the speaker or the chairperson in a democratic institution.

Cycles may present problems for a rational understanding of outcomes and agenda setters may indeed exploit their special positions and seek to control outcomes by manipulating the agenda to their advantage. Yet individuals are not defenseless against agenda setters. Perhaps voters are more skillful and adroit than the earlier models assumed. Maybe legislators or citizens in democracy can anticipate an agenda setter's attempt to manipulate them. An extensive literature in social choice theory has explored this and related questions (Ordeshook 1986; Mueller 1989). The conclusions are not quite as pessimistic as the earlier results, although there is also no cause for jubilation here either.

Voters are not required to always vote for the option they think is best. They may vote for another, less-preferred alternative in order to avoid their least-preferred outcome. When this occurs, voters are engaging in strategic voting. Strategic voting occurs whenever a voter behaves in a way that is 'inconsistent' with his true preferences and his intention is to bring about a choice that is better than if he voted 'sincerely'. To illustrate the advantages of this type of voting, consider the preferences of Voter A in Table 4.3 and the three different agendas in Table 4.4. Agenda 1 in Table 4.4 shows that *z* is the social choice, if the first stage voting order is *x* versus *y*. Although *z* is the social choice, it is the worst outcome for Voter A. If Voter A knows this and also knows the preferences of the other voters, he can influence the majority-rule outcome by voting for *y* over *x*. By voting 'insincerely', Voter A avoids his worst outcome. In the first stage *y* beats *x* and in the second stage *y* beats *z*. Voter A does better by voting strategically.

This example suggests that strategic voting occurs because of cycles, cycles being that unwanted feature of majority-rule decision making. Are there other systems of voting that cannot be manipulated in this way? In an important result, Alan Gibbard (1973) and Mark Satterthwaite (1975) showed independently that no system of voting can preclude strategic voting for all systems in which chance plays no role.

Theorem 4.8   There is no voting system that is strategy proof.

This theorem, when coupled with Theorem 4.7, implies considerable instability in the democratic process with different actors mutually adjusting their strategies to exploit the existence of multiple equilibria. Social choice theory suggests that majority rule will be manipulated by agenda setters who seek to win advantage and by voters who seek to protect themselves. The picture that emerges is unsettling because manipulation and deception seem to be among the best strategies to use in democratic policy processes. Theorem 4.8 suggests that we cannot discriminate among voting systems on the basis of whether or not they are subject to manipulation. This provides additional corroboration regarding the earlier claim about the imperfection of all voting systems. Not only do they all violate some condition of reasonableness or fairness, they also are manipulable.

8.4   Conclusions on social choice for political science

Arrow's theorem casts a very long, dark shadow over democratic politics. Social choice theory shows us that there is no perfect voting system. All voting systems have some normative blemish and all voting systems can be manipulated. Social choices in democracy depend on the particular type of majoritarian voting procedure used by a group, on whether voting is sincere or strategic and on the order in which alternatives are considered. This suggests that it is extremely difficult to infer anything from democratic policy outputs concerning what the people or institution want. In this sense, Rousseau's vision of the general will is illusory.

Voting cycles, according to social choice theory, are endemic to democracy. Social choice theory tells us that for most policy issues, there is some coalition of actors who jointly prefer some other outcome. Whenever they have the power to get this outcome, the social choice may simply reflect their power. Stability in democratic politics may well be an arbitrary feature of an institutional arrangement, with losers attempting to dislodge winners of their temporary authority. If they do not have the power to get this outcome then the status quo choice is a result of something besides individual preferences. Institutional rules can help prevent cycling from occurring and therefore prevent losers from becoming winners (Shepsle and Weingast 1981). Democratic agreements are therefore likely to be the product of a fortuitous intersection of forces.

Social choice research shows that policy agreements in a democracy may simply be the product of agenda manipulation. This need not pose terrible consequences, except when other majorities exist that would have chosen another policy. As we have seen, the converse is also true: when there is strong social agreement, as in the case of the Seventeenth Amendment, there may be no political agreement. It seems that we cannot validly infer anything about the preferences of the society based on the laws produced by a legislature. Nor can we say anything about the preferences of the society when a policy is not produced. This has certainly raised fears among many about the legitimacy of laws in democracy.

But how damning are cycles to democratic politics and policy outcomes? Some scholars argue that the existence of cycles may not be terrible for democracy. The instability results described above merely suggest that no one will always win and that no one will always lose in a functioning democracy. As Miller (1983, p. 744) puts it,

> a pluralist political system does not authoritatively allocate values in a stable fashion. Rather, it sets political competitors – who might otherwise be bashing heads instead of (repeatedly) counting them ... running around 'one of Escher's stairways leading always up yet always coming back to its own foundations'. Not only does each competitor win some and lose some but most wins and losses are themselves reversible. Thus the competitors can never be confident of their victories, nor need they resign themselves to their defeats.

In terms of the distribution of power, cycling may be good. In other ways, however, cycling is not so good.

The existence of cycles in a legislature can lead to extremely inefficient policies. Yet the degree of inefficiency that occurs in democratic politics is a matter of dispute among political theorists and economists (Mueller 1989). Research in social choice theory shows that outcomes depend on the kind of game the legislators face. In policy decisions involving distributional issues, if the game legislators face is negative, zero- or constant-sum, vote trading among legislators can easily result in Pareto-inferior outcomes (ibid., p. 84). However, if distributional and allocational issues in politics are essentially positive-sum games, the situation changes somewhat, and vote trading can lead to Pareto-preferred policy outcomes (Coleman 1966). Any answer regarding the efficiency of democracy partially depends on the assumptions made about the distribution of the payoffs to the game political actors most frequently play.

9 Conclusions

There is an irony associated with popular understanding of social choice and its relevance to economics and political science. Contrary to the understanding of most economists, it is possible to make reasonably strong claims about the welfare of the society based on the welfare of individuals. However, the moral from more recent research in social choice theory is that such judgments cannot be made within the narrow confines of traditional welfare economics. To make such judgments economists need to consider and compare different kinds of information about welfare and the distribution of welfare in society.

The situation is exactly opposite in political science. Contrary to the understandings of many political scientists, it is not possible to make claims about what the society wants, based on what voters decide or would decide across different social issues. All voting systems suffer from some kind of normative defect that can lead to different social decisions across the same profile of individual preferences. This remarkable fact suggests that making claims about the desires of the society based on the outcome of a democratic vote or the procedures of a democratic institution is very unwise indeed.

Social choice theory teaches us to treat claims about collective preferences or welfare with prudence and perhaps even suspicion because those claims normally need to pass through two kinds of conceptual filters. First, unless a person's viewpoint can be understood as a considered judgment, individual preferences over alternatives cannot be taken as given. Studies in social psychology and experimental economics show us that a person's preferences may not be inherently stable. The preferences individuals reveal about their welfare may partially reflect the behavioral means used to elicit them. Second, social choice theory teaches us that democratic institutions, even under the most favorable conditions, express the viewpoints and wishes of individuals in the society only imperfectly.

Notes

1. See McLean and Urken (1993) for a general historical overview of social choice theory.
2. See Hardin (1997) for a more detailed discussion of the implications of these two contrasting views for theories of the origins of the state.
3. This estimate was obtained from a literature search using an online provider service of the University of Michigan known as JSTOR. JSTOR's database includes many popular scientific journals in the social sciences and philosophy.
4. For excellent accounts of this literature see Kelly (1978), Plott (1976) and Sen (1977). Rowley (1993) provides an extensive introduction to a three-volume collection of papers on social choice theory.
5. This viewpoint on rationality is not only plainly evident in the works of Bentham and Mill, but also in those of David Hume and Adam Smith.
6. A choice function $C(S, R)$ defined over X is a functional relation such that the choice set $C(S, R)$ is non-empty for every non-empty subset S of X.
7. 'The concept of a preference ordering or, by extension, of a utility function is related to hypothetical choices. Its usual use is in a complete theory, say of individual behavior, in which the preference ordering and the feasible set jointly determine the chosen alternative. The preference ordering is thought of as given before the feasible set is known and therefore determines choices among all possible pairs of alternatives. The feasible set prescribes which alternatives are in fact available. It makes sense, therefore, to include in our information choices which are not in fact feasible even though they are conceivable' (Arrow [1977] 1983, p. 159).

8. For proofs of this result, see Kelly (1978) and Sen ([1970] 1984, 1995).
9. See the footnote in Arrow ([1951] 1963, p. 103).
10. For a discussion of Arrow's four conditions, see Sen ([1970] 1984) and Seabright (1989).
11. An important exception to this is Sen's (1970) 'liberal paradox'.
12. Given both reflexivity and completeness, a weaker condition than quasi-transitivity, acyclicity, is both necessary and sufficient to generate a choice function defined over R (Sen [1970] 1984, Lemma 1*1, p. 16).
13. Properties of the choice function, related to rationality conditions, turn out to be significant when exploring the robustness of Arrow's theorem. For example, demanding that a choice function satisfies Property α or Property β influences results in social choice theory. For a discussion of these conditions, see Plott (1973) and Sen (1977, p. 169).
14. The proof can be found in Fishburn (1973, pp. 209–10).
15. See Brown (1974) and also Mas-Colell and Sonnenschein (1972).
16. In a penetrating series of papers exploring this and other informational conditions, Roberts (1980a, b, c) shows what this space looks like. See, in particular, Roberts (1980a, p. 437).
17. If the Pareto principle is modified to include Pareto indifference, then it can be shown that all non-welfare characteristics of social states are excluded from the planner's comparison of social states (d'Aspremont and Gevers 1977, Lemma 2).
18. Preferences are lexically ordered when some level of satisfaction must be attained for the first argument of the preference function before we can evaluate the outcome according to the second argument. Earlier arguments have absolute priority, so to speak, with respect to later ones, and hold without exception. For example, suppose that an agent prefers $10.00 and sunshine to $10.00 and rain, but that both are preferred to $9.99 and either sun or rain. If no amount of either good or bad weather can be substituted for the $0.01, then the agent's preferences are lexically ordered with respect to money.
19. This example is from Schwartz (1995).
20. See Garman and Kamien (1968); Niemi and Weisberg (1968); and Gehrlein and Fishburn (1976). Riker (1982, pp. 273–4) cites other relevant articles.
21. For a proof, see Enelow and Hinich (1984, p. 13) or Hinich and Munger (1997, p. 35).
22. Sen ([1970] 1984, Theorem 10*6, p. 184) has shown that analogous results hold for classes of cases where preferences cannot be defined in spatial terms.
23. Opposing groups in the political process sometimes have trouble discussing political issues because of the multidimensionality of the problem. The impeachment process of President Bill Clinton in 1998–99 illustrates this very clearly. Was President Clinton's lying a breach of the law that required action by the Congress or was President Clinton's behavior an excuse for the Congress to move against him? Was his action essentially a private action or a public action? The most appropriate perspective or dimension for understanding this political problem was itself a matter of dispute among the electorate and the legislature.
24. This theorem is discussed using spatial voting models. For any two points x, y there is a finite amendment procedure leading from x to y back to x. See Ordeshook (1986) for an illustrative proof.

PART II

THE CONSTITUTIONAL FRAMEWORK

5   Constitutional choice

Geoffrey Brennan and Alan Hamlin

1   The nature of constitutional choice

Central to the analysis of constitutional choice is a distinction between the 'constitutional' and 'in-period' level of decision making. The latter is choice *within* rules; the former is choice *of* the rules. Or, as James Buchanan sometimes puts it, constitutional choice is the choice *among* constraints in contrast to choice *under* constraints, which is the central preoccupation of ordinary economics. However, neither 'rules' nor 'constraints' should be interpreted narrowly here; the constitutional level of choice is concerned with all those rules, constraints, laws, conventions, customs and institutional arrangements that jointly constitute social order. Equally the idea of 'choice' is not limited to some explicit, deliberative process, but is intended to include a considerably wider range of processes by which social order may emerge from individual decision making.[1]

The idea of 'constitutional choice', so understood, is to be distinguished from the choice of capital-C 'Constitutions', with the latter understood as legal documents that seek to specify some aspects of the political and economic institutions of a political community. Often, capital-C Constitutions are only a small part of the set of rules that govern 'in-period' choices. Equally, capital-C Constitutions often include elements that are not small-c 'constitutional' in our sense at all.[2] Our use of small-c 'constitutional' is, at one level, entirely metaphorical: it gestures at a kind of essentialist conception of capital-C Constitution making, but is neither exhausted by nor exhausts that essentially legal exercise. At another level, the usage is, however, quite literal: it is directly concerned with those things that constitute the social order. These might include emergent norms and conventions and other elements of the social fabric that are entirely extra-legal. As is often the case, our meaning of 'constitutional' here is best understood against the frame of what it is *NOT*: and in this respect, the distinction between 'constitutional' and 'in-period' is central.

Two examples will clarify. Ordinary consumer choice involves the choice among consumption goods subject to the constraints imposed by the chooser's income and the relative prices of the various objects of value (or more generally, subject to the vector of prices and the chooser's initial endowments of goods, productive factors, or both). However, the pattern of initial ownership and the structure of prices and the costs of organizing and enforcing the

various exchanges that constitute the market order are all themselves arte-
facts of the institutional arrangements within which market choices occur –
including the specification of property rights and rules for exchanging those
rights. In this example, 'constitutional economics' refers to the analysis of
alternative property rights specifications, alternative rules for exchange and
other institutional arrangements; and 'constitutional choice' refers to the
choice among such specifications and rules.

Alternatively, consider the choice of a particular public policy among a set
of feasible policy options. Each option will imply a social outcome (or a
probability distribution over a range of outcomes) that will depend in turn on
the behavior of the agents who are affected by the policy. So, for example, the
preferences of agents between goods and leisure will constrain the amount of
revenue that can be collected from any particular income tax regime, and
thereby the redistributive impact of that tax policy. Moreover, as public
choice scholars have emphasized, the choice among alternative policy
regimes may itself be influenced by the direct preferences of those same
agents – with the agents acting here as citizen-voters. In this sense, the
depiction of policies as being explicitly or deliberatively chosen by a distinct
set of policy makers – according, say, to some general normative scheme –
may be largely illusory: policies may simply emerge from the essentially
political interactions among the various interests and values that are at large
in the electoral process. Accordingly, the institutional details that govern such
political interactions – particularly those details that bear on electoral competition, lobbying procedures and the like – are critical constraints on policy
choice. Moreover, these institutional conditions, unlike the constraints that
reflect the preferences of citizens as taxpayers and as voters, are themselves
available for choice at the relevant constitutional level. That is, whether the
political process is representative or direct; whether the deliberative assembly
is bicameral or unicameral; whether the electoral structure is based on single-
member districts or involves some form of multimember district (ranging all
the way up to proportional representation); whether the voting system is first-
past-the-post or preferential; whether the decision rule within the assembly is
simple-majority rule or a more restrictive rule; whether there is some form of
separation of powers among legislators, executive and judiciary and, if so,
what form – all these are matters for determination. The properties of the
alternative institutional arrangements therefore become objects of considerable interest: the role of constitutional economics is to explore those properties.

Some aspects of the constitutional approach are relatively well established
within the traditional domain of narrowly economic institutions: market institutions and structures, for example, as illustrated in the first of our two
examples. In particular, much of the traditional literature on industrial organization, and the more general modern literature on 'mechanism design' may

be conceived as a narrowly economic form of constitutionalism. But even here there is a further distinction worth noting – the industrial organization and mechanism design literatures are often straightforwardly normative in the same way that much traditional economic policy analysis is normative. If traditional economic policy analysis is subject to the familiar public choice critique of operating as if there were a benevolent despot, then equally much of the industrial organization and mechanism design literatures might be subject to the parallel criticism at the constitutional level – that organizational structures and mechanisms are recommended from the abstract normative position of a 'benign founding father' – a sort of 'meta-benign despot'. In short, these literatures are typically concerned with the utilitarian evaluation of alternative economic institutions, while constitutional economics in the sense that we identify it here is both more contractarian in its foundations and more wide-ranging in its subject matter.

One might also note that the exploration of the properties of alternative political and social institutions is no less the agenda of much traditional political theory. What distinguishes constitutional *economics* from constitutional politics or constitutional analysis more generally is that constitutional economics brings to bear the distinctive armoury of presumptions, abstractions and analytical techniques, taken from mainstream economics. Accordingly, in deriving the properties of alternative institutional arrangements, constitutional economics is characterized by its predilection for methodological individualism, a focus on the role of relative prices (or incentive effects), a tendency to equilibrium analysis, the assumption that agents are rational in the pursuit of their goals, and further the assumption that generalized wealth maximization is significant (perhaps predominant) among such goals. Constitutional economics differs from ordinary economics, then, in terms of its subject matter and normative commitments – and from other styles of constitutional reflection in terms of its economistic method.

This characterization invites two questions. First, what *difference* does it make to the analysis of choice if the objects of choice are the rules themselves rather than outcomes within rules? After all, the economic analysis of choice is typically cast at a very abstract level: the objects of choice are typically denominated as Xs and Ys – elements of some feasible set of alternatives. What difference does it make if the objects in question are rules of the game or institutional arrangements rather than widgets or cloth and wine (as in Ricardo's famous example)? And second, following on from this question, do any of these differences have any implications for the proper methods of analysis – analysis either of the working of institutions themselves, or of acts of choice among them?

In what follows, we shall engage both these questions. The argument develops in several stages. In Section 2, we shall identify four aspects of constitutional choice that lend some weight to the idea that constitutional choice is different from the standard conception of in-period choice. In Sections 3 and 4, we shall then explore some of the major ingredients in the analysis of constitutional choice. Section 3 distinguishes a number of 'reasons for rules'. These 'reasons' can be thought of as representing the demand side of constitutional choice. But these demand-side considerations will also point to some supply-side considerations, raising questions about the *feasibility* of rules in various contexts and we discuss these in Section 4. The final section will raise some further questions about how the analysis of constitutional choice is to be seen – whether as descriptive or prescriptive, and indeed whether the positive–normative distinction is not given a new twist in the constitutional choice context.

2   The distinctiveness of constitutional choice

Choice among rules may be regarded as having four important aspects which, taken together, render constitutional choice interestingly different from in-period choice – a motivational aspect, an informational aspect, a social capital aspect and a public goods aspect. We consider each in turn.

2.1   The motivational aspect

As has been familiar since the work of Rawls (1971), and in public choice circles from the time of Buchanan and Tullock (1962), the shift from the in-period to the constitutional level of analysis increases the extent to which agents may be expected to agree to choose in the general interest rather than in their particular self-interest, and therefore increases the prospect for (approximate) unanimity. Individual interests fade into the background and are replaced by the generalized interest of all agents, somehow conceived. The notion underlying this claim is that the constitutional level is characterized by forms of uncertainty that induce a 'veil of ignorance'. The move to the constitutional level reduces the agent's information about her own particular circumstances, or about the impact of the proposed constitutional rule on her own life, and thereby induces her to opt for the set of rules that offers the best outcome *whatever* the particular circumstance she may find herself in at the level of in-period choice.

To appeal to a familiar example, suppose you are to choose the rules of a card game *before* the hands are dealt. The incentives that you would have if you knew which cards you held are removed: you have to choose the rules with an eye to *all* the possible hands you might hold, and you will rationally choose the rules that reflect that generalized perspective. In the same way, if you knew nothing about your own income and preferences, or about what social role you will occupy, but only something about the working properties of alternative institutional arrangements and general information about the level and natural distribution of resources, you would look to the question of which institutions will work best for you from a generalized perspective that accounts for the variety of income levels, preferences, and social roles.

In the Buchanan formulation, the predicament of radical individual uncertainty simply allows an approximation to unanimity. In the Harsanyi formulation, this same predicament is presumed to lead each individual to maximize the *expected* returns to each (and hence total expected utility). In the Rawlsian version, this same predicament is presumed to make individuals behind the veil especially attendant to the situation of the least-advantaged group in society, and to induce agreement on social arrangements that will do the best for a member of that group. Clearly, there is a serious clash of intuitions here – one that can only be resolved by empirical investigation.[3] And equally clearly, the kinds of institutional rules that would be chosen under the expected return and maximin criteria would be rather different.

However, to the extent that individual differences are reduced in relevance and, in the limit, suppressed entirely by the shift to the constitutional level, we might suppose that individual judgments increasingly converge on the set of institutions that should prevail. It is important to note that this apparent shift from private to public interest is not dependent upon individuals being in any sense moral in their underlying motivations – the trick is done entirely by the change in the circumstances of choice. It may be that constitutional choice proceeds *as if* individuals were motivated by consideration of the public interest (in some specific sense of that phrase), but this is very different from any claim that individuals should be modeled as anything other than self-interested. We shall return to this point below. Note also that, in this conception, institutional arrangements are evaluated entirely *consequentially* – by reference to the capacity of those arrangements to maximize variously total income/wellbeing, or the income/wellbeing of the least-well-off group. And, in principle, the effect of alternative institutions on the relevant measure (whether average wellbeing or minimum wellbeing) is a matter of social analysis, not of values. Opinions may differ on the question of whether, say, a unicameral or a bicameral structure is superior, but these differences of opinions behind the 'veil of ignorance' reflect different empirical assumptions or applications of logical reasoning. They are differences that can in principle be resolved in the seminar room, rather than the ballot box.

One can, of course, overstate the case here. If one looks to the veil of ignorance to translate private interests fully into public interest, so that a community of rational egoists is transformed into a community that speaks with a single voice, it seems hard to imagine the amazing alchemy actually working. But equally if one makes the more modest claim that the move to the constitutional level of choice will tend to reduce the effect of individual differences and so soften the conflict of private interests, it seems difficult to disagree. We ought to expect that debate over constitutional matters will be less divergent than debates at the substantive or 'in-period' level of choice. There is, however, a correspondingly greater problem potentially at the constitutional level in securing compromise agreements, and we shall take that up below.

2.2   The information aspect

A further aspect of the move to the more abstract level of constitutional choice among rules is that the informational demands of choice are reduced. Suppose you are called on to advise the government of some distant country on the proper level of production and consumption of bread for the ensuing 12 months. You can adopt either of two broad approaches – an in-period approach or a constitutional approach. To illustrate the in-period approach, you could carefully calculate the nutritional value and the gastronomic and other properties of bread and, on this basis, assess the ideal weekly consumption of bread by individuals of different ages and types. Then, from the demographic data, you could calculate what the annual aggregate bread consumption 'should' be. Production is a little trickier, but it would involve, *inter alia*, an assessment of the country's comparative advantage in the production of bread, the storage properties of imported bread, and the culinary gifts of domestic as compared with foreign bakers.

There is an alternative, more constitutional approach to the problem. Rather than attempt to answer the substantive questions of the optimal levels of consumption and production, you could focus on the constitutional question of the institutional structure under which bread is produced and consumed. You could attempt to assess whether bread consumption or production involved the generation of any externalities, or involved monopoly elements on either the buyer or seller side of any relevant market, or other 'market failures'. These are not trivial tasks, but provided that you were satisfied that bread was essentially a 'private good' (in the sense of Samuelson 1954 and Buchanan 1968) and that markets were tolerably competitive, you could simply recommend the *institutional* solution of leaving markets alone to allow the right production and consumption results to emerge *as if by an invisible hand*, as Adam Smith might have said. The point that we want to emphasize here is not that the institutional solution is necessarily better than the substantive solution, but that it requires less specific and detailed information – a point that derives from Hayek's (1945) argument on the informational demands of alternative social institutions.

Consider another example. Suppose you are to offer advice on, say, environmental policy, and you are persuaded that some aspects of environmental protection are 'public goods' (again, in the sense of Samuelson 1954 and Buchanan 1968). You have read the relevant literature and you know that the optimal conditions involve an 'ΣMRS = MRT' requirement, but you don't know what the relevant 'MRSs' *are*. Perhaps a large-scale questionnaire (along the lines of 'contingent valuation' procedures, say) is called for – but this is costly and you wonder how exactly you could interpret the responses. Once again, as an alternative to substantive policy advice, you could contemplate an *institutional* response. You might think, for example, that if only you can structure political decision making so as to suppress the risks of global cycling, the median-voter result will emerge from electoral competition. In this case, candidates will have to estimate what level of environmental protection to offer in order to maximize the probability of electoral victory – and, if the median-voter theorem applies, this process will result in an outcome that is a good approximation to that which would arise from the ΣMRS = MRT calculation in most instances. You will have assigned the decision-making responsibility to those who have the most at stake in getting the right answer, and you will have established a procedure for selecting those who are best at making such estimates. In this general setting, you might also be able to make some constructive suggestions as to how the electoral process might be made to work better – perhaps by organizing the structure of electorates so that there are only two major rival candidates, or by establishing a specialist environmental committee within the legislature to reduce logrolling, or whatever. The critical point here is that the logic of institutional analysis can indicate how you might best structure the electoral process and the process of political decision making *without any detailed knowledge of the precise preferences of voter-citizens.*

A final simple example in a mainstream area of economics might help. The logic of rational choice tells us that bidders in a sealed-bid auction will, if fully rational, bid their true valuations of the object to be auctioned if the auction is a 'second-price' or Vickrey auction (whereby the price paid by the highest bidder is the *next* highest bid) – whereas they will rationally underbid in a sealed-bid 'first-price' auction (where the highest bidder pays what she bid). We do not need to know what the bidders' valuations *are* to demonstrate the a priori logic of the argument. The shift to the discussion about the auction *process* allows us to draw conclusions and secure the result of allocating a prize to the highest-value user that would require a very great deal more information if we were to pursue the exercise at the level of attempting to choose the outcome directly. Just as constitutional choice is distinctive in the kinds of interests agents bring to bear, so it is distinctive in the kinds of informational demands it makes upon choosers.

2.3 The social capital aspect

Rules of the game, by their nature, are intended to remain fixed in place over relatively long periods of time. Were they to change with more or less frequency after every play of the game, much of their value would be lost. Rules provide information to players about the game and the value of that information is lost if the rules are in a constant state of flux.

This point is most conspicuous in cases where a primary function of the rules is to provide information to agents so that they can coordinate their choices in the arena of action. Road rules are a simple example here. The precise content of the rule – 'give-way-to-the-right' or 'give-way-to-the-left' – may not matter much; what is crucial is that the rule is common knowledge, so that all agents are confident that the rule is known by all. If a rule is subject to change, this confidence would be undermined. Rules that establish systems of weights and measures, monetary units, or languages to be used in 'official circles' are all forms of *social capital*. And almost all rules have this character to some extent.

Rules take time to learn, and they shape decisions that extend far into the future. Individuals want to make decisions about their futures – and cannot make such decisions intelligently if the basic structures within which such decisions are to take effect are unknown or known to be unstable. Securing long-term investment, for example, requires a stable property rights structure – and, among other attributes of constitutional options that commend themselves behind the 'veil of ignorance', stability will be a desirable property. The fact that constitutional rules *are* social capital has two important implications. The first is that expected stability or 'resilience' becomes an important property of constitutional options. To some extent, stability is an artefact of the meta-rules, and hence is itself 'meta-constitutionally' valued. Most real-world (capital-C) Constitutions specify rules under which the provisions of that Constitution can be altered. And such rules are often rather restrictive, involving special, more inclusive decision requirements,[4] or perhaps moratoria that specify that any provision to be altered must lie *un*altered for a further given period. In these cases, stability is expressly chosen.

But expected stability can also be a property that to some extent inheres in the object of constitutional choice. For example, some institutional arrangement may be a matter of controversy – with some believing that arrangement to be in the perceived constitutional interest, others believing that the arrangement is perverse. There is then a manifest danger that this particular arrangement will be 'on and off', as rival opinions gain periodic ascendancy. Some alternative institutional arrangement may, however, be regarded by virtually everyone as reasonably good – though not necessarily regarded as the best by anyone. That institutional arrangement will, however, be more resilient: given some transaction costs involved in changing institutions, the arrangement is likely to prevail for an appropriately long period and to be *recognized* as likely to so prevail by ordinary agents when making their in-period plans. This latter arrangement has a special constitutional virtue – one that reflects the social capital nature of rules.

A further important implication is that constitutional choice does not take place in an institutional vacuum or on a clean slate. It is important to emphasize this point because much of the literature has proceeded otherwise. That is, in an attempt to show the roles that rules play, many authors have followed the Hobbesian line of imagining a world *without* rules, and from that base asking what set of rules rational agents in a veil-of-ignorance setting would have most reason to choose. But that is not the setting relevant for most instances of constitutional choice: in virtually all cases there is a pre-existing set of institutional arrangements, and the relevant exercise is one of institutional *reform* rather than institutional *design*.

To take a simple analogy, there is a significant difference between the house you would build on a vacant lot and the house you would construct on that same lot if there is a house already there. You may choose to raze the existing construction to the ground; but this will typically be a costly exercise. It will usually be better to modify what is already present. In the same way, the social capital nature of rules – the habits of practice, the entrenched expectations about others' actions, the information abroad about others' expectations of you – implies that there will almost inevitably be a path dependency about rules. In constitutional choice, bygones are not bygones. In constitutional choice, the familiar Irishman's response to the question about the best way to get to Dublin – 'well, I wouldn't start from here' – is well taken.

To pick up an example discussed earlier in relation to the provision of bread, it may seem that the best recommendation one might make to the distant government in that example is that it should establish a regime of private property rights and appropriate rules about contracting and exchange, and then simply let the market system rip. But as the experience with post-Communist transition suggests, things may not be so simple.[5] Institutional reform is a matter of going from where you are. That is just a concomitant of the social capital nature of rules. The past necessarily casts its shadow over constitutional choice: the choice among rules is both constrained by the existing rules and constrains future choice among rules, and both aspects must obtrude on any proper constitutional calculus.

2.4   The public goods aspect

With an important exception to be noted below, constitutional choice will typically involve options that are non-excludable and non-rejectable public goods – in the sense that all must 'consume' the chosen rules equally. The institutional arrangements that structure social interaction – whether the basic property rights system, or the rules that govern collective decision-making processes, or the rules that determine what will be subject to these collective decision-making processes and what left to private decentralized determination – are essentially the same for all members of the political community, and are so even when outcomes differ widely among individuals. Your consumption of bread may differ from mine; but the rules that specify ownership of bread, the rules under which bread may be traded, and the processes by which all such rules are enforced – these are the same for us both.

And indeed, if we take seriously the idea that identifiable individual interests disappear in the context of constitutional choice by virtue of the 'veil of ignorance', then one of the interesting features of the constitutional setting is the absence of a basis for interpersonal trade. If, at the constitutional level, all the objects of choice are pure public goods, there cannot be 'voluntary exchange' in the sense of Wicksell and Lindahl, because the parties have no private goods to exchange. This fact is interesting because it implies that where the veil of ignorance is incomplete, there may be genuine limits to the scope for exchange in the constitutional setting. Set against the strong contractarian flavour of much constitutionalist theorizing, this limited scope for exchange presents a puzzle.

Constitutional choice is, in this sense, intrinsically an n-person 'bargaining game' in which the (meta) rules for determining the rules are critical. In the happy case, where all agents' opinions as to the 'best' set of rules converge, then there is no problem – though, as Buchanan and Vanberg (1989) observe, there is no genuine 'contractual' element in this case either. And if, as Buchanan and Vanberg argue, there *is* residual disagreement and so scope for a contractual element in constitutional choice, there does not seem to be anything other than potentially irresolvable argument to oil the wheels of agreement.

At a different level, recognition that the objects of constitutional choice are public goods alerts us to the possibility that agents will have an incentive, where feasible, to 'free ride'. One arena of possible free riding is in the gathering of relevant information: as Downs (1957) notes in connection with ordinary political decision making, voters will be 'rationally ignorant' and this rational ignorance extends to the constitutional level. That is, if everyone is to participate in constitutional choice, then each will have a reduced incentive to acquire relevant information about the options and their consequences. And this is so even if each has a potential veto (that is, even if the decision rule at the level of constitutional choice is unanimity) because each knows that he will be decisive if and only if no other voter exercises the veto. Now, as we have argued elsewhere,[6] the effect of expected non-decisiveness is not just to discourage participants from acquiring (normatively relevant) information, it also induces agents to act 'expressively'. That is, agents tend to treat options not as objects of *choice* so much as occasions for expressing their identity or their values. Accordingly, the 'preferences' of agents over alternative institutional arrangements are likely to reflect not so much careful consequentialist calculation of which arrangements would actually be best, but more an array of ideological passions and morally infused posturing. Popular attitudes to democracy, for example, are instructive here. What seems to count in such attitudes are the things that democratic institutions are taken to *symbolize*: there is rather less attention to the question of what precise outcomes those institutions are likely to *produce* – less attention certainly than the constitutional economics literature might lead one to expect.

This is perhaps not the place to air (again) our views about the relevance of expressive considerations within a coherent account of rational action in collective choice settings. It is, however, worth noting that, within the expressive account, the distinction between in-period and constitutional choice will not be as marked as in the more conventional public choice account in which instrumental behavior is taken as axiomatic at all levels.

3   The demand for rules

The foregoing discussion sets some of the context for the analysis of constitutional choice by pointing up key features of the constitutional setting. We now turn to a consideration of the *demand side* of constitutional choice. Why do we *want* rules – either envisaging ourselves collectively, or as representative agents in our respective political communities? Following, in at least most respects, the lead of Brennan and Buchanan (1985), what is the reason *for* rules, as we might put it?

There are four strands of response discernible in the literature – each associated with a different diagnosis of the problem that rules overcome. The relevant problems can be designated, respectively, as the prisoner's dilemma problem, the coordination problem, the Ulysses problem and the trust problem. Each of these problems provides a reason for rules, and we examine each briefly in turn.

3.1   The prisoner's dilemma problem

The prisoner's dilemma is sufficiently widely known not to require rehearsal here (though see Luce and Raiffa 1957 for an early and influential statement). The key aspect of the dilemma, as it bears on the demand for rules, is that if only each player could somehow adopt a strategy of conditional cooperation – cooperating *if and only if everyone else does* – then this strategy would be both individually rational and Pareto efficient – so dissolving the prisoner's dilemma. In other words, when contemplating a prisoner's dilemma game from the constitutional perspective, a rule that effectively enforces cooperative behaviour would be chosen by every rational agent over the standard alternative: each would in this sense rationally trade her own discretion to defect in return for all others giving up their discretion to defect. This is the central idea in Buchanan's (1975a) *The Limits of Liberty*, which lays out Buchanan's conception of the normative foundations of the state. The Buchanan analysis is decidedly Hobbesian in spirit: the Nash independent adjustment equilibrium for rational agents in the absence of rules is Hobbesian anarchy, and the primary reason for rules is that they permit escape from the Hobbesian jungle. For Hobbesians, the chief benefits of rules are the solitude, poverty, nastiness, brutishness and shortness of life that rules avoid.

But the general argument applies not only to the 'global' choice between anarchy and society. The argument is applicable to the whole range of more 'local' social dilemmas arising from the existence of public goods (and public 'bads'). If a general rule compelling cooperative action from all players is available, then the choice of this rule becomes the choice of the Pareto-dominant optimal outcome over the 'defect–defect' equilibrium that prevails in the absence of a rule. Accordingly, the same logic that argues for a basic structure of private rights and rules for their exchange also argues for laws against littering the beach, or against environmental degradation of other kinds.

Rules provide, at least in principle, an escape from the social predicament that the simple prisoner's dilemma exposes. That escape is one clear source of the demand for rules.

3.2 The coordination problem

Sometimes, the reason for rules is not that they solve a prisoner's dilemma problem so much as that they provide information in contexts where that information is vital in the decision calculus of each player. In pure coordination games, no one may care much precisely which set of rules is put in place, as long as some rules are operative, and each person has reason to think that those rules will be obeyed by others. The classic example here is the case of the rules of the road already mentioned in the context of the social capital aspect of rules. As noted before, the important issue is whether the rules are common knowledge so that each person can expect compliance from all. The only additional point to make here is that, in this case, there may be no need for any enforcement of rules since there is no private incentive to defect from rule-following behaviour: the rule may be self-enforcing.

The self-enforcing nature of rules in the pure coordination case provides a clear contrast to the prisoner's dilemma situation examined earlier. The coordination problem might therefore, in principle, be solved by convention rather than by formal rule. For example, each of us has an incentive to be able to communicate with others around us, and this incentive has, over the course of human history, been sufficient to support the emergence of language – which is, as we now receive it, an extensively 'rule-bound' phenomenon. There is good usage and bad; elegant expression and clumsy; clear speech and confused. We do not here *need* the intervention of a rule maker or rule enforcer (such as the state, or an 'academy') to enforce these rules – and many would feel the intervention of stipulated rule makers/enforcers to be either pointless or perverse. The use and development of language is an example of spontaneous order in that language both emerged spontaneously and is spontaneously self-enforcing.

But not all cases are like language in this respect. Where the cost of failing to coordinate is truly catastrophic (as it is in the case of air-traffic control, say) one might well want to appoint a rule maker/interpreter with explicit enforcement powers – both to give players greater confidence that the rules will be followed and to act to prevent 'accidental non-coordination' where instances loom.

Sometimes, rules once established will be self-enforcing, but their initial establishment may not be 'spontaneous'. Sometimes, to rely on the evolution of conventions may be too slow or costly in other ways. In these cases, there may be a role for an explicitly collective determinative act in setting up the rules, but no further ongoing role. In other cases, the rules may be self-enforcing only if there are fail-safe mechanisms in play that support compliance. In all such cases, there will be a role for the exercise of an explicit constitutional *choice* – either in terms of the establishment of the rule or supportive processes that may never need to be activated.

The demand for rules here springs from the benefits of coordination or, equivalently, from avoiding the costs of failing to coordinate.

3.3   The Ulysses problem

A quite different reason for rules arises from a partial failure of agent rationality. In the standard economic account of the rational actor, the agent is rational if her actions are such as to best satisfy her desires, given her beliefs. Typically, the agent's desires are taken to be unifiable in a non-problematic way, so that though different desires may conflict, such conflicts can be traded off to generate an action that reflects the agent's true preference, all things considered. Economists have never been enthusiastic about disinterring these internal conflicts: we have, for the most part, been content to assume that such conflicts are resolved to the agent's own satisfaction. End of story.

But there seems no reason to assume a priori that the way in which the agent thinks desires *should* best be aggregated will produce the action that the jostling among desires *will* produce. The agent's *meta*-desire to manage his in-period desires properly may not be strong enough to do the relevant management work. Or at least not in all cases. So, for example, when presented with the fifth drink, the agent may no longer desire to stop drinking, even though *ex ante* she holds that four drinks is the optimal number. Or she may discover in herself various apparently 'hard-wired' impulses that she would prefer not to have or that make her life go less well for her overall if she accedes to them. Some scholars regard such problems as endemic. Frank Knight, for example, argued persistently that people do not really want more goods with *given tastes* so much as they want *better tastes*. Other scholars are inclined to see such problems as primarily restricted to particular goods (addictive drugs, perhaps) or to particular people (schizophrenics, say). But whenever the issue of 'desire management' becomes a real issue there is a distinction to be drawn between the constitutional (or meta-) level and the in-period level of choice (between preference and meta-preference) and the rational agent will frequently find herself putting in place *constraints* that will prevent her from doing things she would otherwise choose to do.

The famous Ulysses case exemplifies. At the constitutional level, Ulysses lashes himself to the mast so that he might both hear the sirens sing and live to tell the tale. At the in-period level, his desire for the siren-song is so strong that, in the absence of the self-imposed constitutional constraint, he would leap into the waves and be dashed on the rocks – something that, viewed with a calm constitutional eye, seems to him *not* to be entirely desirable. And in this fabled example we can, as observers, see well enough that being so dashed is not going to make his life go particularly well. In other cases, however, the normative authority of the constitutional choice over the in-period one will not be so clear. Constitutionally viewed, being besotted with love for another may seem ludicrous – even pathological. But from the 'inside looking out', the constitutional view will seem small-minded, un-imaginative, dry – a preference for death over life. In short, it is not an a priori truth that constitutional choices are normatively authoritative simply by virtue of being at the constitutional level. But what *is* clear is that there are at least some cases in which constitutional and in-period preferences over one's own actions diverge – without any reference to the behavior of others or interdependence among different agents. In such cases, the agent will attempt to act *now* so as to confound his future actions, and will in that future struggle against the shadow of earlier, constitutional choices. He will, in short, adopt an essentially *private* constitution.

Note especially the 'private' aspect. Crusoe on his island is no less a candidate for a private constitution than the man in society. Crusoe may rationally store his coconut wine in small bottles with corks deliberately constructed to be very difficult to extract, and almost certainly beyond the capacity of anyone less than totally sober. Or he may acculturate himself to dressing for dinner in the interests of maintaining a certain decorum.

The individual in society will have additional resources to assist her in establishing and maintaining her chosen rules – a wider institutional array, as it were. The individual in society can use the division of labour to this end and enrol others in assisting her to maintain the course on which she has determined. We do not wish to imply by this observation that the coercive powers of the state will necessarily have a comparative advantage in this area. The fact that agents may not always choose the action consistent with their constitutionally considered 'best interests' does not establish an a priori license for state intervention. That A does not always act in her own best interests does not mean that she would do better to place herself under B's control, still less under the control of the 'central committee'. Desired private constitutions may be no less varied than desires themselves. But equally we cannot, on a priori grounds, exclude a role for collective action here. If a sufficient number of individuals recognize a private desire to limit their own behavior in a particular way, it might be the case that a rule limiting the behavior of *all* would be chosen, even if enforcement of that rule might harm some individuals (that is, impose constraints that are not desired by them at the meta-level). This is one important case (*pace* Section 2.4 above) where the constitutional rule in question is *not* a public good – although its enforcement might impose external costs on some.

3.4 The trust problem

The trust problem indicates a reason for rules that lies somewhere between the prisoner's dilemma problem and the Ulysses problem – with elements of both. The trust predicament, which represents the point of departure for the economic analysis of trust, may be characterized as a sequential two-person game, depicted in extensive form in Figure 5.1 (for more detailed discussion see Brennan and Hamlin 2000, particularly Chapters 3 and 5 and references therein). In this game, the first mover (player I) must initially choose between N (no trust) and T (trust). If I chooses the former, then the interaction ceases and both players receive a zero payoff. If I chooses to trust (T), then player II gets to move, and must choose either to reward (R), in which case both players receive a payoff of two, or to exploit (E), in which case the second mover (II) receives a payoff of three and the first mover (I) a payoff of minus one.

In the context of a single interaction, player I reasons that, since II is rational, if I chooses T, II will choose E over R ($3 > 2$); player I would then receive -1 rather than 0, which I would have received if he had chosen N. Ergo, I chooses N, producing the unique equilibrium payoff (0, 0) despite the fact that $T{:}R$, with payoff (2, 2), is technically feasible. This simple game is similar to the one-shot prisoner's dilemma in so far as it has a unique equilibrium outcome that is Pareto dominated by another feasible outcome. What both I and II would prefer is some means of getting the (2, 2) payoff associated with $T{:}R$, rather than the (0, 0) associated with N; but $T{:}R$ is ruled out here by virtue of II's rationality. Player II might *promise* to choose R if I chooses T, but player I has no reason to believe that (rational) II will keep the promise.

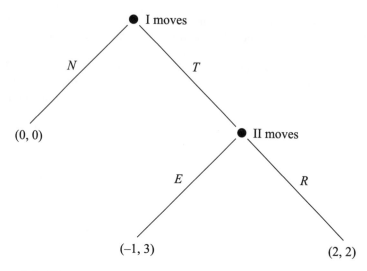

Figure 5.1   The trust predicament

If, however, there were some technology whereby II could effectively bind himself to choose R if I chose T, then both players would be better off. The expanded game would be something like that shown in Figure 5.2. In this augmented game, II can choose a prior move – to remain silent S or 'promise' P, where a promise is costly to break. If II chooses S, then the game is as before (in Figure 5.1); but the choice of P changes II's payoff under E to $(3 - k)$ where $k > 1$, so that it is now rational for II to choose R. Player I knows this and will accordingly choose T if II chooses P. If the choice of P by II is fully observed by I, then it will clearly pay II to adopt the P-technology.

The P-technology can be thought of in terms of a constitutional choice – a choice of rules that will constrain the future conduct of player II and make possible an outcome that would remain inaccessible in the absence of the chosen constraint. The constraint in question might be 'external': P can be conceived as a formal contract, and k as the penalty the courts will impose if II violates that contract. Here, the P-technology depends on the institutional apparatus of the courts: the 'constitution' in question is a '*public* capital good' in the sense indicated in a previous section. Alternatively, the constraint might be thought of as 'internal' – more like Ulysses' self-binding than like the prisoner's dilemma case. Here, the P-technology involves an internal disposition to adhere to promises made, say because of a moral belief that promise breaking is 'bad'. This internal constraint is 'private'; my adopting the constraint does not require anyone else to adopt it. But unlike the Ulysses case, there is a necessary social dimension – my commitment to

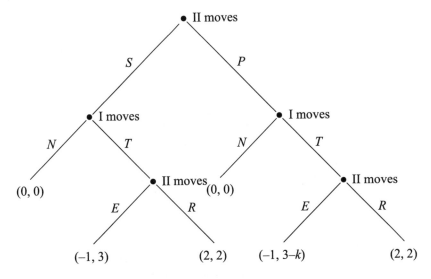

Figure 5.2   The augmented trust predicament

promise keeping only makes sense in the context of others to whom I make promises, and whose behavior my promise giving can influence.

The rationally based reason for rules here is that my adopting the rule induces behavioral changes in others (potential trustors) but there is no direct *exchange* as in the prisoner's dilemma case: I do not adopt the *P*-technology in return for your adopting it, and indeed things may go better for me if I am the only trustworthy agent in town. It is in this sense that the trust problem exposes a reason for rules – a source of demand for constraint – that lies somewhere between the standard prisoner's dilemma account and the Ulysses account, but is not properly captured by either of these cases. Within the *constitutional political economy* tradition, the trust problem has been some-what neglected; we are inclined to think it is an important case.

4   The supply of rules

The foregoing discussion provides, we hope, good reason to think that there may be a widespread desire for rules – with rules here understood as binding constraints on the future conduct of relevant agents. But the desire for rules does not ensure that the appropriate rules will be forthcoming – demand does not necessarily create its own supply. One way to open up the range of issues at stake here is to consider the Hobbesian problem, adverted to above. The thrust of our earlier discussion was to show that, if there were rules of social order (and specifically of private property) such that once instituted, everyone would in fact obey them, then it would be rational for each to choose to invoke such a rule-governed regime. The 'supply-side' analysis in constitutional choice foregrounds the proviso: is such a rule-governed regime feasible?

For Hobbes, the answer was a modified affirmative. The only *feasible* rule-governed regime, Hobbes thought, was government by a single authority: the exchange that each made with each was to establish that single authority – hence, the origins of his Leviathan state. But Hobbes's response here is famously contested, and certainly on its face remains seriously incomplete. In particular, two major questions loom. One relates to the conduct of 'rule enforcers'. Unless the rules are fully self-enforcing (in which case no single enforcement agency, no Leviathan state, is required), someone will have to be assigned the power to enforce and, as Hobbes recognized, that power will be uncontingent and hence liable to exploitation in the interests of the holder. '*Quis custodiet ipsos custodes?*' becomes a central question. As Hobbes's contemporary, James Harrington, puts it, why is submission to an arbitrary despot likely to be any less nasty and slavish a life than that on offer in the state of nature? (Pocock 1977). Hobbes does have available an answer of sorts – of the kind adumbrated by McGuire and Olson (1996) – concerning the nature of the constitution that a rational Leviathan might choose to impose on itself in order to secure maximal returns. The idea here is that a government is likely to secure a larger aggregate discretionary surplus by instituting a system of basic economic and personal rights and instituting a revenue-maximizing tax regime than by attempting to operate the national economy as a single monopoly firm. The constitution so chosen would involve many of the elements of a liberal constitution – a well-defined system of property rights, secured from intrusion *both* by other citizens and by the state itself; rules for the free exchange of such rights; a fiscal system bound by rules such as non-retroactivity; and so on – but there would be no *political* rights as such.

Note that, within the typology set out in the previous section, the logic of constitutional choice would fall into the category of the trust problem. That is, the reason for rules is that the Leviathan finds it profitable to bind himself, so that individuals will have reason to expect to be able to act so as to maximize their own incomes (subject to the revenue-maximizing tax), and the income of Leviathan thereby. Recognizing this, citizens will have reason to empower Leviathan at the relevant constitutional level of choice. The feasibility of rules in *this* particular context (of which more anon) turns out to be significant in ensuring that there is adequate reason for individual citizens to consent to the Leviathan order.

The conduct of rule enforcers, more generally than in the Leviathan case, is, of course, a familiar issue in public choice analysis. The notion that political agents (bureaucrats and politicians) will have interests independent of those of the citizenry, and hence that rules should be designed so as to make politicians' '*interests coincide with their duty*' (as Hamilton puts it in *The Federalist* No. 72; emphasis added) is a cornerstone issue in constitutional analysis. The Hobbesian analysis falls at a yet more abstract level. Even if democratic electoral rules *do* provide incentives for political agents to offer policy outcomes that accord with citizen preferences, there is still the question as to why those political agents will abide by democratic rules. In short, how is it that rule makers and enforcers have the incentive themselves to obey constitutional rules?

A somewhat similar issue arises at the level of compliance for ordinary citizens. In the prisoner's dilemma conception of rules, we might be able to explain why each individual would rationally agree to establish an all-powerful Leviathan. But if Leviathan were *not* all-powerful, if there remained a multitude of cases in which individuals could violate the rules and get away with it, then the logic of the argument suggests that each *would* violate the rules in any instance where the expected return to non-compliance was positive. The very notion of rules implies that this compliance problem can be solved – at least in sufficient measure that the idea of rules makes sense. The thought that I would voluntarily agree to be subject to a binding set of rules in exchange for others doing so depends critically on those rules *being* binding: no such exchange would be possible otherwise. In other words, the rules require some institutional backing through which enforcement is assured.

Note that this is a rather different issue from that which is customary in much contractarian political philosophy, where the central issue is one not of 'power' but of 'authority'. Authority here summons up an unmistakably moral dimension: the quest for authority is a quest for reasons why one ought to obey in cases where resistance is a feasible option. The work the attribution of authority does is to confer moral legitimacy on a regime. And that moral legitimacy provides, one might suppose, grounds for compliance to the regime's edicts that transcend (and augment) the mere self-interest in complying, based on the regime's power. Of course, one might believe that moral considerations do exercise some behavioral clout – so that moral reasons based on a regime's authority will provide an extra element of compliance. But it is outside the economistic spirit (and outside the spirit of Hobbes, arguably) for such moral reasons to fully *determine* behavior. And in any event, one must be careful not to invent moral reasons for compliance to a regime's edicts, which moral considerations are assumed to be entirely ineffective in the situation without rules. If an individual has a morally based inclination to abide by a legal rule not to defect in a prisoner's dilemma situation, why does that individual not have the same inclination not to defect in the absence of that legal rule? If creating a law in itself provides moral reason for compliance to that law over and above any moral reason for performing the act that the law dictates, this moral creativity needs to be explained.

One might, of course, respond to this concern over compliance with the observation that, in fact, most of us live in tolerably well-functioning constitutional orders, with widespread (though not universal) compliance to rules by both ordinary citizens and even by the political and bureaucratic agents who enforce them. Anxieties about rule following and rule enforcement in the face of that experience might seem to be a case of a solution in search of a problem. Perhaps, as H.L.A. Hart (1961) has argued, humans are rule followers by nature. If so, the content and properties of various alternative regimes of rules is an important issue, but neither compliance nor enforcement issues are of much concern. Analysis of constitutional choice can proceed plausibly *as if* all conceivable rule regimes are feasible. Perhaps. But, ultimately, it seems analytically unsatisfactory to take as given something which the nature of the problem exposes as essential: the very reason of rules earlier laid out gives us cause to think that compliance and enforcement issues may be troublesome.

Or at least this is so in that subset of cases in which the reason for rules is connected to *n*-person prisoner's dilemma problems. What, though, of the case in which the reason of rules connects to the trust predicament? Here, we can see clearly that similar problems arise if the solution to the problem involves some external contract-enforcing institution (say, the courts): the law of contract may be a satisfactory solution to the trust problem if those who are assigned enforcement powers use them only to punish agents who violate the terms of some contract, and if the spread of legal contract can plausibly encompass all that players would wish to contract over. There is, however, another possibility in the trust case, as we have noted. This possibility leads us to a solution more redolent of that to the Ulysses problem – a solution that is 'dispositional', in the sense that it involves the agent in having quasi-moral inhibitions about failing to keep promises. If the '*P*-technology' is something that involves an internal psychological change in the agent, we must ask whether that kind of internal psychological change is both plausible *and* relevantly transparent. The transparency property is relatively straightforward. For it to be rational for me to adopt the *P*-technology, it must be the case that adopting it *causes* agents to trust me – and this will be the case only if I am able to be identified by those agents as a trustworthy person. *Total* transparency is not required: that is, agents may make some mistakes about whether those they trust are trustworthy or not. But the correlation between being identified as trustworthy and actually being trustworthy must be sufficiently large that it pays to *be* a trustworthy type. Whether such a degree of transparency exists must be a matter of some conjecture. The extreme case (somewhat attractive to many economists) in which agents' dispositions are totally opaque – so that we can know nothing about each other except the actions we perform – seems implausible (after all, even many economists are willing to assume that rationality is common knowledge), and no less so than the opposite case in which the intentions of each are an open book to all. Presumably, much depends on the social distance between the two parties, and the availability of information about previous behavior. In at least some cases, the relevant degree of transparency seems likely – particularly when we note that trustworthy persons have an interest in the availability of accurate information and a corresponding incentive to develop relatively reliable signals, and that all potential trusters have an incentive to inform themselves about the trustworthiness of potential trustees.

Suppose the relevant degree of transparency is in place. There remains a further issue about psychological plausibility. In the general Ulysses case, there is a conflict between the way the agent wants, at time t_1, to act at time t_2, and the way that same agent predicts she will want, at time t_2, to act at time t_2 (at least in the absence of deliberate action at time t_1 to frustrate those future actions). Various resources are available to the agent at time t_1 to influence her future action. She can develop habits; she may be able to take actions now that make various actions in the future more or less expensive to herself; she may be able to alter her desires (say by developing in herself various aversions). All those resources are, in principle, available to her in the trust case in order for her to develop a disposition to keep promises. But there seems here to be a particular difficulty. To the extent that the reason she acquires the disposition of trustworthiness is in order that people will trust her, and the reason she wants them to trust her is that she can receive higher payoffs thereby, then the reason for acquiring the disposition is the same reason to break with the disposition once someone *has* trusted her: the payoff is yet higher when she actually acts in an untrustworthy manner. This fact creates an internal tension in the agent making the constitutional choice problem one that is not present in the Ulysses case. The situation is rather like that of instrumentally valuable false beliefs. Consider the case (attributable to John Broome) where the recovery rate of a patient is directly related to his optimism: if the patient believes that he will recover in n days, he will actually recover in $n + 1$ days. Clearly, the best thing for the patient is to believe he will recover tomorrow because then he will recover the day after tomorrow. But the accelerated recovery cannot be a *reason* for his holding the profitable belief, because that reason entails the belief being false. It may be good for the agent, but the goodness is not accessible to rational choice. The belief is one of the category of states that Elster (1983) refers to as necessarily incidental byproducts. And so it may be with trustworthiness. That is, one's life goes better for one if one is trustworthy, but choosing to be trustworthy for this reason may be extremely difficult psychologically, and conceivably even impossible.

Here then is a further reason why the supply side of constitutional choice may present interesting problems – why even where rules are feasible, the instrumental *choice* of rules may not be.

5   Positive and normative elements in constitutional choice

The idea of constitutional choice has played a significant role in contractarian political philosophy, at least of the kind practised by Buchanan and those following his lead. It is beyond the scope of the current chapter to explore the full set of connections between constitutional thinking and contractarian *mores*; but it is appropriate that we conclude with some remarks on the nature of constitutional analysis from the viewpoint of the familiar positive–normative distinction.

At one level, the analysis of constitutional choice is strictly positive. Questions about how various institutional arrangements will operate, about what kinds of rule regimes are feasible, and about why rational agents might desire rules at all and if so which ones – these are all questions that constitutional analysis seeks to answer within the positive logic of rational choice. To the extent that real agents fail to be fully rational, or act rationally in the context of false beliefs (say, about the workings of alternative institutions), a normative element might obtrude: explicating what fully rational and well-informed agents *would* choose might be taken to imply what real agents *should* choose. But if rationality is taken purely as an axiom of behavior, scope for that particular normative element is ruled out by assumption.

In that setting, we can explain why agents operating at the constitutional level will (rationally) take a more public-interested view than they will at the in-period level for reasons explored above. But this fact does not allow us to assign greater normative authority to constitutional than to in-period choice – because we have not specified whence the normative authority derives or what the content of the normative scheme is. We do not want to say much about these matters, but it is worth noting that the logic of the public choice approach operates as a discipline on what is allowable. In particular, in the spirit of the opposition to 'benevolent despot' conceptions of political process, we must be careful not to arrogate normatively driven concerns to any particular subset of the population: we must be careful not to replace the monopoly on benevolence often assigned to politicians or their advisors with a similar monopoly held by scholars. Whatever arguments and reasons adumbrated by authors or assumed to be compelling to readers should be generalized to all agents. So, for example, if contractarian norms are taken to be appropriate in evaluating institutional arrangements or the social outcomes such arrangements generate, then those same contractarian norms should be relevant to at least some extent in the in-period behavior of ordinary agents. Those norms may exercise a stronger behavioral influence at the constitutional level, for reasons to do with the veil of ignorance, but will still be relevant at the in-period level. In other words, those norms will not only provide reasons why some institutional arrangements will be *better* than others (rather than simply chosen over others); they will also provide reasons – persuasive in principle – to ordinary agents why they *should* abide by certain rules and help enforce them in the face of violation. Of course, such reasons will not be decisive in many cases: they will simply exercise a marginal influence alongside agents' interests more narrowly conceived. But it seems implausible to imagine that there will be motivations in play at the constitutional level that will not have at least some influence at the in-period level. The attempt to build an analysis of constitutional choice on the foundations provided by a strictly *Homo economicus* conception of agent motivation serves to emphasize the distinctively economic nature of the enterprise, but it may also unnecessarily restrict the institutional scope of the analysis and undermine the attempt to imbue the idea of constitutionalism with any normative significance.[7]

Notes

1. For alternative characterizations of constitutional political economy, and key references, see Buchanan (1987b, 1990), Hardin (1988), Brennan and Hamlin (1995, 1998a), and Voigt (1997).
2. See Brennan and Casas Pardo (1991) for a discussion of one example.
3. Of which there is surprisingly little, though see Frohlich and Oppenheimer (1992).
4. In the style recommended by Buchanan and Tullock (1962).
5. See Elster et al. (1998).
6. In Brennan and Lomasky (1993) and in Brennan and Hamlin (1998b, 1999, 2000).
7. For discussion of this theme at greater length, see Brennan and Hamlin (2000).

6 Monarchies, hereditary and non-hereditary

Gordon Tullock

1 Introduction

Most people in the history of the human race have lived under hereditary monarchies. It should be emphasized at the outset that hereditary monarchies are not regimes where the throne always passes from the beloved dying king to whichever of his children or near relatives is next in line under local law or custom. That does happen frequently, but it is also true that events like the Wars of the Roses happen too.

We tend to exaggerate the difficulties of establishing a firm line of succession to the throne, probably because the English throne was the most contested one in Europe. Thus, Anglo-Saxon history has a good deal more in the way of violent overthrow than is found in the histories of most countries ruled by monarchs.

Today there is one case – North Korea – in which a dictatorship has been made, at least for a time, hereditary. There was a period when the Somozas seemed to have a hereditary monarchy in Nicaragua, and it seems likely that the Trujillo family would have established one in the Dominican Republic had not the US government intervened by arranging not only to have the reigning dictator assassinated,[1] but also by sending in the Navy to keep his family from perpetuating the regime. Note that such ceremonial figures as Elizabeth II are not really monarchs in the old-fashioned sense.

The former European empires frequently maintained sort of semi-puppet kings along their borders, partly as a method of reducing the administrative burden, and partly because the areas were not thought to be worth a great deal. In these cases, although the throne was theoretically hereditary, as a matter of fact the imperial powers or their local agents could adjust lines of succession or actually remove a reigning king if there were difficulties.

Some of these monarchs are still around. There is Morocco, formerly part of the French Empire, and now ruled by a man who originally became king while the country was under French control. Nepal was always rather independent of the rule of the British Viceroy in New Delhi. As the homeland of the famous Gurkhas, it was virtually a British ally. It retains more or less this same relationship with both Britain and India.

Along the South and East of the Arabian peninsula there is a whole collection of minor kingdoms in what used to be called the Trucial States and, of course, Kuwait. It is interesting that the British finally withdrew their last troop units from the Gulf in the early 1970s. One might speculate as to whether the 1973 oil embargo would have been imposed if the British troops had still been there.

Although these are all something of hangovers of late imperial administration, Saudi Arabia was pretty much independent. It was not true that the king would generally speaking take strongly anti-British positions.[2]

A special case is Trans-Jordan. That country was actually set up by the British government as a sort of gift to one of its important Arab clients. It was for some time an independent, but very poor bit of desert with the famous Arab legion commanded by an Englishman as its military forces. The current king is the great grandson of the first one. In view of his father's generally speaking good relations with his powerful next-door neighbor, Israel, it is likely that this throne will stay in the family for a while.

All of these existing hereditary monarchies, except North Korea, are of obvious strategic importance. For special reasons they have foreign protection. A more common form of autocratic government in the world today is dictatorship, which does not at least proclaim itself as hereditary.

My own guess is that the temporary dictatorships that are around today will eventually develop into hereditary monarchies. After all, that was the history of Rome, and of the dissolution of Rome. In believing this I am out of the mainstream. Most people think that we are moving toward universal democracy.

As a matter of fact at the moment a larger part of the world is democratic than in any previous period. Only about half of the world's population lives under dictatorships.[3] Whether this shows a long-run trend for democracy or is a temporary fillip like the ones earlier in history is something upon which there is a difference of opinion between me and the rest of the intellectual community. In any event, the purpose of this chapter is to talk about autocratic government rather than to speculate about whether it will be replaced by democracy.[4]

2   An aside on the definition of democracy

As a digression I should say here that the term 'democracy' traditionally referred to a political system in which large numbers of people could vote. This emphatically did not mean that all adults who were not either insane or in prison were enfranchised. That type of system, the modern form of democracy, is a very recent invention. Before 1900 very few women voted, and governments where only part of the adult male population voted were not particularly uncommon.

Athens, to take one famous example, allowed all adult males who were citizens to vote. This excluded not only the slaves but also people the Athenians regarded as foreigners. These might very well be persons who were brought up in Athens of parents who had been born and brought up in Athens, and who had themselves been born of parents who had been born and brought up in Athens, but they still were not Athenian citizens. As a further problem eligible voters actually had to take the day off and go to the Pnyx in order to vote.

Representative democracy is another recent development. This special kind of democracy in which a large part of the adult male population in a given city could vote if they went to the appropriate place was quite common in the Mediterranean world. Indeed the Mediterranean was surrounded by city-states of this sort, with Rome and Carthage, in the earlier days, being simply very large examples.

It is rather surprising that representative democracy was not invented in this period. Normally in Athens, if some decision had to be taken which was not worth turning out the entire male citizenry, representatives were not elected. Delegates to the 500-member Council (50 from each of the ten 'tribes of Cleisthenes') were chosen by lot instead (Finer 1997, p. 345).[5]

Something like this limited franchise system was the way democracy worked almost everywhere until the twentieth century. It was only in 1918 that all adult males in England were permitted to vote, and not until 1930 did all adult females get the franchise. The power of England was created roughly from 1700 to 1860. The number of people who could then vote was quite restricted; the House of Lords was in those days both hereditary and power-ful.

3   Assuming power

To return to our major subject, dictatorships and monarchies, the important thing to remember about dictatorships is that every dictator lives under the Sword of Damocles: 'uneasy lies the head that wears the crown', or so the saying goes. The adage is particularly true when the crown is not hereditary.

The second thing to be said here is that dictators are always people with greater than normal abilities. In this they differ from hereditary monarchs who can occasionally, as a result of genetic effects, be stupid. George III and Louis XVI, for instance, were clearly somewhat defective mentally. Compar-ing the West and East Roman monarchies, for example, Bryce ([1873] 1904, p. 331) remarks that, in the latter, 'the absence of regular rules of succession had the merit of giving to energy and ambition opportunities for displacing the incapable. Men of force came more readily to the top than they do in hereditary monarchies'.[6] Dictators have climbed the slippery pole, and this shows great talent and ability, but not necessarily great interest in the well-being of others.

Having said that dictators are usually talented and able, I should say that this does not necessarily mean they give their countries good government, although on occasion they have. Caesar Augustus was apparently very popular, and certainly he did well except for the *Teutoburger Wald*. Of course, he set up the hereditary monarchy, and his successors were in general far inferior to him.

The combination of bright people and hereditary succession has rarely been achieved, although China's Manchu dynasty managed it for a few generations. In that case the Emperor who had many sons selected one to be his successor with the aid of their tutors and the High Ministers. This led to a line of four unusually able emperors.[7]

In the more typical case this is not the selection method and the talents of the rulers who are thrown up by the genetic lottery will tend toward the mean of the normal distribution. In those cases in which there are many potential heirs and the early Manchu system is not followed, there are usually disputes over succession which do not help the state. Hereditary monarchs do have the advantage of training as children, but unfortunately this training usually involves how to entertain oneself while waiting for the king to die, as well as how to run the country.

The French monarchists maintained that having a king who actually owned the whole country was from the standpoint of the citizens a good idea because he would have no possible conflicts of interest with his subjects.[8] Indeed, although Versailles is an impressive sight, its total cost was a tiny share of the government budget, as was the imperial palace complex in China. The latter makes Versailles look like a village hut.

The French monarchists also point out that, as a result of childhood training, as long as the House of Bourbon ruled France, Germany and Italy were kept divided. It was only with the emergence of the Republic and Louis Napoleon, who ran a more or less constitutional monarchy, that Italy and Germany were united, thus greatly injuring the strategic position of France. Louis Napoleon actually took a positive role in uniting Italy.

4   Holding on to power

Let us now discuss the problem of maintaining a dictator or king in power. We shall turn later to how transitions of power can be governed. The first thing to be said is that the whole process is very risky. Further, the principal danger to the dictator is not the revolting masses, but the fact that some of his own officials may decide that they would like to replace him.

President Park of Korea, who was shot by the chief of his secret police one night at dinner, is an extreme but not atypical case. That very untrusting person, Joseph Stalin, always locked the door of his bedroom at night so that his personal, carefully selected guard could not get in. Incidentally, this may have been one of the causes of his death. When he failed to appear at the usual time in the morning, the commander of the guard was afraid to break the door down. I suppose that all of us can feel sympathy for the commander's dilemma. Hence, Stalin did not receive medical treatment for several hours later than he would have received it had he been discovered earlier.[9]

The usual procedure here is not to attempt to cultivate complete loyalty among one's immediate followers, but to keep them shifting around so that they are always a little uncertain of their positions. A well-functioning dictatorship is one in which everyone thinks that if a coup is attempted, the dictator will put it down. As long as people think that the dictator's power is secure, he is secure. If they begin to doubt, he lives at risk.[10]

Machiavelli ([1513] 1981) observed that the overthrow of any prince was astonishing because the existence of a conspiracy provided its various members with an opportunity to curry favor. Divulging the conspirators' plans is safe and certain to be rewarded, whereas siding with the organizers of the *coup d'état* is dangerous if it fails.

The problem with this from the standpoint of the dictator is not that the coup may get through without his hearing about it, but that he is surrounded by people who constantly tell him that others are plotting against him. In modern times, the possibility of secret recording devices may make it easier for a person who wishes to betray a coup to convince the dictator that it is a genuine threat and not a product of the informer's ambition.

Note that I have not said anything about popular uprisings. They are rarely capable of overthrowing an established monarch. Karl Marx and Friedrich Engels both thought that a regular military force could always put down a street mob, and as far as I know there are substantially no cases in which the military and police remained loyal to the ruler, and street rioting replaced him.

Street rioting is more apt to be either a symptom of something wrong in the government farther up, or in some cases an incentive for the military and police to turn against the dictator because they have concluded that they can topple him. The Bastille, after all, was under attack by the mob, but it fell to a regiment of regular infantry.

Before turning to the possible overthrow of dictatorships or, for that matter, monarchies, I should pause briefly to point out that the modern totalitarian dictatorship is unlike most historical monarchies. Traditional monarchs and dictators have not striven for total control. Indeed, the degree to which the government attempted to exercise detailed control in, let us say the France of Louis XIV, was probably less than the US government does. Certainly tax collections represented a much smaller share of the national income than they do in the present-day United States. Louis's army did not recruit soldiers. Instead it rented regiments from various private entrepreneurs.

If Karl Wittfogel (1991) is right, back in the early days of history when countries were dependent on elaborate irrigation networks to stay alive, similar types of governments existed. But in modern times the usual South American dictator is far from exercising totalitarian control. Indeed, it should be pointed out that actually even totalitarian governments are not always mass murderers. Joseph Stalin, Adolf Hitler, Mao tse-Tung (or 'Zedong'), Pol Pot, and Ho Chi Minh assuredly were. Slobodan Milosevic may be.

Communist states have a tendency to go in for a lot of executions, but not necessarily on the same scale. Fidel Castro apparently killed only about 30 000 people. Both Benito Mussolini and Francisco Franco killed very few people, and both of them got through almost their entire regimes without any death penalty at all.

As a general matter the ruler, whether a dictator or king, is likely to try to keep people who appear to be too talented out of power. Gonzalo Fernandez de Córdoba won the title 'The Great Captain' by long and successful campaigns for the King of Spain. Once he had been victorious, he was recalled to Spain and exiled to his estates to keep him away from the temptations of power. (This does not mean that he lived in poverty; his estates were very extensive.) Nevertheless, the king obviously thought that Córdoba's popularity made him a potential threat.

Hernando Cortez, after the conquest of Mexico, went to Spain where he became a part of the resident nobility for a time, and obviously had no power to menace the king. When he returned to the New World, the viceroy carefully saw to it that he never had a position of power. He died peacefully and his descendants remained great nobles.[11]

The average hereditary monarch or dictator has not been a wholly nice person. But, hereditary monarchs are probably nicer than dictators, on the average, because they have not had to endure the long arduous climb up the slippery pole. Nevertheless, one should not confuse the phrase 'dictator or monarch' with the phrase 'benevolent dictator or monarch'. Some of them are, some of them are not.

Mainly they should be thought of much as the type of person who either by heredity or intrigue acquires a controlling block of stock in a corporation. The dictator is probably both tougher and more self-centered than his counterpart in the corporation, but they are of the same type. They have the success of the corporation or kingdom firmly in mind because it is after all their property. Furthermore, on the whole, they do not positively want to do nasty things to their citizens or their employees. When the cards are down, though, they do put their own interests above those of the individual employees or citizens.

In both hereditary monarchies and those corporations in which the control is passed from father to son, we have the problem of the son sometimes being incompetent. This is quite a regular phenomenon in the American economy. Normally after the incompetent son has run the company down a good deal, he or his close relatives realize he is not up to the job and he sells out at a much lower price than he could have obtained when he was first in office.

This alternative is not available to the son of a king and normally he would not be safe if he passed the throne on to someone else. There are a few exceptions. Richard Cromwell, after failing to keep his father's protectorate, lived comfortably in England for the remainder of his life.

If we go over history we find a very large variance among people who have inherited thrones. The same is true with people who have simply inherited noble titles. Data on the noble class of England seem to indicate that they are in intelligence, skill, and so on above, but not far above, the average English person. There are fairly radical exceptions both ways. Louis XVI was a dunce, but the seventh Duc de Broglie (1892–1987) was awarded the 1929 Nobel Prize in physics. Charles II also seems to have been very bright and much interested in science.[12] But he was an exception.

It is likely that a collection of kings would have no higher percentage of really outstanding intellects than a collection of, let us say, college graduates. Further, the damage done by college graduates, if they turn out to be hopelessly stupid, will be minimized by competitive market forces, whereas a hopelessly stupid king may continue in power for quite some time.[13]

5 Transfers of power

This raises the questions of how does the actual transfer-of-power process work and why is it apparently much easier for the king's legitimate heir to seize power than it is for anyone else? For this purpose I would like to turn to some work by William Riker (1962) which dealt oddly enough with the institution of the American political party nominating convention back in the days when the nominating conventions actually did nominate the presidential candidates. Today, of course, nominees are determined by a presidential primary system.

Riker pointed out that the bulk of the delegates who were at the convention, although they may have had strongly held beliefs as to who they wanted as their party's candidate, mainly wanted to maximize the returns for themselves. These returns could be maximized by backing the ultimate winner, but not backing him too late (that is, after it was obvious to everyone who was going to win). Delay in joining the winning coalition would likely result in the nominee not offering any reward to the delegates whose support was not needed to put him 'over the top'.

Thus, what we typically see is a large number of delegates carefully waiting and calculating who is going to win. Their intention is to join the winner just at the time when their vote will push him over the necessary vote threshold. Since everybody adopts the same strategy, nominating conventions experienced long periods of apparent inaction, followed by a torrent of delegates rallying around the nominee's banner. The replacement of absolute rulers exhibits much the same pattern, although perhaps not as openly.

The events surrounding a ruler's death pose a similar dilemma. Most of the people know that they have no realistic chance of being selected as the new ruler, and they had better try to make good contacts with whoever will assume power. Determining who that person is in order to back him is very important.

The problem, then, with dictatorship as opposed to a hereditary monarch is that there is no legitimate heir. For one thing there is no accepted set of rules governing succession, but even more important there is a problem from the standpoint of the current dictator. His designated successor, if there is one, will normally be able to protect himself against charges of murder or assassination once he has assumed control. Thus, he is the person who finds murder or assassination of the dictator the safest path to power. Further, since the dictator can always change his mind, he has a strong motive to act. Once a dictator has appointed a successor, he is in danger.

Until the time of the Nixon administration in the United States, there was considerable tension between the president and the vice president. Probably this state of affairs was a civilized variant on the foregoing theme. It is notable that most dictators do not formally appoint a successor. There are only occasional exceptions to this rule.

If no official successor has been designated it is still possible that some relative, preferably the dictator's eldest son, will appear to almost everybody as the likely winner. In that event, he will in fact be the likely winner unless he suffers from a really appalling lack of talent. Thus, there is a tendency for dictatorships gradually to develop into hereditary monarchies and historically this has happened many times.

Dictators, like everyone else, sometimes want to retire. Life at the top of the slippery pole is not entirely a bed of roses. Retiring is risky because if the dictator retires and remains in his own country, he is a standing menace to his successor, and his life is again in danger. Under the circumstances, South American dictators have on a number of occasions solved the problem by creating democratic governments and then continuing to live on their local estates. They apparently find this more pleasant than appointing a successor and taking off to France so that they increase their chances of enjoying their retirement years in full.

The reasons underlying this strategy are fairly clear, but it should be pointed out that it has recently been showing signs of change. Democratic successor regimes to dictatorships used to be grateful to the dictator for setting them up, but in the cases of the last dictator of Korea, the last dictatorial president of Mexico, and Indonesia's deposed President Suharto, new democratic regimes seem bent nowadays on finishing off or at least impoverishing former strongmen. Augusto Pinochet has not yet really been injured, but democratic forces in Chile continually campaign for his punishment. Presumably this will mean that dictators are far more likely simply to stay in power until they die rather than setting up democratic governments and retiring. Revenge is sweet, but it is also expensive.

In general, absolute rulers are deeply concerned about avoiding being overthrown, and being so deeply concerned they pay attention to the opinions of those around them. They will normally also be mildly interested in doing things that will get them public approval. They are like the rest of us and want such public approval, but also like the rest of us, the sacrifice they will make for such public approval is limited.

Hitler, a totalitarian who, one would think, was less concerned than most with such matters, had a whole branch of the secret police whose duty it was simply to find out what people were saying about the National Socialist government. People who criticized the government were not normally arrested, but notes were made as to what policies were apparently approved of and which were not, and Hitler paid some attention to these opinions in making his decisions.

It is even possible that public opinion is more likely to sway a dictator or king than a democratically elected body because the 'public opinion' that autocrats are concerned with is that of the entire population rather than just the majority.

President Bill Clinton, as a result of the twenty-second Amendment to the US Constitution (ratified in 1951), cannot continue in office beyond his second term, but Congress can. It is somewhat ironic that a good many congressmen who were elected recently on campaign promises to vote for congressional term limits proceeded to change their minds. All congressmen worry about the next election just as all dictators worry about the possibility of *coups d'état*.

It is true that a member of Congress, although he or she may be voted out of office, is not likely to be killed. A dictator does face that possibility. Further, congressmen normally do not have elaborate bureaucracies under them, and do not have to worry particularly about the leading members of that bureaucracy deciding to launch a coup. On the other hand, on the whole they have less control over the bureaucracy than either a dictator or a king would have.

What is the net effect of all this? What are the advantages of democracy over dictatorship? The most recent data seem to indicate that dictatorships grow about as fast as democracies, although the variance among dictatorships is greater.[14] I realize that these data are subject to criticism and that there are all sorts of unfortunate characteristics in measurements of growth, including the fact that transfer payments are frequently counted as actual production.

For example, government purchases of agricultural products at prices above market values are transfers to certain farmers, but such purchases appear as real output in the GNP accounts. The available data nevertheless seem to indicate not much difference here, and the most rapidly growing countries recently were the dictatorial Asian 'Tigers', South Korea, Taiwan, Hong Kong and Singapore. Taiwan and South Korea have not been doing so well since they became democracies, but it is harder to have rapid growth when the economy has already become large than when it was still small. Undemocratic Hong Kong, which was the all-time record holder, is currently in a state of considerable disarray for external reasons. Singapore is still dictatorial and now growing quite slowly.

The average person seems to have no strong arguments for favoring democracy over dictatorship except that it is, well, more democratic. Karl Popper used to point out that in democracies, the people vote the government in, or the people can vote the government out, without resort to bloodshed. This is generally speaking true, although it should be said that, gauged in terms of casualties, the largest war the United States ever engaged in was entirely domestic – a war, it bears emphasizing, that was fought not to overthrow the central government, but for the right to secede from it. It should also be said that *coups d'état* may be rather less expensive than the average presidential election.

I should digress here briefly and point out that Mexico, from about 1930 until a few years ago, had a form of government which as far as I know was only duplicated in the Roman Empire during the period of the adoptive emperors. Having no natural male progeny, emperors were succeeded by adopted sons. Marcus Aurelius Antoninus unfortunately had a son who was one of the worst emperors Rome ever had. In Mexico, until recently, the dictator ruled for six years and appointed his successor. On the whole, it seems to have worked quite well.

So far in talking about what might be called hereditary dictatorship, I have been contrasting it with democracy. I have not discussed such forms of government as the rule by civil servants that dominated China.[15] Nor have I dealt with feudalism, a rare form of government found, as far as I know, only in Europe and Japan, or said anything about the true theocracies like Utah and Tibet. I am not going to take them up now, but stick to dictatorships and monarchies.

It should be pointed out that neither dictators nor monarchs are sadists who positively want to make life difficult for their subjects. Further, they normally suspect that making anybody unhappy is likely to make their thrones somewhat less secure. Still, if the ruler makes Smith unhappy by taking his money away and giving it to Jones, the gain of Jones may be greater than the loss of Smith. If Smith is also killed, he is unlikely to try to overthrow the ruler.

While there are exceptions, neither dictators nor monarchs are likely to do wicked things just because they want to. Further, there is some truth in the French monarchist argument, discussed above, that the ruler has no conflict of interest with his country. He may have conflicts of interest with those parts of his country that would like to get rid of him, but the prosperity of the country as a whole is to his advantage (Brennan 1990; Haddock 1994). It must be said, however, that the sovereign's interest in the prosperity of his subjects is not necessarily consistent with overall economic efficiency. One well-known model of autocracy characterizes the ruler as a 'stationary bandit' (Olson 1993; McGuire and Olson 1996) whose objective is to maximize the amount of privately created wealth redistributed to himself and his supporters.[16] The interference in the economy required to achieve that goal can lead to high levels of regulation, taxation, and budget deficits as well as rent-seeking activities by individuals and groups striving to be included among the favored. Mercantilism (Ekelund and Tollison 1981, 1997b), modern *dirigiste* France and Spain, and the regimes of 'Papa Doc' Duvalier, Ferdinand Marcos, and Manuel Noriega are obvious examples. But so is the Leviathan democratic state (Brennan and Buchanan 1980).

There is a significant difference between hereditary monarchies and dictatorships, as mentioned above, which is simply that the monarch is more secure and that there is not likely to be a general outburst of street fighting when he dies. 'The King is dead, long live the King.'

Kurrild-Klitgaard (2000) examined the history of the Danish monarchy. He found that during the period when the throne was not hereditary, civil strife was endemic and kings were overthrown frequently. During the last 400 years, when the throne has been hereditary, domestic tranquility has been the norm. This was true in the days when Denmark was a genuine monarchy as well as now when its queen is a constitutional monarch. That is only one country. Similar studies of other countries would be valuable.

Transitions of power in monarchies are not always peaceful. The ancient Persian Empire, the empire overthrown by Alexander the Great, had almost continuous difficulties with the line of succession to the throne. The problem was that the emperor usually had many sons and he tended to appoint them to administrative posts in various parts of the empire. They rarely attempted to overthrow their father, although sometimes they did, but the emperor's death usually ignited a civil war among contending heirs.

A more extreme example of this occurred in Turkey, after the time of Selim the Grim (1467–1520), who enacted a dynastic law requiring the Padashah to kill all of his brothers. As a result of this rule and other efforts to protect the Padashah, the male heirs were all confined to a palace in the safekeeping of eunuchs. When the Padashah died, a violent civil war immediately broke out within the palace walls. Normally one of the sons survived and became the next Padashah. The system did not produce very good rulers.

Most European states had a simpler rule, which was that the heir to the throne was kept close to his father in the royal capital, but not given any administrative position that might supply him a power base either to overthrow his father or to dispose of his younger brothers.[17] In general, there was a positive effort to inoculate the younger brothers with the belief that they would live well, but not become king.

Traditionally in China, where the emperor once again had many wives and children, there was a rule under which the eldest son of his principal wife was to succeed. The other sons, in essence, were pensioned off generously. Under the Ming dynasty, as a part of their pension agreement the other sons were required to move to South China, a very long way from the capital. There do not seem to have been any cases in which they attempted to overthrow their half-brother.

All of these methods worked, but not perfectly. The Wars of the Roses started when a close relative of an existing, but mentally unbalanced, king successfully replaced him.

Another solution to the succession problem, which was used originally by the Catholic Church but copied by most communist countries, is simple and seems to work in most cases. There was the Great Schism, though. In this case, the dictator, called the Bishop of Rome in the Catholic Church and the general secretary of the Communist Party in Russia, appoints a body to advise him, the College of Cardinals in Rome and the Politburo in Moscow. When the dictator dies, this group elects his successor.[18]

Transitions of power under this system did not always proceed without bloodshed, but on the basis of the rather limited experience of it in communist countries, it has worked pretty well. Perhaps the fact that almost all of the cardinals are elderly men is the reason that it has worked so well in the Catholic Church. Members of the various Communist Party politburos also tended to be elderly.

The end of the reign of a dictator who has climbed the slippery pole rather than inherited his position is rarely as orderly as that of hereditary monarchs. First, he may be overthrown by some of his colleagues or, in some cases, by foreign invaders. Second, as we have mentioned, he may get tired of the burden of office and simply withdraw. In any event, it is usually difficult for a dictator to control the transition of power and the process is apt to be disruptive. There may not be anyone killed during these interregnums, but sometimes many people are.

After seizing power, dictators are apt to feel much less secure than the eldest son of the previous king. This insecurity may also cause difficulties, running from systematic executions of defeated rivals and others whose loyalty is suspect, to simply running a very weak government. On occasions the new dictator has actually had radically different ideas from a predecessor and has imposed them. Sometimes the new dictator is overthrown quite quickly because he does not have the armed support his predecessor did.

6   Political freedoms

We now come to the subject of freedom. First, dictators normally object to anybody suggesting that they be overthrown, and they suppress it. Freedoms of speech, assembly, and the press may be curtailed in the process. Democracies also have a record of suppression of objectors. Socrates was in fact killed by the Athenian democracy and Aristotle found it necessary to leave town hastily in order to prevent Athens from committing 'another sin against philosophy'.[19]

Democratic Germany has a very complicated set of laws that ban the expression of certain right-wing views. Most people, including myself, do not regard this as particularly offensive, although I do think they are vastly exaggerating a minor problem.

Any academic living in the United States is familiar with the problems of 'political correctness' (for example, Bernstein 1994). Confusingly, this particular ideological movement has had grammatical effects. One is not supposed to refer to 'chairman', but 'chairperson', and so on.

This restriction on freedom is not only about minor language matters, though. It has led to a number of American universities wasting a great deal of money and corrupting the education of their students in order to teach certain politically correct courses. Moreover, a lot of total nonsense is being taught as 'history' at the grade school and high school levels.

Restricting freedom is exactly what government, democratic or dictatorial, is about. All sorts of things one can do to injure other people are prevented by the government, it is hoped. These restrictions are not necessarily confined to ordinary crimes. The small homeowners' association that governed the area where I lived in Tucson complained about a person painting a new house the wrong color. He refused to do anything about it; the association sued and collected $7000. In this area one is not free to choose the color of one's own house. The homeowners' association thought that the value of the other houses would be lowered and I believe that this was a correct estimate.

Altogether, the extent to which people have freedom is more or less an inverse function of the number of laws in force. In general, when I talk to people about freedom, what they actually mean is not freedom in the way I have been discussing it here, but freedom to do the things that one can now do in the United States, and not freedom to do things that are now illegal in the United States. Dictatorships have different sets of rules of this sort, and it is always possible to maintain that a given set of them is not consistent with freedom. Ulster's Irish Catholics frequently maintain they are not free and they sometimes even say that Ulster is not democratic. The problem here is simply that the majority disagrees with them about a number of things and proceeds to enforce its opinion.

If it is understood that freedom means the freedom to do the kind of things one can do in the United States, and not freedom to do other things one cannot do in the United States, for example, putting up a crèche on the courthouse lawn, then it must be conceded that there are more freedoms in the United States than in dictatorships. But that is not always true. I lived in Hong Kong at a time when it was run by the colonial office as a straightforward dictatorship. As far as I could see, it was a remarkably free place. More so than the United States because the government was not attempting to enforce any of the moralistic provisions which are part of American law.

Take an earlier example. During the reign of Caesar Augustus,[20] there was substantially nothing that an ordinary free citizen of Rome could say that would get him in trouble. Ovid succeeded in irritating Caesar enough to be exiled, but people without his talent would normally be left alone even if they sharply criticized the emperor.

There are two other famous examples. In one case a member of the Senate, who was a great believer in the Republic, kept going about Rome saying that he was going to kill the emperor. Caesar eventually came to the conclusion that perhaps social pressure would lead him to actually make the attempt, so he passed a special law prohibiting the man from living in Rome. Surely this was not a gigantic infringement on his freedom.

The other case, which is more amusing, occurred while Caesar Augustus was, as Roman dictators did, acting as a judge in a court. In a case originating in Spain one party offered evidence that the other party regularly cursed the emperor. The emperor said 'is that so', turned to the other party and spent the next five minutes cursing him. He then said, 'he has cursed me and I have cursed him, now let's get on with the lawsuit'. It is likely that the object of the emperor's invective was not very happy while the cursing was going on.

Caesar Augustus was an exceptional ruler. Most dictators have not had this kind of freedom from deep worry which permits them to get by with this kind of thing. Hereditary monarchs very commonly have. The crime of lese-majesty is always available for a king to deal with people who criticize him, but it must be said that kings do not use it very often. On the other hand, they are not criticized very much, which may be because of the threat of retribution or simply because their subjects have little to be critical of.

7 Concluding remarks

Much of what I have said in this chapter is contrary to the current conventional wisdom. The reader may recall that during the latter part of the nineteenth century and the early part of the twentieth century, nationalism was one of the great virtues. Austria-Hungary was broken up in its name, Germany and Italy united in it, and there are many other examples. Woodrow Wilson was a firm believer in it. That has changed. Nowadays nationalism is on the whole a bad word, and we have been attempting in Yugoslavia to compel separate groups of people, who do not want to live with each other, to do so peacefully. Apparently, it is to be tried in several other parts of the world as well.

At the moment, democracy has about the same respect that nationalism had in the early part of the twentieth century. Almost everybody is firmly in favor of it. For a very long time people were prepared to die, not for democracy, but for the one true king. The Wars of the Roses is a good example of this kind of thing, but there are many others. The kind of enthusiasm we now have for democracy used to be marshaled in favor of the legitimate heir to the throne. Marco Polo, who was governor of a large Chinese city, remarks that the Mongols were unpopular because the people wanted to be ruled by their own prince.

All of this is not an argument that dictatorship or hereditary monarchy is better than democracy. My view is simply that the matter has not been given much serious thought. When I have talked to people about this they almost invariably think of Hitler or possibly, if they are on the right, Stalin. They then turn to African countries or Muslim countries ruled by autocrats and say that democracy would be an improvement, but it is not obvious that they have good reasons for their preference. Recently, there has been a feeling rather than an argument that democracy will lead to greater economic progress. This is normally based on nothing more than the fact that people believe in democracy and in economic progress, and all good things go together. We badly need serious consideration of the matter.

Turning to my own personal feeling, I was brought up in a democracy and would be rather unhappy living under a dictatorship, although I was perfectly happy in Hong Kong. I see no reason to believe either that today's wild collection of differently organized governments that are called democracy or that the other wild collection of governments that are at the moment referred to as autocratic are the best form of government. They are both thousands of years old and it seems to me that invention is as important in this area as in any other. On the other hand, in spite of having thought about the matter for a long time, I have no third form of government to suggest.

Notes

1. It is ironic that shortly after President John Kennedy arranged the death of Diem in Vietnam, General Trujillo in the Dominican Republic, and Lumumba in the Congo he was himself assassinated. 'They that take the sword ...'. The eventual outcome in the Dominican Republic was that Lyndon Johnson sent in the 82nd Airborne. This led to some

desultory fighting in the course of which a few American soldiers and somewhat more Dominicans were killed.

2. He did award the oil exploration contract to an American company rather than to a British one. This was at the time when the British needed American support in other parts of the world.

3. India accounts for a very large share of the people living in democracies.

4. For an earlier discussion, see my *Autocracy* (Tullock 1987). Wintrobe (1998) is a more recent contribution to a not very large literature.

5. Council members served one-year terms and no one could serve more than twice. The machine used to produce these selections is still on display in the Stoa of Attalus at Athens.

6. While 'there was of course a tendency for the throne to become settled in a family, for an Emperor usually tried to secure the succession for his son or some other relative either by publicly destining him for power, or by associating him as co-Emperor during his own life … when the vigor of a reigning stock began to die out, the stock usually disappeared, and an upstart adventurer set up a new dynasty' (Bryce [1873] 1904, pp. 331–2).

7. The fourth conformed to Chinese rather than Manchu traditions and selected the eldest son of his principal wife to succeed him. The fifth emperor was unusually poor.

8. The absence of private property had disastrous consequences for Russia. See Pipes (1999).

9. Interestingly enough, Stalin was at the time he died planning his own 'final solution' for Russian Jews. He had begun with an attack on Jewish doctors, and it is possible that this pogrom led to his having poorer medical attention than he would have had otherwise.

10. Kinship is one margin of regime stability: 'for example, the French court for most of its history was often a collection of relatives of the various noblemen. Such individuals were obliged to take up residence at the royal court so that noblemen could not rebel against the king without jeopardizing their own kin' (Dugatkin 1999, p. 162). Another strategy is to retain some of the members of the previous ruler's supporting coalition in office, diluting their power but reducing their incentives to oppose the new government (Kimenyi and Shughart 1989).

11. Pizarro, on the other hand, stayed in Peru and apparently was suspected by the king of trying to establish an independent monarchy there. In consequence, his family was wiped out.

12. He attended meetings of the Royal Society. Henry VII was probably equally bright and extremely devious. Both of these kings had to fight for their thrones.

13. Louis XVI did not succeed in holding on to power, and even though George III remained on the throne, he was much less powerful when he died than he had been earlier.

14. Ali (1997, pp. 4–5) collects all of the existing studies. He sums up his findings as follows: 'out of twenty-one studies … nine report a positive relationship between democracy and economic growth and four studies indicate a negative relation between growth and democracy. The remaining eight studies find no significant difference between regimes' (p. 3). There are, of course, no hereditary monarchies in the sample. See also Chapters 28 and 29 of this volume.

15. There was an emperor, of course, but the officials carried out the bulk of his duties.

16. 'Stationary bandits are superior to roving bandits (for example, Chinese warlords) because, being stationary, they have an incentive to preserve the wealth or capital of potential victims' (Wintrobe 1998, p. 131). Wintrobe refers to such a ruler as a 'kleptocrat'.

17. Stalin seems to have done the same thing. Had he had lived longer, he might well have established a dynasty.

18. Electors likewise chose the Germanic monarch, and this system continued to be used after that monarch and the Holy Roman Emperor became united in one person. Bryce ([1873] 1904, p. 246) remarks 'how difficult, one might say impossible, it was found to maintain in practice the elective principle'. While 'the imperial throne was from the tenth to the nineteenth century absolutely open to any orthodox Christian candidate', the fact of the matter was that 'the competition was confined to a few powerful families, and there was always a strong tendency for the crown to become hereditary in some one of these.' Bryce also credits this system with contributing to the Holy Roman Empire's eventual fall:

The power of the crown was not moderated but destroyed. Each successful candidate was forced to purchase his title by the sacrifice of rights which had belonged to his predecessors, and must repeat the same shameful policy later in his reign to procure the election of his son. Feeling at the same time that his family could not make sure of keeping the throne, he treated it as a life-tenant is apt to treat his estate, seeking only to make out of it the largest present profit. And the electors, aware of the strength of their position, presumed upon it and abused it to assert an independence such as the nobles of other countries could never have aspired to. (p. 247)

In the Empire's dying days, the electors were 'driven to the expedient of selecting for the office persons whose private resources enabled them to sustain it with dignity' (ibid., p. 361).

19.   After the establishment of Macedonian control, Aristotle returned to Athens and set up his famous academy.

20.   After he was firmly established in power; when he was consolidating his power things were different.

7 The anatomy of political representation: direct democracy, parliamentary democracy, and representative democracy

*Tim R. Sass**

1 Introduction

One of the most fundamental issues in constitutional design is the degree to which individuals will participate directly in collective decision-making processes. There are two questions to be addressed in this regard. First, will individuals select representatives to act as their agents in group decision making or will all decision-making authority be retained by the individual members of the group? Second, if representatives are to be granted some decision-making authority, how will they be selected and what specific decision-making authority will be delegated to them?

The first choice, between direct democracy and representative democracy, may at first blush seem to be irrelevant. While many townships in the United States and some municipalities in Switzerland are run as direct democracies, most sizeable political jurisdictions employ some sort of system of representation whereby citizens elect representatives to make decisions on their behalf. Despite the relative rarity of pure direct democracies in the political arena, the choice between direct and representative democracy is important nonetheless. While most political entities function as representative governments, the degree of representation can vary considerably. Whether it be approval of school bond issues or constitutional amendments, many representative governments incorporate some elements of direct democracy. Moreover, voting is not limited to the political sphere. Publicly held corporations, homeowners' associations, and private cooperatives all employ direct voting to make collective decisions and may cede little or no decision-making authority to boards of directors or other representatives. Thus, analysis of the polar cases of direct democracy and representative government can lend insight into the functioning of many real-world institutions that lie somewhere in the middle of the representation spectrum.

If a representative democracy is chosen as the primary means of making group decisions, choices must still be made about how representatives are selected and what powers they will be assigned. While a myriad of possible representative government structures exist, the focus here will be on the dichotomy between presidential and parliamentary governments. Under the basic presidential system, both the legislative and executive branches of government are elected directly by enfranchised citizens and they share decision-making authority. While political parties play a role, the identities and policy preferences of individual candidates are relatively important. In parliamentary governments, on the other hand, the electorate only chooses representatives to the legislature directly and it is the legislature that in turn selects the executive, the prime minister. Political parties are afforded a more prominent role in such systems since it is the majority party that ultimately selects the head of government.[1]

As Shugart and Carey (1992) point out, the choice between presidential and parliamentary systems is an ongoing process. Some emerging democracies in the 1980s and 1990s have selected parliamentary governments (for example, Pakistan, Nepal) while many of the fledgling democracies of Eastern Europe have opted for directly elected presidents (for example, Russia, Poland). Some countries have switched from parliamentary systems to presidential ones (for example, Nigeria, Zimbabwe). Given the dynamics of institutional structure within representative democracy, comparative analysis of presidential and parliamentary systems is particularly relevant to real-world collective decisions.

2   The choice of representative versus direct democracy

2.1   Theory

Still one of the best analyses of constitutional design is the seminal work of Buchanan and Tullock (1962). Buchanan and Tullock delineate two costs associated with collective decision making: external costs and decision-making costs. External costs encompass 'costs that the individual expects to endure as a result of the actions of others over which he has no direct control' (ibid., p. 45). Decision-making costs are 'the costs which the individual expects to incur as a result of his own participation … in decisions when two or more individuals are required to reach agreement' (ibid., pp. 45–6). Buchanan and Tullock refer to the sum of these two costs as 'interdependence costs'. They hypothesize that rational individuals will select a decision-making mechanism that minimizes these costs.

One of the fundamental elements of collective decision making that Buchanan and Tullock analyse is the ratio of the number of elected representatives to the size of the entire group, or 'degree of representation'. As the size of a group increases, the total decision-making costs to group members of attending meetings, participating in discussion and casting ballots rises. By reducing the size of the decision-making group, representative democracy economizes on decision-making costs. Thus, the degree of representation is directly proportional to the size of the group. Viewed as a discrete choice, the probability of direct democracy is expected to decline with the size of the group (all else equal).

Barzel and Sass (1990) and Sass (1992) have modified and extended the original constitutional model of Buchanan and Tullock. Buchanan and Tullock's definition of 'external costs' focuses on the costs that an *individual* bears when collective decisions do not go his way.[2] However, such costs are mainly redistributive; a loss to one individual in a group is often a gain to another. The net value of a voting system is determined by the *deadweight* costs associated with attempts to institute or prevent transfers of wealth within the group (that is, 'rent seeking'). Efforts to use the collective decision-making process for the purpose of redistributing wealth are a net loss to the group as a whole and will thus affect the choice of voting system.

In their analysis of decision-making costs, Buchanan and Tullock do not explicitly consider the cost of acquiring information to make decisions. If individuals are to participate in group decisions they will rationally obtain information up to the point where the cost of gaining additional information equals the anticipated marginal benefit from more enlightened choice. The costs of information acquisition can vary across individuals, however. There exist potential gains from trade from having individuals with high information costs cede some decision-making authority to representatives with a comparative advantage in information acquisition and decision making.[3]

In addition to decision-making and rent-seeking costs, a third cost of voting arises in representative governments, namely agency costs. In representative democracies collective decisions are made by elected representatives rather than by the voters themselves. An agency relationship therefore exists wherein elected officials are the agents and the voters the principals. Representatives will seek to maximize their own utilities, which may not coincide with maximizing the utility of voters.[4] The losses imposed on voters will vary directly with the divergence of interests between voters and representatives. If representatives possess superior information they can exploit that asymmetry to impose even greater losses on voters. Faced with the prospect of suffering losses from the decisions of representatives, voters will impose restrictions on the choices representatives have authority to make and will allocate resources to monitor the behavior of elected officials. Following Jensen and Meckling's (1976) analysis of managerial behavior in the modern corporation, agency costs include the sum of the expenditures devoted to monitoring and constraining representative behavior plus the net cost of undesired representative actions that remain.[5]

By appropriately modifying the definitions of 'external costs' and 'decision-making costs', as well as adding agency costs to the list of interdependence costs, one can apply Buchanan and Tullock's model to the choice between direct and representative democracy.

2.2   Empirical evidence

Quantitative empirical analysis of the choice between direct and representative democracy is scant. Only three studies, Sass (1991), Fahy (1998), and Hersch and McDougall (1997), investigate the factors affecting the form of government empirically.

Sass (1991) considers four determinants of the choice between representative and direct democracy: population, population change, income, and group heterogeneity. Decision-making costs are expected to increase with group size. More populous communities are therefore more likely to be governed by representative democracies. Given that changing government structures is costly, growing communities will not instantaneously switch from direct democracy to some system of political representation. Cities with recently expanded populations are consequently less likely to possess representative governments than cities of equal size that have grown more slowly. Whether as a result of a positive correlation between income and decision-making productivity, or a greater impact of political decisions on the wellbeing of the wealthy, it is well known that political participation tends to increase with income. If the demand for participation in group decision making increases with income, then we should observe a negative correlation between income and the choice of representative democracy. Group heterogeneity will affect both the decision-making and wealth-transfer costs of collective decision making. More diverse groups will have higher costs of reaching decisions, making representative democracy, which economizes on decision-making costs, more likely. Wealth-transfer costs may also increase with group heterogeneity since divergent preferences can produce non-uniform effects of group decisions. The relatively high costs of coalition formation and vote trading in direct democracies tend to limit these wealth transfers, making representative government less attractive for heterogeneous voting groups. Likewise, minority groups with strong preferences, which might be on the losing end of group decisions, will tend to have a greater voice in direct democracies because those with milder preferences will choose not to incur the costs of attending meetings and voting. The combination of reduced wealth-transfer costs and higher decision-making costs associated with group heterogeneity leaves the relationship between intragroup diversity and the form of government ambiguous.

Sass's empirical estimates are based on a sample of 102 Connecticut towns with either open-town-meeting or representative governments. The findings generally support the economic model of government choice. As expected, population size is positively correlated with representative democracy and recent population growth is negatively associated with the existence of a representative government. The estimated effect of median income on the probability of having a representative government is negative, but not statistically significant. The standard deviation of income, a proxy for group hetero-geneity, is negatively and significantly correlated with representative democracy.

Fahy (1998) argues that direct democracies can be manipulated by special-interest groups that 'pack' town meetings. In particular, existing coalitions, such as municipal employee unions, could take advantage of low turnout at meetings to push their legislative agendas.[6] This would tend to increase wealth transfers from the majority to the minority. If wealth transfers increase in direct democracy on net balance, this would reinforce the impact of decision-making costs and lead to an unambiguous positive relationship between group diversity and representative government.

Fahy also contends that the effect of population growth on the choice of representative versus direct democracy is uncertain. While she agrees with Sass that transition costs would tend to increase the likelihood that a rapidly growing community would still possess a direct democracy, she also asserts that a community experiencing rapid growth is less likely to have stable and powerful interest groups. If this is true, then the effect of population growth on government form is ambiguous.

Fahy utilizes data on townships in Massachusetts to test her hypotheses. In contrast to Sass, who employs only contemporary data, Fahy estimates the relationship between community characteristics and government form with data from the time of structural change as well as current (1990) data. Con-sistent with previous work, she finds a strong and statistically significant positive relationship between population size and the likelihood of a repre-sentative government with both historical and current data. The impact of population change depends on the vintage of the data, however. Using current data she finds the same significant negative relationship that Sass finds in Connecticut. However, using data from the time of adoption for representa-tive government towns (and current data for open-town-meeting governments), she finds that rapidly growing communities were more likely to possess representative governments. While these findings are consistent with her view that the impact of population change on government form is ambiguous, they could also be a result of the way in which she constructed her data. If population growth was generally higher in the past, then using contemporary data for open-town-meeting governments and historical data for representa-tive governments could bias the estimates toward a positive population change–representative government relationship.

The estimated effects of voter wealth and group heterogeneity on govern-ment form also depend on the data employed. Using 1990 data for all cities, Fahy finds the same negative relationship between wealth and representative government in Massachusetts as Sass found for income and representative government in Connecticut. Using historical data, however, she finds that wealth and representative democracy are positively correlated. In the case of group heterogeneity she finds a positive but insignificant effect of income heterogeneity on the probability of representative government. In contrast, using historical data she finds that both income heterogeneity and a measure of diversity on other socioeconomic margins have positive and significant impacts on the likelihood of representative government. These later results lend support to her view that wealth-transfer costs are lower in representative democracies.

Hersch and McDougall (1997) analyse empirically the choice between purely representative government and a limited form of direct democracy, the voter initiative. Initiatives allow citizens to propose and pass specific laws directly, thereby circumventing the legislative (representative) process. The specific case they study is the 1994 vote by the Kansas legislature to amend the state constitution to allow voter initiatives. Hersch and McDougall view initiatives as a way for legislators to avoid taking stands on potentially divisive legislative issues. They posit that the more heterogeneous the constituency, the harder it would be for a representative to gauge public opinion and the more divisive decisions would tend to be. Thus, they predict that the greater the heterogeneity of the electorate the more likely a legislator would favor adopting an initiative process and moving toward direct democracy. Hersch and McDougall also reason that older and better-educated voters would have lower decision-making costs and thus tend to favor an initiative process. Representatives from districts where such voters reside would therefore tend to support an amendment allowing voter initiatives. Unfortunately, there is at best only modest support in the data for these hypotheses. The winning margin of a legislator in the most recent election is negatively correlated with the likelihood of voting for an initiative process, suggesting that where the electorate is more cohesive, a representative is less interested in transferring decision-making authority to voters. However, the coefficient of variation in district household income, a proxy for voter heterogeneity, is not found to have a significant impact on legislators' votes on adopting an initiative process. Voter age also had an insignificant influence on the vote to permit initiatives, while the percentage of voters with a college education was negatively correlated with voting to permit initiatives.

There is clearly room for more empirical studies of the choice of government form. However, the extant literature does strongly support the idea that decision-making costs are higher in direct democracies and that larger groups are more likely to adopt representative governments. Unfortunately, the existing studies also suggest that results can be sensitive to the data and methodology employed.

3   The impact of government structure on policy outcomes

Another way of viewing the choice between direct and representative democracy is to consider whether there are measurable differences in the decisions that are reached in representative versus direct democracies. Different outcomes could arise for three reasons. First, in a representative democracy elected officials will seek to maximize their own utilities, which may lead to them making decisions that deviate from the preferences of their constituents. This agency problem could lead to higher governmental spending either because representatives themselves value a larger bureaucracy (Niskanen 1975; Romer and Rosenthal 1982) or because they benefit personally from consuming the perquisites of office.

Second, even if agency problems are non-existent, the decisions rendered in representative democracies can differ from those in direct democracies owing to the nature of the voting system used to elect representatives. In a single, at-large election between two candidates the winner will be the candidate preferred by the median voter. However, this may not be the case in a district election format. Depending on the extent of gerrymandering and the geographic distribution of voters, the majority of elected representatives could have preferences decidedly different from those of the (jurisdiction-wide) median voter.

Third, the political outcomes under direct and representative democracy can diverge because the identity of the (participating) median voter is different. Casting a ballot in a single election is less costly than attending periodic town meetings and voting on individual issues. Thus, the median voter in an election to choose representatives may differ markedly from the median participant in a direct democracy. If, as has been found in a number of circumstances, political participation increases with income, then the median (participating) voter in a direct democracy may be wealthier than the median voter in a representative election and thus the collective decisions in each circumstance will differ.

3.1   Government form and expenditure levels

A number of empirical studies have analysed the relationship between government form (representative versus direct democracy) and governmental expenditure. Almost uniformly these studies focus on the issue of agency costs associated with representative democracy and predict that expenditures will be higher in representative governments, all else equal. The first such empirical analysis is Wheeler (1967), who compares town-meeting and city (representative) governments in Maine. Wheeler's empirical model of local per-pupil educational expenditures is parsimonious, containing just four explanatory variables: average daily attendance, attendance duration/proportion of high school students, population growth rate, and a dummy variable representing the form of government. The list of included variables is relatively *ad hoc* and not based on any particular theoretical model. Using decade-long averages over a 70-year span, Wheeler does not find significant differences between school expenditures in open-town-meeting and representative governments.

In a pair of companion studies, Pommerehne (1978) and Pommerehne and Schneider (1978) analyse aggregate expenditures across Swiss municipalities with different government forms. They estimate expenditure functions based on the median-voter model, with expenditures a function of median income, the tax share, and total population. Rather than simply include a shift parameter for representative versus direct democracy, they instead allow all of the model's parameters to vary across governmental regimes by estimating separate expenditure equations for direct and representative democracies. Pommerehne (1978) utilizes expenditure data for 1970 and finds the fit of the median-voter model (measured by $\bar{R}^2$) much better in the 48 Swiss municipalities with direct democracies than in representative democracies without referenda. In contrast, Pommerehne and Schneider (1978) employ average expenditure over the four-year period 1968–72 and find only very modest differences in the fit of the median-voter model between direct democracies with either obligatory or optional referenda and representative democracies with no referenda. Both studies find income and tax elasticities to be much larger in direct democracies, though no formal tests are conducted to determine if the income and tax share coefficients vary across the equations representing different government forms.

Similar to Pommerehne (1978) and Pommerehne and Schneider (1978), Chicoine et al. (1989) compare the performance of the median-voter model in direct and representative democracies. They study expenditures on road maintenance in 102 Illinois townships with representative governments and 119 Minnesota townships with direct democracies. They focus on road expenditures since this is the primary function of the township governments. The data arrangement is somewhat unfortunate, since any differences in expenditure levels could be due either to the form of government or to other state-level effects. Indeed, while the level of road expenditures is lower in the direct-democracy governments of Minnesota, the authors attribute this difference to greater maintenance responsibilities of townships in Illinois (relative to county governments) and higher road maintenance costs in Illinois. They focus instead on differences in the slope parameters across government forms, conducting formal *F*-tests of equivalence. Contrary to the results of Pommerehne (1978) and Pommerehne and Schneider (1978), they find that the tax elasticities are larger for the representative governments of Illinois. Indeed, the estimated coefficient on median income for the direct democracies of Minnesota is not statistically significant. The tax price coefficient is also insignificant in Minnesota, although the estimated tax elasticities are not significantly different across the two states and governmental forms.

Santerre (1989) utilizes a modified version of the median-voter model to examine both municipal and public school expenditures among 90 direct-democracy and representative-democracy townships in Connecticut. Rather than examine individual coefficient differences across governmental forms, he jointly tests the equivalence of all of the slope parameters and fails to reject the equivalence of the slope coefficients across governmental forms. He then proceeds to estimate expenditure models where governmental form is modeled solely as an intercept shifter. Given this functional form, he finds that representative governments are associated with 8–9 percent higher per-capita municipal expenditures, though the effect is only marginally significant at about the 10 percent level. In contrast, per-pupil school expenditures are found to be 3 percent *lower* in representative democracies. Santerre suggests that perhaps a lack of voter control in representative democracies may influence the type of expenditure rather than the overall expenditure level chosen by bureaucrats.

One factor common to all of the aforementioned studies is the assumption that government form is exogenous. A number of the investigations attempt to account for the fact that representative democracies tend to be more populous by estimating samples which include only direct democracies at least as large as the smallest representative government and exclude representative governments more populous than the largest direct democracy. However, Sass (1991) is the only study explicitly to account for the choice of government form when estimating the fiscal impact of government structure. Using data on Connecticut townships similar to that of Santerre (1989), Sass first estimates a probit equation of the probability that a community possesses a representative government. The predicted values from the probit equation are then used to construct a variable that corrects for selection bias in both municipal and school expenditure equations. When government form is treated as exogenous, representative government is associated with 3 percent lower per-student school expenditures and 11 percent higher per-capita municipal expenditures, as in Santerre (1989). However, these differences are no longer significant when government form is treated as endogenous. Further, the selectivity variable has a significant coefficient in the school expenditure equation, indicating statistically significant bias in per-student expenditures when government form is treated as exogenous.

Santerre (1993) provides one possible explanation for the puzzling result that expenditures in representative governments are often the same or sometimes even lower than expenditure levels in direct democracies. Like Fahy, he posits that a well-organized interest group, such as public-sector employees, can more easily influence budget outcomes in direct democracies. In the open-town-meeting governments of New England attendance is often light. Thus a well-organized interest group can get its members to attend town meetings and exert a disproportionate influence on budgetary decisions. If this is true and organized special interests desire more spending, then their disproportionate influence in direct democracies could mimic the budget-inflating aspects of the agency relationship inherent in representative democracy. Using the same data as his earlier work (Santerre 1989), Santerre (1993) finds that public school employee voting power is positively corre-lated with public school expenditure levels in direct democracies, but not in representative governments.

The studies of the relationship between government form and expenditure provide little support for the notion that agency costs in representative gov-ernment produce higher total expenditures. The only strong evidence favoring the hypothesis is that of Pommerehne (1978), although even these results do not appear to be robust when compared to the analysis of the same cities over a different time period by Pommerehne and Schneider (1978). The lack of a strong and consistent correlation between representative democracy and total spending suggests either that electoral competition and voter monitoring are sufficient to constrain representative behavior or that agency costs materi-alize along different dimensions such as the mix of expenditures.

3.2   Initiatives, referenda, and expenditure levels

Initiatives and referenda can be viewed as limited forms of direct democracy. In pure direct democracies all issues are determined by a vote of the citizenry and there is no legislature. Initiatives and referenda are used in conjunction with an elected legislature and provide for direct voter decision making on a limited set of issues. Initiatives allow citizens to propose and pass new legislation. The signatures of some fraction of registered voters usually must be obtained to place an initiative on the ballot. In contrast, referenda give voters the opportunity to approve or nullify laws initiated by the legislature. Referenda can be obligatory or optional and may be placed on the ballot by citizen petition or legislative referral. They may be relatively general, as in budget referenda, or they may apply to a single policy issue. Whatever the particular form, however, to the extent that representative governments with referenda or voter initiatives enhance the decision-making role of citizens, they should perform in a fashion similar to direct democracies. Thus we should observe higher decision-making costs but lower external and agency costs in jurisdictions where referenda are available to voters. In particular, if agency costs take the form of excessive public expenditures we should observe lower expenditures (all else equal) in the presence of referenda.

A trio of studies, Pommerehne (1978), Pommerehne and Frey (1978) and Pommerehne and Schneider (1978), measure the marginal impact of referenda on expenditure in representative democracies in Switzerland. They construct an expenditure equation based on the median-voter model and estimate the parameters separately for representative democracies with referenda and those without. Using data from two different time periods (1970 and 1968–72), they find that the median-voter model of expenditures produces a better fit (higher $\bar{R}^2$) in municipalities with referenda than it does in those without. While the differences are not always statistically significant, the estimated tax and income elasticities of expenditure were higher in representative democracies with referenda, suggesting that referenda may enhance voter control. Consistent with the notion that electoral competition alone provides only a limited check on agency costs, they also find that time until the next election is positively correlated with the level of public expenditure in cities without referenda, but uncorrelated with expenditure in cities with referenda.

In a more recent study of municipalities in Switzerland, Feld and Kirchgässner (1999) find corroborating evidence that referenda serve to constrain local public expenditure. Using cross-sectional data from 1990, they estimate the simultaneous determination of per-capita debt, the median tax-payer's tax rate, and own-government revenue as a fraction of total revenue and total expenditures. Consistent with previous Swiss studies they find that budget referenda are associated with both lower total per-capita expenditures and reduced per-capita debt. Interestingly, referenda are also positively correlated with tax rates and the share of revenues from local sources.

Weck-Hannemann (1990) looks at the impact of referenda from a different perspective. In the mid-1980s, Swiss voters considered two measures proposing protectionist trade policies. One of them passed; the other was rejected. Welfare-reducing government intervention evidently cannot be explained entirely by elected representatives being bought off by powerful special interests. Voters in direct democracies are also vulnerable to special pleading, in the one case facilitated by bundling protectionism with a popular issue.

In contrast to the Swiss studies, evidence on the impact of referenda in the United States is quite mixed. At the local level, McEachern (1978) compares debt levels in states that require a referendum for municipal bond issues and those with no such requirement. He finds no significant effect of referenda on local per-capita debt, suggesting that agency problems are minimal. Similarly, Megdal (1983) finds no significant impact of referenda on local school expenditures. Applying a median-voter-type model to a sample of 177 New Jersey school districts, Megdal finds that the level of spending per pupil is not significantly different between districts with and without referenda. Further, the income elasticity of expenditure is actually larger in districts without referenda.

At the state level, there is conflicting evidence on the fiscal effects of initiatives and referenda. Matsusaka (1995) compares the 27 states that allow voter initiatives with the 23 states where laws must be drafted by the legislature. Using annual data for 1960–90, Matsusaka finds that in initiative states total per-capita government expenditures are 4 percent lower than in non-initiative states, all else equal. While state governmental expenditures are lower in initiative states, per-capita expenditures by local governments are higher. Matsusaka also finds significant differences in the sources of government revenues: initiative states rely less on broad-based taxes for revenues and instead finance a greater proportion of services through user charges tied to the consumption of public services. Thus initiatives are associated with a smaller government sector and less income redistribution among citizens.

Kiewiet and Szakaly (1996) analyse the impact of referenda on state-level indebtedness and obtain results consistent with Matsusaka's findings. Using a similar data set (panel data for the 50 states from 1961 to 1990), they find that states which require referenda for debt approval have lower relative levels of guaranteed and total debt than states without a referendum requirement.

A more recent study by Matsusaka (1998) suggests that the effect of initiatives on expenditures may vary over time, however. Matsusaka essentially replicates his previous study for an earlier time period, 1900–50. For this earlier time period, initiatives are associated with higher per-capita state spending. Matsusaka conjectures that initiatives in the first half of the twentieth century may have served to satisfy voters who wanted higher spending than their more fiscally conservative representatives, whereas these roles were reversed in the later part of the century and initiatives satisfied voters' desires for a smaller government than representatives provided. Consistent with his prior work, Matsusaka also finds that initiative states had higher levels of local governmental expenditure than non-initiative states.

3.3   Referenda and the cost of government services

In addition to constraining bureaucratic incentives to increase expenditures, improved monitoring through direct democracy could push government officials toward more cost-effective provision of public services. Two Swiss studies, Pommerehne (1983) and Pommerehne and Weck-Hannemann (1996), empirically examine the effect of voter control on the efficiency of specific government activities. Pommerehne (1983) finds that the threat of referendum significantly lowers the cost of refuse collection in Swiss municipalities. Costs of production are the lowest in municipalities with direct voter control and a private service provider. They are about 20 percent higher in representative democracies that contract with a private supplier. The costs are around 10 percent higher for either form of government if refuse collection is performed publicly instead of privately. Pommerehne and Weck-Hannemann (1996) argue that in representative governments there will be a greater divergence between actual expenditures and voters' demands for public goods than in direct democracies. As a result, they contend that voters will have a greater incentive to evade taxes in representative governments. Their hypothesis is supported by evidence that 8 percent less income is concealed by residents of Swiss municipalities with either obligatory or optional budget and tax referenda than in municipalities without such direct voter controls. The authors view this result as evidence that representative democracies are more efficient at tax collection than representative governments.

Other, indirect evidence on the relative efficiency of representative and direct democracies is presented by Feld and Savioz (1997). For the year 1989 they estimate a three-factor (labor, human capital, and plant and equipment) Cobb–Douglas production function with government form acting as a shift parameter. They find that, all else equal, Swiss cantons with referenda have a 15 percent higher GDP than do cantons with purely representative governments. Over the period from 1982 to 1993, the difference was more modest, 5.4 percent, but still quantitatively and statistically significant. Feld and Savioz argue that the GDP differential is consistent with public services being supplied less efficiently in representative democracies.

3.4   Government form and land values

An alternative method for investigating the fiscal impact of government structure is to measure the relationship between political institutions and land values. Santerre (1986) argues that the agency costs associated with representative democracy, particularly fiscal decisions that deviate from the median voter's preferences, will be reflected in lower land values. Invoking Tiebout (1956)-type competition, Santerre claims that consumer-voters will shun communities with less desirable fiscal packages. Land prices will adjust until people are indifferent between living in a direct democracy with higher land prices and more desirable fiscal packages and a community with lower land prices but representative governments that supply less desirable fiscal packages. Santerre fails to recognize the decision-making costs associated with direct democracy, however.[7] While agency costs are eliminated in direct democracies, citizen-voters must bear the costs of attending meetings and participating in the decision-making process. If representative democracies are inherently inefficient, as Santerre seems to assume, then it is not clear why they exist. Unless institutional change is prohibitively costly, all communities would simply adopt direct democracies if they were in fact superior to representative governments.

Using data from 91 communities in Connecticut, Santerre estimates the average price of land in a community as a function of the quantity of land, population, household income, spatial location, and government form. Consistent with his hypothesis of the relative inefficiency of representative government, he finds that (all else equal), the price per acre of land in a direct democracy is $2643 higher than in communities with representative governments.

Santerre's work is criticized by Deller and Chicoine (1988). They claim that within a Tiebout (1956) framework consumers will migrate to the community with the most desirable fiscal package. Thus, if representative governments do tend to spend more than direct democracies, citizens who prefer higher expenditures (and more public services) would tend to migrate to representative democracies. Consumers with similar tastes will migrate to the same community, making the population of each jurisdiction homogeneous. Deller and Chicoine claim that this homogeneity would violate the assumptions of the median-voter model since there would be no intragroup diversity and everyone would be the median voter. They suggest that a model where local officials seek to maximize property values would be more appropriate for testing the relative costs of direct and representative democracies.

Following their own prescription, Deller and Chicoine (1993) test the relative efficiency of direct democracy in the context of a property-value-maximization model using a sample of 66 towns in Maine. They hypothesize that if elected officials are maximizing property values (and not deviating significantly from the desires of their constituents), then the marginal effect of changes in public expenditures on property values should be zero. Their empirical findings are consistent with property-value maximization in both direct and representative democracies. Under both forms of government the marginal effect of government expenditure on total property values is not significant. Further, the impact of expenditure on total property value in representative democracies is not significantly different from that in direct democracies.

4 Parliamentary versus presidential systems

Given that most political entities are organized as representative democracies, an interesting and important issue is the structure of representative government and how that structure impacts governmental performance. While there are a myriad possible institutional variations within representative democracies, the focus here is on the general dichotomy of presidential and parliamentary systems.[8]

Despite the fact that the parliamentary form of government is at least as common as the presidential 'separation-of-powers' system utilized in the United States, parliamentary systems have only recently received attention from public choice scholars.[9] As a result, institutional comparisons between presidential and parliamentary systems are relatively new and few in number.

Moe (1990) is one of the first scholars to consider the differences between presidential and parliamentary systems from a public choice perspective. He lays out some basic differences between the US presidential system and the

British (Westminster) parliamentary system. These ideas are later refined and applied to the bureaucratic structure of the two systems by Moe and Caldwell (1994). In his 1990 paper, Moe focuses on the difficulties encountered in adopting new laws and modifying existing ones in the separation-of-powers system. Since laws are relatively difficult to alter in the US system, restrictions imbedded in the law, including those controlling the behavior of executive branch agencies, can enjoy relative permanence. Such formalization would not work well in the Westminster system since a new government, which holds a monopoly position, can readily pass or modify whatever laws it chooses.

The monopoly position of the governing party in a parliamentary government and its ability to pass legislation at will creates significant commitment problems. Deals made today can easily be undone in the future. Rather than relying on formal institutional mechanisms to deal with the commitment problem, Moe argues that parliamentary governments may depend on informal arrangements to limit reneging on deals, thereby facilitating political exchange.

One informal mechanism for limiting *ex post* contractual opportunism is the establishment of a reputation for living up to commitments. The 'brandname capital' of a political party can act as bond that is forfeited if it reneges on deals.

Moe posits that 'cooptation' – bringing interest groups within the ambit of the government bureaucracy – may also reduce commitment problems and reneging on legislative contracts in two ways. First, interest groups can thereby gain access to inside information of strategic value which becomes a transaction-specific asset preventing 'holdups' by the government. Second, by helping to align incentives, cooptation of interest groups can reduce the problems of *ex post* contractual opportunism much like vertical integration can solve 'holdup' problems in the commercial context.

While these cooptative strategies may limit commitment problems for a given government, there still exists the problem that the opposition can win a subsequent election and undo any deals made by its predecessors. Moe claims that the incentive to engage in such behavior may be limited by the ability of interest groups to entrench themselves in the bureaucracy and insulate themselves from changes brought about by shifts in governmental control. Further, the repeated-game nature of interparty competition in a two-party parliamentary framework may promote policy stability. Since each party knows that deals made by one party can be abrogated by the other, both parties may settle on a cooperative strategy where neither party engages in wholesale subversion of the other party's previous commitments.

Given political uncertainty, Moe argues that it may be optimal for the winning party in an election to include the losers in the cooptative arrangements, allowing some bureaucratic functions to be controlled by affected interest groups. This would allow some accommodation of competing interests while maintaining party control. Such an arrangement could enhance stability and prolong the majority party's control of government.

Moe and Caldwell (1994) emphasize the differences in agency design between the US presidential and British parliamentary systems and how these structural differences impact the functioning of the bureaucracy under the two systems.[10] They argue that an ideal government structure is one that promotes 'effective organization' – agencies with expert knowledge and sufficient discretion to use their expertise and respond efficiently to changing circumstances while remaining accountable to the legislature or executive. They claim, however, that political forces within the US separation-of-powers system will prevent the ideal bureaucratic design from being achieved. They consider the incentives of interest groups, legislators, and the president in turn.

Three factors will lead interest groups to push for ineffective bureaucratic structures. First, faced with the prospect of future electoral competition and defeat at the polls, winning coalitions will initially structure agencies to limit future democratic control. This may take the form of limiting agency discretion and flexibility by adopting specific decision-making criteria, procedures, personnel rules, and the like. Second, the need for political compromise will require that losing groups be given some say in agency design. Moe and Caldwell argue that the losers will push for structures that undermine agency performance and thereby further push agency design away from the ideal. Third, they argue that interest groups fear control by public officials who may have policy agendas that differ from their own. This 'fear of the state' will lead interest groups to push for even more formal rules and requirements to impose tighter constraints on agency behavior.

Moe and Caldwell contend that legislators' interests will be closely aligned with those of interest groups. Representatives and senators will have relatively parochial interests and will respond to interest-group pressures to design bureaucratic agencies that have formalistic structures with little discretion. In contrast, Moe and Caldwell argue that the US president's national constituency and autonomy will lead him to champion a more effective, unified and centrally controlled bureaucracy. The fear of presidential interference, however, will provide further incentives for interest groups to design agencies that are resistant to *ex post* control from above.

In Moe and Caldwell's view, two important features of parliamentary government yield very different bureaucratic structures. First, unlike the US system, the executive and legislative branches are unified under the control of the majority party in the British parliamentary system. Thus, there is no need to formalize the structures of agencies to guard against each other's influence. Second, and perhaps most important, under a parliamentary system the ruling party has virtually unchecked power to pass its own legislative agenda. Consequently, formalizing the structure of bureaucratic agencies to insulate them from future influence of political opponents does not work. If the opposition gains power they can readily undo whatever controls have been placed on the bureaucracy. Moe and Caldwell conclude that these differences yield a bureaucratic system that is subject to greater central control by political leaders, is less constrained by externally imposed rules, and generally operates in a more effective and efficient manner.

Moe and Caldwell's depiction of parliamentary government as one that produces a superior bureaucratic system begs a fundamental question. If the parliamentary system produces a more desirable bureaucratic structure, why has the US system not become more like a parliamentary system over time? Indeed, the fact that some countries, such as Nigeria and Zimbabwe, have shifted from parliamentary to presidential systems, while no country has dropped its presidential system in favor of a parliamentary government runs counter to the notion that parliamentary systems are inherently more efficient.

In a comment on Moe and Caldwell, Kirchgässner (1994) suggests that the reason why there has not been a shift toward parliamentary government may be rooted in the desire of the electorate to limit government power. When the potential agency costs associated with governmental discretion are taken into account, the more formal or restricted structure of the US bureaucracy may indeed be optimal. Lupia (1994) adds that the agency costs between legislators and bureaucrats must also be considered. As first noted by Niskanen (1971), bureaucrats may possess superior knowledge about the issues their agencies face and how their agencies operate to deal with those issues. Legislators are thus at an informational disadvantage and may only be able to effectively control bureaucratic behavior through formalistic rules.

Palmer (1995) models government as a natural monopoly in the production of coercion. His analysis of the US presidential system of government and the Westminster parliamentary system in Britain focuses on the different structures of agency relationships in the two systems. The Westminster system is viewed as analogous to the franchise bidding solution to the problem of natural monopoly (Demsetz 1968; Williamson 1976). As with franchise bidding, there is competition *ex ante* between political parties for the right to hold monopoly control of government. When a party is elected to a majority in parliament it is akin to voters accepting the best bid from numerous potential operators of a natural monopoly. Also, just as with franchise bidding, there is a lack of significant *ex post* competition. The majority party controls both the executive and legislative functions of government. Similar to the potential for non-renewal of future contracts, the primary constraint on the majority's behavior is the threat of losing its monopoly control of government in the next election.

Palmer views the agency relationships in the Westminster system as a three-tiered hierarchy. The primary principals are the electorate, who choose a governing party, the governing party, which then selects a cabinet, and the cabinet, which in turn oversees the civil service. The opposition party acts as a separate agent of the electorate, monitoring the behavior of the governing party.

In contrast to the monopoly position of the majority party in the Westminster system, the US separation-of-powers system breaks up the natural monopoly of government into a triopoly organized along functional lines – the executive, legislative, and judicial branches of government.[11] While the Westminster system relies on future electoral competition to limit agency costs, the US system relies on the president's veto power, the legislature's override authority, and judicial review, to hold the others in check. Veto power creates a currency that may be used to bargain with other branches over the distribution of the burden of coercion.

Unlike the straightforward hierarchy of the British Westminster system, the US separation-of-powers system creates a multilateral system of agency relationships. The electorate is still the primary principal, but it elects three agents: the president, the Senate, and the House. All three of these agents interact with one another and all three exert some control over their own agents, the civil service.

In the Westminster system the individual and collective decision-making responsibilities of cabinet ministers are an important component of governmental structure. In Palmer's view there are three key elements of collective responsibility: confidence, confidentiality, and unanimity. The first requires that the cabinet must have the confidence of parliament and will be forced to resign if it loses a vote of confidence. Confidentiality ensures that access to the proceedings of the cabinet and advice given to the cabinet is restricted. Unanimity requires that all members of the cabinet publicly support the decisions of the cabinet or resign their posts. There are likewise three components of individual responsibility. First, individual ministers must report to parliament regarding matters within their portfolios. Second, it is the duty of civil servants to be loyal to whoever is the current minister. Third, cabinet members agree to protect the anonymity of civil servants.

The unanimity principle induces collective decision making within the cabinet. Since each minister must publicly support a cabinet decision, the cabinet can override the individual policy preferences of any minister. This gives ministers an incentive to seek cabinet approval of policies. Collective responsibility also helps ensure that cabinet decisions are not reversed in the future. Since ministers must openly support the policies of the government, they are effectively barred from using electoral pressure to try to reverse a prior cabinet decision.

Palmer also argues that the doctrines of ministerial responsibility serve to enhance monitoring and thereby mitigate agency costs. Members of Parliament may interrogate any cabinet minister in open session. This also applies to opposition members, who have an incentive to get information that may be damaging to the majority party. Thus, the opposition acts as a monitor of the governing party's actions.

The system of ministerial responsibility also makes it easier for the electorate to attribute responsibility for policies. In contrast, the US separation-of-powers system makes it easier for individual actors (the president, senators, and representatives) to shift responsibility to others for unpopular decisions.

Palmer views the civil service as an asset managed by the cabinet. Under the Westminster system, where civil servants do not bear allegiance to any particular political party, the asset is not specific to either party. In a patronage system, however, bureaucrats would be beholden to the current majority party and would have little value to a government formed by another party. As in the case of franchise bidding for public utilities, this asset specificity would create an advantage for the incumbent and reduce subsequent competition.

Palmer contrasts ministerial responsibility in the US and British systems. Palmer claims that decision making in the US civil service is less constrained by hierarchical structures, but is subject to more formal procedural requirements. While there are pressures for the Westminster prime minister and cabinet to establish and maintain formal collective decision-making procedures, the US president has flexibility to utilize whatever decision-making regime he desires. Unlike the central control and hierarchical nature of the Westminster system, decision making in the US system relies on negotiations between the House, the Senate, and the president. Civil servants must respond to all three of these principals while there is but one master in the Westminster system.

Under both the Westminster and US systems electoral competition serves as a check on representative behavior. Given the fractured nature of decision making in the US federal government, however, there is far less party discipline than in the Westminster system. Consequently, monitoring of representative behavior by the electorate is far more individual specific. Also, there is less interparty monitoring of representatives in the US system. Given less party discipline and the varying constituencies of the House, the Senate and the president, representatives in the US system do not monitor one another as closely as the opposition monitors the government in the Westminster system.

Palmer argues that a US president must rely more heavily on political appointees to influence bureaucratic decision making than does the prime minister in a Westminster-type system. This in turn lessens the permanence of civil servants and reduces institutional memory. Since electoral competition is less important in the US system, however, the potential for problems related to such president-specific bureaucrats is less.

In contrast to Palmer, Breton (1991) argues that, while both the congressional and parliamentary systems are internally competitive, the nature of competition is different due to their differing structures. Breton focuses on how the differing structures of parliamentary and congressional government both serve to enhance the stability of intragovernmental transactions. In particular, he analyses the budgetary process in the United States and Canada and considers how the institutional arrangements of each system help to ensure the stability of budgetary deals.

Breton points to four elements of the parliamentary system that stabilize and enforce intragovernmental exchange: the caucus, budgetary secrecy, prime ministerial power, and a non-partisan senior bureaucracy.

The governing party's parliamentary caucus brings together ministers, 'back-benchers' (elected members of the governing party who do not hold ministerial positions), and senators (who are appointed in Canada). Each of these groups represents various constituent interests. Breton argues that the caucus serves as an essential forum for back-benchers (and their constituents) to influence ministers and cabinet officials. Without this forum, back-benchers would have an incentive to put pressure on the cabinet through the media or outside special-interest groups, thereby undermining party discipline.

Breton models the budgetary negotiation process as a set of bilateral negotiations between the Minister of Finance and the other line ministers. The secrecy of these budgetary negotiations is viewed as a key element in achieving a stable bargaining equilibrium. Budgetary secrecy allows the finance minister to negotiate with each line minister independently. This leads to 'softer' bargaining strategies for each of the line ministers and enhances the attainment of Nash equilibrium outcomes.[12]

The incidence of Nash equilibrium outcomes for the budgetary process is also increased by the ability of the prime minister to reshuffle the cabinet. If the prime minister (implicitly) assigns a lower probability of being sacked to the finance minister than to other ministers this strengthens the finance minister's relative bargaining position and increases the likelihood of achieving an equilibrium. Thus, the ability to achieve a stable bargaining outcome will be directly related to the political strength of the prime minister.

In contrast to other authors, Breton argues that political parties do not enforce intragovernmental bargaining outcomes. Rather, in Breton's view enforcement is accomplished by senior bureaucrats who are non-partisan and relatively permanent. Senior bureaucrats have vested interests in existing policies and will try to influence new ministers to adopt policies close to those already in place. This adds durability to agreements, but also can create friction between ministers and bureaucrats. Breton argues, however, that the non-partisan nature of the bureaucracy helps mitigate this tension.

While the US congressional system must also overcome bargaining problems, the nature of the bargaining and the institutional mechanisms for achieving equilibrium are very different. Whereas bargaining is bilateral in parliamentary governments, it is multilateral in the congressional system. In the parliamentary system each cabinet member bargains with the finance minister over budget allocations and related policies. In the congressional system blocs of legislators must strike policy bargains (that is, 'logroll') in order to achieve a majority and get legislation passed.

Relying on the previous work of Weingast and Marshall (1988), Breton argues that two elements of the congressional system are crucial to maintaining a stable equilibrium in a logrolling environment: party leaders' control of committee agendas and the standing committee system. By controlling agendas, the leadership can reduce the temptation for committee members to venture into new legislative territory and renege on past agreements. Similarly, standing committees, which effectively have veto power over legislation in their assigned domains, can prevent senators and representatives from reneging on past legislative bargains. If, for example, legislators from farm states back mass transit legislation to benefit urban areas in exchange for certain farm programs, the urban legislators cannot later renege on the deal because the farm bill will be under the control of the farm-state legislators who sit on the agriculture committee.

Although Breton offers an insightful description of the differences between the US presidential and Canadian parliamentary systems, he never directly addresses the fundamental issue of why one system is used in the United States and another in Canada.[13] Indeed, a similar criticism can be leveled at most of the still young literature on presidential and parliamentary systems. Certainly history plays a large role in the initial constitutional design of governments. Westminster-style parliamentary governments are common in former British colonies while the United States fought to secede from Britain and establish a different form of government. However, institutional structures are not static and significant changes can occur over time as we have seen recently in Eastern Europe and parts of Asia. More can be done in the future to generate testable implications regarding the distinctive features of the presidential and parliamentary systems. Multiple cross-country comparisons could be made to test hypotheses regarding the choice of representative government.

5   Summary and conclusions

As Buchanan and Tullock emphasized nearly 40 years ago, one of the basic issues in the design of collective decision-making systems is the degree of representation – what proportion of group members will participate in group decision making? If representatives are selected to make decisions on behalf of the entire group, how will they be elected, what powers will they have and what institutional controls will be used to constrain their behavior?

In recent years, the theoretical work on representation has been refined and extended to explicitly encompass costs inherent in the agency relationship between representatives and the electorate. Only a small empirical literature on the choice between direct and representative democracies exists, however. Much more attention has been paid to the impact of government form on political decisions. Several papers have analysed the effects of representative government on public expenditures and jurisdictional land values. While much valuable work has been done, empirical consensus has not yet been reached. Scholars have hypothesized that representative governments should produce inflated bureaucracies and excessive expenditures, but few studies find significant differences in fiscal outcomes between direct and indirect (representative) democracies. Studies of referenda, a form of partial direct democracy, are similarly inconclusive.

While still new and in its formative stages, a branch of the public choice literature is beginning to address the choice of institutional structure within representative democracies. In the last few years a handful of papers have begun to analyse the differences between presidential and parliamentary forms of government. Two central themes in these works are the differences in the degree of intragovernmental competition and in the structure of agency relationships in presidential versus parliamentary governments. The monopoly control of government by the majority party in parliamentary systems has been contrasted with the intragovernmental competition between the legislative and executive branches in a presidential system. Attention has also been focused on the relationships between elected officials, ministers or department heads, and civil servants in the two systems of representative government. While the literature has produced some important insights into the structural differences between presidential and parliamentary government, the existing work is largely descriptive. Opportunities remain for formalizing the theories and empirically investigating the choice of representative government among different countries.

Notes

*   I would like to thank Lars Feld, Randy Holcombe, and John Matsusaka for their helpful comments. Remaining errors are solely my responsibility, however.

1. The head of government is not necessarily also the head of state, who may be a monarch or a popularly elected president with ceremonial duties only.
2. External costs are therefore zero only under a rule of unanimity where each person can veto decisions that work against his or her own interests.
3. Frey (1994) argues that in addition to delegating some decision-making authority to the general populace, referenda also serve to stimulate discussion among citizens and between voters and representatives prior to actual voting. This enhanced discourse increases the amount of information available and can facilitate mutually beneficial bargaining and exchange between groups.
4. For a review of the literature on legislator shirking, see Bender and Lott (1996).
5. Institutions will arise that help reduce the agency costs associated with representative democracy. For example, Holcombe and Gwartney (1989) argue that political parties can provide brandname capital that lowers voters' costs of monitoring their agents.
6. Santerre (1993) presents evidence that public school employees have a greater impact on per-pupil expenditures in open-town-meeting governments than in representative democracies.
7. Santerre does recognize the higher decision-making costs associated with direct democracy in his later work (Santerre 1988).
8. For a discussion and empirical analysis of specific constitutional elements within a private representative 'government', see Sass (1992).
9. The traditional political science literature contains a number of analyses of parliamentary democracy (for example, Lijphart 1992). The discussion here is limited to literature that fits within the public choice arena, that is, studies based on rational choice models, whether they appear in political science or economics journals.
10. The literature addressing bureaucratic control and performance in the US system is surveyed in detail in Chapters 11 and 12.
11. See Chapters 8 and 13 for an alternative interpretation of the 'separation of powers'.
12. Breton later modifies his model to account for the Policy and Expenditure Management System (PEMS) adopted by Canada in 1979. Under PEMS, the finance minister negotiates with a set of 'super-ministers' who in turn represent the individual line ministers. Breton argues that this system further enhances the probability of achieving a Nash equilibrium.
13. A related issue, though one that is beyond the scope of this chapter, is the choice between monarchy and parliamentary government. For interesting analyses of the formation of parliament and transfer of powers from the monarchy to parliament, see Barzel (1997) and North and Weingast (1989).

PART III

INSTITUTIONS AND MECHANISMS OF COLLECTIVE CHOICE

8 Institutions, durability, and the value of political transactions

W. Mark Crain*

1 Introduction

Public choice nourished the reunion of economics and political science, disciplines that had become increasingly detached during the first half of the twentieth century. The study of economic policy making in a political vacuum had fatal weaknesses, and the tools of modern economic analysis readily transferred to decision making in non-market settings. Between the late 1950s and the middle 1970s the public choice literature burgeoned with scholarly research stressing the similarities between the market process and the political process – and the interplay between these sectors.[1]

In 1975 William Landes and Richard Posner drew attention to a key difference between market transactions and political transactions. Their seminal paper revealed that a major institutional detail underlying the analysis of politics as an exchange process had been glossed over. The legal system customarily guarantees that parties involved in market transactions will live up to their agreements. In private sales and contracts buyers and sellers have recourse to legal sanctions in the event of non-performance by one of them. Market exchanges occur with limitless frequency because the participants may rely if necessary on the courts to enforce their commitments. Landes and Posner noted that political transactions lack this third-party enforcement mechanism.

In political transactions third-party enforcement is not possible simply because one of the parties to the agreement, the government, can subsequently change the rules or renege without fear of legal sanctions. For example, suppose that an elected representative promises to impose a tariff on imported clothing in exchange for cash contributions, endorsements, and votes from a trade association composed of domestic textile firms. Neither party to this agreement has legal recourse if the other party reneges on its promise. And even if the tariff-raising law were enacted, future legislators would not be bound by past agreements; they could enact a new law amending or revoking the old. The absence of an enforcement mechanism creates uncertainty about whether – and for how long – political agreements will be maintained. This means, of course, that political transactions are less likely to go forward in the first place. A public policy that has little or no assurance of remaining in force has limited value to its proponents.

The value of political transactions and the potential gains from trade depend on the probability that parties live up to the agreement and on its expected durability. The insight of Landes and Posner was to recognize and elevate the role of political institutions as enforcement mechanisms. In hindsight this innovation is perhaps simple and obvious. However, it fueled a considerable body of research that re-examined from an entirely new perspective a host of political institutions. In this chapter I emphasize the rich explanatory power of this analytical tradition and its potential for placing familiar institutions in an entirely new light.

Less than two years after the Landes–Posner paper appeared, Kydland and Prescott (1977) published a seminal article on the topic now known as time-inconsistency or strategic fiscal policy. A variety of important theoretical models followed in this mold stressing that current political regimes might use fiscal variables as means of controlling policy choices by future regimes. In other words, the literature launched by Kydland and Prescott explores how a political majority today may be motivated to 'lock in' a current policy that a future majority would predictably oppose. Note the striking similarity between the problem that motivated the models of strategic fiscal policy and the problem that motivated Landes–Posner. Even more striking is that both of these emerging lines of analysis completely ignored the other. As a second task of this chapter I attempt to stress the fertile common ground between the two approaches.

I organize the remainder of the chapter into four sections. Section 2 presents the Landes–Posner framework and illustrates the simple analytics of mechanisms that enforce legislative transactions. Section 3 surveys key empirical applications that document the explanatory power and versatility of the framework. In Section 4, I turn to the strategic fiscal policy literature, summarize selected models, and then attempt to build a bridge between the models of strategic choice and institutional sources of legislative durability. Section 5 comments briefly on the lessons for future analysis.

2   Enforcement mechanisms and the value of legislative transactions

In their path-breaking article, Landes and Posner (1975) question how it is possible for long-term contracting between interest groups and legislators to proceed if the current legislature can repeal the laws passed by the preceding legislature. This question motivates their analysis of the independent judiciary as an institution that sustains political agreements made with special interests beyond the current terms of the sitting legislature. Landes and Posner's original contribution focused on the purposes and effects of an independent judiciary, but their fundamental insight is much more general: legislative agreements, like market contracts, would be worth little without some type of enforcement mechanism.

The Landes–Posner framework can be described graphically as in Figure 8.1 (adopted from their original version). S_0S_1 is the marginal cost of passing legislation, here for simplicity assumed to be constant. These costs include such activities as holding legislative hearings and debates, commissioning legislative analyses, disseminating information to various constituencies, drafting bills, and negotiating among legislators to assemble a majority coalition (Buchanan and Tullock 1962). The demand curve d_0d_1 represents the value to interest groups of the benefits associated with a given law. Importantly, the benefits represented by d_0d_1 flow only during a single legislative period, that is, the term during which the legislation gets enacted. E_0 shows the equilibrium level of legislation in this case, and $d_0S_0E_0$ measures the net benefits of political exchange that accrue to interest groups.[2]

If the flow of legislative benefits can be assured beyond the term of the enacting legislature, the demand curve shifts outward simply because the present value of the benefits increase. D_0d_1 in Figure 8.1 depicts this case. If

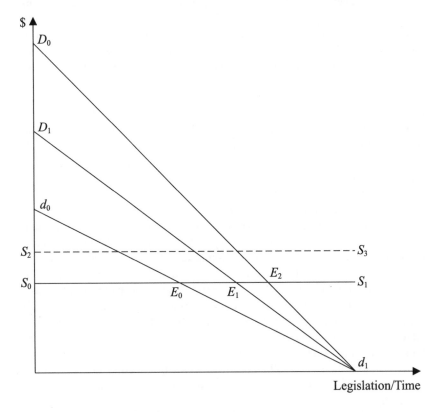

Figure 8.1   Value of legislative transactions

the cost of enacting long-term agreements with special-interest groups is no higher than that for single-period legislation, E_2 represents the new market-clearing level of legislation. Total benefits to special interests rise to $D_0S_0E_2$; the net value of multiperiod legislation obviously exceeds the net value of single-period legislation. This increase in value provides the incentive to devise institutional mechanisms that add durability to political agreements.

Institutional mechanisms that endow political agreements with durability come in two broad forms.[3] One type of institution adds durability on the external margin, for example, the independent judicial branch that Landes–Posner focused on in their 1975 paper.[4] Judicial branch independence typically is due to three factors: judges are not elected, they serve life terms, and their salaries cannot be reduced. A set of independent judges who interpret laws in terms of the intent of the enacting legislature adds durability to legislative outcomes. This result follows because judges rarely nullify or declare laws unconstitutional under these circumstances. Indeed, judges exhibit a pronounced tendency to resolve legal disputes and statutory ambiguities in terms of the expressed intentions of the legislature that originally enacted the law. This sort of behavior by an independent judiciary increases the net worth of bargains reached between legislators and interest groups, especially in contrast to a situation where judges are elected or their tenures are otherwise limited.[5]

This grant of independence does not guarantee that judges will support all past legislative agreements. Figure 8.1 represents uncertainty about the independent judiciary's decisions as a counterclockwise rotation of the demand function from D_0d_1 to D_1d_1. The present value of benefits from special-interest legislation at E_1 will, however, still be above that given by d_0d_1 for reasonable probabilities of judicial nullification.

A second type of institution adds durability on the internal margin by increasing the cost of repealing legislation once enacted. This type of institution presents a double-edged sword. Consider, for example, a restrictive voting rule that requires a two-thirds majority to enact legislation. This rule, on the one hand, raises the cost of passing the original legislation. Graphically, Figure 8.1 shows this effect as an upward shift in the cost function to S_2S_3 from the initial level of S_0S_1. On the other hand, once enacted, the two-thirds voting requirement makes future legislative changes more difficult compared to a simple-majority voting rule. This latter, durability-enhancing effect increases the demand function. The net value of legislation increases as long as the value of the additional impediment to repeal (the increase in demand) more than offsets the additional costs of enacting the legislation. In the next section I highlight several institutions that appear to meet this criterion.

3   Durability-enhancing institutions: examples and evidence

3.1   Constitutional change

The first extension of the Landes–Posner framework stressed the inter-dependence of institutional sources of durability. Crain and Tollison (1979a) developed a positive model of constitutional change and employed the model to explain the pattern of amendments to the constitutions of the American states.

Constitutional rights are an especially durable type of political agreement, evidenced by the observation that constitutional change occurs infrequently when compared to other types of political agreements. A constitutional right is more difficult to retract than a statutory right because the procedures for amending constitutions are so costly and time consuming in comparison to ordinary legislative action.[6]

The Crain and Tollison extension stresses that while a constitutional amendment offers political durability coveted by interest groups, the extent to which interest groups will bear the higher cost depends on what other sources of political contract durability are available. For example, few American states grant life tenure to their supreme court justices, and some states elect rather than appoint them. These differences with respect to the degree of judicial independence provide the basis for a testable hypothesis: state constitutional amendments should vary inversely with the degree of state judicial independence. In other words, judicial independence yields a relatively low-cost source of durability, which should substitute at the margin for the high-cost mechanism of constitutional amendments. The model estimated in Crain and Tollison finds this sort of tradeoff using American state data.

The empirical results in Crain and Tollison also reveal other tradeoffs at the state level as predicted by the Landes–Posner durability framework. For example, controlling for other factors, the Crain–Tollison specification finds state constitutional amendments to be positively correlated with procedural rules that raise the cost of constitutional change, rules such as those increasing the number of legislative sessions required to approve amendments or imposing super-majority voting requirements. Such procedural rules on the surface would seem to increase costs and therefore deter constitutional change. However, these costly procedural rules at the same time erect formidable barriers to repeal once a constitutional amendment is ratified. The value-added associated with ratifying constitutional amendments increases expected durability more than enough to offset the associated procedural costs.

Finally, Crain and Tollison develop the related point that longevity and stability in the legislature branch should also trade off in a predictable way with constitutional sources of durability. Their evidence indicates that longer legislative term lengths and lower legislator turnover retards reliance on costly constitutional changes as a source of durability.[7]

3.2   The executive branch veto

Crain and Tollison (1979b) developed a second application of the Landes–Posner framework to explain executive branch vetoes as a means of enhancing the durability of legislation. This extension turns out to be straightforward given the similarity between the power of the independent judiciary to interpret and nullify laws and the power of the chief executive to veto them.

Consider the analogy between the executive veto and the independent judiciary. Nullification of a law by the courts is analogous to the casting of a veto by the government's chief executive. In both cases the legislature may try to override the decision but usually with limited success. Veto power is a means of enhancing the durability of legislation, performing the same function as the independent judiciary and the procedural rules of the legislature in the Landes–Posner theory. In effect, executive veto power, like judicial review, raises the costs of reneging on previous legislative bargains between special interests and legislators. Empirically this framework explains quite well the pattern of gubernatorial vetoes across the American states. Vetoes as an external source of durability are positively correlated with aspects of the political environment, such as legislative term lengths and legislator turnover, that tend to reduce the expected lifetime of laws.

In summary, Landes and Posner (1975) offered a novel perspective on the role of institutions as mechanisms for enforcing and enhancing the durability of political agreements. The success of this perspective in developing predictive models of political behavior should not be confused with its broader and perhaps disturbing normative ramifications. The American political system may be better described as collusive rather than one based on a 'separation of powers'. The Landes–Posner perspective undermines any semblance of a separation-of-powers argument in favor of a tripartite system of government. The legislative–executive–judicial nexus becomes analogous to a vertically integrated seller of long-term legislation to interest groups.

3.3   The independence of central banks

Miller (1998) subsequently drew upon the Landes–Posner framework to explain the creation and role of independent central banks. Miller argues that an independent central bank serves a function analogous to the independent judiciary, namely to promote the adoption of monetary policies with long time horizons detached from volatile political influences. In the Miller analysis, politicians delegate monetary policy decisions to an independent central bank in order to make credible commitments to interest groups that their gains from currently enacted programs will not be devalued by subsequent inflation. For example, interest groups such as labor unions and creditors that benefit from stable wages and prices stand to gain from the inflationary safeguard that an independent central bank provides. In effect, interest groups demand not only nominal transfers from government, but also monetary stability to preserve the future real values of these transfers.

In the absence of central bank independence no enforcement mechanism exists to prevent politicians from inflating away the gains and reopening the bidding for new special-interest legislation. If control over monetary policy is politicized and current politicians have the power to inflate, interest groups will be less inclined to enter into legislative deals with politicians. An independent central bank thus increases the durability of legislative deals by removing the threat of inflationary *ex post* contractual opportunism. Finally, Miller notes that because interest groups have much to gain from central bank independence, the adoption of independence should be associated with the presence of concentrated interest groups that benefit from stable wages and prices.

3.4 The committee system and other institutional sources of durability

The value of maintaining policies beyond the current legislative regime provides a novel way of thinking about a number of familiar legislative institutions. I briefly describe a few examples beginning with the committee system, the ubiquitous and most important institution in American legislatures. Two aspects of the committee system enhance the durability of legislative bargains. First, legislative party leaders use their power over committee assignments to maintain party discipline and thereby exercise control over policy decisions, present and future. By assigning non-conforming party members to committees with jurisdictions over relatively minor policy areas, the leadership can exclude them from participating in prominent policy debates. The reverse also holds as party leaders offer the carrot as well as wielding the stick: party members most loyal to the leadership's policy preferences get assigned to the plum committees where the most important legislation gets formulated.[8] Coupled with a seniority rule, the leadership's power to select and sort legislators among committees means that like-minded legislators stand in line to succeed departing members and assume control over key policy areas. This filtering process imparts continuity to policies and thereby reassures interest groups that current agreements are likely to be maintained.

The second aspect of the committee system that enhances the durability of legislative bargains has come to be known as 'universalism'.[9] Under the norm of universalism, legislators logroll and defer to each other's preferences regarding legislation with geographically targeted benefits. If the division of committee jurisdictions allows legislators to specialize in particular subjects tailored to their constituents' interests, legislation usually associated with pork-barrel projects tends to be protected from meddling by non-committee members. The stylized version of the process goes as follows. Legislative proposals that would affect the status quo and alter existing projects must be referred to the committee overseeing the project. That committee's monolithic membership protects the status quo by bottling up bills at the committee stage.[10] Exercise of committee gatekeeping power means that proposed legislative changes never proceed to the floor where consideration by the full legislative chamber would include a broader cross-section of legislators. Legislators who might otherwise oppose a particular pork-barrel measure acquiesce and defer to the committee members' policy preferences because they can expect similar treatment when it comes to their pet projects. In short, the committee system protects past legislative agreements even if a majority in the legislature would favor change given the opportunity to express their preferences in an up-or-down, unbundled vote.

Of course, the stability of committee members and party leaders varies over time depending on such factors as electoral turnover and reversals in majority-party control. Doernberg and McChesney (1987) analyse the effects of variations in committee stability in the US Congress on the durability of federal tax laws. Their findings link the reduction in the permanence of congressional committee chairmen to the rapid acceleration in federal tax reform legislation. Crain and Muris (1995) examine a similar thesis at the American state level, finding that the stability of legislative committee chairmanships influences the level of state government spending. Garrett (1996) focuses on the role of term limits as impairments to the durability of legislation. From an interest group's perspective, term limits result in increased turnover rates and thereby create ineptitude and confusion that reduces the predictability of the legislative process. Interest groups find unpredictable promises less reliable than the potent guarantee of durability provided by an entrenched committee system coupled with a strong seniority norm. Term limits thus lower the expected value of any legislative bargain. As Garrett notes, however, the impact of term limits on durability may not be as large as expected simply because the affected parties, legislators and interest groups, would seek to develop alternative durability mechanisms. For example, term limits might inspire an expanded role for political parties as conduits between interest groups and legislators over multiple electoral cycles.

3.5   Legislative majorities and implicit political contracts
Several studies examine the role of legislative majorities as an enforcement mechanism based on the theory of implicit contracts. An implicit contract in private market transactions refers to a self-enforcing mechanism, or one that does not rely on third-party enforcement. For example, a seller accumulates brandname capital the value of which would be eroded or destroyed by

abandoning contractual obligations or simply not fulfilling buyers' expectations. More directly, a seller might post a monetary bond that would be forfeited in the event of non-performance. The loss of the investment in brandname capital (or bond forfeiture) provides potential buyers with an implicit contractual guarantee that the seller will perform and thereby facilitates market transactions.[11]

A somewhat puzzling phenomenon is the large majorities that political parties hold in American state legislatures. In fact, the intuitively powerful minimum-winning-coalition model developed by Riker (1962) predicts a razor-thin margin of majority-party control.[12] Crain et al. (1988a, 1991) and Sass and Saurman (1991) apply the theory of self-enforcing contracts as a plausible explanation for this paradox. The argument is straightforward: demanders of legislation view a narrow majority as risky because the current majority party's control of the next legislature hinges on the loss of just a few seats. Despite the reduction in per-capita benefits from an increase in the size of the majority, the party benefits because the assurance of long-term control increases the present value of current legislation, and thus the demand for it shifts out as illustrated in Figure 8.1. The studies cited above provide evidence supporting the implicit contract framework using regression models to explain the variation in the size of majority parties in American state legislative chambers. The empirical specifications posit that the implicit contractual guarantees reflected in the size of the majority party is another margin along which the value of political transactions can be optimized. The size of the optimal majority thus predictably increases as alternative sources of durability decrease, and the state evidence supports this hypothesis.

3.6 Durability-enhancing budgetary rules and government spending
Poterba (1996a,b) summarizes the budding literature that evaluates the impact of budgetary institutions on fiscal policy outcomes, and concludes that the preponderance of evidence indicates that 'fiscal institutions do matter'. Crain and Crain (1998) analyse alternative budget baseline rules from the durability-enhancing perspective. The two main choices for a budget baseline are the dollar amounts spent the year before or the level of services that those dollars bought, which is labeled a 'current services' baseline.[13] A current services baseline and a last year's budget baseline create different reference points, and based on prospect theory and experimental evidence, Crain and Crain posit that legislators may exhibit loss-averting behavior in voting on budgetary proposals.[14] This means that future spending levels on programs enacted under a current services baseline are more secure than spending levels on programs enacted under a budgetary rule that uses last year's spending as a baseline. The present value of programs enacted under a current services regime is thus higher than under the latter budgetary regime.

This increase in present value in turn raises the expected return to investments in lobbying by pressure groups to secure wealth transfers and thereby fuels an expansion in public-sector spending. Controlling for a host of institutional, economic, and demographic factors, the findings show that over the course of the 1980s a current services baseline rule added about 5 percentage points to the growth in real state government spending.

4   Strategic behavior and durable fiscal policy

The pure theory of strategic fiscal behavior abstracts from the institutional sources of durability such as those described in the preceding section. Importantly, the very absence of legal or institutional mechanisms to maintain long-term policy commitments stands behind the motivation to make strategic fiscal choices. The inability of present-period voters (or their representatives in the present political regime) to make binding contracts with voters in the next period (the future regime) creates the basic dilemma. Policy makers respond by making fiscal choices designed in part to prevent the undermining of current programs and to bind the policy choices of future regimes.

As long as the current government can affect some policy variable that enters into its successor's decision calculus, it can influence to some degree the policy carried out by the successor government. In the process of binding future fiscal outcomes, however, the current government selects a different (and suboptimal) policy relative to what it would have preferred if it expected to remain in power. This occurs when the current and future regimes have different, or time-inconsistent, fiscal policy preferences. Three models illustrate the problem.[15]

Perrson and Svensson (1989) develop a model in which a current government uses the level of the public debt as an instrument for controlling the level of spending by a future government. They construct a principal–agent model in which government (or the decisive voter) today is the principal and government in the next period is the agent. The intuitive example in their model posits an incumbent conservative regime that expects to be replaced in the next election by a liberal regime. The current regime will put in place a fiscal policy that features lower taxes and higher deficits than it would otherwise prefer in order to control the ability of the future liberal government to embark on large spending programs. As long as public debt enters negatively into the policy preferences of the future liberal regime, it responds to the conservative regime's legacy of deficit financing by spending less than it otherwise would prefer.

Alesina and Tabellini (1990) develop a related model, the key difference being that succeeding regimes champion different spending priorities. For example, the current regime favors large defense budgets and minimal welfare budgets, and the future regime favors the opposite policy mix. Alesina

and Tabellini also assume that public debt enters negatively into the preference functions of both regimes. In the case of time-inconsistent spending
preferences, the current regime moves to constrain future spending (on the
welfare programs it detests) by running a larger deficit than it would if it were
assured of remaining in power.

Glazer (1989) develops a strategic model in which voters have a bias
toward capital-intensive projects in the absence of durability-enhancing institutions. Rational voters show a consistent bias in favor of capital projects,
which they would oppose were the decision theirs to make individually in a
private-market environment. I do not repeat Glazer's formal derivation here;
an intuitive understanding is straightforward and sufficient to illustrate the
durability-motivated strategic fiscal choice.

Because current-period voters cannot make contracts with next period's
voters, one possible strategy is to limit future policy options by constructing a
long-lived capital project.[16] This maneuver eliminates from the next period
the option to renew or reject the services from the capital project. An inefficiently large public capital stock is predicted under majoritarian rules,
irrespective of the cost efficiency of the capital project.[17]

As this brief summary indicates, strategic fiscal policy models are based on
the idea that choices in a given electoral period take into consideration
expectations about preferences of decision makers in succeeding periods.
Fiscal variables such as spending, taxing and borrowing are used strategically
as devices to control future choices if current policy makers expect the
preferences of future policy makers to differ from their own. The process of
binding future fiscal outcomes causes the current government to select second-
best (and suboptimal) policies relative to what it would have preferred if it
expected to remain in power.

Because these policy choices are second best from the standpoint of the
current regime, political conditions and the presence of institutions that
enhance policy longevity should reduce the motivation to use fiscal variables
strategically. Political conditions and institutions that facilitate policy durability predictably lower the incentive for strategic fiscal policy choices. In
effect, strategic fiscal choices substitute for institutional sources of policy
durability, such as those I describe in Section 3 above.

Crain and Tollison (1993) examine the tradeoff between strategic fiscal
choices and institutional sources of durability using American state data.
They find that such factors as term limits and the stability of the majority
party controlling the state legislature reduce strategic behavior of the type
described in the Perrson and Svensson (1989) and Alesina and Tabellini
(1990) models. Crain and Oakley (1995) specify an empirical model to
investigate implications of the Glazer model. Specifically, political conditions and institutions that facilitate policy durability predictably lower the

capital intensity of government spending. Also using American state data, the findings indicate that institutions such as term limits, citizen initiative, and budgeting procedures significantly affect infrastructure spending across states. The results further indicate that political conditions such as majority-party stability and voter volatility are systematically related to infrastructure differences across states. These two empirical studies indicate a fruitful common ground between models of strategic policy behavior and the institutional models. This ground remains largely unexplored, particularly in formal theoretical models, and represents a promising area for future research.

5   Concluding remarks

Perhaps more than any other social science, public choice champions the idea that institutions matter. Yet despite the impressive array of evidence about the importance of institutions in mediating choices, a sometimes-healthy and sometimes-knee-jerk resistance to the idea remains. The intellectual battle is far from over.

The Landes and Posner (1975) perspective on the institution of the independent judiciary raises an important question. Institutions may matter, but how? A checks-and-balances, separation-of-power thesis yields implications quite different from the collusion-of-power thesis. A vision of a constitution as an institution that protects the rights of electorally weak minorities differs sharply from a vision of an institution that maintains long-term interest-group deals. The message is this: exploring radically different perspectives on the function of institutions may prove more constructive than rejecting the role of institutions *per se*.

The interplay between political forces and institutions adds a layer of complexity that should not be taken lightly. The term-limits movement provides a good case in point. As term limits remove an institutional source of political durability, legislators respond by seeking suitable alternatives that may produce even more inefficient policies. The value of enforcing long-term political agreements will not disappear, and the role of enforcement mechanisms deserves a central place in the study of political economy.

Notes

*   I am grateful to Nicole Crain and Bill Shughart for highly constructive comments. All errors remain my responsibility.
1.   Mueller (1985) describes the five seminal works that launched the field of public choice. Mueller (1989) presents an introduction, survey, and broad overview of contributions to the field.
2.   More generally, with increasing costs, legislators will also obtain benefits from legislating in the form of inframarginal rents (producer surplus). The precise distribution of the benefits of exchange between interest groups and legislators is unimportant to the analysis.
3.   In the next section I add to the analysis the relationship between institutional sources of

durability and durability gained from using fiscal policy variables strategically. Certain fiscal choices can bind future politicians to continue current fiscal policy regimes. The institutional mechanisms I examine here substitute for the use of fiscal variables as a source of durability.

4. See Shughart and Tollison (1998) and Chapter 13 of this volume for a more complete discussion of these issues.

5. In essence, Landes and Posner attack the idea that a separation of powers appropriately describes how the US political system functions. Rather than acting as a brake on the actions of the legislature or acting to represent electoral minorities that cannot achieve representation elsewhere in the system, the independent judiciary acts to enforce long-term contracts between interest groups and legislators.

6. Landes and Posner (1975, p. 892) offer a valuable discussion of constitutional versus other statutory agreements, although they do not provide any empirical analysis. Macy (1986) provides a related analysis.

7. Anderson et al. (1990) replicate and extend the Crain and Tollison specification, confirming the central points described above.

8. Crain (1990) describes the role of the committee system as a mechanism for maintaining party discipline and control. Crain and Coker (1994) offer empirical evidence for the loyalty-filtering theory of committees using data for the US House of Representatives.

9. The norm of universalism is described in Weingast (1979), Emerson and Ordeshook (1985) and Collie (1988).

10. In the stylized version, members self-select on to committees that most closely match their constituents' policy interests: the representatives of coastal districts seek appointment to maritime committees, farm state representatives seek appointment to agriculture committees, and so on.

11. See Klein and Leffler (1981) for the main paper on the theory of implicit contacts in private transactions.

12. The reason, of course, is that the smallest possible majority coalition maximizes the per-capita benefits to individual members of the coalition and minimizes the per-capita costs of reaching agreements.

13. For example, in the United States the procedure for computing the current services budget takes what was spent the year before, adjusts it for inflation and, in the case of programs such as Social Security or unemployment compensation, for the number of people projected to be eligible in the year ahead. That becomes the federal budget baseline. Any amount in excess of that level is defined as a spending increase, lesser amounts a spending cut.

14. For discussions of loss-aversion behavior, prospect theory and relevant experimental results see Kahneman and Tversky (1979, 1984), Quattrone and Tversky (1988), Tversky and Kahneman (1986), and Myakov and Plott (1997).

15. Models of strategic fiscal behavior generally trace to the seminal papers by Kydland and Prescott (1977) and Fischer (1980). For survey articles, see Perrson (1988) and Alesina (1988). An interesting and important wrinkle in strategic fiscal policy analysis is that inefficient government policies are driven by the representative voter and not by pressure group demands for wealth redistribution.

16. These deals can sometimes unravel, of course. See Basuchoudhary et al. (1999).

17. This conclusion does not require any assumptions about the cost structure of the projects. Suppose that the benefits of two short-lived projects are equivalent to the benefits of one durable project, yet the costs of constructing two short-lived projects are less than the cost of building the long-lived (durable) project. Suppose further that the decisive voter in period 1 would like the services of the project in both periods. However, if the decisive voter in period 1 expects the short-term project to be rejected in period 2, he prefers the more expensive durable project in period 1. This would be the case if the benefits derived from the short-lived project over the two periods exceed the costs of the relatively more expensive durable project. In other words, the decisive voter selects a second-best outcome to prevent the worst-case outcome: no project in period 2. Glazer labels this source of capital bias a 'commitment effect'. Alternatively, suppose that the decisive voter in

period 1 has no strict preference for either the durable or the single-term project and that he expects the decisive voter in period 2 to choose the short-term project. If building the durable project is cheaper than building two successive short-term projects (that is, there are economies of scale), the decisive voter in period 1 may select the durable project, even though the benefits are less than the cost, because it is less costly than the two short-term projects. This is what Glazer calls the 'efficiency effect', which motivates a capital bias under collective choice as long as the difference in the benefits and costs of the single short-lived project exceed those of the durable project.

9 Voting

Michael C. Munger

1 Introduction

The use of voting to guide public decisions is very old. It was clearly well established in Athens, as Plutarch reported in his *Lives*, in the story of Aristides. Consider his account of the ostracism, or banishment, of Aristides about 480 BCE.

> It was performed, to be short, in this manner. Every one taking an *ostracon*, a sherd, that is, or piece of earthenware, wrote upon it the citizen's name he would have banished, and carried it to a certain part of the marketplace surrounded with wooden rails. First, the magistrates numbered all the sherds in gross (for if there were less than six thousand, the ostracism was imperfect); then, laying every name by itself, they pronounced him whose name was written by the larger number, banished for ten years, with the enjoyment of his estate. As, therefore, they were writing the names on the sherds, it is reported that an illiterate clownish fellow, giving Aristides his sherd, supposing him a common citizen, begged him to write *Aristides* upon it; and he being surprised and asking if Aristides had ever done him any injury, 'None at all', said he, 'neither know I the man; but I am tired of hearing him everywhere called the Just'. Aristides, hearing this, is said to have made no reply, but returned the sherd with his own name inscribed. At his departure from the city, lifting up his hands to heaven, he made a prayer (the reverse, it would seem, of that of Achilles), that the Athenians might never have any occasion which should constrain them to remember Aristides. (Plutarch [1517] 1932, p. 396)

Plutarch's story is interesting for a couple reasons. First, it establishes that one main focus of voting scholarship, *behavior*, may be hard to predict unless one understands the way people think about voting. The 'clownish fellow' was voting to ostracize Aristides because Aristides was a good man! Obviously, votes can be a mechanism for coercion and petty retribution, as well as a means of achieving good. Second, we see that the *institutions*, or the way votes are counted, can determine the outcome. Ostracism used the simplest form of plurality rule; whoever got the most votes lost, and had to leave the city in disgrace. It will turn out that plurality decision rules have particular properties that may not be very attractive. The use of a different rule might well have let Aristides stay in Athens. Of course, whether he wanted to stay or not is quite a different question.

In this chapter, I shall consider both of these questions, the 'how do people choose?' (behavior) question, and the 'how do choice rules affect choice?'

(institutions) question. But before I begin, I would like to consider some of the classical political theory that underlies the idea that voting is the way to decide for a group, even in the face of profound disagreement within the group.

2   Classical theory

In the United States, we live in a democracy, in an advanced industrial society, with well-developed political parties and ways of choosing candidates and enacting laws. Suppose that this were not true. Imagine that we had only rudimentary definitions of rights and rules of behavior to guide us, but that we face problems of deciding what to do. How would we decide policies that affect the whole nation?

Philosophers and social scientists call this conjectural thought experiment the 'state of nature'. Different people have had very different ideas about what 'natural' life would be like. One of the most famous is Thomas Hobbes, who was not (to say the least) optimistic. As he put it,

> the nature of War, consisteth not in actuall fighting; but in the known disposition thereto, during all the time there is no assurance to the contrary. ... Whatsoever therefore is consequent to a time of War, where every man is Enemy to every man; the same is consequent to the time, wherein men live without other security, than what their own strength, and their own invention shall furnish them withall. In such condition, there is no place for Industry; because the fruit thereof is uncertain: and consequently no Culture of the Earth; no Navigation, nor use of the commodities that may be imported by Sea; no commodious Buildings; no Instruments of moving, and removing such things as require much force; no Knowledge of the face of the Earth; no account of Time; no Arts; no Letters; no Society; and which is worst of all, continuall feare, and danger of violent death; And the life of man, solitary, poore, nasty, brutish, and short. (Hobbes [1651] 1991, ch. 13, p. 186)

Hobbes (p. 187) recognizes that his dark portrayal of the condition of humankind in the state of nature may not be realistic ('It may peradventure be thought, there was never such a time'). But that is not his point. What Hobbes (p. 188) is analysing are the conditions or conventions that enable a society to avoid the cataclysmic 'war of every man against every man'.

In Hobbes's view, societies are able to avoid the state of nature by vesting power, and the legitimate ability to focus force, in the person of the *sovereign*. As democratic theory has progressed, we have adapted Hobbes's notion of sovereignty into something more abstract and at the same time more concrete. That 'something' is the *will of the people*. This is really quite an astonishing intellectual achievement: we start with (i) a *state of nature*, move to (ii) the *person of the sovereign*, who embodies the power and legitimacy of the state, and then (iii) mentally divorce the literal person (king, sultan, or chieftain) from the function of that office, which is to carry out the *will of the people*. In this construction, the sovereign *is* the will of the people, which (in theory, at least) is the anthropomorphized ruler of the society. Add to this formulation the next step, (iv) the will of the people can be discovered by *voting*, and you have modern democracy.

Not everyone would accept this formulation, not by a long shot. For some, it is not the state of nature that is to be avoided, but rather the rule by the general will that we should fear. Edmund Burke, speaking perhaps facetiously,[1] makes this argument most clearly:

> In vain you tell me that Artificial Government is good, but that I fall out only with the Abuse. The Thing! The Thing itself is the abuse! Observe, my Lord, I pray you, that grand Error upon which all artificial legislative power is founded. It was observed, that Men had ungovernable Passions, which made it necessary to guard against the Violence they might offer to each other. They appointed governors over them for this Reason; but a worse and more perplexing Difficulty arises, how to be defended against the Governors? (Burke ([1756] 1982, pp. 64–5)

In this passage, Burke would appear to argue that nature, or 'natural society', may be preferable to government, since there is no way to ensure that the will of the people is obeyed. 'The thing' is government; saying 'the thing itself is the abuse' means that Hobbes had it all wrong, and humans in the natural state would be just fine. It is the power of unjust government we should fear, and guard against.

I am not going to pretend to resolve this debate, but it is useful to think about where governments, and societies, come from. Consider Aristotle's account, from Book I, chapter 2 of the *Politics*:

> When several villages are united in a single complete community, large enough to be nearly or quite self-sufficing, the state comes into existence, originating in the bare needs of life, and continuing in existence for the sake of a good life. And therefore, *if the earlier forms of society are natural, so is the state.* ... Hence it is evident that the state is a creation of nature, and *that man by nature is a political animal.* And he who by nature and not by mere accident is without a state, is either a beast or a god. (Aristotle [c. 350 BCE] 1979, p. 8; emphasis added)

This passage leads to a hard question: is it true that 'man by nature is a political animal'? If the answer is yes, then collective decision-making institutions are required. More simply, humans will have to make decisions as a group that somehow embody, or at least account for, the desires of the individuals who make up the group.

Many people have worked on the problem of how to make collective choices out of individual desires. One of the most important early efforts was by Jean-Jacques Rousseau ([1762] 1973). Rousseau's thought was complex, so any attempt to summarize it briefly here will not do it justice. However, it is clearly true that Rousseau believed in the superiority of some idealized 'natural' condition of humanity, where people are free to delight in liberty and enjoy the gifts of nature. On the other hand, he recognized that some mechanism is required for generating binding collective choices, and for governing the otherwise unavoidable tendency for inequalities among citizens to arise. These two competing ideas (complete freedom of the individual set against the need for submission of the individual to the general will) are not fully reconciled in Rousseau, but he certainly recognizes the problem. In a celebrated and controversial passage, Rousseau makes his argument:

> As long as several men in assembly regard themselves as a single body, they have only a single will which is concerned with their common preservation and general well-being. ...
>
> A State so governed needs very few laws; and, as it becomes necessary to issue new ones, the necessity is universally seen. The first man to propose them merely says what all have already felt. ...
>
> There is but one law which, from its nature, needs unanimous consent. This is the social compact, for civil association is the most voluntary act in the world. Since every man is born free and master of himself, no one can, under any pretext whatsoever, subjugate him without his consent. ... Apart from this primitive contract, the vote of the majority is always binding on all the others; this is a consequence of the contract itself. But it may be asked how a man can be free while he is forced to conform to wills that are not his own. How are the opponents free while they are bound by laws to which they have not consented?
>
> I reply that the question is not put properly. The citizen consents to all the laws, even to those that pass against his will, and even to those which punish him when he dares violate any of them. The unchanging will of all the members of the state is the general will; through it they are citizens and free. When a law is proposed in the assembly of the people, what they are being asked is not precisely whether they approve or reject the proposal, but whether or not it is consistent with the general will that is their own; each man expresses his opinion on this point by casting his vote, and the declaration of the general will is derived from the counting of the votes. When, therefore, the opinion that is contrary to my own prevails, this proves neither more nor less than that I was mistaken, and that what I thought to be the general will was not so. If my private opinion had prevailed, I would have done something other than what I had willed; it is then that I would not have been free. (pp. 150–51)

This reasoning may seem a little tortuous, but the argument is important. As a citizen, you want government to do the right thing. However, citizens may disagree about what the right thing is. We could vote, as a way of deciding what 'we' think, as opposed to insisting that we must all think the same thing. Provided that each of us renders a judgment about what is best for society, rather than just what is in our self-interest, this process of voting is a means of discovering the collective wisdom, or general will. Each member of a society must agree, in the abstract, to accept specific decisions he may not agree with. Rousseau is arguing that this submission to the general will (paradoxically) is the price of freedom.

In mentally creating the general will out of some combination of individual desires, we have also created something else, the 'society'. In fact, the very essence of the general will is the notion that there is some group larger than the individual whose welfare we can measure, or at least compare. Public choice theorists, however, have come to question the existence of anything like the 'general will'. It turns out that we cannot confect the organism called 'society' quite so easily as Rousseau would have us believe.

The basis of much of this criticism is the apparent incoherence of collective choice, under quite general circumstances. While, as will be seen later in this chapter, much of the theory behind these 'paradoxes' of collective choice is based on work by Kenneth Arrow ([1951] 1963), perhaps the clearest intuitive statement of the public choice position is that of Riker (1982). Riker calls the Rousseauvian idea 'populism', and contrasts this view with a more modest, and value-neutral, conception of the state, which he calls 'liberalism'.

> What is different between the liberal and populist views is that, in the populist interpretation of voting, the opinions of the majority *must* be right and *must* be respected because the will of the people is the liberty of the people. In the liberal interpretation, there is no such magical identification. The outcome of voting is just a decision and has no special moral character. (p. 14; emphasis in original)

Riker's interpretation of voting is simple: elections are a way to control officials, and nothing more. Some observers have called this conclusion unduly pessimistic, or have objected that the normative conclusions make citizens skeptical about government.

These criticisms of Riker's conclusions, however, ignore the *positive* character of his argument, as we shall see. The non-existence of a single best alternative, or a coherent general will, is not in itself good or bad. Rather, cycles are a generic, *scientific*, property of majority-rule decision-making processes, under some circumstances. As long as the 'middle' either does not exist, or exists conditionally and ephemerally, faith in the ability of majorities *always* to discover objective truth is dangerous and misleading. Although he was hardly a mathematician, H.L. Mencken intuitively mistrusted the idea that there was always wisdom in the collective voice of many individuals.

> It [is impossible] to separate the democratic idea from the theory that there is a mystical merit, an esoteric and ineradicable rectitude, in the man at the bottom of the scale – that inferiority, by some strange magic, becomes superiority – nay, the superiority of superiorities. ... What baffles statesmen is to be solved by the

people, instantly and by a sort of seraphic intuition. ... This notion, as I hint, originated in the poetic fancy of gentlemen on the upper levels – sentimentalists who, observing to their distress that the ass was overladen, proposed to reform transportation by putting him in the cart. (Mencken 1926, pp. 3–4)

3   Behavior: the voting decision

To predict and explain voter behavior, public choice theorists have broken down the voting decision into basic components. We have to recognize that the voting decision itself is only the last in a series of decisions, or reactions to costs and constraints, by the citizen. To see this, consider the results of Fort (1995), who elaborates and tests a 'sequential barriers' model of turnout suggested by Cox and Munger (1989, 1991). The point is that the 'participation rate' of voters in any given election j is *definitionally* the product of four ratios:

$$\underbrace{\frac{\text{Vote}_j}{\text{Population}}}_{} \equiv \underbrace{\frac{\text{Enfranchised}}{\text{Population}}}_{(a)} \times \underbrace{\frac{\text{Registered}}{\text{Enfranchised}}}_{(b)} \times \underbrace{\frac{\text{Enter Booth}}{\text{Registered}}}_{(c)} \times \underbrace{\frac{\text{Vote}_j}{\text{Enter Booth}}}_{(d)} \quad (9.1)$$

In words, for a citizen to vote in election j, (a) the citizen is part of the population enfranchised by the laws and practices of the society, (b) the enfranchised citizen has chosen to register, (c) the registered citizen has chosen to enter the voting booth, and (d) the citizen in the voting booth has chosen to cast a vote in election j.

The right-hand side of this identity simplifies to the left-hand side, of course, because most of the terms cancel out. Nonetheless, each of the intervening steps affects the measured turnout rate at that point. Attempts to analyse turnout empirically in any one election must account for all of the choices the citizen makes or has made for her by the rules of her nation, state, or city. For example, if the political jurisdiction that makes voting rules restricts enfranchisement by race, sex, age, literacy, or income, then ratio (a) in equation (9.1) may be small. If registration is expensive, time-consuming, or complicated and intimidating, ratio (b) may be small. Finally, there is an important interaction between ratios (c) and (d): the number of registered people who vote may depend on how groups of elections are packaged. If elections are held separately, it may be that few people vote (ratio (c) will be small), but that everyone who enters the booth casts a vote in election j (ratio (d) would be near 1.00).

Having broken voter participation into components, it turns out that several different explanations are required to understand the process. The task of explaining variation in ratio (a) (legal enfranchisement) across countries is an interesting question, but is primarily institutional rather than behavioral.

Explaining the variation in ratio (b) (registration) across nations, or US states, is an interesting policy question, but deciding whether to register is clearly different from deciding whether to vote (although, as Erikson (1981) points out, registration may be the more important decision overall).[2]

If we are to analyse individual voting decisions, we must restrict our attention to ratios (c) and (d). The simplest case is to assume that the race in question is the only one on the ballot. The reason is not that most elections actually look like this (they do not; ballots are often quite long). We already *know* that multiple elections have complicated effects (Burnham 1965; Cox and Munger 1989; Fort 1995; Hamilton and Ladd 1996). By considering a single race and a single decision about whether to go to the polls and vote, we isolate the logic of the citizen's choice. In the next section, the two major reasons the classical spatial model gives for abstention, indifference and alienation, are addressed.

4 The classical model: indifference and alienation

There are at least two circumstances where enfranchised citizens might not choose to vote in an election. One of these is *indifference*, or the perception that there are no important differences (in terms of citizens' welfare) among the alternatives presented on the ballot. The other is *alienation*, or a voter's sense that the issue positions of the candidates are far removed from what she cares about. One candidate may be closer to the voter's preferred position, but all candidates are outside the range of policy alternatives where the voter has any interest in participating.

The classical spatial model can handle either indifference or alienation.[3] To understand the meaning of, and distinction between, the concepts, it is useful to portray indifference and alienation graphically. In Figure 9.1, panel (a) depicts a single voter's ideal point x_i and two sets of positions for candidates A and B. Notice that the voter is indifferent between x'_A and x'_B. She is also indifferent between the much closer x''_A and x''_B. Of course, if the candidate positions were x'_A and x''_B, the voter would choose candidate B. But paired as the platforms are, she finds herself indifferent in each case, although at two very different levels of utility.

Panel (b) contains the analogous diagram for alienation. If the race is between x''_A and x''_B, the voter will cast her vote for candidate B. But if the race is between x'_A and x'_B, both alternatives are so far away that the voter sees no point in participating. It does not matter which is relatively closer; both are too distant, in an absolute sense, for the voter to care about the election. More precisely, abstention inspired by alienation requires that beyond some threshold distance (defined here as δ) the voter loses interest in the election. She may perceive herself as lacking efficacy because she is so remote from the campaign she hears about in the media.

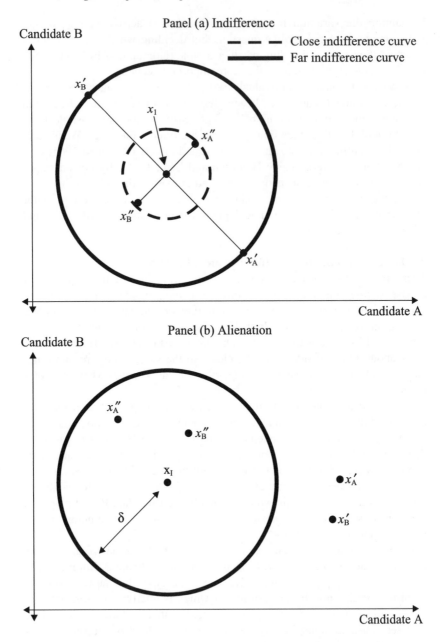

Figure 9.1   Indifference and alienation as explanations for abstention

These effects are observed in actual elections in at least two ways. First, polities have widely varying rules governing the number of polling places and how long the polls stay open. If the polls open late and close early, many 'almost indifferent' voters will not make it to the precinct.[4] Second, the weather on the day of the election may determine turnout. If it rains, the almost indifferent voter stays home.[5] If it snows, she laughs at the very idea of going to the polls. However, if she prefers A to B by a wide margin, she will brave storm or snow to cast her ballot. Consequently, the impact of bad weather is not random, because it drives down turnout from voters who are nearly indifferent. To put it another way, costly registration or bad weather ensures that choices are made by relatively extreme voters.

The classical spatial model's depiction of the decision to abstain is useful, because it identifies circumstances when citizens are less likely to vote from the perspective of a particular election. Since turnout varies across elections, it is important that we can identify variables (such as voter perceptions of candidate locations) that differentiate elections. The problem with the classical model, however, is that it is deterministic and does not allow for the possibility that voters consider what other voters will do before deciding whether to abstain.[6] In the next section, this 'paradox of not voting' is addressed.

5 Voting is a collective action problem

I said earlier that no one's vote matters, and in a sense that is true: mass elections are almost never decided by a single vote. But suppose that a group of voters all agree on who would be the best candidate. If that group can persuade its supporters to go to the polls, then all members of the group benefit when 'their' candidate wins. On the other hand, any one voter might prefer to stay home and let everyone else do the work.

This 'free-rider' problem was recognized by Mancur Olson, particularly in his *Logic of Collective Action* (1965). Olson claims that the key to success in providing collective goods is to induce people to contribute to the creation of collective benefits. Free riders are people who enjoy collective benefits provided by the efforts of others, without contributing any effort or resources themselves. Olson makes the free-rider argument explicitly for voters:

> Though most people feel they would be better off if their party were in power, they recognize that if their party is going to win, *it will as likely win without them, and they will get the benefits in any case.* ... The point is that the average person will not be willing to make a significant sacrifice for the party he favors, since a victory for his party provides a collective good. (pp. 163–4; emphasis added)

To analyse turnout as a collective action problem, we need to consider the 'Downsian' model of voting, from Downs (1957). This model was elaborated by Riker and Ordeshook (1968).[7] According to this model, an individual will vote if and only if:

$$P \times NCD + D \geq C, \tag{9.2}$$

where P is the probability that this individual's vote will affect the outcome of the majority-rule election; NCD is the 'net candidate differential', or perceived net benefits of one candidate over another in the eyes of the individual; D is the individual's sense of civic duty, or the utility derived from voting, regardless of the outcome; and C is the marginal cost associated with the act of voting, including the opportunity cost of the voter's time, the chance of inclement weather, and so on.

The logic of this model turns on a comparison of costs and benefits: if the (expected) returns exceed the costs, the citizen becomes a voter and casts a vote for the candidate he most prefers. Otherwise, he abstains. But notice how complex the model truly is. The decision of *whether* to vote is made simultaneously with the choice of *for whom* to vote. Imagine that the duty term is negligible (that is, $D \approx 0$). Then the citizen votes if and only if $P \times NCD \geq C$. We know that $C > 0$, because voting entails some identifiable costs, including time spent filling out registration forms, traveling to the polls and waiting in line. This leads us to predict that $P \times NCD \neq 0$ is a *necessary condition* for voting.

To put it another way, if either P or NCD is zero, the simple Downsian model predicts abstention. The P term is the individual's belief (in probability terms) that her vote will transform a loss into a tie, or a tie into a victory for her preferred candidate. If an individual knows how everyone else will vote, she knows the outcome: P is either 1 (her vote changes the outcome) or 0 (it will not). Such accurate information is implausible, even in small electorates, because no one knows how everyone else will vote. Furthermore, everyone is wondering whether everyone else will vote.

Now, suppose that $D > 0$. While this seems like a simple matter, the intuition behind the D term is actually very intricate. As John Aldrich points out,

> adding a D term is the same as subtracting a C term. Thus, C can be thought of as 'net costs', that is, as costs of voting, less any positive values, such as doing one's duty. A positive C says that duty only partially outweighs costs of voting. ... Thus, the D term does not change the fundamental analysis, unless $D > C$, in which case it is better to vote for [the more preferred candidate] than to abstain in all circumstances. (Aldrich 1993, pp. 251–2)

This is a very important point: if $D > C$, the voter *always* votes, regardless of the locations of the candidates. Whether the motivation is the avoidance of guilt or the enjoyment of the act of voting itself, the point is the same. But then voting is simply a *consumption* activity, more like attending a baseball game than an act of rational investment.[8] Imagine: you go to a baseball game, you stand in line, you pay for tickets and parking. When your team comes to bat, you stand up and yell, 'hurray!'. Do you really believe that your shout, amid all the others, changes the outcome of the at-bat, or of the game? Probably not. Yet you do it; you express your sense of belonging and your pleasure in participating. Obviously, the costs of going to a ballgame are higher than the costs of voting. Furthermore, the chances of influencing the outcome of an election, or a ballgame, by 'participating' as a voter or a fan are about the same: zero. The desire to explain, at all costs, the *investment* (as opposed to *consumption*) value of voting may have led public choice scholars astray.

Nonetheless, it is not strictly impossible to rationalize voting from a purely investment perspective. The logic goes like this: in terms of Downs's model, who would vote if the P term is zero? The answer is obvious: no one. Of course, this answer is also obviously wrong. One is reminded of Yogi Berra's famous *bon mot* about a New York restaurant: 'No one goes there anymore, it's too crowded!' In our case, if no one votes because it will not matter; it *will* matter. If no one votes, then one vote determines the election. But then P is not really zero. In fact, $P = 1$, because *anyone* who did vote determined the outcome!

Ferejohn and Fiorina (1974) call this the 'paradox of not voting': if everyone knows that the chances of affecting the outcome are trivial, no one votes. But then any one voter's chance of affecting the outcome if she *had* voted is very large. Game theory provides a way out, by allowing us to see if any level of 'rational' turnout can be sustained in the face of Ferejohn and Fiorina's paradox. Ledyard (1981, 1984), building on the probabilistic voting model of Hinich et al. (1972), demonstrated that such a game among voters has a 'mixed strategy' equilibrium.

Mixed strategies require the voter to randomize over pure strategies (in this case voting and not voting). Ledyard showed that each voter might plausibly choose to vote in any given election with only a small probability. But then it will turn out that some voters will actually vote in any given election, and turnout exceeds zero in equilibrium.

This was an important achievement, because the act of turning out was rationalized: positive levels of political participation were shown to be consistent with purposive, self-interested behavior. Palfrey and Rosenthal (1983, 1985) showed, however, that as the size of the electorate rises, equilibrium turnout shrinks, even in Ledyard's game. In the limit, as the potential electorate goes to infinity, the 'rational' level of turnout goes toward zero. Palfrey and Rosenthal show that the maximum level of turnout predicted in equilibrium (for plausibly sized electorates) is about 3 to 5 percent. But actual rates of turnout in the United States exceed 30 percent, and may be much higher in US presidential races or elections in other countries.

This conflict between theory (no more than 5 percent) and fact (more than 30 percent) suggests that something else is going on. Parties and other political elites play the role of getting voters to turn out. Securing the 'right' policy from government is a collective good, so that my actions in voting 'correctly' benefit everyone who agrees with me, but did not feel like voting. Somehow, groups (large groups!) of citizens are overcoming the free-rider problem. More people are participating than would be predicted by a purely self-interested investment strategy. Incorporating groups into an individual decision-making calculus is difficult, but some progress has been made (Uhlaner 1989a, 1989b; see Aldrich 1993 for a broader review). Still, attempts to use private returns,[9] or Olson's (1965) 'selective incentives', have not solved the problem of explaining observed levels of voter turnout. After all, if people vote because they like to vote, then what is the point of calling the decision 'rational'?

There is a pretty useful point in all of this. We have used the model of narrowly self-interested behavior to generate hypotheses about turnout rates. Those hypotheses, that turnout will not exceed 5 percent in any reasonably large electorate, have been proven false. This has led analytical political theorists to look to mechanisms by which pure self-interest motives are overcome and collective action problems are solved. Further, although the *levels* of turnout are hard to explain, we can make useful predictions at the *margins*. Voters respond to costs of voting, opportunity costs of time, and other factors as the 'rational' model predicts, namely by being less likely to vote.[10] As was noted earlier, rain or bad weather drives turnout down (Morton 1991; Knack 1994) because traveling to the polls is more onerous. Difficult or time-consuming registration procedures make people less likely to vote (Kelley et al. 1967; Wolfinger and Rosenstone 1980; Nagler 1991). People with few resources find it hard to take time to vote (Tollison and Willett 1973; Wolfinger and Rosenstone 1980).

There are two other important insights from the early game-theoretic literature on strategic influences on turnout (Ledyard 1981, 1984; Palfrey and Rosenthal 1983, 1985). These results hark back to our earlier concern with elections as a means of eliciting 'truth', the 'best' policy, or the 'general will'. I shall simply present the results in the form of theorems, without proofs, and refer the interested reader to the original sources for the details.

Theorem 9.1   Under some conditions, one equilibrium to the game among voters choosing whether to vote or abstain, is for no voters to turn out. However, under the assumptions of the classical spatial model (if a median in all directions exists), the locations parties are expected to have chosen in such an 'election' are optimal from the point of view of the median citizen. More simply, candidates act as if all voters were going to vote, but if candidates act that way voters may, in equilibrium, not vote (Ledyard 1984).

Theorem 9.2   The proportions that split the vote among two alternatives is a biased measure of the actual distribution of preferences in the population of enfranchised voters. Majorities have greater incentives to free ride, so large majorities will be harder to sustain if victory seems certain. Elections can be fairly close, even when one alternative is actually supported by a large majority of the citizenry (Palfrey and Rosenthal 1983).

The verbal paraphrasing of the two sets of results seems obvious at first glance, but both are substantively important. Further, each demonstrates the importance of formal analytical reasoning applied to politics. Theorem 9.1 addresses a common concern among observers of democracies, who complain, 'Turnout is too low!'. Presumably, the object of elections is to ensure a coincidence between the desires of the people and the actions of government. Ledyard showed that low turnout could be a sign that parties and candidates are occupying the positions in policy space that would win the most votes even if everyone voted. Ledyard did warn that the outcomes of such a process were not necessarily Pareto optimal, but this problem would exist even if turnout were universal.

Theorem 9.2 calls into question the use of polls and other forms of election prognostication, based on sample proportions in populations. Sample proportions in populations may be very different from election percentages, because turnout is itself a strategic choice. The reverse is also true, of course: using percentages of the vote as signs of a 'mandate', or the lack of one, represents an unsupportable conclusion about the opinions held by various segments of the population. Election results may be all that politicians or the media have to go on, but the rational turnout model suggests that extreme care should be taken in assuming election results are meaningful for anything other than the simple selection of one alternative over another.[11]

6   Institutions: social choice and other voting models

We started with a brief overview of how people choose. Let us now consider the implications of how those choices are 'added up'. One of the conventions of social choice theory is to describe each of several important results as a 'paradox', a term deriving from *paradoxon*, a Greek word meaning 'beyond opinion or belief'. Thomas Schwartz described the role of paradox in analytical politics: 'Deduce a contradiction from reasonable-looking, widely held assumptions, and you have a paradox; the better entrenched the assumptions, the more paradoxical the paradox' (Schwartz 1986, p. 116).

But there is no need to start with paradoxes; rather, I shall begin with some more encouraging results. The 'median-voter theorem' (MVT), and the corollary stated here, establish a benchmark in the study of collective choice. There is a determinate, positive answer to the 'what will a group of people do?' question, and there may even be a normative basis for saying that this is the *right* thing to do. In other words, under certain assumptions, the 'middle', or median on a single dimension, may correspond fairly closely to what Rousseau meant by the 'general will'.

> *Theorem 9.3* (median-voter theorem)   If the issue space is a single-ordered dimension, and preferences are single-peaked, a median position cannot lose to any other alternative in a majority-rule election (Black [1958] 1987).

The MVT implies that the middle of the distribution of citizen preferences in a society holds a privileged position in political competition. If the median position is unique (identified with just one voter), this very important person is called the 'median voter'.

> *Corollary to the MVT*   In a comparison of alternatives that are not median positions, the alternative closer to the median wins.

The corollary shows that under certain conditions (unique median and symmetric preferences), closeness to the middle is the basis of political power. Consequently, even if the status quo differs from the median, there are pressures for new alternatives to move toward the center until a median position is reached.

But what if preferences are not single-peaked? Well, that question takes us back to paradox. This problem, recognized and solved by Black, dates to the Marquis de Condorcet, who published a lengthy discussion of the mathematical properties of sequences of pairwise majority rule contests in his *Essai sur l'application de l'analyse à la probabilité des décisions rendues à la pluralité des voix* (1785). Condorcet himself considered the result to be merely a feature of majority rule, rather than a paradox. Nonetheless, 'Condorcet's paradox' has become part of the language of modern social choice theory. What is the deduced implication that is 'beyond belief'?

It is useful to define a technical term before proceeding further. That term is 'transitivity'. Suppose that a person is asked to rank three alternatives, A, B, and C. Imagine that she responds with the following two comparisons:

1.   C is better than B.
2.   B is better than A.

Now, it is tempting to conclude that anyone who likes C better than B and likes B better than A must also like C better than A. But, from a technical perspective, the conclusion 'C is better than A' is not at all obvious. In fact, we can deduce that C is preferred to A in our example if and only if the preferences of the person in question are transitive.

> *Transitivity*   Preferences are *transitive* if, for any three alternatives, C preferred to B preferred to A necessarily implies that A is not preferred to C (weak transitivity) or that C is preferred to A (strong transitivity).

Note that transitivity is a concept that might be applied to a preference ordering of an individual or a society choosing among alternative policies.

We are now in a position to state Condorcet's paradox.

> *Condorcet's paradox*   Suppose that all individual preferences are transitive, but not necessarily single-peaked. Then the social preference ordering under majority rule may be intransitive.

The paradox is that the aggregation of *individually* transitive preferences leads to an *aggregate* intransitivity.[12] The society finds itself in an endless cycle of 'best' alternatives, none of which commands a majority against all other alternatives.

Consider an example. Suppose that the only three foods in the world were apples, broccoli, and carrots. Each type of food is sold only in large crates. Consider three people who, if they cooperate, will have *just enough* money to buy one, but only one, crate of food. The preference profiles of the three people, Mr 1 (who loves apples), Ms 2 (who loves carrots), and Mr 3 (who loves broccoli), are listed in Table 9.1.

The premise of the example is that choice is collective: if the three people cannot agree, all will go hungry, because no one of them has enough money to purchase a crate of food. They must pool their resources, but they disagree about what to buy. After discussing the choices endlessly, they realize that they will never reach a consensus, and no one is going to change his or her mind (if you do not like broccoli, you just do not like it; there is little room for persuasion). So, our three people decide to vote. They learned in ninth-grade civics that voting is the only 'fair' way to make collective decisions. Besides, they are all getting hungry.

The alert reader may feel sympathy at the naive hope that voting will yield the 'seraphic wisdom' to solve the problem of fundamental disagreement.

Table 9.1   Preference 'lists' of three voters over apples, broccoli, and carrots

| | Person | | |
Ranking	Mr 1	Ms 2	Mr 3
Best	Apples	Carrots	Broccoli
Middle	Broccoli	Apples	Carrots
Worst	Carrots	Broccoli	Apples

The reason faith in voting is naive is that the preferences profiled in Table 9.1 do not admit of a Condorcet winner. By majority rule, apples are preferred to broccoli is preferred to carrots are preferred to apples, always by 2 to 1 margins. Say, for example, apples are voted against broccoli first. Mr 1 and Ms 2 both prefer apples to broccoli; Mr 3 vainly dissents, and apples are selected. Apples are then compared with the remaining choice, carrots; Mr 1 votes for apples, Ms 2 votes for carrots, and Mr 3 votes for carrots. It is quite possible that the three stop there, if they do not think things through. On the face of it, the 'carrots preferred to apples preferred to broccoli' group preference seems fair enough. But the fact of the matter is that there is no unique choice that is defensibly the 'general will' of this group. The general will does not exist.

It turns out that Condorcet's paradox is an example in a general class of paradoxes arising from using *any* social choice mechanism, except dictatorship. The results are called 'paradoxes' because the general problem seems so simple, yet turns out to be insoluble.

The meaning of collective choice   Suppose that all citizens are perfectly informed about all policies. We then solicit citizens' ordered 'lists' of policies, ranking all feasible alternatives from best to worst, assuming that the information on the list is accurate and not strategically misrepresented to manipulate the outcome. Then, given sincere, accurate information about each individual's relative valuation of policies, compose the aggregate list for the society. The aggregate list looks like an individual's list, again ranking polices from best to worst. The difference is that 'best' now is defined from the collective perspective.

Social choice theorists have repeatedly demonstrated that there is no sure way of choosing a transitive aggregate list if all citizens' preferences count. This is true even under the best circumstances (perfect information, no manipulation), if no restrictions are placed on the form of individual lists. The objections made by some that these assumptions are unrealistic miss the point. If social choice is not tractable under idealized circumstances, then adding imperfect information and manipulation makes the problem *even harder*. What is beyond belief about paradoxes of social choice is that even the simplest kinds of voting schemes yield surprises.

We shall briefly examine the best known of these paradoxical results, Arrow's ([1951] 1963) impossibility theorem. Arrow laid out a set of properties or conditions that (arguably) are desirable features of a social choice mechanism. The impossibility theorem is a deduction that no social choice mechanism can possess all of these features. In particular, all voting procedures must violate at least one of the conditions Arrow demonstrated to be mutually inconsistent. Since Arrow's paradox applies to *any* non-dictatorial aggregation mechanism, it encompasses all of what we might label 'democratic' decisions by societies. Let us consider briefly a variety of ways of choosing collectively and discuss some of their advantages and disadvantages.

7   Choosing how to choose

Decisions may be made by one person, by some people, or by everyone. The set of citizens required to make a decision or choice is called the 'decisive set'.

> *Decisive set*   A set C of citizens is 'decisive' if for two alternatives **y** and **z** the fact that all members of C like **y** better than **z** is sufficient to ensure that **y** is selected over **z** by the society, regardless of the opinions of citizens not members of C. We shall call $K(C)$ the 'size' of C, or the minimum number of people required to be decisive.

An easy example of a decisive set is suggested by majority rule: C is any group of $(N/2) + 1$ citizens. Of course, there are many different potential Cs, each of which must have $K(C) \geq (N/2) + 1$ citizens.

Both the inclusion of a given person's preferences in a decision (enfranchisement) and the decision to use a particular means of summarizing these preferences (aggregation mechanism) can affect the decision. Generally we think of 'private' decisions (What will I have for breakfast? What shirt will I wear with these pants?) as being very different from 'group' decisions (What is the appropriate budget for national defense? What is the right speed limit in school zones?).

But distinguishing private and group decisions begs the question. Apparent differences among 'kinds' of choices may be caused by differences in enfranchisement and aggregation mechanisms, not necessarily by inherent properties of the choices themselves. Breakfasts and clothing could plausibly be chosen collectively (as in the military or in a school with a compulsory dress code).

Similarly, spending levels and speed limits might be picked by individuals, at least in principle. Government vouchers could be applied toward local private armies, which provide defense against those aggressors on the next block. Drivers might drive as fast as they like in school zones, with private groups hired to transport children in armored personnel carriers across the streets.

Thus, 'social choice' has two elements:

1. *Public decision*   The choice will have a significant public impact, affecting more than one individual. This might be because the choice affects others; this effect is called an 'externality'. The effect is called a 'positive externality' if others benefit, or a 'negative externality' if others are harmed. Alternatively, the choice might involve the level of provision of a 'public good'. Public goods (for example, national defense) are characterized by zero marginal cost of production and high cost of exclusion from consumption.
2. *Collective decision*   It is mandated, by rule or practice, that the choice will be made by more than one person. Technically, all this means is that $K(C) > 1$. If collective decisions are made by majority rule, $K(C) \geq (N/2) + 1$. If the rule is unanimity, the decisive set may be all enfranchised citizens: $K(C) = N$.

The two aspects of choice may appear to go together, but they are distinct. Choices might be public but not collective: suppose that I build a factory that produces sooty smoke and my downwind neighbors suffer. There may be no institution that *enfranchises* in the decision to build the factory those who will be harmed.[13] Their preferences receive zero weight in the public (but not collective) decision, because $C = 1$. In the extreme, *all* decisions might be made by one person (a dictator), with no collective enfranchisement whatsoever, although all of the dictator's choices might be 'public' in the sense that others are affected.

Conversely, choices may be collective but not public: a society may decide to outlaw some consensual sexual practice involving two mentally competent adults. Another society might require that skateboarders wear helmets. In both cases, people's choices are being regulated, even though these activities affect no one else.[14] In this case, other people are enfranchised to decide individual behavior: the sexual partners and the bareheaded boarders get voices in the collective decision, but their preferences count only as a few among many. It is no longer true that $C = 2$ (for the consensual sexual activity) or that $C = 1$ (for the skateboarder).

Enfranchisement rules are clearly an important part of voting, but are beyond the scope of this chapter. I shall focus on the implications of different aggregation mechanisms.[15] The following section lays out the limits of the abilities of aggregation mechanisms to solve collective choice problems.

8   Arrow's paradox and the limits of social choice

Condorcet showed that majority rule may be intransitive, even if each individual has transitive preferences over the alternatives. Intransitivity is a kind of system meltdown, assuming that some choice is required. That choice may be to preserve the status quo and do nothing, but the choice itself must be clear and determinate. Intransitivity means that the society is incapable of choosing among several mutually exclusive outcomes, without resort to random or imposed 'choice'. One might ask whether this potential for incoherence extends to other aggregation mechanisms. The definitive answer is 50 years old and dates to Arrow ([1951] 1963).

That answer is disturbing for defenders of democracy or for advocates of any particular form of collective choice. We shall present a simple overview of Arrow's technical result, but it is worth beginning by summarizing the intuition of the result:[16]

> *Arrow's paradox*   The only collective choice mechanism that is always transitive, allowing for any possible fixed set of pairwise preferences over alternatives, is dictatorship.

The 'paradox' is that the only transitive collective decision rule that obeys the technical criteria Arrow sets out is dictatorship, or rule by one. Such a decision rule is not 'collective' at all! Dictatorship resolves disagreements by restricting the decisive set to contain only one person. How did Arrow arrive at this conclusion?

8.1   The 'impossibility' result

I shall consider only a simplified paraphrasing of Arrow's theorem and will not consider the technical aspects of the proof. The reader interested in pursuing this subject more deeply can find an introduction to the literature in Mueller (1989, especially chs 19–20) and treatments in depth by Schwartz (1986) and Kelly (1988). Arrow's result can be summarized this way:

1. Specify a set of desirable characteristics for an aggregation mechanism, or a way of 'counting' preferences registered by enfranchised citizens.
2. Determine the set of collective choice mechanisms that have these desirable characteristics.
3. Ask how many of these choice rules are *not* dictatorial. The answer: not one! Any social choice mechanism exhibiting all of the characteristics Arrow listed as desirable *must* be dictatorial.

Some scholars have questioned the merit of Arrow's list. Others have suggested substitute axioms that are weaker or quite different, but Arrow's original set of desirable characteristics is not implausible. The version of these characteristics used here is adapted from Mueller (1989), adapted in turn from Vickrey (1960). To describe the list of desirable characteristics for social choice mechanisms, it is useful to begin by defining some terms and concepts.

Consider three different states of the world, S_1, S_2, S_3, representing discrepant policy vectors 1, 2, and 3, respectively. We can then describe the set of desirable characteristics as follows:

1. *Unanimity (also, the Pareto criterion)*   If all enfranchised citizens agree (for example) that S_1 is better than S_2, then S_1 is selected by the collective choice rule over S_2.
2. *Transitivity*   The collective choice mechanism is transitive, so that if S_1 is selected over S_2, and S_2 over S_3, then S_1 is selected over S_3.
3. *Unrestricted domain*   For any individual, and for any three alternatives S_1, S_2, S_3, any of the following six preference orderings (from best to worst) is possible:

	1	2	3	4	5	6
Best	S_1	S_1	S_3	S_2	S_2	S_3
Middle	S_2	S_3	S_1	S_1	S_3	S_2
Worst	S_3	S_2	S_2	S_3	S_1	S_1

4. *Independence of irrelevant alternatives (IIA)*   The social choice between any two alternatives must depend only on the individual rankings of the alternatives in question in the preference profile of the group. Thus, if S_1 is socially preferred to S_2, then it will still be socially preferred if we rearrange the orderings of the other alternatives while leaving the paired rankings of S_1 and S_2 the same. For example, the following two sets of preference profiles of three citizens must yield the same social ordering for S_1 and S_2, if the social choice rule is IIA:

Preference profile set I

	1	2	3
Best	S_1	S_2	S_1
Middle	S_2	S_1	S_3
Worst	S_3	S_3	S_2

Preference profile set II

	1	2	3
Best	S_1	S_3	S_1
Middle	S_3	S_2	S_2
Worst	S_2	S_1	S_3

Notice that the relative rankings of S_1 and S_2 are the same in profile sets I and II. All that is different is the position of S_3 in the rankings. For example, in set I, person 1 ranks the alternatives in the order S_1, S_2, S_3. In set II, person 1 ranks them S_1, S_3, S_2. In both cases, person 1 likes S_1 better than S_2. Independence of irrelevant alternatives requires that this pairwise comparison of rankings does not depend on the position of other, 'irrelevant' alternatives (such as S_3 in our example).

The final 'good' characteristic of mechanisms for the democratic aggregation of preferences is probably the most obvious: no one person possesses unilateral power to decide.

5. *Non-dictatorship* There is no dictator. If person 2 (for example) is a dictator, then if that person ranks S_1 above S_2, then 'S_1 better than S_2' is the social ranking, regardless of how anyone else, or even everyone else, ranks S_1 compared to S_2.

With these conditions established, a version of the 'impossibility' theorem can be stated.

Theorem 9.4 (impossibility theorem) Consider the set of all collective choice rules that satisfy requirements 1–4 (unanimity, transitivity, unrestricted domain, and IIA). Every element of the set of collective choice mechanisms satisfying these requirements violates requirement 5, implying the existence of a dictator.

What does the impossibility result leave us? A menu of choices: any mechanism for aggregating individual preferences must lack at least one of the desirable properties, 1–4. We have listed non-dictatorship separately because tyranny is incommensurate with democracy. To put it another way, non-dictatorship is a starting point if the goal is to compare ideal forms of democratic government. A similar argument (for restricting the menu of choices for ideal forms of government) applies to the Pareto criterion, though on more practical grounds: it is hard to imagine adopting a rule that would prevent change if literally *everyone* favored the change. If nothing else, all members of society could unanimously change the rules![17]

If we insist on non-dictatorship and the Pareto criterion in our social choice rules, we are left with three options: decision rules that allow *intransitivity*, rules that allow *independent alternatives* to affect pairwise choices of other alternatives, and rules that restrict the set of *preferences* that will be allowed (that is, violate universal domain). A complete discussion of the implications of relaxing the postulates of the impossibility theorem is beyond the scope of this chapter; the interested reader should consult Schwartz (1986) or Kelly (1988).

What I shall do instead is look at some alternatives to simple majority rule. People have come up with many different ways to choose. Each of these methods of aggregating preferences has some advantages and some drawbacks. The search for an 'optimal' method is very difficult, however, because all methods of aggregating preferences have potential problems with fairness, and all of them can be manipulated. In its starkest form, that is what Arrow's theorem is all about.

9   Alternative decision rules

There is a difficulty with majority rule as a normative prescription for all members of society. That difficulty is that the majority's 'will' must serve all, though it is only determined by most. Such a process must rely for its legitimacy on the majority's forbearance: 'To be governed by appetite alone is slavery, while obedience to a law one prescribes to oneself is freedom' (Rousseau [1762] 1973, Book I, ch. 8, p. 41). If the majority does not act on 'appetites', but rather enacts only good laws, *the same policy would be chosen* by one person, by a group, or by the whole society, provided the choosers are wise, well informed, and well intentioned. Such an approach begs the question of collective choice by assuming the problem away: the collective is organic, not composed of many individuals with potentially different ideas.

This moral force of unanimity can be achieved for majorities by artifice, as is done behind Rawls's (1971) 'veil of ignorance'. Rawls proposes the following thought experiment: suppose you did not know what your position would be in the society; then what laws, rules, and policies would you select? The answer, Rawls (p. 140) claims, is that 'each is forced to choose for everyone'. Since you do not know what your self-interest is, you must choose for society, rather than for your own 'appetites'. If each chooses for everyone, the distinction between private and collective choice vanishes.

But what if the majority decides to act on its appetites? Suppose, for example, that most of society simply wants to enslave the rest. Even on a smaller scale, it is perfectly possible that the majority may want to enrich itself at the expense of the minority, and ultimately at the cost of virtue and order for the society. How can we choose rules that determine how we choose policies and have any faith in the justice of the choice? By advantaging certain alternatives, the choice of aggregation mechanism will determine, in part, the nature of the society. I shall consider three major sets of alternatives to simple majority rule: (1) optimal majority rule, (2) the Borda count and approval voting, and (3) proportional representation.

9.1 Optimal majority rule

The first variation on majority rule is some form of majority rule itself, allowing the size of the required 'majority' (that is, the decisive set) for an affirmative decision to be different from the simple majority $C = (N/2) + 1$. After all, what is so special about 50 percent (plus one voter) as the minimum group in favor? In theory, as was discussed above, the size of the group making a decision can vary from one person to the whole society.

In practice, lots of normal collective business is done by majority rule. But even within the context of real-world collective decisions, the size of the proportion of enfranchised voters required to make a decision varies widely. In many legislative assemblies, unanimous consent is required to alter or suspend temporarily the rules of procedure. To amend the US Constitution, two different supermajorities (two-thirds of a national assembly to propose, three-quarters of state assemblies to ratify) are required. There are examples of decisive sets smaller than even simple majority, including the US Supreme Court's practice of affirming a writ of *certiorari* based on a vote of less than one-half of the seats on the court (four out of nine). What is the 'best' decisive set as a proportion of the polity? The answer to almost all important questions, of course, is that 'It depends'. But what does the answer depend on?

The classic analytical treatment of optimal majority is Buchanan and Tullock's *Calculus of Consent* (1962). Taking an economic approach, Buchanan and Tullock note that there are *costs* of widely shared decision power as well as *benefits*. The costs of *including* more people in the required majority entail defining and amending the proposal, explaining it to the voters, providing payoffs to solve strategic maneuvering of swing voters, and so on. These are called 'inclusion costs', because the costs fall on those whose preferences count in the decision. The costs of *excluding* members of society from the required majority can be thought of as the costs of being forced to obey a policy that one opposes. Buchanan and Tullock call these costs 'external costs'.

We can depict the problem of optimal majority graphically, as in Figure 9.2. Inclusion costs rise dramatically as we near a rule of unanimity, because each voter becomes a potential swing voter. Anyone can threaten to withhold

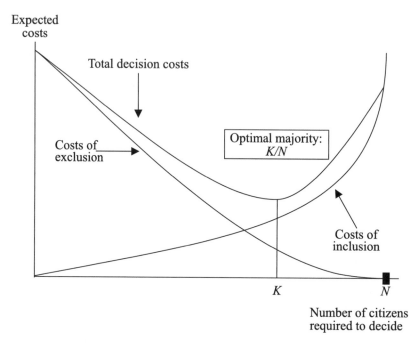

Figure 9.2   Buchanan and Tullock's 'optimal majority' analysis

approval unless certain concessions or payoffs are made. Similarly, exclusion costs fall as we near unanimity, because by definition there is less chance a policy can be enacted without approval of everyone affected.

The optimal majority is K/N, because it minimizes the sum of the costs of inclusion and the costs of exclusion, that is, total decision costs. These costs, though hard to quantify, clearly figure in how we choose how to choose, as public decisions fall into three categories:

1. *Allowing access*: $K < [(N/2) + 1]$ Just a single member of the US House or Senate is required to introduce a bill. If no one introduces the bill, it is completely blocked. Alternatively, four or more members of the US Supreme Court are needed to grant *certiorari*, or petition for a case to be heard. Neither of these decisions by any means ensures *success*; all that is granted is *access*.

2. *Routine decisions*: $K = [(N/2) + 1]$ The smallest strict majority is a very common value for the decisive set in democracies, from tiny private clubs to the US Congress and Supreme Court. This value for K is the smallest value that ensures no simultaneous passage of two directly

contradictory measures. Consequently, both inclusion and exclusion costs are moderate. For simple majority rule to have such wide real-world application, it must minimize the (perceived) costs of making everyday collective decisions.

3. *Rule changes*: $K > [(N/2) + 1]$ The rules governing the decision process itself affect the kinds of outcomes that the choices represent. A decision to change the rules has more far-reaching and unpredictable effects than a decision made under a fixed set of rules. Consequently, the costs of excluding enfranchised members is higher for rule change decisions, and the optimal majority for rule changes is more than 50 percent + 1.

In most cases, there is no single decision rule used for all choices; it depends. For example, in the US Congress the introduction of a bill requires the support of just one member. The passage of a bill requires 50 percent + 1 of the members present and voting. A resolution to propose an amendment to the Constitution requires a two-thirds majority. A motion to suspend the normal procedural rules requires unanimous consent. Business in the Senate can be held up almost indefinitely by dilatory tactics or 'filibustering', unless three-fifths of the membership vote for a resolution of 'cloture', cutting off further debate.

If there is a general rule, it would appear to be that we require larger majorities for larger questions, just as Buchanan and Tullock suggested. This conclusion is also quite consistent with some of Rousseau's thought, although his justifications are very different from those given by Buchanan and Tullock.

> A difference of one vote destroys equality; a single opponent destroys unanimity; but between equality and unanimity, there are several grades of unequal division, at each of which this proportion may be fixed in accordance with the condition and needs of the body politic.
> There are two general rules that may serve to regulate this relation. First, the more grave and important the questions discussed, the nearer should the opinion that is to prevail approach unanimity. Secondly, the more the matter in hand calls for speed, the smaller the prescribed difference in the numbers of votes may be allowed to become: where an instant decision has to be reached, a majority of one vote should be enough. (Rousseau [1762] 1973, Book II, ch. 2, p. 278)

Equilibrium for larger majorities   It appears that different decisive sets are appropriate for different choice situations. But now we must ask what effects these differences may have on the existence and nature of equilibrium. We will still face the generic failing of majority-rule systems, of course: the society may cycle among alternatives within a subset of the overall space of feasible political choices. But given this caveat, is there a generalization of the MVT that applies to optimal majorities, K/N, where $K > N/2$?

The answer is yes.[18] Define N_1 as the number of points on one side of a hyperplane H (*including* points on H), and N_2 as the number of points on the other side (again, including points on H). For example, assume that the policy 'space' is a line and that there are three voters, A, B, and C. If the voters have distinct ideal points, ordered alphabetically, then $N_1 = 2$ (A and B) and $N_2 = 2$ (B and C). Notice that B, the median voter, 'counts' in both sets. This seems cumbersome, but is necessary to account for all possible preference configurations.

The *K*-majority theorem (KMT) is then just a fairly obvious generalization of the median-voter theorem.[19] The KMT can be stated as follows:

> *Theorem 9.5 (K-majority theorem)*   An alternative **z** is a *K-majority equilibrium* for the society if and only if $N_1 \geq (N - K + 1)$ and $N_2 \geq (N - K + 1)$ for every H containing **y**.

Interestingly, the KMT reduces to the median-voter theorem for majority rule, since for majority rule $N - K + 1 = N/2$, where $K = N/2 + 1$.

The real problem, or advantage (it is actually just a feature!) with supermajority rules is the dramatic increase in the number of possible equilibria for the society. There is no way of choosing one over another at the outset. Further, there is no way of changing the choice once any equilibrium position

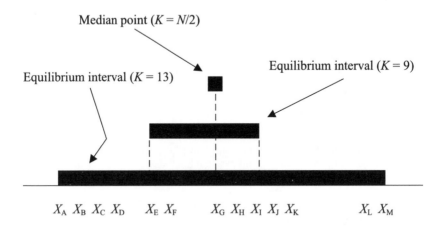

Ideal points for 13 committee members

Figure 9.3   *An example of supermajority rule: many equilibria, little change*

is established as the status quo. Another way to think of the KMT, as Figure 9.3 shows, is to realize that supermajority rules profoundly advantage the status quo position. The larger the required majority, the more difficult is any kind of change, *once a status quo is established.*

As the figure shows, larger majorities imply broader equilibrium intervals, illustrating why the KMT is a generalization of the MVT. If $K = N$, the set of equilibria is the Pareto set. For $N > K > N/2$, the set of equilibria is an interval. As K shrinks to $N/2$, the set of equilibria is the median ideal point (as in our example), or a median interval containing two ideal points (if the median is not unique).

If any point in the set of possible equilibria is established as the status quo by accident, practice, or strategic action, it is protected from change under supermajority rules. Consequently, supermajority rules ensure stability, but at the expense of flexibility. The status quo is immutable, even if most citizens want something else.

Runoffs and pluralities   One other consideration remains in our discussion of majorities. We have required that votes be conducted in a series of pairwise comparisons. That is, although the set of alternatives may be quite large, our consideration of majority rule has required that each new proposal be voted against the status quo, with the winner becoming the new status quo. Majority rule can also be applied to more than two alternatives, but the analysis becomes much more complex. Further, the existence of equilibria (particularly 'centrist' equilibria) becomes problematic. One solution is to have a modified form of majority rule over three or more alternatives: if any alternative receives more than half the vote, that alternative wins and becomes the status quo. Otherwise, the top two alternatives (in terms of votes received) are selected for a *runoff* election.

An apparently similar (but very different) procedure is *plurality rule*. In plurality-rule systems, whichever party or candidate receives the most votes wins, regardless of whether the top vote-getter garners a simple majority. To see the difference, consider the following vote shares for a four-candidate election: candidate 1, 27 percent; candidate 2, 26 percent; candidate 3, 24 percent; and candidate 4, 23 percent.

In a majority rule with runoff election, candidates 1 and 2 would have to stand for election again. The outcome is very much in doubt, since we have no idea how the 47 percent who cast ballots for candidates 3 or 4 compare 1 and 2 (or even if they will vote in the runoff election). Importantly, the candidate who wins will be the one who appeals to more of the 47 percent of the voters who did not vote for candidates 1 or 2 in the first round. Under plurality rule, the leftover 47 percent are irrelevant: candidate 1 wins the election outright, and the other three candidates get nothing.

While majority rule with runoff and plurality rule are fairly widely used in the real world of politics, it is interesting to note that neither has quite the direct centralizing tendency so apparent in the two-alternative, majority rule world of the median-voter result. Plurality rule, in particular, may lead to the non-existence of equilibrium if candidate entry or movement is free and unrestricted. Plurality rule may also lead to equilibria that are 'decidedly noncentrist' (Cox 1987). Cox shows that some candidates (if there are several) will take positions outside the two central quartiles of the distribution of voter ideal points even in equilibrium. This point is elaborated, for a variety of voting systems, in Cox (1990).

9.2   Borda count and approval voting

Majority rule and its variants are based on the premise that each person gets one, and only one, vote. It is simple, easy to understand, and technically defensible when the polity is seeking a choice of a single 'best' outcome from the set of proposed alternatives. The blunt and decisive quality of majority rule is a disadvantage, however, if the goal is to select a set of alternatives, or if the polity is trying to rank alternatives in a way that reflects voters' preferences from best to worst, rather than just choosing a single outcome or candidate.

In this section, aspects of two types of voting over 'lists' of alternatives (or candidates) will be considered, with the presumption that the number of alternatives may be much larger than the two assumed so far. These two voting rules are the *Borda count* and *approval voting*.

Borda count   Jean-Charles de Borda (1733–99) anticipated some of the observations of Condorcet, whose achievements were outlined earlier. His objection to majority rule was different from Condorcet's, however (see Black [1958] 1987 for discussion and background). Condorcet's criterion for value in elections was that if a majority preferred an alternative, that alternative should be selected. Borda was concerned that majorities might pick the *wrong* alternative, even if Condorcet's criterion were satisfied.

Suppose that there are 21 voters, who must choose over three alternatives, A, B, and C. Suppose further that the preference rankings of voters fall into three categories, as in Figure 9.4. If we use a majority (actually, plurality) choice rule, only first-place votes count. We do not know the second- and third-place preferences of voters in the first group. All we know for sure is that they like alternative A best and that they are the most numerous (eight first-place votes for A). Since B receives seven votes and C gets only six, A is the chosen policy.

Borda's point was that 13 voters, a clear majority, may actually like alternative A *least*. The problem with plurality rule, he felt, was that it counted

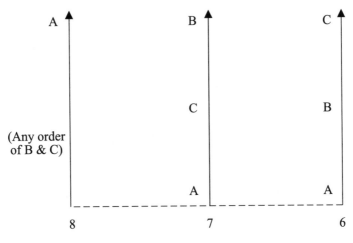

Source: Black ([1958] 1987, p. 157).

Figure 9.4 Borda's example of how majority rule picks the 'wrong' alternative: A wins, but either B or C is better

only first-place votes. Borda suggested several possible alternative decision rules, but the one most often associated with him is the 'Borda count': let each voter assign to each alternative a number corresponding to his or her rank ordering of that alternative.

Thus, each voter in the middle group in Figure 9.4 gives alternative B a rank of 1, C a rank of 2, and A a rank of 3. (If there were more alternatives, say *q* of them, then the ranks would go down to the worst, or *q*th, alternative on each voter's ballot.) The authority conducting the election then adds up the scores, or 'marks', for each alternative, and the alternative with the *lowest* number (for Borda, the most 'merit') wins.

Borda left the exact distribution of preferences for C and B in the first group unspecified (again, see Black [1958] 1987). For the sake of illustration, let us suppose that four of the eight voters like B better than C, and the others prefer C over B. What would be the result of using the Borda method? Alternative A has eight first-place votes, zero second-place marks, and 13 third-place marks, for a Borda count of 47. Alternative B has seven first-place votes, ten second-place, and four third-place, for a count of 39. Alternative C has six first-place marks, 11 second-place, and four third-place, for a count of 40. Using the Borda count, then, B wins over C in a close race, with A well back in the voting.

We might change the preferences of the first group for B over C in the example, but the basic result would be the same: no matter how voters rank those two alternatives, A always comes in *last*, rather than first as under majority rule. When the preferences of voters beyond their first-place rankings are considered, A is eliminated from serious consideration in this example.

Approval voting   The Borda count has been criticized as requiring of citizens too much character and information. Borda requires voters to rank all alternatives. If some do not, the outcome will depend on the way abstention is counted. Further, although Borda noted that 'my scheme is intended only for honest men',[20] the Borda count provides opportunities for voting strategically, misrepresenting one's preference ordering to change the outcome.[21]

An alternative that preserves some of the qualities of the Borda count is *approval voting*: each voter votes for as many of the candidates as he or she deems acceptable, and the candidate with the most votes wins.[22] Another way of thinking about approval voting is to imagine that each voter composes a list of candidates, ranked from best to worst. The voter then draws a line between the worst acceptable candidate and the best unacceptable candidate. Every candidate the voter approves of gets a vote, but those below the line get nothing.

Returning to the example in Figure 9.4, suppose that voters in the first group think that only A is acceptable. Imagine that voters in the middle and last groups consider both B and C acceptable. What will be the result under approval voting? Candidate A will receive eight votes, just as under plurality rule. Candidates B and C will each receive 13 votes, so that the specific outcome will depend on how ties are broken. The point is that A will not have a chance as long as A is judged not acceptable by a majority of voters, which is the spirit of Borda's example.[23]

Both the Borda count and approval voting must violate one of Arrow's axioms, but which one? The answer is independence of irrelevant alternatives (IIA). The social choice under either the Borda rule or approval voting may depend on the relative positions of two alternatives compared with other (irrelevant) alternatives. Violation of IIA is the basis of the manipulability of the Borda count. This may be more of a disadvantage in small-group settings than for mass elections, of course. In any case, IIA is almost always violated for choice rules that require scoring an entire list of alternatives rather than making a single best choice.

A simple example (adapted from Arrow [1951] 1963, p. 27) illustrates another property of the Borda count: it is not *independent of path*.[24] This is actually a separate problem from independence of irrelevant alternatives, since it involves the presence or absence of particular alternatives, not their relative rankings in the preference orderings of voters. The interesting thing about Arrow's example is that it reveals an access point for strategy: for the Borda count and related social choice rules, outcomes can be sensitive to the set of alternatives that appear on the ballot, even in a single-stage decision.

Imagine that there are three voters (A, B, and C) and four alternatives (x, y, z. and w). Further suppose that all voters use the Borda count and vote sincerely. Consider two different ballots, one with four alternatives and another with only three.

Ballot 1:   A comparison of x, z, *and* w *with* y *also considered*

Rank of alternative	Voter			Borda count
	A	B	C	
x	1	2	2	5
z	4	1	1	6
w	2	4	4	10
y	3	3	3	9

Clearly, x wins, because it has the lowest Borda count. Now, however, suppose that one alternative, y, is eliminated from the contest.

Ballot 2:   A comparison of x, z, *and* w *without* y

Rank of alternative	Voter			Borda count
	A	B	C	
x	1	2	2	5
z	3	1	1	5
w	2	3	3	8

The outcome is now different: x and z tie, although nothing about their *relative* ranking has changed. All that is different is the decision context: for vote 1, y was on the ballot, and for vote 2, y is not an option. Furthermore, if there is now a runoff between x and z, z actually wins. Dropping y from consideration consequently changes the outcome. This sensitivity to the inclusion or exclusion of other alternatives is different from the relative rankings of irrelevant alternatives, having more to do with how alternatives are retained, or dropped, in the early stages of elections or amendment procedures. That is the reason the 'path' is important in this example.

9.3   Proportional representation

A wide variety of collective decisions, particularly choices of political representatives in national assemblies for geographic districts, are made using 'proportional representation' (PR) rules. There are many such rules, but they share the characteristic that *each party's share of seats in the assembly is approximately that party's share of votes in the last election.* The ideal for a pure PR system, then, would be:

$$\frac{\text{Party's seats}}{\text{Total seats}} \approx \frac{\text{Party's votes}}{\text{Total votes}}.$$

In practice, this ideal is violated in many ways and for very practical reasons. One of the most common modifications made to pure PR systems is the *threshold*, or minimum vote required for a party to seat members in the assembly. For example, Greece requires that a party receive at least 15 percent of the votes. Israel, by contrast, has an 'exclusion threshold' of only 1.5 percent (Sartori 1997). Such rules have two effects. First, there is a departure from the ideal of pure proportionality, since a party can receive support up to the vote threshold, minus 1 vote, yet get no legislative representation. Second, people may therefore vote strategically, eschewing sincere votes for small parties that have no chance and concentrating on one of the larger parties.

Table 9.2   Plurality rule and proportional representation compared

Party	%vote received	Pluralities won	Seats (plurality)	Seats (PR)
Green	45	55	55	45
Red	30	45	45	30
Blue	25	0	0	25
Totals	100	100 elections	100 seats	100 seats

To compare a PR system with a plurality-rule system, consider Table 9.2.[25] In the table, we see a sharp difference between one-seat allocations under plurality rule and a pure PR rule for three parties. The implications of plurality and PR rules for the distribution of power in a 100-seat assembly, even given identical vote totals in both cases, are strikingly different.

Notice that the table does not give individual election results, but only nationwide totals. The number of pluralities won was chosen arbitrarily, but represents one possible outcome: the Green Party comes in first in 55 races, the Reds come in first 45 times, and Blues do not win any races outright. Under a plurality rule, these are exactly the proportions of seats the two parties hold: Greens 55 percent, Reds 45 percent, Blues 0 percent. (The Blue Party is presumably out in the street, organizing riots in support of electoral reform.)

Under a pure PR system, the Blue Party would get fully 25 percent of the seats, corresponding to its 25 percent of the votes cast in the election. There is no clear majority party, since the largest number of seats is held by the Greens, who have only 45 percent of the assembly under their control. The Greens will be obliged to form a coalition if they want to govern, or face the possibility that a Blue–Red coalition government (the Purple) will form and control 55 percent (the Red's 30 percent plus the Blue's 25 percent) of the seats, a working majority.

The process of coalition government formation is complex and quite beyond the scope of this chapter; the interested reader should consult Laver and Schofield (1990). The key point is simply that once a PR election has been held, it is by no means clear that a government has been selected; in fact, the process may have barely begun. Any two of the three parties in the example are capable of joining together and forming a government. On the other hand, no one party can govern. Consequently, the nature of the government is very much in doubt. Cycling over coalition partners simply moves the incoherence of democratic process from voter choice to bargaining among elites.

In some ways, the consideration of whether plurality or majority rule (sometimes called 'first past the post' elections) is better than PR mimics our earlier discussion concerning the optimal size of majorities. If a single decision among several mutually exclusive alternatives is required, then plurality rule, or majority rule with runoff, has clear advantages. The polity may simply need to decide something *right now*, so the costs of delay from deliberation and negotiation in a PR system may not be worth paying.

On the other hand, questions of far-reaching consequence for all citizens may require a representation of many points of view. In such decisions, representation may even be an end in itself, since not just the decision but the legitimacy of the decision is crucial to the survival of the society. For such decisions, voters may want to be sure they have a representative of their own choosing. PR systems are appealing in such circumstances because the deliberative process of the legislative assembly mimics, in proportions of perspectives, the population as a whole.

10 Strategic voting

It has been assumed up to this point that participants in political decision-making processes have reacted to each choice situation by casting votes that reflect their 'true', or sincere, preferences. More specifically, given a vote between alternatives A and B, voter i votes for the alternative he most prefers. Of course, this makes sense if the present vote is the last one and no further choices will be presented.

Such a stopping rule is rarely in force, however. More often, a vote is really a choice between a set of future votes, the sequence of which depends on the 'agenda' rule adopted by the organization. If political actors are sophisticated, they can recognize that a vote leads not to an outcome, but to another vote. Their preferences over outcomes can plausibly induce preferences over branches of an agenda 'tree'.

Recall the earlier apples–broccoli–carrots decision. If the first vote were between apples and carrots, then broccoli would be the collective choice (carrots beat apples, but lose to broccoli, in pairwise majority voting). If carrots and broccoli are the first comparison, then apples emerge as the favored food. The point is that there exists *some* agenda leading to *any* given outcome. Interestingly, this result is surprisingly general, as McKelvey (1976a, 1976b, 1986), Schofield (1978, 1984), and McKelvey and Schofield (1986) showed. This result can be stated in the form of a (very much simplified) theorem, which is more restrictive (but easier to understand) than the actual result.

Theorem 9.6 (chaos theorem)   Imagine a continuous policy space P. Let the number of dimensions in P be at least three, assume that decisions are by simple majority rule, and let there be at least three voters with proposal power. Let voting be sincere. If there is not at least one 'median in all directions', it is possible to construct an agenda, or sequence of comparisons of pairs of alternatives, that leads to any alternative in the space.

Intuitively, this theorem simply means that given a status quo $\mathbf{y}$ and any other alternative $\mathbf{z}$, there exists an agenda (sequence of pairwise votes) that leads from $\mathbf{y}$ to $\mathbf{z}$. Under some circumstances, in fact, this agenda has only one intermediate step, $\mathbf{w}$, so that a sophisticated agenda setter can go from $\mathbf{y}$ to $\mathbf{w}$ to $\mathbf{z}$, no matter what values of $\mathbf{y}$ and $\mathbf{z}$ are chosen. We can illustrate such a 'trajectory' in Figure 9.5. Beginning with $\mathbf{y}$, a majority (B and A) prefers $\mathbf{w}$. But then a majority (A and C) prefers $\mathbf{z}$ to $\mathbf{w}$. What the chaos theorem says is that for any $\mathbf{y}$ and $\mathbf{z}$ there exists a $\mathbf{w}$ (where neither $\mathbf{z}$ nor $\mathbf{w}$ are necessarily contained in the Pareto set) that allows the agenda setter to go from $\mathbf{y}$ to $\mathbf{z}$.

But hold on a minute. This result requires voters to be completely ignorant of politics! Let us go back to our apples–broccoli–carrots problem. It is true that if no one knows social choice and an agenda is constructed at random by our peckish deciders, the choice could be *any one* of the three foods. In a way, this is 'fair' because if the *agenda* is chosen at random, the implied

Issue 2

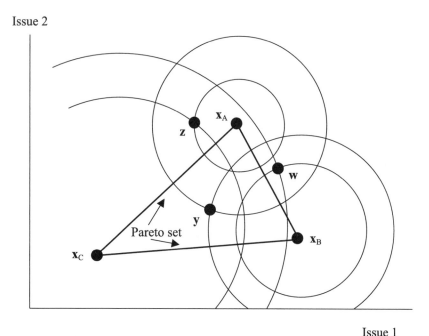

Issue 1

Figure 9.5   The existence of an agenda from **y** *to* **z**

outcome is (in effect) also randomly selected. If there is no median in all directions, a *naive choice over agendas* is tantamount to a *lottery over outcomes*.

If this kind of choice is routine, however, it seems unlikely that people could really fail to understand the underlying correspondence: choosing an agenda implies a choice of an outcome. As Riker (1980) pointed out, if people disagree about outcomes and understand politics, their disagreement will take the form of a disagreement over the agenda, or institutions of choice more generally.

More fundamentally, what can be said from an ethical perspective about the 'fairness' of the outcome if some people understand agendas, but others do not? The answer is disturbing: if only one person gets to pick the agenda and enforce a stopping rule, and if participants vote sincerely, there is no important difference between majority rule and dictatorship. Figure 9.6 contains the agendas selected by Mr 1, Ms 2, and Mr 3. In each case the outcome is the same as if that person were dictator and had sole decision-making power. There is one sinister difference between dictatorship and a 'monopoly agenda setter', however. Dictatorship is openly, and definitionally, undemo-

Panel (a): Mr 1 wants apples to win

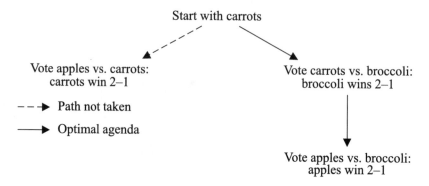

Panel (b): Ms 2 wants carrots to win

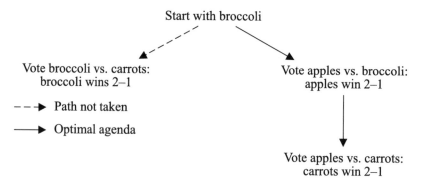

Panel (c): Mr 3 wants broccoli to win

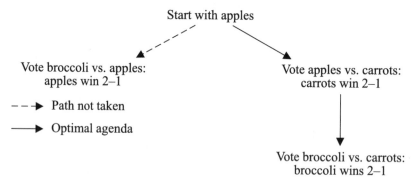

Figure 9.6   My agenda means my outcome

cratic. By contrast, people naively voting on alternatives whose order is decided by an agenda setter may be unaware that the choice of outcome is, in effect, dictatorial.

Each alternative in the agenda is 'considered', it is true, but the order of consideration dictates the outcome.[26] Getting to vote does not mean choice is democratic, although letting people go through the motions may imbue the choices of the agenda setter with an aura of legitimacy. To put it another way, there is nothing inherently 'fair' about a sequenced majority-rule decision. The trappings of democracy (people get to vote) may simply be the mechanism of manipulation.

There is some evidence that control of the agenda does confer just this sort of power on the 'setter'. Agenda control can be imbedded either in the rules of parliamentary procedure (see, for example, Denzau and Mackay 1983), or in proposals made by bureaucrats to elected officials (see, for example, Niskanen 1971; Romer and Rosenthal 1978b, 1979; Rosenthal 1990). On the other hand, there have been claims that elected officials would not allow the sort of rules that really give bureaucrats proposal power (Weingast and Moran 1983; McCubbins and Schwartz 1984; Shepsle and Weingast 1987a). More fundamentally, if 'institutions' give real power to an agenda setter there may be a contest over choice of institutions themselves (Riker 1980); cycles over outcomes could be transformed into cycles over institutions. Still, if there is a monopoly agenda setter, that person can act as something close to a dictator if other participants vote their true preferences.

But then hold on another minute: why assume that people vote their sincere preferences in the face of agenda manipulation? What if the other participants know the power of the agenda setter? What if they recognize that voting over alternatives in the first stage is really voting over future agendas? Cannot the *voters manipulate their votes*, in just the way the *setter can manipulate the alternatives*? The answer is obviously yes.

For that matter, why preclude strategic or sophisticated voting in any circumstance, not just when the agenda is set by someone else? Until we admit the possibility that voting might not be sincere, we *still* will not have captured the reality of collective decision making in committees. One of the first scholars to treat the difference between 'sincere' voting (that is, vote your true preferences) and 'sophisticated' voting (vote strategically, in effect choosing over agendas rather than outcomes) was Farquharson (1969). There is considerable theoretical work (for example, McKelvey and Niemi 1978; Denzau and Mackay 1981; Enelow 1981), and empirical evidence (Enelow and Koehler 1980; Denzau et al. 1985) that claims sophisticated voting may be part of real-world political processes.

How would sophisticated voting work in our simple example of collective food purchase? We shall suppose that Mr 1 is the setter, for simplicity, since the exposition is the same for each participant. Mr 1, of course, wants an outcome of apples, so he has the process begin with broccoli against carrots. Since he knows broccoli beats carrots, but loses to apples, this ensures the 'right' outcome if the other participants cooperate by voting sincerely.

But suppose that Mr 3 has read Farquharson (1969) and recognizes that a first-stage vote for broccoli over carrots is not the end of the process. Mr 3 mentally looks ahead on the agenda tree in Figure 9.6 and notes that a first-stage vote for *broccoli* is really just a vote for *apples*! Mr 3 detests apples. He decides to vote strategically for carrots. Ms 2 is happy to vote for carrots (her sincere preference is for carrots over broccoli, anyway). Consequently, carrots win the first round. Since Mr 1's agenda specifies that the first-round winner is then voted against apples, the result is that carrots win again, this time on (sincere) votes by both Ms 2 and Mr 3. The agenda and new outcome is shown in Figure 9.7.

The point of this example is that the power of the agenda setter to dictate the sequence of votes may not be enough to ensure the setter his or her most

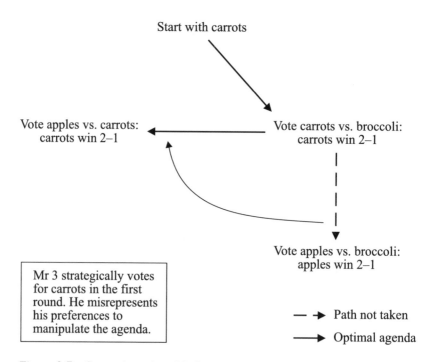

*Figure 9.7   Strategic voting: Mr 3 votes strategically, and Mr 1's agenda
leads to carrots, Mr 1's least-preferred outcome*

preferred outcome. If there are specific rules that force elected officials to accept a take-it-or-leave-it proposal, as the Romer and Rosenthal (1978b, 1979) work assumes, then the setter has broad power. If the other participants are not clever enough to recognize the need to choose sophisticated votes, then again the setter has his or her own way. But is it not a little silly to base a theory on the presumption that people systematically make mistakes? Successful politicians understand politics. They recognize chances to vote for a particular sequence of future votes instead of the apparently simple issue at hand.[27]

The example in this section has dealt with simple-majority rule. The logic of the example can be generalized to any voting procedure in an important theorem called the 'Gibbard–Satterthwaite theorem'. First, however, we shall give a definition of a technical term, 'strategy-proofness', adapted from Mueller (1989, p. 395).

Strategy-proofness Suppose that voter i is trying to decide how to vote. Let M_i be the 'message' i gives the voting procedure when he/she states his/her true and sincere preference (so M_i could be a vote, a list of votes, or whatever is required by the voting procedure to register a preference). Let M_i be any distortion or strategic misrepresentation in M_i, so that $M_i \ldots \text{M}_i$. Now consider two outcomes of the actual application of the voting procedure, whatever it is:

- x is the outcome when voter i states M_i, and all other voters state their true preferences;
- y is the outcome when voter i states M_i, and all other voters state their true preferences.

Then a voting procedure is strategy-proof, or immune to strategic voting, if and only if there is no achievable alternative y voter i prefers to x, regardless of the distorted message M_i that i chooses.

More simply, a voting procedure is strategy-proof if and only if the voter's best strategy is *always* to be sincere, regardless of what other voters do.

There is an important logical connection between voting procedures that are strategy-proof, and social choice rules that obey the IIA axiom.[28] Vickrey (1960), in his proof of Arrow's theorem, offered two conjectures. First, social choice rules satisfying IIA are also strategy-proof. Second, strategy-proofness implies satisfaction of IIA.[29] This conjecture was correct, as was shown by Gibbard (1973) and Satterthwaite (1975).[30] A simple summary of the theorem is:

Theorem 9.7 (Gibbard–Satterthwaite theorem)   No voting rule that can predictably choose one outcome from many alternatives is strategy-proof, unless it is dictatorial.

'Predictably' here means that the voting rule is not random, so that the voter can see some correspondence between the message or vote she reveals and the outcome. The Gibbard–Satterthwaite theorem is a classic social choice good news, bad news result. On the one hand, it means that all voting procedures (at least, all those that are not trivial or useless) are manipulable under many circumstances. Further, we cannot trust the particular votes or messages that voters deliver to represent their true preferences. This is bad news, because it means that voters often do not vote honestly, and the reasons have to do with the voting procedure itself, not the character of voters.

The good news is that 'manipulation' (that is, strategic voting) may be the mechanism that gives voters countervailing power over agenda setters. The apparent dictatorial power of those who manipulate the agenda is ameliorated by the ability of voters to manipulate their votes. Consequently, while the *means* of manipulation seems dishonest, strategic voting may actually ensure the 'right' *end*. As we saw in our apples–broccoli–carrots example, simple agenda manipulation did not determine the outcome.

11   Summary and conclusions

In this chapter, I have outlined some intuitions behind voting behavior, and behind alternative voting institutions. The essence of the problem is the genuine need of human societies to make collective decisions that are both *correct*, in the sense that the causal models on which they are based are true, and *legitimate*, in the sense that citizens accept the choice, even if they themselves did not support it. In public choice theory, behavior and institutions come together in an integrated model of the political process. Gary Cox (1987), in discussing alternative voting institutions, notes that

> another way to organize the findings herein is along a 'degree of centrism' axis. Holding down one end of this axis would be the Condorcet procedures, under which candidates have a dominant strategy to adopt the position of the median voter. Other procedures (such as Borda's method and approval voting) under which the unique convergent Nash equilibrium is the situation in which all candidates adopt the median position would come next, followed by systems (such as negative voting) under which there are multiple convergent equilibria. Finally, holding down the other end of the centrism axis would be procedures such as plurality rule, under which candidates will not converge at any point, instead spreading themselves out more or less evenly along the policy dimension. (p. 99)

Dictatorship, for most of us, is unacceptable as a way of organizing government. In the weighing of order versus liberty on the scales of choosing a 'good' society, dictatorship provides only order. But liberty without order may lead to chaos. The contribution of Arrow and the social choice theorists that have followed him has been to show that there is no perfect alternative to dictatorship. Ultimately, dictatorship may be with us always, for order *sans* liberty may be better than liberty *sans* order. The construction of institutions that can preserve order for the society and still protect liberty for the individual is at once the most challenging and useful research agenda in the social sciences.

Notes

1. This passage is from a work of fiction, published anonymously by Burke, as a very young man. It is by no means clear that Burke is arguing in his own voice here. Still, the argument is concisely and starkly stated, and therefore serves the purpose of exposition well.

2. If the registration decision is actually the key decision, analysis of turnout without accounting for differences in voter registration rates is misleading. Also see Kelley et al. (1967).

3. Downs (1957) and Riker and Ordeshook (1968) model indifference. Ordeshook (1969), Hinich and Ordeshook (1969, 1970), and Hinich et al. (1972) extend the Downsian model to account for alienation.

4. For a review of this literature, see Cox and Munger (1989).

5. Knack (1994) considers a variety of explanations for the effect of weather on turnout and outcomes.

6. We have also given short shrift to an important empirical perspective on the factors voters use in deciding among candidates: *retrospective* voting. According to this view (Key 1966; Fiorina 1989), voters evaluate the performance of the party or candidate now in office. If the incumbent has performed well (in the voters' judgment), he or she is returned to office. If the incumbent has botched things, voters vote for someone else, punishing poor performance after the fact. Retrospective voting is not completely contradictory to the classical spatial model, because there is an implicit comparison between the actual performance of incumbents and the expected performance of challengers. Still, the emphasis in the retrospective voting approach is clearly on the evaluation of the effectiveness of incumbents.

7. Also see Barzel and Silberberg (1973).

8. Hinich (1981) goes further, and conceives of voting as if it were an act of contribution. Contributions are usually thought of as monetary, but the time and effort required to vote can be thought of as a sacrifice by the voter for the sake of the candidate. Fiorina (1976) compares the 'expressive' and investment-oriented, or 'instrumental', motives for voting.

9. One noteworthy attempt in this regard is Crain et al. (1988b).

10. See Tullock (1967c), Tollison et al. (1975), and Silberman and Durden (1975). For a review, see Matsusaka and Palda (1993).

11. An interesting, and potentially important, new result is the 'swing voter's curse' (Feddersen and Pesendorfer 1996). They show that if other voters have private information (that is, not all information about the alternatives is common knowledge), voters may be strictly better off abstaining than voting for either candidate, even if the costs of voting are not taken into account. This result hinges on the set of conditions that must be true about the world if the voter turns out to cast the 'swing' vote, or the vote that determines the outcome. For some policy implications on using polls, rather than votes, to determine public policy, see Brehm (1993). A more ambitious approach to 'deliberative' decision making using polls is Fishkin (1991).

12. It is possible to question whether the 'individually transitive, collectively intransitive' contradiction is a genuine paradox. Buchanan (1954, 1975a), Tullock (1970), and Plott

(1972) argue that the 'paradox' simply results from an indefensible insistence on an organic conception of societies. For a review, see Mueller (1989, pp. 388–92).

13. Coase (1960) points out that markets may allow enfranchisement of the downwind citizens, assuming transaction costs and wealth effects are negligible, and that distributional equity can be ignored. Coase's argument is that such arrangements can be non-collective, yet solve public problems. But this observation actually proves our point: such a 'market' requires a well-developed set of institutions for defining, enforcing, and transferring property rights, as well as a currency or accepted medium of exchange for effecting the transfer. Obviously, some collective decision, if only to define rights and afford some means for enforcing them, has taken place if a market solution can work.

14. It is commonly argued that both such activities do affect others, of course. 'Immoral' sexual practices may offend others. If some people refuse to use helmets the result may be higher insurance rates for everyone. However, each of these arguments may also be a *post hoc* rationale. The point is that it is clearly possible, in principle, for the larger group to *determine* whether an action is private, quite separate from what the actors themselves believe.

15. The reader interested in pursuing public goods, externalities, and enfranchisement rules may find an extensive review in Mueller (1989).

16. There are many statements of Arrow's paradox. Ours is closest in spirit to that of Riker (1982, p. 18). An important general discussion, and some extensions, can be found in Sen (1970).

17. This statement is too strong. It is quite possible that societies are locked into conventions that nearly everyone knows are not Pareto optimal. The most common example given is the QWERTY keyboard, which (arguably) is not cost minimizing in the sense of offering combinations of letters in the most useful sequence for someone typing in English. The costs of changing, however, would include changing all keyboards and having everyone relearn how to type! Another example, given by Brian Arthur (1989), is the competition between steam engines and internal combustion engines. Steam engines might have won, but there was a shortage of distilled water at a crucial period in history. Consequently, people worked on internal combustion technology, which developed an insurmountable lead in costs of production. See Schelling (1960), Lewis (1969), North (1981, 1990), and Denzau and North (1994). The QWERTY story is debunked effectively by Liebowitz and Margolis (1990).

18. It is important to note that rules requiring approval by a fixed $K < N/2$ plurality apply only to access, and can allow but two alternatives: reject the proposal or pass the proposal along for further consideration. There is no inherent problem with access decisions if multiple alternatives 'pass', since all this means is that the alternatives (bills, court cases, and so on) then continue through the process for disposition. The subject of concern in this chapter is for making a single choice from a set of mutually exclusive alternatives. Consequently, we shall restrict our attention to $K > N/2$.

19. The KMT we present is greatly simplified, compared to the more rigorous treatments in Slutsky (1979). Slutsky's analysis has a different object, however, in that it compares mechanisms for achieving Pareto optimality in public goods provision with endogenous tax shares. The reader interested in the properties of different majorities required for decisiveness should also consult May (1952) and Sen (1970).

20. J. Mascart's *La Vie ... de Borda* (1919), quoted in Black ([1958] 1987, p. 182).

21. Strategic voting is generally beyond the scope of this chapter. See Cox (1997) on the importance and breadth of strategic action in politics.

22. For an in-depth treatment of approval voting, see Brams and Fishburn (1984) and Brams and Nagel (1991). For some interesting background on approval voting, see Cox (1984).

23. On the other hand, if each group considers only its first alternative to be acceptable, A will win, receiving eight votes compared to seven for B and six for C. Consequently, one might expect the middle and last groups to vote strategically by including B and C in the acceptable category. This would ensure at worst a second-place result for voters in those groups.

24. On 'independence of path', see Plott (1973), Parks (1976), and Ferejohn and Grether

(1977); on 'multi-stage choice processes', see Schwartz (1986). For quite a different interpretation of the problem of social choice in general, see Nitzan and Paroush (1985).

25. For a variety of comparisons between PR and presidential systems, see Grofman and Lijphart (1992).

26. An important related result is the Romer and Rosenthal (1978b, 1979) 'setter' model, where the setter gets to choose a reversion level and then make a take-it-or-leave-it proposal.

27. One difficulty with this claim, of course, is that politicians may have to explain their vote on a specific issue, and it may prove difficult to explain that the vote was strategic. On the other hand, however, legislators who have won the trust of constituents may not need to make such explanations very often. For more on 'trust', see Bianco (1994). Denzau and Munger (1986) describe the importance of different constituencies and levels of information in determining how voters' interests are represented.

28. For a more general discussion of the topics in this section, see Mueller (1989).

29. In fact, the result can be *derived* directly from Arrow's 'impossibility' theorem and its proof, as was shown by Blin and Satterthwaite (1978) and Schmeidler and Sonnenschein (1978). For a useful and intuitive review of the technical basis of manipulability, see Kelly (1988, pp. 101–18). On the other hand, there are important differences between Arrow's result and the Gibbard–Satterthwaite impossibility conclusions (see, for example, Border 1984).

30. In his review of this literature, Schwartz (1986) points out that the Gibbard–Satterthwaite theorem applies to 'resolute' voting rules, or rules that choose a single outcome from the choice set. Schwartz (1982) extends the theorem to (as he might say) 'irresolute' collective choice processes.

10 On legislatures and legislative efficiency wages

Robert E. McCormick and Chad S. Turner

1 Introduction

The legislatures of the states in the United States are an interesting study in political economy. They are as varied as the people, land, and property they represent. Governed by constitutions written and rewritten, some so often as hardly to be called constitutions, their functions are similar, but their operations are not. In this chapter we summarize some of the salient facts about state legislatures and offer some new evidence on the determinants of legislator pay. We are motivated primarily by an interest in the diverse sizes, structures, and operating rules of the legislative bodies across the land.

It was little more than a quarter century or so ago that economists began to colonize the study of legislatures in an empirically meaningful way, an area previously left mostly to the political scientists. Tollison, Crain, and others blazed this trail by pointing to the wealth of data available about the structures and outputs of state legislatures.[1] Research topics since that time have included the role of legislative committees, their chairs, the impact of political parties, or lack thereof, and the causes and consequences of constitutional constraints determining such matters as the disparity of a legislature's chamber sizes and the length and regularity of its sessions.[2] As is often the case after a gold rush, most of the ore has been extracted from the mine, but improved technology allows us to recover a few remaining nuggets. Some questions will probably remain forever unanswered. Why, for instance, does Nebraska, alone among the 50 states, have a unicameral legislature? With that caveat in mind, this chapter provides some background information on state legislatures, much of which is admittedly not unique or new here.

We then consider the relation between state economic performance and the compensation of legislators. Using data on changes in state income per capita from 1970 to 1996, we find that higher legislative pay begets greater economic growth. A similar link is found for the salary of the state's chief executive. These findings, which suggest that states offering more liberal compensation packages to their elected officials tend to be better off economically, are consistent with an efficiency-wage theory of politics (Barro 1973; Becker and Stigler 1974). Rewarding politicians for 'good' behavior *ex ante*, rather than punishing them for malfeasance *ex post*, seems to help align their interests more closely with those of the polity at large. A carrot seems better than a stick.

2   Some basic facts

Each of the 50 states has a legislature prescribed by the state constitution but influenced by the constitution of the United States and its interpretation by the federal judiciary. For instance, rulings of the US Supreme Court require, at least since the 1960s, what amounts to equal representation ('one man, one vote') in each state legislature.[3]

All states, save Nebraska, have bicameral legislatures. Table 10.1 lists the states and the sizes of their representative bodies. (These data are plotted in Figure 10.1.) Some legislatures meet once every two years; others meet every year. Almost all have time limits on their regular sessions, but almost all can and do meet in special sessions.[4] Notice the vast differences in legislature size, even in neighboring states. New Hampshire has the largest state legislature (424 seats); that of its neighbor Vermont is considerably smaller (180 seats).[5]

Owing to the large differences in the sizes of state legislatures across states, the closeness of the relation between representative and voter varies a great deal. In populous states, such as California, each member of the legislature represents more than a quarter of a million people, obviously not on a first-name basis. In smaller states, such as Vermont, Wyoming, or North Dakota, representation is far more personal – on the order of 3000 to 5000 people per representative. Assuming that about half of the population turns out to vote on a typical election day, this means that in a state like New Hampshire, a state representative might only have to know the names of about 1350 voters to know them all. In neighboring New York, where a member of the legislature represents more than 43 000 voters, this is obviously far less likely. While it is certainly true that television, e-mail, and fax machines bring representatives and voters closer in large and small states alike, the handshake is still far more likely to occur in states that are less populous, have larger legislatures, or both.

This diversity raises a number of questions about the similarities, if any, between legislatures and classical capitalist firms. The orthodox literature of industrial organization asks, for example, whether small firms use the same production and sales techniques as larger organizations. Do they employ the same mix of labor and capital? Do the careers of the managers of differently sized firms follow similar paths? Are the age and gender profiles of management the same across large and small firms? If so, that is, if ordinary firms have characteristics that vary with sheer size, can we find similar patterns in legislative firms?[6]

State legislatures also differ markedly in the disparities of their chamber sizes, as is apparent from Table 10.1's listing of the ratios of lower to upper

Table 10.1   *State legislatures, 1996–97*

	Senate	House	Total	Ratio	State population	Persons per representative
Alabama	35	105	140	3.00	4 273 000	30 521
Alaska	20	40	60	2.00	607 000	10 117
Arizona	30	60	90	2.00	4 428 000	49 200
Arkansas	35	100	135	2.86	2 510 000	18 593
California	40	80	120	2.00	31 878 000	265 650
Colorado	35	65	100	1.86	3 823 000	38 230
Connecticut	36	151	187	4.19	3 274 000	17 508
Delaware	21	41	62	1.95	725 000	11 694
Florida	40	120	160	3.00	14 400 000	90 000
Georgia	56	180	236	3.21	7 353 000	31 157
Hawaii	25	51	76	2.04	1 184 000	15 579
Idaho	35	70	105	2.00	1 189 000	11 324
Illinois	59	118	177	2.00	11 847 000	66 932
Indiana	50	100	150	2.00	5 841 000	38 940
Iowa	50	100	150	2.00	2 852 000	19 013
Kansas	40	125	165	3.13	2 572 000	15 588
Kentucky	38	100	138	2.63	3 884 000	28 145
Louisiana	39	105	144	2.69	4 351 000	30 215
Maine	35	151	186	4.31	1 243 000	6 683
Maryland	47	141	188	3.00	5 072 000	26 979
Massachusetts	40	160	200	4.00	6 092 000	30 460
Michigan	38	110	148	2.89	9 594 000	64 824
Minnesota	67	134	201	2.00	4 658 000	23 174
Mississippi	52	122	174	2.35	2 716 000	15 609
Missouri	34	163	197	4.79	5 359 000	27 203
Montana	50	100	150	2.00	879 000	5 860
Nebraska	49	unicameral	49		1 652 000	33 714
Nevada	21	42	63	2.00	1 603 000	25 444
New Hampshire	24	400	424	16.67	1 162 000	2 741
New Jersey	40	80	120	2.00	7 988 000	66 567
New Mexico	42	70	112	1.67	1 713 000	15 295
New York	61	150	211	2.46	18 185 000	86 185
North Carolina	50	120	170	2.40	7 323 000	43 076
North Dakota	49	98	147	2.00	644 000	4 381
Ohio	33	99	132	3.00	11 173 000	84 644
Oklahoma	48	101	149	2.10	3 301 000	22 154
Oregon	30	60	90	2.00	3 204 000	35 600
Pennsylvania	50	203	253	4.06	12 056 000	47 652
Rhode Island	50	100	150	2.00	990 000	6 600
South Carolina	46	124	170	2.70	3 699 000	21 759
South Dakota	35	70	105	2.00	732 000	6 971
Tennessee	33	99	132	3.00	5 320 000	40 303
Texas	31	150	181	4.84	19 128 000	105 680
Utah	29	75	104	2.59	2 000 000	19 231
Vermont	30	150	180	5.00	589 000	3 272
Virginia	40	100	140	2.50	6 675 000	47 679
Washington	49	98	147	2.00	5 533 000	37 639
West Virginia	34	100	134	2.94	1 826 000	13 627
Wisconsin	33	99	132	3.00	5 160 000	39 091
Wyoming	30	60	90	2.00	481 000	5 344

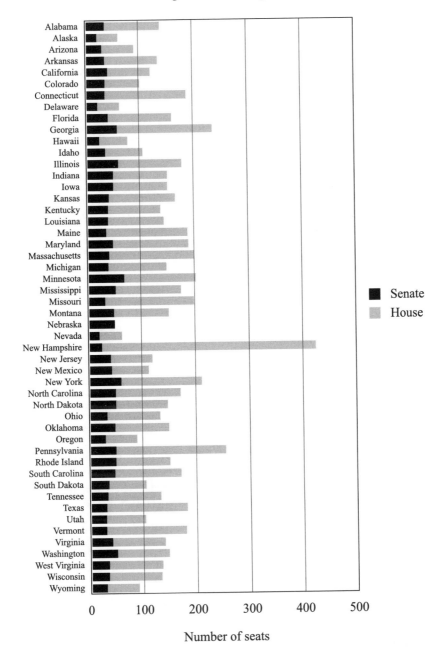

Figure 10.1. Sizes of state legislatures

house memberships. New Hampshire again stands out, with nearly 17 state representatives for every state senator. In Colorado, by contrast, this ratio is less than two.

The structure of a state's legislature impacts its performance (McCormick and Tollison 1981, pp. 33–4). Total size, by itself, has an ambiguous effect in this regard. On the one hand, by reducing the average number of constituents per member, larger legislatures tend to lower voters' costs of monitoring their elected representatives. On the other hand, because each member of a large legislature can be expected to have less influence on the legislative process, such monitoring will pay fewer benefits. By diluting the value of each legislator's vote, large legislatures also lower the price at which interest groups can buy influence. The effect of legislature size on the price of influence is offset to some extent by the logic of collective action (Olson 1965), which suggests that it will be more difficult in large legislatures for a majority of the members to reach the agreement necessary to enact legislation. Votes are cheaper in large legislatures, but to assemble a majority coalition more of them must be bought.[7]

While the impact of legislature size on legislative outcomes is uncertain, increases in the disparity of chamber sizes unambiguously raise the total cost of enacting legislation (McCormick and Tollison 1981, pp. 44–5). This is because a majority in both houses is required to secure the passage of a bill. If chamber sizes are unequal and the legislature's cost of making collective decisions increases at an increasing rate, a lobbyist's cost of buying an additional vote in the larger chamber will exceed the savings from buying one less vote in the smaller chamber. It follows that the total cost of securing a bill's passage will be greater the more unequal are the sizes of a bicameral legislature's chambers.

Examined through the lens of the interest-group theory of government, in short, the structure of the legislature 'matters'. Its total size and degree of bicameralism affect the cost of legislating and, hence, the expectations of success by the groups that seek to influence the legislative process.

2.1   Lengths of legislative sessions

Table 10.2 reports the length of the regular legislative session, by state, for 1995. Some legislatures did not meet that year because their legislative sessions are scheduled only once every two years.

To explore the determinants of the time spent legislating, we regressed the length of a state's regular legislative session during the 1994–95 biennium on state population and state personal income per capita.[8] The results, not shown in detail here, suggest little in the way of a systematic relation between session length and the population of a state (the estimated coefficient is positive but not different from zero at standard levels of statistical significance). The business

Table 10.2   Regular legislative sessions, 1995

Alabama	30L*
Alaska	121C
Arizona	95C
Arkansas	89C
California	39L*
Colorado	120C
Connecticut	155C
Delaware	49L
Florida	60C
Georgia	40L
Hawaii	60L
Idaho	68C
Illinois	61L
Indiana	61L
Iowa	116C
Kansas	89C
Kentucky	60L*
Louisiana	52L*
Maine	70L
Maryland	90C
Massachusetts	100L
Michigan	352C
Minnesota	61L*
Mississippi	90C
Missouri	129C
Montana	86L
Nebraska	90L
Nevada	169C
New Hampshire	23L
New Jersey	105L
New Mexico	60C
New York	152L*
North Carolina	S109L, H108L
North Dakota	67L
Ohio	S188L, H89L*
Oklahoma	65L
Oregon	153C
Pennsylvania	66C*
Rhode Island	77L
South Carolina	40L*
South Dakota	40L
Tennessee	48L
Texas	140C
Utah	45C
Vermont	63L
Virginia	46C
Washington	105C
West Virginia	60C
Wisconsin	365C*
Wyoming	37L

Note: L = work days; C = calendar days; S = Senate; H = House; * refers to the previous term, not 1995. Some states did not hold legislative sessions in 1995.

of government, using this metric, does not seem to be affected by the size of the governed body, perhaps indicating that, in more populous states, more of the legislature's work is delegated to legislative staff members. On the other hand, there is some weak evidence that legislative sessions are longer in richer states: the estimated coefficient on state personal income per capita is significant at the 10 percent level, and the coefficient is positive. The R^2 is very low, though. Be that as it may, the coefficient produced by a regression of session length on income alone is statistically significant at the 6 percent level, and its algebraic sign remains positive. We have also estimated this simple regression in logs and the results are nearly the same. The elasticity is about one. A 10 percent increase in income is associated with a 10 percent increase in legislative calendar days, but the coefficient of determination is once again small. Less than 10 percent of the overall variation in session lengths is explained by differences in income across states.

It appears that the lengths of regular legislative sessions have more to do with the idiosyncrasies of individual states than with the demands of conducting the routine business of government, at least as measured by the size of the polity and the amount of income available for redistribution. The determinants of the time spent legislating certainly merit additional study. One is tempted to speculate that larger, more populous and richer states have larger bureaucracies and legislative staffs, but that guess is not yet confirmed, at least not here.

There are nevertheless two reasons for not being too surprised by the empirical results. First, one might find the same thing in the private sector. The boards of directors of large corporations may not meet for longer periods of time than the boards of smaller companies with less income or value. Second, however long the regular legislative session may be, in order to help enforce logrolling bargains, most of the formal (voting) business of legislatures takes place at the end of the session (Crain et al. 1986). The results do suggest, however, that much of the work of government is done outside of regularly scheduled legislative sessions.

2.2   Legislator compensation

The methods of compensating legislators vary widely across the states. Some lawmakers are paid biennially, some annually, some by the day. The perquisites of legislative office vary as well. Some legislators have expense accounts, and these also exhibit considerable diversity. Cross-state comparisons are thus rendered somewhat cumbersome, but despite these complications Table 10.3 reports legislative salaries for the states as provided for in the law. Given special sessions, per-diem travel and meal allowances, and other salary supplements, these are not necessarily the exact amounts legislators actually receive in any given year.

Table 10.3   Compensation of legislators

	Legislative salaries ($)	
	1996–97	1994–95
Alabama	10/C salary plus 2280 monthly living expenses	
Alaska	24 012	24 012
Arizona	15 000	15 000
Arkansas	12 500	12 500
California	72 000	52 500
Colorado	17 500	17 500
Connecticut	16 760	16 760
Delaware	26 000	24 900
Florida	23 244	22 560
Georgia	10 854	10 641
Hawaii	32 000	32 000
Idaho	12 360	12 000
Illinois	42 265	38 420
Indiana	11 600	11 600
Iowa	18 800	18 100
Kansas	63/C salary plus 80 per diem living expenses	
Kentucky	103/C salary plus 88 per diem living expenses	
Louisiana	16 800	16 800
Maine	9 975 9975 (1995), 7500 (1996)	7 125 9975 (1995), 7125 (1994)
Maryland	28 840	28 000
Massachusetts	46 410	30 000
Michigan	49 155	47 723
Minnesota	29 675	27 979
Mississippi	10 000	10 000
Missouri	24 313	22 863
Montana	58/L salary plus 70 per diem living expenses	
Nebraska	12 000	12 000
Nevada	130 per diem salary plus federal per diem vote for capitol area	
New Hampshire	200	100
New Jersey	35 000	35 000
New Mexico	163 per diem living expenses	
New York	57 500	57 500
North Carolina	13 951	13 026
North Dakota	2 160	2 160
Ohio	42 427	42 427
Oklahoma	32 000	32 000
Oregon		13 104
Pennsylvania	47 000	47 000
Rhode Island		10 250
South Carolina	10 400	10 400
South Dakota	4 267 4267 (odd year), 3733 (even year)	4 267 4267 (odd year) 3733 (even year)
Tennessee	16 500	16 500
Texas	7 200	7 200
Utah	Annualized salary will be 7680–8160 depending on weeks in session in 1995	
Vermont	7 920	7 680 7680 (1993), 8160 (1994)
Virginia	18 000 (S), 17 640 (H)	18 000 (S), 17 640 (H)
Washington	25 900	25 900
West Virginia	15 000	6 500
Wisconsin	38 056	35 070
Wyoming	125/C salary plus 80 per diem living expenses	

Table 10.4   Summary statistics, legislator salaries, recent years ($)

Year	N	Mean	Standard deviation	Minimum	Maximum
1992	31	22 850.87	12 494.38	7125.00	52 500.00
1994	31	23 497.52	12 642.08	7125.00	52 500.00
1996	30	25 647.07	15 248.75	7200.00	72 000.00

Legislative salaries are the lowest in Maine and the highest in California. The average over all states is about $25 500. (See Table 10.4 for summary statistics on the most recent data.)

A variety of processes exist for setting the compensation of state legislators. Table 10.5 lists the current methods. One of the mysteries not yet solved by public choice and political science is how these methods are chosen and why they vary so much. It is also true, of course, that the process by which private companies set the salaries of their senior executives is not completely understood either. Some firms have compensation committees, others delegate this responsibility to specific individuals, and others rely on rules-of-thumb. In this light, legislative wage setting is not as far removed from private wage setting as it might first seem.

2.3   Legislator salaries over time

Table 10.6 reports, on a biennial basis, the average wages of legislators across the states from 1962 through 1996. State legislator salaries have grown at an average annual rate of about 1.9 percent over this period. Figure 10.2 plots these changes. Over a comparable period, 1975–98, the growth of wages in executive, administrative, and managerial occupations has averaged 0.001 percent per year.[9] The differences between these two wage series, in somewhat similar lines of occupation, are not statistically different.[10] In real terms, legislator salaries have grown at about the same rate as executive wages for the past 25 years.

2.4   Legislative and gubernatorial salaries

Legislative salaries are quite a bit lower than gubernatorial salaries on a per-person basis. Over the period 1956 through 1996, the average legislator's salary was $25 773 (in constant 1996 dollar terms) and the average governor's salary was $111 751. However, the cross-time and cross-state correlation between these real wages is very high, 0.42. (See Figure 10.3.)

To explore the factors that might explain the relative compensation of the executive and legislative branches of government, we regressed the ratio of governor's salary to legislator's salary on state personal income per capita

Table 10.5 Determination of legislator salaries

	1996–97 Set in Constitution?	Legislatively determined?	Set by commission?		Related to state employee compensation?
Alabama	1	0	1		Tied to sate employees' salary schedule for non-salaried employees
Alaska	0	1	1	Alaska commission makes recommendations but does not have the force of law	
Arizona	0	0	0	Arizona commission recommendations are put on ballot for a vote of the people	
Arkansas	0	1	0		
California	0	1	0		
Colorado	0	0	1		
Connecticut	0	0	1		
Delaware	0	1	1	Delaware legislature must reject recommendations within 30 days by joint resolution or pay recommendation becomes effective	
Florida	0	1	0		Tied to average percentage increase of state career service employees for the fiscal year just ended
Georgia	0	1	0		Automatic cost-of-living increases equal to ½ of percentage approved for state employees
Hawaii	0	0	1	Hawaii commission recommendations effective unless legislature or governor disapproves by official action	
Idaho	0	1	1	Idaho commission recommendations effective unless rejected by the legislature prior to 25th day	
Illinois	0	0	1	Commission's recommendations take effect unless rejected by a resolution of both the House and Senate	

Table 10.5 continued

	1996–97 Set in Constitution?	Legislatively determined?	Set by commission?	Related to state employee compensation?
Indiana	0	1	0	
Iowa	0	0	1	
Kansas	0	1	0	Legislators receive margin of increase given to all state employees
Kentucky	0	1	1	Commission must make a continual study of all matters relating to compensation and must report on or before December 1 of the year preceding regular session
Louisiana	0	1	0	
Maine	0	0	0	The Statutory Compensation Commission was repealed in 1993. Currently there is no statutory provision for changing legislators' salaries
Maryland	0	0	1	Maryland commission meets before each four-year term of office and presents recommendations to General Assembly for its action
Massachusetts	0	1	1	
Michigan	0	0	1	Michigan commission recommendations take effect unless rejected by two-thirds vote in each House
Minnesota	0	1	0	Compensation council makes recommendations by April 1 of odd-numbered years. These are subject to modification or rejection by a bill enacted into law
Mississippi	0	1	0	

State			Comments
Missouri	0	1	Legislators receive all cost-of-living increases given to state employees
Montana	0	1	Tied to state employee pay schedule
Nebraska	1	1	
Nevada	0	0	Legislature considers recommendations and may take any action deemed appropriate, except for increasing compensation for members during their present term in office
New Hampshire	1	0	
New Jersey	0	1	
New Mexico	0	0	A proposed citizens' legislative compensation commission was defeated in 1992
New York	1	0	
North Carolina	1	0	Amount of increase equal to the average increase received by state employees
North Dakota	1	1	
Ohio	1	0	
Oklahoma	1	1	Any change in compensation becomes effective on the 15th day following the succeeding general election
Oregon	0	0	
Pennsylvania	1	0	
Rhode Island	0	1	
South Carolina	0	0	
South Dakota	0	0	
Tennessee	0	0	
Texas	1	1	
Utah	0	1	
Vermont	0	0	
Virginia	1	0	
Washington	0	1	
West Virginia	0	1	Approved by Joint Committee on Employment Relations
Wisconsin	1	0	Tied to pay plan of classified non-represented employees
Wyoming	0	0	

Table 10.6   Average state legislator salaries over time*

Year	Average ($)	Standard deviation ($)	Maximum ($)	Minimum ($)	Annual growth rate (%)
1962	15 419	10 642	36 854	2 750	
1964	16 607	11 442	41 886	2 685	3.85
1966	18 719	13 991	51 479	2 574	6.36
1968	20 943	18 643	77 253	362	5.94
1970	27 833	19 736	69 139	324	16.45
1972	29 639	19 151	76 893	300	3.24
1974	29 906	16 358	66 419	4 151	0.45
1976	29 156	15 940	62 506	3 551	−1.26
1978	28 481	14 607	60 438	7 798	−1.16
1980	25 775	13 691	52 459	8 622	−4.75
1982	25 061	12 990	54 280	7 354	−1.39
1984	26 905	16 811	77 378	6 771	3.68
1986	29 819	16 231	71 617	7 345	5.41
1988	29 665	14 343	56 593	6 811	−0.26
1990	28 365	14 342	60 582	8 701	−2.19
1992	27 220	14 883	62 538	8 487	−2.02
1994	26 500	14 257	59 208	8 035	−1.32
1996	27 268	16 213	76 552	7 655	1.45
				Average	1.91

Note: *All figures are 1996 dollars.

and state population. Using data from 1964 through 1996 and converting nominal salaries to real 1996 dollars using the consumer price index, we find that the gubernatorial–legislator salary ratio is significantly lower in states with larger populations and higher per-capita incomes. That is, when a state's per-capita income is high, its population is large, or both, the compensation of legislators tends to be closer to that of the governor. When legislators represent people that are more numerous and richer they receive wages that are similar to those of the state's chief executive.

3   Legislative efficiency wages

Some time ago McCormick and Tollison (1978) reported what now seems obvious, namely that, because constitutional change is everywhere more costly than legislative change, state legislators tend to be paid more where they set their own salaries than where their salaries are set by the state's

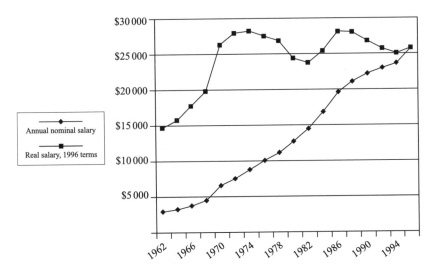

Figure 10.2   Average salaries of state legislators

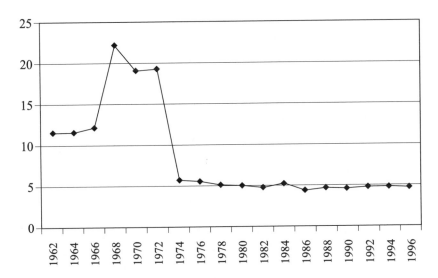

Figure 10.3   Ratio of governors' to legislators' salaries

constitution.[11] Left begging was the question of the overall impact of this finding on economic activity in a state.

It is easy to construct arguments on both sides of the fence here. On the one hand politicians, like ordinary human beings, are utility maximizers. The myth of politician-as-Jekyll-and-Hyde has long been buried. So, given the chance, they will line their own pockets. Hence, where salaries are set legislatively rather than through more cumbersome and costly procedures for amending the constitution, which normally require ratification by voters, legislator pay will be higher, *ceteris paribus*. In this world, pay does little to motivate or otherwise affect performance. It goes to one and all, regardless of their attendance records, their policy positions, or their influence on the legislative process. Legislative pay, in other words, is a zero-sum game. Whatever legislators get, taxpayers lose. If politicians vote to increase their own pay, some programs may suffer or some taxes may be higher, but little else will be different. This view is consistent with the public outcries that visit almost any discussion of political compensation as if it were nearly all stealing.

The hypothesis that legislative salary determination leads to higher legislator pay is broadly consistent with the facts. In 1972 the salary of Delaware's legislators was set by the state's constitution at $6000 per annum. By late 1975 Delaware had converted to statutory salary determination, and the yearly compensation of the state's legislators had risen to $9000 (McCormick and Tollison 1981, p. 77).

By contrast, neoclassical economic theory teaches that wages equal the value of labor's marginal product. Taxpayers get what they pay for from this point of view. Low legislator pay implies little legislative output or output of low quality.[12] High pay attracts more highly qualified people to legislative office, stimulates more legislative output and perhaps even produces better legislative decisions. The theory of labor supply is the foundation of this arm of the argument. The important question then becomes, do constraints on the competitiveness of political markets preclude the classical competitive outcome?

A third possibility emerges from the work of Barro (1973) and Becker and Stigler (1974). They observe that one way to control the behavior of individuals in positions of trust, such as legislators, is to pay them more than would otherwise be justified on marginal productivity grounds. High pay substitutes for direct voter monitoring of legislator performance. It does so by imposing 'a cost of dismissal equal to the present value of the difference between the future earnings stream' in legislative office and the legislator's next best employment opportunity (Becker and Stigler 1974, p. 6). The prospect of losing the pay premium disciplines behavior – promotes trustworthiness – by creating a penalty for malfeasance. As long as that penalty is large enough to offset the gains from corruption, rational legislators will avoid abusing the public's trust, at least up to the limits of detection. Or, put somewhat differently, Becker and Stigler (p. 12) argue that 'trust calls for a salary premium not necessarily because better quality persons are thereby attracted, but because higher salaries impose a cost on violations of trust'.

If political corruption (bribe taking, attentiveness to the demands of special-interest groups at the public's expense, and so on) reduces the incentives for private wealth creation, then one implication of this theory of efficiency wages is that rates of economic growth should be higher in states where politicians are paid more. Are there any discernible differences in the economic features of states that are linked to the wages of their governors and state legislators?

We tackled this problem empirically by alternately regressing the changes in state per-capita personal income and state population over the period from 1970 to 1996 on the salaries of the state's governor and legislators. The results suggest that there is a positive and significant relation between changes in income and population and both legislator and gubernatorial salaries. States that pay their governors more have higher growth rates of income and population. The same is true for legislators, but with lower statistical confidence.[13]

To explore this issue further we regressed an index of state economic freedom developed by Byars et al. (1999) on gubernatorial and legislative salaries as well as on their ratio.[14] We find that there is more economic freedom where the ratio of governor salary to legislator salary is higher, and where legislator salary is higher. This seems to suggest that states with higher salaries are better off, at least as measured by the freedom index.

4   Conclusions

Legislatures affect our lives in too many ways to count. Our approach to exploring the determinants of legislator compensation suggests that some rational forces are at work, but considerable research remains to be done. Why, for instance, are legislators paid so little in comparison to their private-sector counterparts? Dividing 1996 state personal income by the number of seats in the legislature reveals that the average state legislator has an impact on over $2 billion, an amount comparable to that for which the chief executive of a medium-sized corporation is responsible. Why are legislators not paid in some fashion based on performance outcomes? In the private sector, raises, bonuses, and stock options are used to motivate efficient resource use and to help align management's incentives with those of the firm's owners. In legislatures, politicians are motivated only by the goal of continued employment (re-election). Are bonuses and the like too hard to structure?[15]

These and other important questions about the structure of legislatures and the compensation of legislators merit further study not only in the laboratory of the US states, which has been the myopic focus here, but in the international arena as well. An efficiency-wage theory of legislative pay, pointing to the conclusion that rates of economic growth are higher where politicians are paid more, may play a role in explaining why some nations are rich and others are poor.

Notes

1. See, for instance, the work of Stigler (1976b), McCormick and Tollison (1978) and Crain (1979), where the sizes of, payments to, and outputs of legislatures are analysed.

2. Important contributions to the literature on the industrial organization of legislatures include Crain (1977), Shepsle (1978), Crain and Tollison (1980), Leibowitz and Tollison (1980), and Weingast and Marshall (1988). For additional theory and applications, see McCormick and Tollison (1981) and Crain and Tollison (1990).

3. The key precedents are *Baker* v. *Carr*, 369 US 186 (1962), *Gray* v. *Sanders*, 372 US 368 (1963), and *Reynolds* v. *Sims*, 377 US 533 (1964). In these and a series of related cases, the Supreme Court ruled that, in order to comply with the equal protection clause of the Fourteenth Amendment, states must apportion their legislative seats on an equal population basis. Among other things, these rulings, which applied to both houses of US state legislatures, meant that the legislative branches of state governments could no longer model themselves on the US Congress, where population is the basis of representation only in the lower house. While state legislatures have more flexibility in meeting the Court's 'one man, one vote' mandate than does the US House of Representatives, where between-district population deviations amounting to less than seven-tenths of one percent of the average district population have been declared unconstitutional (*Karcher* v. *Daggett*, 462 US 725 (1983)), the upshot is that regional interests unrelated to population get less representation in state legislatures than they do in the federal legislature.

4. The diversity of state legislatures along these and other dimensions defies convenient summary. A data appendix listing legislative session limits and many other characteristics of the state legislatures over the past 35 years is available from the authors. These data are also available online in spreadsheet format at http://sixmile.clemson.edu/researchtopics.htm. Virtually all of the information reported herein is taken from the *Book of the States*, published biannually by the Council of State Governments.

5. There are also pronounced differences in tax policy between these two neighboring and seemingly similar states. See Byars et al. (1999) for details on these differences and others across all of the states.

6. McCormick and Tollison (1981, ch. 5) have made some preliminary inquiries in this direction. For instance, the New Hampshire legislature, which is very large, has an unusually large number of female representatives, and interestingly, very few lawyers. But the provocative questions about tenure, campaign finance, legislative output, its scope, and the like remain unanswered at this point.

7. The model summarized herein also yields a testable implication about campaign finance. In particular, because each seat in a large legislature is less valuable, other things being the same, fewer resources will tend to be invested in campaigning for legislative office in states with large legislatures than in those with small ones.

8. Some states report legislative sessions in calendar days (C) met and some in legislative days (L). We converted legislative days to calendar days by assuming that there were five work days per calendar week, that is, $1L = 1.4C$.

9. The data on executive wages were obtained from http://www.economagic.com/em-cgi/data.exe/blsec/ecu21112i.

10. The average difference is N0.001 with a t-ratio of N0.18.

11. The salary demands of politicians are constrained by the fact that they must stand for re-election prior to receiving a raise. This creates a game of sorts that has been called the 'wish fairy' problem. You can ask for as much as you like, but the more you ask for, the less likely you are to get it. See McCormick and Tollison (1978) for more details.

12. Of course, there is more than a little disagreement in the literature about just what it is that legislatures produce. On the one hand, if one subscribes to the public-interest theory of government, then less output is bad. There is more inefficient or inappropriate provision of public goods. But if one believes that government's chief function is to redistribute income, then less government and more inefficient government is good, and low pay is a reflection of the polity's demand for little redistribution. This debate is not resolved here.

13. There is, of course, the issue of the total compensation of voters' legislative agents, which

may include *sub rosa* payments. If there are illegal payoffs to legislating, the Becker–Stigler approach implies that such payoffs will be larger where legislator pay is lower. Bribery and political corruption are therefore inversely related to the legal compensation of legislators. The problems of obtaining information on illegal payments mean that this proposition must be tested indirectly. See Chapter 5 of McCormick and Tollison (1981).

14. The full study can be accessed at http://freedom.clemson.edu.
15. Michael Jensen and his colleagues dispute the conventional wisdom that incentive compensation is an important motivating tool in the private sector. See Baker et al. (1988) and Jensen and Murphy (1990a, b). Perhaps the compensation of legislators differs less from managerial compensation than one might think.

11 Bureaucracy

William A. Niskanen

1 Introduction

Most government services are supplied by bureaus, so any comprehensive theory of government must include a theory about the behavior of bureaus in the broader political environment. This chapter summarizes the development of the economic theory of bureaucracy. As I made a major early contribution to this theory (Niskanen 1971), my review of this literature reflects a continuing interest but, possibly, some personal bias. This review also borrows broadly from my two prior reassessments of this literature (Niskanen 1991, 1994), since my perspective on this topic has changed little in recent years. For other recent reviews of this literature, see the fine articles by Ronald Wintrobe (1997) and Terry Moe (1997).[1]

2 Building blocks

2.1 Contributions from other traditions

The study of bureaucracy, like the broader study of politics, was the almost exclusive domain of sociology and political science until several decades ago; as of 1968, for example, the article on 'Bureaucracy' in the *International Encyclopedia of the Social Sciences* did not cite one study of bureaucracy by an economist. At that time, the modern scholarly literature on bureaucracy was dominated by the writings of Max Weber, a German sociologist. Weber recognized bureaucracy as the characteristic form of public administration for a state with extended territorial sovereignty, using the term bureaucracy largely as a synonym for a system of relations based on rational–legal authority. The modern literature on public administration was also strongly influenced by Weber's writings, with occasional infusions of Confucian and Platonist guidance on how a good bureaucrat, now civil servant, ought to behave. An important contribution by James Q. Wilson, *Bureaucracy* (1989), is the best recent book in this general tradition.

Although the scholarly literature usually represented bureaucracy as a desirable, or at least necessary, form of public administration, popular attitudes reflecting personal experience are often critical of the methods and performance of bureaucracy. These popular attitudes are probably best reflected in the irreverent and sometimes caustic form of literary satire, ranging from Honoré de Balzac's observations on the mentality and behavior of minor bureaucrats to Cyril Northcote Parkinson's mock-scientific observations on the behavior and performance of bureaus. The late Joseph Heller's *Catch-22* will probably become the modern classic in this tradition.

2.2 *The distinctive nature of economic theory*

As has since become clear, economics offers a valuable new perspective on bureaucracy – one based on the distinctive nature of economic theory. The compositive method of economics develops hypotheses about social behavior from models of purposive behavior by individuals. The individual consumer, entrepreneur or, in this case, bureaucrat is the central figure in the distinctive method of economics. He is assumed to face a set of possible actions and to choose that action within the possible set that he most prefers. The larger environment influences the behavior of the individual by constraining the set of possible actions, by changing the relations between actions and outcomes and, to some extent, by influencing his personal preferences. The economist develops models based on the purposive behavior of individuals, not to explain the behavior of individuals but to generate hypotheses about the aggregative consequences of the interaction among individuals in specific institutional arrangements.

The central insight of conventional economics is that the provision of private goods and services is an *incidental* effect of the incentives and constraints of consumers, entrepreneurs and employees. In other words, the provision of private goods and services is an effect, but is not the primary objective, of any participant in the private economy. Similarly, the central insight of the literature now described as public choice is that the provision of government services is an incidental effect of the incentives and constraints of voters, politicians and bureaucrats. Although this perspective on government services is now more broadly shared, one should recognize how radical this perspective was first regarded and how radical it still seems among some groups.

2.3 *Early contributions by economists*

As of the late 1960s, only a few venturesome economists had taken on the bureaucracy as a subject for scholarship. Ludwig von Mises's book, *Bureaucracy* (1944), was more a forceful polemic against socialism than an analysis of bureaucracy, but it provided some of the first critical insights for a theory of bureaucracy. Specifically, Mises recognized that bureaus specialize in the supply of those services that are not sold at per-unit prices. He concludes, however, that the problems often attributed to bureaucracy are inherent in the scope and scale of government. One of Gordon Tullock's first sorties into the poorly defended province of political science was his *The Politics of Bureaucracy* (1965). Based on his own experience in the US Department of

State, Tullock focused on the information flows and advancement procedures within bureaus, providing an entertaining guide to the maximizing bureaucrat. I especially liked his comparison of a bureau to a gaseous diffusion plant. Similarly, Anthony Downs's book, *Inside Bureaucracy* (1967), focused primarily on the behavior within and among bureaus. Downs builds on the insight by von Mises that bureaus do not receive most of their revenues from the per-unit sale of output, but his typology of bureaucrats leads to the awkward conclusion that the behavior of a bureau is dependent on the motivation of the specific person who heads the bureau. One interesting characteristic of these early contributions, as well as my own, is that they were each written by an economist working outside the academy.

2.4   *The distinguishing characteristics of bureaus*

From Weber to Downs, each of the major writers on bureaucracy developed his own list of the characteristics of bureaus and the bureaucracy. Paring down these lists to the smallest common set, one is left with a definition of bureaus as those organizations that have the following characteristics:

1. The owners and employees of these organizations do not appropriate any part of the net revenues as personal income.
2. A major part of the recurring revenues of the organization derive from other than the sale of output at per-unit prices.

In a single sentence: bureaus are non-profit organizations that are financed primarily by a periodic appropriation or grant.

The first characteristic includes all government agencies, most government enterprises, most educational institutions and hospitals, and the many forms of social, charitable and religious organizations. This characteristic clearly excludes corporate businesses, partnerships and sole proprietorships. Many staff units in profit-seeking organizations, however, have both of the critical characteristics of bureaus. The more difficult it is to identify a unit's or a division's contribution to a firm's profits, the more likely that the unit will behave like a bureau. The first characteristic also excludes mutual financial organizations, cooperatives and families; although these organizations are normally classified as non-profit organizations, the identity of owners and consumers permits the appropriation of residual revenues either in the form of personal income or in lower prices for certain goods and services.

The second characteristic includes most non-profit organizations. Some government enterprises (such as electric power, bridge and toll-road authorities) and some private non-profit organizations are excluded by this characteristic, as their recurrent operations are financed entirely by the sale of output at a per-unit rate, even though these organizations may have been established initially by an appropriation or grant.

The appropriate definition of a bureaucrat or a bureaucracy follows directly from the above definition of a bureau. A bureaucrat is best defined as the head of a bureau with a separate budget. And a bureaucracy is some set of bureaus with a similar role or other common feature. None of these terms, of course, has any inherent normative connotation.

2.5   The contemporary economic role of bureaus

Given the above definition of bureaus, what is the economic role of bureaus in the United States and how has it changed? No one indicator, unfortunately, adequately reflects the scope and scale of the activities of bureaus. The three indicators presented in Table 11.1, however, provide rough estimates of the relative magnitude of the economic activities of bureaus.

Table 11.1   Relative size of economic activity by bureaus (percent of US GDP)

	1929	1949	1969	1989
Factor payments				
Non-profit	1.1	1.4	2.5	3.8
Government	4.3	7.8	13.2	12.1
Government purchases	8.6	19.9	22.8	20.1
Government expenditures	10.0	23.2	31.4	33.9

The top two rows of numbers indicate the payment for factors employed by non-profit institutions and general government (primarily the compensation of employees) as a percentage of the gross domestic product. This aggregation includes some non-profit institutions and government enterprises financed entirely by the sale of services but, of course, excludes the bureaucratic components of profit-seeking firms. By this measure, assuming the value of the services supplied by bureaus is equal to their cost, the share of GDP originating in bureaus increased rapidly through 1969 and has since been a relatively stable 16 percent.

The third row indicates the total purchases by government, the sum of factor payments plus purchases from private firms. This is the broadest measure of the cost of services supplied by the government. By this measure, the relative size of government bureaus increased rapidly through 1949 and since then, except during wars, has been a relatively stable 20 percent of GDP.

The fourth row indicates the total expenditures by government – the sum of government purchases, transfer payments, interest payments and subsidies. All of these expenditures pass through government bureaus, but the final expenditures financed by these transfer and other payments are largely determined by the recipients. By this measure, the relative size of expenditures made by or through government bureaus increased rapidly through 1969 and since then has been a relatively stable 33 percent of GDP. More interesting, perhaps, the increase in transfer payments accounts for almost all of the increase in the relative size of government in the United States since 1949.

One other dimension of the role of bureaus is not reflected in Table 11.1. Government regulatory bureaus also impose substantial costs on the private sector – an amount, including paperwork costs, which may be 5 to 10 percent of GDP. Although the costs of the older forms of price and entry regulation have declined since the late 1970s, this has been more than offset by the rapid increase in the regulation of health, safety, and the environment.

3   The budget-maximizing bureaucrat

3.1   A personal note

At the time I began writing *Bureaucracy and Representative Government* (Niskanen 1971), I had worked a dozen years as a defense analyst at the RAND Corporation, the Pentagon and the Institute for Defense Analyses (IDA). That experience shaped my perspective on bureaucracy in several ways that I was slow to understand. Most important, it was a frustrating but maturing experience, the transformation of a technocrat into a political economist. Gordon Tullock, when working briefly at IDA in 1966, helped shape my still inchoate views on bureaucracy and urged me to distill them in a professional article. And since the opportunities for career advancement in the military are almost exclusively limited to one's own service, I carelessly assumed that was also the case in other bureaus. The book that developed from this perspective provided the first formal economic analysis of the supply of government services, a framework that proved to be important but conspicuously flawed.

3.2   The core elements of the initial framework

Any theory of the behavior of bureaus must be based on the relationship between bureaus and their sponsors, usually some group of politicians. This relationship, in turn, is shaped by the distinctive incentives and constraints faced by bureaucrats and politicians. The primary elements of my initial framework that have survived subsequent analysis and comment are the following:

1.   Bureaucrats are much like officials in other organizations. Their behavior will differ, not because of different personal characteristics but because

of the incentives and constraints that are specific to bureaus.

2. Most bureaus have a monopoly buyer for their service. The effective demand for the output of the bureaus comes from this sponsor, rather than from the ultimate consumers of the service.

3. Most bureaus are monopoly suppliers of their service. More specifically, most bureaus face a downward-sloping effective demand function, even if there are alternative actual or potential suppliers of the same or similar service.

4. The bilateral monopoly relation between a bureau and its sponsor involves the exchange of a promised output for a budget, rather than the sale of output at a per-unit rate.

5. As in any bilateral monopoly, there is no unique budget–output equilibrium between the preferences of the sponsor and those of the bureau. The sponsor's primary advantages in this bargaining are its authority to monitor the bureau, to approve the bureau's budget, and to replace the senior bureaucrats. The bureau's primary advantage is that it has much better information about the costs of supplying the service than does the sponsor.

6. Finally, neither the members of the sponsor group nor the senior bureaucrats have a pecuniary stake in the outcome of this bargain. The effect is that the outcome will serve the interests of the sponsor and the bureaucrats in different ways, but not as direct compensation.

My initial framework, in addition, included three assumptions about the behavior of bureaucrats and their political sponsors that proved to be the focus of most subsequent criticism. Specifically, bureaucrats were assumed to act to maximize the expected budget of their bureau. Second, the sponsors were assumed to be 'passive' in accepting or rejecting the bureau's budget–output proposal without any careful monitoring or evaluation of alternatives. A third implicit assumption that I did not recognize at that time was that bureaucrats and their sponsors bargain over the full range of the possible combinations of budget and output.

3.3 The implications of the initial framework

The primary implication of the initial framework is that both the budget and output of a bureau are larger than optimal; more precisely, the marginal value of the bureau's service to the constituents of the median voter in the legislature is lower than the marginal cost, the bureau appropriating the potential surplus to this group by expanding output beyond the optimal level. This outcome also generates a larger surplus to any labor or capital resources that are specific to the production of the service.

This framework also led to an awkward two-region solution to the budget–output outcomes. In the 'budget-constrained' region, the budget is equal to the minimum total cost of producing the output promised to the sponsor; here the service is produced efficiently but at a higher-than-optimal level of output. At a sufficiently high level of demand, however, the resulting budget–output outcome is in a 'demand-constrained' region. In this region, the marginal value of output is zero, and the budget is larger than the minimum total cost of producing the promised output. In this region, the waste due to bureaucratic supply is some combination of both allocative and productive inefficiency.

At the time that I developed this framework, I recognized that it was incomplete. Specifically, the framework did not develop the other side of this market – the behavior of the sponsors in monitoring the bureau and bargaining over the budget. Over time, I also came to recognize that the several behavioral assumptions in my initial framework led to conclusions that are both theoretically inelegant and inconsistent with the available evidence.

4   The major criticisms of this framework

4.1   What do bureaucrats maximize?

Fortunately, the most important early comment on my book, by Jean-Luc Migué and Gerard Bélanger (1974), suggested an approach that both generalized and simplified my initial framework. They made an assumption, more consistent with that of a profit-maximizing firm, that bureaucrats act to maximize the bureau's discretionary budget, defined as the difference between the total budget and the minimum cost of producing the output expected by the bureau's sponsor. This assumption leads to somewhat different conclusions: the budget of a bureau is too large, the output (again in terms of the demand revealed by the sponsor) is generally too small and that inefficiency in production is the normal condition. My 1975 article, 'Bureaucrats and politicians', incorporated this important modification.

The superiority of a slack-maximizing model was reinforced by several other considerations. In their 1975 article, Albert Breton and Ronald Wintrobe observed that the incentive for budget maximizing is likely to be limited to those bureaus, such as the military, in which the opportunities for promotion are limited to that bureau. Subsequent empirical work by Ronald Johnson and Gary Libecap (1989) and by Robert Young (1991) also indicated that the salaries of bureaucrats are only weakly related to the level and growth of their bureau's budget. And the accumulation of empirical studies indicates that inefficiency in production is a more general condition than suggested by my initial model.

4.2   The behavior of sponsors

A bureau's sponsor, of course, is not passive. I knew that, having served as a policy and budget review official in the Pentagon and later in two other federal review positions.

The first review of my book, by Earl Thompson (1973), correctly observed that a sponsor has both the authority and the opportunity to monitor a bureau by means that would reduce the inefficiency of bureaucratic supply. Breton and Wintrobe (1975) expanded on this point with a simple model of the review process that determines the optimal amount of control devices and the consequent effects on the budget. The behavior of the sponsor was further developed in the political science literature by Gary Miller and Terry Moe (1983) and by Jonathan Bendor et al. (1985 and 1987).

I acknowledged the early contributions by Thompson and by Breton and Wintrobe in my 1975 article, but pointed out that their model did not reflect the specific institutions of the review process or the incentives of the legislators. In the United States, for example, legislative review is mostly conducted by specialized legislative committees that are largely self-selected. This introduces two powerful biases in the review process: most of the costs of effective review are borne by members of the committee, but almost all of the benefits accrue to a broader population; this creates a substantial free-rider problem internal to the legislature and the expectation that monitoring activities will be undersupplied. The study by Morris Ogul (1976) confirmed the general perception that members of Congress engage in very little oversight. Second, self-selection for committee assignment leads to committees that have a higher relative demand for the services of the bureaus subject to their oversight than the demand of the broader legislature. A high-demand committee, thus, is less likely to monitor oversupply by the bureau than would a randomly selected committee.

Several recent articles explore the institutions of the review process in more detail. Glenn Parker and Suzanne Parker (1998), for example, conclude that party leaders in Congress are more effective in influencing floor votes than committee decisions, but that obligations to interest groups will be more immune to leadership influence because of the incentives for committee members to adhere to their bargains. Hirofumi Shibata (1998) develops the implications of the budget-review process in the government of Japan and other parliamentary systems.

4.3   What is the range of budget bargaining?

One implicit assumption of my initial framework is that a bureau and its sponsor bargain over the whole range from a zero budget to the bureau's proposed budget. As I had previously served as a budget review official, this was a mistake for which I had no excuse. An important article by Thomas

Romer and Howard Rosenthal (1978b) fortunately provided a better framework for analysing each step in this process. They define the *reversion level* of the budget in a specific year as the level that will be maintained if there is no agreement on a new budget. If the sponsor's preferred budget is higher than the reversion level, a bureau has an incentive to propose an even larger budget that the sponsor values only slightly more than the reversion level. This framework leads to a conclusion that the excess budget will be roughly equal to the difference between the sponsor's preferred budget and a lower reversion level.

The rule for defining and changing the reversion level is thus very important. In many cases, for example, the reversion level in the annual budget review is the prior year's budget for that bureau. Sometimes, the reversion level is the budget for which the benefits to the sponsor are so low that it leads the sponsor to replace the managers of the bureau. Romer and Rosenthal estimated the results of school budget referenda in which the school board was the agenda setter and the reversion level was the budget at which the schools would have to be closed. The more general practice of setting the reversion level at the prior year's budget may seem to minimize the excess budget that year, but that may be misleading because the accumulation of the excess budgets in prior years is included in this year's reversion level. I have not worked out the long-term implications of a series of such annual budget reviews, however; nor, to my knowledge, has anyone else.

4.4   What group is the effective agenda setter?

My initial framework, in which the bureau is assumed to act strategically and the sponsor is passive, provoked a productive reaction among political scientists, initially led by Barry Weingast and his colleagues. Weingast and Mark Moran (1983) and Weingast (1984) assert that congressional committees have as much control over bureaus as they desire – by use of their legislative and appointment powers and by shifting the burden of monitoring to constituency groups. This position, in turn, was challenged by Terry Moe (1989) and Murray Horn (1995), who emphasized the incentives of the current effective coalition to bind a subsequent legislature from breaking promises that the current coalition has made to their favored constituents. Reflecting on this controversy, Moe (1997, p. 466) concludes that 'the theme of this literature ought to be that Congress has a difficult time controlling the bureaucracy, and that the latter has much autonomy. This is precisely what mainstream work by political scientists has long maintained'.

Back to square one. What group or groups are most effective in setting the budget agenda? On this issue, I also agree with Moe (p. 472) that 'attention to institutional context … should be central to any theory of bureaucracy'. In the American political system, I suggest, the bureau and the specialized committee effectively collude to set the budget agenda, with the executive and the body of the legislature as the nearly passive sponsors. The bureau and the committee agree on the budget and program to be submitted to the whole legislature. The reversion level is the budget for which the benefits to the decisive voter in the legislature are so low that the legislature will discipline the committee (by changing its leadership or by removing some authority from the committee) or the executive will similarly discipline the bureau. The committee will submit the largest budget that the legislature will approve and not be vetoed by the executive, a budget that the legislature prefers only slightly to the reversion level. Again, the lower the reversion level, the larger the excess budget. Members of the legislature tolerate the agenda-setting powers of the committees because of the costs of monitoring, the necessity of a division of labor, and to avoid their own committee from being similarly disciplined. Most of the bargaining between the bureau and the committee is specific to the division of the excess budget between activities that serve the interests of the bureau and those that serve the interests of the committee. The committee is likely to threaten or initiate monitoring only when the bureau breaks its promise concerning the division of the spoils.

Barry Weingast was correct to assert the dominance of the legislature in the American political system, but the committees, in effective collusion with the bureaus, are the groups that exercise this power. And, as Terry Moe suggests, the powers of the bureaucracy are likely to be different in a different political system. Future scholarship on the supply of government services, I suggest, should focus on the relation between a committee and the legislature in the American political system and on the characteristic institutions of the budget review process in other political systems.

5 The current state of the economics of bureaucracy

5.1 Empirical evidence

My initial framework and the major criticisms of this framework provoked a wealth of empirical studies that bear on the hypotheses derived from the developing economic theory of bureaucracy. An article by Roderick Kiewiet (1991) provides the broadest recent summary of these empirical studies. A range of indirect, but not very discriminating, tests of the oversupply hypothesis provides little evidence in support of this hypothesis. On the other hand, there are now dozens of studies that support the inefficiency hypothesis. Almost all such studies find that the production cost of private firms is significantly lower than that for bureaus supplying the same or a similar service. A part of the problem may be due to the poor information on the cost of government services that is available to the political sponsor. In a recent letter to Congress summarizing an audit of the first consolidated financial statements for the federal government, for example, the acting controller general of the General Accounting Office reported that, 'significant financial systems weaknesses, problems with fundamental record-keeping, incomplete documentation, and weak internal controls, including computer controls, prevent the government from accurately reporting a large portion of its assets, liabilities, and costs' (Hinchman 1988). The fact that most federal services have yet to be privatized, however, suggests that some amount of 'waste, fraud, and abuse' may be just what Congress ordered.

A growing body of studies also supports the hypothesis that competition among bureaus, both within and among jurisdictions, reduces production inefficiency. The earlier studies in this group were unfortunately subject to an alternative interpretation that the lower local government expenditures in a multijurisdictional metropolitan area result from the intercity competition for tax base rather than from bureaucratic competition. Later studies were more careful to focus on inefficiency rather than expenditures and to control for a variety of socioeconomic characteristics. A recent study of school districts in New York State (Duncombe et al. 1997, p. 15), for example, concludes that 'efficiency is negatively related to school district size, percent tenured teachers, district wealth, nonresidential property values and labor intensity and positively related to the percent of adults who are college educated'. A recent study of Illinois cities (Hayes et al. 1998, p. 1) yields similar results, concluding that 'inefficient behavior is associated with richer communities, lower education levels and a lack of competition for residents among municipalities'.

Several types of studies also confirm the hypothesis that government expenditures are higher than preferred by the median voter. My own study of presidential elections (Niskanen 1979) finds that the popular vote for the candidate of the incumbent party is a negative function of the increase in real per-capita federal expenditures since the prior election. The classic studies of school district referenda by Romer and Rosenthal (1979, 1982), the numerous studies of the 'flypaper effect' (such as by Courant et al. 1979 and Wyckoff 1988) and the occasional popular vote for a supermajority rule on major fiscal decisions (Olmsted et al. 1988) all confirm the general hypotheses of the agenda-setter model.

Reflecting on the empirical studies of bureaucracy, Kiewiet (1991, p. 161) observes that 'Niskanen's model is more one of legislative failure than of bureaucracy chicanery', and he concludes (p. 166) that this model 'has fared at least as well as any other model in political economy of comparable generality'.

5.2   Theory

Sorting out the major criticisms of my initial framework and the developing empirical literature has led to a broad consensus for two major changes to this framework:

1. Maximizing the discretionary budget is a better description of bureau-cratic behavior than budget (or output) maximizing.
2. The reversion-level budget is very dependent on the institutions of the budget review process but, in general, is not zero. In the limiting case, the reversion level is that for which the benefits to the sponsor are so low that the sponsor exercises its authority to replace or otherwise discipline the bureau.

The implications of this modified framework are summarized efficiently in an article by Paul Wyckoff (1990), from which Figure 11.1 below is drawn. On this figure, the vertical axis is the level of private goods and services (P), and the horizontal axis is the level of government services (G). The point A is the optimal combination of P and G for the decisive voter in the sponsor

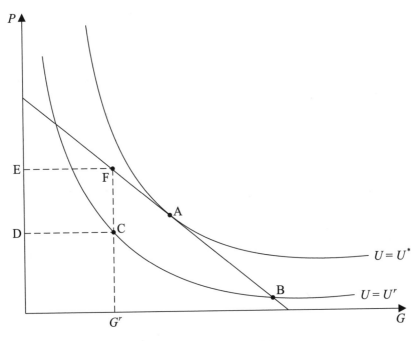

Figure 11.1   Slack and budget-maximizing models

group, given the budget constraint, yielding the utility level U^*. Wyckoff posits that the reversion utility level for the decisive voter is U^r, below which he or she will vote against the public official or leave the community. For these conditions, the budget- (or output-) maximizing bureaucrat will propose an output indicated by the point B, an output that is too large but is produced efficiently. For these same conditions, the discretionary-budget-maximizing bureaucrat will propose an output indicated by the point C, an output that is generally too low and yields an excess budget ('slack') of CDEF. Figure 11.1 also illustrates that a bureau's output will be higher and the excess budget will be lower, the higher is the reversion utility level. Since the consequences for the bureau of underestimating the reversion level can be quite severe, a risk-averse bureaucrat is likely to opt for a higher output and a lower excess budget.

There is less agreement on two other major issues, in part because these issues are very dependent on the institutional details of the political system. Most important, and peculiar to the US political system, do the specialized review committees act as agents of the broader legislative membership or are they in effective collusion with the bureaus? As noted above, my judgment is that the review committees are the effective agenda setters, and their interests are largely in common with the bureaus except for the division of the excess budget. In this case, the body of the legislature should be considered to be the sponsor, and my initial assumption that the sponsor is passive may not be far off the mark. I encourage other scholars to weigh in on this issue, including how to test this hypothesis. Second, how much of a difference from the budget–output combination preferred by the decisive voter in the legislature is necessary to trigger special investigative hearings and possible disciplining of the normal review committee or the bureau? It is important to identify the conditions that determine the reversion level and how much the reversion level may be increased by changes in voting rules, committee organization and monitoring by the broader sponsor group.

In summary, those of us who have worked to formulate and refine the economic theory of bureaucracy have made major progress, but there is still a lot of productive work to do.

Note
1. The next chapter surveys rational choice models of bureaucratic control and performance.

12 Rational choice theories of bureaucratic control and performance

Kelly H. Chang, Rui J.P. de Figueiredo, Jr and Barry R. Weingast

1 Introduction: the Wilson challenge

Perhaps the most salient feature of government agencies is their inherent complexity. As with most organizations, the behavior of public bureaucracies is difficult to unpack. The complexity of bureaucracy calls into question the efforts by political scientists to develop deductive theories of bureaucratic performance and behavior. If a complex set of interactions among a plethora of variables characterizes government agencies, then the rational choice theorist's intention to predict agency behavior with (simple) models might be chimerical.

Perhaps the most forceful statement of this view has been advanced by James Q. Wilson in *Bureaucracy: What Government Agencies Do and Why They Do It* (1989). In his criticisms of the institutional theories of bureaucracy, Wilson points to two related failures of such theories: the ignorance of variation and complexity, and the consequent failure to recognize the importance of internal organization. In terms of the former, Wilson argues that bureaucracies vary dramatically in the nature of the tasks they perform, their interest-group environments, their political context, and their institutional constraints. These variations, he points out, lead to vastly different behavior and performance. In terms of the latter, Wilson points to a number of features of the internal organization of agencies which vary: organizational cultures, missions, incentives of agents at different levels of hierarchy, and reporting relationships and task assignments all determine what kind of outputs an agency will produce.

In an earlier work, Wilson (1980, p. 393) argues that government agencies are not a single phenomenon, and as a result, '[a] single-explanation theory of regulatory politics is about as helpful as a single explanation of politics generally, or of disease. Distinctions must be made, differences must be examined'. For example, Martha Derthick (1990) notes that the Social Security Administration has a strong service orientation while, according to Wilson (1989, p. 86), the United States Post Office, before it became semi-private, focused on cost reduction and containment at the expense of service. All agencies, in sum, do not behave alike.

271

Wilson does not stop at a call to recognize and explain variation in the dependent variable, bureaucratic behavior. He goes further, to demand that descriptions and explanations incorporate a range of independent variables. He states firmly that the variation in bureaucratic behavior is not monocausal. Theories which ascribe behavior of agencies to dyadic relationships are therefore inadequate: to Congress and agency (for example, Weingast and Moran 1983; McCubbins and Schwartz 1984), to the president and agency (for example, Moe 1985, 1989), to a single interest and agency (for example, Stigler 1971; Peltzman 1976; Moe 1980). Wilson makes this point in *The Politics of Regulation* (1980) with thick descriptions of the origins and development of many regulatory agencies. In Wilson's book, each government agency seems to have a unique genesis and evolution. Each account adds a new variable to explain behavior, and it is this variation in a number of variables that leads to variations in agency behavior. If one examines patterns of influence on agencies, Wilson identifies a myriad of possible cases. As he points out,

> there is no distinctive pattern of influence at all in the case of the [Federal Trade Commission] and the Antitrust Division [of the Department of Justice]; the relationship is more bilateral ... in the case of the [Office of Civil Rights] rulemaking (the agency and civil rights organizations) and quadrilateral in the case of the [Environmental Protection Agency, Occupational Safety and Health Administration and the Food and Drug Administration] (agency, committee, pro-industry group and anti-industry group). (p. 391)

In his later work, Wilson provides a more systematic account of relevant variables, perhaps responding to the criticisms of his purely descriptive approach (for example, Shepsle 1982). In the later rendering, Wilson still concludes that almost everything matters: the nature of institutions, interests, policy tasks, technological change, ideas and beliefs, and individuals in organizations.

As an example of Wilson's approach, consider his interpretation of the behavior and evolution of the antitrust policy of the Federal Trade Commission (FTC). How can one understand the development of the commission, Wilson asks, without noting the role of the president, Congress and the courts? Wilson claims further that it is impossible to understand which cases will be brought without noting the composition of the FTC's professionals: while economists seek cases that promise improvements in economic efficiency, lawyers seek cases that clearly violate the letter of the law. Similarly, for most of its history, the FTC was characterized by a broad coalition that 'left it confronting an environment devoid of important interest groups'. When it attempted changes in the reporting requirements for funeral prices, for example, this environment shifted to one in which there was a fierce group in opposition to the FTC (funeral directors). And finally, Wilson argues that it is impossible to understand the development of the FTC without also tracking changes in ideas about what kinds of activity should be regulated. As the Chicago-school approach to the appropriateness of focusing on conduct versus structure in regulating competition rose and then partially fell, so did the pursuit of cases which regulated structure versus conduct (Wilson 1989, pp. 60–61, 82–3, 207–8, 247–56; Wilson 1980, ch. 5; Weingast and Moran 1983; Moe 1987a).

According to Wilson, the task for deductive theory is even more formidable. Wilson points out that the seeming chaos of bureaucracy stems from the fact that the large set of potential causal factors is highly interactive. Everything affects everything else. Thus, theories that explain only part of the picture will lead to incomplete and even misleading explanations. Returning to Wilson's interpretation of the history of the FTC, he asks: how was it that Caspar Weinberger was able to imbue the FTC with a new mission during the Nixon administration, for example, but Michael Pertschuk was largely unable to do so during the Carter years? His answer has to do with what he argues is the interaction between the nature of the tasks the two chairmen set out for the agency and how those tasks interacted both with the professional orientation of the FTC staff and the interest groups that were mobilized in response to those tasks. Weinberger charged the agency with policing and penalizing deceptive national advertising, which was acceptable for lawyers at the FTC to follow and generated support from both consumer and business interests who would benefit from costs imposed on those advantaged by weak enforcement. Pertschuk, on the other hand, sought to reorient the mission of the FTC from one focusing on changing the practices of individual companies, such as deceptive advertising, to enforcement of industry-wide rules of fair practice, such as the regulation of television advertising on Saturday mornings. In Wilson's view, this led not only to a broader-based opposition externally, among business interests, but also to internal resistance from lawyers who found it much more difficult to attack the conduct of whole industries (Wilson 1989, pp. 207–8; Heymann 1987, pp. 14–85). In this case, and many others, then, the interaction of a multiplicity of variables creates enormous difficulty in trying tractably and deductively to predict agency behavior.

One of the main sources of variation and complexity which deserves special mention in Wilson's argument is the role of organization itself. As Wilson concisely puts it, 'organization matters'. While obvious to public administrationists, organizational sociologists, and organizational economists, this point seriously challenges deductive theorists' use of institutional variation as their primary vehicle for explaining agency behavior. As Wilson points out, institutional relationships are only part of a complete explanation: who populates an agency, how they define their mission, what values they hold, how they report to one another, and the way tasks are assigned all affect policy choice. Institutionalists who focus on an agency's external environment tend to ignore internal factors. '[S]tudying the goals, resources and structure of an agency is not always a helpful clue to what it will do', Wilson (1989, p. 13) concludes. For this reason, he advocates not only a 'top-down' approach to studying agencies but a 'bottom-up' one as well; taking a 'worm's-eye' as well as a bird's-eye view of agencies, as many scholars have done (ibid., ch. 2).

Wilson's view poses significant challenges to the current school of positive, rational choice theorists.[1] Figure 12.1 summarizes the challenge. First, the new institutional school has focused on panel A, the relationship between formal institutions such as Congress, the president and the courts, and government agencies. In Wilson's estimation, rational choice theory is too simplistic even in this area; it leaves out too many institutional players and details. Second, rational choice has contributed very little to our understanding of agency organization (panel B) – how they are structured, rules that govern them, norms of behavior, who populates them. Third, since organization matters, a full-blown theory must simultaneously account for institutional players *and* the effects of organization (panel C).

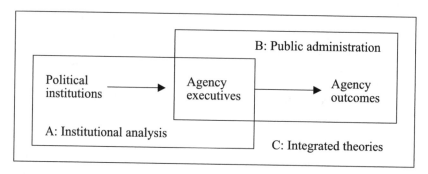

Figure 12.1   Theories of government agencies

Simply put, rational choice theories must confront the *Wilson challenge*: that complete theories of bureaucratic behavior must simultaneously include all of the external factors – such as the president, Congress and the courts; all relevant interests; and technological, economic and social changes – and the multiplicity of internal factors – differences in the nature of agency tasks, organizational structure, and the backgrounds of individuals. The Wilson challenge questions whether, given the complexity of American bureaucracy, a unified, positive theory is possible. In our estimation, Wilson's descriptive approach implies a pessimism about the prospects for deductive theory (ibid., ch. 1).

We are more optimistic. In this chapter, we argue that rational choice models of bureaucratic structure and performance have deepened the understanding of American bureaucracy. Although positive theories of agency behavior initially were too sparse, and therefore legitimately subject to the first part of the Wilson challenge, they have subsequently developed more nuanced, richer theories that have led to a number of important insights about American bureaucracy. To illustrate this point, in the next section we outline the development of positive theories and, in particular, rational choice approaches for studying bureaucratic behavior. This section shows that the development of deductive theories is an ongoing process: scholars in this tradition have enriched models in precisely the way Wilson might advocate. At the institutional (or what Wilson calls the contextual) level, the study of dyadic relationships between single institutional actors and monolithic agencies has expanded into richer studies of agencies located in a context of a system of shared powers between branches. This enrichment has broadened the understanding of agencies in precisely the way Wilson advocates, with two added benefits. First, positive theory provides the rigor and clarity necessary to understand which interactions are important, and how institutional constraints impact agency behavior. Second, positive theory provides predictions of agency behavior that allow for tests of the validity of alternative explanations. Despite this progress, the task is not nearly complete. In Section 3, therefore, we outline some of the future directions in which rational choice might fruitfully address other aspects of the Wilson challenge. In particular, we emphasize ways in which Wilson's focus on internal organization might be integrated fruitfully into positive institutional theories of bureaucracy. We begin by examining exemplary early steps in this direction and then highlight future extensions of this work. In Section 4, we offer conclusions.

2   The development of rational choice models of bureaucratic politics

The study of political organizations has its roots in public administration and the behavioral tradition best represented by James March and Herbert Simon, but it has since deviated significantly from its roots. Public administration has traditionally concentrated mainly on the efficient organization of the executive branch. In particular, public administration scholars have viewed bureaus as effective vehicles for administering public policy. To many scholars in this tradition, politics is an unfortunate feature of government that impinges on bureaucratic effectiveness: 'An organization structure that provides access for particular groups within the community is not necessarily flawed, unless it prejudices policy outcomes, prevents teamwork, and permits private groups to exploit public institutions for their own benefit' (Seidman and Gilmour 1986, p. 329). Public administration scholars have a normative interest in finding solutions to ineffective administration.

The behavioral tradition is rooted in a more positive approach. March and Simon sought to explain the structure of organizations as a result of human cognitive limitations. They first point out that the attention span, information-gathering capabilities, and the multitasking abilities of individuals are quite limited. In response to their inherent limitations, individuals rationally choose certain organization structures that deal with their limitations, structures that are required to achieve goals. Division of labor, for example, solves the problem of the inability of individuals to multitask. In some ways Wilson's work is a culmination of this behavioral tradition; March and Simon look inside bureaucracies at the physical limitations of individuals, and while Wilson does not go quite so far as to look inside at the individuals themselves, he does advocate a bottom-up approach that examines the organizational structure of bureaucracy as a result of individuals' interactions inside the bureaucracy (March and Simon 1958; also see Simon [1945] 1976; Scott 1992; Perrow 1986; Nelson and Winter 1982; March 1978; Selznick 1948; Kaufman 1975; Lindblom 1959; Williamson 1975, 1985; Alchian and Demsetz 1972).

The new institutional approach to bureaucracy in political science also takes a positive approach, but its concerns have been different from those of both public administration and behavioral scholars. First, in contrast to public administrationists, studying the political causes of ineffective administration is exactly the focus of the new institutionalists, for whom bureaucratic ineffectiveness is a stark reality underpinned by actors with strong, consistent, political motivations. Who has these political motivations, their sources, and the processes by which they are translated into bureaucratic structure and policy are the questions that occupy their interest. Second, whereas the behavioralists focused on the bureaucracy itself, the new institutionalists view bureaucracy as shaped and influenced by its interaction with other actors in its political context such as the president, Congress, and the courts.

The new institutional work on bureaucracy has used advances in game theory and econometrics to gradually develop more complete theories of bureaucracy that rise to Wilson's challenge. The newer models break out of the dyadic prison of the 1980s that examined bureaucracy and its interaction with one other institution, such as Congress. One by one, these models have incorporated an impressive range of the elements that make up the Wilson challenge. But the new models represent more than incremental developments. They form a new way of thinking about American politics and about bureaucratic performance in particular: the modeling of political choice as a function of an integrated separation-of-powers system.

We start this section by examining the earlier institutional theories that featured dyads of a bureau and a government institution, and then move on to more recent theories that incorporate multiple government institutions.

2.1 Dyads

Congress and the bureaucracy The first rational choice attempts to place the bureaucracy within the separation-of-powers context began with applications of the principal–agent theory from economics. A typical example of the principal–agent problem is that of an employer, the principal, who hires a worker, the agent, to accomplish some tasks. The employer would like the worker to work hard while the worker would rather not if she does not have to. One way to verify the worker's efforts is through monitoring, and then dock her wages or fire her if she slacks off. But monitoring can be costly; the employer's time might be better spent on other tasks. The solution is to design a contract with proper incentives for high levels of employee effort. A profit-sharing plan is one example; the idea is that if the workers work hard, the company's profits increase, and the workers reap a share of the profit gains – everyone wins.[2]

William Niskanen (1971) pioneered the application of the principal–agent theory to bureaucratic politics. In his model, the sponsor or principal seeks certain non-market services from the bureau or the agent, who is the monopoly supplier of those services. In return for a budget, the budget-maximizing bureau will perform a certain set of functions specified by its sponsor. The key is that the sponsor cannot actually observe the agency's true need for funds to perform the tasks it requires. The key insight of Niskanen's model is that owing to the asymmetric information between the sponsoring legislature and the agency, as well as the monopoly supply of services by the agency, agencies can extract rents from the sponsor. In this way, Niskanen provides a formal basis for understanding the stylized fact of bureaucratic inefficiency.

Although Niskanen's theory represented a promising start toward formalizing a bureau's interaction with its superior, it concentrated almost exclusively on the bureau. The bureau is a strategic actor, while the sponsor is completely passive. The bureau maximizes its budget subject to constraints imposed by the sponsor. The model is therefore decision theoretic rather than game theoretic; that is, one actor makes decisions given the relevant parameters of the situation at hand rather than each actor making decisions contingent on the other actor's actions. In addition, both the bureau and the sponsor are monolithic actors in Niskanen's model. They are examined on the aggregate level without reference to the individuals, their motivations, and internal structures of the collective bodies.

In the early 1980s, Weingast and Moran (1983) looked more carefully at the internal organization of Congress and how it affects bureaucratic behavior. Weingast and Moran assert that certain congressional committees have rights over particular policy areas and that these committees perform oversight on agencies that deal with the policy area (see also McCubbins and Schwartz

1984). In their model, the committee is the principal, and the bureau, the Federal Trade Commission in their particular case, is the agent. Weingast and Moran's key proposition is that lack of overt committee oversight does not necessarily mean lack of influence. Rather, 'the threat of ex post sanctions creates ex ante incentives for the bureau to serve a congressional clientele' (Weingast and Moran 1983, p. 769). They predict and find evidence for changes in FTC policy with changes in committee membership. Their results consequently lend support to Mayhew's (1974, p. 135) claim that 'there is every reason to believe that the regulatory agencies do what Congress wants them to do'.

Later studies developed and extended the Weingast and Moran framework. McCubbins and Schwartz (1984), for example, extended Weingast and Moran's control hypothesis by pointing to alternative mechanisms by which Congress influences bureaucratic behavior. Their theory is that agencies do not need to be constantly policed. As long as the agency makes decisions within bounds set by Congress, no intervention is required; but when decisions fall outside these bounds, the agency sets off 'fire alarms'; members of Congress respond to the alarms with oversight. They show, therefore, that Congress need not keep a vigilant eye on all agency activity; instead Congress ensures that their informational environment is rich (that the fire alarms are installed and functioning) and then can manage by exception (see also Lupia and McCubbins 1994; de Figueiredo et al. 1999; McCubbins et al. 1987, 1989). Grier (1987) applies the principal–agent model to the Federal Reserve and finds evidence of congressional influence. However, in contrast to Niskanen, these later works concentrated on the powers of Congress and black-boxed the agency; they do not delve into the bureaus' structures. Owing to that emphasis, this approach has often been referred to as the 'congressional dominance' approach.

Miller and Moe (1983) swung back in Niskanen's direction by looking inside the bureau and by incorporating a more strategic role for the bureau with their examination of the role of bureaucratic expertise. Bendor et al. (1985, 1987) looked at the role of bureaucratic as well as legislative expertise in the context of asymmetric and imperfect information on the part of both the bureau and the legislature. They conclude that, depending on the quality of monitoring by Congress, the bureau will either reveal its true budget needs or exaggerate its costs.

The president and the bureaucracy   Terry Moe (1987a) has strongly criticized the congressional dominance approach for its absence of emphasis on the presidency under whose branch most agencies reside. Moe makes two main arguments for the importance of the president in bureaucratic politics. Both stem from the idea that presidents are motivated by larger, history-making concerns rather than the narrow, particularized, parochial concerns characteristic of members of Congress. The first argument is motivational: presidents want to control agencies because they are essential to whether presidents achieve or do not achieve policy goals (Moe 1989). The second argument has to do with capabilities: the president is, Moe argues, far better equipped to deal with agencies than Congress. As chief executive, the president is a single actor who does not, like Congress, suffer the problems posed by the need to act collectively (Moe and Wilson 1994).

Rather than congressional dominance, Moe claims presidential dominance in the area of agency appointments. The Constitution grants the power of appointing federal office holders to the president, but only with the advice and consent of the Senate. Although the Senate technically has veto power over appointments, Moe argues that there exists a Senate norm of deference to the president; senators have other battles to fight with the president (Moe 1987b). Keech and Morris (1996), Grier (1987), Havrilesky (1995), and Chappell et al. (1993, 1995) also examine the president's powers to appoint members of the Federal Reserve Board of Governors without reference to the Senate, and find empirical evidence to support presidential dominance.

Another area in which Moe has argued for significant presidential influence is in what he calls 'the politics of structural choice'. In several papers, Moe (1989, 1991) develops a theory of agency creation in which interest groups, legislators, and the president all play a role in shaping a bureau, which is not necessarily the most efficient in terms of administration. Moe and Wilson (1994) and Moe and Howell (1998) argue that presidential influence is strong. Moe emphasizes his argument about the president's advantages over Congress by constructing an analogy of the president as a chief executive officer and Congress as the corporation's board of directors. The president is the agenda setter and the executor of laws passed by legislators. As such, the president can sometimes quickly and coherently direct what new organizational structures look like, just as a manager can in the absence of direct board approval.

Interest groups and the bureaucracy   Rather than examining the relationship between Congress or the president and the bureau, a number of works on the bureaucracy have examined the direct relationship between interest groups and bureaus. Stigler's (1971) groundbreaking contribution is best known for this approach. Stigler starts by challenging the two most popular notions of economic regulation, namely that (i) regulation is for public benefit, and (ii) rationality cannot be used to understand politics. His is a cynical view; industry controls regulation and basically uses the state apparatus to obtain benefits for itself. Regulatory agencies are 'captured' by the very industries they are supposed to regulate. Peltzman (1976) deepened the theory of 'capture' by formalizing Stigler's argument and deriving conditions under which such capture is most likely to prevail.[3]

Despite their contributions, neither Stigler nor Peltzman make the concrete procedural connection between interest groups and the captured bureaus. As Wilson points out, both use very simple models in which the world consists of regulators and the regulated. The actors maximize in a world abstracted from political processes. In their setups, interest groups provide votes and resources to a regulator that will support their interests through legislation. These regulators are bureau agents appointed by legislators or the executive, whose interests and powers are subsumed in the regulators' utility functions and constraints. However, like Niskanen's early attempts, the Stigler–Peltzman capture theory provided the basis for later rational choice work on bureaucracy and its principals.

Dyads: summary and conclusions   By bringing political principals into the study of bureaucracy, dyadic models began to rein in the popular and academic idea of the runaway bureaucracy. One of the most forceful statements of the runaway bureaucracy comes from Dodd and Schott in *Congress and the Administrative State* (1979); they point to the pervasiveness and power of the bureaucracy and state that it is often thought of as a fourth branch of government. The theories discussed here have demonstrated that bureaus operate in a broader context, interacting with the president, Congress, or interest groups, all of which constrain a bureau's policy decisions.

According to these works, what looks deceptively like a runaway bureau actually operates within limits set by its principals. Weingast and Moran's (1983) discussion of the FTC is an important example: they point to numerous instances in which changes in the composition of congressional oversight committees corresponded to changes in FTC policy. As long as the FTC complied with congressional preferences in its various activities, the committees had no need actively to oversee the agency. Similarly, Ferejohn and Shipan (1990) show how the lack of congressional legislation in the battles between the Federal Communications Commission (FCC) and Congress does not mean that Congress had no influence on the FCC. When AT&T was dismantled in the early 1980s, long-distance companies needed a way to reach local customers. The FCC decided to make customers pay an access fee; the fee did not represent new costs to customers since they had paid such costs to 'Ma Bell' in the past. However, the fee would have appeared on phone bills as a separate charge to customers, and members of Congress were concerned that customers would view the charge as emblematic of higher prices in the new, deregulated telecommunications environment. Over the next few years, Congress threatened to pass legislation to halt FCC actions.

However, Congress never went very far with its threats because the FCC backed off and delayed imposition of the access charges.

Whereas Weingast and Moran and others show why the lack of *ex post* control activity (such as oversight) does not necessarily imply a runaway bureaucracy, Moe concentrates on the *ex ante* control of an agency exercised by the president through the appointment process. After the creation of the National Labor Relations Board (NLRB) by the Wagner Act in 1935, the NLRB became a frequent object of attack by business interests and the Republican Party. Each time a group of business interests sought to get rid of the NLRB, labor resisted, and for many decades these sides remained at loggerheads over labor legislation. Over time, both business and labor began to understand the futility of fighting over legislation – neither seemed to have the support necessary to radically change labor laws or the NLRB. Moe claims that this truce led to a shift in focus to NLRB appointments, and that while Republican presidents are more accommodative to business than to labor interests, they do not completely ignore the latter; Democrats favor labor interests, but they too must strike a balance. Moe points to an equilibrium in which both sides influence the NLRB when one is in power.

Bureaus do not operate in a vacuum, and these dyadic models represent the first attempts to locate them in the political context. They are relatively simple and were criticized as such, but they laid the foundations for more complex models of bureaucratic behavior that incorporated multiple institutional actors (see Wilson 1989, ch. 13 appendix and Moe 1987a for criticisms of the Weingast and Moran approach). By examining the relationship between bureaus and various principals one by one, scholars began to sense which actors mattered for bureaucratic action. The most prominent were the president, Congress, interest groups, and the courts. The next set of models moved beyond dyadic relationships between the bureau and these actors.

2.2   Beyond dyads

A frequent criticism of the earlier institutional models was their lack of both multiple principals and multiple channels of political influence: in other words, these models suffered from a general lack of the complexity that makes up political reality. In response, theories have moved past narrow dyadic models to triads and beyond.

Politicians, interest groups, and the bureaucracy   The first attempts to move beyond dyadic models involved politicians, interest groups, and bureaus. Recognizing the problems inherent in the non-institutional framework created by Stigler and Peltzman, later works added politicians, usually legislators, to the Stigler–Peltzman model. Bendor and Moe (1985) develop a dynamic model of interaction between the legislature, bureaus and interest groups in which there is a constant, circular, adaptive process between the actors; interest groups influence the legislature, the legislature influences the bureau, and the bureau influences interest groups. Banks (1989) and Banks and Weingast (1992) start with a simple budgeting model of true strategic interaction between a politician and an agency. In this model, interest groups are possible providers of information about a bureau's true budget needs and therefore lower the costs of auditing the agency for the politicians.

In a similar fashion, works on central bank independence examine the connection between voters, politicians, and central banks (Rogoff 1985; Lohmann 1992; Waller 1992a; Waller and Walsh 1996). In these models, voters' expectations based on politicians' and central banks' actions determine macroeconomic conditions. The voters vote for a politician who decides whether or not to delegate policy making to the central bank. Here, too, appointment power of the politician is very important since the politician can appoint conservative central bankers after the power to determine monetary policy has been delegated.

These models added an important element of political accountability to the previous dyadic models. Voters or interest groups are the true principals who must work through politicians to obtain the policies they want. In some models, if the politicians do not comply with their wishes, voters can kick the politicians out. The earlier models often did not formally incorporate this explicit motivation for the politicians.

Who are the politicians in these models? In all of the aforementioned models, politicians are theoretical and generic; they could be the president, Congress as a whole, a congressional committee, and so on. It is not clear, nor is it necessarily meant to be clear, who the politicians should be. Sometimes they are specifically legislators, but they are not necessarily members of the US Congress. The advantage of the generic nature of the politicians is that the models are then applicable in a variety of governmental contexts other than the American system. However, the disadvantage is that the models require some adaptation to real characters in a political setting in order to test the models' predictions. Partially in response to this problem, in a parallel line of development, other scholars pursued models with more realistic politicians.

Congress, the president, and the bureaucracy   Another avenue of research parsed the politicians into real institutional actors. These models started with the previous dyadic models, president–bureau or Congress–bureau, and added either the president or Congress as a veto player.

For example, Ferejohn and Shipan (1990) included the president as a veto player in congressional dominance models. They formally explored the effects of the presidential veto on agency policy making. Their model includes judicial review as well (see below). Morris (1994) examines the role of legislative override and the presidential veto in Fed decision making. Morris and Munger (1997) show that the president's veto of congressional legislation is binding when a congressional coalition for a veto override does not exist. They apply this logic to legislation passed by Congress to counteract Federal Reserve policy.

Second, others added Congress to the presidential dominance models. In the area of appointment politics, recent works by Calvert et al. (1989), Hammond and Hill (1993), Nokken and Sala (1996), Snyder and Weingast (1996), McCarty and Ragazhian (1998), and Chang (1998) look at the president's appointment power in the context of Senate advice and consent and bureaucratic structure. Their conclusions are that although the president has agenda-setting power with appointments, he must keep in mind the Senate's preferences and procedural powers of delay, as well as the effects on bureaucratic policy. In addition to these works, a number of studies on appointments have examined the Supreme Court in the same fashion (Segal et al. 1992; Cameron et al. 1990; Lemieux and Stewart 1990; Moraski and Shipan 1999). Epstein and O'Halloran (1999) take a different tack. They model policy implementation as a choice on the floor of Congress to delegate authority to either an agency dominated by the president or a committee. The choice to delegate is contingent on the policy preferences of the president, the committee and the members on the floor. Their results enhance the framework to determine when agencies will even be given an opportunity to make policies.

By adding real institutional actors to the models, scholars could proceed relatively quickly and logically to test the models' implications empirically. Nokken and Sala (1996), Snyder and Weingast (1996), McCarty and Ragazhian (1998), Chang (1998), Moraski and Shipan (1999), and Bailey and Chang (1999) all test for presidential and senatorial influence on appointments and find influence by both sets of actors not only on appointments but also on policy. Similarly, Epstein and O'Halloran (1999) provide detailed analysis of delegation decisions by Congress as evidence in support of their delegation model. With real actors in the models, they could avoid the often-difficult step of adapting a generic formal model to real situations.

Congress, the president, the courts, and the bureaucracy   The courts are the newest addition to the models of bureaucratic influence.[4] These models try to capture the following sequence. Once an agency rules on regulatory policy, Congress can pass legislation to counteract the decision. The president can veto the legislation, and if he does so, Congress can override the veto. If the legislation is passed, the Supreme Court can strike down the statute, after which Congress can pass another law that overrules the Supreme Court decision. This sequence has implications for the types of decisions made by each of the actors in the sequence.

A number of recent models, often called 'separation-of-powers' models, try to capture some or all of this sequence. In these models, multiple principals influence the bureau but only in the fixed sequence prescribed by the Constitution. Each principal or branch has certain powers that provide a basis for interbranch squabbling. This approach has its roots in the late 1980s with McCubbins et al. (1987). They informally examine administrative procedures as a vehicle for congressional and presidential control over agencies which constituents and the courts help to enforce. Ferejohn and Shipan (1990) explicitly model the above sequence in a one-dimensional space by starting with the agency and Congress, then adding the president and, finally, the courts. Eskridge and Ferejohn (1992) build on the earlier work by Ferejohn and Shipan. They examine a slightly different sequence in which the courts can review agency policy under the Administrative Procedures Act (APA). After the courts review the policy, Congress can legislate against the judicial decisions or let them stand. By adding the possibility of congressional reversion, they temper earlier models in which the Court's last move was a binding constraint on legislative action at an earlier stage.

Others have extended these basic separation-of-powers models. Bawn (1995) develops a model in which politicians have a choice of ways to influence the bureau: *ex ante* statutory control and *ex post* oversight. Hammond and Knott (1996) examine the basic separation-of-powers model in an *n*-dimensional space. Resolving an old debate, they identify the conditions under which congressional or presidential dominance of the bureau prevails and when both institutions truly share powers.

Hammond and Knott's and Bawn's models provide examples of how rational choice work on bureaus has developed to meet Wilson's challenges. Starting with simple models of the bureaus themselves, rational choice scholars have added multiple principals, policy dimensions, and channels of influence. In short, they have slowly but surely added complexity in a systematic manner starting with the same, simple assumptions: actors that maximize their interests subject to their environmental constraints. These recent separation-of-powers models are a hopeful basis for yet more complex models in the future.

Beyond dyads: summary and conclusions   These studies focus more on political processes compared to earlier studies and place bureaus in a more realistically complex political setting. Whereas earlier works focused on the existence of influence *per se*, these works look at how that influence occurs as a process of ongoing interaction between several sets of actors, all with different institutional constraints. Furthermore, they have not just examined any interaction between actors, but particularly the institutional interaction in the American system of separated powers. In these attempts, they have done much to illuminate how that peculiar legal–constitutional and routinized system really works. Each institution has a set of its own actors with their own preferences who act within constraints set by the institution, but the institution itself has to deal with constraints set by other institutions' preferences and actions.

A number of recent papers on appointments provide excellent examples of the application of these models. Going back to the NLRB example, Snyder and Weingast (1996) dispute the finding that Republican presidents appoint pro-business members and Democratic presidents appoint pro-labor members. They point out that whether such appointments take place depends on the majority party in the Senate, which has veto power over presidential appointments. When the president and the Senate are of the same party, then the earlier predictions may play out, but not with certainty. Snyder and Weingast show that the structure of the NLRB itself also determines whether certain appointments are made since politicians are reasonably concerned with changes in policy which may require several appointments to accomplish. Thus, they show how the interaction of the president, the Senate and the NLRB lead to changes or lack of changes in policy. One institutional actor, the Senate for instance, or even two of them together, may limit the actions of the other actors, such as the president's ability to make his desired appointments.

Not only have these models been used to understand how the separation-of-powers system works, but also how its functioning has changed, and what that means for normative conclusions. Eskridge and Ferejohn (1992) use formal models to analyse the interaction of agencies, courts, Congress, and the president and demonstrate how a 1980s Supreme Court case transferred lawmaking power from the Congress to the president, thereby undermining Article 1, Section 7 of the Constitution. In that case, *Chevron USA, Inc.* v. *Natural Resources Defense Council, Inc.*, 467 US 837 (1984), the Court ruled that the APA did not require courts actually to challenge an agency's rulemaking; instead, the Court ruled that the courts should defer to the agencies (Ferejohn and Shipan 1990, p. 182). Ferejohn and Shipan then proceed to show how, even compared to the legislative veto, strong judicial scrutiny of an agency's interpretation of legislation upholds the separation of powers between the president and Congress when the courts are fairly clear on how the other two branches wish policy to be set.

These examples demonstrate how separation-of-powers models are readily applied and helpful in understanding policy making by the bureaucracy in the American system. However, this style of work is hardly limited to that system. A number of recent works have examined how a multi-institutional system works in other countries. Lohmann (1997) shows how monetary policy in Germany was determined by the federalist structure of Germany and of the German central banking system. Moser (1997) looks at the variation in checks and balances in governmental systems across countries and concludes that more checks and balances are associated with more independent central banks. Undoubtedly, cross-national comparisons of institutional interaction in government and its effects on policy represent a promising future area of study for separation-of-powers scholars.

3   Incorporating internal organization

Over 15 years ago, Terry Moe (1984) pointed to the potential of the new organizational economics for the study of bureaucracy. His key insight was that the choice of *internal* organizational structure could have as much to do with final policy outcomes as policy definition that occurred at the institutional level. The new economics of organization, he argued, allows us to understand how the design of organizations will affect outcomes, and this understanding would allow for predictions of the choice of structure given the policy objectives of institutional actors. To achieve this, he therefore argued, required two things: modification of models of private bureaus to incorporate the features and constraints of public ones ('B' in Figure 12.1) and a *linking* of models of institutional policy choice and internal organizational choice ('C' in Figure 12.1). As pointed out in the previous section, while approaches such as agency theory, transaction-cost economics, and contract theory increasingly have been applied successfully to study the organization of institutions other than bureaucracy and to the various interactions between them (see, for example, Banks and Weingast 1992; Weingast and Marshall 1988; Gilligan and Krehbiel 1987, 1989a; Austen-Smith 1992; Epstein and O'Halloran 1999; Williamson 1999), less sweeping progress has been made in analysing the internal organization of bureaucracy and its implications for institutional choice. Recent work applying the new economics of organization to the internal organization of bureaucracy, however, has shown the continued promise of this approach.

3.1   Rational choice models of internal agency structure and performance

To understand policy outputs from government agencies it is critical to understand how different organizational forms impact on these outputs. In other words, taking the organization to be *exogenous*, what outputs can one expect from different types of organizations? As Moe (1984) points out, in the past, the primarily normative study of organizations by public administrationists de-emphasized differences between private and public organizations. But as Wilson (1989), Moe (1984), and Williamson (1999) insist, government agencies do not operate under the same objectives or constraints as private, commercial organizations.[5] Thus, both organizational sociology and organizational economics must be modified to examine the impact of unique structural configurations on the outputs of government agencies.

One of the primary differences between government and private organizations is that between the punishments and inducements which can be offered to executives, managers, and operators. In the latter case, high-powered incentives are available to motivate subordinates and align interests. Often, however, that is not the case for government agencies. In particular, allocating shares of residual rents is not as easy or even possible in the context of government agencies. Here, a number of theorists have provided important insights into an alternative theory of incentives in government agencies. Two recent projects illustrate the usefulness of these efforts.[6]

Banks and Sundaram (1998) examine how civil servants might behave when only replacement and career advancement are available as a means of motivating action. Their model combines two types of informational asymmetries between a political principal and an agent: both the agent's competence or capability (or type) and the agent's precise effort are unknown to the principal. The only thing that the principal observes is the final output from the agent. In the traditional model of this form, the best that the principal can do is to design an incentive scheme which encourages the agent to both reveal her type *and* exert effort in doing so. But when such a scheme is not available, the principal's problem is harder. In this case, the only incentive the principal can provide is a promise of future employment. The insight that Banks and Sundaram provide is that this incentive must also be credible; but it is difficult for the principal to precommit to re-employment or advancement. How then can such a device work at all to motivate effort? They answer that it will be in the principal's interest to re-employ an agent if the outcome from the agent's early-stage work reveals a sufficiently high type (higher than what the principal could obtain by employing an unknown individual from the external labor market). Since the principal prefers more capable types and her estimate of a particular agent's capability depends on past performance, she is better off rewarding good outcomes with a new (contractual) term. This insight about the credibility of promises of career advancement allows for a strong prediction about the nature of outputs from agencies in which only 'low-powered' incentives are available: weaker types of agents will not exert much effort, because even if they do, it is unlikely that they will be retained; stronger types of agents will work hard in the hope of also showing their types and gaining re-employment.

A second example of useful modification of models from the new economics of organization is the examination of agency 'missions' by Tirole (1994).[7] Tirole starts with a logic similar to Banks and Sundaram, adapting the traditional principal–agent model to account for career concerns. In his model, however, there are multiple tasks. The question Tirole asks is what types of 'missions' are feasible as equilibrium behavior? In particular, Tirole examines three types of equilibria. The most basic is what he calls a 'simple', 'clear', or 'single' mission: each agent pursues one task and performance is rewarded based on the output that is produced. But as Wilson (1989) points out, particularly in public bureaus, these types of single missions are rare. More often, agencies are charged with multiple objectives which must be navigated by the agent. What effects do multifaceted, or 'composite' missions have? Tirole generates two results that address this question. First, if performance is only measurable for a subset of the tasks, then agents will not pursue all the tasks at the desired level. Instead all of their efforts will be focused on tasks in which measurement is possible. However, a composite mission equilibrium, one in which the agent pursues multiple tasks, can exist if the agent's capability is revealed precisely by the fact that she can be successful in more than one task. Second, Tirole also demonstrates that under certain conditions there will exist 'fuzzy mission' equilibria. In these equilibria, the political principal has an incentive not to reveal *ex ante* how performance will be rewarded. Instead, she acts probabilistically, sometimes rewarding performance on some tasks and at other times rewarding performance on the others. The reason is that under these conditions, agents will 'hedge', splitting effort among multiple tasks. Tirole therefore uses the logic of agency theory to understand both the conditions under which the different types of missions Wilson describes can be rational and, what is more important, explains a mechanism whereby these missions can actually affect outcomes.

3.2   Linking institutional choice, structural choice, and agency performance

Having understood the way that different organizational forms map incentives and objectives into policy outcomes, it is possible to understand how these forms can be used as political tools. In the rest of this section we review four examples, two formal and two informal, of how rational choice models can help understand the mechanisms whereby internal organization affects policy outcomes, and how organizational design affects the interbranch policy games described in Section 2.

In a series of papers, Moe (1984, 1987a, 1989, 1991) develops a theory of how rational political actors use organizational design as a means of obtaining preferred policy outcomes. Moe argues that two factors – political uncertainty and political compromise – lead holders of public authority to structure government agencies in ways that are not economically efficient. Each of these factors has a different implication. Political uncertainty – the fact that today's holders of public authority might not be tomorrow's – leads elected officials to set up government agencies that are resistant to change by potential future saboteurs. For example, when the Environmental Protection

Agency (EPA) was formed, environmentalists, who were enjoying a 'moment in the sun' in the early 1970s, were fearful of losing power. They therefore organized the agency using detailed procedures and staffed it with lawyers rather than scientists to make sure that, if and when the opponents of the environmental movement took power, the agency would 'stay the course' despite attempts to redirect it.[8] Moe argues that if environmentalists had not been concerned with the future, they would have structured the EPA so as to more effectively make and carry out policies. But because of political uncertainty, this agency was designed suboptimally.

The second factor Moe identifies is 'political compromise'. Moe argues that since majoritarian institutions require interested parties to strike compromises over both policy and structural decisions, 'losers' in public debates obtain some say in the design and structure of agencies. They use this opportunity to design a structure of policy implementation that tempers vigorous enforcement of the 'winner's' policies. A clear example of this strategy is the design of formal implementation of the Occupational Safety and Health Act in the early 1970s. According to Moe, although business interests failed to completely prevent the development of workplace health and safety regulation, they succeeded in having some say in the design of policy implementation. Specifically, they split standard setting from enforcement – by creating two separate agencies, the National Institute for Occupational Safety and Health (NIOSH) and the Occupational Safety and Health Administration (OSHA) – delegating much of the implementation to state government administration. They also created lax standards for judicial review of OSHA rules (Moe 1989, 1990, 1991). Thus, opponents of the law successfully limited the effectiveness with which it could be implemented. Although aspects of Moe's argument are vulnerable to criticism (see, for example, de Figueiredo 1998a; Epstein and O'Halloran 1999; de Figueiredo et al. 1999; Zegart 1996; Williamson 1999), Moe takes a large step by demonstrating that organizational choice can be manipulated to achieve policy objectives.

In their book, *Bureaucratic Dynamics: The Role of Bureaucracy in Democracy*, Wood and Waterman (1994) argue that the dynamics of government agencies can be understood by applying principal–agent theory from the economics of organization.[9] Wood and Waterman argue that simple comparative statics about institutional change provide an insufficient picture of how bureaucracies react to political changes. They argue that when the political context of an agency shifts, the *dynamic agency adjustment process*, or how the agency responds to a political shift, depends on the internal organizational of the agency. In general, agencies will respond to the incentives provided by political principals, but the exact nature of this response depends on a number of organizational as well as institutional factors. In other words, the way an agency responds to a particular political 'stimulus' will depend on the nature of the stimulus (in the more traditional parlance, the type of control mechanism) *and* the nature of the agency organization. As Wood and Waterman comment on one example of how organizations might respond differentially to the same technological stimuli, 'Technological factors can affect the bureaucratic response dynamic through interorganizational dependencies and inertial effects. For example, some bureaucratic activities depend on others for completion. ... Obviously, the exact nature of the technological factor varies with the agency and the process' (1993, p. 503).[10]

Both Moe, and Wood and Waterman use non-formal applications of the economics of organization to show how the organization of agencies affects the political calculus of policy implementation. Recent approaches have formally explored these interactions.[11] For example, Snyder and Weingast (1996), Havrilesky and his coauthors (Havrilesky 1995; Chappell et al. 1993; Havrilesky and Schweitzer 1990; Havrilesky and Gildea 1992) and Chang (1998) demonstrate how the internal decision-making processes *within* agencies can affect the interbranch struggles over appointments. For agencies that are *voting bodies*, such as the NLRB, Snyder and Weingast (1996) distinguish between appointments that move the median voter within the agency and those that do not. Consider a simplified example of the appointment process to the NLRB. Suppose that the median member of the Board is pro-business. If a pro-labor coalition is forged between the Senate and president, their ability to influence the future decisions of the Board will depend on *whom* they are replacing. If the member to be replaced is pro-labor, they cannot move the median: the best they can do is replace the pro-labor member with another pro-labor member, which will maintain the median as pro-business. Alternatively, if the retiring member is pro-business, they can move the median: appointing a pro-labor member will move the median in the direction of greater labor bias, thus shifting policy outcomes. Chang (1998) uses a similar examination of voting and organizational procedures in the Federal Reserve Board (FRB) to demonstrate empirically how the organization of the FRB conditions appointment decisions to that organization. In both of these cases, the structure and procedures of the NLRB and FRB condition the political strategies pursued by elected officials to influence policy.

A second example of how formal models linking politics and structure can fruitfully be applied is the current work that links the nature of internal incentives within an agency to the assignment of policies to particular agencies. De Figueiredo (1998b) uses multitask agency theory – pioneered by Holmstrom and Milgrom (1991) – to show that the assignment of tasks to an agency can be used as a political tool (see also Ting 1998; Feltham and Xie 1994; Itoh 1993). The key insight of multitask agency theory is that the performance of an agent on a particular task depends not only on the characteristics of the task to be performed and the incentives provided by a principal, but also on the characteristics and incentives of the *other tasks* an agent is charged with performing. In politics, this has important implications, for it implies that 'political principals' can use jurisdictional groupings for political purposes. In his most stark result, de Figueiredo shows that this implication of the internal organization of government agencies means that elected officials will assign tasks in a way that not only achieves the implementation of policies they support, but also distracts attention *away* from implementation of policies they oppose. As with Moe's arguments, this theory shows how structural choice is an important driver and constraint on the political interaction between elected officials and government agencies.

4 Conclusion

Understanding government agencies is not easy. They are complex and differentiated, making the development of a unified, coherent theory of American bureaucracy a difficult, potentially insurmountable challenge: theories must account for a range of possible agency outputs by taking account of the interplay between all of the external variables – including all of the formal institutions and interests – and internal variables, including organizational factors. As we noted earlier, this is the crux of the Wilsonian view that scholars applying rational choice methods must address. In many ways, so far, Wilson's critique has been well founded: rational choice methods have not developed a single, unified theory of American bureaucracy.

As we have outlined in this chapter, however, while not yet having fully met the challenge, recent developments have indicated that rational choice approaches are being fruitfully applied to meet the Wilson critique. In particular, models of separation of powers have expanded the range of actors and their institutional interactions in extremely promising and deep directions. At the same time, a number of rational choice models have begun to be developed which also link the internal organization of bureaucracy to the political choices of elected officials. Just as enormous progress has been made in the field of economics in applying economic methods to understanding the internal performance of private firms, agency theory, contract theory, transaction-cost economics, and game theory have all been applied to enhance our understanding of how the 'black box' of a firm performs (see Williamson 1996; Milgrom and Roberts 1992). These approaches have begun to uncover how the 'black box' of government agencies operate and influence actual political outcomes. In this way, the deep literature on public administration, which is primarily concerned with how government agencies should be organized, is being integrated with the positive approaches of the new instutionalism in the field of bureaucratic performance and behavior.

Notes

1. Notably, as we discuss later, 'positive', 'deductive', 'formal', and 'rational' theories are obviously distinctive concepts. In the context of this literature, for the purposes of the current exposition, we use these terms relatively interchangeably. Later in this survey, we offer a more variegated discussion of the distinctions.
2. A very clear exposition of the principal–agent theory is contained in Milgrom and Roberts (1992).
3. Notably, Wilson's famous two-by-two matrix, in which he outlines the different interest-group environments an agency might be subject to, also focuses exclusively on the nature of dyadic interest group(s)–bureau relations.
4. Notably, the traditional view that the courts 'move last' was motivated primarily by constitutional rulings: in that domain, Supreme Court rulings are the final word and other institutional actors must, at least constitutionally, comply with these decisions. In the area of statutory interpretation, however, this is not the case: Congress and the president can revise interpretations through follow-on legislation (see McCubbins et al. 1994; Schwartz et al. 1994).
5. See also De Alessi (Chapter 2, this volume).
6. For other examples see also Hammond (1986, 1994); Maskin et al. (1997).
7. See also Dewatripont et al. (1999).
8. Moe's argument has been further strengthened by others who have studied how administrative procedures, as determined by Congress, the president and the courts, are important determinants of policy outcomes. McCubbins et al. (1987, 1989) for example, explain how the design of agency procedures – through methods such as the standing of interest groups, informational and reporting requirements, and interest-group subsidies – have a major impact on the dynamic control of agencies.
9. See also Wood and Waterman (1993).
10. Indeed, this interaction between political and institutional change and agency structure was echoed in Moe's (1987b) work on the National Labor Relations Board.
11. These examples highlight the fact that there is an important distinction between two traditions which traditionally are perceived to 'go together': a tradition of formalization and the assumptions of rationality. In the context of organizations, the latter often is attacked (see, for example, Perrow 1986; Williamson 1985, 1996, 1999; March and Simon 1958; March 1978; Simon [1945] 1976). In fact, it is the former that has the greatest power in exploring the complex interactions between internal and external factors determining agency outputs. As the formal technology has become more sophisticated, the need to pair rationality with formalization has diminished. Exciting new work on boundedly rational agents and the implication for organization has just begun to explore this promise (see, for example, Bendor and Moe 1985; Bendor 1999; Ting 1999).

13 The judiciary

Gary M. Anderson

1 Introduction

A cursory examination of the judiciary might lead one reasonably to conclude that the legal rulings rendered by judges are essentially unaffected by outside influences. This relative independence of the judiciary is usually assumed to derive from the institutional insulation of sitting judges from those interested parties who may be significantly impacted by their rulings. For example, laws against bribery and corruption are strict and zealously enforced. At the federal level, judges are granted lifetime tenure, albeit subject to the sanction of impeachment in extreme cases; at the state level, judges typically serve for more limited periods but generally enjoy high security of office. Therefore, judges seemingly are well protected against political threats designed to influence their decisions in favor of particular interested parties.

The independence of the judiciary is sometimes portrayed as necessary to ensure that this branch of government functions as an effective counterweight to the legislative and executive branches. Many scholars have defended the 'independence' of the judiciary on normative grounds, arguing that the welfare of society is thereby enhanced (see Buchanan 1977). According to this view, the role of the judiciary is to protect society from unconstitutional actions by the other branches, the judges being motivated to behave in this way by their concern for the public interest. Consistent with this view, the independent judiciary might be regarded as an agent representing the interests of groups which would otherwise be unrepresented (or underrepresented) in other political forums.

A large and important literature has emerged which models legislatures as firms supplying wealth transfers to competing interest groups, packaged by those political bodies in the form of legislation (McCormick and Tollison 1981). In this model, legislatures assign property rights in wealth transfers to the highest bidder by means of contracts termed 'laws'.

What is the relationship between the operation of this market for wealth transfers and the operation of the judiciary? One interpretation would suggest that judicial rulings as well as the general behavior of judges are simply functions of the short-run interests of the pressure groups who successfully bid for political influence. Accordingly, the judiciary would not actually be 'independent' at all, but would instead tend to behave in a manner reflecting the shifting tides of interest-group competition.

However, when long-run effects are taken into account, a degree of judicial independence may be consistent with, and indeed an integral component of, the interest-group theory of government. In a path-breaking article, William Landes and Richard Posner (1975) developed an economic model in which the independent judiciary plays an important role in the operation of the political market for wealth transfers. They argue that the function of judges is to impart stability to the bargains struck between the legislature and organized interest groups. Because of its effective independence from the current legislature, the judiciary can resolve disputes involving the interpretation or constitutionality of a law or regulation in terms of the intentions of the originally enacting legislative body. Thus, legislative contracts with interest groups will not be abrogated simply because the political winds have shifted; the durability of such contracts is instead enhanced. Legislation transferring wealth becomes more valuable to interest groups than would be the case if it were vulnerable to changes in the political composition of the legislative body.

In this chapter I examine this theory of the independent judiciary, explore its implications, and review the relevant empirical literature. Are the findings of these empirical investigations supportive of, or inconsistent with, the Landes–Posner model?

The chapter is organized as follows. Section 2 examines issues related to the problem of specifying the objective function of judges, and considers the advantages and disadvantages of alternative behavioral models of the judiciary. Section 3 outlines the interest-group theory of government and explores its implications for multibranch representative democracy. Section 4 discusses the subtleties of judicial 'independence'. Section 5 explores the functioning of the independent judiciary in the context of the interest-group model of government. Section 6 reviews the recent empirical literature on the relationship between current political coalitions and judicial behavior. Section 7 concludes and summarizes the key arguments.

2   What do judges maximize?

Until fairly recently a view of judicial motivation held by many legal scholars and political scientists was that judges act in ways designed to preserve the integrity of the legal system, maximizing the abstract concept of 'justice' and, at the same time, the welfare of society. In other words, judges are not merely ordinary mortals but are instead motivated to pursue more noble goals. Nor, according to this view, are judges subject to influence, even at the margin, by parties whose economic interests stand to be affected by judicial rulings. Economists, even while extending the model of rational self-interest beyond the domain of ordinary commercial exchange into the realm of governmental decision making, long neglected the problem of judicial behavior and motivation.

An exception to the evident lack of interest in this question among economists was Adam Smith, arguably the original 'economic imperialist'. Smith assumed as a matter of course that judges were self-interested actors, and proceeded to analyse the implications of various sorts of constraints on judicial behavior.[1] Later economists, however, largely ignored Smith's seminal contributions in this regard.

Applications of the neoclassical model to the behavior of judges can proceed down one of two paths. First, judges might be seen as rational actors who maximize something other than their own pecuniary wealth. Adherents of this view argue that since the judiciary is insulated from monetary pressures, judges maximize along other margins, for example by basing their legal decisions on their personal ideological preferences, by seeking greater power or prestige by way of those decisions, or both. But judges are supposedly prevented from acting or deciding cases in ways that garner them greater financial benefits.

Interestingly, a prominent exponent of this view is Richard Posner. In his widely respected *Economic Analysis of Law* (1998, pp. 581–4), he argues that judges are not motivated by personal economic interests which lead them to behave in ways consistent with pecuniary wealth maximization. They instead indulge their ideological preferences through their judicial decisions, acting 'to impose their policy preferences on society' (p. 583). Thus, in Posner's view, judges are self-interested but only in a utility-maximizing sense, and do not behave as simple wealth maximizers. They decide cases not on the basis of their personal economic interests, but instead as ways of expressing their personal philosophical and political beliefs.

The second model of rational self-interest applied to judicial behavior views judges as actors who do in fact maximize simple pecuniary wealth. They may pursue this objective explicitly in the form of salary, perquisites, and so on, or implicitly in the form of accomplishments strongly correlated with future potential earnings, such as promotion to a higher court.

The question of the nature of judicial motivation has recently received quite a bit of attention from empirical economists. There is substantial evidence supporting the proposition that judges are self-interested at the margin, and that simple pecuniary wealth maximization is a dominant factor.

Cohen (1989) based his study on a rich source of data, examining the dispositions of over 600 Sherman Act antitrust indictments issued between 1955 and 1980. He hypothesized that self-interested judges would tend, *ceteris paribus*, to decide cases based on how they thought their rulings would affect their chances for promotion to a higher court. This is indeed what Cohen found. In cases where deciding judges saw opportunities for promotion, rulings tended to favor the prosecution (the US Department of Justice) which, of course, makes recommendations to the president on judicial appointments and court assignments. Antitrust defendants also tended to receive longer jail sentences and stiffer fines, and *nolo contendere* pleas were less likely to be accepted by the court over the government's objection, when vacancies existed on the next higher court.

In addition to enhancing his prospects for promotion, a self-interested judge should be concerned with minimizing his burden of work. Cohen reported evidence suggesting that such judicial behavior was occurring as well. He found that the larger the backlog of cases on a court's docket, the more severe were the penalties imposed on defendants who elected to plead 'not guilty' but who were subsequently convicted of the crime charged. Defendants who increased the judge's workload by refusing to settle out of court were selectively penalized. By so altering the structure of incentives facing defendants awaiting trial, the judge's workload is substantially reduced; when guilty defendants expect to face relatively more severe penalties, they will be more likely to accept pre-trial settlements.

In another paper, Cohen (1991) utilized a different data source to consider similar questions. He examined federal district court rulings as to the constitutionality of the criminal sentencing guidelines promulgated by the US Sentencing Commission. Cohen again argued that the economic model of self-interested judicial behavior suggests that, *ceteris paribus*, judges will tend to prefer lighter workloads and to decide cases in ways likely to enhance their prospects for promotion to a higher court.

Cohen found strong empirical support for these propositions in the data. By reducing prosecutorial discretion, stricter sentencing guidelines would tend to increase the number of criminal defendants going to trial. Judges with very heavy dockets should therefore be more inclined to rule the Sentencing Commission's guidelines unconstitutional and this correlation was statistically significant. Judges enjoying superior prospects for promotion to an appeals court position – measured by several 'promotion-potential factors', including the current number of vacancies on the appeals court, the number of district court judges per circuit court seat, and the age of the oldest appeals court judge from the judge's state – were, other things being equal, less likely to rule particular guidelines unconstitutional. In other words, judges facing better prospects for promotion tended to rule more often in favor of the government's preferred outcome.

In short, Cohen found that judicial rulings appear to be influenced in part by personal career ambitions. Promotion to a higher court tends to increase the present discounted value of a judge's lifetime income stream owing not only to a higher judicial salary, but also to the greater earnings prospects in private practice following (voluntary) retirement from the bench. These findings suggest that, other things being the same, judges will tend to decide cases in a manner that promotes their own self-interest, maximizing their pecuniary wealth subject to constraints.[2]

Of course, as mentioned above, rational self-interest might conceivably express itself in the form of the pursuit of personal ideological agendas by individual judges. Kimenyi et al. (1985) subjected that proposition to empirical testing. They reasoned that if judicial decisions merely reflect personal ideological preferences, judges would tend to try more cases in jurisdictions where judicial pay is lower. Judges with an ideological bent would want to try more cases because each additional decision affords them an opportunity to increase their level of personal satisfaction by imposing their ideological preferences on society. This source of utility would tend to be relatively more important to judges operating in low-pay jurisdictions than in jurisdictions where the financial returns to judgeships are higher.

For the purpose of exploring this possible relationship, Kimenyi et al. looked at the behavior of US state courts during 1980. They found that where the salaries of state supreme court judges were higher, *ceteris paribus*, the number of cases those judges decided was significantly higher, too. Therefore, lower-paid judges do not seem to compensate for lower salaries by pursuing additional opportunities to express their ideological preferences more aggressively (that is, hearing more cases). Rather, judges appear to behave as simple wealth maximizers, hearing cases as a positive function of their remuneration. The supply curve of judicial decisions thus seems to be upward sloping.

In sum, recent empirical studies support the hypothesis that judges are at least partly motivated in their judicial behavior by the pursuit of personal wealth, and not merely by a desire to express their ideological preferences or to maximize the welfare of society. Judges therefore seem potentially subject to influence from other branches of government exerted in the form of tangible rewards, including salary but also including other kinds of wealth enhancement, offered with the intention of modifying the content of judicial rulings.

3   The interest-group theory of government

At the core of neoclassical economics is the concept of rationally self-interested maximization, the assumption that personal behaviors represent consistent efforts to enhance the individual's wealth and wellbeing. Traditionally, the application of this self-interest model stopped at the boundary of the private sector. Public policy formation was widely seen as a different animal, a process by which benevolent government actors made decisions aimed at the goal of increasing society's welfare. This view implied that government intervention follows from the unselfish efforts of politicians and bureaucrats to correct various market failures, either to provide efficient levels of public goods, to correct externality problems, or to redistribute income in the direction of greater equity.

The 'public-interest' theory of government is obviously very implausible, given that it fails to relate the resulting distribution of benefits to the motivations of individual actors. By coercively intervening in private markets, government benefits some groups and individuals at the expense of others. Laws, programs, regulations, and other public policies serve to transfer wealth (sometimes in the form of cash payments, sometimes in the form of opportunities to earn restriction rents) within society. The availability of such transfers provides an incentive for individuals to band together with those having similar economic interests in order to influence the transfer process in their favor. Competition between different groups of organized potential recipients of such transfers explains the pattern of government policies that we observe.

The interest-group theory of government (see Stigler 1971; Peltzman 1976; McCormick and Tollison 1981; and Becker 1983, 1985) is founded on this simple logic. As is the case with an ordinary, private, voluntary market, the precise public policy outcome will reflect the equilibrium interaction of demand and supply. But whereas a voluntary private market will necessarily be a positive-sum game in which both demanders and suppliers mutually benefit, the public policy 'market' is a zero- (or negative-) sum game wherein the marginal benefits enjoyed by the winners are at best equal to (and frequently less than) the marginal costs suffered by the losers. Prospective recipients of the transfers are the 'demanders', while the previous owners of the wealth being transferred are the 'suppliers'. Politicians act as brokers in this market, matching the recipients of the transfers with the sources of the wealth required to finance them, in accordance with the goal of maximizing their own political support.

A considerable body of research demonstrates the usefulness of the interest-group model of government (compare Alesina and Rodrik 1994; Grossman and Helpman 1994; and Leidy and Hoekman 1994 for a sampling of the recent literature). If government is modeled as a firm specializing in the production and distribution of wealth transfers to competing pressure groups, public policy decisions can be understood as the operational manifestation of this production process. Because all policy decisions potentially have implications for the distribution of wealth in society, interest groups will rationally seek to manipulate the policy agenda of government in ways designed to influence this redistribution of wealth in favor of their own members (see McCormick and Tollison 1981).

From this perspective, legislation is the primary mechanism by means of which government transfers are organized and distributed. The legislature functions as the broker of wealth transfers produced and marketed to pressure groups, although certain legal devices are available which permit interest groups access to wealth transfers without the intervention of that legislative body. One of these alternatives is the constitutional amendment, which has been shown to provide wealth transfers of greater durability, other things held equal, than ordinary legislative enactments (see Anderson et al. 1990).[3]

4   How 'independent' is the independent judiciary?

The judiciary can be described as 'independent' to the extent that the decisions rendered by courts are uninfluenced by the sorts of factors and political pressures which tend to affect legislative deliberations. Individual judges in such a setting would render decisions solely on the basis of relevant legal principles (precedent, constitutionality, and so on) and would be essentially unaffected by pressures exerted by interested parties. Those who espouse this view often go on to argue that an independent judiciary plays a key role in guaranteeing the smooth operation of a representative democracy. The functional independence of the judiciary is often merely presumed by these thinkers, who devote little or no effort toward explaining what would possibly motivate judges to act in such a public-spirited manner. Thus, it is possible to conceive of the independent judiciary as a kind of non-economic artifact, exhibiting a pattern of behavior on the part of individual judges which benefits the overall society despite the absence of a plausible motivational model explaining that behavior.

This economically unmotivated model of judicial behavior has been criticized by political scientists, some of whom have long argued that the judiciary is in reality not 'independent', but is instead buffeted by the same kinds of political pressures to which other branches of government are subject (compare Dahl 1957 and Shapiro 1964).

A major difficulty for this variant of the interest-group story is that the existing judiciary seems to be highly independent of day-to-day partisan political pressures in actual practice.[4] In part, this independence is built into the structure of the judiciary. Take, for example, the federal judiciary. Article III of the US Constitution imparts a substantial degree of independence to the courts by requiring federal judges to be appointed for life terms rather than being elected (partially insulating sitting federal judges from electoral politics), and prohibiting Congress from reducing their salaries while they are serving on the bench (stymieing possible efforts by the legislative branch to punish federal judges by lowering their pay).

Although a number of studies conducted by political scientists have reported finding evidence of a relationship between the political party affiliation of judges and the decisional tendencies of those jurists (Goldman 1966 and Tate 1981), recent econometric studies cast doubt on this hypothesized relationship. For instance, consider the empirical investigation conducted by Ashenfelter et al. (1995). They analyse nearly every federal civil rights and prisoner appeals case filed in three federal court districts during fiscal year 1981, and investigate the possibility that various characteristics of the presiding judge (including his or her political party) play a significant role in explaining judicial decisions. (Civil rights cases were included owing to the greater likelihood that these politically sensitive cases would allow judicial partisanship to affect the outcome.) They report no significant results from including the party affiliation of the ruling judge, however.

This finding, namely that there appears to be no statistically significant correlation between political party affiliations and the actual rulings issued by judges, nevertheless leaves room for ordinary 'patronage politics' in the judicial appointment process, evidence of which has been reported by a bevy of political scientists (for example, see Barrow et al. 1996). Federal judgeships are still plum appointments, which provide the fortunate appointee with a large capital gain in connection with his or her legal career. In the context of the interest-group theory of government, political party organizations represent competing wealth-transfer brokerage services, and the party faithful must be rewarded for their contributions of various resources (time, effort, money, and so forth). Assuming that the political market for transfers is efficient, the behavior of suppliers should be identical regardless of party affiliation, other things held equal. Hence, while patronage politics may determine the identities of judges, it does not necessarily follow that, once they have been elevated to the bench, their decisions will be swayed by partisan political considerations. Regardless of the precise identities of the 'winners' in this patronage game, the pattern of investments by relevant interest groups will remain the same.

But judicial independence also tends to benefit participants in the market for transfers by protecting the durability, and hence the value, of agreements reached between legislators and interest groups. This suggests that a relatively independent judiciary plays a crucial role in the functioning of an efficient market for wealth transfers.

5   The independent judiciary in an interest-group perspective

At first blush, it might seem that the judiciary should be subject to the momentary whims of interest-group politics. The production of wealth transfers requires the joint efforts of all three branches of government, the legislative, the executive, and the judicial. Decisions about the interpretation of, and implications following from, particular legislative acts play a pivotal role in determining the practical effect of such laws, and hence their value to interest groups. Thus, according to this reasoning, judicial rulings should be the expression of interest-group equilibria, for the same reasons that legislation takes the precise form it does. Each new Congress would therefore have a compliant and supportive judiciary.

Landes and Posner (1975) challenged the notion that the interest-group theory of government implies a judiciary that automatically supports the momentary bargains struck between the legislative branch and high-bidding interest groups seeking governmentally brokered redistribution. They proposed a model in which the efficient functioning of the market for wealth transfers is significantly enhanced by a judiciary that operates in a highly independent manner.

They define an *independent judiciary* as 'one that does not make decisions on the basis of the sorts of political factors (for example, the electoral strength of the people affected by a decision) that would influence and in most cases control the decision were it made by a legislative body such as the US Congress' (ibid., p. 875). Such a judiciary would be functionally autonomous, insulated (at least in part) from the day-to-day political pressures exerted by the shifting coalitions of organized interest groups. As a result, past legislative contracts are protected from being easily abrogated.

The element of continuity and stability that is necessary for interest-group politics to operate in the context of the legislature can be provided either by the *procedural rules of the legislature* (including the committee system, parliamentary rules of order governing bill introductions, floor debates and votes, and so on), by the *independence of the judiciary*, or both (ibid., p. 878).

Landes and Posner argue that protecting the integrity of the courts will be to the advantage of the legislature because this independence will help to preserve the value of wealth-transfer programs; such benefits would obviously be worth less if such programs, once enacted, were threatened by judicial interference. 'If we assume that an independent judiciary would … interpret and apply legislation in accordance with the original legislative understanding … it follows that an independent judiciary facilitates … interest-group politics' (ibid., p. 879). Consequently, they predict that a legislature will take steps to provide itself with an independent judiciary in order to protect the value of legislative contracts with interest groups.

If judicial independence is valuable to the legislature as a source of durability for the wealth transfers it brokers, then the legislature presumably should reward the judiciary for providing that 'service'. In other words, the legislature should be observed to foster judicial independence. An effective device for encouraging any form of behavior is to pay for it. This suggests a possible direct test of the Landes–Posner theory: are judges who exhibit greater independence rewarded by the legislature?

There are two avenues for approaching such a test: the operating budget of the judiciary and the salaries paid to individual judges. Anderson et al. (1989) selected the latter reward mechanism for empirical testing. They investigated whether there was any statistically significant relationship between the annual salaries of state Supreme Court judges and the degree of independence exhibited by the judiciary in that state, after controlling for other relevant factors which might be expected to influence salaries. (The exogenous factors included measures of the opportunity cost of service on the court and of the prospective workload on that court as well as measures of statutory constraints on judges, such as lengths of judicial terms of office.)

They employed a measure of substantive due process reviews as an indicator of judicial independence. Substantive due process review is an evaluation by the court designed to determine whether a legislative act or other government regulation violates the constitutional guarantee of due process. In other words, does the legislation or regulation have the effect of violating an individual's freedom of contract, or otherwise interfere with his due process rights, without there being a vital public interest served by the law in question? The classic substantive due process case was *Lochner* v. *New York*, 198 US 45 (1905), in which the US Supreme Court ruled that a state law restricting the number of hours bakers could work violated the Fourteenth Amendment to the US Constitution. Although the Supreme Court refused to hear further 'substantive due process' cases beginning in early 1937, this did not foreclose state courts from continuing to undertake such reviews. All state constitutions contain due process provisions similar to that forming the basis for earlier reviews in the federal courts.

Anderson et al. argued that the willingness of state courts to overturn legislative acts on constitutional due process grounds provides a strong indicator of the effective independence of that judiciary. Courts that demonstrate a greater readiness to subject acts of the current legislature to due process review are more 'independent' of that body, better protecting the durability of all legislative contracts with interest groups. Provision of this valuable service by the judiciary should be rewarded by the legislature: other things being equal, judges who are more independent should be paid higher salaries.

Using state data, Anderson et al. found that judicial pay indeed tends to be significantly higher, *ceteris paribus*, in states where the courts have a stronger record of challenging legislative acts on substantive due process grounds. This suggests that judges receive financial rewards for behaving independently. The functional independence of the state judiciary provides a valuable service to the state legislature by enhancing the durability of past (and the expected durability of future) contracts with interest groups. Greater independence results in higher salaries for state judges, *ceteris paribus*.

Other factors were also found to be significant in determining the remuneration of state judges. Salaries tended to be higher where the opportunity cost of service on the bench was higher, where prospective judicial workloads were heavier, and where judges' terms of office were shorter and, hence, less secure. State legislatures act to reward the exercise of judicial independence at the margin, but other factors beyond the direct control of the lawmaking body also appear to affect judicial pay.

In short, the judiciary is apparently populated by rational individuals who respond in predictable ways to salary incentives offered by the legislative branch to encourage judicial independence. This implies that a degree of such independence benefits the legislature, the broker of wealth transfers to favored parties. Yet a completely independent judiciary would likely jeopardize the production of new wealth-transfer contracts between the current legislature and high-bidding interest groups. We now turn to a review of this problem.

6   Partisan politics and judicial independence in political equilibrium

In a government driven by interest-group politics, the existing degree of judicial independence represents an equilibrium outcome, and is therefore not necessarily absolute or total. There is a tension between protecting the durability of wealth transfers to interest groups brokered by past legislatures and the ability of the present legislature to enact new special-interest measures. The same judicial independence that serves to protect the value of past legislative contracts tends to conflict with the ongoing operation of the legislative wealth-brokering process. The rulings of a completely independent court may interfere with the ability of a legislature to enter into new contracts or to undertake the recontracting necessary to maintain political equilibrium. Efficiency requires that a balance be struck between these two competing influences.

Therefore, from the perspective of the legislature, there is an *optimal degree of judicial independence*. That optimum equates marginal cost and marginal benefit, where the costs associated with the tendency of an independent judiciary to impede the functioning of current redistributional activity just balance the benefits of enhanced durability. One implication of this equilibrium condition is that simple partisan politics may in fact exert a marginal influence on the behavior of judges. The actual equilibrium outcome may well reflect such political pressure.

The possibility that partisan political considerations may interact with the behavior of judges has been studied extensively by political scientists. Consider the recent contribution by Barrow et al. (1996). They examine data describing the careers of US federal circuit and appellate court judges from 1789 to 1992. They report finding that partisan politics appears to correlate with the decisions to appoint and promote federal judges – that presidents overwhelmingly nominate members of their own party to federal judgeships. This 'same party appointment rate' tends to fall when the president is 'politically vulnerable', or when his party does not control the Senate, a majority of which must vote to confirm all federal judicial appointments. Voluntary departures from the federal bench tend to occur more frequently when the judge's party occupies the White House. 'Divided government' (that is, control of the presidency and Congress by different parties) seems to induce the president to make concessions to the opposition party in the form of cross-party appointments (ibid., ch. 2).

The president has the constitutional authority to nominate prospective judges to the federal bench. But the Senate must approve the actual appointments. The Constitution prohibits Congress from reducing judicial salaries, but the legislative branch is free to manipulate salaries in the other direction, determining the rate of increase. Moreover, any expansion of the federal judiciary requires legislative authorization, and Congress must appropriate funds for the administrative budget of the federal courts.

New judgeships must be authorized by Congress, and that body has a strong incentive to carefully assess the implications of possible expansion of the judiciary in terms of the patronage opportunities available to the majority party. When Congress is controlled by a majority from one party and the presidency controlled by the other, the legislative branch will be less likely to approve new judgeships (which would amount to giving patronage away to the other party).

For example, in 1954 the Democrats won the majority in both houses, and for the rest of the Republican Eisenhower administration, only four new judgeships were authorized (and three of these came about as a result of granting statehood to Alaska and Hawaii). But after the election of the Democrat Kennedy administration, the Democrat majority in Congress promptly passed a huge Omnibus Bill that added 70 new federal judgeships. In fact, all but four of the 251 judgeships authorized by Congress over the period 1933–68 came during years when the president's party controlled Congress (ibid., pp. 52–6).

In other words, when Democrats control the executive and legislative branches they tend to elevate Democrats to the federal bench, whereas when Republicans are in control they tend to elevate Republican judges. Barrow et al. offer no evidence, however, that this partisan pattern in appointments has resulted in any significant differences in actual judicial rulings. It is possible, in principle – and likely, in theory – that Democrat-nominated and Republican-nominated judges issue similar rulings, *ceteris paribus*.

Thus, the protection of judicial independence is constrained by political realities: judges may need to appease currently dominant interest-group coalitions at the margin, at the same time exhibiting a general 'independence' in the sense of maintaining the quality and integrity of judicial review applied to legislative contracts with interest groups.

Clearly, Article III of the US Constitution goes a considerable distance toward protecting the independence of the federal judiciary (for example, by granting judges lifetime tenure), but that protection is imperfect. The other branches of government (the executive and the legislative) do, however, still have access to possible influence over the judiciary, for example by controlling the process of appointment and confirmation. Other margins of potential congressional influence include the size of the judiciary (which affects judicial workloads), and the fact that judicial rulings can be overturned legislatively or by means of amending the Constitution. However, these particular control devices are relatively costly, and in principle only allow a crude level of control (at best).

However, there *is* a margin that in principle permits closer and less costly control of the courts by the current Congress, namely the annual budget of the federal judiciary. Although the US Constitution forbids the legislative branch from using actual judicial salaries as a control variable, there is no such constitutional restriction placed on the appropriation of funds for purposes of covering court operating expenses in a given year. It is possible, then, that the current Congress might employ this margin to influence federal judicial decision making. Whether such influence is actually exerted represents an interesting empirical question.

In her provocative study of recent US Supreme Court decisions, Toma (1991) reported evidence that the Court is subject to sanctions based on the degree to which it pursues a different ideological agenda than Congress prefers. Ideological differences on the part of the Court resulted in a reduced budget allocated by the Congress.

Toma calculated the absolute value of the difference between the mean ideological ranking for a sample of Supreme Court decisions and the mean ideological ranking of the members of Congress for the period from 1946 to 1977. This allowed her to address the question whether ideological differences between the Court and the Congress resulted in lower budgetary appropriations from that legislative body. If the answer were 'yes', then this would suggest that Congress was employing budgetary appropriations to influence the ideological complexion of the Court's rulings.

That is exactly what Toma found. As the Supreme Court rulings became more consistent with the ideological preferences of members of Congress, that legislative body responded by awarding the Court a larger budget. Given that the members of Congress were generally more conservative in their ideological rankings than justices on the Supreme Court during this time frame, this meant that the budgetary incentives rewarded the Court for deciding cases in a more conservative light. Other things held equal, as the Court's rulings became relatively more conservative, the Court's budget grew faster, but as those decisions reflected a more liberal bent, budgetary appropriations fell (or at least grew more slowly than they would have otherwise).

Toma's empirical finding is consistent with the possibility that congressional pressure (exerted in the form of budget appropriations dedicated to the Court) may influence actual Court decisions at the margin, but this is not precisely what she found. As she acknowledges (ibid., p. 145), the answer to

the question of whether the Court alters its decisions in the direction preferred by Congress would have required an examination of specific case
decisions. Instead, she tested whether the Court's budget was a determinant
of the overall *liberal–conservative rating* of Court decisions and found that
this influence was significant.[5]

Congressional control is not limited to the margin of the judiciary's budget;
there are a number of other means by which it can potentially exert influence
on the federal judiciary. Congress can, for example, manipulate the rate at
which the judiciary expands. Although the employment of particular judges
is strongly insulated from political pressure (for example, Congress cannot
simply fire or otherwise replace a federal judge with whom the majority party
disagrees), the creation of new judgeships *does* require joint action by the
Congress and the president. The US Constitution gives the president authority to nominate and the US Senate to vote to confirm new judges; the Congress
must vote in favor, and the president must sign legislation authorizing expansions of the federal judiciary.

This relationship has been studied carefully both by economists and political scientists. Consider the recent article by de Figueiredo and Tiller (1996).
While caseload pressure would presumably in part explain moves by the
legislative and executive branches to expand the judiciary (since more judges
imply a lower caseload per judge, *ceteris paribus*), this would constitute the
sole determining factor only if these political decision makers were single-
minded in their dedication to the pursuit of the 'public interest'. Assuming
that a given expansion in judgeships and concomitant reduction in average
caseload leads to the improvement in the quality (measured in some objective
sense) of judicial decisions, then the legislation would be *institutionally
efficient*. On the other hand, to the extent that political calculations figure in
the process of judicial expansion, then new judgeships would come about
independently of the objective 'need' for such growth, reflecting the differential
pursuit of *political efficiency*.

De Figueiredo and Tiller subjected this hypothesis to econometric testing.
They divided the problem into two parts, the *timing* of expansion and the
magnitude of expansion. They employed data on judicial expansion for the
Federal Appellate Court covering the period from 1869 to 1991.

In one set of regressions, de Figueiredo and Tiller addressed the question
of whether political factors influence the timing of bouts of judicial expansion. Their dichotomous dependent variable was defined as one if the federal
judiciary expanded in a given year, zero otherwise. Independent variables
included the average caseload per judge, the length of time since the last
expansion (to control for trend effects), growth in the overall federal budget,
and 'political alignment', another dummy variable set equal to one if the
House of Representatives, Senate, and the presidency were all controlled by

the same political party, zero otherwise. Using probit analysis, they found that the only independent variable of (high) significance was 'political alignment', which had a positive sign – indicating that successful judicial expansion was significantly more likely when the same party controlled both the legislative and executive branches.

In a separate set of regressions, designed to explain the *number* of judgeships added, that dependent variable was regressed on the following independent variables: caseload growth since the last expansion, judicial makeup, and political alignment (as defined above). The results indicated that 'political alignment' was again positive and highly significant. ('Caseload growth' was also positive and highly significant.) De Figueiredo and Tiller (ibid., p. 458) concluded that these results support the hypothesis that political alignment is a 'decisive factor' in determining both the timing and the size of expansions in the federal appellate judiciary.

Spiller and Gely (1992) approached the judicial independence issue from the perspective of another limited subset of court decisions, cases involving the interpretation of the National Labor Relations Act (NLRA) by the Supreme Court – a sample consisting of 249 cases decided between 1949 and 1988. They categorized each decision according to whether it was 'pro-union'. In order to measure the preferences of members of the House and the Senate, they used the relevant ideological rankings of Americans for Democratic Action (ADA). They discovered that the ADA score of the relevant House member appeared to affect the Court's probability of a pro-union decision. (Senate ADA rankings were insignificant, however.) Similarly, a pro-union decision was significantly more likely if the percentage of justices serving on the Court appointed by Democratic administrations was higher, and (sometimes) significantly correlated with the fact that the sitting president was a Democrat.[6]

7   Conclusion

For many years, the consensus among legal scholars was that judges were not ordinary self-interested maximizers, but instead simply and directly served the 'public interest' in the rendering of their decisions. More recently, some analysts have argued that although judges can in fact be modeled as rational maximizers, the principal argument in their objective function takes the form of the expression of personal ideological preferences.

As we have seen, another view of judicial motivation has attracted strong support: judges are self-interested actors who consistently seek to maximize their pecuniary wealth. They tend to respond in predictable ways to incentives in the form of salaries, budgets, workload reductions, and various other perquisites. Thus, the legislative branch in principle possesses the necessary means to influence judicial behavior: tangible rewards.

Landes and Posner offered a key extension of the interest-group theory of government by arguing that an independent judiciary performs a crucial role in protecting and preserving contracts between the legislature suppliers and the interest-group consumers of legislated wealth transfers. Institutions that increase the level of independence of the judiciary from the political process do not place the court system outside the market for political wealth transfers but rather provide that market with the contractual infrastructure necessary to ensure its efficient operation. In sum, self-interested judges can be shown to behave in a manner consistent with the functioning of efficient markets for coercive wealth transfers for the same reasons that other rational actors participate in these markets.

However, this model of the role of the independent judiciary in an interest-group perspective must take into account the impact of such 'independence' on the ability of the current legislature to successfully orchestrate wealth transfers in the present. The more independent the judiciary, the less likely it is to be amenable to enforcing new agreements with interest groups, rendering wealth-transfer contracts more difficult to negotiate and raising the cost of the legislature's brokering function. Thus the optimal degree of judicial independence (from the perspective of the legislature) necessarily represents an equilibrium outcome, with the marginal cost of potential judicial interference equated with the marginal benefit associated with the enhanced durability of wealth-transfer agreements.

Notes

1. Smith concerns himself with assessing various proposed schemes for defraying the expenses associated with providing court services. He argues that a system of 'user fees' charged to litigants can be an effective option, assuming that the fees of court are well regulated. 'Those fees', he writes, 'might be rendered fully sufficient for defraying the whole expence of justice. By not being paid to the judges till the process was determined, they might be some incitement to the diligence of the court in examining and deciding it ... [and] those fees might give some encouragement to the diligence of each particular judge. *Public services are never better performed than when their reward comes only in consequence of their being performed, and is proportioned to the diligence employed in performing them*' (Smith [1776] 1976, Bk V, Ch. 1, Pt 2, pp. 240–41; emphasis added).
2. Judges behave in another way consistent with their own self-interest: damage awards in tort cases are larger, *ceteris paribus*, in states where members of the judiciary are elected rather than appointed. Such behavior tends to transfer wealth from out-of-state defendants to in-state plaintiffs, providing benefits both to voters and to trial lawyers, major contributors to judges' re-election campaigns (Tabarrok and Helland 1999). Maloney et al. (1984) showed earlier that, for similar reasons, state public utility regulators who must stand for election to office tend to set higher prices for electric power sold to out-of-state customers.
3. Another device potentially available (at least in some states) is the voter initiative. This form of 'direct democracy' is a mechanism by means of which voters can, within limits, directly implement laws. See Anderson (1999) and Chapter 7 of this volume.
4. For evidence that the decisions of Japanese judges are not so independent of the political preferences of the Liberal Democratic Party, for many years the Diet's majority party, see Ramseyer and Rasmussen (1997).
5. In a more recent article, Toma (1996) explored the precise mechanism by means of which

the Congress exerts influence over Supreme Court decision making. Utilizing data in the form of budgets allocated to the Court and the decisions reached by that Court over the period from 1946 to 1988, she found support for the hypothesis that the Chief Justice of the Supreme Court functions as an agent of Congress and coordinates the Court's reactions to the budgetary signals sent by that legislative body.

6. Spiller and Gely (1992) also include various macroeconomic performance variables, such as the unemployment rate and the inflation rate, in some of their regression specifications. If Supreme Court decision making is strongly influenced by the personal ideology of the individual justices (as opposed to partisan political calculations), this should presumably show up here. Neither independent macro variable is found to be consistently significant, however.

14 Money

*Kevin B. Grier**

1 Introduction

Are campaign contributions free speech or bribery? Are elections for sale to the richest or biggest spending candidate? Does accepting interest-group money inevitably mean that legislators will abandon their constituents and serve Mammon? The role of money in politics is hotly debated, with few accepted conclusions. Views range from Thomas Ferguson's (1995) claim that interested money is the driving force in American political life, to several statistical findings suggesting that campaign contributions do not influence congressional voting and that campaign spending does not help House incumbents get re-elected. The study of money in politics is fascinating because of its intrinsic importance, the existence of high-quality (and free!) data, and the potential for using empirical studies of money in politics to test broader theories.

In this chapter I tackle two topics. First is the raising and allocation of campaign contributions by interest groups. Second is the effect of campaign expenditures on election outcomes. We shall see that, in the first case, econometric problems are manageable, and a general empirical consensus exists, although many important areas remain untouched or at least understudied. In the second case, we shall see that while campaign contributions have been found to have positive and significant effects on the election prospects of Senate incumbents, to date no one has demonstrated convincingly the same commonsense results for House incumbents. I shall argue that the econometric problem inherent in these models is generally misunderstood and that the differences between Senate and House elections may give us some clues about how to improve our models of the effect of campaign spending in House elections.

The scope and importance of the themes of this chapter are so great that I feel compelled to offer a disclaimer in advance. Each one of my themes could easily merit two or three distinct review essays. My goals here are to give the big picture, look for common ground, try to retain the general reader's interest and cite a lot of my own work! I thus apologize in advance for the omissions and self-aggrandizement that will surely follow.

2   The raising and allocation of interest-group contributions

2.1   Introduction: a primer on PACs

I begin by thanking the Supreme Court for not letting Congress ban interest-group contributions, Congress for creating the Federal Elections Commission (FEC), and the FEC for maintaining a comprehensive database on contributions! I shall not spend much time on the historical vagaries of government regulation of campaign finance, but shall at least give a brief sketch of the process and a description of what political action committees (PACs) can and cannot do before jumping into the literature.[1]

In 1907, with the passage of the Tilman Act, the US Congress banned any 'money contributions' by corporations in federal elections. This ban did not apply to labor unions and was rationalized as shareholder protection. Interestingly, the Tilman Act argued that shareholder interests could well be damaged as a result of corporate officials directly using company funds for political purposes![2] The Corrupt Practices Act of 1925 removed the word 'money' and simply banned corporate 'contributions'. The Smith–Connally Act of 1943 and, upon its expiration, the Taft–Hartley Act of 1947 added the word 'expenditures' to the list of proscribed activities and extended the corporate contribution ban to labor unions.

However, many unions continued to be politically active, leading to a series of complaints accusing unions of violating Taft–Hartley (as it had amended the Corrupt Practices Act of 1925). In the cases addressing that issue, *United States* v. *CIO* (1948), *United States* v. *Painters Local #481* (1949), *United States* v. *Construction & General Laborers Local #264* (1951) and *United States* v. *UAW* (1957), the courts generally failed either to enforce or overturn the statute. Rather, they repeatedly found that the statute did not apply in cases where, to the naked eye, it surely did. In reference to the CIO case it has been noted that 'history's verdict is that the Court was wholly mistaken'.[3]

The 1970s brought a renewed legislative initiative to campaign finance regulation. The Federal Election Campaign Act (FECA) of 1971 proscribed corporate and union campaign contributions and regulated individual contributions. However, almost at the same time, in *Pipefitters Local #52* v. *United States*, the Supreme Court upheld the legality of the union's campaign fund, dealing a mortal blow to the 1971 FECA legislation. The Court's decision paved the way for the explosive growth of PACs that we have observed over the past 25 years.

Many of the original regulatory provisions of FECA were repealed after the decision in *Pipefitters*, and the law was amended in 1974 to comply with the Court's ruling. This legislation created the FEC, imposed reporting requirements on contributors and on campaigns and set limits on PAC contributions. The limit, which still stands today, is $5000 per candidate per election for a 'qualified multi-candidate committee'.[4] Parts of the 1974 legislation were also struck down by the Supreme Court's famous *Buckley* v. *Valeo* ruling in 1976 that equated contributions with political 'speech', protected by the First Amendment. *Buckley* also permitted PACs to make unlimited 'independent expenditures' for or against candidates for federal office, provided that such expenditures are not coordinated with the candidate's own campaign. In the 1997–98 election cycle, PACs gave about $220 million to federal candidates for the House and Senate and made an additional $9.4 million in independent expenditures.[5]

2.2   Determination of the level of interest-group expenditures

The PAC is a strange beast. Its funding must be separate from that of the general funding of its sponsoring organization, and contributions to it cannot be coerced or made mandatory. Literally, then, PACs are not direct extensions of their sponsoring organizations.[6] It was these features of the original Pipefitters Local #52 campaign fund that the Court pointed to approvingly in protecting its existence.

It is thus entirely possible that PACs march to the beat of a different drummer than their sponsoring organization or, in other words, that PACs do not act to maximize the self-interest of the sponsoring organization. This point is advanced both by Handler and Mulkern (1982) and Wright (1985; 1990a, b). As a first step, then, it is important to see whether or not the political activities of a firm or an industry can be predicted from self-interest. If the raising and allocation of PAC money is idiosyncratic, or random, then we should not expect to see an effect of contributions on politicians' behavior. While there are a host of studies on whether the allocation of PAC monies is consistent with self-interest, there is much less research on whether the scale of interest-group activity is predictable by self-interest. Most of what literature does exist debates the effect of industry structure (mainly concentration) on corporate political activity.

One group of papers (Andres 1985; Masters and Keim 1985; Grier et al. 1991; Humphries 1991; McKeown 1994) studies the choice by firms whether or not to sponsor a PAC. Pittman (1976, 1977) studies individual contributions at the industry level in 1972 and argues that industry concentration spurs political contributions. However, Esty and Caves (1983) and Zardkoohi (1985) find much weaker evidence to support this conclusion.

Surprisingly, there are no published comprehensive studies of the determinants of trade association or labor PAC sizes. All of the existing work concentrates on corporate political activity, and of these papers only one, Grier et al. (1994), tests a broad model of corporate PAC activity with a panel of data.

Grier, Munger and Roberts (GMR) study 'corporate PACs as if they were directly controlled by their sponsors in cooperation with other corporations in the industry'. They develop and test an 'organizationally constrained profit maximizing model' of the determinants of industry political activity using data from five election cycles (1978–86). On the theoretical side, they show that the effect of concentration on political activity, a major point of previous research, should be non-linear. They argue that there is an inverse relation between the ability to solve the collective action problem and the need to make political contributions. For example, in a competitive industry, firms are earning zero profits and could benefit tremendously from a price-raising government intervention. However, the large number of firms makes the collective action problem severe. On the other hand, a monopolist has no collective action problem, but also has little need for profit-raising government intervention, as maximal profit is already being earned. Thus, while increased concentration makes collective action easier, it also makes it less necessary.

The type of data employed in these studies present econometric problems. For example, there are firms and industries that have no PACs and thus make no recorded contributions. Several authors (Pittman 1976; Esty and Caves 1983; Zardkoohi 1985) only study industries or firms making contributions. However, if the factors that determine the existence of political activity are correlated with the factors determining the extent of political activity, we have a classic case of selection bias where least squares regressions using only the politically active industry data are biased and inconsistent. Several authors (for example, Boies 1989) include the firms or industries with no contributions in their sample and, by using the TOBIT estimator, treat the problem as one of censoring. GMR instead treat the problem as one of selection and use the two-stage Heckman (1976, 1979) selectivity correction model often referred to as the HECKIT model. Here, the probability of becoming politically active is estimated in an initial probit equation, and then the extent of political activity is estimated using selectivity corrected least squares on the politically active subsample. Heckman has shown that under the restrictions that the independent variables, coefficients, and error terms are all identical in both equations, the HECKIT model simplifies to TOBIT. GMR test and reject the restrictions implied by the TOBIT model, implying that previous studies which used TOBIT may be in error.

Empirically, then, GMR find that concentration has a powerful, non-linear effect on the probability that an industry will be politically active, and a smaller, but still significant non-linear effect on the extent of political activity. They also find that industries with significant regulation, sales to the government and a history of antitrust problems contribute significantly more, while industries with greater internal diversity (in geography or product lines), and more risky profits, contribute less.

Of all the areas to be discussed in this chapter, the one focusing on the determinants of the level of political activity by interest groups is the least developed. GMR's work points to the importance of considering a wider range of explanatory variables and of using HECKIT selectivity models, but only scratches the surface of what can be done in this field. There are no studies of the scope of labor's political activity, or studies of whether corporations and labor in the same industry cooperate or compete in their political activities.

2.3   Allocation of interest-group money

The allocation of PAC funds can be used to investigate interesting and controversial theories. I shall organize this section in four parts: (1) What do PACs try to accomplish? (2) Do congressional committees 'matter'? (3) Does being in the majority party 'matter'? and (4) Overall observations.

What do PACs try to accomplish?   The issue here is whether or not one can uncover the strategic intent of PACs by analysing their contribution patterns. In Section 2.2 above, I argued that the scope of industry PAC activity is reasonably well explained by an institutionally constrained profit-maximizing model. However, the question remains as to how exactly a PAC should allocate its funds to improve the profitability of its sponsor. The question is most frequently posed as: what do PACs maximize? The answers most often given are (i) the election of friendly candidates, (ii) an explicit quid pro quo, most often taken as a roll-call vote on a particular bill or amendment, and (iii) 'access', or a guarantee of a sympathetic ear from the person receiving the contribution.[7]

Early work (Welch 1981; Eismeier and Pollock 1988) favored the idea that PACs support their friends (possibility i) and cast doubt on the idea that PACs rationally allocate contributions to influence policy (possibility ii). The reasoning here is that if you are trying to buy a majority, or a policy outcome, there is little need to pay someone who will vote or work for your desired outcome already, independent of your contribution. To maximize support, scarce resources should be concentrated on the marginal legislator. Yet these first studies showed that the most natural supporters of a PAC's policy agenda received the largest contributions.

However, as pointed out by Denzau and Munger (1986), Grier and Munger (1991) and Stratmann (1992a), what may look like an unsophisticated strategy of supporting one's friends (preaching to the choir) can actually be effective policy influence, if one's friends are the low-cost providers of the service desired. Here, of course, we must discard the usual (and in my view erroneous) assumption that the service desired is one vote on one bill. It is obvious that what is in (or left out of) a bill, or what happens in a regulatory agency overseen by the Congress can be as important (if not much more so) as how one legislator votes on the bill, yet this basic insight is all too often ignored in the literature. The focus on a roll-call vote as what is bought by a PAC is misguided and causes unnecessary confusion.

Another common and problematic assumption is that the amount of a PAC's contribution is too small to ever affect the probability of re-election or even to influence a congressional vote. Authors often take the $10 000 per election cycle (primary plus general election) limit as the extent of the PAC's influence. However, most government policies are not so narrowly tailored that only one organization benefits from them. For example, a bill or a regulatory decision or a campaign that featured limits on imported steel could mobilize two large groups of interests each with many PACs, namely domestic steel producers and domestic steel consumers.[8] If ten steel PACs give $10 000 each to a legislator, we are quickly talking Dirksenian 'real money'. In this context, the work of GMR discussed in the preceding section, where the industry is the unit of analysis and its incentive to contribute combined with the degree of its collective action problem determine its level of political activity, is especially relevant.

In any event, it is not so obvious that PACs unsophisticatedly give to their staunch supporters, as is still frequently claimed in the literature (for example, Levitt 1998). Stratmann (1992a) shows for the case of farm PACs that, *ceteris paribus*, PACs give more to marginal legislators. Stratmann uses the rural population percentage in the district to measure how friendly a legislator intrinsically is to PAC interests. He estimates a switching regression model to see whether PACs distinguish between marginal and intrinsically friendly legislators, and finds that there is a cut-off point in farm PAC behavior. Once a district reaches 28 percent rural, the positive association between pro-farm voting by its representative and contributions from farm PACs is significantly attenuated.

Instead of a switching regression, Grier and Munger (1993) allow the effect of intrinsic friendliness on contributions to be non-linear. They study three broad groupings of PACs – corporate, trade association, and organized labor – and use the incumbent legislator's Conservative Coalition vote score as the measure of intrinsic friendliness (hostility) to business (labor) interests. They argue that moderately supportive legislators should, *ceteris paribus*, receive more contributions than either staunchly unfriendly or staunchly supportive ones. Their study demonstrates the predicted effect strongly for trade association PACs, a bit less strongly for corporate PACs, and not at all for labor PACs.

Even if PACs do tend to target marginal legislators, they may also contribute in order to try to influence election outcomes. My contention is that there is simply no way to disentangle these two activities with the common research design used in the literature. Instead, a focused dynamic analysis of a group or interest class before, during, and after a critical legislative event would be far more effective. Stratmann (1998) makes some headway in this direction by studying the timing of individual farm PAC contributions. He finds that contributions tend to cluster around important legislative events and election dates. He also shows that the clustering near the election is not due to a PAC cash-flow problem, but rather represents a deliberate PAC strategy.

Do congressional committees 'matter'?   It is hotly debated whether or not congressional committees 'matter', which is to say whether or not committee members or leaders have the ability to move outcomes away from what would be preferred by the decisive member of the full House. Shepsle (1979), Shepsle and Weingast (1987a, b), and Weingast and Marshall (1988) are perhaps the best-known exponents of the 'committees matter' theory. At the risk of drastically oversimplifying, the Shepsle–Weingast–Marshall (SWM) argument goes like this: Congress is organized to routinize and institutionalize logrolling. Representatives come from diverse districts and seek committee assignments where there is a match between jurisdiction and constituent interest. Each representative trades off a little influence over every issue for a lot of influence over a few important issues controlled by the committee(s) where she sits.

From this point of view, committee members have more than proportionate power over the issues that come before their committee and thus should, *ceteris paribus*, receive more than proportionate contributions from groups seeking to influence decisions in the area.[9]

Almost the opposite conclusion follows from the work of Thomas Gilligan and Keith Krehbiel (1987, 1990), hereafter G&K. G&K argue that the committee system arose to maximize the information available to the Congress by encouraging representatives to specialize and develop expertise in their jurisdictions. The committee system raises the level of information and improves the quality of congressional decisions in an uncertain world, but policy decisions are made by the median voter of the full chamber and are not influenced disproportionately by committee members.

While often portrayed as such, these are not two directly competing, comprehensive theories. The SWM model arose from efforts to explain how, given the generic instability results for policy choice in a multidimensional space, there is so much stability in congressional policies. Thus they emphasize how the institutionalized logroll can in effect create N, one-dimensional spaces instead of one, N-dimensional space. G&K assume a unidimensional policy space and show how uncertainty about the real effects of policy choices can lead to a demand for legislator specialization. The two theories differ on what is the driving principle of legislative organization: the avoidance of cycling and policy instability due to multidimensional policy spaces (SWM) or the avoidance of poor decisions due to uncertainty (G&K). Unfortunately, each ignores the other's fundamental axiom, in my view to their own detriment. Uncertainty is important in politics, but so is multidimensionality. In any event, one obvious differing prediction between them is whether or not PACs tailor their contributions to members of committees with jurisdiction over policies of interest to their sponsoring organizations.

No paper in the vast empirical literature on the allocation of PAC funds explicitly presents its results as a test to distinguish between SWM and G&K. Yet, on the whole, the results are largely consistent with the SWM view of legislative organization. There are studies of individual PACs where the sponsor-interest-to-committee-jurisdiction linkage is weak to non-existent, but at the industry level or at the broader corporate–labor–trade association level of aggregation, the evidence is overwhelmingly pro-SWM. Below I briefly outline the results of several different studies.

Using individual PACs as the unit of analysis, Gopoian (1984) finds a strong link between each of nine PACs whose sponsor is a firm in the defense industry and incumbents who sit on the Armed Services Committee. However, of the other 20 PACs he studies, including labor, automotive, and oil industry PACs, there is a positive and significant relationship in only seven instances. Grenzke (1989) finds a positive relationship between the interest of the PAC and a 'power index' that includes jurisdictionally relevant committee assignments for only four of the nine PACs she studies.

However, when industry or interest class groupings of PACs are used as the unit of analysis, the results are very different.[10] Stratmann (1998) shows how farm PACs concentrate their contributions on members of the Agriculture Committee. Kroszner and Stratmann (1998) show the strong relationship between banking and insurance PAC contributions and membership of the Banking Committee.

At the interest class level, Grier and Munger (1991, 1993) show a strong connection between the committee jurisdiction and the allocation of PAC money, especially for corporate PACs. Dummy variables for membership of the Banking, Energy and Commerce, and Ways and Means committees are significant in both subsamples of their 1993 analysis, and no other committees are. Their results are about as strong for the trade association–committee link and more mixed for labor PACs.

One caveat in this good news is that the experimenter is choosing which committees should be relevant in a preliminary step and then testing whether or not committee jurisdictions shape PAC contributions. Romer and Snyder (1994) make this criticism and then present an alternative strategy that examines what happens to contribution patterns when committee assignments change. That is, they look at how transfers affect the sources of an incumbent legislator's PAC money. Interestingly, their results largely confirm those of Grier and Munger. Corporate and trade association PACs concentrate contributions on the Energy and Commerce and Ways and Means committees. Romer and Snyder also show that 'large' PACs increase contributions to new members of these committees, while continuing to support previous members who transfer off them. Romer and Snyder do not investigate the significance of important labor committees (Education and Labor, Post Office) to labor PACs in their work.

It is also possible to examine the real effects of procedural or jurisdictional changes by looking at what happens to the flow of interested money after the change. Milyo (1997) does exactly that for the Gramm–Rudman–Hollings (GRH) Deficit Reduction Act of 1985 and the Tax Reform Act of 1986. While the results are somewhat mixed, he does show that GRH increased the power of the Budget Committee relative to the Appropriations Committee and that the Tax Reform Act constituted a financial windfall for members of the tax-writing committee (Ways and Means).

Roberts (1990) presents another novel use of PAC money to test for committee power. He considers a dramatic unforseen event, the sudden death of Henry 'Scoop' Jackson, ranking Democrat on the Senate Armed Services Committee. He shows that firms that had contributed to Jackson but not to the new ranking Democrat (Sam Nunn) in the past show a negative and significant stock price reaction, while firms that had contributed to Nunn previously show a positive stock price shock. At least in this instance, the stock price reaction of defense firms to an unforseen event in the defense oversight committee significantly depended on their PACs' contribution histories.

Does being in the majority party 'matter'?   Here again we have a situation where PAC allocation data can provide evidence on competing theories and, thanks to Newt Gingrich, recent data allow a much cleaner test than before.[11] There is a considerable literature arguing that party affiliation is largely irrelevant in the legislature. This is certainly the tone of David Mayhew's important book (Mayhew 1974), where he argues that Congress is run by a group of incumbents who have developed its institutions to promote re-election. It is also an implication of recent work by Keith Krehbiel (1990, 1993) (see especially his 'Where's the party?') and by Schickler and Rich (1997a, b). In contrast stands the partisan view of legislative organization (for example, Rohde 1991; Cox and McCubbins 1993; Aldrich and Rohde 1998), where majority-party status is argued to provide systematic advantage in the procurement of policies.

Under the assumption that PAC contributions are at least partly given to pay for services of some type, a natural test of the importance of party affiliation for the delivery of services is whether, *ceteris paribus*, majority-party incumbents receive more contributions. Unfortunately, during the 1970s and 1980s, the majority party in the House was always the Democratic Party and it was thus impossible to cleanly separate ideologically based contributions from majority-party contributions.

Grier and Munger (1993) wrestle with this issue, largely unsuccessfully, due to the Democratic stranglehold on the House during the period they study. However, Cox and Magar (1999) show that the shift in majority-party control that occurred in the House in 1994 is associated with an average increase of around $35 000 in the sum of corporate and trade association PAC contributions to a Republican incumbent. However, labor PAC money did not change significantly. Thus, there is mixed support for the idea that majority-party status is important for the provision of legislative services.[12] Overall, the claims that committee assignment and majority-party status matter to PACs are supported much more strongly by business PAC behavior than by labor PAC behavior.[13]

Overall observations   Studying PAC behavior is fun, which may explain the huge number of papers in the field. I think that, at the end of the day, there is a set of general principles we can take away from the existing literature. First, individual PAC behavior can be idiosyncratic. This is not surprising given the loose legal connection between the PAC and its sponsoring organization. However, at the industry or interest class level PAC behavior appears purposive, though collective action problems are important. The question of what is the optimal level of aggregation to use in the study of PAC behavior remains important and wide open.

Second, there is no mono-causal theory of PAC goals that can successfully explain behavior, nor should we expect there to be. PACs sometimes give to influence policy, sometimes to influence elections, and undoubtedly sometimes because the treasurer's sister-in-law is running for Congress. However, given that some PAC contributions are systematically designed to elicit a quid pro quo, we can investigate hypotheses about the organization and the location of institutional power in Congress by following where specific interested money goes. This has been done in two cases, and the results, on balance, show that committee assignment and majority-party status affect the ability to influence policies.

Third, the stylized fact, still much used by theorists, that PACs give overwhelmingly to their staunch supporters and thus are not trying to influence policy is (like most stylized facts) false. To try to identify when PACs target elections and when they target policies, the experimental design of empirical work must change. Consider the steel quota issue mentioned above. Here we can envision an experimental design as follows. (i) Was the issue raised by legislators with a history of receiving contributions from the domestic steel industry? (ii) Once on the table, what is the dynamic nature of contributions from producers and consumers? (iii) If there is a vote or a significant regulatory decision, how does that affect contribution patterns? (iv) If there is an election involving a key legislative player, how do the competing PAC groups address the race? The dynamic dimension used by Grier and Munger, Romer and Snyder, Milyo, and Cox and Magar has much wider and important uses.[14]

3   Campaign spending and election outcomes

3.1   Introduction

The central irony in the academic literature on money in politics is the difficulty of reconciling the frequent assumption that PAC contributions involve a quid pro quo with the common finding that campaign spending does not help House incumbents. Why would an incumbent do anything that is not in the interest of her voting constituency if the contributions her action would attract do not give an electoral advantage and it is not supremely easy to use the funds for personal consumption?

We shall see that people have been extremely reluctant to accept this negative result, and have proposed a series of solutions or econometric fix-ups to eliminate or ameliorate the problem. These attempts are hurt by the often ignored empirical result that in Senate elections, even simpleminded least squares regressions show clearly that increased incumbent spending is associated with improved incumbent electoral success. It is not widely appreciated that these Senate results mean that technical econometric problems are probably not responsible for the 'perverse' House results.

In the rest of this section, I review the first generation of results on the effect of campaign spending in House elections, examine the solutions to the perverse House results offered in the literature, discuss the current state of the art empirical work, and speculate about how progress might be made.

3.2   Gary Jacobson: 'da man' or demon?

The person who started all the trouble is, of course, Gary Jacobson. In a pioneering empirical paper, Jacobson (1978) showed that while challenger spending improves their electoral prospects, incumbent spending does not help them.[15] Jacobson does not take the finding of increased incumbent spending having a zero or negative impact at face value, but argues that it is an artifact of simultaneous equations bias.

Jacobson estimates equations of the form:

$$CV = a_0 + a_1 C\$ + a_2 I\$ + a_3 Party + a_4 CPS.$$

Here *CV* is the challenger's share of the two-party vote, *C$* is challenger spending, *I$* is incumbent spending, *Party* is a dummy variable equal to 1 for Democrat challengers and *CPS* is the challenger's party's vote share in the previous election. In the 1972 House election (sample of 296 elections), Jacobson finds a positive and significant effect for challenger spending and a much smaller and statistically insignificant effect for incumbent spending, using least squares to estimate the model. In 1974 (sample of 319 elections), *C$* is still positive and significant, and while *I$* attains significance at the 0.05 level, its effect is only about one-fifth the size of *C$*.

Jacobson argues that this startling result is probably due to unmodeled simultaneity: that spending and votes are jointly determined. He then uses *Seniority*, a dummy for whether the challenger held a previous office, and a dummy for whether the incumbent ran in a primary to overidentify *I$* in the *CV* equation. However, the new results are that *I$* is not significant in either 1972 or 1974. Jacobson makes the argument that incumbent spending is reactive. When there is a strong challenger, and the incumbent is in trouble, then he raises and spends more money. With a weak challenger, the incumbent will not take the time and trouble to raise and spend a large amount of money. This is not an argument for simultaneity; rather it is an omitted variables argument. If we could only control for challenger quality, then incumbent spending would, *ceteris paribus*, be revealed to help the incumbent. This argument is inconsistent with Jacobson's two-stage least squares analysis, because he uses challenger quality there to overidentify spending. That is, he assumes that challenger quality is correlated with incumbent spending, but *not* with the challenger's vote.

Jacobson performs a least squares analysis on the 1972 (sample of 25 elections) and 1974 (sample of 22 elections) Senate elections, finding a significant effect for *I$* in the first, but not the second data set. He mentions that using two-stage least squares to correct for simultaneity does not change the results.

In a subsequent paper, Jacobson (1985) shows that using the same basic model, incumbent spending is almost never correctly signed and significant in House elections.

3.3   But the Senate is a different story

However, other authors (Abramowitz 1988; Grier 1989b; Gerber 1998) show that incumbent spending is almost always correctly signed and significant in Senate elections. For example, Grier estimates a model of the form:

$$(1 - CV) = a_0 + a_1 C\$ + a_2 I\$ + a_3 Scandal + a_4 (1 - CPS).$$

The variables are defined as above, and *Scandal* is a dummy variable for incumbents with serious scandals. Grier finds that while challenger spending has a bigger effect on the election, incumbent spending is positively and significantly related to the incumbent's vote. He also tests for diminishing returns to spending by including the squares of $C\$$ and $I\$$. Grier finds strong evidence of diminishing returns for both incumbent and challenger spending, but that the effect of challenger spending peaks earlier. In his 1978–84 sample (101 elections), he finds that the average challenger spent around $0.20 per capita for a yield of almost 12 percentage points, while the average incumbent spent almost $0.40 for a yield of around nine percentage points.

Gerber (1998) studies Senate elections from 1974 through 1992. Using least squares, he finds, like Grier, that both incumbent and challenger spending are correctly signed and significant, but that challenger spending is much more effective. Gerber uses challenger wealth, state population, and total spending in the previous Senate race in the state to overidentify both incumbent and challenger spending in the vote equation. He finds that in this instrumental variable model, both incumbent and challenger spending are correctly signed, statistically significant and equally productive. Interestingly, Gerber includes a variety of controls for challenger quality, a series of dummy variables detailing the challenger's level of political experience, but these variables are collectively and individually insignificant. Gerber concludes that both incumbent and challenger spending are important in Senate elections, and once one controls for the endogeneity of spending in the vote equation, the effects are equally powerful.

3.4   Post-Jacobson empirical work on House elections

Thus, for Senate elections, incumbent spending matters, and the debate is over how much, while in House elections incumbent spending seems not to matter. The study most often cited as showing significant incumbent spending effects in the House is Green and Krasno (1988), hereafter GK. GK argue that Jacobson's work has two major shortcomings, namely lack of adequate controls for challenger quality and lack of adequate instruments for the simultaneous equations analysis. To control for challenger quality, GK develop an eight-point quality scale, and to improve the two-stage least squares analysis, GK introduce lagged incumbent spending as an instrument. They argue that lagged spending represents the incumbent's propensity to raise funds and is correlated with current spending but not with the current vote.

GK estimate a Jacobson-style least squares regression for the 1978 House election (289 observations). They show that their eight-point quality scale is significant when added to Jacobson's $I\$$, $C\$$, *Party*, and *CPS* variables, but that the inclusion of challenger quality does not make incumbent spending significant. GK then stratify the sample, estimating separate regressions for 85 low-spending challengers (<$10 000), 129 medium spenders (between $10 000 and $100 000), and 75 high spenders (>$100 000). However, incumbent spending is correctly signed and significant only in the low-spending challengers subsample (coefficient of –0.021, standard error of 0.008) and even here it is *twenty times smaller* than the coefficient for challenger spending. However, when they use lagged incumbent spending as an instrument for current spending (which reduces the sample to 236 observations), challenger and incumbent spending are both correctly signed, statistically significant, and roughly equally sized.[16] GK then produce results for the House that accord with Gerber's for the Senate. However, GK have not escaped criticism.

Jacobson (1990) returns to protect his turf by arguing, first, that GK inappropriately restrict incumbent spending to be linear and, second, that GK have chosen the only election where their model provides strong results. Jacobson shows that with the GK data for 1978, enforcing diminishing returns directly on the spending variables by logging them raises the R^2 of the model from 0.57 to 0.70 and the null hypothesis of linearity (constant returns) is rejected at the 0.001 level. In his diminishing returns model, though, the coefficient for incumbent spending, though correctly signed and significant, is only about half the size of the challenger spending coefficient. Further, Jacobson estimates a version of the model for the 1976, 1980, 1984 and 1986 elections as well, showing that incumbent expenditure is significant only in the 1986 election. He concludes that, at best, incumbent expenditures have a much smaller effect than do challenger monies, and that the effect is significant in only two of the five elections he studies.[17]

Much of the debate between GK and Jacobson revolves around controlling for challenger quality. Levitt (1994) makes an important contribution in that regard. Levitt also argues that controlling for challenger quality is crucial in estimating the effects of campaign spending, but does not think that quality can adequately be measured with the simple variables used in the literature.

Instead, Levitt assembles a panel of data on House elections where the same two candidates face each other more than once. Assuming that candidate quality is constant over time, one can difference the data, estimating the effect of changes in spending on changes in the vote, removing individual candidate-specific effects from the equation. Levitt shows that estimating a traditional Jacobson-type cross-sectional regression on his data produces Jacobson-type results: challenger spending is important, incumbent spending not. However, in his experimental design with fixed effects eliminated by differencing, neither incumbent nor challenger spending is statistically significant.[18]

Levitt thus encounters results diametrically opposed to GK, who find significant and sizeable effects for both incumbent and challenger spending. In his work, neither type of spending matters much. Levitt concludes that campaign spending limits are probably a good thing, and that the importance of money in elections and politics is greatly exaggerated.

3.5   *Different approaches to the puzzle*

Rather than attempting to change Jacobson's non-results on the efficacy of incumbent spending, some authors have argued that the result is actually to be expected because Jacobson simply starts with a regression instead of a theory of how spending and campaigning works. These authors claim that spending does matter, but regressions like Jacobson's are too crude or ill-specified to show the effect.

For example, Lott (1991) agues that as incumbents amass more 'brand-name capital', additional investments in such capital in the form of new campaign expenditures will have less and less of an effect. One can think of the argument as saying that incumbent spending is subject to diminishing returns, but the proper base to measure the accumulated amount of spending stretches over the entire political history of the politician in question.

Lott argues that from this perspective, Jacobson-style regressions showing small effects of current incumbent spending, or coefficients that vary from election to election are not at all surprising, since incumbent brandname capital is missing from the equation.

Scott Thomas (1989) presents a model where challenger spending is on negative advertising that reduces the probability that a voter will vote for the incumbent, while incumbent spending is used to rebut the negative challenger advertisements. In the model, challenger spending raises the challenger vote but at a diminishing rate, incumbent spending lowers the challenger vote at a diminishing rate, challenger spending is more effective than incumbent spending, and incumbent spending becomes more effective as the level of challenger spending rises.[19]

Thomas's model thus signs the first, second and cross-partial derivatives of campaign spending. He tests the model using data from the 1978 and 1980 elections and the following regression equation:

$$CV = a_0 + a_1 C\$ + a_2 I\$ + a_3 Party + a_4 CPS + a_5 [C\$/(C\$ + I\$)].$$

While the estimated signs of the partial derivatives in question vary for each observation in the data, Thomas provides the distribution of results and argues that the results largely validate his model's predictions.

Coates (1998) argues that if House incumbents can raise money at low or zero marginal costs, they will spend it until it has a low or zero marginal product. He develops a model where the marginal product of expenditure is a function of a complicated set of interactions between candidate characteristics, constituency characteristics, and both incumbent and challenger spending.[20] Coates shows that, for the 1984 election, his model fits the data well. Further he finds that 86 percent of the incumbents in the sample have marginal productivities of expenditure insignificantly different from zero, while 91 percent of challengers' marginal productivities are significantly positive. Coates argues that this is to be expected if incumbents are relatively unconstrained in their fundraising while challengers have more trouble raising campaign contributions.

3.6   What does it all mean?

The literature contains almost any possible result. Incumbent spending does not matter (or only a little bit) according to Jacobson and Levitt. Incumbent spending matters, but less than challenger spending, according to Grier and Thomas. Incumbent spending matters and is about equally effective as challenger spending according to GK and Gerber. It is enough to create despair over the possibility of progress in empirical social science.

However, in my view there actually is some progress here. In Senate elections incumbent spending has a sizeable and significant positive effect on their vote shares. Abramowitz, Grier and Gerber all show this. While Jacobson does not, Grier shows that the reason for this non-result is an extremely inappropriate data transformation. Therefore, the real puzzle to be explained is not 'why is it so hard to find that incumbent spending matters?', but rather 'why does incumbent spending seem to matter in Senate, but not House, elections?'.

I think that the existing literature points to two possible answers. The first possibility is that there are far fewer lopsided or uncompetitive elections in the Senate than in the House. The problem is usually thought to be that secure incumbents may not spend so much, but still do well. This is partly why controlling for challenger quality is so important. It is correlated both with incumbent spending and incumbent vote percent. To the extent that challenger quality is hard to measure correctly, having a greater variation in challenger quality may degrade the House results relative to the Senate results.

However, a complicating factor that is seldom considered is that we also see secure House incumbents spending a fair amount on their campaigns even when running virtually unopposed. That money is not going to matter very much. Thus we have secure incumbents facing low-quality challengers, doing well in the election but spending very different amounts of money. There are both the low spenders considered by Jacobson and GK, and the higher spenders that I mention here. This phenomenon of secure incumbents getting high vote shares while having a large variance in spending levels should occur much less often in the Senate, making the desired results easier to uncover.

The second possibility is that both sets of results are actually correct. Recall that Coates argues that incumbents with a low opportunity cost of raising funds will do so until their marginal impact on the election is close to zero, and finds that House incumbents often come close to this point, while challengers rarely do.[21] It may then be possible that incumbents of all stripes face a slowly rising marginal cost of funds, but due to the generally larger constituencies and spending in Senate campaigns, Senate incumbents reach the marginal cost equals marginal benefit point later, at a higher marginal cost and correspondingly higher measured marginal benefit. In this regard it is interesting to note that Grier finds evidence of zero or negative marginal products of incumbent spending in the Senate mostly in low-population states.

Future empirical work in this field would do well to consider and test alternative functional forms for the effects of spending, continue to work on measuring challenger quality, and consider variables that can measure the differences in the underlying propensity to spend in campaigns (model why some secure incumbents spend a lot anyway).

4   Conclusion

While there has been a tremendous amount of work done on money in politics, with a wide variety of results and considerable controversy, there is a consensus of results in broad areas of the literature.

Consider first the PAC. At the industry or interest-group level, PACs raise and spend money purposively, and a new wave of research has taken the study of PAC allocations further, testing important competing theories about congressional organization. Further, more-focused studies of PAC behavior over the life cycle of an important issue hold much promise for furthering our understanding of what PACs try to do and how well they do it.

Concerning the effect of spending on election outcomes, there is a consensus of results that campaign spending in a traditional Jacobsonian equation is effective for Senate incumbents, Senate challengers, and House challengers, with difficulties arising only for House incumbents. Here we need to establish whether this to be expected due to maximizing behavior under different constraints by the two types of incumbents or whether a more carefully specified model, as discussed above, would alter these findings.

Notes

*   I thank Robin Grier, Mike Munger, and Doug Nelson for their comments on this chapter and Bill Shughart for not taking no for an answer. I also wish to thank Art Denzau and Bob Tollison who, for better or worse, created and built my interest in political economy.
1.   This section relies heavily on Bolton (1980).
2.   Obviously public opinion of what political contributions do has changed considerably since 1907.
3.   Bolton (1980, p. 389). It should be noted that in individual opinions, Supreme Court Justices Rutledge and Douglas both argued that the statute was indeed unconstitutional, on First Amendment grounds.
4.   A 'multi-candidate committee', which is what we generally mean when we say PAC, is one that has been registered for at least six months, has received contributions from at least 50 persons, and has made contributions to at least five candidates for federal office.

See Sproul (1980) for a survey of what sponsoring organizations can and cannot do and what PACs must do to comply with FECA.

5. It is an interesting question as to whether $230 million is a lot or a little. I make $80 000 a year, so by that metric it is a lot. The federal budget is over one trillion dollars per year, so by that metric it is a little.

6. The sponsoring organization can use its own funds to establish, administer and solicit contributions to its PAC. However, contributions cannot be mandatory and solicitations are supposed to inform the target that a failure to make a contribution will not have adverse consequences.

7. Hall and Wayman (1990) is probably the best piece on access.

8. The strategies of interested parties with competing interests is developed and tested for the case of the financial services industry in Kroszner and Stratmann (1998).

9. Note that the first part of the Shepsle–Weingast–Marshall argument is not really needed. It is not necessary that the committee have jurisdiction over an area important to the representative's constituents to arrive at the conclusion that interest groups will give more to committee members.

10. The one well-known aggregate study where committees are found not to matter is Poole and Romer (1985). However, from the point of view of whether PACs give to the specific committees in charge of their jurisdictional interests, Poole and Romer's test is not well constructed.

11. Despite his personal or ideological shortcomings, Newt Gingrich and the congressional Republicans have done a lot for empirically minded students of Congress.

12. Of course, those who argue against partisan theories of legislative organization can take comfort in the fact that while the $35 000 coefficient estimate is significant, it is not very large, especially since it represents the average increase from all business PACs to each Republican incumbent.

13. See Snyder and Groseclose (1999) for recent evidence of party influence on House roll-call voting.

14. Ironically, these authors estimate their dynamic models in differenced form and act as if that was the key element of the model. It is not. One could achieve the same results with a conventional panel of data in the levels allowing for individual effects. The key is to isolate how big events affect behavior.

15. Glantz et al. (1976) demonstrate the same basic result.

16. This is reported in the first regression of Table 6 in GK. Surprisingly they do not focus in on this result, preferring instead to interpret their 'non-additive, nonlinear, equation', which logs challenger spending and interacts it with *CPS* and their quality scale. I prefer to concentrate on the more straightforward aspects of GK's empirical work.

17. Green and Krasno (1990) return to refute the Jacobsonian attack, but do so only with their non-intuitive interaction term model. It is thus not a convincing rebuttal.

18. To be more precise, the null hypothesis that both coefficients are jointly insignificant cannot be rejected. In two of the three functional forms, challenger spending is just barely significant, with very small coefficients compared to Jacobson or GK.

19. This is because incumbent spending only works to rebut challenger attacks. If challenger spending were zero, the effect of incumbent spending would also be zero because there is nothing to rebut.

20. Coates's model is an extension of Denzau and Munger (1986) and is similar to Thomas (1989).

21. Levitt's results can be similarly interpreted. In repeat contests, he regresses the change in the vote on the change in spending, which could be thought of as looking for the marginal effect of new spending in what is basically the same election. He finds coefficients close to zero for both incumbents and challengers. Of course, his challenger sample is selected: repeat challengers are either (a) crazy, or (b) people who ran a close race last time.

15 Ideology

Paul H. Rubin

1 Introduction

Public choice scholars have addressed two major questions related to the influence of ideology on political behavior. One is essentially an existence question: is there an influence? The second concerns the role of the ideology of the elected representative himself versus the role of constituent ideology. This has been addressed as a form of 'shirking': do elected representatives evade responsibility by voting their own ideological preferences instead of the interests of their constituents? We now have answers to these questions. First, ideology does matter. Second, politicians do not shirk; rather, elected representatives follow their constituents' interests rather faithfully. However, in the process of answering these questions, the analysis of ideology has been markedly advanced and its empirical relevance has been extensively explored. This analysis shows that ideology may be a fundamental building block of political behavior. I discuss each of these issues: existence, shirking, and current and new problems related to ideology.

If the question of the importance of ideology were raised today, it is unlikely that there would be much of a debate. Important political controversies seem to deal with matters, such as abortion and homosexual rights, which are far removed from economic interest as normally understood. Often the perception of an official's 'liberalism' or 'conservatism' is independent of his views on economic issues, and determined solely by his position on issues such as abortion. Moreover, positions on social and economic issues seem to be melded together: it is difficult or impossible to find an elected politician who is in favor of less economic regulation and also in favor of abortion rights, and conversely. As we shall see, both of these observations – the importance of non-economic ideological issues, and the linkage of issues so that the ideological space is one-dimensional – are consistent with what we have now come to understand is the nature of ideology in politics.

2 Existence

George Stigler (1971) created interest in ideology, although inadvertently. Stigler took an extremely strong stand *against* the importance of ideology, and argued that virtually all economically relevant political behaviors could be explained by economic self-interest (see also Posner 1974 and Peltzman 1976). This notion was appealing to economists for two reasons. First, the hypothesis was sharp and was subject to empirical test. Second, the nature of the hypothesis was one that created sympathy among economists; economists are happy to believe that economic self-interest is the prime motivator of human behavior. This may be because such a belief creates a stronger position for economics as a discipline, and hence is in the economic self-interest of economists.[1] On the other hand, it may be because economists themselves behave this way, and expect others to do so as well (see Carter and Irons 1991). In other words, economists liked this hypothesis for reasons related both to their own self-interest and to ideology.

However, as much as we might like the hypothesis, it is fair to say that the results are in, and the hypothesis has been falsified. There has been a substantial body of empirical analysis of congressional voting and it has shown that ideological factors have considerable power in explaining congressional voting.[2] The major initial contributors to the literature were James Kau and Paul Rubin (1979, 1982).[3] Joseph Kalt and Mark Zupan (1984) also made an important contribution. These scholars have found that ideology, measured as a score on a voting scale such as one compiled by the Americans for Democratic Action (ADA) or measured by the presidential vote in the congressional district, has significant explanatory power in predicting voting by individual congressmen. These results may be considered as confirming Schumpeter's (1950) claim that ideology is important in economic affairs (although not his claim that it would lead to the fall of capitalism, which has recently been falsified).

The basic method has been to use congressional voting on issues as the dependent variable and a list of factors aimed at measuring constituent economic interests and also ideological variables as the independent variables in probit or logit regressions. The constituent characteristics typically include income, age, urbanization, race, education, unemployment, industry of employment, unionization, measures of government spending in the district, and sometimes measures of particular types of economic activity in the district. Following Kau and Rubin (1979), it is common to regress these measures on a measure of ideology, such as ratings assigned by the ADA or other ideological pressure groups, and then use the unexplained regression residual as the measure of 'pure' ideology. Sometimes a simultaneous model is used where campaign contributions are also controlled for (for example, Chappell 1982; Kau et al. 1982; Kau and Rubin 1982, 1993; also see Stratmann 1992a for a careful analysis of this issue). Logrolling is also taken into account in some specifications (for example, Kau and Rubin 1979; Stratmann 1992b). In such analyses, the measure of ideology is invariably statistically and economically significant.

What has perhaps been equally influential in convincing many scholars that ideology is an important variable are the results of the relatively unsuccessful attempts to challenge the hypothesis. Indeed, the original work by

Kau and Rubin was intended to show that ideology did not matter, and was unsuccessful. Peltzman (1984, 1985) later engaged in a determined effort to show that ideology was not important. Peltzman (1984) first controlled more carefully than others had for constituent characteristics, specifically by measuring the characteristics of those who actually voted for US Senators rather than by measuring characteristics of all voters in the electoral district (here, the state). In this way he was able to reduce the impact of the ideological variable, but not, in general, to eliminate it. In other words, Peltzman found that ideology mattered, although perhaps not as much as others had suggested. Indeed, in a subsequent paper (Peltzman 1985), he found much the same result as others: while economic factors matter in explaining congressional voting, and, in particular, trends in such voting, non-economic factors also are extremely significant. Peltzman generally calls these non-economic factors 'history', but he indicates that 'one could allude to regional differences in ideology as easily as to "historical inertia"' (ibid., p. 666). In his 1985 paper, Peltzman himself relegates the results of his 1984 paper to a footnote. Thus, the existence of ideology as an important determinant of congressional voting has survived a concerted attack by an accomplished econometrician.[4]

Additional evidence supporting the importance of ideology is provided by studies examining campaign contributions. Changes in campaign finance laws led to a large increase in the ability of various organizations to contribute to political campaigns by creating Political Action Committees (PACs). Historically, labor unions had contributed significantly to campaigns. However, changes in the law enabled business and ideological groups to form PACs and use contributions to attempt to achieve their goals. (It is interesting to note that the changes in the law which triggered the rise of the PACs were endorsed by labor unions, apparently because they failed to forecast the effects of these changes on the ability of businesses to contribute to campaigns.) Both business and ideological PACs now contribute substantially to political campaigns. The structure of these contributions is analysed more fully in Poole and Romer (1985), who show that there is an important ideological component to contributions in general.

The large volume of contributions generated by ideological PACs is itself evidence against the strong economic interest hypothesis. These contributions show that many individuals and groups are willing to spend money to achieve non-economic goals. This apparently demonstrates that these contributors have a taste for public goods. This observation is of course not inconsistent with economic theory (where the elements of the utility function are left unspecified), but it is inconsistent with the strong claim that political action is aimed only at increasing money income. If some are willing to contribute money to change public policy for non-economic reasons, then it is not surprising that people are willing to use their votes to achieve these same goals. It would not be surprising if people were willing to vote for candidates who promised to support legislation which would satisfy their ideological, as opposed to economic, preferences.

This is especially true when we recall that the act of voting is itself not explicable in terms of economic rationality, since the probability of any one vote changing the outcome of an election is minuscule and voting does have positive costs (Downs 1957). However, Nelson (1994) has recently presented a model, discussed more fully below, in which political activity, including apparent ideological activity, serves a private goal (see also Morton 1991).

Even if we believe that the ideological PACs actually achieve economic goals, economic theory still has difficulty in explaining their existence. This is because such PACs must overcome substantial free-rider problems, as discussed by Olson (1965). Even for a potential contributor who believes in the goals of these organizations, the optimal strategy would be to refrain from contributing and to free ride on the contributions of others. Thus, when we observe individuals voluntarily contributing to ideological PACs, we have already observed a phenomenon that is inconsistent with the narrow view of self-interested rationality. It may be that, in addition to tastes for policies, individuals also have tastes for feeling that they themselves have influenced those policies. However, whatever theories may be evolved to explain these organizations, their existence and size do present a puzzle for the strong versions of the economic theory of politics.

3 Shirking

Even if it is conceded that ideology 'matters' in congressional voting, an important question remains. That is the issue of whose ideology counts. Congressmen voting ideologically might simply be reflecting tastes of constituents. Alternatively, they might be indulging their own preferences (Wittman 1977, 1983). This is essentially a principal–agent question: are legislators good agents for their constituents' (principals') ideological views, or are they shirking and representing their own views?

This question has been addressed thoroughly in the literature. There has been some confusion in many analyses, however. The initial work (Kau and Rubin 1979) was concerned with the issue of whether non-economic factors (called ideology) influenced legislation; this work did not attempt to distinguish between the ideology of the representative and that of his constituency.[5] But others have conflated the question of ideological impacts on voting with the question of ideological shirking. Peltzman (1984), for example, views his analysis as testing between the impacts of constituent interest and ideology. It is possible for a representative to represent constituent ideological interest, so Peltzman's categories are not mutually exclusive.

Conceptually, issues of ideology and of shirking should be separated. It is possible to have ideologically based voting without shirking. It is also possible to have shirking without ideologically based voting. For example, a representative might vote in response to contributions received from various special interests, and thus shirk with respect to his constituents' desires, but in a way unrelated to ideology. Indeed, Kau and Rubin (1993) find exactly this form of shirking. This last possibility has not been carefully studied in the literature, which has focused on ideological shirking (see Bender and Lott 1996 for an analysis).

Kalt and Zupan (1984, 1990) argue strongly that the observed voting behavior of representatives comports well with representatives' own ideologies, and therefore represents shirking. Nelson and Silberberg (1987) test the responsiveness of their measure of shirking to changes in its relative price. However, as Bender and Lott (1996) indicate, their measure (relative strength of ADA ratings in explaining voting on general versus special-interest bills) is flawed. A better measure is the behavior of legislators in periods when re-election is not an issue; using this measure, Lott (1987) finds that legislators shirk by voting less often, but do not change their ideological positions when they do vote. Dougan and Munger (1989), following Downs (1957), argue that what appears to be ideology is actually an investment in brandname capital – a signal of reliability and commitment providing voters with assurance that representatives will not behave opportunistically. They argue that past votes create a valuable reputational asset that makes promises of future voting behavior credible. Both Kalt and Zupan, and Dougan and Munger present empirical evidence that they argue is consistent with that hypothesis.

In a recent and important paper, Lott and Davis (1992) have criticized the methodology both of Kalt and Zupan and of Dougan and Munger. More importantly, Lott and Davis (1992) and Bender and Lott (1996) have shown that voters punish shirking, to the extent that it exists, and that they are empirically quite sensitive to wandering in ideological space. One result is that senators who deviate from the interests of their constituents by as little as 1.27 percentage points are ultimately defeated. Thus, they conclude that whether or not shirking exists is unimportant since if there is shirking it is strongly punished by political markets. Kau and Rubin (1993) also find that if there is ideological shirking, it is strongly and quickly punished. The key argument is that political markets do a good job of sorting legislators. That is, a representative must be in ideological agreement with his constituency to be elected to office.

If ideological voting is based on constituent ideology, this also has created a puzzle for economists. We have had no theory of constituent ideology. Indeed, we have had no theory of political behavior in general by individuals. Revealed theory cannot explain why rational individuals vote.

Recently, however, Nelson (1994) has presented a theory that relies on ideology to motivate voting. Nelson begins with the standard Downsian observation that, because the chance of any given voter influencing the outcome of an election is trivial, there is no private motive for voting related to the expectation that any one vote will be decisive. Nelson goes on to argue, however, that there is a private motive for voting and for expressing a political (ideological) position that is distinct from 'instrumental' considerations. In particular, he suggests that 'political positions are ... chosen not because these positions are the desired outcome for voters, but rather because one wants to associate with certain people and they have certain positions. People imitate others in choosing political positions' (p. 92).

Nelson presents empirical evidence, relating to political behavior of ethnic groups, which is consistent with his hypothesis. For example, he shows that membership in various ethnic groups is significant in determining political affiliation (after adjusting for economic variables) and that the income of the ethnic group's members 60 years ago is significant in explaining its political orientation today. Thus, Nelson has presented a theoretical and empirical basis for constituent ideology based on private motives and normal utility maximization. This model should make the use of variables related to constituent ideology less controversial among economists.

4 Current research and outstanding questions

Any future work on ideology must begin with a very important analysis of ideology that is probably the most significant public choice analysis of the US Congress. This is Poole and Rosenthal (1997), a book-length treatment of roll-call voting by the House and Senate for all roll calls from the first Congress in 1789 to 1985. It is based on numerous articles by these authors and others; I shall refer to the book rather than to the articles. Poole and Rosenthal find that what they call ideology is the basic organizing principle behind all such voting. By their definition, 'voting is along ideological lines when positions are predictable along a wide set of issues' (ibid., p. 4). They show that individual congressmen can be arrayed along a unidimensional continuum for most roll-call votes. Almost everyone to one side of a 'critical point' on this continuum will vote one way and almost everyone to the other side will vote the other way, with errors being clustered near the critical point. The winner in any vote is then determined by the location of this critical point.

Ideology as so defined is more important than constituent economic interest in explaining voting by legislators. Moreover, it is even more important in explaining the policies that are actually selected than in explaining voting *per se*. Policies adopted tend to be systematically biased away from the center of the distribution of legislators and toward the ideological center of the majority party. Ideology is more important in influencing the outcome of the legislative process than in influencing voting by legislators, even though voting is what has most often been studied.

A major issue raised by Poole and Rosenthal is the nature of the voting continuum. They characterize it in several ways. It is roughly defined in terms of conflict over economic redistribution. It also generally reflects party loyalty. A key point is that the continuum reflects logrolling. That is, votes are structured so that coalitions are maintained across most issues. This explains in part why the economic interests of constituents are not significant in any one vote. The vote trading reflected in the continuum in part accounts for these interests. One theoretical treatment consistent with these arguments is Hinich and Munger (1994). However, as discussed below, the nature of this continuum is one of the most important research questions in the contemporary study of ideology.

Poole and Rosenthal also show that for most of American history, a single ideological dimension is all that is required to array votes. During two periods (the 1830s–40s and the 1940s–60s) a second dimension dealing with race was also useful. From the New Deal until the 1970s, they find that there was actually a three-party system in the United States (Republicans, Northern and Southern Democrats). More recently, the country has returned to a single ideological dimension and a two-party system.

This is not a logical necessity. For example, Poole and Rosenthal point out that it would be possible for two dimensions to be required, and the actual number needed is an empirical matter. They give the example of social and economic ideology, with economic liberals favoring government intervention in economic matters and social liberals opposing intervention in social or behavioral issues. It would then be possible for two dimensions to be needed to explain voting. But the fact that one dimension is sufficient is because social conservatism and economic liberalism are highly correlated, and the reverse. Other than readers and writers of this book, there are relatively few libertarians, and also relatively few individuals who favor both social and economic interventionism.

The procedure used to estimate the continuum is called 'NOMINATE'. It is an iterative procedure, aimed at maximizing the probabilities assigned to the observed votes.[6] They also develop a dynamic procedure, 'D-NOMINATE', based on assuming that each legislator moves at most along a linear trend over his career. This assumption and resulting trend line enables Poole and Rosenthal to estimate a common issue space for all US history. (Groseclose et al. 1999 estimate a similar function.) Because of the volume of data involved (11 473 legislators, 70 234 votes and 10 428 617 total decisions), the estimation requires the use of a supercomputer. A two-dimensional model (that is, an issue space allowing for two ideological dimensions) and a linear trend for each legislator provide as good a fit (about 85 percent of individual votes predicted correctly) as higher-order models (with either more dimensions or a more complex polynomial time path for legislators). Indeed, a one-dimensional model assuming that each legislator maintains a constant position predicts about 80 percent of the votes correctly.

Poole and Rosenthal show that the NOMINATE variable is highly correlated with more traditional measures of ideology, such as the ADA rating. This is a nice result since many researchers have used these scores in measuring ideology. NOMINATE is a preferred rating scale since it is more comprehensive and since traditional interest-group ratings are subject to 'folding' problems. That is, a legislator just a little more liberal than the ADA would get the same rating as a representative who was more conservative by the same amount. However, many of the major interest groups (for example, the ADA and the American Conservative Union) are at or very near the (opposite) ends of the political space, so this problem is not acute.

The major theoretical issue regarding ideology is the low dimension of the ideological space, as found by Poole and Rosenthal. (This is consistent with others who have examined ideology, but Poole and Rosenthal document the result much more carefully and completely.) Indeed, it appears that the US political system can only handle a one-dimensional space. In those two periods when the space increased to two dimensions, catastrophe followed. The first was the Civil War. The second was the chaos of the 1960s. Thus, it appears that our institutions may have difficulty with a policy space of more than one dimension. This of course would not be surprising; many of the theoretical results following Arrow show that the only guarantee of stability is a unidimensional, unimodal issue space. But what has not been fully explored is the mechanism that constrains the US to remain in such a space.

The work of Poole and Rosenthal shows that such a mechanism must exist and that it is exceedingly important. Poole and Rosenthal have measured the issue space for congressional voting. However, the results discussed above on the absence of evidence of shirking show that the congressional issue space is congruent with the issue space of voters as well. In other words, if the ideological space for Congress is one-dimensional and unimodal, and if Congress faithfully reflects preferences of constituents, then the issue space of voters must also be one-dimensional and unimodal. This conclusion raises the question of which comes first – does the issue space facing Congress come from the underlying preferences of constituents, or does the political process somehow define the issue space for individuals?

Beyond this, there are fundamental questions of the nature of ideology itself. North (1990) has raised this issue and stressed its importance. He believes that the basic direction of society is determined by its ideological preferences and that we do not sufficiently understand these preferences. This means that, in addition to determining the mapping between constituent and representative preferences, the underlying structure of these preferences itself is an issue of fundamental importance.

5   Summary and implications for future research

The initial interest in ideology was an effort to determine whether non-economic factors influenced economic legislation. The conclusion is that they do. The emphasis on shirking following this initial analysis has, in my view, been misguided. Constituent ideological preferences do have impacts on legislative outcomes, and the profession should devote its efforts to determining the source and nature of these beliefs. The recent work of Nelson (1994) is a good attempt at beginning this effort, and future research on ideology should focus on this issue, rather than on devising ever more scholastic tests to measure the relative strength of constituent and legislator ideology. In addition, the factors that make the issue space unidimensional and unimodal are worthy of attention because these factors serve to eliminate problems of cycling and instability. Finally, the work of North (1990) tells us that the underlying structure of ideology is itself of crucial importance in ordering an economy, and we have no good theory to explain this structure.

Notes
1. The downside of this argument is, as Stigler (1976a) indicates, that economists will have little influence on policy decisions.
2. See also Mueller (1989, p. 213, note 14) for a discussion essentially agreeing with this conclusion.
3. The first paper using ideology as a determinant of congressional voting was Kau and Rubin (1978). However, the economics profession's attention was initially drawn to this issue by Kau and Rubin (1979). Also see Kau et al. (1982).
4. I do not offer a complete analysis of the economic literature relating ideology to passage of legislation. There are numerous papers providing such analysis. Lott and Davis (1992, footnote 1) cite 18 such papers. Kalt and Zupan (1990, footnote 2) cite 20, only partially overlapping those listed by Lott and Davis.
5. Kau and Rubin (1979, p. 366) stated explicitly that, 'the representative (or his constituency) may be ideologically in favor of the bill'.
6. The program and data are available at Poole and Rosenthal's web site, http://voteview.gsia.cmu.edu/.

16 Clubs and club goods

Gary M. Anderson, William F. Shughart II and Robert D. Tollison*

1 Introduction

Club goods occupy the middle ground between private goods and public goods. Whereas private goods are both rivalrous and excludable, pure public goods are neither. Private provision and collective consumption mean that club goods are a little of both. On the one hand, only those individuals who want to consume a good in a club setting and are willing to finance its provision join; others can be excluded from enjoying the benefits of the club at relatively low cost. On the other hand, club goods are subject to crowding, and this rivalry in consumption limits the number of people who want to become club members. Nonetheless, the provision of a collective good in the setting of a private club has all the problems attending public goods production, such as truthful preference revelation and free riding, which must be handled simultaneously with the problem of determining the optimal club size.

In effect, individuals must optimize both output and group size simultaneously in the theory of clubs. A pure public good in the Samuelsonian sense is a polar case of the theory of clubs in which the optimal group size is all-inclusive. So, technically at least, the theory of clubs deals with so-called 'impure' public goods, which are not equally and costlessly available to all users.

This chapter assesses the empirical relevance and applicability of the theory of clubs. This is not an easy task because there has not been very much in the way of direct empirical testing of the theory of clubs, at least outside of the economics of alliances (see below). Moreover, the effort here is not intended to be copious. The chapter will summarize areas where the theory of clubs has been applied, at least in an analogous fashion, and outline the major results and problems involved in these applications. A reasonable number of areas and examples will be covered, but the reader will undoubtedly be able to think of others. Hopefully, the exercise will produce a preliminary understanding of the extremely useful nature of the theory of clubs.

We begin in Section 2 with a summary of the relevant theory. We then proceed in Section 3 to a discussion of the economic theory of alliances. Section 4 addresses the related problem of interest groups and their impact on government policy. Section 5 considers the issue of political coalitions in democracies. In Section 6 we describe developments in the economics of law firms from the perspective of club theory. In Section 7 we outline an application of the theory to the problem of the behavior of organized religions. Finally, we discuss possible future extensions of the theory of clubs to some economic problems not yet subject to such consideration.

2   The economic theory of clubs

Clubs are ubiquitous. From the country club to the Explorers' Club, individuals associate in order to achieve benefits from collective production, consumption, or both, that they could not achieve (or could achieve, but only at substantially higher cost) by acting unilaterally. Club goods typically have high fixed costs relative to variable costs, which means that the average cost of production falls sharply as additional members join, output is increased, and the financial burden is spread more broadly. This reduction in the per-member cost of provision supplies the economic motivation for forming clubs. But the necessity of cooperating with others to take advantage of the scale economies of collective provision also means that clubs are laboratories of public choice principles.

As articulated by James Buchanan (1965a), the economic theory of clubs applies to goods having three key characteristics.[1] As mentioned at the outset, club goods are both excludable and congestable. They are also divisible in the sense that once a club's membership has reached its optimal size, individuals who want to join but have been excluded can form a new club to produce and consume the same good. Clubs can be cloned or 'hived' as the demand for them warrants.

Under these assumptions, the determination of the optimal club size is, in theory at least, a straightforward exercise of equating costs and benefits at the margin. The marginal calculus yields three conditions that must be satisfied simultaneously for optimal clubbing. The first is the *provision condition*, which states that the optimal club size (in terms of capacity) is found by setting the summed marginal benefits to members from reducing congestion costs equal to the marginal cost of capacity. Holding membership constant, larger club capacity means less crowding, but supplying additional capacity is costly. Hence, the club must balance benefits and costs on that margin. It must also see that this capacity is utilized optimally. The *utilization condition* accordingly contemplates the charging of user fees, which will ensure optimal utilization if they equate a member's marginal benefit from consumption of the club good with the marginal congestion costs that member's consumption imposes on others. If the fee is set too low, the club's capacity will be overutilized; it will be underutilized if the fee is too high. Optimal capacity utilization therefore requires that consumption of the club good be priced to reflect members' tastes for crowding. Finally, new members should be added to the club until the net benefit from membership (in terms of lower pro-rata provision costs for existing members) is equal to the additional congestion costs created by increasing the club's size. This is the *membership condition*.

These three conditions help explain the prevalence of two-part pricing of club goods. Fixed up-front membership ('initiation') fees defray the club's cost of capacity provision while per-unit charges for use of the club's facilities ensure optimal utilization. When two-part pricing is not feasible – when the club exists primarily to provide its members with a pure public good such as political lobbying, for instance – clubs may also be able to price their services by bundling them with a private good. Calendars, group life insurance, and group travel arrangements are examples in this regard. But in any case, the pricing of club goods is disciplined by a 'voting-with-the-feet' mechanism (Tiebout 1956; Hirschman 1970). As long as clubs can be cloned freely and the members of existing clubs are free to exit, club prices will be kept in line with costs. 'Voting-with-the feet' also helps overcome preference revelation problems as individuals sort themselves among clubs. Those with high demands for club goods (and corresponding willingness to pay for them) join clubs that supply high levels of output; low demanders join organizations that offer levels of output closer to their liking.

But while the exit option helps prevent clubs from charging prices that are too high, jointness in consumption and shared responsibility mean that free riding remains the most troublesome economic problem facing club members. Individuals have incentives to understate their benefits from joining (in order to have their fees lowered appropriately),[2] to reduce the effort they contribute toward the club's operations opportunistically (in order to consume their pro-rata share of the collective benefits without bearing their pro-rata share of the costs), and to otherwise take advantage of their fellow members. Apart from the three conditions for optimal clubbing stated above, the logic of collective action (Olson 1965) suggests that successful clubs will tend to be relatively small in size and composed of individuals having relatively homogeneous interests. Not only does small club size raise the per-capita benefits of club membership, thereby giving individuals a greater stake in the club's success, it lowers the costs of monitoring and controlling free riding. If the lower costs of coping with free riding in smaller groups more than offset the correspondingly higher per-capita costs of club-good provision, the optimal club will have fewer members than otherwise.

Small groups also have lower decision-making costs (Buchanan and Tullock 1962), an outcome that is facilitated by homogeneity of members' interests. Group heterogeneity creates differences of opinion that raise the club's decision-making costs, making it more difficult to reach agreement on common courses of action, and creates opportunities for the membership's majority to take advantage of the minority (what Buchanan and Tullock call the external costs of collective decision making). Voluntary association, voting-with-the-feet, and the ability to clone organizations as demand warrants mean that diversity of tastes and preferences amongst individuals will tend to promote diversity amongst clubs rather than diversity of club membership. People will tend to associate with others who are like-minded in the sense of having similar tastes for crowding and similar demands for club-good provision.

As this brief summary indicates, the analysis of clubs and club goods raises virtually all of the problems encountered by governments in the provision of public goods. The differences between these two arenas of collective action are more matters of degree (presence of 'voluntariness' and absence of coercion) than of kind. Both must grapple with issues of size (capacity), utilization, and membership. Careful study of how actual clubs deal in practice with preference revelation, free riding, and pricing can therefore shed considerable light on the public sector's responses to similar problems. That is the subject to which we now turn.

3   Alliances

Perhaps the most extensively investigated topic in the literature pertaining to the theory of clubs has been the economics of international alliances. In his recent survey article, Sandler (1993) reviews 23 published empirical studies devoted to this topic, and since then several additional studies along these lines have been published. While the literature on alliances has been extensively and competently reviewed elsewhere, it is instructive to summarize the main empirical issues briefly here, given that alliances are in a sense the paradigm for further extensions of the theory of clubs.

From our earlier discussion we know that clubs form to fill the space between the polar cases dealing with the provision of purely public goods and purely private goods. In the provision of purely public goods the optimal club size is all-inclusive because of the non-rivalrous nature of the good in question (national defense, for example). In the case of purely private goods, an apple, say, the optimal club size is one. The rivalrous and excludable nature of such goods dictates that it is optimal to limit the size of the club to just one individual.

In the theory of alliances the observational unit shifts from the individual person to the individual country.[3] Sovereign nations voluntarily establish international organizations to achieve goals that are either unattainable or too costly to attain were they to act on their own.[4] Olson and Zeckhauser (1966) introduced the economic analysis of such organizations, which they call alliances. Whether they are created for the purpose of promoting mutual defense, common markets (which might be thought of as multiproduct clubs), harmonious law, supranational regulation of common pool resources, or other collective benefits, the formation and functioning of international alliances mirrors that of clubs.

The main difference between the analysis of international alliances and more pedestrian clubs resides in the cost-sharing scheme. Olson and Zeckhauser provide a cost-sharing analysis of the North Atlantic Treaty Organization (NATO) and identify the conditions under which it would be in the interest of the alliance's members to increase the size of the 'club'. Should a country in the neighborhood of any of the member countries apply, the additional benefits to the alliance may well outweigh the additional costs of protection. The scenario changes if the applying country is either too large or too distant from the existing members. In this case extending NATO's defense umbrella may be too costly, because of the need to disperse existing military forces across a broader geographic area.

Individual members in a club arrangement bear their pro-rata shares of the costs of operating the club. In the absence of price discrimination, cost shares are computed based on the club's total costs and group size. It is thus plausible to argue that, given the voluntary nature of club formation, members' costs are of similar magnitude. In the case of NATO, though, Olson and Zeckhauser point out that the United States is by far the single largest contributor to the alliance's coffers. As we shall see, however, the disparities in members' shares of NATO's total costs can be viewed as reflective of each member country's valuation of the good provided by the alliance rather than as representative of some unjust or unfair distribution of the total costs.

Olson and Zeckhauser devise and test five hypotheses related to the NATO alliance.[5] They find empirical support for the following propositions:

- There exists a positive correlation between the size of a member country's national income and the percentage of that income spent on defense.
- In a voluntary organization with quota assessments (cost shares) that are not always fulfilled, there exists a positive correlation between a member country's GNP and the percentage of fulfillment or overfulfillment of its quota.
- Among a group of developed nations, there exists a positive correlation between foreign aid expenditures as a percentage of national income and the size of the national income.
- In an alliance in which the marginal costs of some activities are not shared and the marginal costs of other activities are shared, the ratio of a member's share of the costs of the activities of the latter type will have a positive correlation with national income.
- In NATO, there exists a significant negative correlation between national income and the percentage of that income devoted to infrastructure expenses.

Olson and Zeckhauser's empirical results suggest that, overall, richer countries bear 'disproportionate' shares of NATO's costs. It is worth reiterating, however, that independently of existing discrepancies in contributions, each member willingly contributes based on its marginal valuation of the alliance's benefits. It becomes clearer, then, how the last proposition links with the other propositions. Smaller European member countries exhibit a greater willingness to participate in infrastructure expenditures simply because the buildings will remain on their soil after the alliance dissolves (if it does). The contributing scheme of each member country thus appears to follow a rational cost–benefit analysis in determining whether or not to contribute to a particular venture and, if so, how much to contribute.[6]

Side payments could, in theory, work to diminish the discrepancies in members' contributions. If offered by the larger countries, they would encourage the smaller countries to increase their contributions. Side payments only make sense, however, if it is in the interest of larger countries to be party to an alliance characterized by roughly equal contributions.[7] As Tollison and Willett (1979) suggest, side payments are more difficult to observe at the country level than at the individual level. They stress instead the mutual interest basis of 'issue linkages'. Linking international trade relations and 'human rights' or defense assistance and foreign aid, to give two examples, provides room for striking mutually advantageous bargains that move an alliance closer to the aggregate efficiency frontier. Tollison and Willett suggest that issue linkages should promote potentially beneficial agreements.

The more general point raised by the theory of issue linkages is that international cooperation on one margin cannot be understood in isolation from other issues. Direct side payments are not very likely among countries, but issue linkage is. Thus, the United States may bear a disproportionate share of NATO's costs, while other members of the alliance contribute relatively more to foreign aid or to humanitarian relief efforts in Africa. The point is simply that the traditional discussion of the theory of alliances does not account for the possibility of issue linkage as a way to increase the overall level of efficiency in the realm of foreign affairs and international cooperation.

The economic theory of alliances is an application of the theory of clubs. The individual members are countries, and the desired collective good is defense. As duly noted by a variety of sources dealing with NATO, there exists a non-negligible discrepancy between the contributions of larger countries and those of smaller (poorer) countries. There have been suggestions that the smaller member countries have had a free ride. Contending that Europe has been the main beneficiary of keeping the alliance functional, there have been calls for the United States to curtail its contributions to NATO.

However, the observed discrepancies in contributions may merely be reflective of each country's valuation of membership benefits and of the tradeoffs made on other issue margins. Had the United States not valued the existence of NATO, it is doubtful that it would have contributed over half of the alliance's operating costs for nearly half a century. Smaller European countries have also expressed their preferences. They exhibit a rational willingness to share the costs of infrastructure investments taking place on their soil. These two observations lead to the conclusion that the current arrangement is optimal in the sense that each member country is 'buying' what it values most. So, too, with NATO's recent expansion. The benefits of adding former Eastern European satellites to the alliance may be low, but the costs may be lower still.

4   Interest groups

A special-interest group is the direct analog of a club. The interest group produces a public good for its members in the form of political lobbying and, like a club, the interest group faces the fundamental problem of controlling free riding. That is, it must be able to form and to finance its lobbying activities, and to do so, it must find means of reducing to a cost-effective minimum club members' incentive to shirk. In other words, interest groups must guard against the prospect that an individual will be able to collect his or her share of the collective benefits of group political action without supplying his or her share of the effort required to produce those benefits.

One way to think about legislation is in terms of the interest-group theory of government.[8] Keep in mind that the use of the term 'interest group' as a modifier in this context is not meant to be pejorative. Individual citizens can want or demand laws for any reason – because it makes the world a better place, promotes the production of a public good, and so forth – but they will generally act in some group context to obtain the passage of a desired law or the defeat of an undesired law.

A basic principle – and conundrum – underlies the demand for legislation. The principle is that groups able to organize for less than $1 in order to obtain $1 of benefits from legislation will be the effective demanders of laws. The conundrum is that economists have little idea how successful interest groups are formed. That is, how do groups overcome free-rider problems and organize for collective action so as to be able to seek $1 for less than $1? The plain truth is that economists know very little about the dynamics of group formation and action.

One attempt to solve the puzzle is Olson's (1965) byproduct theory of collective action. According to this theory, an association ('club') provides a private good or service to its members that cannot be purchased competitively elsewhere. By monopolistically pricing the good or service above cost, the association can raise money to finance its lobbying activities. Political action becomes a byproduct of the organization because start-up costs have already been borne in the process forming the association for some other (non-political) purpose.

Indeed, for whatever reason organization is undertaken, lobbying for special-interest legislation becomes a relatively low-cost byproduct of being organized. A business firm is an example of an organization whose resources can be redeployed for political lobbying purposes (not necessarily in the context of an industry lobbying effort). Workers may organize to bargain collectively with employers and then find it relatively easy to open an office in Washington to advocate higher minimum wages.[9] Lawyers may agree collectively to a code of ethics to address such matters as attorney–client privilege and then proceed to adopt provisions in their code that, by banning advertising, for example, restrict competition among lawyers.

Olson's byproduct theory was originally dismissed by Stigler (1974), who argued that there is no good reason for assuming that interest groups will have monopoly power over the provision of particular private goods to their members. How, then, could they raise monopoly rents for the purpose of lobbying?

The basic point, however, is that Olson's hypothesis about the use of selective incentives is a testable hypothesis; it simply cannot be dismissed as a theoretical curiosity. It is entirely plausible, for example, to argue that the demand for calendars sold by the Sierra Club, one of the most venerable organizations of American 'greens', is downward sloping and that the Sierra Club has sufficient monopoly power in the calendar market to finance many of its lobbying activities with the associated rents. And the point goes well beyond the perhaps trivial example of calendars to such selective benefits as group insurance policies, a variety of discounts to members, and, in some cases, such as the American Medical Association, the right to practice one's profession.

As it turns out, there has been some empirical work on the use of selective incentives by interest groups. Mulvey (1994) investigated the use of selective incentives by the American Association of Retired Persons, and found that they are directly related to association membership, which is a proxy for interest-group clout. In short, Olson's byproduct theory of interest-group formation seems to be more empirically relevant than commonly assumed.

The formation of interest groups has received the attention of Kennelly and Murrell (1991). They attempt to identify factors of relevance to the process with international data. Using observations on 75 industrial sectors in ten countries, they examine the way in which variations in interest-group formation are explained by variations in selected industrial and political variables. Their results indicate that industry characteristics such as the proportion of the industry's sales purchased by households (+) and the industry's concentration ratio as a proxy for free-rider effects (–) are significantly related to interest-group formation. Insofar as such industry characteristics measure the private advantages available to firms from joining a trade association that then can engage in organized lobbying, these results provide indirect evidence for Olson's byproduct theory.

There is a tendency in the public choice literature to neglect non-American, non-OECD applications of the interest-group model. Exceptions are Kimenyi (1989) and Kimenyi and Mbaku (1993), which are relevant here. Kimenyi argues that each permanent interest group can be viewed as a kind of club that produces goods for its members in the form of wealth transfers obtained through the political process. In order to maximize its share of available transfers, each group will engage in competitive strategies to gain control of the political machinery that mediates those transfers. Such competition will tend to be more intense the larger the number of permanent interest groups in a given country and the greater the likelihood that the competition will involve non-democratic means of achieving the required control. He predicts that the more intense the competition for transfers, the less democratic the system of government will tend to be in a particular country. He reports international cross-section regression results that support this prediction.[10]

5 Political coalitions

The theory of public choice has evolved a theory of optimal coalition size that has straightforward links to the theory of clubs. In 1962, William Riker postulated his famous minimum winning coalition theory in which he stressed that a winning coalition's pro-rata gains would be maximized with a bare majority. This theory was challenged by Stigler (1972) in an approach which argues that the optimal political coalition is larger than $(N/2) + 1$. Political competition is not 'all or nothing', according to Stigler, but rather 'more or less': larger coalitions tend to be more effective in the political process.

Riker and Stigler essentially ask the question, namely, what is the optimal club size? The size and stability of political coalitions are crucial issues for public choice scholars given the well-known instability of simple-majority collective decision-making rules. Why is so much stability observed in the face of the theoretical prediction that winning coalitions will form and reform, producing a never-ending 'cycle' of political outcomes (Tullock 1982)?

Without enforcement mechanisms, agreements between interest groups and legislators would be worthless. Political exchanges, like private transactions, require some assurance that agreements will be honored. Interest groups are not likely to invest resources to secure the passage of legislation if laws once enacted are easily altered or repealed. Mechanisms to maintain political bargains are the central focus of the interest-group theory of the independent judiciary developed by Landes and Posner (1975).

Landes and Posner address two relevant margins through which the durability of political agreements is promoted.[11] Their primary focus is on the judicial margin, which is analogous to an explicit contract enforced by a third party. The independent judiciary, because of its methodology in reviewing cases, increases the durability of interest-group deals with the legislature. Thus, if a legal dispute arises with respect to the validity or constitutionality of a law or regulation, the independent judiciary resolves the dispute by interpreting the law, basically, in terms of the intent of the enacting legislature. By following this methodology, the promises made to interest groups by one legislature are made to endure beyond the elected representatives' terms of office. The durability of laws and, hence, the present value of political benefits to interest groups are thus impacted by the structure and the behavior of an independent judiciary.

Whereas the independent judiciary is analogous to an explicit, third-party enforcement mechanism, legislators can adopt implicit or self-enforcing mechanisms to promote durable agreements. (The constitutive rules of the legislature on such matters as majority voting, committee hearings, and floor action are examples in this regard.) As the degree of independence of the judiciary falls, contracts between interest groups and legislatures become more incomplete in the sense of being less enforceable by a third party. In such cases, we would expect greater reliance on implicit mechanisms to maintain a given level of enforcement in the pricing of special-interest contracts.

In the literature on private contracting, Klein and Leffler (1981) have analysed the role of implicit contracts between buyers and sellers when explicit contracts enforced by third parties are incomplete or too costly to write. One form of an implicit enforcement mechanism is for the potentially defecting seller to make an investment in a firm-specific, non-salvageable asset. This investment serves as an implicit guarantee that the seller will not cheat the buyer because cheating will render the investment worthless. That is, the seller will lose future business, and the investment in the non-salvageable asset is thereby forfeited. The purchase of a non-salvageable asset is equivalent to posting a bond that assures non-cheating behavior. For their part, buyers pay a price premium for the product to induce the seller not to cheat. In equilibrium, the value of the investment in the non-salvageable asset just dissipates the 'protection money' offered by buyers so that the seller earns only a normal rate of return.

The analogy we draw to political contracts is the investment by a political party in the size of its majority control of a legislature. Larger majority sizes are costly to achieve and to maintain – more legislative races must be won, more resources must be devoted by the party's leadership to monitoring and managing the rank and file, and so on. As such, parties would prefer third-party enforcement of legislative agreements by the judiciary, if the latter mechanism were complete or costless. A larger-than-minimum winning majority (*à la* Riker) is analytically equivalent to a non-salvageable investment that a political party can make to guarantee non-cheating behavior. The size of the non-salvageable investment is related to the extent of incompleteness in enforcement by the independent judiciary. Where the judiciary is less independent, the analysis predicts that a larger investment will be made on the legislative margin, that is, that a larger legislative majority will be maintained as a means of self-enforcement of political contracts. Thus, if a political party has invested in a larger-than-minimum majority size and it subsequently reneges on an agreement it reaches with an interest group, the interest group will turn its future support toward another party. The past expenditure on the party-specific brandname capital is forfeited.

In essence, the majority party is a supplier of legislative output, and the value of its brandname capital is a function of keeping its word. If it cheats on its commitments to interest groups, this capital is devalued. This means that in future elections it will be harder for the party to sell its program to prospective supporters. A supermajority (or superclub) is a way that a party signals that it has more to lose by cheating in terms of its investments in brandname capital, that is, cheating would mean that the party could incur losses in excess of short-run gains.

With respect to the demanders of legislation, interest groups are willing to pay the majority party not to renege on bargains struck in the past. This 'protection money', which may take the form of additional campaign contributions, extra efforts to deliver voters to the polls, and so on, would in turn be dissipated by the party's investment in a larger-than-minimum legislative majority. In other words, a normal rate of return to contracting would tend to prevail in political equilibrium. The effect, however, is that the possibility of reneging is reduced on both sides. The political party would lose the value of its investment in a larger majority, and a capital loss would also be imposed on the interest groups that have paid a price 'premium' in the form of political support.

In the above way, control of the legislature, the implicit enforcement device, can be traded off at the margin against the explicit enforcement mechanism offered by the independent judiciary. There will be less investment in larger legislative majority proportions where the degree of independence of the judiciary is strong, and vice-versa.

As stressed above, the margin of enforcing political contracts by implicit means will not be as necessary where explicit mechanisms such as judicial independence are stronger. This perspective suggests a theory of optimal legislative majority sizes. Specifically, larger majorities will trade off in a predictable way against measures of judicial independence and other variables across states. Thus, where judges have longer terms and have more independence, there is less call for the interest group and the political party to be concerned about the size of the latter's majority in the legislature. Jurisdictions with more judicial independence should exhibit smaller majorities, all else equal. This empirical implication is borne out in testing by Crain et al. (1988a) and Sass and Saurman (1991), casting considerable doubt on the proposition that winning coalitions will be bare majorities.

6   Law firms

The theory of team production, as articulated by Armen Alchian and Harold Demsetz (1972), represents a potential application of the theory of clubs. In this approach inputs are organized into productive teams, and the key problem of production becomes the monitoring of team members when it is not feasible to allocate rewards as a function of the marginal productivities of inputs.[12] Alchian and Demsetz note that partnerships are the most likely form of team production in professions requiring hard-to-evaluate artistic or intellectual abilities and that the partnerships will tend to be small and formed by relatives and old friends to help avoid shirking problems. How might this theory be applied to derive useful implications about the organization of legal practices?

Sole practitioners in this approach are monitored directly by the market for legal services. In individual law practices, however, there are not only limited amounts of entrepreneurial capacity, but limited amounts of professional labor that are complementary to the firm's other inputs. A sole practitioner wishing to expand his practice finds that he has a limited number of hours per week to achieve this goal and that the substitution of other inputs such as paralegals is possible only up to a point (paralegals can do research and draft briefs but are not allowed to argue in court, for instance). If a sole practitioner wishes to add another lawyer to his firm, he may have to offer him a share of the rewards because that lawyer has the option of forming his own firm. The fact that we do not observe all law practices organized as sole proprietorships suggests that there must be benefits to larger size.

Following Alchian and Demsetz, law partnerships involve more principals, each with less incentive to monitor and more incentive to capture returns personally in terms of perquisites, on-the-job leisure and other amenities that increase the partnership's costs. There is thus scope for free riding and shirking in partnerships, and it will be more of a problem where there is equal sharing of residual returns unrelated to productivity.

Despite these theoretical expectations, the fact that larger firms continue to exist indicates that there are factors offsetting the increased costs of free riding and shirking. Several other aspects of partnerships could be sources of efficient operation and offset the potential costs of this form of legal practice. First, there is the possibility of economies of scale where teams of lawyers share the same capital (for example, a law library). We do not expect such technical economies to be important, however, since law firms do not employ much physical capital. Second, until the Supreme Court ruled on the issue, the ban on professional advertising by lawyers implied that larger partnerships facilitated in-firm referrals of business. However, referrals cannot be the sole explanation of large partnerships since we observe many large firms that are completely specialized in one area of legal practice (for example, corporate law). Third, lawyers sell a product whose quality is unknown prior to purchase. Brandname capital is therefore valuable in this industry, and large partnerships may emerge because clients are willing to pay more per unit for legal services from firms with good reputations. Clients can buy the services of more aggregate legal experience from a partnership, and even if the work is actually done by an associate rather than by a partner, the client may feel that the partnership has screened complementary inputs for high quality.

In an initial empirical test, Leibowitz and Tollison (1978) sought to determine the optimal size of legal partnerships with respect to controlling free riding. They regressed operating and payroll expenses divided by receipts on measures of law-firm sizes, notably the number of partners and that number squared. They found an initial range over which partnerships passed an efficiency test. That is, they observed a U-shaped relationship between the share of operating expenses in receipts and the number of partners, with a cost minimum at five partners. Up to this point adding partners is like adding monitors; beyond it, each partner's interest in controlling costs is so diluted and the costs of monitoring other partners' behavior rises sufficiently that the operating cost ratio begins to creep up.

The recent literature has extended Leibowitz and Tollison's empirical work. In-house attorneys – lawyers permanently employed by (mostly) large corporate clients – have also become more important in recent years. In-house lawyers tend to handle legal issues short of trial, which is normally left to outside litigators who typically have more courtroom experience. This vertical integration of legal services has brought with it the possibility of expert monitoring of the performance of legal firms by the clients who hire them. Thus, direct monitoring increasingly seems to be supplementing the indirect monitoring of law-firm performance in the form of tracking the market reputations of those firms. This development seems to be driven by the increasing complexity of litigation, as in-house counsel, while although lacking the necessary skills actually to supply the required legal services, are equipped to monitor the hired outside law firms to protect their corporate employers from legal malfeasance or opportunism.

Carr and Mathewson (1990) consider this problem, and report evidence suggesting that while larger law-firm size promotes more monitoring by corporate clients, more monitoring by these corporate clients in turn produces smaller law firms. All else equal, larger law firms tend to facilitate appropriation of more quasi-rents by opportunistic partners.

In any event, team production in general and the problem of the organization of legal and other professional practices as partnerships, in particular, seem to be very fruitful applications of Buchanan's theory of clubs.

7   Religion

The application of economics to the study of religion has been around a long time. Adam Smith wrote extensively about the role of religion in human affairs, and approached the problem assuming that the faithful were what we would today call rational maximizing actors. But following Smith there was a long hiatus in similar applications of economics to religious questions. This dry spell was broken by Azzi and Ehrenberg (1975). They argue that participation in religion is a rational activity predicated on the assumption that there exists an 'afterlife', and that individuals pursue the maximization of consumption opportunities in that afterlife. Azzi and Ehrenberg helped spawn a recent resurgence of interest in religion among economists.

More recently, Iannaccone (1990, 1992, 1998) has extended the theory of clubs to religious organizations.[13] He starts by noting that religion in modern pluralistic societies is a market phenomenon, and that competing faiths live or die according to how successful they are in convincing potential adherents that they offer a superior 'product'. This vision of near-perfect competition is seemingly marred, however, by the existence of an obvious anomaly. Although the behavioral burdens most major religious faiths impose on their adherents tend to be relatively light, as the competition for customers has become more intense in recent years, the religions that appear to have been most successful, somewhat surprisingly, are the relatively small ones that make the strictest behavioral demands. For example, Krishnas shave their heads, wear robes, and chant in public; Orthodox Jews wear side curls and yarmulkes; and so on. Fundamentalism is on the rise. These religious groups seem to flourish despite their strict requirements, which not only involve the sacrifice of earthly pleasures but, in some cases, significant social stigmatization as well.

Iannaccone maintains that the explanation for this seemingly peculiar twist in market dynamics relates to the collective nature of religious activity. He argues that a religion is a kind of club which produces an 'anticongestible' club good. By this he means that each member's participation confers benefits, not costs, on other members; in other words, there are positive returns to crowding.

There remains the problem of ensuring an efficient level of participation among adherents to a particular faith. Participation rates may tend to be non-optimal because individual group members have an incentive to free ride in the collective enterprise. After all, rational actors will prefer to obtain desired benefits at lower personal cost. If even those who participate minimally can expect to receive full benefits (salvation), the collective good will likely be underprovided. This is the classic free-rider problem. It tends to be difficult to monitor, and therefore to regulate directly, the particular types of free riding available to the members of religious organizations. While it is fairly easy to observe certain measures of participation, like frequency of attendance or dollars placed in the collection plate, the nature of collective religious goods is such that many of the relevant costs borne by individual members take the form of intangibles, like 'devotion'. Free riding in the form of a failure to make a full emotional investment in the 'club' will tend to detract from the ability of that organization to produce certain collective goods, but be inherently unobservable. What the organization needs is some form of member 'self-monitoring'.

Religious clubs may be able to minimize this free-rider problem by requiring their members to follow strict rules of behavior. Personal sacrifices (keeping kosher, shunning buttons, wearing turbans, and so on) tend to be more readily observed than levels of participation (that is, motivation), and this is an important advantage. But also making the required sacrifice public knowledge and the individual adherent subject to the resulting social stigma raises a barrier to free riders. Only those with a high level of motivation and emotional commitment to the 'club' will participate.

Iannaccone tests his model using data on denominational characteristics. He finds that sect-like religions, which impose stricter behavioral requirements on their members, indeed seem to induce greater levels of participation. Sect members attend more religious services, contribute more money, and choose more of their closest friends from within the congregation than do otherwise comparable members of more 'mainstream' religions.

8 Conclusion

The past 35 years have seen the emergence of a plethora of empirical applications of the modern theory of clubs. This theory has provided a fruitful framework for exploring the inner workings of non-market economic phenomena. Moreover, further extensions of the basic framework to additional examples of non-market decision making and organization seem possible as well.

Consider some possibilities. Cartels might usefully be modeled as clubs, in which cartel rents represent a form of impure public good (to the cartel members), and in which the same basic tension exists between group size and average returns (assuming positive transaction costs). The military presents another potential empirical opportunity for the theory of clubs.[14] Armies are like clubs in so far as the entire group obtains benefits from sharing an impure public good in the form of the gains from the effective exercise of military force. Winning a war is a cooperative effort, victory deriving from the shared costs of expressing military power in a regimented context. There seem to be diminishing returns to larger armies owing to congestion effects; armies are subject to size constraints. Since Chandler (1977) suggests that the US Army was an important organizational model for the modern business corporation, the extension of the theory of clubs to this particular arena of collective action may generate dividends in the form of greater understanding of the working of the modern corporation as well.[15]

Or consider the application of the theory of clubs to the problem of federalism. Impure public goods characterized by excludability, but only partial rivalry, are at the heart of the theory of clubs. This, for example, describes the case of the swimming pool at the country club, the library on the college campus, and many other similar instances.[16] Therefore, the question of the optimal size of the relevant club can be related straightforwardly to the problem of fiscal federalism. For some public goods, the optimal size of the club is the entire nation; for others, it is a more delimited jurisdiction.

Casella and Frey (1992) introduce the example of determining optimal currency areas. Money as a means of transaction is a fully non-rivalrous public good, and the optimal currency area is as large as possible. But if money serves more as a source of public finance or as a stabilization tool, then the optimal currency area might be much smaller (consistent with the requirement that preferences over the use of money be homogeneous within the club). These results suggest a clear-cut empirical agenda with respect to, say, the debate over European monetary unification.

The modern theory of clubs provides a rich framework with many significant empirical applications to a variety of important problems. This model will surely be remembered by future historians of economic thought as one of James Buchanan's key contributions to his chosen profession.

Notes

* We are grateful to Todd Sandler for comments on an earlier version of this chapter.
1. A more technical exposition of the theory can be found in Mueller (1989, pp. 150–54). Cornes and Sandler ([1986] 1996) is a highly useful reference.
2. The American Economic Association (AEA) posts a membership fee schedule that rises with the member's faculty rank and annual income. According to the AEA's secretary, there are many more members claiming to be assistant professors and pleading poverty than warranted by national statistics on the economics profession. For systematic evidence in this regard, see Laband and Beil (1999).
3. 'Countries' do not make choices, of course; individuals do. The following discussion suppresses consideration of the domestic collective decision-making processes that gener-

ate national policies with respect to the terms and conditions of participation in international alliances.

4. For an excellent survey of the literature on the economic approach to international organizations, see Frey (1997).

5. Also see Sandler and Forbes (1980).

6. Hence, France's decision to withdraw from the alliance can be understood as a rational calculation that, because of its strategic location in Western Europe, NATO would come to its defense even if French taxpayers do not contribute their 'fair' share of NATO's costs. French forces still participate in NATO military exercises, though.

7. This might be the case if taxpayers in the larger countries object to what they view as free riding by smaller countries and threaten to reduce their contributions.

8. See McCormick and Tollison (1981) and Chapters 17 and 18 of this volume for more complete expositions of the interest-group theory.

9. Indeed, Olson (1965) devoted an entire chapter to the collective action problems of labor unions. The main point of contention in the literature seems to be whether workers can be motivated to join unions in the absence of coercion (for example, laws mandating 'closed shops'). See Akerlof (1980) and Booth (1984, 1985). The theory is summarized succinctly in Sandler (1992, pp. 113–14).

10. In related work, Kimenyi et al. (1988) find a positive relationship between the intensity of interest-group competition for wealth transfers and population growth.

11. Also see Chapters 8 and 13 of this volume.

12. Holmstrom (1982) and Rasmusen (1987) extend the analysis of team production to principal–agent models with multiple agents. Also see Sandler (1992, pp. 124–6).

13. Also, see Ekelund et al. (1996). Sandler (1982) characterizes religions as 'intergenerational clubs'.

14. For fascinating application of the theory of clubs to military operations, see Brennan and Tullock (1982).

15. The theory of clubs describes the behavior of voluntary organizations, and most armies have been coercively recruited organizations. However, various studies of the behavior of soldiers suggest that regardless of the coerced nature of the recruitment into the service, soldiers can typically choose to shirk on their assigned duties; you can lead a soldier to battle but you cannot make him fight. Therefore, the production of military force requires the active, voluntary participation of the army's personnel. See Anderson et al. (1996) for a more extensive discussion of this problem.

16. Foldvary (1994) provides applications of club theory to homeowners' associations and to the provision of local 'public' goods and services.

PART IV

PUBLIC CHOICE PERSPECTIVES ON GOVERNMENT AND THE ECONOMY

17 The interest-group theory of government

Robert B. Ekelund, Jr and Robert D. Tollison

1 Introduction

The interest-group theory of government seeks to explain governmental behavior on the basis of the costs of organizing interest groups in order to seek wealth transfers through the aegis of the state (or, what is analytically the same thing, the costs of organizing interest groups to resist governmental expropriation of wealth). As such, interest groups have long commanded the attention of scholars who sought a better positive understanding of how government works or a better normative understanding of the possible social costs of interest-group behavior. In this regard, for example, one need look no further than Adam Smith's writings on the mercantile system or James Madison's commentaries on factions for early trenchant analyses of interest groups. Moreover, in the scholarly literature of political science, there is a strong tradition of interest-group analysis, dating back at least to Bentley (1908) and clearly illustrated in Truman (1951).

Economists were latecomers to the idea that interest groups are important analytical units, which form the basis for a positive–predictive theory of government. Nonetheless, when economists did turn their attention to interest groups, they did so with an analytical toolkit that has spurred the development of a more formal and more easily testable theory of government. George Stigler began such analysis in his 1971 paper on the theory of economic regulation, and this tradition has been carried forward in the literature by numerous other scholars, including Sam Peltzman (1976), Robert McCormick and Robert Tollison (1981), and Gary Becker (1983). Taking a slightly different tack, Mancur Olson began a lifelong study of interest groups and their impact on economies in 1965, a study which parallels and complements the Chicago-school approach of Stigler et al. And, finally, Gordon Tullock's (1967b) essay on what has come to be called the theory of rent seeking blazed an important new trail to understanding how to assess the social costs of interest-group behavior. We thus have both a positive (Stigler–Peltzman) and a normative (Olson–Tullock) theory of interest groups.

In any event it is this modern literature on interest groups, primarily exposited by economists, which has come to constitute what is called the interest-group theory of government and which will constitute the subject matter of this chapter. We begin with the positive–predictive aspects of the theory, and then consider the possible social costs of interest-group behavior.

In each case we do not seek a full explication of the relevant analysis, but only a short, readable summary. Finally, we analyse conflicting theories and some contemporary criticisms of interest-group analysis.

2   Interest-group formation

In a fundamental sense the interest-group theory lacks a proper theoretical foundation, in that there is little that economists have had to say about how interest groups are formed. Interest-group formation is like a traditional public goods problem wherein the benefits of lobbying are non-rivalrous and non-excludable, so that it is narrowly rational for individuals to free ride on any efforts to lobby. Thus, in this sense economic theory predicts that there will be no interest groups formed, yet any perusal of the entry under 'Associations' in the Washington, DC *Yellow Pages* (or those of any other seat of government) would belie this prediction.

The plain fact of the matter is that we do not know very much about how public good problems are solved and, hence, about how interest groups are formed. There have been some limited attempts to deal with this issue in the literature (Stigler 1974), but the only remotely rigorous approach to the problem was exposited by Olson (1965), who articulated a byproduct theory of interest-group formation. In this approach the interest-group provides certain private goods as a byproduct of its lobbying activities. Olson postulated that the interest group has monopoly power in the provision of these byproducts and that it uses the monopoly rents so earned to finance its lobbying efforts. A calendar or group life insurance policy would represent examples of such byproducts.

Olson's theory has been criticized on the grounds that there is no reason to expect an interest group, such as the environmentalist Sierra Club, to have monopoly power in, say, the calendar market. Nonetheless, this is a testable proposition that deserves its day in court. In other words, empirically, is it true that interest groups finance most of their lobbying activities with revenues from the sale of byproducts? It is possible that there is monopoly power in some of these relevant markets due to pooling economies for insurance (for example, the American Association of Retired Persons) and other reasons. Olson's theory thus deserves a rigorous test that would involve the examination of the revenue sources of interest groups and, perhaps, the elasticities of demand for the private goods provided by interest groups.

To say the least, however, interest groups exist, so that even without an analytical basis for interest-group formation, the effects of given groups and changes in the number of groups can be explored. Perhaps the simplest way to frame the issue is to say that once free riding has been overcome and a group has been organized, the marginal cost of using that organizational capital to lobby is essentially zero. So when firms, unions, churches, and the like form for other reasons, the fact that they then engage in lobbying for or against wealth transfers should not be surprising.

3   Interest-group analytics

The economic analysis of an interest-group economy is relatively straightforward, and can be stated more or less in conventional demand and supply terms (McCormick and Tollison 1981). The demand for transfers is based upon the organizational costs facing potential interest groups. Net demanders of transfers will be those groups that can organize for collective action in a cost-effective fashion. In other words, net demanders will be those groups that can organize to lobby for $1 for less than $1. Net 'suppliers' are simply the inverse of the demand function for transfers, namely, those for whom it would cost more than $1 to organize to resist losing $1 in the political process. 'Suppliers' is in quotation marks because individuals clearly would not engage in such a 'transaction' voluntarily without being coerced by the state.

The equilibrium amount of transfers is determined by the intersection of the demand and 'supply' curves, and this equilibrium is facilitated by the actions of the agents of the political process, such as elected officials. The incentives of these agents are to seek out 'efficient' transfers by targeting 'suppliers', who will generally be unorganized with low per-capita losses from transfers and regulation (why spend $1 to save $0.10?), and by targeting demanders who will be well organized and active in the political process. If political agents miscalculate and transfer too much or too little wealth, the political process will discipline them, for example, through elections.

There are various testable implications of this framework, which boil down to predictions about the costs and benefits of lobbying. When the benefits of lobbying are higher and the costs lower, there will be more transfers and more lobbying (and lobbyists). Cross-sectional empirical research on the American states (McCormick and Tollison 1981; Shughart and Tollison 1985; Crain and Tollison 1991) and on the OECD countries (Mueller and Murrell 1986) have illustrated many such results. For example, larger legislatures have been shown to be more costly environments in which to lobby; so too bicameral legislatures with more disparate house and senate sizes (McCormick and Tollison 1981).

Note that the interest-group theory is envisaged here as a theory of government. As pointed out earlier, the theory arose from the Stigler–Peltzman–Chicago tradition of studying economic regulation, which represents both a subset of government activity and a subset of regulatory activity. In Peltzman's (1976) articulate formulation of this approach, consumer welfare is brokered against producer welfare by the political process to produce a regulatory equilibrium price and profit pair. There are many refutable implications of the

Stigler–Peltzman approach which have been identified and tested. For example, regulated prices are likely to be lower in jurisdictions in which regulators are elected rather than appointed (Crain and McCormick 1984).

Peltzman's model is summarized in Figure 17.1. Here, the regulator's 'indifference' curves ('iso-majority' curves, in Peltzman's terms) represent the political process at work. Each curve traces out combinations of price and profit that yield the same level of political support. Curves that are higher or more northwesterly denote greater support. The iso-majority curves are positively sloped, indicating that, in order to maintain a given level of support, votes lost through price increases must be compensated by increases in profits. The conventional profit hill shows the amount of wealth that is available for redistribution. The regulator seeks to mediate between producers and consumers and establishes political equilibrium price and profit levels at point E. Notice that the regulator does not choose either the competitive optimum or the monopoly optimum, but rather some intermediate price–profit pair.

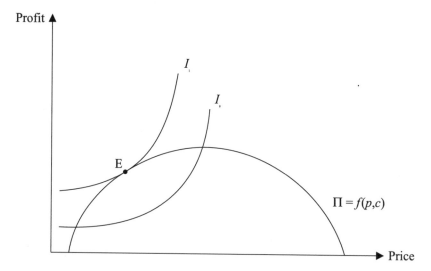

Figure 17.1   Peltzman's model

Peltzman's model is typical of the Chicago approach to public choice. The political process is secondary to obtaining an allocative result. In fact, the political process is reduced to the iso-majority curves, or *I*-functions, in Figure 17.1, which represent price–profit pairs yielding the same political majority or level of political support. Although these *I*-functions drive the result in Figure 17.1, they are basically unexamined in Peltzman and treated as being stable in the face of changing constraints. Thus, the *I*-functions embody some monolithic summary of political preferences, the determinants of which are left as an open question. It should also be stressed that one can begin to form an idea from the Peltzman approach of the origins of regulation. The profit hills in Peltzman's model, in other words, come from somewhere. Anything that causes these hills to emerge or to change measurably invites regulation and regulatory change as a consequence. Thus, the advent of inventions and new technologies, a sudden shift in relative prices due to cartel formation, the aftermath of a hurricane, and the like, can all lead to the establishment of new regulatory regimes.

Becker (1983) generalized the Chicago-school model of economic regulation to encompass all of government. First, he pointed out in a comment on Peltzman (Becker 1976a) that the same rent-seeking forces that explain economic regulation could also explain social regulation (for example, job safety). This has proven to be a rich prediction, and perhaps the best illustration in the literature is Marvel's (1977) paper on the British Factory Acts.[1] There, Marvel shows how economic forces (certain mill owners) and not some general concern for the 'public interest' shaped legislation regulating the hours worked by women and children in the British textile industry. Also, more recent environmental and occupational safety regulations in the United States have been usefully explained by the interest-group approach (Maloney and McCormick 1982). These contributions rely upon a heterogeneous-firm model of regulation in which different cost structures lead some firms in an industry to seek regulatory advantages over others.

Imagine, for example, an upward-sloping industry supply function. Under less-elastic configurations of the industry demand and supply curves, lower-cost firms can seek increased inframarginal rents through the imposition of uniform, cost-increasing regulations on all firms in the industry. Such regulation increases the wealth of the relatively lower-cost firms at the expense of their rivals. This is the model that Marvel (1977) applies to the British Factory Acts and that Williamson (1968) applies to collective-bargaining agreements.

Second, Becker (1983) offers a theory of pressure groups in which the demand and supply process for transfers results in what he calls an 'efficient' set of transfers. Becker's approach suggests that the conventional deadweight costs of these transfers are minimized; otherwise, corrective competition by Nash-like maximizing interest groups will seek out a more efficient political equilibrium. Needless to say, Becker's result has stirred up a great deal of controversy (see, for example, Wittman 1995). Much of this discussion is, however, misplaced if Becker and others are interpreted as offering a testable hypothesis. In this case two questions are critical: is the proposition that existing transfers are efficient testable, and why are the cost–benefit ratios for some transfer programs (for example, sugar import quotas) so high? Most of the debate over Becker's result, however, concerns its normative implications. For example, is it futile for economists to lobby for 'better' policies? We shall return to this issue below.

The undergirding principle of the interest-group approach is nonetheless organization costs. The theory begins and ends with this principle. Organized groups gain political wealth transfers at the expense of unorganized or less-well-organized groups. These are, of course, very general statements. Other building blocks involve the formulation of models of lobbying production functions, and analyses of how specific conditions in and among interest groups lead to specific political outcomes. Peltzman (1976), Becker (1983), and others have worked on these problems, but much remains to be done if the interest-group model is to yield precise predictions about government behavior. Not the least of the problems with the interest-group theory is that virtually no sooner than it was fully articulated, a movement began away from regulation and government enterprise toward deregulation and privatization. The challenge of these movements is clear: how does one explain deregulation with the same model employed to explain regulation? Somehow, the interest groups representing genuine consumer welfare have lately gained the upper hand in political processes around the globe. This is obviously an important problem for the positive interest-group theory, with only a few inklings of how the model can handle such issues (Shughart and Tollison 1985; Sullivan 1994).

Think of the issue in terms of Peltzman's model in Figure 17.1. What sort of change in the regulator's 'preferences' or the profit hill might cause the system to collapse to a competitive solution? One possible explanation is found in the theory of unintended consequences. Some other change in the political process sets off a chain reaction in which deregulation ensues as an unforeseen byproduct. In the United States, for example, court rulings in the early 1970s mandating legislative redistricting to ensure 'one man, one vote' led to an increase in the political power of urban constituencies in the US House of Representatives. The chain reaction set off by this institutional change could have represented the basis of, for example, the deregulation of airline pricing. Old-style economic regulation incorporating cross-subsidies to rural interests could not be sustained in the new political equilibrium. In any event, we need more work along these lines; the interest-group theory must be able to explain both the rise and fall of government with the same theory.

4   Long-term contract enforcement

A key feature of the modern interest-group theory is the role of the independent judiciary as an enforcer of contracts between interest groups and the legislature.[2] This theory of judicial behavior was first exposited by Landes and Posner (1975). They asked the following basic question: why does the next legislature not renege upon the interest-group deals made by the present legislature? Based upon an explicit interest-group theory, Landes and Posner suggest that independent (life tenure and fixed nominal pay) judges facilitate long-term contracting between legislators and interest groups. They do so by adhering to a judicial methodology wherein legal disputes are decided on the basis of what the enacting legislature originally intended. 'Intent' is divined, of course, by reading the contemporaneous legislative record of particular legislative acts. If disputes are resolved in favor of the original legislators, this has the effect of stabilizing and shifting to the right the present value demand function for rents from legislation. Thus, the independent judiciary increases the durability of legislative contracts with pressure groups in the interest-group theory of government.

The Landes–Posner theory is a testable theory which also suggests other margins of long-term contracting in politics. For example, long-lived and stable majority-party coalitions in the legislature would represent a substitute for independent judges in that political parties can thereby signal their willingness and ability to keep their bargains with interest groups over time. This is, in fact, what one observes across American states (Crain et al. 1988a). The constitutional amendment process in the American states has also been shown to be a function of the independence of state judiciaries (Crain and Tollison 1979a; Anderson et al. 1990).

In the interest-group theory, as extended by Landes and Posner, there is no 'separation of powers' as is commonly thought to characterize governmental institutions in the United States. There is rather a collusion of powers designed to set up and perpetuate an interest-group economy over time. The judicial branch is a cooperating agent with the legislative branch in this approach, not a separate watchdog institution, guarding against excesses by the legislative or executive branch. Indeed, even the executive branch has been brought within the ambit of this theory (Crain and Tollison 1979a). This linkage of the legislative and judicial branches is facilitated by the self-interest of the participants. For example, judicial pay and budgets are higher where judges are more 'independent' in the Landes–Posner sense (Anderson et al. 1989).

5   Political agents in the interest-group model

Political agents facilitate the process of wealth transfers. Elected politicians operate as brokers pairing demanders and 'suppliers' of transfers (McCormick and Tollison 1981). Judges function as long-term contract enforcers of interest-group bargains with legislators (Landes and Posner 1975). Executive branch officials participate in the interest-group model by resisting attempts to overturn previously enacted legislation through the selective use of the presidential veto (Crain and Tollison 1979b) as well as by allocating transfers across jurisdictions in ways that enhance the president's prospects of re-election (Wright 1974; Anderson and Tollison 1991a, b; Couch and Shughart 1998). Using their budgetary and oversight responsibilities, specialized congressional committees see that bureaucrats implement the legislature's policy preferences so as to ensure the political equilibrium amount of transfer activity (Weingast and Moran 1983).

Explaining the behavior of political agents as part of a wealth-transfer process has been one of the most fruitful aspects of the interest-group approach. This research has yielded new and useful insights into political behavior. For example, the executive branch is now modeled as an electoral vote maximizer subject to constraints. In this approach the president seeks re-election by allocating spending and other governmental benefits on the basis of a political 'closeness' criterion applied to electoral votes. Results in this spirit have been derived for New Deal emergency relief programs (Wright 1974; Anderson and Tollison 1991a; Couch and Shughart 1998), Civil War causalities (Anderson and Tollison 1991b), and executive vetoes (Grier et al. 1995). The point is that the president is a careful shopper. He ranks states by the number of electoral votes at stake weighted by the probability of victory at the polls. He then allocates his time, efforts, and programs according to this closeness criterion. It should come as no surprise to anyone that such a model works very well empirically. New Deal spending by state, for example, was much more directly linked to closeness-weighted electoral votes than to the perceived 'need' for New Deal programs.

Of course, this example, and perhaps the interest-group theory in general, is overly adapted to the US political landscape. There has been important research on other systems (Mueller and Murrell 1986; Weck-Hanneman 1990), but there is clearly room for expanding the interest-group theory beyond political institutions in the United States. Along these same lines, there is more useful work that can be done on the role of interest groups in autocracies (Tullock 1987; Wintrobe 1998).

6 Compared to what?

As a positive theory of government, the interest-group model has proved to be empirically robust in explaining a large variety of historical and contemporaneous governmental activities. For example, our earlier work (Ekelund and Tollison 1981, 1997a, b) develops a rigorous theory of mercantilism and the types of politicized economies that were propagated by interest groups in combination with divine-right monarchies over the period roughly 1550–1700 in England, France, and Spain. The creation of protected monopolies for favored interest groups became a central fund-raising ploy by these monarchs, so there is no mystery in explaining (as opposed to critiquing) mercantile policies and regulations.

In a modern context, interest groups have come to play a critical role in scholarly thinking about topics such as the size and growth of government (Mueller and Murrell 1986; Shughart and Tollison 1986) and economic growth generally (Olson 1982). Olson's famous hypothesis, for example, is that the longer interest groups have been around to advance their agendas, the more regulation-bound is the economy and the lower is the rate of economic growth. This idea and the work of Olson in general have revived modern scholarly interest in the causes and consequences of interest groups. (Below, we devote a section of the chapter to a discussion of other historical and modern applications of the interest-group theory.)

A key question, of course, is compared to what? The interest-group theory has proven helpful in explaining particular legislative episodes, but as a general theory of government, what is the alternative theory? In terms of the literature of public choice, the answer would have to be the median-voter theory. How does one go about evaluating the explanatory–predictive power of the two theories? In the literature this has generally been achieved by positing models of governmental expenditures (social security, for instance) in which the effects of interest groups (the elderly; civil servants) and me-dian-voter measures (income) are estimated in the same empirical model (Congleton and Shughart 1990). Although the record is mixed, it is fair to say that in most of these cases, the median-voter variables outperform the inter-est-group variables. However, it is also fair to say that these tests have not been very extensive and in some respects are not entirely satisfactory. For example, interest groups may be endogenous to income, a fact not controlled for in these tests.

The point is, however, that we do not have a definitive test for unraveling the relative explanatory powers of alternative theories of government, or, indeed, a definitive regime for conducting such a test. There are numerous median-voter results in the literature (Hinich and Munger 1997), and there are numerous applied examples of interest-group politics (Davidson and Ekelund 1997). For now, we have various theories of government, and additional research will continue to ferret out which theory works best. We are not yet at a stage where we can say that one approach definitively outperforms all others. The task will be to find methods of confronting the predictions of the alternative theories in ways that can be tested.

7   Conflicting theories: an example
A good example of how theories of government can make conflicting predictions concerns the distribution of income and wealth. The median-voter theory essentially predicts that democracy works so as to level the distribution of

income, redistributing wealth from the top and bottom of society to the middle class. This leveling arguably leads to a smaller Gini coefficient in the observed income distribution. This theory has been discussed in the literature under the heading of 'Director's Law' (Stigler 1970). Without a rigorous demonstration we argue, for illustrative purposes, that the median-voter theory suggests that government acts to reward the middle class at the expense of the lower and upper classes and in the process reduces the amount of disparity or skewness in the distribution of income.

By contrast, as stressed above, the interest-group theory simply states that well-organized groups win transfers through government at the expense of the less-well-organized or unorganized segments of the polity. In this case, some metric of organizational costs would do a better job of predicting the *pattern* of the post-government-intervention income distribution than measures of the median voter's or middle class's position in that distribution. This metric might, for example, be group size, which will in general be unrelated to median-voter characteristics.

The two theories thus make conflicting predictions about the impact of government on the distribution of income. These conflicting predictions set up a possible test of which theory does the better job of explaining outcomes. Clearly, setting up such a test would not be easy since the impacts of government on the distribution of income would be hard to untangle. Moreover, individual positions within the income distribution change over time, so that income mobility must be accounted for in both theories. Nonetheless, this is an example of one possible means of conducting tests of conflicting theories. Some agreed-upon and reasonable tests would, in short, be quite useful.

8 Some examples of positive interest-group analysis

A growing literature on interest-group analysis, most of it using empirical tools, is under development. Historical experience provides an especially rich laboratory for such tests of the theory. While a number of examples are given elsewhere in this book (see Chapter 25), we briefly consider only two cases: the development of factory legislation in the nineteenth century and the origins of antitrust policy in the United States in the nineteenth and early twentieth centuries.

Consider factory legislation. Historians and economic historians attributed public-interest motives to agitation to foreclose children and, later, women, from textile industry jobs. The acts of 1814 started the process, but the Factory Act of 1833 (Althrorp's Bill) was the first with enforcement provisions (children nine years old and younger were banned from the factories and those between 9 and 18 years of age were restricted in the number of hours worked). The tool of public choice as interest-group analysis has exploded the myth. Rather than protection for the 'exploited', Marvel (1977) argued, with evidence, that owners of steam-driven mills increased their wealth by restricting competition from water-driven mills (the water mills operated long hours when water was available and employed more children). But, in addition to capital interests, labor interests participated in the interest-group process. Corollary provisions in the act relating to health and education meant that physicians and teachers benefited as well (Anderson and Tollison 1984). Male operatives, especially the spinners, also acted as an interest group opposing the employment of 'children', who were viable competitors for their jobs (Anderson et al. 1989). These labor interests became more politically effective when the Reform Act of 1932 extended the voting franchise to adult male operatives. The voting rights granted to spinners (which, of course, also demands explanation) enabled them to bring greater pressure to bear on Parliament. Male-dominated labor groups were so effective in fact that, in 1844, they were an important element in spurring legislation prohibiting the employment of women in factories.[3]

Other important areas of special-interest legislation, regulation, and institutional change have been subjected to interest-group analysis with considerable success. Indeed, one of the most effective thrusts of public choice analysis directed to historical episodes has been in the areas of antitrust and regulation. The new technologies and sources of power that led to heavy industry, manufacturing, and metallurgy brought many issues to the fore. The very idea of 'competition' began, as a result, to diverge sharply from Adam Smith's characterization of England as a 'nation of shopkeepers'. In particular, the emergence of all-weather railway transportation (under way in both the United States and Britain by the 1830s) altered Smith's central notion of 'atomism'.[4] The result, for railroads and large manufacturing industries, was a public policy focus on income-distribution 'problems' created by these so-called monopolies.

Interest groups coalesced around these capital-intensive industries with the predictable result that, with proper conditions in place, legislation redistributing wealth and income could be expected. In the United States these interests were first felt at the state levels where interest-group analysis has been used to describe antitrust policy *before* the Sherman Act (Libecap 1992; Boudreaux et al. 1995) and its relation to the passage of various state antitrust statutes. Interest-group methodology and empirical evidence is marshaled to show that the impetus for early antitrust legislation came from state agricultural lobbies of the American Midwest, particularly rural cattlemen. The Sherman Act itself has been scrutinized from a public choice perspective (Stigler 1985; DiLorenzo 1985), the latter revealing clear evidence that the very industries accused of being monopolized in the mid-1880s were in fact expanding output and lowering prices.[5] The political and interest-group underpinnings of the Clayton Act of 1914 have also been suggested

(Ekelund et al. 1995) in an analysis of the Senate vote on this legislation. In short, as these examples illustrate, interest-group theory has wide applicability in explaining historical episodes of institutional change in economies, society, and government.

And, as discussed in the first part of this chapter, modern applications of the interest-group model are also numerous and interesting. Across the gamut of political and regulatory policies, from modern antitrust (Microsoft) to social security reform (American Association of Retired Persons), from tax reform (accountants) to global warming (scientists), from educational reform (the National Education Association) to reform of campaign finance (incumbents), and on and on, the interest-group theory is alive and well in American politics. And so too could the same point be made about other countries, both developed and less developed. The world is awash in interest-group activity.

9   The social costs of interest groups

Thus far, we have focused primarily on the positive economic theory of interest groups. As noted earlier, there is also a normative economic theory of rent seeking, which is quite novel and which was invented by Tullock (1967b). 'Normative' here simply refers to the recognition that lobbying for transfers imposes costs on society.

Tullock's point was simple and profound. In addition to the traditional deadweight costs of government programs, such as economic regulation, Tullock pointed out that any scarce resources used to compete for a transfer were also a social cost. In other words, the act of lobbying itself produces social costs. This result follows because lobbying for $1 is at best a zero-sum game and is usually negative sum in that traditional deadweight costs are associated with transfer programs. Even if a program is zero sum (a cash-transfer program), however, there are social costs of transfer seeking because the resources employed to seek transfers are drawn from positive-sum activities elsewhere in the economy. The opportunity costs of resources used in lobbying constitute the social costs of lobbying or rent seeking.

Given that Tullock's idea is relatively new in the literature, there are many issues about the concept of rent seeking that are not yet fully resolved. For example, does rent-seeking competition exactly dissipate the available rents or is more or less than the value of those rents spent in an effort to capture them (see, for example, Higgins et al. 1985)? Several general observations are in order.

First, Tullock's concept of rent seeking complements Olson's (1982) hypothesis concerning interest groups. Interest groups result in social costs that can become an impediment to economic growth. As more and more resources become allocated to transfer seeking, increasingly valuable productive opportunities in an economy are sacrificed. Growth and development suffer as a consequence.

Second, the empirical magnitude of rent-seeking costs is hard to estimate, and estimates run from low to high, depending upon the economy under study (Tollison 1997). The key point, however, is how to assess any measure of the costs of rent seeking. If we say that 10 per cent of an economy's GDP is absorbed by rent-seeking expenditures, how should this result be interpreted? This question brings us back to Becker's (1983) efficiency hypothesis. To say that rent seeking constitutes 10 percent of GDP does not actually say very much unless it is accompanied by some Pareto-feasible suggestions as to how the economy might be reorganized so that rent-seeking costs would constitute less than 10 percent of GDP. Only if there is a way to reorganize the economy to increase output and reduce rent seeking that is Pareto feasible can we claim that there is a net social cost of rent seeking. In the absence of such a showing, 'what is' is efficient, as Becker argued.

Third, a related point is that political agents have incentives to convert rent-seeking costs into transfers. This competitive force should to some extent mute the costs of rent seeking, although if the rules of the game permit agents deployed in rent seeking (lawyers) to write the rules, this check on rent seeking may not be as strong as it otherwise would be.

Fourth, the above discussion is related to the prospects for reform of rent-seeking processes. The two inherent problems here are, first, that rents get capitalized so that many regulated firms are not extraordinarily profitable (Tullock 1975) and, second, that at any rent-seeking equilibrium, rent recipients will fight to protect their rents. In Tullock's formulation, the social costs associated with expenditures to keep a transfer are every bit as costly to society as expenditures to capture a transfer. Hence, any utilitarian approach to reform would count the costs of resistance against the expected gains from reform or deregulation, and the value of the reform process itself would be lessened (McCormick et al. 1999).

Such an analysis, which is akin to Becker's efficiency hypothesis, is generally disturbing to economists and other would-be reformers. The message is that the world might indeed be efficient as is, and that efforts to change it may be a waste of social resources. On the other side of the coin, however, is the message that even though the job is harder, efforts to find a way out of the rent-seeking equilibrium remain worthwhile and all the more so if the results find their way into higher rates of compound economic growth. This makes the burgeoning literature on the relationship between property rights and economic development all the more important in so far as it establishes what a growth-friendly set of economic policies and social institutions look like (see Chapters 28 and 29). The role of the economist as reformer is to show societies what are the cost-effective ways to get from growth-retarding to growth-friendly institutions.

Like other parts of economic analysis, then, there are positive and normative aspects of the behavior of interest groups. And the normative aspects are useful in helping to assess the productivity of institutional processes across economies.

10   Criticisms of the interest-group theory

The public choice approach to the study of interest groups has not gone unchallenged. Much of the criticism is misdirected and may easily be dismissed. One writer, in an unbalanced analysis of taxing institutions, attacks the theory of rent seeking as recognizing 'only the waste caused by government, ignoring the waste entailed in the relationships among firms and among employers and employees', noting that 'the disjunction between private costs and social costs is what is really at issue' (Levi 1988, p. 24). This criticism is, of course, incorrect. The early 'capture theorists' might have had in mind something like a monolithic cooptation of government administrative agencies by special pleaders, creating a public sector constantly at odds with the public interest. However, Peltzman (1976) clearly indicated that an 'interest group' may well lobby on behalf of consumers.[6] More pointedly, Becker (1983) noted that both parties to a governmentally created regulation – that is, both losers and winners – would support wealth-increasing policies so that market failures that reduce economic efficiency are more likely to be addressed.[7] (This is so because both groups would gain from government intervention in such cases.)

Other critiques are even more intractable. Some writers, espousing a sociological–historical perspective, criticize public choice and neoclassical economics as 'too mathematical in form and, thus, too abstracted from the empirical realities it is presumably attempting to explain' (for example, Levi 1988, pp. 26–7). Neoclassical economics is no longer simply the economics of Alfred Marshall. It encompasses transaction and information costs, legal change, property rights assignments, and a wealth of contractual relationships based on assumptions of rationality, self-interest, and economizing behavior.

10.1   Self-interest in the dock?

An equally confused literature attacks the self-interest postulate within the interest-group (rent-seeking) approach. The poison dart supposedly is the charge that models based on self-interest are tautological in nature. Coats (1985, p. 31) directly criticizes the public choice approach by asking, 'what evidence, if any, would constitute falsification of … [the] theory, or what counterexamples, if any, would persuade' adherents to abandon it?[8] Clearly, the rent-seeking, interest-group theory of government would have to be jettisoned if another theory better fit the essential facts of institutional change. For instance, a public choice analysis of mercantilism or of some particular modern regulation would be seriously challenged if critics could show that the policies enacted by political representatives consistently increased the general welfare at the expense of narrow special interests. The theory has the power of *explaining* real-world events, with the best empirical methods available, in terms of self-interest, transaction-information costs, and political processes. It is based on economic foundations, not on the legerdemain of 'ideas', 'ideology', 'error', 'ignorance', or 'surprise' typically invoked by historians and critics of the interest-group approach to the description of institutional change.

A prime criticism of the interest-group theory (and presumably market analysis in general) is that the postulate of rational self-interest, as fuel for interest-group activity, is limited in applicability. Individuals and groups, in other words, are assumed by many to be guided by other motives. Rutherford (1994, p. 119), for example, speaking of government wealth transfers 'corresponding to the interests of small groups', appears to believe that 'non-economic' motives drive results. As he put the matter, 'norms of fairness and social justice seem to play a role both in which redistributive programs are adopted and which are not'.[9] North (1990) goes even further by identifying what he believes to be the failure of the economic view of human behavior to explain particular categories of human activities. According to him,

> the broad range of human actions characterized by such activities as the anonymous free donation of blood, the dedication to ideological causes such as communism, the deep commitment to religious precepts, or even the sacrificing of one's life for abstract causes could all be dismissed (as many neoclassical economists dismiss them) if they were isolated events. But obviously they are not and they must be taken into account if we are to advance our understanding of human behavior. (pp. 25–6)

The literature is awash in such views (for example, Magnusson 1993), despite factual errors by some writers.[10]

A central point is that economics is not, at bottom, a science of wealth maximization. Utility maximization is the source of all analysis of markets, both explicit and implicit. One may well be motivated to be altruistic or to marry for love or to support communism or old-time religion. Markets and interest groups are very much alive in these areas, however, no matter the difficulty in calculating prices and quantities. That one is dedicated to ideological causes such as communism may indeed represent some kind of philosophical maximization. It may also represent the calculation of one's (or a group's) prospects within the income distribution under that system.

Contemporary research, moreover, continues to place many heretofore 'non-economic' phenomena within the reach of economic analysis (for example, Becker 1981; Azzi and Ehrenberg 1975).

The suggestion, however, that rational self-interest is somehow a defective premise for use in a theory of interest groups and institutional change because of 'extra-economic' influences or for that matter informational problems (including bounded rationality, outcome uncertainty, and path dependence) must be dealt with directly. The fact of the matter is that no one has yet produced a cogent and testable theory of interest-group activity, government, and institutional change that places non-rational elements at the *center of analysis*. Careful analyses of the emergence of the US Constitution and the First Amendment to it in particular (Landes and Posner 1975), child labor legislation (Davidson et al. 1995), and New Deal programs providing relief to the 'needy' (Couch and Shughart 1998) all reveal huge doses of private-interest influence on policy outcomes. That motives other than rational self-interest *might* be involved in some models or explanations is indisputable. But science demands a fair test of their influence and position in any theory or application.[11]

10.2   The institutionalist critique of interest-group theory

A particularly vacuous attack on interest-group analysis is that of the 'new Veblenians' (NVs). Stripped of its camouflage in new terminology and in contorted usage of 'law and economics', the NV critique of modern economic analysis (of which interest-group theory is a part) is no more cogent than that of its predecessors.

Thorstein Veblen's *fin de siècle* assault on economic theory rested on so-called explosions of the natural law (1899–1900) as a basis for theorizing, attacks on utility and price theory as the focal point of economic science (1909), and lack of the use of Darwinian principles by Marshall and the neoclassicals (1898).[12] In place of neoclassical economics, Veblen espoused an institutional economics that, unfortunately, contained no discernible theory of institutional change.[13] Further, although Veblen hailed Humean empiricism as opposed to the kind of 'animism' found in Smith's theory of markets, he undertook no empirical work to support his sociological–anthropological theory of human behavior. While Veblenian economics, in both its old and new variants, has never posed a serious challenge to orthodox economic analysis (as elaborated by Marshall or his successors), Veblen's ideas have rearisen to sponsor critiques of end-of-twentieth-century economic theorizing, including interest-group analysis.

Studies of institutional change by some economists have led to the admission of non-rational elements into the discussion. These elements include such notions as 'path dependence',[14] the elevation of ideology to the level of self-interest as a motivator in markets, and 'bounded rationality'. The new Veblenians also seem to eliminate what they regard as 'economic imperialism' from consideration. They have seized upon these themes, but have melded them with artifacts of the old institutional economics. The hostility toward standard microeconomics exhibited by Veblen is not easily reproduced in Veblen's own context, but the NVs follow in a modified tradition – that of John R. Commons, who supported governmental regulation and interference in markets from a peculiar, non-scientific, and highly speculative context of law and economics. Modern partisans of these views, like the Veblenians of old, reject the dominant paradigm in economics. Positive and normative microeconomics – of which interest groups are an integral part – is rejected on a number of grounds. Almost all of the critique involves bringing sociology and normative concepts of 'justice' into the analysis to replace rationality and utility as the foundation of economic science.

10.3   Interest groups and the new Veblenians

Like their predecessors, the NVs adhere to any and all arguments that promise new market failures commanding new and enlarged roles for government. These arguments possess little of substance or logic. Samuels and Mercuro (1984, pp. 58–9), for example, attack the assumed given structure of rights. Excoriating the analytical views of James Buchanan, they eschew a scientific approach entirely by arguing that the interest-group, rent-seeking theory

> deliberately or inadvertently postulates the preeminence of some given, status quo structure of rights – and the nature of the bundle of commodities that make up the pie together with the rights-specific market prices. By giving such preeminence to the status quo structure of rights it has the effect of ruling out of analytical bounds most if not all efforts to change rights. Indeed, such efforts are selectively denigrated as wasteful. The effect is to perpetuate status quo rights. If the only permissible change is through exchange, the price structure will reflect the high reservation demands of the already wealthy *vis-à-vis* all other persons. (p. 63)

It appears from such criticism that somehow interest-group analysis ignores institutions (that is, ignores the past use of the state by treating received institutions as exogenous). Rather, the NVs believe that economic society and growth (undefined by the NVs) *follow* laws and legislation promulgated by the (impartial) state to promote 'justice'. Samuels and Mercuro emphasize legal change and insist that exponents of interest-group analysis 'are more interested in limiting the right to try to change the law than looking openly at the society that could emerge under changing law' (p. 64).

What are these 'narrow and myopic' principles (p. 67) of analysis to be replaced with? They, like their predecessors at the end of the nineteenth century, are short on answers to that question. They assert that an economic system is to be based on 'justice', 'a just ideology', or an 'evolving concept of "rights"' – hardly a scientific or useful approach to analysis of policy or institutional change. They ignore the fact that economists are interested in the effects of *changes* in policies or institutions. Naturally, past institutions are taken as 'givens' for such analytical purposes. The world may be evolutionary (or Walrasian) in nature, but the only manner of getting a handle on the nature of change is through scientific methods that have served economists well for over a century. Like their Veblenian and Marxist predecessors, the NVs are theological and sociological in approach.

Rent-seeking forces *change* law and legislation in evolutionary fashion. That is, law and legislation tend to follow rent-seeking activity (Rubin 1977; Priest 1977); they do not lead it as suggested by the NVs (Samuels and Medema 1997).[15] A stylized Pareto optimum – in the absence of some concept of dynamic efficiency – is used as a starting point in assessing the normative effects of policy change. There may well be legitimate objections to such use, especially over the long run, but short-run welfare calculations are excellent indicia of *change* in economic wellbeing from interest-group activity (as a sample of the host of studies we have cited above indicates). It is also the case that abandonment of some maximand (welfare, utility) throws economics open to the kind of redistributive charlatanism espoused by both old and new Veblenians.[16] With 'justice' as the ideological objective, there is no reason to prefer capitalism to communism on efficiency grounds or to prefer government involvement in 40 percent, 10 percent, or 100 percent of an economy.

10.4 Economic 'imperialism' and NV totalitarianism

The heart of the NV criticism of interest-group economics appears to be that it is some kind of exercise in 'economic imperialism', defined by one writer as the 'application of economic analysis to traditionally noneconomic areas such as political science, law, sociology, and biology' (Medema 1998). (Never mind that Darwinian biology is actually an application of economics.) This criticism is, in effect, that scarcity, choice, and economizing behavior are somehow inapplicable beyond the realm of ordinary markets. Not only does such criticism neglect the large and growing successes of economic models of religion, sex, anthropology and, most particularly, public choice, it is uninformed. Economic motivation is not based solely on nominal prices and homogeneous quantities. It is based on utility and demand. The laws of economics are not rescinded when considering marriage or the demand and supply of regulation or 'social' legislation. Economic tools are just as applicable – and have with much empirical testing been *shown* to be applicable – in dealing with such phenomena.[17]

The use of extraeconomic explanations for policies, institutions, and behavior is the hallmark of the NV attack on interest-group analysis and general economic theory. The attempt – in politics and elsewhere – to find exceptions to the 'rational actor model' has, moreover, produced some peculiar conclusions. One example (ibid.) is an assault on traditional law and economics which pretends to offer evidence that the Coase theorem is 'often' inapplicable in the face of 'community norms' or concepts of 'justice'. The 'evidence' offered will not convince anyone of the superiority of such approaches to exchange.[18]

Ultimately, the introduction of normative, untested, and untenable behavioral models to replace those of economic analysis could create a new totalitarianism. Whose 'norms' are to be adopted? Is 'justice' not simply another term for someone's or some interest group's self-interest? Possibly, it is the outcomes produced by market processes in the many aspects of life that NVs do not accept. But in order to thwart or to retard the takeover by economics of other social sciences, including public choice and interest-group analysis, the NVs will have to produce evidence that outperforms economizing behavior in formal empirical tests. That evidence does not yet exist. However, plentiful evidence for the interest-group theory of government as opposed to the reified categories of 'public interest' or 'justice' does exist. And the dossier grows in length with each passing day. Thus, the foundations of the new Veblenian critique of interest-group analysis are unscientific and untenable. Propositions derived therefrom, especially those regarding law and economics (Mercuro and Medema 1998), are likewise lacking in substance. This new assault on orthodox economic theory is destined for the same fate as that of the 'old Veblenians'.

11   Conclusion

The interest-group theory of government is young and robust with a growing number of adherents. And it has an advantage not as well possessed by the major alternative competing theories of government (median voter, Leviathan, and public goods) in that most of its exponents are dedicated empiricists who insist not just upon *testable* theories but upon *tested* theories. Predictably, certain academic interest groups resist the use of evidence, especially if evidence subjected to widely accepted standards of science is at variance with preconceived notions of 'justice' or acceptable 'culture'. There is naturally much yet to be done, both with respect to theory (for example, principles of interest-group organization) and to empirical testing (for example, the nature of comparative tests) relating to the interest-group theory of government. But if evidence matters to social scientists, there is a good chance that the interest-group model will emerge over time as the primary method of understanding government organization, its social costs, and how special interests affect ongoing institutions of many types.

Notes

1. Marvel's analysis is discussed further below.
2. Chapters 8 and 13 of this volume provide detailed reviews of the literature on political contract enforcement.
3. Interest-group analysis of this type has also been used to explain twentieth-century child labor legislation (Davidson et al. 1995) and compulsory school attendance laws (Edwards 1978).
4. For a discussion of important aspects of this development, see DiLorenzo and High (1988) and Ekelund and Hébert (1990).
5. The complexity of the institutional changes wrought by legislators and interest groups is also revealed in DiLorenzo's (1985) paper. He suggests that the Sherman Act of 1890 was in part a political smokescreen for the McKinley Tariff that was passed by Congress only three months later (with Senator Sherman as the sponsor).
6. Institutionalists, such as Rutherford and Eggertsson, do not appear to have a firm grip on the interest-group approach to institutions and policy change. Rutherford (1994, p. 119) notes that 'a final, and important line of criticism, is that the interest group theory seems to imply that those in control of the state apparatus have no interests (other than the social interest) of their own'. Rutherford goes on to quote Eggertsson (1990, p. 279), who argued that 'in much of the rent-seeking writings there seems to be a presumption that the state will somehow supply output-maximizing property rights, if only special interest groups can be contained'. These views are of course exactly the opposite of those advanced by leading contributors to the interest-group literature. Even a cursory reading of Peltzman (1976) reveals that a *central proposition* of the theory is that politicians are rational economic actors, striving to maximize dollars, votes, or other measures of political support. Far from being solons or lawgivers, politicians are as driven by their own self-interests in supplying wealth transfers as special-interest groups are in demanding them.
7. It is, of course, difficult empirically to show that regulation evolves in an efficient manner, although there have been some arguments to that effect (Rubin 1977). There is some evidence that, even in the case of genuine market failures, government does not necessarily increase social welfare over that produced under initial private or less-centralized arrangements (for example, Johnson and Libecap 1982; Libecap and Wiggins 1984).
8. That question appears to permeate the critical literature on the interest-group theory of government, certainly as it relates to the analysis of mercantilist institutions. The question of tautology is important. Posed in the form of what facts would cause us to abandon interest-group theory in this case, there are some clear responses. If, instead of creating monopoly rights for favored groups, we observed Elizabeth I employing a Tudor 'Alfred Kahn' to deregulate the British economy, an alternative to the neoclassical, public choice approach to regulation would have to be sought. If the business and political interests of the time took to heart the quantity theory of money or the price-specie-flow mechanism and reduced or eliminated trade protectionism, the public choice theory of the mercantile period would have to be displaced. If local trades and professions (as enshrined in the Statute of Artificers) were not 'regulated for revenue' but were left open to unrestricted entry, an interest-group theory of mercantilism could not be maintained. Finally, if we observed more robust growth rates in France than in England, despite more intense regulation in all areas of the French economy, confidence in the public choice view of history would be shaken. At a minimum, the public choice, interest-group theory has the advantage of being falsified. The confused and meaningless Marxian approach to history, exemplified in the works of Coats (1985) and Magnusson (1994), requires a suspension of science and a simple belief in stories weaved to fit a particular political ideology.
9. North (1984, p. 39) adds that 'if ideology is not important, then economists must explain the enormous amount of resources that political units and other principals in political and economic activity devote to attempting to convince participants of the justice or injustice of contractual arrangements'. However, such activities are observationally equivalent to 'mitigating opposition' or 'encouraging support' for redistributions of wealth. The aim of

economics, after all, is utility maximization. Religion, from the dawn of time, has been sold based on the natural fear of death and the demand for 'assurances of eternal salvation'. North seeks to separate ideology from 'product'. For a discussion that places ideology firmly within the boundaries of the public choice model, see Rubin (Chapter 15, this volume).

10.   Rutherford (1994, p. 119), for example, is incorrect in assuming that only 'small' groups gain in politico-economic wealth redistributions. As Stigler and Peltzman clearly showed, small groups may have an advantage, but redistribution, incomplete except in extreme cases, will go to those who, *ceteris paribus*, can generate the most political support in terms of both money and votes. Naturally, organizational costs and a host of transaction-cost factors also enter the picture, but the supposition that only 'small' groups or 'producer' groups always win is demonstrably false. Eggerston (1990) also makes this mistake (see Rutherford, p. 119).

11.   The simple observation that some people donate blood does not negate the regularity and predictability with which rational self-interest shapes policy outcomes. Do tax deductions for donations to museums increase, decrease, or remain the same when the gifts are valued at current prices versus original cost? Actual results (after a change in the law in 1993) unequivocally favor the former. Government displacement of property rights has served to discourage the private provision of transfused blood, all in order to benefit the Red Cross and hematologists (Kessel 1974). Increase the market reward by offering monetary inducements, changing liability rules, or both, and more blood would be 'donated'.

12.   On the latter, Veblen simply did not understand or make an effort to understand Marshall's actual position on evolution. See Marshall (1887).

13.   In Veblen's writings, habits and institutions are in fact exogenous and, although he recognized 'a specific sociological–anthropological variant of economizing, he failed to identify how the cost–benefit mechanism applied to real wealth or utility maximizing behavior to explain change under conditions of instinctually-determined goals' (Ault and Ekelund 1988, p. 42). Pecuniary values were not associated with material progress. For example, Veblen *did* argue that 'pecuniary behavior' was primarily responsible for creating institutions such as the corporation, common and preferred stock, and corporate finance generally (Raines and Leathers 1993, pp. 256–8), but he did not believe or understand that these new and evolving institutions produced *real* wealth. This is, of course, not a general theory of *endogenous* habit formation, and Veblen did not describe a utility-maximizing view of institutional change outside an ill-understood 'pecuniary context'.

14.   See the discussion of path dependence in Chapter 25 of this volume.

15.   We agree with one position of the NVs, namely that the role of empiricism is never more important than at present in economics, a point clearly made (with reference to Coasian economics) by McCloskey (1997). Whether government intervention to correct 'externalities' can or cannot improve on unregulated solutions is the test of whether they should be supported. The Coasian solution encompasses such a commonsense approach. This, however, is different from *asserting* the superiority of government solutions, as so many NVs are wont to do. The fact is that much evidence seems to show that private solutions to externality issues are in fact preferable (Cheung 1973; Johnson and Libecap 1982; Libecap and Wiggins 1984). Further, the convoluted view of the 'post-modern' law and economics advocates calls for 'recognizing the multiplicity of potential solutions and underlying value premises' (Mercuro and Medema 1998, p. 129), hardly a fruitful agenda for finding answers to important questions concerning economic wellbeing or efficiency. Some NVs, moreover, have sought to interpret Coase as positively *favoring* government regulation (Samuels and Medema 1997). Such a conclusion is highly doubtful (for example, Coase 1964).

16.   The 'brain trusters' of the New Deal sponsored (what has turned out to be) legislation having critically negative effects on society. Further, to argue that the 'needy', as opposed to politically powerful special interest groups, were the primary beneficiaries at the time is to ignore mounting evidence on the issue (Anderson and Tollison 1991a; Couch and Shughart 1998).

17. Many writers have missed the real source of this view. It appears in writings of the French engineer, Jules Dupuit, long before Marshall's delineation of the realm of neoclassical economics or of Becker's 'imperialistic' extensions of it. As Dupuit expressed it in 1853:

> We extend its [utility's] domain over all things which men desire, over all that they seek to acquire or to conserve through sacrifice. That is to say, the domain of utility exists not only over material objects susceptible to exchange, but over natural wealth, over the pleasures of the mind and heart, which also have the property of satisfying our desires even at a higher degree and, consequently, of being useful. ... [Not all wealth has] an exchange value susceptible to market analysis, but it all has utility. Since utility is susceptible to a common measure, the general principles of science may be applied to [such goods]. ... [T]he beauty, the youth, wit or good breeding of a woman takes the place of a dowry; reciprocally, a fine dowry takes the place of what is missing in her. ... Doesn't the consideration which a magistrate receives form part of his salary? Give to this consideration a value in exchange and then you would no longer be surprised that society gives less money to the magistrate than a dancer. If political economy aims to explain social phenomena, it must necessarily understand all that causes them. Now, it is a mistake to believe that man attaches a price only to material things. (Dupuit 1853, pp. 13–14)

18. Medema (1998, pp. 136–8) cites Landa's (1994) study of contracting forms among Chinese traders of Southeast Asia. Medema would have us believe that somehow the code and its 'norms' – which include kinship, clan relations, and 'distance' – are evidence that trade does not take place in the framework of an economizing process. He concludes that 'given these Confucian norms, the most reliable group with which to trade will be one's kinsmen, and the least reliable non-Chinese' (Medema 1998, p. 137). But, contrary to Medema, the absence of posted prices does not mean that the law of demand and economizing principles are not at work. The use of other categories is question-begging. Ultimately, the economics of benefits and costs determines the categories of trades. The use of Confucian codes is observationally equivalent to the laws of demand and supply, where the information costs of dealing with 'distant' traders is a 'tax' on exchange. Medema's (pp. 127–33) use of one-shot experiments to 'explode' the rational behavior model is likewise unconvincing.

18 Rent seeking and rent extraction

Fred S. McChesney

The Army can't make you do something. But it sure as hell can make you wish you had. (Saying of US Army drill-sergeants, Second World War; Ambrose 1997, p. 331)

1 Introduction

Use of the single label 'public choice' risks suggesting that there is only one prism for viewing the role of government in the otherwise private ordering of affairs. And indeed, as a subset of public choice, the economic theory of regulation began by adopting such a monocular perspective. Particularly in the University of Chicago public choice tradition (for example, Stigler 1971; Peltzman 1976), politicians were viewed as working to shift wealth from consumers to producers. That approach was enormously influential in analysing conventional economic regulation (the regulation of railroads, public utilities and other sectors of the economy, for instance).[1]

A synoptic view may once have sufficed. But the economic model of public choice from which the theory of regulation derives is hardly limited to describing politicians' transfers of wealth from consumers to producers. The wider public choice model, deriving from the different tradition of the Virginia school (see, most notably, Buchanan and Tullock 1962) begins with a much broader focus on the interplay between public (political) and private actors and activities. The differences from the narrower Chicago tradition might be described as both 'vertical' and 'horizontal'.

Vertically, the Virginia approach emphasizes that one cannot fully analyse any particular set of political (legislative, bureaucratic) activities without understanding the anterior constitutional rules that constrain legislative and bureaucratic choices. Horizontally, the Virginia perspective emphasizes the complexity of relationships among politicians, bureaucrats, producers, consumers, and input suppliers – in short, all the different groups affecting and affected by non-market (political) decision making. These richer vertical and horizontal dimensions mean that no one 'economic model of regulation' will do in analysing all public choices (Aranson 1990).

But, running through the various models necessarily employed to analyse myriad aspects of regulation, there are some constants. One of these is the fundamental importance of presuming rational maximizing behavior on the part, not just of private actors, but of politicians and bureaucrats as well.

Individual incentives, the prospect of personal gain and loss, motivate public-sector actors just as they do those in the private sector. What distinguishes public from private choice, though, is the extent to which individual political decisions retard rather than advance overall social welfare. The particular contribution of Virginia-based public choice has been its 'theory of the failure of political processes', as one observer summarized more than a decade ago:

> Essentially the theory [of public choice] is focused on the perverse incentives embedded in rules of collective choice that necessarily enable redistribution to dominate efficiency. ... Accordingly, inequity, inefficiency, and coercion are the most general results of democratic policy formation. For more than twenty-five years, Virginia economists have developed and related these themes to a variety of institutional and policy settings. (Mitchell 1988, p. 107)

That is the setting, then, for the rent-extraction model summarized in this chapter. The model considers a subset of all 'institutional and policy settings', a subset in which 'inequity, inefficiency and coercion' are prominent, most notably the last: coercion. In effect, rent extraction represents a political strategy to extort private wealth. The rest of the chapter explains how the extraction (extortion) strategy works. To highlight what the rent extraction model adds to public choice, however, it is useful to begin with the older rent-*seeking* model of public choice.

2   Rent seeking and rent creation: regulation as contract

Although hardly the first public choice analysis of government activity in private markets, George Stigler's (1971) article was the first to gain recognition for demonstrating how elementary economics could explain otherwise puzzling phenomena in the realm of politics. The puzzle concerned the oldest sort of economic regulation, which applied to entities such as railroads and public utilities. Regulation was popularly seen as something imposed on private firms against their will, so as to constrain prices and profits that allegedly these firms would otherwise earn as natural monopolies. Such was the theory. In practice, however, it was observed that regulation did not actually restrain firms; indeed, firms actively sought to be regulated. How to explain this divergence between the theory of regulation and its actual practice?

Stigler's answer was elegant in its simplicity. One observes that private actors seek (demand) regulation, and in response government provides (supplies) it. In that sense, political markets function like private markets, where demand also elicits supply. The difference is in the 'product' demanded and supplied. In the political realm, private producers demand cartel-type rents; if payments sufficient to compensate politicians for the costs of creating rents are sufficiently high, they will supply the regulation demanded.

By definition, then, the Stiglerian demand–supply model is essentially one of contract. Admittedly, this did not nullify Tullock's (1967) point that rent seeking was a negative-sum game. The parties were contracting for redistribution (transfer) of existing wealth: higher producer prices through regulation were achieved at the expense of consumers, and in the process imposing deadweight losses. There were, moreover, other possible victims of regulation whose influence might be reflected in the regulatory contract between rent seekers and politicians (Peltzman 1976). But to the extent that rent-creating regulation was actually achieved, it reflected a mutually advantageous contract between regulation's private beneficiaries and the politicians who supplied it.

The impact of Stigler's contribution was enormous, eventually contributing to his winning the Nobel Prize in economics. With the model of regulation redefined in Stiglerian terms, economists had no difficulty (using econometric techniques such as stock-market event studies) locating the gains to private rent seekers. The gains to the other contracting parties, the politicians, remained less well identified and quantified. (Indeed, as discussed further below, the role of the politician was rather poorly defined in the early economic models.) But under the contract-based model of regulation posited by this first version of the economic theory of regulation, politicians received recompense for creating private rents in any number of ways: 'campaign contributions, contributions of time to get-out-the-vote, occasional bribes, or well-paid jobs in the political afterlife' (Peltzman 1989, p. 7).

3   Rent creation *versus* rent extraction: regulation as extortion

The notion of regulation as essentially a bilateral contract explains the observed frequency of rent seeking. Like any contract, regulation must leave both demanders (rent seekers) and suppliers (politicians and their bureaucratic agents) better off. Thus is solved one puzzle, the spectacle of the regulated imploring politicians for regulation.

But viewing regulation as a contract raises a new question: might not other sorts of relationships exist between the two groups, private citizens and politicians? After all, voluntary contracts do not make up the complete set of real-world human interactions. Game theorists, for example, study and model both cooperative (for example, Axelrod 1984) and non-cooperative (for example, Schelling 1960) behavior in society. The law governing human interaction includes not just rules concerning cooperation (including contracts) but also rules concerning non-cooperative behavior such as torts, theft, and murder.

In other words, contract is not the only form of human relationship. 'In the general case, the individual will observe two ways to persuade: by a threat and by a bribe' (Gunning 1972, p. 20). In the typical day at my house, I will combine contract-type bribes to my wife (if you cook dinner I'll do the dishes) with simple threats to my children (if you don't clean your room your friends can't come over tomorrow). On the job, bosses motivate workers by a combination of carrots (for example, high performance earns bonuses) and sticks (poor performance causes termination).

One would thus expect politicians to use the same dual strategy in their dealings with people. Private beneficiaries would predictably pay bribes (legal or illegal) to a politician who can create rents for them. That is the essence of Stigler's model of rent creation, derived from Tullock's points about rent seeking. But a politician (like a parent or a boss) can also make demands on private parties, not by promising benefits but rather by threatening to impose costs.

That is the essential insight of the rent-extraction model. If the expected cost of the act threatened exceeds the value of what private parties must give up to avoid legislative action, they rationally will surrender the tribute demanded of them. With constant marginal utility of wealth, a private individual will be just as willing to pay legislators to have rents of $1 million created as she will to avoid imposition of $1 million in losses. (With declining marginal utility of income, the individual will pay even more to avoid the losses than she would to obtain the gains.)

In the wider public choice approach to government action, rent creation is to rent extraction as, more generally, bribery is to extortion. With the former (rent creation–bribery), the beneficiaries of political action compensate the politician for increasing their welfare. With the latter (rent extraction–extortion), persons whose welfare would otherwise be diminished by political action compensate the politician for not effectuating that diminution. Of course, the ultimate implications for the payers themselves are completely different; the politician is enriched either way, though.

4   Rent extraction: the formal model

Figure 18.1 presents graphically the essence of the rent-extraction model. Assume an industry in which producers have different amounts of some firm-specific, fixed-cost asset (including entrepreneurial ability). The industry supply curve in the absence of regulation (S) thus is upward sloping, intersecting the demand curve (D) so as to produce market price P_m. Returns to specific assets come out of producers' surplus ($0P_mB$). Those returns are rents, returns to the asset's owner above the returns necessary for the owner to continue the asset in its current use.[2] Critically, the producer's surplus consists of privately created rents, not governmentally created ones as in the Stiglerian model of regulation. Economically, they are 'good' rents, ones resulting from sources such as innate productive ability, prior investment, and gains from mutually beneficial exchanges. Allowing asset

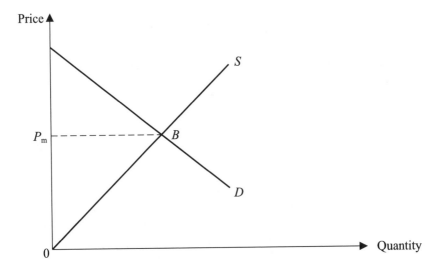

Figure 18.1   Rent-extraction model

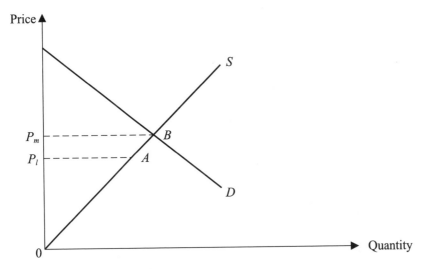

Figure 18.2   Extracting rents by threatening to lower price

owners to realize the returns (rents) to their assets is of course necessary to induce optimal levels of investment.

But the very fact that the investments must be made first and the returns realized only afterwards means that the rents are subject to threats of later extraction. In Figure 18.2, suppose that a bill is submitted in the legislature to lower price from its market-determined level (P_m) to some legislatively dictated level (P_l). By lowering price, the law would decrease producers' surplus by P_mBAP_l per period. Rather than suffer such a loss, producers would offer up to the discounted present value of P_mBAP_l per period over the relevant time horizon to have the bill *not* enacted into law. In the process, no legislation would actually pass but some of the rents that producers would have earned will have been extracted.

Artificial lowering of price is not the only way to threaten producers. Regulations that threaten to increase costs imperil private rents just as much as proposals to legislate price decreases. Figure 18.3 illustrates the effects of a threatened increase in excise taxes ($0E$), or any other proposal that would increase per-unit marginal costs of production, such as a higher minimum wage. With higher costs, the supply curve rises from S to S', resulting in the higher price P_t. The per-period net loss in producers' surplus that would result is shown by area I minus area II ($0BGE - P_tFGP_m$). Rather than suffer such a loss, those who would earn that surplus would offer to compensate legislators, up to the discounted present value of area I minus area II. If producers are successful in buying off the legislators, the producers will nonetheless have had some of their rents extracted.

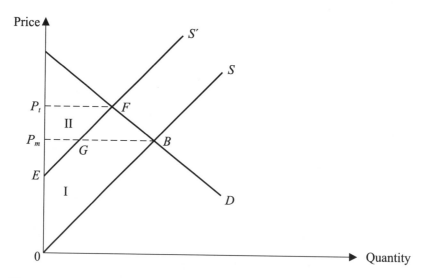

Figure 18.3   Extracting rents by threatening to increase a tax

While usefully illustrated graphically, the rent-extraction potential open to politicians is not mere blackboard economics. Indeed, politicians talk about rent extraction among them themselves as routinely as they practice it. 'Milker bills' is one term used to describe legislative proposals submitted just to 'milk' private producers for payments not to pass the legislation.

> Early on in my association with the California legislature, I came across the concept of 'milker bills' – proposed legislation which had nothing to do with milk to drink and much to do with money, the 'mother's milk of politics'. ... Representative Sam, in need of campaign contributions, has a bill introduced which excites some constituency to urge Sam to work hard for its defeat (easily achieved), pouring funds into his campaign coffers and 'forever' endearing Sam to his constituency for his effectiveness. (Stubblebine 1985, pp. 1–2)

Reporting on such 'milker bills' in California, *Time* listed several tax bills introduced (but not passed) only for 'the thousands of dollars of lobbyist lucre' that such legislative threats elicit.[3]

Such bills go by other names in other parts of the United States: 'cash cows' or 'juice bills'. *Newsweek* describes what are known in the Midwest as 'fetcher bills', which are 'bills introduced solely to draw – fetch – lavish treatment from lobbyists. Usage: "Let's toss in a fetcher on prohibiting the sale of Japanese-made Christmas-tree lights"'.[4] Another source reports an incident from the United States Congress:

> Rep. Jim Leach quietly introduced a bill a few days ago aimed at reducing speculation in financial futures. Barely 24 hours later, the Iowa Republican learned that Chicago commodity traders were gunning to kill his proposal. Rep. Leach said one Illinois lawmaker told him the bill was shaping up as a classic 'fetcher bill', a term used in that state's Legislature to describe a measure likely to 'fetch' campaign contributions for its opponents. Sure enough, one of the first to defend the traders was Democratic Rep. Cardiss Collins of Illinois, recipient of $24,500 from futures-industry political action committees. She called on colleagues in the Illinois delegation to beat back the Leach bill and watch out for similar legislation.[5]

To an outside observer, distinguishing rent extraction from rent creation may be difficult. 'Bribery and extortion substantially overlap and have for centuries. ... The same envelope filled with cash can be both a payment extorted under a threat of unfairly negative treatment and a bribe obtained under a promise of unfairly positive treatment' (Lindgren 1993, p. 1700). The agents of the Union government who occupied the American South during Reconstruction were notoriously corrupt, but bribery was indistinguishable from extortion: 'Much of the corruption of the Grant era involved payments to public officials by businesses seeking state aid, and in the Reconstruction South it often proved difficult to tell where bribery left off and extortion began' (Foner 1988, p. 486).

The point is an important one. There is a tendency, perhaps fueled by facile press reports, to ascribe all payments to politicians as made to purchase special favors. 'PAC excesses' routinely provoke editorial hand-wringing, with fat-cat lobbyists portrayed as corrupting upright but weak legislators. Maybe. Sometimes. But the press has no way of knowing why payments are made. And clearly, much of the money crossing palms is not for special advantage but to avoid being especially disadvantaged.

5   The economic costs of rent extraction

Superficially, political extortion may seem to be a mere transfer, of distributional importance to the politician–extortioner and the citizen–victim but of no allocative consequence. But the economic implications of political threats to private wealth are subtler. Even when no regulation is imposed, buying off the politician to forestall the threat reduces the value of the capital threatened. Several sorts of true economic loss ensue.

First, most obviously, diminished capital values reduce the incentives to invest in the first place. As Tullock (1967b, p. 229, n. 11) summarizes, 'One way of minimizing loss by theft is to have little or nothing to steal. In a world in which theft was legal we would expect this fact to lead to a reduction in productive activities'. Similarly, the specter of rent extraction will induce greater investment in capital that is less valuable socially but also less likely to fall prey to political extortion. These investments are second-best socially, but first-best in a world of rent extraction. They include investments made in the 'underground economy', where they are less likely to be taxed or otherwise taken (Alm 1985).

Citizens of more-developed countries sometimes shake their head at the antics of Third-World governments, in which 'the treasury is indistinguishable from the sovereign's pocket' (Shleifer and Vishny 1993, p. 603) and payments to avoid nationalizations or other depredations are just a way of life. But economically, what real difference is there between capital expropriations in less-developed countries and 'mere' regulation in developed nations? Regardless of the setting, the sovereign's ability to take outright or 'merely' to take through regulation (including taxation) has the same implication: loss of private investment that would have been made otherwise, and investments in assets that are less valuable but also less expropriable.[6]

Full accounting of the costs of rent extraction must also register the transaction costs (including bargaining costs) necessarily entailed in the threat-mitigation sequence. Richard Posner suggests these costs are the reason that private blackmail and extortion are made illegal:

> although ostensibly a voluntary transaction between consenting adults, [blackmail] is likely to be, on average, wealth-reducing rather than wealth-maximizing. ... [Extortion threats] are intended to transfer wealth from the person threatened to the threatener. Such a transfer does not, on its face, increase social wealth; indirectly, it diminishes social wealth by the sum of the resources employed by

the threatener to make his threat credible and of the victim to resist the threat. So, prima facie at least, it is a sterile redistributive activity, like (simple) theft. (Posner 1993, pp. 1818–20)

Transposing the private extortion process into a political setting, one reaches the same conclusion. To the extent that politicians' time has a positive opportunity cost, it is costly for them to negotiate over division of the rents generated by private investments. Private capital owners incur the same sort of opportunity cost, as do their lawyers.

The costs of rent extraction are measured along any number of other margins as well. Studies, meetings, legislative hearings, and floor debates are all part of the political process needed to make expropriation threats credible whenever milker (fetcher, juice) bills are proposed. Hiding resources to avoid their expropriation likewise imposes deadweight losses. As Gunning notes (1972, p. 22), there are different incentives to hide resources when the objective is bribery (rent creation) as opposed to extortion (rent extraction). In the case of bribery, the payer's strategy is a relatively complicated one of convincing the other party (politicians) that he has some resources, enough to pay the other party's reservation price but no more. But with possible extortion, the payer's strategy is the simpler one of hiding the existence of assets altogether.

6   Rent extraction in action

What sorts of political threats will induce payments of private wealth to politicians?[7] Most generally, the threats fall into three categories: threats to legislate lower prices, threats to legislate higher costs, and threats to expropriate wealth. It is useful to consider each separately.

One way to threaten private wealth available to private individuals is to mandate by law lower prices than would otherwise prevail in the market. Any measure that reduces price necessarily reduces the level of revenues that a producer would earn. Thus, one straightforward way to threaten private wealth is to threaten price controls. Such a threat would predictably evoke a response (offers to pay) from affected producers in exchange for legislative forbearance against price controls.

That scenario describes well what happened when the Clinton administration proposed its radical restructuring of the health-care industry in 1993, shortly after President Clinton's election. The Clinton plan did not use the term 'price controls', but as dozens of economists pointed out at the time, the plan was organized around widespread controls in several sectors (doctors, insurance companies, pharmaceutical firms) of the health-care industry. The legislation envisioned in the Clinton plan would have set fees charged by doctors and hospitals, capped insurance premiums, and restricted prices on drugs.[8]

Following due debate and consideration, Congress killed the Clinton plan in 1994. None of the price controls threatened ever passed. Yet, as the rent-extraction model would predict, the threats were quite effective in inducing private contributions to politicians to ward off the threats. Under the head-line, 'Medical industry showers Congress with lobby money', the *New York Times* reported 'vast campaign contributions', the total amounts running up-wards of 30 percent more than in 1991, the prior non-election year.[9]

More sophisticated empirical techniques have been used to identify and measure rent extraction in practice. Capital-market event studies are particu-larly useful, because they allow researchers to isolate the two parts of the extraction sequence, the initial threat followed by mitigation of the threat – for a price. If rent extraction is at work when a milker bill is proposed, for example, submission of the bill should have a negative impact on the share prices of the firms affected. Alleviation of the threat would either

- restore none of the wealth initially lost, if the price of purchasing inaction on the bill were the same as the wealth threatened by the bill (or if the price of purchasing forbearance were accurately estimated at the time); or
- restore only some of the wealth lost, if the price charged for inaction on the bill was less than the wealth threatened (or if the price of purchasing forbearance were overestimated at the time).

In either event, the extraction sequence would leave the threatened firm worse off, once the extraction sequence was completed.

That is what empirical attempts to test rent extraction have found. For example, a study of stock-market returns for pharmaceutical firms during the period when President Clinton's health-care program was under discussion discovered a significant, negative impact on pharmaceutical stocks starting when Clinton was elected and continuing until Congress abandoned attempts to pass the Clinton program.[10] But alleviation of the threatened price controls on pharmaceuticals did not restore the wealth that had been lost when the threat was made. The entire sequence thus resulted in no legislation but loss of private wealth and increases in politicians' wealth – the essence of rent extraction.

Other statistical inquiries have revealed the same pattern. Beck et al. (1992) studied a series of threats to impose new costs (including new taxes) on firms in Canada. None of the threats ever resulted in actual imposition of the costs, however, as the government ultimately withdrew the threatening proposals. As with the threat of price controls in the Clinton health-care plan, the announcement of the threatened costs in Canada caused a significant, nega-tive decline in stock-market returns for the Canadian firms affected. But removal of the threats did not cause a significant restoration of any of the lost wealth. The governmental threats never actually materialized into actual legislation, but the process was wealth reducing to firms nevertheless. As Beck et al. conclude (p. 224), 'existing estimates of the social welfare loss from regulation are understated – they ignore the costs of persuading the government not to regulate'.

An empirical example of this last point is presented in Mixon and Wilkinson (1998). They test a model of campaign contributions which includes *inter alia* variables for government spending and taxation (the latter captured as the size of the government budget deficit). Not surprisingly, campaign contributions are a positive function of government spending, *ceteris paribus* (see also Lott 1998). That is, rent seeking pays off. More interesting, however, campaign contributions also rise as taxation rises (deficits fall), all other things equal. At the same time that government is raising taxes overall, it is selling tax relief to some individuals and groups.

Much empirical work remains to be done on rent extraction. But episodes providing research opportunities arise constantly. Observers (for example, Sidak 1998; Yandle 1989b) note that antitrust initiatives, the welter of attacks on tobacco companies, and various environmental initiatives all have important rent-extraction components. As government grows, so does the area for profitable threats. One writer likens the extraction process to payment for 'safe passage' through a powerful king's territory, namely

> Between the White House and the Congress and all the agencies under their control as incumbents, we have many kings who can grant or deny you safe passage. ... [T]heir powers have grown enormously. Over the past two decades, starting roughly with the enactment of the Great Society legislation, the federal government has acquired an ever more expansive role in the affairs of business, industry, professions and institutions than it began to have before.[11]

Government's push into new policy arenas reflects the Constitution's wanting vitality in protecting property from taking (Epstein 1985), including taking by taxation. The credibility (and so the political attraction) of expropriation threats is a function of constitutional rules protecting private property and contract rights. Legislative threats to expropriate returns to private capital elicit fewer payments for political forbearance, the more probable it is that capital owners can have any legislation voided constitutionally in court. Rent extraction waxes as constitutional protections wane. In effect, as courts have shrunk from shielding citizens from legislative depredations, potential private victims must use self-help remedies, buying off politicians to avoid even more costly regulation.

390

7   The expropriating politician: rent extraction *versus* rent defending

The model of rent (or wealth) extraction differs importantly from the standard rent-creation model in the role assigned to the politician. Rather than supplying rents in response to demands therefore (as in the consumer-sovereignty construct of private markets), the politician in the rent-extraction model is an independent actor, seeking increased returns of his own. He finds them, not just in transferring rents from one group (for example, consumers) to another (producers), but in threatening the privately created wealth held by any group and agreeing – for a price – to forbear from having government take it.

There is a similarity, but not a complete identity, between rent extraction and what has come to be called 'rent defending' (for example, Davis and Reilly 1998a). The idea of rent defending derives from Peltzman's (1976) extension of Stigler's (1971) original model of regulation. In Stigler, producers gain and consumers lose from regulation. Producers are fewer than consumers. Therefore, producers face fewer free-riding problems in organizing to secure regulation; their gains are concentrated, while the losses of consumers are dispersed over larger numbers, reducing any incentive to organize.

Peltzman noted, however, that consumers are never completely inactive politically. At a minimum, their votes outnumber those of producers, and votes matter to politicians. Thus, at the margin, consumers will exert some influence in the regulatory auction. Producers will predictably not get all that they want; consumers will not lose all they have.

In the Peltzman model, though, consumers function essentially as voters only.[12] But producers seek rents in ways other than by voting – indeed, as voters alone they typically would obtain no regulation, being outnumbered by consumers. Producers seek rents by providing favors (including pecuniary favors like campaign contributions) to politicians. But if so, would consumers not try to respond likewise? Predictably, rent seeking by would-be victors will be matched, at least partly, by rent defending on the part of their intended victims.

Recognition of rent defending by regulation's victims reinforces two important points. First, *à la* Peltzman, victim resistance reduces the overall amount of social loss from regulation itself, because it results in less regulation being imposed. Second, however, the social costs of rent seeking (as opposed to the costs of regulation) are higher than would otherwise be the case, because increased rent seeking will predictably be matched by increased rent defending. Both these implications, namely lower social loss from regulation but higher rent-defending expenditures, have been tested and validated experimentally (Davis and Reilly 1998a).

Again, as Beck and his co-authors point out (1992, p. 224), 'existing estimates of the social welfare loss from regulation are understated – they ignore the costs of persuading the government not to regulate'. In that sense, it is easy to confuse rent defending with rent extraction. In both settings, holders of private wealth pay politicians to maintain the surplus that they have earned themselves. The negative impacts on investment incentives discussed above for rent extraction apply just as well to the need for rent-defending payments.

But the settings in which rent-extraction and rent-defending payments are made are quite different. Rent defending is the reaction elicited in a Stigler–Peltzman framework when rent seekers importune government for regulation. The politician in the rent-seeking, rent-defending model is a passive broker among competing private demands, with no utility or wealth function of his own. He is a 'mystery actor' (Tollison 1982, p. 592). His role is 'subsumed' (McCormick 1984, p. 14), as there is little consideration given to the ways in which the politician can benefit himself.

One of those ways, as illustrated above, is by making credible threats of his own to extract private wealth, then withdrawing the threat (for a price). The point is not that the rent-seeking, rent-defending model is wrong. It is, rather, that in maximizing his own wealth the politician has strategies available other than being paid to create rents for favored groups. As an independent actor, he can and does initiate threats himself – fetchers, juice bills, milkers. Total gains to the politician involve both rent creation (including attempts to defend one's own surplus) and rent extraction.

8   Extensions: interest-group organization in a rent-extraction model

The rent-extraction model helps to explain several puzzles in economics. For example, the criminality of victimless activities (gambling, prostitution, drugs) makes more sense when one realizes that criminalizing such mutually beneficial contracts sets the stage for political extraction of some of the gains from trade. The current obsession with drug-related crimes, for example, has proven a boon for police budgets. Laws allowing the police to keep assets seized in fighting drug crimes allow the police to expand their budgets directly. Off the books, of course, police shakedowns of those buying and selling in criminal markets (for example, prostitution, drugs) is commonplace.

More fundamental aspects of the rent-seeking model are altered when the potential for complementary rent extracting is appreciated. For example, just as rent creation focuses a different light on politicians' activities, so does it entail a new set of implications for interest-group organization. In the rent-seeking, rent-defending model, organization is an unambiguously good thing. But it is costly and fraught with free-rider problems (Olson 1965). Stigler himself explained regulation in terms of differential costs of organization faced by producers versus consumers. Because the former group is less numerous, its costs of organization are lower, free riding is reduced, and so producers are better able to lobby successfully for rent-creating regulation. In effect, regulation in the standard model reflects a Coasian lesson. As in any Coasian analysis, the issue is identifying the relevant set of transaction costs. These include the organization costs that Olson and Stigler discuss.

The rent-extraction model, focusing as it does on regulators themselves, draws attention to the *politicians'* transaction costs. To maximize the benefits available to them, politicians must engage in costly negotiation with private groups over the amount and form of consideration to be paid for regulatory action – or inaction. Accounts of how politicians spend their time make this clear.[13] Politicians operate under budget and time constraints, just as private actors do. They thus have an incentive to minimize the transaction costs of transferring wealth or, alternatively, of threatening it and then forbearing from transferring it. That is, politicians will spend more time regulating or threatening in markets where the amount of surplus at stake, net of the transaction costs, is greatest.

This in turn means that the net surplus or wealth that politicians predictably will threaten or transfer is a function of the extent of private groups' organization. Organization is therefore a two-edged sword. Greater organization allows a group to make higher pecuniary offers to politicians (that is, seek more rents). But it also lowers the cost of politicians' threatening the group's existing wealth. Because private organization facilitates higher offers to politicians at lower negotiation costs, politicians' costs of threatening and forbearing fall, thereby increasing the returns from rent extraction.

Politicians in effect make two choices: *whether* to regulate or threaten a particular market and *how* to regulate. In the latter respect, they can benefit themselves either by transferring surplus from one group to another or by threatening one group's surplus but ultimately not transferring it. But this choice – how to regulate – is only posed once politicians have decided to be active in a particular market in the first place. And that decision is a function of the costs of negotiating with affected groups.

In sum, a well-organized group represents more extractable surplus than disaggregated individuals would. Once it is organized and its fund-raising ability is demonstrated, a consumer group like the NRA (National Rifle Association) represents to politicians a lower-cost source of expropriable surplus. Savvy politicians therefore are more likely to adopt a rent-extraction strategy than if the group had never organized. Recognition of the rent-extraction option available to politicians alters the standard perception of interest-group organization. Organization advances rent seeking, which benefits the organized group, but it also increases the chances of rent extraction, which harms the group.

9   Conclusion

Rent extraction is a hoary process. As one columnist writes concerning the growth of campaign contributions, the procedure 'has been familiar since ancient times as a tributary system. Those who pay tribute are (or believe they are) buying the right to function as they wish, to be left alone, not to be set upon by those with official power to harm them'.[14]

Although the process is ancient, integration of rent extraction into formal economic models of political behavior is relatively recent. But its integration into the formal analysis of regulation has been called (Sidak 1998, p. 657) 'one of the most influential [developments] in law and economics of the last decade'. While the rent-extraction model leaves many puzzles unsolved (McChesney 1997, ch. 8), it has proven to be a useful complement to models of rent seeking in explaining the full range of activities undertaken by politicians.

Indeed, in appraising the overall importance of rent extraction versus rent seeking, one realizes that the orthodox economic model of regulation is just a special case of the rent-extraction model. The conventional model has been of admirable utility and undeniable influence since its inauguration by Tullock (1967b) and Stigler (1971). Nevertheless, the orthodox model necessarily depends on unspecified assumptions about transaction costs and political-market failure. In the absence of transaction costs, all regulatory activity would be rent extraction. The deadweight costs of regulation mean that existing owners of rights to future capital flows or present wealth will always pay more to keep what they have than would-be transferees of that surplus or wealth would pay for its transfer. Regulation occurs only when the transaction costs of avoiding expropriation – of reaching a rent-extraction agreement – prove prohibitive.

Notes

1. McChesney (1997, ch. 1) summarizes some of the principal contributions along these lines.
2. More technically, some of the returns to producers are true economic returns (for example, the returns to entrepreneurial ability) while others are quasi-rents (returns to prior capital investments). In the rent-extraction model, however, the distinction is unimportant. It is not the type of rent but its source – political versus non-political behavior – that is of interest.
3. W.F. Doerner, 'California's political gold rush', *Time*, 3 February 1986, p. 24.
4. 'Buzzwords', *Newsweek*, 20 November 1989, p. 6.
5. Brooks Jackson and Bruce Ingersoll, 'Chicago futures industry, to fend off attack, rallies lawmakers who received PAC funds', *Wall Street Journal*, 12 November 1987, p. 64.
6. It follows that any increase in the sovereign's ability to expropriate, tax or impose costs through regulation will decrease the value of the *existing* capital stock as well. Again to quote Tullock (1974, p. 67), 'if private property depends on the payment of bribes, then the bribe to be extorted can be the full value of the property and, hence, the property has no value'.
7. The discussion of rent-extracting strategies that follows should be distinguished from

threats to deregulate an industry already enjoying rents created by regulation. If politicians threaten to deregulate, shareholders suffer a wealth loss. Rather than suffer the costs of deregulation, shareholders will pay politicians an amount up to the total expected wealth loss threatened to purchase a continuation of regulation. But these payments are made to continue rents created by regulation, not to safeguard private wealth created in private markets, outside the political process. It is the protection of privately created wealth on which the rent-extraction model focuses.

8. Details of the Clinton health-care plan and sources on which this discussion is based may be found in McChesney (1997, pp. 56–8, 83–5).

9. N.A. Lewis, 'Medical industry showers Congress with lobby money', *New York Times*, 13 December 1993, p. A1.

10. McChesney (1997, ch. 4). Clinton's campaign had included numerous statements about the need to 'reform' the health-care market, and it was understood that he and Mrs Clinton would make this their first major legislative initiative if he were elected.

11. Meg Greenfield, 'The king's protection', *Washington Post*, 5 January 1998, p. A19.

12. Hirshleifer (1976) criticized Peltzman for limiting consumers' role in the politics of regulation, noting that it necessarily implied that politicians were vote maximizers. Politicians should be modeled as wealth maximizers like other people, Hirshleifer (p. 241) pointed out: 'If wealth is the ultimate goal, majority maximization can only be an instrumental and partial aim'.

13. One report (Jackson 1988, p. 193) describes a politician who spent 'an hour in the morning and another hour in the afternoon, every day, calling anyone who might be good for a contribution. It was too little; successful fund-raisers spend much more of their time personally soliciting donations'.

14. Greenfield, 'The king's protection'.

19 Public choice and public finance

Randall G. Holcombe

1 Introduction

Public choice can be defined as the application of economic methods to the analysis of political phenomena. This definition fits well with some of the early classic works that launched public choice as a separate subdiscipline, such as Black ([1958] 1987), Downs (1957), Buchanan and Tullock (1962), and Olson (1965). By this definition, and in the context of those works just cited, public finance has a distinctly peripheral relationship to public choice, and is relevant only to the extent that it is one of the activities taken on by the public sector. Yet public finance does have a close relationship to the fundamental ideas of public choice. Buchanan (1987a) gives substantial credit to Knut Wicksell ([1896] 1967) for laying the foundations for what has become modern public choice theory, but Wicksell's goal was not to analyse political phenomena with economic tools. Rather, he wanted to develop an efficient and just system of taxation and public expenditures. Building on Wicksell's insights, modern public choice theory shows that one cannot fully understand the government's taxing and spending activities without also understanding the political decision-making process that determines those policies.

A complete understanding of the process of public finance requires an analysis of the political decision-making process that determines how governments will both raise and spend revenues. In other words, a complete understanding of public finance requires that it be analysed from a public choice perspective. The importance of public choice considerations to the study of public finance appears so reasonable at the end of the twentieth century that it is worth recalling that half a century earlier, economic analyses of the public sector almost never took political institutions into account. Furthermore, although the merits of the public choice approach are well recognized, much of the current study of public finance, and especially taxation, ignores politics altogether. This chapter provides an overview of public choice as applied to public finance, and concentrates on the area of taxation, where there is substantial room for public choice to make further inroads. Before describing and applying these principles of public choice, the chapter first considers the relationship between public finance and public choice.

2 The methodology of public choice

Is public choice a methodology or an area of inquiry? If the definition in the first sentence of this chapter is accepted, it is a methodology. The discipline that studies political phenomena is political science, and public choice applies the methodology of economics to the same area of inquiry. Following this line of reasoning, public choice is a methodological approach to the study of political science. The public choice methodology, in a sentence, applies the rational choice model of individual behavior to analyse political institutions and political decision-making processes. The rational choice methodology has its origins in economics, but public choice, as an analysis of political decision making, is more a methodology for the study of political science than a subdiscipline within economics.

Economists, by virtue of their training, have had a comparative advantage in undertaking public choice analysis, but political scientists have been a part of the public choice movement since its inception,[1] and increasingly, the rational choice methodology is becoming a part of the standard training of political scientists.[2] Combined with the fact that the training of political scientists gives them a much more extensive knowledge of political institutions, this means that as the rational choice approach becomes a part of the standard toolbox of political science, political scientists should naturally acquire a comparative advantage in applying economic methodology to the study of political phenomena.

This economic methodology, referred to as rational choice modeling in the disciplines outside of economics, is becoming more common not only in political science but in sociology, criminology, and throughout the social sciences.[3] The model of rational choice behavior subject to constraints can be applied generally to all human action. As it happens, rational choice modeling began in economics, but is now an accepted part of political science and is increasingly making inroads into social science in general. As rational choice modeling becomes incorporated into the training of all social scientists, the comparative advantage of economists in studying human behavior will decline, and public choice will more and more become the province of political scientists who not only have a rational choice background but a deeper knowledge of the operation of political institutions.

When mathematics became a common part of the methodology of economics around the middle of the twentieth century, people trained in math and physics were able to make contributions to economics because of their familiarity with mathematical methods. Now that economists are routinely trained in those methods, they have the advantage again, because economists also have the requisite training in economic institutions.[4] Similarly, when rational choice modeling invaded political science, economists temporarily had an advantage over political scientists, which is rapidly being eroded.

Because of their stronger grounding in political institutions, one would expect that the public choice analysis of voting as a preference aggregation mechanism, of legislative decision making, and of political institutions in general, will become almost exclusively the domain of political scientists. From the standpoint of economists, this means that the economics of public choice is likely to return to its Wicksellian roots; that is, back toward analysing public taxing and public spending policies.

Looked at in this way, public choice at the end of the twentieth century can be divided into two branches: political science and public finance. The political science branch of public choice uses the rational choice paradigm to analyse political phenomena. The public finance branch of public choice applies the rational choice paradigm to the taxing and spending decisions taken by government. If the conjectures in this section are warranted, one can expect the study of public choice within economics to narrow, and for the economics of public choice to become increasingly concerned with public finance issues, leaving the analysis of political decision making more generally to the social scientists who specialize in politics. In short, for economists, public finance should become an ever more important part of public choice. But because the methodologies are the same, political scientists and economists who take the public choice approach can draw much from each other, and perhaps in the end public choice analysis will draw economics and political science closer together, creating a unified field study reminiscent of nineteenth-century political economy.

3   Public finance before public choice

In the 1950s, after the conditions for allocating resources Pareto optimally were formulated mathematically,[5] a market failure was defined as occurring whenever these mathematical conditions for welfare maximization were not met.[6] From a policy perspective, the presumption was that if the market failed to allocate resources optimally, government should intervene either through regulation of market activity or more directly through government ownership of the means of production. For example, Paul Samuelson (1954) observed that the market faces a revealed preference problem with public goods, resulting in a market failure, and as a result he advocated government production of public goods. But Samuelson never explained how government would overcome the same revealed preference problem, and so never considered the possibility that there could be a government failure, analogous to market failure, that would prevent the public sector from allocating resources Pareto optimally.[7]

Buchanan (1975b) notes that until that time, public finance theory assumed that participants in the market responded to incentives, and if the incentive structure led them to allocate resources inefficiently, market failure ensued.

Public choice simply applied the same types of assumptions regarding behavior in the market sector to the behavior of individuals in the public sector. Thus, there was no presumption in public choice theory that in the face of market failure, government intervention would necessarily improve matters. Rather, the incentive structures in the public sector and the private sector would have to be compared, and it might be that even though there were incentive problems in the private sector, incentive problems in the public sector would also result in a failure to allocate resources optimally. Thus, in order to select the appropriate policy, market allocation would have to be compared with government allocation to see which would produce the better result.

Before public choice analysis, the deck was stacked against the private sector because the real-world problems with market allocation of resources were being compared with the theoretical standard of Pareto optimality. Public choice unstacked the deck by using the same behavioral assumptions to model both public-sector and private-sector behavior. Thus, in normative analysis, public choice attempts to compare the real-world results of market allocation with the real-world alternative of government allocation, rather than with some unattainable theoretical ideal.

The development of public choice analysis has at least made economists aware that political considerations can stand in the way of the efficient allocation of resources through the public sector. Curiously enough, despite Wicksell's interest in taxation, public choice analysis has been applied much more frequently to problems of public expenditures than it has to problems on the revenue side of the budget, and applications on the revenue side of the budget have focused more on borrowing than taxation. Buchanan has emphasized Wicksell's work as a major part of the foundation for public choice analysis, and Wicksell was explicitly concerned with taxation. In the Wicksellian tradition, most of the remainder of this chapter will deal with taxation, because it has been relatively neglected and because other chapters in this volume deal with the expenditure side of the budget in more detail. However, the next section gives a brief overview of the public choice analysis of public expenditures.

4 Public choice and public expenditures

Much of the early public choice analysis of public expenditures consisted of studies showing how majority-rule voting acted as an allocator of economic resources. Barr and Davis (1966) demonstrated that the characteristics of voters, as demanders of public-sector output, were correlated with the level of public-sector expenditures, and Inman's (1978) frequently cited study finds the same result with a more sophisticated analysis. Barlow (1970) compared the actual level of public expenditures with a calculated median-voter demand to compare political allocation of resources with the

Pareto-optimal allocation, and discovered inefficiencies. McEachern (1978) and Holcombe (1980) also offered tests of the correlation between voter preferences and public-sector output. While most empirical studies of the median-voter model concluded that there is a close correspondence between the preferences of the median voter and public-sector output, that did not necessarily mean that the level of output that the median voter preferred was Pareto optimal. Indeed, the median voter's preferences would in general not be consistent with Pareto optimality. Hence, even at its best, simple majority-rule voting would not yield an optimal allocation of resources. Democratic decision making consequently also leads to government failure, where the term 'failure' is used in the same sense as in the literature on market failure.

Romer and Rosenthal (1978b) applied a similar logic to argue that public expenditures would be systematically larger than what the median voter preferred, if agenda setters were budget maximizers. Their analytical framework followed the median-voter model, however, and their conclusions illustrated another possible reason why public-sector allocation of resources would deviate from Pareto optimality. The potential for cyclical majorities in democratic decision making was emphasized much earlier by Arrow ([1951] 1963), providing yet another reason why democratic decision making might lead to government failure.

This literature on voting and public expenditures points to some general conclusions. Even when majority-rule voting works at its best, it produces the outcome desired by the median voter, but in general the median voter's preferences will not align with the allocation of resources that is consistent with Pareto optimality. Thus, democratic decision making will not efficiently allocate resources, resulting in a government failure that parallels the notion of market failure. If one extends the definition of market failure used by Bator (1958) to the public sector, resource allocation by majority rule will in general lead to a government failure, so there is no reason to believe that intervention by a democratic government could transform a market failure into an optimal allocation of resources. However, the literature has shown that there may be other problems with voting institutions as well, creating further deviations from Pareto optimality and additional sources of government failure. Most of the empirical literature on the subject has found that public-sector output does tend to conform with the median voter's preferences, but virtually all of the literature has dealt with data from state and local government expenditures. There are reasons to believe that federal expenditures correspond even less with voter preferences than state and local expenditures. In short, majority-rule voting will not, in general, result in an optimal allocation of resources even under the most optimistic assumptions.[8]

The political process does not necessarily produce what voters want, however. If voters tend to be ignorant of most of the legislature's activities, while special interests are well informed about those issues that affect them most directly, then the political process will produce outcomes that benefit the special interests rather than the general public interest. A substantial body of literature, including McCormick and Tollison (1981), Weingast et al. (1981), and Holcombe (1985), has analysed this interest-group model of government, and has uncovered yet another reason why political institutions may fail to allocate resources efficiently. There is another side to this argument, however. In what amounts to an application of the Coase theorem to political decision making, Becker (1983) and Wittman (1989) contend that whatever government does, it has the incentive to do it efficiently in order to maximize the benefits to those who receive them. This is an argument more general than just disputing the inefficiency of the interest-group model of government; it suggests that the government failure analogy to market failure is false. Of course, applying the same framework to the private sector, Coase showed that in the absence of transaction costs, market failures will be negligible also.

Public choice analysis has also been applied to the incentive structure associated with bureaucratic decision making, beginning with the analyses of Tullock (1965) and Niskanen (1971). This literature examines the incentive structure facing bureaucrats in the same way that microeconomic theory has examined the incentive structure of individuals working in firms, and has found that, unlike in markets, bureaucrats do not have the incentive to produce the output that the consumers of their services demand. This is yet another potential source of government failure. The public choice approach has also been applied to regulation, beginning with Stigler (1971), and has similarly concluded that regulators do not have the incentives to create welfare-maximizing regulations. Rather, they tend to cater to those they regulate, turning regulation from a constraint facing the targets of regulation into special-interest benefits.

The analysis of rent-seeking behavior has been another significant area in which the application of public choice theory has informed the study of public finance. Tullock (1967b) and Krueger (1974) pointed out that when individuals can gain from government policies, they have an incentive to expend resources up to the expected value of that gain in order to get the benefits, creating substantial welfare losses in the process. Thus, when government undertakes spending projects, the possibility for transfers is created, triggering rent-seeking activity that, from society's point of view, dissipates some, and perhaps all, of the potential gains. The transformation of transfers into social costs is yet another reason why government allocation of resources can fail to reach Pareto optimality. Indeed, rent seeking is likely to cause government intervention to move away from Pareto efficiency rather than toward it.[9]

This brief summary indicates that the ideas of public choice have been applied to the whole range of political decision making to determine the level and composition of public expenditures, beginning with majority-rule voting and extending through legislative decision making, regulation, and bureaucratic supply. Indeed, considering the Wicksellian origins of public choice, it is ironic that public expenditures have been analysed more extensively in the public choice framework than have public revenues.

5   Public choice and public revenues

Government can finance its expenditures in three ways: through taxing, borrowing, and creating money.[10] Public choice analysis has lent insights into the study of all three methods of public finance, demonstrating the general conclusion that one cannot fully understand the public finance process without taking into account the political decision-making process that determines policy outcomes. Taxation will be discussed most thoroughly below, partly because it is most solidly a part of the subdiscipline of public finance. Borrowing and money creation are more often considered under the headings of macroeconomics or monetary theory, but it is still worthwhile to consider briefly how public choice analysis has been applied to those areas of public finance.[11]

With regard to money creation, one must recognize that those who are in charge of a nation's money supply have incentives with regard to their own welfare that may be at odds with the making of optimal public policy decisions. Thus, as Toma (1982) argues, central bankers do not always pursue the monetary policy that best serves to promote stable prices, full employment, and economic growth, but rather have an incentive to pursue inflationary policies. The inflationary bias in the incentives faced by the central bank comes from several sources.[12] First, the central bank is often in a position to capture the seigniorage revenues that are produced by inflation. In the United States, the Federal Reserve gets its revenues entirely from the interest earnings on the monetary base, providing an incentive for inflation, as Shughart and Tollison (1983) argue. In countries where the central bank is a branch of the treasury, or falls directly under the control of the government, the incentives are even more direct. In addition, with progressive income taxes and taxes on nominal capital gains, there is even more of an inflationary bias faced by the central bank.

The larger point is that one cannot fully understand monetary policy outcomes without examining the private incentives facing the monetary authority. What would be optimal monetary policy with a monetary authority that had only the public's interests at heart will differ when the monetary authority has incentives of its own and, as the public choice literature on the subject has shown, the incentives facing the monetary authority often lead to a less than optimal monetary policy. These problems can be dealt with by changing the incentives – for example, by tying the salaries of those in charge of monetary policy to inflation targets – or by imposing some kind of constitutional constraints on the ability of the monetary authority to exercise discretion.

Similarly, public choice analysis has been brought to bear on deficit finance, and has shown that the incentives of those who make the decisions to run deficits may be at odds with socially optimal macroeconomic policy. Buchanan and Wagner (1977) argue that prior to the 1960s the US federal government was bound by an implicit balanced budget constraint that could be violated only under extenuating circumstances. During normal times, the government was expected to balance its budget and, for the most part, it did. In the 1960s, Keynesian economics became politically acceptable as an operating principle of fiscal policy. The idea was that budget deficits should be run to combat unemployment whenever the economy was threatened with insufficient aggregate demand, and that surpluses should be run to combat inflation whenever the economy was threatened by excess aggregate demand. Despite the symmetrical nature of surpluses and deficits in theory, the incentives facing policy makers led them to favor deficits over surpluses, and the result was a persistent budget deficit. Indeed, the federal government in the United States ran deficits in every year but one from 1960 to 1998.

The incentives to engage in deficit finance come from several sources. First, when an economy is plagued by both inflation and unemployment, as was the case during the 1970s, one might honestly believe that it is more important to combat the unemployment problem first, putting people back to work, and then tackle inflation. Of course, the fact that both problems ('stagflation') loomed at the same time should – and did – cast doubt on the underlying theory. Can an economy simultaneously have both too little aggregate demand and too much aggregate demand? Beyond this source of bias in favor of deficit finance, however, lies a deeper one. Legislatures are always pushed by interest groups to spend more for the benefit of their members, but are limited in the amount they can spend by a budget constraint. They can spend no more than the sum of government's revenues from taxes, inflation, and borrowing. If the borrowing constraint is relaxed because Keynesian ideas become more palatable, that gives the legislature more freedom to increase government expenditures to finance programs demanded by interest groups. Thus, the political system naturally creates a bias toward budget deficits.

Holcombe and Mills (1995) note that when the electoral security of legislators rises, the legislature tends to authorize larger budget deficits. The logic behind this is that citizens favor government expenditures, but oppose taxes, and so spending bills are easier to pass through the legislature than tax measures. The deficit is a residual: the amount by which spending exceeds taxes. The primary place where politics constrains deficit finance is at the ballot box. If legislators are more secure electorally, they will have less to fear politically from running deficits, and so deficits will predictably increase.

Again, an analysis of the incentives decision makers face when deciding when to run deficits and how much to borrow shows that their own interests do not coincide with the general public's interest. One way to address the problem would be to adopt a constitutional amendment restricting the ability of the legislature to run deficits. Almost all of the American states have such constraints (although they vary in their effectiveness), for example. Whether such a constraint would be desirable for the federal government, all things considered, is really beside the point for present purposes. The key idea is that once one takes into account the incentives facing political decision makers, optimal public policy regarding budget deficits is not the same as when one assumes that government decisions will always be made in the public interest. This idea that the incentives faced by policy makers are important determinants of public finance outcomes applies to taxation as much as it does to deficit finance and money creation.

6   Optimal taxation

Taxes are the explicit price people pay for government goods and services, and the idea behind the concept of optimal taxation is to keep the costs of raising revenues through the tax system as low as possible. With the advent of modern welfare economics, the concept has been broadened somewhat so that optimal taxation can mean designing a tax system to produce the highest amount of social welfare given the amount of revenue the system raises. The public choice approach does not take issue with the goals set out by optimal taxation, but rather finds that when the incentives of political decision makers are taken into account, what would be optimal if the tax system were designed and administered by a benevolent despot is no longer optimal when the tax system is run by utility-maximizing individuals.

Any analysis of optimal taxation first addresses the 'excess burden' of taxation that arises because taxes distort relative prices in the economy. As Browning (1976) has shown, the excess burden of taxation can be substantial, and so there are good economic reasons to try to design a tax system that minimizes the excess burden of taxation, given the amount of revenue raised. Economists have also recognized that compliance costs and administrative costs are social costs of taxation that must be added to the traditional excess burden in order to calculate the total welfare cost of taxation. Slemrod and Sorum (1984), for example, calculate that compliance costs for the US individual income tax are about 5 to 7 percent of revenues collected, which is a not insubstantial amount. Administrative costs, which are the costs to the government of administering the tax system and collecting the revenues, are undoubtedly lower than compliance costs for most taxes, but still must be considered when assessing the full welfare cost of taxation.

A public choice analysis of the tax system adds political costs to the analysis. The political costs of taxation are those costs involved in designing the tax system and in modifying it once it is in place. Some of the political costs are borne by the government in the form of the collective decision-making costs of tax policy making. But surely the bulk of the political costs of the tax system materialize in the form of rent-seeking activities by interest groups that want either to modify the tax system to their advantage or to defend the status quo against a competing interest group's demand for favorable tax treatment. As Tullock (1967b) and Krueger (1974) have shown, these political costs of the tax system can be substantial, and unless they are taken into account, the welfare cost of taxation will be seriously underestimated. In addition, political considerations can transform the whole notion of what constitutes an optimal tax system.

7 The political costs of taxation

Before public choice, economists rarely considered the political environment within which tax policy is made. The process, in brief, goes as follows. The legislature, perhaps through the auspices of a specialized legislative commit-tee, designs the structure of taxes and writes it into law. Legislators may have their own ideas about how the tax system can be modified, but most often it is modified through a process described by Becker (1983) in which interest groups approach their legislators to lobby for changes they would like to see made. Opposing interests also weigh in, and the legislature acts as a kind of marketplace in which the competing demands are balanced and policy deci-sions are made. There are some incentives for efficiency in the process, as Becker (ibid.), Hettich and Winer (1988), and Wittman (1989) note. The more efficient the resulting tax structure, the more surplus there is available to divide among the competing parties. This approach to the analysis of the tax system essentially applies the Coase theorem to suggest that if there were no transaction costs, resources would be allocated to their highest-valued use. But there are transaction costs, and they are likely to be higher in the political system where markets are less well developed than in the private sector. Efficiency is an unlikely outcome.

One factor weighing in favor of high political costs is that the tax system is always subject to change. Thus, unlike in markets, where one can own prop-erty and determine how it is used, one can never 'own' a particular political outcome. An interest group can invest in lobbying to change the tax code to its benefit this year, but unless it remains vigilant, the legislature could change the provisions again next year. Because property rights in political outcomes are never secure, people must continually invest resources in rent seeking even if they just want to maintain the status quo. As Tullock (1967b) and Krueger (1974) have shown, there is a tendency for rent seeking to dissipate the entire gain that can be produced by government intervention.

Taxpayers could always profit from having their taxes reduced, so will weigh the costs of undertaking rent seeking to reduce their tax burdens against the expected benefit. If the expected benefit is at least as great as the expected cost, it pays to enter the political marketplace to lobby for a tax reduction. Even if a group is not now being taxed, however, it still may pay to undertake lobbying activity to avoid being taxed in the future. When the tax system is perpetually subject to negotiation, current and potential taxpayers always have an incentive to incur political costs in order to prevent changes in the tax code that could adversely affect them. One way to reduce the political costs of taxation is to increase the difficulty of revamping the tax code. The harder it is to modify the tax system, the lower the incentive to incur political costs to do so. Thus, as Buchanan (1967) argues, there are merits in a fiscal constitution that defines the basic tax structure, and can be changed only if there is a substantial consensus in favor of doing so. An old tax is a good tax.

The political costs associated with the tax system are undoubtedly substantial, but there are no good estimates of the magnitude of these costs. Holcombe (1997a) estimates the annual political costs of a selective excise tax on soft drinks to be in excess of 10 percent of the revenues raised, based on the lobbying expenditures undertaken by the industry, but this estimate is imprecise, and uses a very limited data set. If this estimate is even remotely accurate, however, the political costs associated with the tax system exceed both the administrative and compliance costs combined. Hence, political costs, while mostly ignored by economists who study the tax system, are a substantial component of the welfare cost of taxation. One can see how these costs can be formidable for existing taxes, but even the process of considering a new tax will generate political costs, despite the fact that no revenue will be collected if the proposal is defeated. Potential taxpayers must take action to protect themselves from having to pay the new tax. The excess burden of taxation, as well as compliance and administrative costs, exist only for taxes that are actually being levied, whereas political costs are generated whenever taxes are being considered, even if the taxes do not yet exist and produce no revenue.

The application of public choice principles to tax policy suggests two ways of minimizing the political costs of taxation. One is to levy taxes according to the benefit principle of taxation. The other is to embody the tax structure in a fiscal constitution, making it difficult to modify the tax system, and therefore making rent seeking for tax benefits uneconomical. The next two sections consider these two ways of minimizing the political costs of the tax system.

8 Political costs and the benefit principle

The idea of using the benefit principle as the foundation of an optimal tax structure goes back at least to Knut Wicksell ([1896] 1967), who built his just system of taxation around it. Wicksell is a good place to start because his ideas are often cited as an inspiration for the modern public choice paradigm. Wicksell, anticipating Lindahl ([1919] 1967) pricing, wanted to create a tax system that allocated tax shares corresponding to each taxpayer's benefit share of the output financed by taxation. Applying the benefit principle, Wicksell thought that such an outcome would result in a just system of taxation. The problem is how to identify each taxpayer's benefit share, and here Wicksell suggested a collective decision-making process wherein all taxpayers would vote on whether they favored the tax and the associated expenditure.

A proposal would be advanced pairing a spending plan and a tax dedicated to financing it. If the proposal were defeated, Wicksell's system would adjust the distribution of tax shares, lowering those of individuals who voted against it because their tax cost exceeded the perceived benefits of the expenditure. This process would be repeated until the distribution of taxes resulted in approximate unanimity among taxpayers. Wicksell advocated a voting rule approximating unanimity so that the result would approximate a Pareto improvement, but did not insist on absolute unanimity because he recognized the potential for the holdout problem it would create. More generally, there are decision-making costs associated with unanimous agreement, as Buchanan and Tullock (1962) noted, that may make absolute unanimous consent too costly.

Wicksell applied the benefit principle to produce a just system of taxation, but it has the additional advantage of providing a mechanism for discovering the optimal amount of public expenditures. When, more than half a century later, Samuelson (1954) asserted that no voting process ensures truthful revelation of preferences for public goods, he did not consider the device of pairing tax and spending initiatives that Wicksell invented. Subsequently, Tideman and Tullock (1976) showed that there are other voting systems that may be able to reveal even more accurately the Pareto-optimal quantity of a public good. The point is that when the benefit principle is applied, public choice mechanisms can reveal preferences for collectively provided goods, leading to the socially optimal quantity of output.

The benefit principle offers another advantage in minimizing the political costs of the tax system. If taxes are levied in proportion to the benefits received, then all taxpayers have the same incentives with regard to raising or lowering taxes. If the benefit principle is not applied, then the tax system is redistributional, and some taxpayers might favor tax increases even when higher taxes would lead to inefficiency, because those taxes would provide benefits to the individuals who favor them, financed by taxes levied largely on other taxpayers. When taxes do not conform to the benefit principle, political divisions automatically exist in which some people will favor more taxes while others favor fewer. Thus, deviation from the benefit principle creates the potential for political costs because it encourages some people to impose taxes on others.

Because the benefit principle is not redistributional, the cost of reaching political agreement on the level of taxes and public expenditures is reduced. The benefit principle means that Lindahl ([1919] 1967) prices will be charged to each taxpayer. It follows that if the level of a public good financed through a tax corresponding to the benefit principle is too low, all taxpayers will agree that taxes should be raised so that more of the public good can be produced. Conversely, if the level of public-good provision is too high, all taxpayers will favor a tax cut and less of the good. Thus, political agreement will be reached with the benefit principle, and the level of output agreed upon through the political process will be Pareto optimal.

One way to find tax shares that correspond with the benefit principle is to require approximate unanimous political agreement, but if this is not feasible (or desirable) because the decision-making costs are too high, taxes approximating the benefit principle can still be designed. User charges and fees are examples of taxes that approximate market prices, and so would roughly correspond to the benefit principle. If it is possible to tax complementary private goods, the tax will more closely correspond to the benefit principle than if some unrelated tax is used to finance the good. For example, a motor fuel tax will be closer to the benefit principle than a sales tax or income tax to finance roads. Using a tax that more closely approximates the benefit principle provides many advantages. In addition to embodying a widely accepted principle of tax fairness, it is easier to reach political agreement on the level of public output to produce, and the level agreed upon is likely to be closer to the Pareto-optimal quantity than if some other tax were used. Furthermore, because a tax based on the benefit principle is not redistributive, it will reduce the political costs incurred when some people want to tax others to provide themselves with public-sector output. Application of the benefit principle has much to recommend it, including the fact that it can help minimize the political costs associated with the tax system.

9   The fiscal constitution

Building on the insights of Wicksell, Buchanan has been the main proponent of a fiscal constitution to minimize the political costs of the tax system. The basic framework appears in Buchanan and Tullock (1962), who make the distinction between constitutional and post-constitutional decision making. Optimal constitutional rules require consensus among those governed by them, but Buchanan and Tullock show that it may be optimal for a group to undertake clearly specified post-constitutional decisions with less-than-unanimous agreement. In the Buchanan and Tullock framework, this can result in making post-constitutional decisions by majority rule, or some other decision rule less inclusive than unanimity. It also might mean delegating some decisions to elected representatives or even to a non-elected individual or group. Buchanan (1967) applies this framework to suggest the advantages of a fiscal constitution in which most of the tax structure is difficult to modify. Those aspects of the tax structure that might generate significant political costs if they could be modified would be a part of the fiscal constitution, leaving some flexibility at the post-constitutional level to modify the tax system in ways that would incur only small political costs.

Within this framework, constitutional rules may be those provisions that are actually in the constitution, but more generally they refer to provisions that are generally accepted as a part of the rules within which government decisions are made. At the federal level, for example, Buchanan and Wagner (1977) argue that a balanced budget constraint was a part of the fiscal constitution in the United States until the 1960s, although there was no explicit constitutional provision requiring a balanced budget. When deficit finance became the norm, the fiscal constitution was effectively modified, leading some to call for amending the US Constitution to codify explicitly the implicit balanced budget provision.

This division between tax rules in a fiscal constitution and tax policy decisions made post-constitutionally can be illustrated by the motor fuel tax, the most common method of financing highway expenditures in the American states. If this is accepted as a part of the fiscal constitution, then there will be few political costs incurred in trying to change it. At the post-constitutional level, interested parties can debate whether the tax should be raised to finance more highways, lowered to save money for taxpayers, or left alone. If the tax generates revenues approximately in proportion to the benefits received from highway use, then there should be a substantial consensus on the appropriate level of the tax. Some people do not drive much, so have a low demand for roads, but those people also do not pay much in the way of motor fuel taxes. This example shows how establishing a part of the tax structure as a component of the fiscal constitution has the potential for lowering political costs associated with the tax system.

While the use of motor fuel taxes to finance highways is generally accepted among taxpayers, there are exceptions, and these exceptions can give rise to political costs. On the one hand, revenue sources other than motor fuel taxes can be used to finance roads. One revenue source used in Florida is a local-option general sales tax that can be approved by voters at the county level. Those who buy large quantities of gasoline would favor the sales tax, because it would shift the tax burden for building roads on to others, whereas consumers who buy sales-taxable items but drive relatively little would favor the gas tax. Thus, political costs are incurred as interest groups have the opportunity to shift some of their tax burden on to others. On the other hand, motor fuel taxes can be diverted away from roads. Also in Florida there is a debate about whether to use motor fuel taxes to finance a high-speed rail project connecting Tampa, Orlando, and Miami. Those who anticipate taking the train rather than driving have an opportunity to have highway users subsidize their rail use, but those who use the highways have an incentive to prevent those potential highway expenditures from being diverted to finance another mode of transportation. Again, political costs are incurred because of potential changes to the tax system.

The fuzzy division between tax provisions that are a part of the fiscal constitution and those that are not can be illustrated by state income taxes. Between 1961 and 1971, nine states established personal income taxes for the first time. New Jersey added a personal income tax in 1976, but the public sector was held in higher regard then than it has been subsequently, and no states added the personal income tax to their tax bases until Connecticut created a personal income tax in 1991. Connecticut's personal income tax was quite controversial, and it would be easy to argue that its creation violated the state's implied fiscal constitution. In 1993, Texas, which never had a personal income tax, but also did not have an explicit provision in its constitution prohibiting a personal income tax, passed a constitutional amendment prohibiting one. The prohibition of personal income taxation in Texas had always been a part of the state's fiscal constitution, in that it was generally agreed that the state would not raise revenue in this way, even though there was no statement to that effect in the state's written constitution. After Connecticut's experience, however, Texans decided to make explicit what they had always believed was a part of their implicit fiscal constitution by passing the constitutional amendment.

The case of the Texas income tax illustrates that tax provisions do not have to be a part of the written constitution to be a part of the fiscal constitution. It also illustrates that when tax provisions are a part of the fiscal constitution, political costs can be minimized, but that if it appears that tax provisions may be vulnerable to post-constitutional modifications, political costs will be incurred to further the interests of those on all sides of an issue. Prior to the passage of Connecticut's income tax in 1991, Texas incurred virtually no political costs related to personal income taxation, because everyone believed the absence of an income tax was a non-negotiable provision of the fiscal constitution. After Connecticut moved to tax personal incomes, Texans incurred political costs to prevent what happened in Connecticut from happening in Texas. Once the amendment passed, political costs related to personal income taxes in Texas again fell to a negligible level.

The main source of the political costs of taxation is from interest groups trying to change the tax structure for their benefit, or trying to maintain the status quo in the face of threatened changes that could harm them. By fixing the tax structure in a fiscal constitution, these political costs can be minimized because then the tax structure cannot be changed without a broad consensus, so individuals have little to gain by trying to push changes that do not produce widespread benefits. Without a fiscal constitution, rent-seeking activity will produce substantial political costs related to the tax system.

10 Taxation and redistribution

One of the things a tax system does is redistribute income. Taxes can be used to finance wealth transfers, but even when they are not, there is always a distributional element in tax policy because the allocation of tax shares is inherently redistributional. This is the origin of the bulk of the political costs associated with the tax system. The reason why the application of the benefit principle and the creation of a fiscal constitution limit political costs is that they reduce the distributional issues in tax policy. The economics literature on taxation and redistribution typically starts out with the idea that some welfare-enhancing redistribution of income is possible, and then continues to design a tax system to achieve this result. This is the line of reasoning taken by the optimal tax literature begun by Mirrlees (1971), for example. This approach ignores public choice considerations, however. Stigler (1970) argues that in the real world income tends to be redistributed from those who have income or wealth toward those who have political power. Thus, Stigler argues, there is a considerable overlap between taxpayers and the recipients of the redistribution financed by those taxes.

When the political environment is taken into account, the use of the tax system as a method of redistribution makes less sense, because those who are truly in need also tend to be those with minimal political power, so they are unlikely to reap the bulk of the benefits from redistribution. The social security program in the United States, which is the nation's largest income redistribution program, illustrates the point well, because it taxes a group that is, on average, less well-off than the group that receives the benefits. A look at the social security program also illustrates that the recipients of the benefits have demonstrated their willingness to incur substantial political costs to maintain their entitlements.

Problems associated with the redistributional nature of the tax system arise even if the tax system is not explicitly used as a vehicle for redistribution. Meltzer and Richard (1981) argue that under a majority-rule political system, there will always be a push to redistribute income because the bottom half of the income distribution has the same political power as the top half, but has less income. They argue that greater income equality reduces the degree to which democracies will be inclined to redistribute income, because the poor stand to gain relatively less the closer their incomes are to those of the rich. Peltzman (1980), in contrast, argues that greater income equality increases the propensity of democracies to redistribute income, because more must be redistributed to have a given impact on the income distribution. Whatever the effect of the distribution of income on the degree of income redistribution, without a fiscal constitution in place to constrain the redistributive activities of government, democratic decision making is not likely to produce a stable pattern of income redistribution.

If redistribution is a zero-sum game, as suggested by Atkinson (1995, pp. 80–84), then no system of income redistribution is stable under majority-rule decision making, because for any redistribution scheme there is always an alternative proposal that could command the approval of a majority. A majority coalition could form at any time to redistribute income away from the minority toward themselves, and may temporarily succeed in giving themselves a larger-than-average share of the redistributed income. However, this makes the coalition a tempting target for a realigned majority coalition. The current minority can entice some members of the majority coalition to leave by offering them an even better deal than they get under the current arrangement, creating a new majority coalition, but again this creates an opportunity for another realignment. Imagine three people trying to decide how to divide a dollar among themselves by majority rule. No matter how the dollar is divided, there is always another division that would be favored by two of the three.

In light of this theoretical source of instability, Tullock (1982) asked why it is that redistributive institutions appear to be so stable in practice. Before addressing that question, it is worthwhile observing that the use of the tax system for redistributive purposes indeed can be destabilizing. If the amount of money available for redistribution grows, that could increase the political pressures for creating a coalition to receive tax-financed transfers that would overwhelm the stabilizing forces in the political system. Thus, the use of taxation for redistribution could potentially destabilize the political system. However, the public choice literature has offered two explanations for how a stable redistributive outcome might be produced by democratic institutions. One explanation is that political institutions restrict the ability of coalitions to form and encourage agreement on a stable outcome. The other explanation is that redistribution is not, in fact, a zero-sum game, and a stable outcome is therefore produced by the incentives to minimize the costs of redistribution.

Weingast et al. (1981) argue that political institutions create an incentive for a universal coalition in which everyone receives a roughly equal share of the redistributive pie. When one considers the possibility that anyone left out of the majority coalition has an incentive to lure defectors to create a new majority coalition, the cost-minimizing approach to redistribution through politics is to let everyone into the redistributive coalition. In the context of American politics, the ability of legislators to generate benefits for their constituents is a key element in political competition, and all incumbents have an incentive to create an inclusive coalition to reduce the risk that they might be left out. This universal coalition creates a prisoner's dilemma situation for its members, however, in that they always find it in their interest to remain in the coalition even if they would be better off if the coalition did not exist. That is because their decision on whether to remain in the coalition will not affect the survival of the coalition. In a majority-rule democracy, a majority coalition requires only a bare majority to survive, and a universal coalition has more than enough members. Thus, each member must choose between remaining in the coalition and continuing to receive his share of the coalition's benefits, and leaving and continuing to pay for redistribution to others without getting anything in return. The individual always has an incentive to stay.

This creates a situation in which everyone could agree to a redistributive program that makes everyone in the program worse off. As Holcombe (1986) notes, if unanimous agreement were required in such a situation, everyone would vote against the coalition, but under majority rule, the coalition garners unanimous support. Quite simply, when one casts a vote under majority rule, it is unlikely to determine whether an issue passes or fails, but it always determines whether one is in the majority coalition or the minority. Individuals often have an incentive to vote with the majority even when they prefer the alternative outcome. The larger point is that political institutions, including legislatures, and even majority-rule voting itself, may produce a stable political environment.

Another possible source of stability is the incentive to minimize the total costs of redistributive programs in order to make the largest possible amount available for redistribution. Becker (1983) models the legislature as a political marketplace in which competing groups register their demands, and the legislature attempts to meet these demands at the lowest possible cost in order to satisfy as many constituents as possible. Hettich and Winer (1988) apply this approach to taxation to argue that, given the competing demands of constituents for taxes and expenditures, the total cost of the tax system, including the excess burden, compliance, administrative, and political costs, is minimized. Legislators have an incentive to create a cost-minimizing tax system in order to maximize the total benefits they are able to allocate. The minimum-cost system maximizes voter support, so produces the greatest benefit to the legislators who create the tax system. More generally, Wittman

(1989) has applied this approach to political decision making of all types to argue that democratic decision making produces economically efficient outcomes. Following this logic, the same forces that lead to a stable equilibrium in a competitive market also lead to a stable political equilibrium.

The public choice approach suggests several problems with using the tax system as a method of redistribution. First, regardless of what one views as the optimal system of redistribution, the political system tends to redistribute from those who have income and wealth toward those who have political power. Second, the use of the tax system for redistributive purposes invites an escalation of political costs as people either find it worthwhile to engage in rent seeking rather than productive activity as a method of gaining income or find it necessary to engage in rent seeking to protect their incomes and wealth from predation by others. While it is true that there are incentives for efficiency, as Becker (1983) notes, transaction costs tend to be higher in the political arena than in markets, preventing many potentially mutually beneficial exchanges from being made and resulting in the types of welfare losses described by Tullock (1967b), Usher (1992), and many others.

11   Optimal excise taxation

Thus far, the discussion of public choice concepts as applied to public finance has been undertaken at a fairly abstract level. This section gets more concrete by applying public choice concepts to the idea of optimal commodity taxation. The conventional wisdom in public finance, following Ramsey (1927), is that under certain assumptions, the welfare loss from commodity taxation is minimized when goods are taxed in inverse proportion to their elasticities of demand. However, a straightforward application of the Ramsey rule ignores the fact that if different excise tax rates are imposed on different goods, those rates will be a product of the political system rather than the result of the best estimates that could be made regarding the elasticities of demand for taxable goods. As a result, interest groups will have an incentive to get involved in the process of determining what tax rates should apply to various goods, inviting the escalation of political costs, and producing a tax structure that will not adhere to the Ramsey rule in any event.

Following the Ramsey rule, economists would be able to minimize the excess burden of commodity taxes if they knew the elasticities of demand for all goods, and if the tax structure actually adheres to the rule. However, demand elasticities cannot be determined by inspection; rather, they have to be estimated by somebody. It does not require much imagination to see that even if a law requires commodity tax rates to follow the Ramsey rule, special interests can weigh in on the process in order to get the estimated elasticities for their goods raised. The result will be that the structure of excise tax rates will be determined by political interests rather than by any type of objective measurement.

Even if a law were written to set excise taxes according to the Ramsey rule, the realities of the political decision-making process would lead taxes to be determined according to the political power of those being taxed, so in reality differential excise tax rates would be unlikely to be close to those dictated by the Ramsey rule. In addition, because excise tax rates on individual goods would be subject to change through the political process, attempting to set taxes according to the Ramsey rule would lead to an escalation of political costs. When public choice considerations are taken into account, it may be preferable to set all excise taxes to a single uniform rate in order to minimize political costs. The uniformity of the excise tax rate should be a part of the state's fiscal constitution to insulate commodity taxation from rent-seeking activity and minimize political costs.

How about creating different categories of goods with different excise tax rates for each? Which goods would go into which categories could then be made a part of the fiscal constitution in order to minimize political costs, but allow a closer approximation to the Ramsey rule. This might be feasible, but then the possibility arises that producers would engage in rent seeking to try to get their products moved from one category to another. For example, some states do not include food in their sales tax bases. In some cases, milk and orange juice count as food (if sold in grocery stores) and are not taxed, but soft drinks do not count as food and are taxed. Even under the current system soft-drink manufacturers and retailers have incurred political costs to test the political feasibility of having their products treated the same way as other beverages. Any kind of differential excise tax rates would raise this possibility, again pointing to the conclusion that when political costs are taken into account, optimal excise taxation is likely to imply a single excise tax rate for all goods.

This examination of optimal excise taxation shows that when public choice considerations are taken into account, radically different conclusions with regard to optimal tax policy can be drawn.[13] The conventional wisdom in public finance is that optimal excise taxation requires setting tax rates in inverse proportion to the elasticities of demand for various goods, so each good would have a different tax rate. When public choice considerations are taken into account, the political costs that would be associated with varying tax rates on different goods point toward the conclusion that excise tax rates across goods should be uniform.

12   The breadth of the tax base

The conventional wisdom in public finance is that the welfare loss from the tax system is minimized when the tax base is as broad as possible. The reason is that a broader tax base can raise a given amount of revenue with lower tax rates, and the welfare loss of taxation increases more than proportionally as rates are increased. This conclusion was challenged by Brennan and Buchanan (1980), who argue that narrowing the tax base can limit the amount of revenue the government can raise without increasing the excess burden of taxation. Their analysis rests on the assumption that the government wants to raise as much revenue as possible, but offers some interesting and more general insights.

One general insight is that the conventional wisdom about broad tax bases is based on a particular set of assumptions, and if the assumptions are changed in a plausible way, the policy conclusions differ dramatically. A second insight is that one can better understand the motives of taxpayers who try to limit the tax bases on which they are taxed. This chapter earlier considered the example of Texans codifying the unwritten provision of their fiscal constitution that prohibited personal income taxation. Following the conventional wisdom, this narrowing of the tax base would have raised the excess burden of taxation in Texas. But within the framework of the Brennan and Buchanan model, it is a sensible constraint on the revenue-raising powers of government, if taxpayers are concerned that those in government might try to collect more than the optimal amount of tax revenues.

A third insight arises from considering the general approach that Brennan and Buchanan follow in their analysis. They assume that those in government are motivated by their own narrow self-interest, not necessarily because the assumption is always true, but rather because when one is designing public policy, it is important that incentives should be created so that those who make and carry out public policy find it in their own self-interest to further the public interest.

A fourth insight parallels that of the previous section on commodity taxation. When one takes into account the political process within which tax policy is made, public choice analysis leads to conclusions that may be remarkably different from the conventional wisdom. Because tax policy is undertaken through the political process, no analysis of tax policy can be complete without an understanding of the political environment within which that policy is made.

13   Optimal income taxation

There is an extensive literature on optimal income taxation, summarized by Mirrlees (1976), that tries to find the optimal tax structure by maximizing social welfare subject to constraints, where social welfare is a function of the individual utilities of all individuals in the society. The assumption of diminishing marginal utility of income would lead to the conclusion that the tax system should redistribute income until everyone had the same income, were it not for the excess burden of taxation. But if everyone's incomes were equal, nobody would have an incentive to work. Thus, there must be some reward left for those who work harder or who have more productive capacity in order to give them an incentive to produce income that can be redistributed to others. In this literature, the purpose of taxation is to redistribute income, and the whole notion of using taxation for the purposes of redistributing income was analysed in an earlier section of this chapter. One might also find fault with this literature based on its use of a social welfare function that requires the questionable practice of making interpersonal utility comparisons. In addition, Buchanan (1976) criticizes this literature for not taking into account how the tax revenues will be spent, which he argues is crucial to determining the optimal tax structure.

Despite the possible criticisms that might be levied against this literature, it is interesting to note that even though the purpose of taxation in this literature is to redistribute income to maximize social welfare, the literature concludes that the optimal tax structure would be a system of roughly proportional income tax rates. The assumptions behind the model would appear to be stacked against such a conclusion, because everyone's utility is weighted equally, and because the tax system serves only to equalize the distribution of income. Nevertheless, even under these assumptions, proportional income taxation appears approximately optimal, in order to preserve the incentive for upper-income people to earn income that can then be redistributed. Even those who favor using the tax system for redistributive purposes should oppose progressive income taxation.

This analysis leaves out any public choice considerations, but when public choice considerations are added to the analysis, the conclusions of that literature are reinforced. If different people are charged different income tax rates, this by itself creates a system in which different income groups have an incentive to engage in rent seeking to lower their tax shares, or raise the tax shares of others. Thus, any system of progressive taxation creates political costs. Hayek (1960, p. 313) observes that, 'unlike proportionality, progression provides no principle which tells us what the relative burden of different persons ought to be'. When different people face different rates, taxpayers always have an incentive to try to alter the rate structure in order to make their own tax treatment more favorable. Thus, following Hayek, when political costs are factored into the analysis, the optimal income tax structure is proportional.

The two previous sections showed how public choice conclusions about optimal tax policy often differ radically from those produced by conventional approaches to public finance. In the present case, a public choice analysis of optimal income taxation yields conclusions that are remarkably compatible with the conventional wisdom, even though the models and methods that produce those conclusions are completely at odds with each other. Because analyses from vastly different points of view lead to similar conclusions, some reassurance regarding the merits of proportional income taxation is warranted.

14   The revealed preference problem

One of the problems frequently addressed by public finance economists is how to discover the preferences of citizens for public goods. The tax system is often studied without considering how tax revenues will be spent, but for many reasons, the characteristics of a system of optimal taxation cannot be determined without considering what those tax revenues will buy, as Buchanan (1976) has argued. Most obviously, it may be that some system of user charges could be devised so that taxes have the same efficiency characteristics as market prices, eliminating the deadweight loss of taxation altogether. However, with public goods, as defined by Samuelson (1954), the revealed preference problem becomes more difficult, but not necessarily insurmountable. In response to Samuelson, for example, Tiebout (1956) showed that if citizens have a choice of jurisdictions, they can 'vote with their feet' by moving to one more closely satisfying their preferences for public-sector output, revealing their preferences in the process.

The revealed preference problem has been recognized for a long time in public finance. Indeed, that was the problem Wicksell ([1896] 1967) and Lindahl ([1919] 1967) were trying to solve. Lindahl and Wicksell took a public choice approach to show how voting systems could be used as preference-revealing mechanisms, and Tideman and Tullock (1976) extend the public choice approach to show that it is possible to design voting systems that produce a Pareto-optimal allocation of resources. However, public choice analysis also shows that democratic political processes do not always reveal the true preferences of voters, and may even be biased.

Holcombe (1978) notes that without a fiscal constitution to fix tax shares, majority-rule voting in a representative democracy tends to be biased in favor of larger-than-optimal public expenditures. The reason is that candidates compete for election by trying to satisfy the preferences of the median voter. One way this can be done is by targeting public expenditure programs at the median voter. Another way is to offer to reduce the median voter's tax burden. Either way, the median voter's tax price per unit of government output is lowered, and a simple application of the law of demand shows that the quantity of public-sector output demanded by the median voter will increase. Thus, when political competition can include changing the tax shares of voters, the size of the public sector demanded by the median voter will be larger than optimal.

While Samuelson may have given up too soon in his search for preference-revealing mechanisms in the public sector, the actual system of majority-rule voting and representative democracy in the United States is unlikely to do a good job of revealing true preferences for public-sector output. This suggests another reason for stabilizing the tax structure within a fiscal constitution. When tax shares approximate the benefit principle, and are not subject to political negotiation, the political system is more likely to reveal the true preferences of voters for public-sector output.

15 Conclusion

The theme of this chapter is that public choice has much to offer for the study of public finance, yet public choice considerations are often ignored in the analysis of public finance issues. In many areas, public choice ideas have made considerable inroads into the study of public finance, whereas in other areas the analysis of public finance is undertaken without much awareness of the political environment within which public finance decisions are made. Considering Wicksell's ([1896] 1967) analysis of taxation as a well-known forerunner to the modern theory of public choice, it is ironic that public choice analysis seems to have had less of an impact on the study of taxation than on other areas of public finance.

In the area of public expenditures, public choice has made significant contributions to modeling the problems of bureaucratic supply, led by Niskanen's (1971) seminal analysis, and has extensively analysed resource allocation by democratic political institutions, including majority-rule voting and legislative institutions. In addition, public choice theory has also been applied to the analysis of government regulation. Public choice analysis has also been applied to the revenue side of the budget, although less extensively. The incentives facing the central bank have been analysed in a public choice framework, as have the incentives legislators face regarding deficit finance. These areas are analysed mostly as a part of macroeconomics and monetary theory, yet even here economists tend to recognize the incentives of decision makers regarding these types of public finance decisions. The economists doing the analysis are for the most part not public choice economists, but they do apply public choice ideas to their research. It is the area of taxation that remains most unaffected by public choice analysis, despite the fact that there has been much public choice analysis applied to the tax system.

For the most part, the economic analysis of taxation is undertaken as if the tax system is imposed on the economy by a government that wants to create the best possible system of taxes. The economist's role is then to design the best tax institutions possible. When one realizes that a tax system is not just imposed exogenously on an economy by a benevolent government, but rather is a product of the political process, the whole notion of optimal taxation takes on a different slant. In addition to the excess burden of taxation, economists also recognize that compliance and administrative costs should be counted as welfare costs of the tax system. The public choice approach also recognizes political costs, which include the costs the government incurs to create tax laws, but more importantly, also include the rent-seeking activities that interest groups undertake to try to shape the tax code to their liking. While no good estimates of political costs are available, they almost surely exceed the compliance and administrative costs of taxation combined. These political costs can be reduced by creating a tax system that adheres to the benefit principle of taxation, and by imbedding the tax code in a fiscal constitution that is relatively immune to changes due to rent seeking.

Public choice analysis also illustrates that the type of tax system created through democratic procedures is unlikely to be the type of tax system that an economist would recommend as optimal in the absence of political consid-erations. Thus, the actual process by which the tax code is created must be taken into account in any analysis of optimal taxation. For example, if the tax code allows flexibility in excise tax rates so that rates on individual goods can be adjusted to conform to the Ramsey rule, the outcome is likely to be low tax rates on goods produced by those with more political power and high tax rates on those with less political power. By trying to create a tax code that can conform to the Ramsey rule, the result would be a tax code that invites rent seeking and an escalation of political costs, but that still does not conform to the Ramsey rule. Thus, the fiscal constitution should impose a tax structure that is relatively unchangeable except when there is a strong consensus that change is warranted.

While public choice is often treated as a field of study within economics, it is really a methodology that can be applied to the study of social science, including economics. Much of what the public choice literature currently studies falls under the heading of political science, but there is a substantial role for public choice in the study of public finance. Ironically, public choice analysis plays a relatively insignificant role in the analysis of taxation, despite Wicksell's pioneering work, now more than a century old. This chapter has outlined some fundamental public choice principles that can be applied to taxation, and has shown some interesting applications that in some cases support the conventional (non-public choice) wisdom, but in other cases generate conclusions that are surprisingly different from the conventional wisdom. This chapter is more a summary of early work on the subject than a summary of well-established results. The basic ideas are there, but there is a great deal more to be done applying public choice ideas to the analysis of public finance.

Notes
1. See Riker (1962) for an example.
2. Downs (1957) has often been used as a political science textbook, and Shepsle and

Bonchek (1997) is a textbook written by political scientists that is developed from the ground up to expose undergraduates to political science from a rational choice perspective.

3. See Coleman (1990) for a development of the theory of sociology based on rational choice models. Gary Becker has been a leading figure in the application of rational choice models outside of economics. See, for examples, Becker (1981) for an application to the family, Becker (1974) for an application to criminology, and Becker (1976b) for a more general application to the subject matter of social science.

4. Of course, one might lament that economists are not better trained in institutions, but the development of the new institutional economics addresses that issue. See Williamson (1990) for an interesting methodological discussion.

5. See Graaf (1957) and Bator (1957) for the conventional wisdom on this subject in the 1950s.

6. Bator (1958) sets out a concise statement of the causes of market failure.

7. Tiebout (1956) did discuss how government institutions help overcome the revealed preference problem, and Minasian (1964) discussed the ways in which markets can overcome this revealed preference problem. Holcombe (1997b) suggests that much of public goods theory was formulated in a manner designed to help justify government intervention into market activity.

8. There is another literature that questions whether majority-rule voting is even capable of arriving at a unique and stable equilibrium. McKelvey (1976b) raised the initial questions, but Tullock (1982) doubted the generality of McKelvey's conclusions. While this chapter relegates the issue to a footnote, Holcombe (1985) discusses it in detail. See also Chapters 4 and 9 of this volume.

9. Usher (1992) presents a good analysis of the resource-allocation problems that can be caused by rent seeking.

10. A fourth possibility is the sale of goods and services produced in the public sector. Because the government rarely competes on an equal footing with private enterprise, however, this amounts to a type of taxation. Still, the author will not quarrel with those who want to include public enterprises and user charges as a fourth method of government-revenue generation.

11. See Chapters 20 and 21 of this volume for more detailed discussions.

12. For additional applications of public choice analysis to monetary policy, see Toma and Toma (1986), Anderson et al. (1988b), and Chapter 21 of this volume.

13. See Holcombe (1997a) for a discussion of this excise tax example and an elaboration of the importance of public choice considerations for purposes of determining tax policy.

20 Politics and the macro economy

Richard E. Wagner

1 Introduction

Do macroeconomic conditions influence the electoral prospects of candidates? Do governing incumbents use their powers of office to influence macroeconomic conditions so as to improve their electoral prospects? The evidence currently available seems pretty strongly to support an affirmative answer to the first question. There is more controversy about the second question, and for good reason. If the second question is answered in the affirmative, it is possible that the very process of democratic competition for office might interject instability into the economy. This possibility contrasts starkly with the traditional view of macroeconomic policy, where a central role of the state is construed as acting to keep stable what would otherwise be an unstable market economy. Rather than being an antidote or corrective for economic instability, politics might be a source of instability.

This chapter explores some recent scholarship on the relation between political competition and economic stability. It starts by setting forth the traditional, Keynesian vision of the corrective or stabilizing state. This vision located the state as outside or exogenous to the economic process. Public choice scholarship has relocated the state to an endogenous position within the economic process, and in so doing has raised the prospect of the destabilizing state. The resulting hypothesis of a political business cycle starts from a consideration of the impact of macroeconomic conditions on the electoral support that incumbents can expect to receive. At this point the literature on the political business cycle reaches a fork. One branch of scholarship explores the theme that incumbent politicians may act opportunistically to manipulate macroeconomic conditions in a search for electoral support. The other branch explores how election outcomes, particularly in tightly contested elections, might inject exogenous shocks that upset the macro economy. The existing literature on politics and the macro economy overwhelmingly adopts such conventions of modern macroeconomics as the presumption that the standard macro variables are simple objects of choice and that macro variables operate upon one another. This convention contrasts sharply with an alternative vision, where macro variables are not objects of choice but rather are simply emergent outcomes of complex patterns of human interaction, and where macro variables do not act upon one another because they are simply aggregate representations of some traces of human interaction. The final section of this chapter explores some lines of inquiry that stem from this alternative, coordinationist approach to macro phenomena (and which are explored more fully in Wagner 1999), and which do not seem to fall out of the conventional, choice-theoretic approach to macro phenomena.

2 The traditional vision of politics and the macro economy

Prior to the Keynesian revolution in economic thought, the vast preponderance of economists thought that a market economy possessed self-corrective forces. Movements away from price stability and full employment would set those forces in motion, reversing those movements and restoring price stability and full employment. For instance, if people generally decided to increase their money balances, aggregate spending would initially fall and unemployment typically increase. But corrective forces would also be set in motion. Falling demands would lead to falling prices. With falling prices, the real value of money balances would rise, which would increase people's desires to spend. The best that government could do in this case was to act as a wakeful night watchman in maintaining an orderly institutional framework within which people organized and conducted their commercial activities. Disorder at the macro level was self-correcting within the framework of the market economy, provided only that the state do its part to maintain that framework.

The proper relationship between politics and the macro economy was tightly confined in the classical system of thought. The characterization of this relationship changed dramatically with the emergence of the post-war Keynesian consensus that a market economy did not possess powerful self-corrective forces. According to this consensus, which took great support from the deep depression and slow recovery that plagued the 1930s, a stable, fully employed economy is a fragile state which self-correcting forces do not guarantee will remain in equilibrium. With a market economy being inherently unstable, the obligations of the classical night watchman state were expanded to incorporate an obligation actively to secure stability and full employment.

This Keynesian formulation of the relation of politics to the macro economy came to command such an overwhelming consensus during the 1940s, 1950s and 1960s that it is now reasonable to denote this as the traditional or received formulation, which in turn will be contrasted below with some more recent formulations. This traditional formulation entails both economic and political presuppositions. A market economy is presumed to be highly volatile, due primarily to sudden and unpredictible shifts in spending on capital goods. If the animal spirits suddenly surge, spending on capital goods will expand and the economy will boom. But when those spirits abate, investment spending will plummet and a bust will ensue. Such classical mechanisms as the real balance effect and price adjustments were regarded in the traditional post-war consensus as ranging between non-existent and weak.

The promotion of a stable and fully employed economy became the province of the state, as the sole repository in society of both the knowledge of what was required to maintain stability and of the will to take the required action. The role of the state was to calm the animal spirits, to lean against the wind. With its acute economic antennae placed throughout the economy, the state would recognize the surging or ebbing of the animal spirits nearly instantly, and soon thereafter would follow with the proper corrective antidote. In the face of ebbing animal spirits, the state would increase its spending by running budget deficits; the state would counteract a sudden outbreak of lethargic spending among private citizens by becoming an eager spender. Alternatively, should private citizens suddenly become excessively spendthrift, the state would absorb the harm that might otherwise result by becoming a lethargic spender through accumulating large budget surpluses. Where the self-corrective tendencies of the market process were slow and unreliable, the state was smart, reliable, and quick.

The traditional approach to macroeconomic policy entails presumptions both about the knowledge politicians or their agents possess and about the incentives they have to use their knowledge. The traditional approach presumes that politicians can acquire knowledge that would be necessary to promote economic stability. It further presumes that such knowledge will always and necessarily be put to good use, as illustrated by the pursuit of a program of the state acting to counteract the forces of instability that would otherwise destabilize a market economy. These traditional economic presumptions have come under strong challenge from what is now known as the new classical macroeconomics, which represents a reaffirmation of the classical presumption of a strongly self-correcting market process, though formulated with contemporary analytical tools and techniques. While I shall return to some of these issues in the final two sections of this chapter, these macroeconomic issues lie mostly outside the scope of this discussion.

What is central to this chapter are the political presumptions regarding the conduct of macro policy. The public choice literature in this regard has proceeded along several lines, not all of them mutually consistent, but all of them coming to generate a substantial shift in scholarly orientation concerning the relation between politics and the macro economy. What emerges in one fashion or another in this revisionist literature is a recognition that political forces and processes may inject instability into an otherwise stable economy, in sharp contrast to the traditional formulation of the state stabilizing an otherwise unstable economy. The reason for this is that the promotion of instability may present higher political rewards than the promotion of stability. Rather than the state acting to stabilize an otherwise unstable market economy, the state may act to destabilize an otherwise stable market economy.

While early statements of how political processes might generate economic instability were articulated by Kalecki (1943) and Akerman (1947), substantial interest in the topic emerged only in the mid-1970s. A sample of writings from this period, arranged chronologically, includes Feiwel (1974), Ben-Porath (1975), Meltzer and Vellrath (1975), Frey and Schneider (1975), Nordhaus (1975), Gordon (1975), Lindbeck (1976), Frey (1976), MacRae (1977), Wagner (1977), Fair (1978) and Tufte (1978). While these writings differ over a number of particular details regarding the impact of politics upon the macro economy, they are united by a recognition that the actual conduct of public policy will be governed by the interests of those who occupy positions of power. Public policy is conducted by political realists and not by disinterested philosophers.

3 Macro conditions and electoral success

Should an incumbent politician look forward fearfully or zestfully to the next election? There have been a large number of scholarly efforts, some of which have been cited above though many others have been published as well, which have sought to gauge electoral success against such common macroeconomic indicators as the rates of inflation, unemployment, and economic growth. There is a simple intuition behind such studies: people do not like inflation or unemployment, but they do like rising incomes. If citizens are thought to blame or credit politicians for the state of those macro variables, it might seem as though a politician's electoral prospects would be strengthened by falling inflation and unemployment prior to an election, as well as by rising economic growth.

By now, a large body of evidence has been accumulated in support of the claim that macroeconomic conditions prior to an election seem to exert some influence over electoral prospects or outcomes. Two approaches have been taken to describing the connection between macro conditions and electoral success. One approach, illustrated by Frey and Schneider (1978), has focused on measures of political popularity prior to an election, and has sought to relate variations in such popularity to variations in macro conditions. The general tenor of these studies is that incumbent popularity varies negatively with the rates of inflation and unemployment and positively with the rate of economic growth. Changes in macroeconomic conditions would seem to bring about changes in the evaluation of incumbent politicians by citizens.

An incumbent who receives a higher popularity score than his challenger may not win when the votes are counted, for any of a number of reasons, and a good number of other studies have sought to assess the effects of these aggregate variables upon actual election outcomes. Once again, the same general pattern emerges, only the dependent variable is some measure of vote share or seats won. Whether measured by popularity prior to an election or by votes cast in an election, reductions in inflation and unemployment would seem to be good for incumbents, as would an increase in the rate of growth. To be sure, not all the studies achieve identical results. Some authors have found only two of the three macro variables to be statistically significant. For instance, Kramer (1971) examined the share of the vote received by the incumbent party in American congressional elections between 1896 and 1964, and found only inflation and growth to be significant. Unemployment was not found to exert any significant effect. Meltzer and Vellrath (1975) likewise found only two of the three macro variables to be statistically significant in their examination of voting in presidential elections. These were inflation and unemployment, indicating only one variable of significance – inflation – common to both Kramer and to Meltzer and Vellrath.

There are also studies that have found only one of the macro variables to be statistically significant. In his examination of voting in presidential elections, Fair (1978) found only the rate of economic growth to be statistically significant. Alternatively, Stigler (1973) found only the rate of inflation to be statistically significant in his examination of congressional elections. This pattern of variability in the details of the findings can be found across the wide range of studies that have been conducted. For instance, Schneider and Frey (1988) survey and summarize a large number of such studies conducted across many nations. As Schneider and Frey report, some authors found all three macro variables to be significant, others found only two to be significant, and a few found only one to be significant. There were also differences over which one or two of the macro variables were found to be significant.

There are obviously differences in the details of these particular studies. Nonetheless, a uniformly strong general impression emerges from an examination of these studies as well. There is nearly unanimity in the signs of the estimated coefficients. An increase in inflation is found to decrease incumbent vote share or popularity, even if some studies find this effect to be statistically significant while others do not. It is the same for an increase in unemployment, as well as a decrease in the rate of growth. These studies overwhelmingly tell the same tale. An incumbent who faces an upcoming election while inflation and unemployment are decreasing and growth is increasing should sense his prospects to be rising, even if he cannot be sure of which of the variables to thank for his good fortune.

4   Politics and the control of macro conditions

To find that popularity or votes vary with macroeconomic conditions in the manner specified above carries no implications for politically generated business cycles unless politicians can control, or at least influence, those conditions.

The literature on political business cycles has accepted such a presumption, at least as a short-run matter, though the ability of incumbent politicians to generate desired macro conditions might be quite limited.

Macro variables are not direct objects of anyone's choice, but are simply incidental byproducts of the interactions among the choices of individual market participants. A price level or a rate of inflation is not an object of direct choice. A central bank can choose how many government bonds it holds, but the effect on prices of an increase in central bank holdings of government bonds depends also on the interactions among market participants along many dimensions. Similarly, a rate of unemployment is not a direct object of choice. A government can choose to modify the conditions according to which unemployment compensation is granted, and changes in government bond holdings by a central bank may change the volume of economic activity, but the connection between policy measures and unemployment will be intermediated in various ways through the interactions among market participants. Any political effort to manipulate macroeconomic conditions would surely be an inexact art and most certainly not an exact science. Nonetheless, so long as there might be some scope for incumbents to manipulate macro conditions to enhance their electoral prospects, it is plausible that such efforts at manipulation would occur.

The main vehicles for exerting political influence over macro variables are through monetary and fiscal measures. Suppose an incumbent party wanted to lower the rate of unemployment prior to an election. Under contemporary monetary systems, this would be accomplished by having the central bank increase its holding of government bonds. In a parliamentary system of government where the central bank is a branch of the treasury, this might be relatively simple to do. But in a presidential system with an independent central bank, this would be much more difficult to accomplish.

Fiscal measures are an alternative for securing a reduction in unemployment. In this case, a budget deficit would be created, either through increasing spending or through reducing taxes. Again, such a policy change would surely be generally easier to accomplish in a parliamentary system of government than in a presidential system, particularly if the presidential system operates with a bicameral legislature. The expansionary impact of any budget deficit also depends on taxpayer reactions to the deficit. In the limiting case of complete Ricardian equivalence, an expansionary fiscal policy will be impossible, as the increase in government spending will be offset by a reduction in private spending.

5 A simple model of opportunistic macro manipulation
Models of political business cycles assume that incumbents can influence aggregate economic variables and will seek to do so, at least if their electoral

prospects are insecure. Of the many formulations of political business cycles, the one developed by Nordhaus (1975) is particularly notable for its expository completeness in setting forth a model whereby democratic politics induces economic instability. To be sure, Nordhaus's model has come under strenuous criticism for both its economic and political elements, and I shall explore these criticisms below. Still, a consideration of this simple model of a politically induced business cycle provides a nice point of departure for exploring a wide range of considerations concerning the relation between politics and the macro economy.

The central features of a simple model of a political business cycle are illustrated in Figure 20.1. The figure combines the two primary ingredients noted above: the impact of macro conditions on electoral prospects and the ability of the incumbent party to generate alternative values for macro variables. The impact of macro variables on electoral prospects is illustrated by the three curves O_l, O_m, and O_h. These denote the odds of success in the forthcoming election. O_h denotes relatively high odds of success, say as illustrated by 56:44. O_m denotes moderate odds of success, say as illustrated by a 50:50 chance of success. O_l denotes low odds of success for the incum-

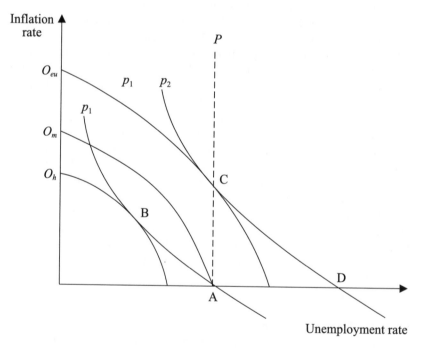

Figure 20.1   Political business-cycle model

bent government, perhaps only 44:56. The shape of this odds function shows that inflation and unemployment are both evaluated negatively by voters. It also shows that there is a tradeoff in voter evaluation of macroeconomic conditions. An increase in unemployment by itself will reduce the odds of electoral success for an incumbent. But there is some reduction in inflation that will offset the vote-losing impact of the increase in unemployment.

The ability of the incumbent government to influence macroeconomic variables is illustrated by the two sets of Phillips-curve relationships, with p_1 and p_2 denoting the idea that there is a tradeoff between inflation and unemployment in the short run, while P denotes the absence of any such tradeoff in the long run. From here, it is a simple matter to illustrate the claim of a political business cycle, as laid out by Nordhaus. Suppose the macro economy is characterized by position A prior to an election. There is no inflation, and unemployment is at its natural rate. If these macro conditions carried forward to the election, the incumbent would face 50:50 odds of success. This situation might, for instance, describe a vision of a well-working economy with a well-performing night watchman state in a two-party system. Each party is regarded as equally competent in organizing the provision of night watchman services, voters are indifferent between the parties, and electoral outcomes are random – and presumably with some voters showing up to cast their indifferent ballots for any of several reasons that have been discussed in the literature on the paradox of voting.

If the incumbent party could undertake a well-timed inflationary program, it could move the economy to B and increase its odds of electoral success to 56:44. The increase in inflation would lose the incumbent fewer votes than the reduction in unemployment would gain for it. However, this reduction in unemployment is only temporary. Once the economy has adjusted to the inflationary surprise, the natural rate of unemployment will be restored. The macro economy will now be described by C, with a higher rate of inflation than at A but with no change in unemployment. If the election were held in the presence of these kinds of macro conditions, the incumbent's odds of success would be only 44:56. Alternatively, the incumbent party could conduct a deflationary program after the election. The initial impact of this program would be to lead to macro conditions described by D, with unemployment well above its natural rate but with no inflation. An election at this time would be disastrous for the incumbent. But if the incumbent has a good or a lucky sense of timing, the natural rate of unemployment will have reasserted itself prior to the next election, as illustrated by a return to the macro conditions described by A.

This simple model thus generates a pattern of recurrent expansions and contractions, of booms and busts, whose timing coincides with the electoral cycle. In the traditional Keynesian formulations of the role of the state, the promotion of economic stability was seen as an important task of the state. The market economy was regarded as inherently unstable, and it was viewed as the task of government to provide the ballast necessary to maintain stability. The idea of a political business cycle stands this traditional claim on its head. The state is no longer viewed as the ballast to be used to promote stability, but rather is seen as injecting instability into the economy because such injection enhances the electoral prospects of incumbents. The original formulations that are characterized by Figure 20.1 have been disputed in several respects, which in turn have led to a number of revisions and reformulations of the relationship between politics and the macro economy. Most of these reformulations can also be addressed in terms of Figure 20.1. Some of them question the odds functions, and dispute the proposition that the ABCD cycle offers the electoral gains that Figure 20.1 portrays. Other lines of reformulation question the ability of incumbents to manipulate macro conditions to their liking, and also dispute the adequacy of the macro-dominated foundations of the various explanatory efforts.

6   Political cycles through partisan politics

Most of the formulations of a political business cycle that are captured by such a construction as Figure 20.1 assume that the predominant interest of politicians is to be re-elected. Much of the basis for this assumption lies in the median-voter proposition deduced from the spatial model of voting and political competition. In that model, voters are arrayed along some single-dimensioned, left-to-right spectrum. Under a wide variety of circumstances, two competing candidates will tend to locate close to one another in an effort to secure the median voter's vote. The median-voter model, which was given its modern articulation by Anthony Downs (1957), assumes that competing parties in a two-party system are nearly identical. The pursuit of electoral success leads the two parties to seek the support of the median voter, which draws the two parties close together. In this formulation, parties are construed as selecting and designing their programs so as to secure support from the median voter. The content of programs is chosen instrumentally in the hope of reflecting more fully than the opposition party the pre-existing preferences of the median voter.

Political programs in this formulation are adopted opportunistically. If one of the candidates thinks the preferences of the median voter have shifted, he will shift his proffered programs in response. In articulating their programs, candidates are trying simply to guess the location of the median voter. Knowledge is always incomplete, of course, and some divergence between candidates may result simply because those candidates make different judgments about the probable location of the median voter. Nonetheless, the specific content of the programs of competing political candidates is adopted opportunistically to secure the support of the median voter. The generation of a business cycle of the form described by Figure 20.1 is a plausible outcome, in light of the presumptions of that model. This can be accomplished directly by treating Figure 20.1 as a representation of the median voter's choice between candidates. If macro conditions are those described by A, the median voter will flip a coin to decide between the candidates. If macro conditions are those described by B, the median voter will make his selection by drawing from an urn that contains 100 tickets, 56 of them containing the incumbent's name.

An alternative conceptualization of political candidates is that they start with desired programs they would like to implement, and then seek to get elected. In this conceptualization, politicians are viewed as holding programmatic beliefs and then seeking election to implement those beliefs. If they are elected, they will proceed with that implementation. If they are defeated, they may run again, they may try different ways of articulating and explaining their program, or they may try any of a number of other things to improve their subsequent prospects. What they will not do, however, is abandon the core of their programmatic beliefs. In this formulation, politicians are partisan but are not opportunistic. They would not violate their ideological presuppositions in an effort to enhance their electoral prospects. Hence, they would not use their powers of office to generate a business cycle of the form described by Figure 20.1.

This does not mean that partisan politics will be free from destabilizing tendencies. An alternative branch of literature about politically induced business cycles is summarized by the notion of partisan business cycles, and is illustrated nicely by such works as Alesina and Rosenthal (1995), Alesina and Roubini (1997), Hibbs (1987), and Keech (1995). While partisan models of political competition can generate an election-oriented cyclical pattern similar to that of the opportunistic models, the partisan cycles are generated by a different process.

In keeping with the character of partisan models, suppose that economic growth can be described by the simple expectation-augmented Phillips relationship

$$Y_t = \bar{Y} + \gamma(\pi_t - \pi_t^e). \tag{20.1}$$

In this expression, Y_t is actual growth in output during period t, $\bar{Y}$ is the natural rate of growth in the economy, and the remainder of the equation shows that deviations of the actual from the natural rate of growth depend on the direction and size of the deviation of actual from expected inflation. Save for deviations of actual from expected inflation, the rate of growth would be steady at its natural rate. With reference to the opportunistic model described by Figure 20.1, so long as actual and expected inflation continued to be zero, the economy would remain at the natural rate of unemployment represented by A, and with a corresponding natural rate of growth in output.

In the opportunistic model of the political business cycle, the approach of an election encourages the incumbent party to inject an inflationary surprise into the economy. This leads to the initial movement to B in Figure 20.1, and would lead to an actual rate of growth that exceeded the natural rate in equation (20.1). The same type of cycle results in the partisan model, only for a different reason. In the partisan model, incumbent politicians do not inject inflationary surprises to enhance their electoral prospects. Politicians remain faithful to their core ideological beliefs, and it is the election itself, in conjunction with some characteristic features of the organization of economic activity, that generates electorally related cycles.

The idea behind a partisan business cycle can be seen most easily by assuming that a forthcoming election is widely regarded as dead even. This locates the initial situation as similar to that illustrated by A in Figure 20.1, where the forthcoming election would be dead even as well. Only in the partisan framework the contending politicians differ in their ideological beliefs and values, and do so in a way that translates directly into implications for macro variables. To maintain the expected inflation rate of zero that characterizes A in Figure 20.1, suppose that one party's program calls for a mild inflation while the other party's program calls for a mild deflation. With the election being dead even, the expected value of the rate of inflation after the election would be zero prior to the election.

The partisan models usually ground alternative programs regarding inflation between the two parties in terms of the implications of changes in unemployment for the distribution of income. Suppose the two parties differ in the income levels of their supporters. The party of the left, L, draws its support from the lower part of the income distribution. The party of the right, R, draws its support from the upper part of the income distribution. The reason why the L party would enact an inflationary program after the election is that this would transfer income to its supporters, under the presumption that reductions in unemployment inject greater equality into the distribution of income, and also because L supporters tend to be debtors. Likewise, the R party would enact a deflationary program because the resulting increase in unemployment would inject more inequality into the distribution of income, and also because R supporters tend to be creditors. (To be sure, no party promotes a deflationary program these days. With respect to macro variables, contests are over alternative rates of inflation and not over inflation or deflation. Whether the expected value of post-election inflation is zero or some positive number, however, is analytically irrelevant, and I have used the zero expectation simply to maintain conformity with the construction in Figure 20.1. For a cogent statement in support of falling prices as output expands, see Selgin 1997.)

Prior to an election that is generally regarded as dead even, the expected value of post-election inflation is zero. (More generally, the expected value would be an average of the different inflation rates attributed to the two parties, as weighted by the probabilities attached to each party's chance of winning the election.) The election thus acts as an inflationary surprise to expectations. If L wins the election, actual inflation will exceed expected inflation, unemployment will fall, and growth will exceed its natural rate. If R wins the election, actual inflation will fall short of expected inflation, unemployment will rise, and growth will fall short of its natural rate. The election of L generates a post-election boom while the election of R generates a post-election bust. As time passes and inflationary expectations adjust to the electoral surprise, the natural rates of unemployment and growth are restored, only with a higher rate of inflation if L is elected than if R is elected.

Besides differing in the process by which elections induce cycles, the opportunistic and the partisan models differ in the weight of their normative implications. In the opportunistic models, electoral contests are waged for the support of the median voter. Opportunistic cycles feed the median voter a diet of boom and bust. Analogizing from the life-cycle and tax-smoothing hypotheses, there would be strong grounds to claim that the median voter would prefer stability to periodic cycles of boom and bust. The booms and busts are shocks injected into the economy that serve only to promote the electoral prospects of incumbents, and to do so in a context where both candidates are nearly identical. Opportunistic cycles represent efforts by incumbents to manipulate voter assessments. To be sure, a good deal of the argument against opportunistic cycles has rested on the claim that voters who supported opportunistic incumbents would be acting with irrational myopia. The construction in Figure 20.1, after all, has a voter continually supporting an incumbent whose policies diverge from those he prefers.

In contrast, partisan cycles involve no manipulation but are an unavoidable byproduct of contested elections whose outcome is in doubt until the ballots are counted. So long as election outcomes are uncertain, an election will inject surprise into the economy. This will generate the macro consequences noted above, only in this case as an unavoidable facet of a democratic process. Partisan cycles are consistent even with the presumption of fully efficient democracy associated with Donald Wittman (1995). They are a cost of democracy, pretty much as voting machines and poll watchers are costs of democracy. There is no reason to think those costs are excessive, and it is hard to see how they could be eliminated without eliminating democracy as well.

It is safe to say that most of the empirical work at this time finds stronger support for partisan models of electoral cycles than for opportunistic models. Alesina and Roubini (1997) provide a clear examination of this literature, using data from both the United States and the OECD nations. The weight of their evidence, and that of much of the other literature, favors the partisan model, though supporting evidence can also be found for the opportunistic model (see, for instance, Haynes and Stone 1990 and Kiefer 1997).

Furthermore, there would seem to be no necessary reason to frame the issue as one model or the other being the right one. Frey and Schneider (1978) offer a blend of the opportunistic and partisan models. This formulation allows politicians both to aspire to hold office so that they can enact their preferred programs, as the partisan model holds, and to be willing to resort to electoral manipulation if they are otherwise facing a vigorous electoral challenge, as the opportunistic model holds. In this setup, partisan forces would always be present, and opportunism in turn would enter the picture ever more strongly as the incumbent's electoral prospects became ever more doubtful.

7   Interest-group politics and macro conditions

One influential body of public choice scholarship on rent seeking and interest groups has characterized the political process as primarily involving competition among interest groups, where winners in this competitive process are able to gain advantages through imposing costs on losers (Buchanan et al. 1981; McCormick and Tollison 1981; and Rowley et al. 1988). This focus on the centrality of interest groups does not rest easily with the literature on politics and the macro economy. Or at least the place of interest groups is largely a missing ingredient in that literature.

The standard macro formulations embody a kind of neutrality proposition, according to which what matters is the aggregate size of the measure but not to whom in particular it accrues or is distributed. In keeping with the literature on political business cycles, an incumbent might face a 55 percent chance of electoral success if the unemployment rate is 5 percent while facing only a 45 percent chance of success if the unemployment rate were 10 percent. There are, however, many different ways that unemployment can be reduced by five percentage points. The macro-neutrality proposition would hold that how this is accomplished is politically irrelevant. The interest-group formulation would claim that how this is accomplished is highly relevant politically.

To be sure, the details regarding relevance would depend on some particular features of the election system. Suppose that unemployment is distributed equally across nine electoral districts. Three of those districts are considered safe for the incumbent party and three safe for the challenging party. It would make no sense for an incumbent party to be concerned with the unemployment rate in the three districts safe for the challenger, and perhaps only modest sense to be concerned with the three districts considered safe for the incumbent. The incumbent party rather would rationally seek to concentrate the program in the three contested districts. If the program is successful, the aggregate rate of unemployment will fall. But that aggregate decline will have been driven by an interest-group process of rational discrimination and not by macro neutrality.

The change in the rate of unemployment, or other macro variables, would be just incidental byproducts of the microeconomic process of attempting to construct winning coalitions. Any relationship found between macro conditions and electoral success will conceal more than it reveals. What it would appear to reveal, a direct link between macro conditions and electoral success, would be misleading because it would mask the real link between economic conditions and electoral success. This real link would stress the construction of winning coalitions through shifting the structure of relative prices, on both product markets and factor markets, in favor of supporting interest groups, by imposing disabilities upon the remainder of society.

The literature on partisan business cycles moves a short distance away from the presumption of macro neutrality through its focus on parties differing according to the segment of the income distribution to which they appeal. In these formulations, the party of the left appeals to people in the lower part of the income distribution, while the party of the right appeals to people in the upper part. Different policies toward inflation are regarded as ways of rewarding these different constituencies. An unexpected increase in inflation will temporarily transfer income downward, while an unexpected reduction in inflation will temporarily transfer it upward. There are some troubling features to this formulation. For one thing, it is not apparent that variations in unexpected inflation are the best means of implementing these partisan programs. If the interest genuinely resides in modifying the shape of the distribution of income, a far more direct means to do this would be through changes in general taxes and subsidies. In this case, the party of the left would increase fiscal progressivity while the party of the right would reduce it. This kind of partisan politics would carry only second-order implications for macro conditions.

More than this, the stylized fact that in two-party systems the median income of supporters of the party of the left is lower than the median income of supporters of the party of the right does not warrant the conclusion that the central political fault line resides at the middle of the income distribution, with everyone below that line being supporters of the left and everyone above that line being supporters of the right. The leading political figures from all parties are well educated and relatively wealthy. People in the top two income quintiles can be found who support either party, and it is the same for people in the bottom two income quintiles. Income levels do not provide a sufficient basis for the formation of political coalitions.

An army must have generals and privates, and lots of people in intermediate grades. A political coalition must likewise have high-powered organizers as well as common clerks. The generation of political pressure, as well as the execution of a military campaign, requires a wide variety of talents and capacities. Some of those will be rare and highly desired, and so command a high price. Other of those talents and capacities will be in generous supply and of relatively low importance, and so command a low price. The generation of political pressure within an interest-group framework will cut across income lines.

8   Coordination, cycles, and emergent macro phenomena

The expectation-augmented Phillips curve illustrated by equation (20.1) conceals the emergent character of macro phenomena, and perhaps leads to an excessive focus on cycles as the point of contact between politics and the macro economy. Coordination and not cycles may be the more appropriate point of contact, and with cycles forming just one type of miscoordination. The formulation of the equation would seem to be troubling for any recognition that macro phenomena simply emerge out of the interactions among the constituent units that comprise the macro universe. A rate of growth emerges out of the interactions among market participants and their choices. If we ask what are the objects of expectation that are relevant for market participants, probably only rarely would we find that a rate of inflation would be an object of anticipation. Bond traders and other dealers in financial paper might place high importance on anticipations of future price levels. But these kinds of activities comprise only a small part of the universe of economic activities. For someone who owns an auto repair shop and is trying to decide whether to expand the facility or to move to a new location where a larger facility is already in place, his expectation about the future general price level is surely far down his list of concerns, and I doubt whether it would appear at all. And it would surely be the same for the vast preponderance of commercial decisions where people are making choices to commit resources today when the results of those choices will not be known until some future time. There would be different particular objects of expectation, depending on the particular activity about which expectations are being formed.

A modern economy is constituted as a dense network of generally, though not universally, coordinated transactions. A rate of growth emerges out of the interaction of individual plans of action. There is no reason to expect smooth stability in all this, as Joseph Schumpeter ([1912] 1934, 1939) recognized. Indeed, the abandonment or revision of plans is evidence quite to the contrary. Moreover, there is a great deal of complementarity among plans, which means that individual decisions to revise or abandon plans would not be independent of other people's decisions. In practical terms, this means such things as that carpenters will not just be involved with building structures (as part of the execution of a plan), but will also be engaged in various remodeling activities (as part of the revision of a plan) that would not have been necessary had things proceeded as originally planned. Further, much of the injection of new plans, as well as revision of previous plans, will stem from the creation of new products, methods for marketing products, and the like. There will be many reasons why plans do not fit together perfectly, and thus call for continual revision.

An emphasis on coordination and emergent phenomena reduces the importance of a focus on cycles and leads to two propositions: (1) variability in economic time series is not necessarily a sign of poor economic performance and (2) constancy in economic time series is not necessarily a sign of good economic performance. The first claim means that observed instability might be a sign of avoidable and correctable miscoordination, but it might also be a sign of progress in an interdependent world with capital complementarity. There would thus be two types of cycles, one that was consistent with the orderly coordination of economic activities in a complex environment and another that emanated from disruptions to the processes of orderly coordination.

The second claim means that just because stability is observed in aggregate variables does not mean coordinative processes are working as well as they might. Consider first of all a simple micro-level illustration of what I have in mind. A ceramicist makes tile murals. Suppose that by working hard she can assemble 1000 tiles in a month. In one case, everything goes well and at the end of the month she has 1000 useable tiles to put into her murals. There are also many things that can go wrong in this process. The clay may dry too quickly and crack. The kiln temperature may not rise exactly as anticipated, with the result being that some glazes do not show the colors that were intended. As a result the ceramicist has to divert some of her time away from making finished tiles into responding to the various exogenous shocks to her studio. For instance, rather than putting some clay tiles into a kiln to be fired, she may have to rehydrate that clay and start over. Because of these diversions required to respond to the shocks that disrupted her anticipations, she may be able to make only 700 tiles. But this does not mean that she is 30 percent unemployed. Rather it means that she has shifted into a different pattern of activity.

Suppose that we analogize the ceramicist's situation to standard macro formulations of shocks to the economy. The first instance is one of full-employment equilibrium. In the second instance, her studio is hit with negative shocks that she had not anticipated. Yet full employment continues to exist, only with a different pattern of activities in the face of disruptions than when those disruptions are absent. Miscoordination implies errors in plans, at least as regarded from a posture of omniscience. A rise in the volume of miscoordination means that there will be some shift of human activity away from executing original plans into activities that revise or reorient plans that have proven unsatisfactory.

An economy can be represented by a network of human activity, some of which is engaged in executing original plans and some of which is engaged in rectifying plans that have been judged unsatisfactory. This distinction between types of activity is, of course, an analytical and not an empirical distinction. There is no way, at least so far as I know, that a census could be taken to determine how many people are employed in executing plans and how many are employed in revising plans that have been judged unsuccessful. Yet this analytical distinction follows from the claim that the degree of coordination is a variable that can be influenced, for good or for bad, depending on a variety of institutional arrangements and policy measures. An increase in the volume of miscoordination in a society will shift the pattern of activity in a society, but it need not alter the total volume of activity. It is conceivable that miscoordination could increase without any impact on aggregate time series. Miscoordination induces revisions in plans. Labor is shifted from the execution of plans to the revision of plans. It is conceivable that this shift of labor can be accommodated within an unchanged aggregate volume of employment.

Using a normative language, cyclical variability may be either good or bad. It depends on the source of the cyclicity. In like manner, the absence of cyclical variability can be either a good thing or a bad thing. It depends on the degree of coordination that is present. A benevolent policy maker would seem to face an insoluble problem of knowledge. It would be necessary to be able to distinguish good cycles from bad, a task rendered even more difficult by recognizing that both features may be present at the same moment. It would also be necessary to know when aggregate stability is a sign of a smooth coordination of plans and when it rather means merely a rapid movement between the execution of plans and the revision or reassembly of plans.

The active promotion of stability in aggregate time series is neither *per se* desirable nor is it possible. Aggregate outcomes are emergent outcomes and not direct objects of choice. There is no sense to a policy aimed to prevent cycles, any more than it would be sensible to prevent traffic delays. What is sensible is to seek to preclude unnecessary cycles or disturbances to the coordination of economic activity. Policy for a coordinationist macroeconomics would be of the same genre as policy generally, and would be concerned with providing and maintaining a framework within which people can order their activities. The pursuit of a truly activist stabilization policy will be both impossible and mischievous. Appropriate macro policy cannot aim to achieve particular values for macro variables, for these variables are not objects of choice. Appropriate macro policy would thus seem to be indistinct from appropriate micro policy, with both involving the creation and maintenance of a constitutive framework within which people can generate orderly patterns of economic activity. Whether such policy measures are, or could be, consistent with rational political conduct is a topic that will surely continue to animate public choice scholarship.

21 Monetary policy

Mark Toma

1 Introduction

The money market of modern theory is plagued by problems. The traditional economic solutions have been magic wand ones – magic monetary wands.

For instance, monetary theorists have devoted much attention to the problem of a determinate general price level. The problem here is that holders of money cannot establish their current demand without knowing the current supply and whether it will be augmented in the future. The upshot is that today's price of money and, hence, the general price level, depends on current and all future supplies. So the problem of a determinate price level is fundamentally an issue of whether money holders are able to anticipate the future time path of money.

The monetary economist is quick to supply the magic wand: assume a deterministic process for generating current and *all* future money supplies. More imaginatively, the magic monetary wand may take the form of Milton Friedman's famous helicopter or a conservative central banker who comes pre-equipped with a well-defined and immutable set of anti-inflation preferences (Rogoff 1985). These solutions are alike in that they solve monetary problems by introducing a supply factor from outside the model.

A major theme of this chapter is that the public choice approach to monetary policy offers more satisfactory solutions because it does not involve wand waving. By modeling the incentives that real-world central bankers confront, the public choice approach is able to make the supply of money endogenous. This is real progress. A key measure of the success of economics as a scientific endeavor is its willingness to leave wand waving to the magicians.

A second major theme takes the form of a conjecture – the close of the twentieth century represents the 'end of monetary policy'. At the most fundamental level, monetary policy implies that there is a supplier, or a group of suppliers, able to choose from a menu of money supply time paths. Using the terminology of microeconomics, monetary policy is about monopoly power; it rules out 'price-taking' money producers. The deathbed conjecture rings true to the extent that national governments in coming years will be less able to insulate their central banks from competitive pressures arising both domestically and internationally. If so, the public choice approach to monetary policy may well have helped to write the final chapter.

2   The public choice approach to monetary policy

2.1   A principal–agent framework

The defining characteristic of the public choice approach is that it brings government decision making inside the model. With respect to monetary policy, the objective is to develop and test theories that explain the origin, evolution and operation of money supply institutions. The public choice approach does not simply assert the existence of a money supplier with certain tailor-made behavioral attributes, but instead insists that monetary policy be derived from more primitive assumptions, concerning the costs and benefits to those agents assigned the task of supplying money.

My starting point is to suggest that all public choice approaches to decision making by 'complex' government units can be subsumed within a principal–agent framework.[1] This framework has been applied to an assortment of public choice issues, including the public choice approach to monetary policy. It is not, however, a theoretical device that has been used extensively in the study of monetary policy. For this reason, the remainder of this section will outline the general principal–agent model in some detail.

A simple principal–agent framework might have three layers. At the top would be the general public, or at least some subset of the public. At the bottom would be an agency or bureau that produces some output for the public. The government, or head of state, stands in the middle. Because my interest is in the behavior of the bureaucratic agency, I shall downplay the relationship between the public and the government and instead focus on the principal–agent problems that might arise between the government and the unit responsible for producing the desired policy output.

The public, as principal, hires the government to control the operation of the bureaucratic production unit. If the head of state could costlessly signal the preferences of its principal and costlessly monitor the bureau, then the output desired by the public would necessarily be supplied, regardless of bureau type. When these costs are positive, however, the type of bureaucratic organization adopted becomes important and the public may assign the government head the responsibility of choosing between the alternatives. Generally, the government can create an in-house (dependent) production unit or delegate production to an independent franchisee. The prototypical in-house bureau receives a budget in exchange for output and is headed by an appointee of the government. The franchisee has a residual claim to an independent source of revenue, chooses its own output, and is headed by someone chosen through a selection process internal to the organization.[2]

There are advantages and disadvantages associated with each type of production unit. An advantage of the in-house arrangement is that the appropriations process gives the head of state a relatively low-cost method of intervening within and between budget periods to influence policy (Weingast and Moran 1983; Weingast 1984). Lacking a residual claimant, however, the in-house unit will have a tendency to employ a production technique that causes actual costs to exceed least costs (Meone 1986). One simple way of modeling the advantages and disadvantages is to assume that the unit produces an output that is close to what is wanted, but at a budgetary cost that may be inflated by the tendency of in-house workers to shirk. To control production costs generally requires that the government head first devote resources to monitoring the production process. The information so gathered can then be brought to bear on agency decision making through the budget and the appointment process.

The government may reject production by an in-house firm and instead delegate production to an independent franchisee. Most simply, the government could enter into a contractual relationship that grants residual claimant status to a private organization. There are several ways that contracts between the government head and the franchisee could be structured. The head of state could use an auction to award production rights to the franchisee that makes the largest up-front lump-sum payment to the government. One advantage of this scheme is that the payment produces revenue immediately for the government. Another advantage is that once the contract is awarded, the franchisee, as residual claimant, has an incentive to choose the least-cost production technology. In particular, the prospect of a larger residual induces the franchisee to devise internal rules and adopt labor contracts (such as piece-rate and contingency-wage contracts) that minimize production costs.

The disadvantage of delegation is that there is no assurance that the franchisee will choose the optimal output level. The government could specify an output level in the contract with the winning bidder, but with this more complex contract, a post-contractual monitoring problem would emerge that is similar to the type of problem that the government faces with an in-house organization. The government would have to monitor the production process to ensure that the franchisee did not deviate from pre-specified contract terms. To make the sharpest contrast between production by an in-house organization versus a franchisee, assume that, when dealing with the franchisee, the government head chooses to avoid monitoring costs by delegating output decisions to its agent.

2.2   The Fed's institutional environment

The Federal Reserve System can be used to illustrate the principal–agent framework. The institutional environment at the birth of the system was defined by the Federal Reserve Act of 1913. The key issue of interest is how the Act specified the relationship between the Fed and the US government. In other words, which agency prototype – an in-house agency, an independent franchisee, or perhaps some hybrid of the two – best describes the central bank as it opened its doors for business in the early days of 1914?

Consider the key attributes of agency type that were suggested by the principal–agent framework. With respect to financing, the Federal Reserve Act forcefully rejected the typical budgetary arrangement (Toma 1982). Instead, the Act gave reserve bank management first call on earnings from discount loans, open-market operations, and fees charged for providing clearinghouse services to member banks. These earnings were to be used to defray 'all necessary expenses'. Next, member banks were to receive a dividend payment on the paid-in capital stock. Finally, 'after the aforesaid dividend claims have been fully met, all the net earnings shall be paid to the United States as a franchise tax, except that one-half of such net earnings shall be paid into a surplus fund until it shall amount to forty per centum of the paid-in capital stock of such bank'. One thing the Act did not do was to authorize transfer payments from the general government treasury to the individual reserve banks in the event of a shortfall in earnings. In this sense, the reserve banks faced a bottom line somewhat akin to that faced by for-profit firms in a private-market setting.

With respect to ownership rights, the Federal Reserve Act nominally designated the system's member banks as shareholders. They were required to subscribe to the capital stock of their reserve bank in an amount equal to 'six per centum of the paid-up capital stock and surplus of such bank'. Stock ownership, however, did not convey voting rights. Nor were there secondary markets where the member banks' shares could be traded.

With respect to selection of the Fed management team, the Federal Reserve System established an interesting blend of government appointment versus 'stockholder' appointment. Every member of the Federal Reserve Board was to have a government connection. In addition to five political appointees, the Board included the Secretary of Treasury and the Comptroller of the Currency (Federal Reserve Act §10). Discount policy was perhaps the most important power the politically appointed Board exercised. Discount rates set by the individual reserve banks were 'subject to review and determination of the Federal Reserve Board'. Thus the government, through the Board, could influence, if not control, money created through the discount window.

The Federal Reserve Act contained one important loophole, however, which tended to undermine the Board's control over aggregate Fed money. According to the Act, the one margin of money supply adjustment over which individual reserve banks unambiguously could exercise discretion was the amount of government securities to buy and sell. These open-market operations were to take place at the initiative of the individual reserve banks and each bank was to have first claim to the earnings generated by the government securities in its portfolio.[3] Clearly, the appointment process could not be used as a means by which the government could control money creation by way of open-market operations.

The Banking Acts of 1933 and 1935 changed the institutional environment of the Federal Reserve significantly. Most importantly, these acts closed off the open-market operation loophole. Open-market operations were now centralized under the authority of a new agency, the Federal Open Market Committee, a majority of whose members were political appointees. In addition, the Federal Reserve was no longer required to make a transfer payment to the Treasury; the interest earnings from the Fed's asset portfolio could be spent exclusively on itself. The Federal Reserve, at its own initiative, changed the financing arrangement in the aftermath of the Second World War. In 1947, the Federal Reserve instituted a policy of transferring excess revenue to the Treasury on an annual basis. These transfers have continued up to the present time. Currently, the Federal Reserve transfers over 90 percent of revenue to the US Treasury.[4]

The overall picture of the Federal Reserve that emerges can perhaps best be characterized as a hybrid between an in-house agency and an independent franchisee. On the one hand, the franchise analogy seems appropriate in that the Federal Reserve is owned by member-bank shareholders that receive annual dividend payments. The Federal Reserve also has an independent source of revenue rather than being funded by a budget. Finally, the annual transfer payments can loosely be construed as a franchise payment to the government in return for the exclusive right to produce money.

On the other hand, the in-house analogy seems appropriate in that there are both implicit and explicit mechanisms that the government can use to control monetary policy. The president, with the consent of the senate, appoints members of the central management team, the Board of Governors. Moreover, member banks are not shareholders in the ordinary sense of the word. Shares cannot be traded, ownership conveys no voting rights, and dividend payments are fixed by statute.

Given that the Federal Reserve does not fit neatly into either of the two organizational prototypes, the fact that a consensus public choice model of monetary policy making has failed to emerge is not surprising. To be sure, public choice theorists seem to be more comfortable with the in-house model. After all, the typical government bureau seems to be of this type. But an important literature has emerged which takes seriously the Federal Reserve's lack of budgetary dependence. In a public choice sense, 'serious' means that care is taken in modeling the incentives Federal Reserve decision makers confront. The next two sections describe the evolution of the two types of Federal Reserve models – the in-house agency and the independent franchise – in the public choice literature.

2.3 The Fed as an in-house agency

The head of government plays an important role in monitoring the operation of the in-house production unit.[5] Yet to this point I have not posed the question, 'Who is the government's head?'. Democratic governments commonly are divided into at least two branches – the legislature and the executive. If one of the two branches controls both the budget and the appointment process, then that branch can be viewed as the head of government. If one branch controls the budget and the other the appointment process then control over the production agency is split. Government is two-headed in this case.

The early public choice literature on Federal Reserve policy focused on the possibility of executive control, presumably with the power of appointment serving as the lever.[6] One strand of this literature examined monetary policy under conservative and liberal presidential administrations and another directed attention toward monetary policy around election time, regardless of the political affiliation of the incumbent. The standard empirical approach taken by the contributors to this literature was to construct and estimate a Federal Reserve 'reaction function' (Grier 1987, 1989a). A proxy for monetary policy, such as the Federal funds rate or the growth rate in some monetary aggregate, was entered as the dependent variable in a regression model. The key right-hand-side variable typically would be a dummy variable that controlled for the political party of the administration in office or for the period immediately preceding a presidential election.

The results from this early executive control literature were mixed. An empirical consensus failed to emerge on the issue of party influence as well as on the possibility of a political–monetary election cycle. Viewed in hindsight, the ambiguous results should not be too surprising. Both approaches to the problem failed to delineate the specific mechanism through which the executive was able to control the Federal Reserve. Also, the model underlying the effects of monetary policy on the economy was either left unspecified, or worse, predicated on the existence of a myopic general public.

Congressional oversight hearings in the 1970s prompted a wave of academic interest in the possibility of legislative influence on the Federal Reserve. A series of invited papers on congressional influence was published in the *Journal of Monetary Economics* in 1978. The overall conclusion was that congressional influence had been minimal. Congressional oversight may have been long on talk but produced little in the way of an observable monetary policy effect.[7]

In the early 1980s, a 'revisionist' theory of congressional control gained popularity. The leading proponent of this camp was Barry Weingast. His work tended to downplay the importance of explicit congressional oversight activities. Less-visible mechanisms (McCubbins and Schwartz 1984), such as 'who gets appointed and reappointed' (Weingast and Moran 1983, p. 769) would be more effective margins of control. The major implication of the revisionist theory was that an agency's policy changes whenever the preferences (composition) of its oversight committee change, even if there are no overt indications of oversight. The revisionists applied their model to an assortment of government agencies ranging from the Federal Trade Commission to the Securities and Exchange Commission.

Encouraged by this early success, proponents of the revisionist theory turned their attention to the Federal Reserve (Hetzel 1990). A student of Weingast's, Kevin Grier (1991) found that a proxy for the preferences of members of the Senate Banking Committee was statistically significant in explaining money growth over the period 1961–80. In particular, a shift in the composition of membership toward the Democratic Party was associated with monetary expansion. Related work (Beck 1990a, b) has called into question the strength and robustness of the party effect on Federal Reserve policy, as measured by the standard monetary aggregates.

A recent book by Thomas Havrilesky (1995), *The Pressures on American Monetary Policy*, advances the early work on executive and legislative control by detailing the specific mechanisms through which the two branches influence policy. At the most basic level, the power of appointment is the source of executive influence and oversight hearings are the source of legislative influence. The executive branch signals its monetary policy preferences ('tight' versus 'loose') primarily through the news media. Congress threatens Federal Reserve power primarily through legislative bills (which seldom pass). Havrilesky provides evidence that is consistent with the hypothesis that signals and threats affect monetary policy. He also finds evidence for the influence of a special-interest group – the financial sector. Monetary policy responds to signals from the banking industry as reflected in the directives issued by the Federal Advisory Committee.

I would be remiss if I closed this section without commenting on what is perhaps the most provocative work in the government control literature. In 1988, Gary Anderson, William Shughart and Robert Tollison published an article in *Public Choice* entitled 'A public choice theory of the great contraction' (Anderson et al. 1988b). Their work is noteworthy for two reasons. First, they focused on what is arguably the major unresolved puzzle in twentieth-century macroeconomic history. Second, they attempted to explain the restrictive monetary policy pursued from 1929 to 1933 on the assumption of 'rational, self-interested behavior' by policy makers.

Contrasting their approach to the orthodox economic approach (Friedman and Schwartz, 1963, ch. 7), which contends that the Fed was distracted by internal power struggles, Anderson et al. (1988b, p. 4) argue that the 'real question should not be "why was the Fed so inept", but rather why have economists been so inept in interpreting the evidence that has been under their noses all along?'. The overlooked evidence was the high failure rate of non-member banks relative to member banks. Their simple hypothesis was that

> the Fed pursued an intentional policy of achieving the widescale demise of non-member banks by failing to engage in appropriate expansionary policies. ... In so doing, the Fed was acting as the agent of the oversight committees, who in turn were representing the interests of the Fed member banks in their states. (pp. 10–11)

The presumption here is that non-member banks would be a relatively impotent lobbying force.[8]

Subsequent work by others (Huberman 1990; Santoni and Van Cott 1990) called into question their empirical results. Still, I see their work as standing as a monument to what is best about the public choice approach to monetary policy. Anderson et al. do not flinch from taking their 'simple hypothesis' seriously. In so doing, their work suggests an explanation that while unsettling offers a new window through which the puzzle of the Great Depression may be examined and ultimately resolved.

2.4   The Fed as an independent franchisee

In modeling the government as delegating monetary policy to an independent franchisee, care must be taken to distinguish between a traditional and a public choice interpretation of central bank 'independence'. A simple, but I would argue apt, characterization of the traditional view is that independence insulates monetary policy from the whims of day-to-day politics and gives the central banker the opportunity to pursue a policy that is more in tune with the long-run interests of the general public. Implicit in this view is the notion that the central banker is of a certain behavioral type – one who has no motive other than operating on behalf of the fictitious representative individual. It is as if independence creates an economic vacuum. Lacking any personal incentive to choose one policy over another, the default strategy of this economic automaton is to pursue the public interest.

Milton Friedman's 1968 article entitled, 'Should there be an independent monetary authority?' represents a first step away from the model of the central banker as economic automaton. Friedman's concern was that policy made in an economic vacuum gives rise to the possibility of 'bad' as well as 'good' outcomes. And because the bad outcomes could be really bad, Friedman concluded that true independence would not be tolerated in a democratic setting. 'Certainly no government to date has been willing to put that much power in the hands of a central bank' (Friedman 1968, p. 185). Governments, in particular the US government, have experimented with nominal independence. But even limited independence has its disadvantages since 'policy is thereby made highly dependent on personalities' (p. 186).

From a public choice perspective, the element missing from Friedman's warning of the potential abuse of Federal Reserve independence was a modeling of the constraints and therefore the incentives confronting Fed decision makers. My paper, 'Inflationary bias of the Federal Reserve System' (Toma 1982), and the paper 'Preliminary evidence on the use of inputs by the Federal Reserve System' by Shughart and Tollison (1983) represented the first formal steps in this direction.[9] Both works, while using the independent firm as a motif, noted that the Federal Reserve was special in that the claims on the firm's residual were attenuated. Federal Reserve management could use excess revenue to finance on-the-job amenities, but neither they nor the member-bank shareholders could 'take the profits home'. In this sense, the Federal Reserve operated as an independent *non-profit* organization.

The model in 'Inflationary bias of the Federal Reserve System' (Toma 1982) compared the policy of an independent non-profit Federal Reserve with the policy of a dependent in-house Federal Reserve. Using the budget as a control device, the head of government induces the in-house Federal Reserve to produce the desired monetary policy, which in a simple representative agent economy would be a deflationary one that reduced the nominal interest rate to zero. The disadvantage is that this optimal policy would not be produced efficiently. In the limit, the budget that the Federal Reserve might realize would exhaust the representative individual's benefits from monetary policy.

The independent non-profit Federal Reserve in my paper does not receive a budget but instead finances its operations out of the income generated by the assets it acquires in creating money. What is it that motivates the Federal Reserve's management team? In a deliberate attempt to move outside the traditional public-interest model, and at the same time provide a clear contrast to the in-house model, I assumed that management did not derive any special benefits from serving others, that is, the so-called 'representative' individual. And while management could not take revenue home it could enjoy on-the-job amenities, the amount of which would tend to be directly correlated with revenue produced in excess of minimum operating cost. The bottom line is that the independent non-profit Federal Reserve would undertake the same monetary policy as a residual claimant Federal Reserve. The rate of money production would be pushed beyond the benchmark optimal level to the point that maximized profits.

While Toma (ibid.) used size of system spending as the empirical indicator of Federal Reserve payoffs, Shughart and Tollison (1983) used system employment. Their empirical findings were provocative. They concluded that, 'every time the Fed hired one more worker, the stock of high-powered money rose by $362,000' (p. 300). The attempt to expand the size of the Fed's empire, in other words, would directly lead to an expansion in the monetary base.

Evidence that this approach was having an impact on the rest of the economics profession surfaced at the 1982 meetings of the Western Economic Association.[10] There, Milton Friedman presented a paper on 'Monetary policy: theory and practice', which represented a turning point in his views concerning the motivation and behavior of Federal Reserve officials. Friedman was willing to entertain the possibility that what he had in the past viewed as inept policy arising from the happenstance of personality may have arisen from something more fundamental. He now emphasized the Federal Reserve's incentives, as conditioned by the lack of budget oversight. As Friedman explained,

> I believe that the fundamental explanation for the persistence and importance of bureaucratic inertia in the Federal Reserve System is the absence of a bottom line. The Fed is not subject to an effective budget constraint. It prints its own money to pay its expenses. The Federal Reserve does not have to face the voters. (p. 115)

Friedman further compared the public choice approach to the approach that he and Anna Schwartz earlier had pursued in their *Monetary History of the United States, 1867–1960* (1963):

> In the analysis of monetary policy in our book, we paid only passing attention to the self-interest of the people conducting the policy. More recently, we have all become familiar with the idea of applying to governmental performance the same approach that we apply to private business enterprises. The social function of business or government is one thing; the forces that control behavior may be very different. (Friedman 1982, p. 115)

By introducing the pubic choice theme to a wider academic audience, Friedman's comments seemed to jump-start research on the Federal Reserve. In particular, Friedman's call to apply 'the same approach that we apply to private business enterprises' led to further research on two fronts. First, there was a flurry of work that re-examined the theoretical underpinnings and the empirical results of the original business enterprise model (Allen et al. 1988; Mounts and Sowell 1990, 1996; Crihfield and Wood 1993).

A second line of research used standard microeconomic tools to analyse the *internal* operations of the Federal Reserve. This work emphasized that the Board is the primary group within the system that conducts monetary policy and is in the best position to appropriate excess revenue for itself. Board employment (or spending) and not system employment represents the key payoff, or rent-seeking, variable (Mounts and Sowell 1986). Also, the Board, acting as a chief executive officer, has an incentive to reward individual reserve banks for (research) activities that enhance Board rents (Toma and Toma 1985).

An article by Gary Santoni (1984) provides a case study of the early Bank of England, which serves as a benchmark for placing the research on the Federal Reserve as a business enterprise in proper context. From its inception in 1694 until the early 1930s, the Bank of England was a privately owned for-profit central bank, albeit one that 'was immersed in a set of institutional arrangements that related the wealth of the Bank's owners inversely to the rate of inflation' (ibid., p. 13). Control of the money supply by the Bank's owners was interrupted from 1793 to 1821, however, 'when the government seized the Bank's monetary control function' (ibid.). During this period, the Bank was effectively transformed into a dependent in-house firm commissioned to help finance military expenditures. Empirically, Santoni finds that money growth rates were significantly lower with the independent for-profit Bank of England during times of peace than with a dependent in-house Bank of England during times of war. While this finding is not too surprising in itself, Santoni's work makes clear that a for-profit central bank need not lead to excessive rates of money production. Indeed, given the appropriate institutional constraints, a for-profit central bank may be a way of insuring against excessive monetary expansion.

Santoni's work on for-profit central banking brings to the forefront a fundamental question – 'why not competition?' – that is only latent in the emerging literature on the Federal Reserve as a business enterprise. Because a competitive monetary equilibrium is one where economic rents are reduced to zero, politics and therefore policy does not matter. Political game playing presumes the existence of economic rents that can be divided among competing interests. And economic rents require the imposition of legal restrictions (Wallace 1983), perhaps in the form of reserve requirements or restrictions on note issue, which transform the industrial organization of money supply from competitive to monopolistic.

So the answer to Santoni's query is a public choice one – competition is no longer tenable once the government has a desire to impose legal restrictions for the purpose of generating and distributing rents. This basic insight has spawned an extensive literature on 'optimal seigniorage' that has much to offer the public choice theorist. According to this literature (Mankiw 1987), a major justification for a monetary monopoly is to provide the government with a source of revenue that supplements regular taxes.

Faced with a funding requirement the government has two choices. It can establish an in-house central bank and pressure it to engage in inflation. Or it can create an independent franchisee and charge it a 'franchise fee' for monopoly rights to issue money. What it cannot do, at least from an optimal seigniorage perspective, is establish a competitive central banking system (Toma 1997).[11]

3 Contract theories: breakthrough or dead end?

The modeling of central bank incentives recently has received attention, as economists have become concerned with the possibility that a policy maker's plans may not be consistent over time. The time-consistency problem was first outlined in a general context by Finn Kydland and Edward Prescott (1977) in the 1970s and then applied by Robert Barro and David Gordon (1983) to monetary policy in the 1980s. Barro and Gordon posit a policy maker (central banker) who chooses the inflation rate on a period-by-period basis so as to maximize a present-value payoff function. Central banker payoffs are negatively related to actual inflation and positively related to inflationary surprises. Inflation in this model tends to be higher than optimal because the public must choose their real money holdings before the central banker chooses each period's actual inflation rate. Replacing the discretionary central banker, who chooses on a period-by-period basis, with some mechanism that would fix inflation at zero, could increase present-value payoffs.

A key assumption underlying the time-consistency problem is that the central banker perfectly reflects the preferences of the government's head. Indeed, the central banker and the government head can be viewed as one. Also, the central banker is assumed to have an infinite time horizon. Policy makers do not suffer from shortsightedness.

The monetary economics literature has proposed what appears to be a straightforward solution to the time-consistency problem: monetary policy should be spun off from the general government. Such delegation may be of two types. First, the general government may delegate monetary policy to a special central banker (Rogoff 1985; Waller 1992b), one with a bias that works against the inflationary pressures inherent in the time-consistency problem. Second, monetary policy may be delegated to an 'independent' central banker who is given a contract specifying that his payoffs will be reduced if inflation increases (Canzoneri 1985; Lohmann 1992; Walsh 1995).

While each of these has a superficial appeal, I argue that neither provides a satisfactory solution to the time-consistency problem. The conservative central banker is no more than an economic automaton or sky-hook device, essentially introduced from outside the model. Who is this non-representative individual who comes equipped with a built-in preference for price stability and who does not enjoy the pleasures of surprise inflation? How do we identify this special person? More importantly, how do we construct the economic vacuum, where incentives do not exist and where the conservative central banker will be free to implement his own brand of anti-inflation policy? Constructing a true economic vacuum may be just as problematic as constructing a true physical vacuum and may be even more misleading as an assumption upon which to develop theories which purport to explain the way the world works. The bottom line is that to the extent the conservative central banker solves the time-consistency problem, he does so only in a very crude non-economic fashion.

The contract solution also fails a public choice test. Referring to the alleged optimality of contracting, Bennett McCallum argues that

> The problem with this result is that such a device does not actually overcome the motivation for dynamic inconsistency, it merely relocates it. Specifically, under the proposed arrangement the government has to enforce the contract – e.g., reduce the CB's [central bank's] financial rewards when inflation is high – but the government has exactly the same incentive not to do so as is identified by the Kydland–Prescott and Barro–Gordon analysis. (1995, p. 7)

McCallum's critique is based upon a 'state-contingent wage contract' that resembles a 'legislated budget' (Walsh 1995) to the central banker. The head of government is responsible for enforcing the contract, that is, adjusting the 'legislated budget' on a period-by-period basis. But if the government's head has the power and will to make the appropriate budget adjustment, then there is really no time-consistency problem in the first place. If the government's head does not have the power and will, there is a problem but contracting does nothing to solve it. The contract will simply not be enforced.

The distinction made earlier between an in-house agency and an independent franchisee becomes relevant at this point. Although seldom made explicit, contract theorists implicitly view the government as dealing with an in-house central bank. I would argue that this is only pseudo delegation, since an in-house central bank is by its very nature subservient to the head of government. True delegation involves turning over monetary policy to a franchisee that makes its own output decisions without oversight from above. Compared to a budgetary in-house firm, the establishment of a truly independent central bank – one that operates more or less on automatic pilot – provides a surer way of locking in policy.

My conclusion, which I think McCallum shares, is that contract theory in its present manifestation is a dead end. Contract theorists have not really grappled with the issue of what counts as a commitment technology. From a public choice perspective, this is an issue in constitutional economics. To say that monetary policy can be precommitted is tantamount to saying that rules of the monetary game can be laid out which cannot be easily revoked once the game commences. Delegation to an in-house central bank is pseudo commitment. In contrast, delegation that is faithful to the franchising motif holds out the promise of true commitment and may be one component of a binding monetary constitution.

4 Origin and evolution of central banking

The focus to this point has been on the *conduct* of monetary policy. Implicitly, a set of institutional rules has been assumed and the operation of monetary policy within that rule set has been predicted. I now turn to the origin and evolution of the rules themselves. More to the point, is there a public choice rationale for the founding of a central bank?

Generally speaking, economists have focused on financial stability (Miron 1986) as the key rationale. In the absence of a central bank the financial system allegedly will be subject to recurring banking crises. The central bank's role in this setting is to serve as a lender of last resort.

The Federal Reserve System represents a case in point. Financial crises before 1913 are generally attributed to the National Banking System, which tied national bank note issue to the amount of federal government bonds in circulation. As a result, the supply of notes tended to be inelastic in the face of seasonal fluctuations in money demand. The solution was to create a central bank rediscount facility in the form of the Federal Reserve that would suffuse the payments system with greater elasticity.

Lawrence Broz (1997) has identified a fundamental problem with this narrow economic rationale for the founding of the Federal Reserve. From a public choice perspective, the broad-based benefits associated with financial stability are unlikely to spur political action. The problem here is the one identified in Mancur Olson's (1965) pioneering work, *The Logic of Collective Action*. No single individual or group will have the incentive to mobilize politically since the benefits of mobilization will be spread out over the rest of the community. Broz's way out of the dilemma is in the spirit of Olson. The broad-based benefits of domestic financial stability must be joined with private benefits to some interest group. Broz's claim, which he forcefully defends,

> is that the Federal Reserve Act was an example of joint production, in which the private output (internationalizing the currency) could not feasibly be separated from the associated collective output (improving the domestic payments system), creating the necessary convergence between the private and social costs of institutional change. (1995, p. 7)

Broz identifies Wall Street banks as a private interest group that benefited from internationalization and thereby served as a potent lobbying force on behalf of the Federal Reserve.

Broz's work represents a major advance over traditional rationales for the founding of the Federal Reserve in that he isolates the political forces that must be mobilized to overcome the free-rider problem associated with providing a public good. I think, however, that Broz may have been too quick to accept the basic premise of the traditional rationale – that financial stability was the primary economic rationale for the founding of the Federal Reserve.

At the most fundamental level, the problem with the nineteenth-century banking system was a legal restriction in the form of a bond-backing requirement that discouraged financial institutions from issuing currency. The most direct solution would simply have been to eliminate the restriction. Alternatively, the government might have given a monopoly privilege to one of the existing financial institutions. Finally, the government could have founded a national clearinghouse. Any of these institutional changes could have enhanced financial stability.

So the question remains, why did politicians in 1913 choose the Federal Reserve and not one of the other solutions to the financial stability problem? The public choice approach, with its principal–agent underpinnings, points to the head of government as the central figure in the story. With focus directed toward the government's head, the possibility arises that fiscal considerations may have been paramount in the founding of the Federal Reserve, or any central bank for that matter. Indeed, as Broz himself recounts, the fiscal rationale has a long history that predates the Federal Reserve.

> Unlike the Federal Reserve, the early forerunners of modern central banks were not born of society's need for a lender of last resort or monetary services. For early central banks, like the Bank of England and the First and Second Banks of the United States, the main societal public good was *fiscal* in nature and involved improving government credit-worthiness during wartime. (p. 206; emphasis in original)

Creation of a central bank serves a twofold fiscal function. It reduces the administrative cost of issuing government debt on short notice and provides an institutionalized mechanism for generating seigniorage. Using tools familiar to public choice theorists, there has emerged a small but growing literature that explores each of these fiscal functions.[12]

5   The end of monetary policy?

If not yet dead, monetary policy is dying. I base this claim on casual empiricism and reflection on the meaning of 'policy'. Consider the definition in Webster's *Dictionary*: 'the course or general plan of action adopted by a government or party or person'. Accordingly, *monetary* policy would be defined as 'the general money supply plan adopted by a central bank'. Here I have identified the central bank as the relevant monetary institution and not, say, a gold standard, a currency board, or a system of note-issuing private banks. The presumption embodied in the definition is that the central banker can choose from a range of options. His behavior is not so tightly constrained that outcomes can be predicted with complete certainty, given the state of the economy. Monetary policy is based on the concept of a decision maker who can exercise discretion; that is, can wield monopoly power. If there is no monopoly power, then there is no policy. This is why currency boards and the like are not included in the monetary policy definition.

To take seriously the claim that monetary policy is on its deathbed, one must first identify the source of its past vitality. What, in other words, accounts for the strength of central banking institutions, particularly in the twentieth century? Public choice theorists have made a persuasive case that the durability of central banks involves more than financial stability. One interesting line of inquiry is that central banking may serve as an efficient means of financing certain types of government outlays – wars, for instance.

In the nineteenth and twentieth centuries, government financing considerations at least in part drove monetary policy. With some justification, changes in financing conditions (that is, wars) could be viewed as exogenous shocks. Governments had little choice but to respond by making more intense use of all its revenue sources. With respect to seigniorage, this meant imposing legal restrictions on the note-issuing industry, which tended to make it more monopolistic.

As the twentieth century comes to a close, technological innovation in the information sector has made competition an international phenomenon. Even if a national government is able to protect a domestic central bank from domestic competition, it may be unable to insulate the central bank from competition by money producers outside national boundaries. In this setting of worldwide competition, the opportunities for a national government to produce seigniorage are severely limited.

In this new world order, monetary policy is less important in that the monopoly central banking institutions that thrived in the nineteenth and twentieth centuries will have poor survival prospects in the twenty-first century. There will be no monetary policy, but simply monetary economics; an economics that has as its primary task the modeling of the competitive constraints within which money-producing firms must operate. Issues that in the past have defined the domain of monetary policy – central bank independence, the personality of the central bank's head, rules versus discretion – are irrelevant in the face of binding competitive constraints. If I am right, then the high tide of the public choice approach, indeed any approach, to monetary policy has passed. I am an optimist.

Notes

1. See Fratianni et al. (1997) and Weingast (1984) for a discussion of the political principal–agent framework.
2. See Toma and Toma (1992) for a comparative analysis of in-house agencies and independent firms with respect to the collection of taxes.
3. See D'Arista (1994, p. 2) and Toma (1997, ch. 5).
4. See Toma (1982) for a discussion of the evolution of the Fed's financing structure.
5. See Woolley (1984) for a general account of the political influences on the Federal Reserve.

456 *The Elgar companion to public choice*

6. See Munger and Roberts (1990) for a summary of the early literature and Chappell et al. (1993) for a specific application.
7. In particular, see Pierce (1978) and Weintraub (1978).
8. Skaggs and Wasserkrug (1983) explore the banking–Congress–Fed nexus in a more general context.
9. A decade earlier, Chant and Acheson (1972) and Acheson and Chant (1973) presented an informal bureaucratic theory of the Canadian central bank's choice of policy instruments. In a similar vein, Kane (1980) applied a bureaucratic theory to the choice of the Fed's policy instruments.
10. More recently, Cukierman's (1992) encyclopedic study of central banking contains numerous insights, which at least implicitly use a public choice methodology.
11. Note that once optimal seigniorage considerations are introduced, there no longer is the presumption that in-house monetary policy will be deflationary. See Goff and Toma (1993) for an application of the optimal seigniorage approach to a gold standard regime versus the Federal Reserve.
12. For example, North and Weingast (1989) discuss the debt function with respect to the founding of the Bank of England and Toma (1997) discusses the seigniorage function with respect to the founding of the Federal Reserve.

22 The politics of government growth

Roger D. Congleton

1 The scope of governance

Fundamentally, government is the organization that governs: that creates and enforces the laws within a particular geographic territory. The range of what may be governed within a particular territory is very broad, and extends well beyond the basic civil and criminal codes of conduct that first come to mind. Regulations limit the range of goods that can be produced and sold, the hours that can be worked, and the wages that can be paid. Tax laws determine the portion of earned income that employees are allowed to keep, and the portion of sales revenues and profits that merchants may retain. Beyond the laws that determine how economic resources may be used and what claims individuals may have on them are laws that *define* life and death, marriage and divorce, parental rights and obligations, and even the bounds of proper public and private intimacy. Perhaps even more potentially intrusive are rules that mandate particular types of public education or genetic screening. Such rules may, in principle, attempt to determine the *kinds* of human beings that reside within a government's jurisdiction in an even more fundamental way than efforts to regulate immigration and emigration do.

The potential scope of governmental rulemaking and rule enforcement extends even beyond the human species. Rulemaking includes efforts to regulate nature as well as humanity. Legislation may reroute streams, drain swamps, create forests, promote the interests of some species over others, attempt to control the composition of the air, or aim to regulate the average temperature of the earth as a whole. The welfare and relative populations of other species may be targeted directly in environmental laws and agricultural policies, or indirectly through land-use regulation and the sponsorship of programs of scientific research. Clearly, the potential scope of governance is enormous.

On the other hand, government's reach has almost everywhere exceeded its grasp: not everything that could be undertaken by the public sector has anywhere been undertaken in fact. Although it is clear that technological bounds have limited the size and scope of governance in the long term (Dudley 1991), the lack of a clear trend suggests that non-technological factors are also significant determinants of the public sector's boundaries. The evidence suggests that politics rather than technology determines the scope of governance at the margin. The scope of governance has varied as legislation has been adopted or repealed, as governments have risen and fallen, and as empires have expanded and collapsed. The technology of governance appears to have been essentially increasing monotonically for much of history as improved monitoring, organization, and information-processing technologies have been developed and increasingly capital-intensive methods of coercion have been applied.

2   Public choice and government growth

The political determinants of the ebb and flow of governance are complex. Political decisions are made by a diverse collection of individuals within the formal organizations of government. These decisions are bound by techno-logical feasibility – by the real and imagined resources within a government's reach – and by political feasibility – by the organizational, legal, and consti-tutional constraints faced by government decision makers. Although it may be said that the former are results of past natural resource endowments and productive human activities and the latter are results of past political deci-sions, it bears noting that political decision-making procedures and technological bounds are not entirely independent of one another in so far as current and past political decisions can affect resource endowments and political organizational structures. Changes in either the real possibilities or political incentives may, and have, led to changes in the scope of governance – to government growth or contraction.

Public choice scholars have studied the process of government policy making in order to isolate essential relationships that shape the complex multidimensional web of formal and informal personal relationships that characterize actual political decision-making processes. The models of col-lective choice that emerge from those analyses are necessarily simplifications of the real world confronted by actual political decision makers. They are models, after all. Yet Occam's razor potentially allows scholars to discover systematic patterns in political decision making and thereby to isolate the fundamental determinants of the scope of governance.

Public choice analyses have generally relied upon atemporal static models of political equilibria rather than truly dynamic models, although a time element can be introduced into the models after the fact. For example, observed political equilibria may be characterized as steady-state solutions to long-term government policy objectives which are changed only when sub-jected to unanticipated shocks of one kind or another. Such an interpretation is suggested by, for example, Barro's (1974) analysis of government debt. Alternatively, one may regard the static models as characterizing discrete elements of a series of temporary political equilibria that change fairly often (Mueller 1987). Here government growth emerges as relevant changes in the economic and political circumstances of decision makers occur through time.

A series of temporary equilibria may be regarded as fully rational solutions to intertemporal optimization problems whose solutions are intertemporally separable (implying that decision makers maximize instant by instant or year by year) or as myopic responses to changes in circumstances from year to year. This chapter relies upon a Mueller-type sequential equilibrium approach to explaining government growth.

All public choice analyses shed light on various aspects of government policy formation and, therefore, all contribute to our understanding of government growth. It bears noting that the politics of government growth is nearly synonymous with the term politics itself, in so far as *decisions to control the scope of governance are essentially what we mean by political decision making*. Consequently, the analysis of government growth undertaken in the present chapter will necessarily be less detailed and less complete than that of the volume's more narrowly focused chapters.

The approach taken here is to show how well the core models of public choice account for government growth. The analysis is organized into sections that focus on the main insights of four areas of research generally thought to be relevant for explaining changes in the scope of democratic governments. In the short and medium run, (i) elections, (ii) bureaucrats and (iii) interest groups are thought to largely determine policies. In the long term, (iv) fundamental political institutions, rights assignments, and culture are also considered to be important determinants of the growth of government in so far as they specify procedures for making political and economic decisions, impose limits on such procedures, or both. Empirical tests of the various models are included in order to illustrate their ability to explain recent changes in the scope of government in the United States.

3 The growth of government: a short overview

Broadly speaking, modern Western governments have been increasing in size and expanding in scope for the past two hundred years. Government budgets and tax receipts generally have grown substantially during this period. For example, census data indicate that federal spending in the United States increased in nominal terms from 5.08 million dollars in 1800 to 1.25 trillion dollars in 1990. A similar trend is evident in most of the developed world as both absolute and relative government expenditures have risen during the past two centuries. Moreover, the growth of government outlays has been accelerating. Tullock (1998) notes that a significant increase in the growth rates of several Western democracies occurred in the first half of the twentieth century. Prior to that time, peacetime government expenditures had grown at more or less the same rate as their respective economies.

The growth of governance has been substantial during the past two centuries but it has not been unremitting. On a year-to-year basis, government size measured in *absolute* terms has fallen on a number of occasions during the past two hundred years. For example, both government expenditures and intrusiveness tend to decline after major wars. Government expenditures also tend to decline with the collapse of national economies, and with significant changes in political regimes. Several such episodes of absolute governmental decline have occurred in the United States (Higgs 1987). More radical changes in the scope of governance have been associated with political regime changes within the former Soviet Union, Germany, Japan, and China during the past century. Measured relative to national output rather than in absolute terms, episodes of negative governmental growth have been even more common-place.

Figure 22.1 presents a short fiscal history of the United States covering the last three decades of the twentieth century using data from the *Statistical Abstract of the United States 1997* (US Department of Commerce 1998). Measured in absolute dollar terms, the growth of government has been continu-ous, although not steady throughout this period. Real (inflation-adjusted) outlays and tax collections increased essentially every year over the entire period. On

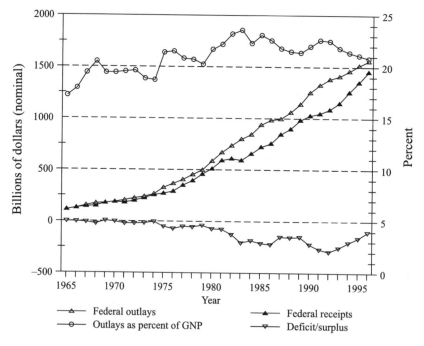

Source: Based on data from US Department of Commerce (1998).

Figure 22.1   US federal government fiscal growth

the other hand, measured relative to what might be considered to be the upper bound of that which might potentially be directly controlled (that is, gross national income), there have been several reductions in the (relative) size of government outlays. In fact, Figure 22.1 suggests that federal government outlays as a fraction of GNP have been declining for about a decade.

This recent pattern departs from the general trend of US federal government outlays, which have generally been increasing relative to national income throughout the twentieth century. Government accounted for about 4 percent of GNP at the beginning of the century, a figure which is only about a fifth of the current ratio for the federal government alone.[1] The recent pattern of decreasing relative levels of government control over the economy may be an important new fiscal development or simply an historical aberration.

It is worth emphasizing that fiscal measures of the size of government always understate the extent to which governments control economic and other resources because other less complete or less direct forms of control are neglected. Only a fraction of the resources controlled or affected by modern democratic governments are *directly* transferred to government and *directly* allocated by it during a given year. As the introduction makes clear, measuring the true scope of governance is not an easy task. Just as a proper measure of an individual's choice set would include many assets omitted from an accountant's balance sheet, the scope of governance extends well beyond what is attributed to government by GNP accounts. For example, both fiscal and regulatory policies may reallocate resources by mandating 'private' expenditures or redefining the use rights of property owners. Less complete control is also very commonly exercised as with building codes and occupational safety standards; preferential and punitive tariffs, taxes and land-use restrictions; and with policies regarding the relative intensity with which these many laws are enforced.

Although these other areas of governance are more difficult to quantify than direct government outlays are, it is generally agreed that the extent of off-budget governance has also grown significantly over this period. For example, the *Federal Register* has lengthened dramatically as the intrusiveness of federal regulation in the United States has increased manyfold.

Another possible proxy for the scope of governance is non-defense federal government employment. New regulations are implemented and enforced, at least in part, by federal employees. Administering tax and expenditure programs, and creating and enforcing regulations appear to be tasks that exhibit only modest economies of scale. As the scope of regulation and enforcement increases, the government consequently demands more inputs, and the federal labor force is necessarily expanded.[2]

Figure 22.2 displays recent trends in US federal government employment based on data reported in the *Statistical Abstract of the United States 1997*.

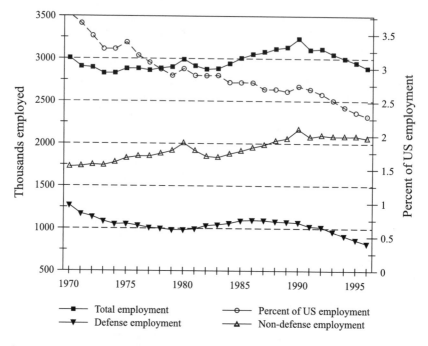

Source: Based on data from US Department of Commerce (1998).

Figure 22.2   US federal government employment

Total federal employment has been fairly stable during this period although
the composition of the federal workforce has changed significantly. Defense
employment has been falling for a decade or more, while non-defense
employment has been steadily rising for the past three decades. The latter
trend is of particular interest here. The expansion of the federal labor force
devoted to administering federal policies suggests that both the fiscal and
regulatory reach of the federal government have been increasing during this
period.

The similarities in the patterns of non-defense employment and federal
outlays during this period suggest that fiscal measures of the scope of government can serve as a reasonable proxy for the government's overall reach.
That is to say, to the extent that the resources directly and indirectly controlled by central governments are correlated with the public sector's revenues
and expenditures, those financial measures provide a summary statistic for a
more complete assessment of the scope of government, although the budget
numbers themselves should be regarded as lower-bound estimates. While
measures of the financial resources transferred from private to public coffers

only directly measure what is collected and spent by government, they seem to be highly correlated with the overall scope of governance.

4 Government growth and electoral equilibria

Within modern democracies, government growth evolves from a series of policy decisions involving many different persons, each with their own private interests and particular institutional constraints. Voters select representatives, who select policies, which are implemented by a professional bureaucracy. Institutions determine electoral incentives, the powers accorded representatives, and the bounds of bureaucratic authority. As demonstrated throughout this volume, each link in the chain from voters to final policies may affect government policy and thereby the size of government.

The first link in the democratic policy-making chain is the one where the demand and supply of government services is connected most directly to the desires of ordinary citizens. This is where the politics of government growth may be said to begin.

4.1 Elections and government growth

In the most parsimonious public choice models of elections, candidates compete for the votes of a well-informed electorate. Competition to secure public office leads candidates to make campaign promises or to adopt platforms which converge to essentially identical policy positions. Candidate positions converge to the median voter's ideal point in non-stochastic voting models (Black [1958] 1987; Downs 1957) or to the average voter's ideal point in stochastic voting models (Coughlin and Nitzan 1981; Coughlin 1992).[3] Increases in government's fiscal scope in electoral models of policy formation are therefore an indirect result of increased median- or average-voter demands for government services.

Voter demands for government services are affected by many of the same factors that affect demands for ordinary private consumer goods. The level of government services demanded increases if the relative price of government services falls through time, as would be the case if relevant factors of production in the private sector become increasingly scarce or if changes in technology favor public over private provision of services. Similarly, the demand for government services increases as personal income increases, leading consumers to demand more of all normal goods and services, including those produced by government. Voter preferences over goods and services (or ideology) may also change through time in a manner that increases demands for government services relative to non-governmental services. In a setting where votes are cast by a well-informed electorate and stable electoral equilibria exist, government growth is entirely the result of continually increasing voter demands for government services.

4.2   *Empirical support for the median-voter model*

An electoral model of government growth can be developed as follows. Suppose that voter *i* maximizes a utility function defined over his consumption of a private good, C_i, and a government service, G, with $U = u(C_i, G)$. Suppose further that voter *i*'s personal income, Y_i, is not affected by policy choices and so can be treated as an exogenous variable for the purposes of his policy preferences. Tax obligations, T_i, clearly rise with government service levels, that is, $T_i = t_i(G)$, so voter *i*'s after-tax income and private consumption, C_i, fall as G increases, that is, $C_i = Y_i - t_i(G)$. Substituting this budgetary relationship into the utility function yields $U = u(Y_i - t_i(G), G)$. Differentiating with respect to G and setting the result equal to zero characterizes the government service level, G^*, that maximizes voter *i*'s utility, for example,

$$U_C(-T_G) + U_G = 0 \text{ at } G^*, \text{ with } T_i^* = t_i(G^*) \text{ and } C_i = Y_i - t_i(G^*).$$

Each voter prefers the government service level that equates the marginal utility of government services with its opportunity cost measured in terms of lost utility from reduced private consumption. Another implication of this first-order condition is that voter *i*'s demand for government services can be represented as a function of his income,

$$G_i^* = g_i(Y_i).$$

The usual assumptions about utility functions and tax schedules imply that the demand for government services may *rise or fall* with personal income:

$$G_{iY_i}^* = -[U_{CC}(-T_G) + U_{GC}]/[U_{CC}T_G^2 - U_C T_{GG} - 2U_{GC}(T_G) + U_{GG}].$$

However, this ambiguity may be avoided if we assume that voter *i*'s utility function is separable, as often assumed in applied work (that is, $U_{GC} = 0$). In that case, voter *i*'s demand for government services unambiguously rises with his personal income, namely $G_{iY_i}^* > 0$.

If the spectrum of voter demands for government services (ideal policies) is assumed to be generated by differences in voter characteristics, such as income in the above model, 'the' median voter will be the voter with approximately median characteristics: median income, median age, and median marital status. The median-voter model implies that this median voter gets the government service level he desires, and government growth occurs when the voter desires a broader range of services than previously supplied by government.

Such very lean electoral models do fairly well at explaining the general time series of aggregate federal expenditure levels during relatively stable

Table 22.1   The median voter and government growth

Independent Variable	Dependent variable		
	Real federal outlays	Real federal outlays	Change in real federal outlays
Constant	−1112.386	−15 191.38	18.512
	(9.24)	(3.295)	(4.105)
Real median income	0.0363	0.0197	
(married, age 40–64)	(15.687)	(2.95)	
Age of median voter		105.626	
		(2.414)	
Education of median voter		71.960	
(years)		(2.476)	
Average sex of electorate		17 803.45	
		(3.22)	
Δ Real median income			0.000956
(married, age 40–64)			(0.269)
R-square	0.907	0.97	0.003
F-statistic	246.079	56.394	0.072
No. of observations	27	11	26

historical periods. The explanatory power of such models can be illustrated by regressing real median-voter household characteristics on total real government outlays. Table 22.1 reports results of such ordinary least squares estimates using data from 1970 to 1996 obtained from the *Statistical Abstract of the United States 1997.*[4]

The good fits of the estimates reported in the table's first two columns indicate that government expenditures and median family income are positively correlated. The *t*-statistics (shown in parentheses under the coefficient estimates) indicate that the estimated coefficients are sufficiently accurate to be distinguished from zero at conventional levels of statistical significance. The estimated Engel curve for government services reported in column 1 demonstrates that some 90 percent of the growth of aggregate real government outlays can be explained by changes in the median voter's real income during this time period.

The estimate reported in column 2 embodies a richer characterization of the median voter, which includes non-income characteristics such as age, education level, and 'average sex'. These election-based data are available only biennially; the number of observations is thus reduced by about one-half. For most of this period, the median voter has been a woman about 40 years of age with a high school education. There is a cycle in turnout that causes the median voter to be older in off-year elections than in presidential election years, and a similar electoral cycle that causes the average sex of voters to be 'less feminine' during presidential election years because relatively more men vote in those contests. The median voter's education level has recently increased, and he now has a year or so of college. Note that the augmented model explains more of the variation in real government outlays than the simpler model, which suggests that the median voter's assessment of public policy is influenced by more than real family income. The latter result is consistent with other electoral studies of particular federal programs (see, for example, Borcherding 1985 or Congleton and Shughart 1990).

Of course, the high and positive correlation found in the regressions between government outlays and median income need not have been found even within a median- or average-voter model. Governments might, for example, produce mainly income-inferior goods. Voters might demand only highly specific, narrowly defined government services, and government growth might cease at the point where tax receipts are more than sufficient to fund desired levels of those services, as might be true of an idealized 'night watchman' state. In such cases, the correlation between government spending and median income might become insignificant or even possibly negative once satiation levels for government services have been reached. Thus, besides suggesting that the median voter 'gets his way', the regression results suggest that government services are income-normal goods. That is to say, the results are consistent with the hypothesis that the scope of governance increases because the median voter demands more extensive government services as his income rises.

4.3   Can electoral equilibria be manipulated?

Even if one accepts the idea that the median or average voter determines government policies in a democracy – and there is much disagreement about this as evidenced throughout the present volume – there remains the question of whether voters are susceptible to influence by groups with policy agendas of one sort or another.[5] There are clearly many people and organizations that stand to gain from policies that differ from the median voter's ideal, but it is by no means obvious how this could be accomplished if voters are perfectly informed and stable electoral equilibria exist. Any candidate who breaks his promises to the median voter would simply be replaced in the next election by a more perfect agent.

However, in cases where voters are not perfectly informed about possible policies or the effects of alternative policies, changes in information can induce changes in policy preferences. New information may affect voter expectations about the consequences of alternative policies, the voter's own costs and benefits associated with those consequences, or alter the perceived range of services that might be provided by government. The demand for government programs would increase if voters are persuaded to expect greater benefits, lower costs, or become aware of new, valuable but previously unconsidered government services.

The predictable effects of information on voter policy preferences also allow the possibility of manipulating electoral outcomes by systematically affecting the relative price of information. Organized groups whose policy interests differ from the median voter's would like to induce voters to prefer policies which better advance the group's interest. To this end, information may be subsidized in order to persuade voters to prefer new policies, as with campaign advertisements, press releases, conferences, and other sponsored publications and forums (Congleton 1991). Alternatively, information may be made more costly, as with obfuscation and secrecy, in order to increase monitoring costs for voters and thereby increase the policy discretion of elected and non-elected government officials and employees.

The success of such information-manipulation strategies requires voters to have imperfect methods of filtering out the biases the strategies are intended to promote. Whether this is plausible or not depends on one's view of the information-processing capacities of voters, the opportunity cost of engaging in information processing, and the incentives for such efforts to be made. If voters invest in policy information only for the purposes of casting a vote, it seems unlikely that they would invest much time and energy in a careful analysis since they ordinarily face a choice between just two (fairly similar) policy alternatives. Survey evidence suggests that voters are often ignorant of many of the details of governance, and thus that they may be susceptible to some persuasive political messages. Moreover, recall that the median voter, as noted above, has only modest educational achievement. In any case, we certainly do see sustained efforts by both political candidates and policy advocates to influence voter opinions.

If such efforts are successful at the margin, it is possible that the median voter gets his preferred policy, but that his 'preferred policy' is a consequence of efforts to persuade relevant government decision makers by manipulating the relative price of policy-relevant information. In such cases, government growth at the margin would be at least partly a consequence of activities aimed at *creating* voter opinions, sowing confusion and ignorance, or both. How such non-electoral political forces may arise and influence government growth rates is the subject of the next two sections of this chapter.

5   Bureaucracy and the size of government

The implementation of public policy is a task that requires significant expertise, oversight and coordination. It is partly for this reason that modern governments are the largest organizations within the territories they govern. Public choice models of bureaucracy imply that these same government employees may be partly responsible for the size and scope of governance within those territories. Such a possibility is neglected in pure electoral models, which implicitly regard government agents as either faithful public servants of the pivotal voter or, equivalently, as so constrained by political institutions that only policies advancing the pivotal voter's interests can be adopted. However, it is quite possible that existing institutions allow representatives and the bureaucracy to act in a manner that is at least occasionally contrary to the median voter's interest.

5.1   The bureaucratic principal–agent problem

Public choice models of bureaucracy were among the many political precursors of what is now called principal–agent theory by economists, where a conflict between the interests of the principal (the 'public' or median voter) and its bureaucratic agents has long been taken as a stylized fact. These early models assumed that bureaucrats have a personal stake in the size of their agency's budget. Budgetary discretion, reinforced by the bureaucracy's informational advantages over its legislative sponsors, leads to greater levels of spending than is optimal from the median voter's point of view (see, for example, Niskanen 1971 or Breton and Wintrobe 1975).

The reasoning goes as follows. As an agency's budget increases, every public-spirited bureaucrat expects to be able to do a better job of advancing the agency's policy agendas and fulfilling its responsibilities. As an agency's budget increases, every bureaucrat must also realize that personal opportunities for advancement and perks tend to improve. Moreover, in so far as monitoring individual performance becomes more difficult as agencies expand in size, larger budgets tend to be associated with wider discretion. As discretion increases, the ability of bureaucrats to use bureau resources to satisfy their own preferences for policy, travel or leisure increases. In sum, bureaucrats have many reasons to prefer larger to smaller budgets, other things being equal, and larger budgets imply larger governments.

Of course, wanting a larger budget is one thing, and getting one is quite another as we all know with respect to our own private budgets. In order for bureaucracy to affect the growth of government services, there must be a method by which the bureaucracy can affect government policy. Clearly, mere hired hands would have a difficult time doing this (Weingast and Moran 1983). The original arguments, and many recent ones (for example, Shleifer and Vishny 1993; Hopenhayn and Lohmann 1996), assume that the same expertise that justifies much of the personnel of government agencies also implies that bureaucrats have an informational advantage over the elected legislature, the voting public, or both. This informational advantage allows the bureaucracy to negotiate for and secure larger budgets or to promote more stringent regulation than would have been chosen by a fully informed principal.

In such cases, the bureaucracy contributes to government growth by increasing the budgetary and regulatory scope of governance beyond that implied by median (pivotal) voter preferences. However, in so far as the scope of bureau discretion remains limited by voter monitoring, albeit fairly indirect monitoring, the median (pivotal) voter continues to control the budget at the margin. Thus, rather than increase government growth directly, bureaucratic discretion tends to amplify the pro-growth impulses of the electorate. That is to say, in models where bureaucrats have a private interest in larger budgets or more stringent regulation, as the median voter increases his demand for services, the increase tends to be magnified by the bureaucracy's pursuit of larger budgets.

5.2 Some evidence of the effect of bureaucracy on government size

Evidence of the effect of the bureaucracy on government growth can be developed by modifying the median-voter model estimated earlier. The lean median-voter model shown in Table 22.1 is augmented below with a new variable to capture the effect of bureaucratic efforts to secure greater budgets. Lagged non-defense federal employment is used as a proxy for bureaucratic influence on government growth. The literature on bureaucracy suggests that bureaucracy itself tends to cause government to grow, and this effect is borne out in the estimates reported in Table 22.2. The data, again, are from the *Statistical Abstract of the United States 1997*. Estimated in levels, government outlays tend to increase as median family income increases and as the bureaucracy expands in size.

Estimated in first differences, we find that changes in real outlays in a given year are larger than would otherwise have been the case if non-defense federal employment increased in the previous year.[6]

6 Interest groups

The same informational problems that allow bureaucracies to have an effect on government growth also empower other organized groups with policy agendas. There are many points in the process of determining policies within a democracy where individuals, firms, and associations can participate in or subsidize the informational strategies that policy makers utilize in order to influence policy and thereby the scope of governance. For example, interest groups may provide candidates for elective office with resources so that they can more effectively get their message(s) to voters. If candidates compete for funds as well as for votes, the policy preferences of campaign donors may be

Table 22.2   Bureaucracy and government growth

	Dependent variable	
	---	---
Independent variable	Real federal outlays	Change in real federal outlays
Constant	−1351.297	22.670
	(9.14)	(5.73)
Real median family income	0.026	−0.0124
	(4.99)	(3.12)
Non-defense federal employment (−1)	0.404	0.258
	(2.53)	(2.506)
R-square	0.913	0.316
F-statistic	116.068	5.072
No. of observations	25	25

expected to affect policy at the margin (Clark and Thomas 1995). Once elected, legislatures may reward their supporters by tailoring legislation to advance contributors' interests or by providing contributors with advance notice of relevant legislative proposals and prospects. Legislation may also strategically open or close the process of regulatory rulemaking to public scrutiny. These informal channels of influence allow contributors and lobbyists to have a wide variety of 'persuasive' effects on policy formation and thereby on the scope of governance.

For a variety of economic and political reasons, individuals and firms generally organize themselves into associations of one kind or another – special-interest groups – in order more effectively to make use of the various 'non-voting' methods of influencing public policy. Since Mancur Olson's (1965) early work on the logic of collective action, there has been a presumption that relatively small groups with relatively intense common interests are more likely to be organized and, therefore, to be more effective than groups which are large and have relatively diffuse interests. The former will have an easier time raising funds and securing other resources from their members with which to influence policy because incentives to free-ride are weaker and solutions more readily applicable. Within the political arena, Olson's analysis implies that producers, especially those in concentrated industries, are more effective at organizing and lobbying for favorable policies than are ordinary consumers who tend to be far more numerous and to have much smaller private stakes in public policy outcomes (see also Tullock 1959; Stigler 1971; Becker 1983).

The interests in public policy outcomes that motivate politically active organizations are often complex. Many, perhaps most, pressure groups are organized to promote the financial interests of their members. Others are organized to promote particular normative conceptions of the proper role of government in what might be called the 'good society'. Many times these amoral (profit) and moral (ideological) motivations are intermingled as economic and ideological interest groups join forces on particular issues (Yandle 1983), or as the staff members of such interest groups promote their own agendas at the margin.

The overall effect of interest groups on the growth of government depends on the interests of the groups that organize and on the effectiveness of their efforts to alter policy. If only groups favoring government growth organize and are effective at achieving their policy aims, then clearly government will become larger as a result. Moreover, if such groups become increasingly effective because of learning-by-doing, or are able to establish more or less permanent institutional changes (such as social security and other so-called entitlement programs) where government obligations expand automatically through time, those interest-group activities may affect government growth rates as well as levels. In other cases, the effect of interest groups on governmental size remains unclear, becoming a matter of the shifting balance of interest-group effort and effectiveness.

6.1   A rent-seeking model of interest-group politics

A simple contest model from the rent-seeking literature can be used to illustrate some relevant aspects of the interest-group model of policy formation. Modeled in the large, interest-group activity is a political struggle over the nation's income flow, Y_t. Suppose that some portion of national income remains 'off the table' as a consequence of constitutional restrictions on 'takings' and other constraints faced by the central government. If we denote this non-governmental domain as $(1 - \alpha)Y_t$, the balance of national income, αY_t, is to be allocated by government.

The interest-group literature argues that the distribution of that portion of national income controlled by the government is affected by the relative efforts (or influence) of interest groups. A well-organized interest group will invest the level of resources, R_{it}, in the political allocation game that maximizes its net receipts, N_{it}, from participating in that policy-making process. Every group's relative success falls as the efforts of the other groups, R_{ot}, participating in the policy-making process increase.

For purposes of illustration, we interpret the Tullock (1980a) lottery formulation as a 'sharing rule' which characterizes the manner in which interest-group efforts, R_{it}, yield private net payoffs, N_{it}, namely

$$N_{it} = [R_{it}/(R_{it} - R_{ot})]\alpha Y_t - R_{it}.$$

Differentiating with respect to R_{it} and solving allows the interest group's ideal investment in political influence to be characterized as

$$R_{it}^* = -R_{ot} + (R_{ot}\alpha Y_t)^{1/2}.$$

Other things being equal, the greater the prize (or pool of resources to be divided up, here αY_t), the more resources a typical contestant is willing to invest. Contrariwise, the more opposition that will be encountered, the less a particular group gains by participating (the smaller the share of total resources that are acquired), and the less the effort in the political conflict tends to be.

In a symmetric contest between N_t interest groups, this reaction function implies a Nash equilibrium investment level of

$$R_{it}^{**} = (N_t - 1)\alpha Y_t / N_t^2$$

by each politically active group. Equilibrium investments in political influence depend upon the number, $N_t - 1$, of other politically active groups and upon the value of the prize, αY_t, to be distributed.

In this very standard formulation of an interest-group-based political influence game, the political stakes are assumed to be exogenous to the contest. Consequently, the standard rent-seeking model provides little direct insight into the process of government growth where the 'prize', government transfers, changes through time. However, a minor extension of this model allows it to be used to characterize government growth. Suppose that rather than being given, the fraction of national income to be divided, α, is affected by the total expenditures in the contest at hand, $\alpha_{t+1} = a(N_t R_{it}^{**})$. Conflict within the domain of transfers may well expand that domain at the margin by affecting the balance of support for the rule of law generally or constitutional constraints, or by raising voters' monitoring costs. In this case, the same variables that affect political or rent-seeking expenditure levels and the distribution of government expenditures *also affect the scope of governance*.

6.2   *Some evidence of the effect of interest groups on the size of government*
Evidence of the empirical relevance of interest-group models of government growth can be developed by regressing the number of politically active interest groups and national income on real federal outlays. The number of political action committees (PACs) reporting to the Federal Election Commission is used to approximate the number of politically active interest groups. Real federal outlays are again used as the dependent variable. Data are from the

Table 22.3   *Interest groups and government growth*

Variable	Real federal outlays	Real federal outlays	Real federal outlays
Constant	512.753	−161.193	−411.004
	(17.408)	(1.43)	(3.211)
Number of PACs	0.099	0.0575	0.052
	(11.37)	(6.71)	(6.99)
Per-capita real GDP		0.0497	0.0360
		(6.045)	(4.30)
Non-defense employment (−1)			0.250
			(2.93)
R-square	0.866	0.954	0.969
F-statistic	129.344	197.9	187.428
No. of observations	22	22	22

FEC web page and the *Statistical Abstract of the United States 1997.*[7] The results are displayed in Table 22.3.

The data set used for the special-interest group model is slightly more limited than that used above for the median-voter and bureaucracy models because PAC counts first began being reported as a result of election finance regulations introduced in the early 1970s. Consequently, the proxy for the number of politically active interest groups is available only beginning in 1974. Nonetheless, it is striking how well the interest-group model can account for the broad pattern of government finances over the last quarter of a century. As the number of PACs has increased and as per-capita national income has increased so has the scope of governance. Augmented with a bureaucracy variable, the interest-group model explains about 97 percent of the variation in the real magnitude of government outlays during this period.

7   Institutions and government growth

The effects of voters, interest groups and the bureaucracy on public policy reflect particular institutional arrangements under which they operate. Formal institutions within a democracy grant eligible voters a direct say in choosing the legislature that writes governmental policies. Election laws specify who can run for office, who can vote, and the manner in which votes will be counted. Formal procedures within the legislature determine the extent and kinds of legislation that can be adopted by specifying an orderly process of collective decision making and review. Formal grants of authority or discretion to the bureaucracy are defined by law and further restricted by internal and external review. Opportunities for individuals and groups outside government to influence legislative and regulatory processes also are determined by rules governing campaign contributions, public hearings, and bribery. Rules define the electoral process, the process of making new laws by legislation, the authority of the bureaucracy, and opportunities for interest groups. All of these formal political institutions affect government policy choices and thereby the scope of governance.

7.1   Electoral cycles and government growth

Perhaps the most fundamental procedural institution of a democracy is the election cycle. It may be a bit surprising that even this most essential institution of democracy can have several effects on public policy formation. First, prior to an election, incumbents seeking re-election have incentives to remind voters of their meritorious service. Incumbents may seek voter approval by sending out glowing accounts of their accomplishments, by promising to continue superior job performance, or by announcing new programs or tax cuts in so far as voters (and others) monitor their representatives more intensively during election years than during non-election years (Rogoff 1990). In this manner, the electoral cycle may promote government growth through the process by which incumbents campaign for re-election. Second, pre-election uncertainties may affect the durability of public policy commitments legislated by incumbents. For example, candidates and parties that fear losing office may attempt to 'lock-in' programs in areas of particular interest (Glazer 1989). To the extent that 'lock-ins' introduce new programs or expand existing programs, they provide another mechanism by which the electoral cycle may affect governmental growth rates.[8]

In addition to *procedural* institutions that define the process by which policy decisions are made, other *constraining* institutions define the permissible domain of political choice. In most cases, restrictions on the domain of public policy making tend to reduce government growth by ruling out areas of policy expansion. For example, the US Bill of Rights places a number of areas of potential government intervention out of bounds. In other cases, the creation or modification of constraining institutions can be a device for implementing durable programs sought by special-interest groups or temporary majority coalitions which may induce government growth (for example, Landes and Posner 1975).[9]

In the latter case, legislatures and bureaus may attempt to institutionalize programs or weaken existing institutional constraints to promote the long-term interests of politically active groups. In so far as they succeed, the basic outlines of future policy decisions are limited by the initial program design. For example, the obligations assumed by the US government for the elderly and for global security have fundamentally been unchanged for decades and have had very significant effects on government growth for much of the past half-century.[10] Alternatively, it is also occasionally possible to amend or weaken previous institutional constraints in a manner that promotes government expansion. For example, the sixteenth Amendment to the US Constitution was adopted in 1913. That amendment greatly increased the scope of federal governance by replacing one long-term fiscal constraint with a less restrictive one that allowed an income tax to be levied to finance federal programs.

In either case, significant government growth can be generated by policy commitments made long ago and only occasionally modified. A good deal of the acceleration in the growth rate of government budgets observed by Tullock may be the result of a handful of quasi-constitutional policy decisions that expanded tax bases and made long-term commitments to provide government services in policy areas like social and global security which have proven to be engines of public-sector expansion.

7.2   Evidence of the impact of electoral cycles on the size of government

Although a wide range of institutions may affect government growth, the empirical analysis focuses on the effects of two American electoral institutions: the electoral cycle and (very) 'lame-duck' congresses. Electoral cycles have recurrent effects on routine government policy making which allows them to be used to estimate the effect that institutions have on government growth. The ruling party of a (very) lame-duck congress, or a lame-duck congressional median voter, knows that policy will be determined by a different set of decision makers in the next congress. Consequently, the members of such congresses may be expected to behave differently compared with those who expect to retain policy-making authority in the next congress. For example, a lame-duck congress may attempt to 'lock-in' programs that would otherwise be reduced by the next congress (Glazer 1989), or to 'lock-out' programs which might adversely affect them in the future (Besley and Coate 1998). Data on the lame-duck congresses and the election cycle are, again, taken from the *Statistical Abstract of the United States 1997*. Estimates for institution-augmented 'combined models' are reported in Table 22.4.

Column 1 reports a combined interest group, electoral model of government outlays as a reference point. (It bears noting that the combined model does a better job of explaining the growth in real federal outlays than either pure model did by itself.) Column 2 reports similar estimates augmented with binary, 0–1, variables for the years in which the majority party of the senate and house changed. Column 3 reports estimates of a first-difference version of the model estimated in column 2 augmented with an election cycle variable.

Again the results are broadly consistent with the comparative statics interpretation of mainstream public choice models. A lame-duck house generates

Table 22.4   Determinants of government growth

	Real federal outlays	Real federal outlays	Change in real federal outlays
Constant	−520.020	−445.387	19.485
	(2.80)	(2.601)	(3.02)
Number of PACs	0.053	0.0573	0.592
	(5.17)	(6.16)	(2.55)
Real median income	0.011	0.0091	−0.0038
(married, age 40–64)	(2.34)	(2.136)	(1.12)
Non-defense employment (−1)	0.302	0.312	0.1067
	(2.75)	(3.15)	(1.24)
Lame-duck house		86.697	50.939
		(2.37)	(1.92)
Lame-duck senate		−47.530	−23.844
		(2.17)	(1.71)
House election year			−18.582
			(1.83)
R-square	0.952	0.966	0.44
F-statistic	118.43	91.4	1.73
No. of observations	22	22	22

increased government expenditures in the following year (lock in), and a lame-duck senate reduces government expenditures in the following year (lock out) – other things being equal – for the period studied. Overall, the estimates indicate that institutional considerations, here the electoral cycle, as well as day-to-day political influences, affect both the magnitude of government outlays and the extent to which they change from year to year.

8   Conclusion
Political policy making is a complex process involving a very large number of individuals each with their own very diverse interests and constraints. That such a process can be characterized with a few relatively simple models must strike those engaged actively in politics as nearly absurd. Yet the fundamental relationships identified by public choice scholars not only make a tangled process understandable in terms of individual incentives to be elected, to administer policy and to lobby for preferential treatment, but, as the empirical evidence provided in this chapter demonstrates, do a good job of predicting the broad outlines of continually changing government programs. It is sur-

prising how well these parsimonious but sophisticated models of political processes perform.

The estimates reported in this chapter are not intended to be – and should not be – interpreted as thorough empirical studies, but are included to provide the reader with some idea of the predictive power and limits of the core models of public choice at explaining short-term variations in the scope of governance. Nonetheless, the estimates demonstrate that the core models of public choice can do a good job of accounting for government growth. Both the pure electoral model and the pure interest-group model of political decision making explained a substantial portion of the growth of government outlays. In addition, a model that combines aspects of both interest-group and electoral models has been shown to explain satsifactorily the growth of real government outlays within the period examined. (This chapter has not attempted to differentiate empirically between the alternative public choice explanations of the policies of democratic governments. Which perspective is correct is left to the reader's intuition and to future research.)

That political models account so well for the growth of government does not imply that other non-political factors are irrelevant. Just as the long-term growth of private markets reflects innovations in products and production technologies, improved understanding of consumer demands, and the evolution of consumer preferences, such long-term phenomena may be expected to affect the opportunities and demands for governance by all parties concerned. Many of these factors are indirect determinants of interest-group and electorate demands in the models developed in this chapter. In addition to such market-like phenomena, the long-term demand for governance is also affected by political innovation – by new insights affecting the organization of elections, political parties, interest groups, the bureaucracy, and constitutions.

Nonetheless, with these caveats acknowledged, it remains clear that the recent path of government expenditures is explainable in the political and economic comparative statics terms used by the core public choice models of public policy formation.

Notes

1. Historical data prior to 1930 are all taken from US Department of Commerce (1975).
2. Baumol (1967) suggests that the production of government services is less amenable to innovation than private-sector production. Consequently, government *expenditures* may increase relative to private expenditures if the demand for public services is relatively inelastic or if the price of government services increases relative to private services. In this case, government outlays would not necessarily reflect government's scope as posited here, but rather simply reflect increases in the cost of a more or less fixed bundle of government services produced by means that do not gain in productivity as rapidly as production in the private sector. (The employment numbers discussed below nevertheless suggest that the supply of government services is growing.)
3. In their recent synthesis of many strands of electoral theory, Besley and Coate (1997) characterize two-candidate equilibria where the electoral outcome is stochastic (each

candidate has a 50/50 chance of winning), but the expected electoral outcome is the median-voter outcome.

4. Data on the median voter's age, education, and sex are computed (interpolated) from voter turnout tables which are available only for election years. The median voter's income is assumed to be the family income of a voter of median age and marital status.

5. Although the correlation between median income and government outlays is consistent with the predictions of electoral models, and suggests that voter demands for new or expanded services account for the general outline of government policy, other theories of governance are also consistent with this result. For example, such a correlation is also consistent with models of government based on the existence of significant political agency problems (Romer and Rosenthal 1978a) or, at a somewhat different extreme, models of democratic decision making where voter demands simply constrain what manipulative agents and interest groups may achieve.

6. 'First differences' estimation use changes in, rather than levels of, the regression's dependent and independent variables.

7. Data for the number of PACs are taken from the Federal Election Commission's PAC count on the worldwide web at http://www.fec.gov/press/pacchart.htm. Data for federal outlays and gross national product are taken from the *Statistical Abstract of the United States 1997*.

8. Elections themselves generate information about future public policies. Estimates of the next several years of government policies have a higher variance prior to an election than after an election when it is known who will be making policy decisions. Alesina et al. (1993) argue that this electoral information allows for the possibility of electoral business cycles in Western democracies.

9. Also see Chapters 8 and 13 of this volume.

10. The difficulty of providing a given level of global security has recently declined with the collapse of the Soviet Empire. This allowed geopolitical security commitments to be implemented with fewer resources. Consequently, although security commitments have continued, defense expenditures ceased being an engine of government growth around 1990.

23 Is trust in government compatible with trustworthy government?

Dwight R. Lee and Jeff R. Clark*

1 Introduction

Public trust in government has been declining since the 1960s, and concern over this decline has been increasing. Data from University of Michigan opinion polls, which began in 1958, show trust in government peaking around 1964, when about 75 percent of the respondents answered 'always' or 'most of the time' to the question, 'How much of the time do you think you can trust the government in Washington to do what is right – just about always, most of the time, or only some of the time?'. Trust has declined significantly since then (although not monotonically). Only about 25 percent of the respondents answered 'always' or 'most of the time' in 1994.[1] Numerous organizations and scholars see this decline in public trust as a threat to the proper functioning of our representative democracy. A brief search of the Internet turns up 20 to 30 websites devoted to the issue.[2] Major studies addressing the problem have been conducted recently by the John F. Kennedy School of Government, the University of Virginia, and the Pew Research Center for the People and the Press.[3]

Pundits located at all points on the ideological spectrum worry that the decline in trust can undermine government's ability to perform essential tasks. Joseph Nye (1997, p. 4), Dean of Harvard's Kennedy School of Government, who leans at least moderately to the left, argues that 'If people believe that government is incompetent and cannot be trusted, they are less likely to provide [it with critical] resources. Without [these] resources, government can't perform well'. Conservatives William Bennett and John DiIulio, Jr have likewise cautioned against the public's 'delegitimating the idea of government'.[4] Even leading scholars in the public choice tradition, who favor only a limited role for government, have worried about declining trust in it. For example, Geoffrey Brennan and James Buchanan (1988) express concern that the public choice premise that government action is motivated primarily by private interest may undermine public trust in government. They ask, 'Is public choice immoral?', and answer in the following terms:

> Even if the explanatory power of public choice models of politics is acknowledged ... the moral spillovers of such models on the behavior of political actors may be deemed to be so important as to negate any purely 'scientific' advance

479

made in our understanding of how politics actually works. The maintenance of the standards of public life, it could be argued, may require a heroic vision of the 'statesman' or 'public servant', because only by holding such a vision can the possibility of public-interested behavior on the part of political agents be increased. (p. 184)

The argument that government performance is positively influenced by public confidence is plausible and can be traced back to the nation's beginnings. For example, Benjamin Franklin worried that 'Much of the Strength and Efficiency of any Government, in procuring & securing Happiness to the People, depends on ... the general Opinion of the Goodness of that Government'.[5] But an equally plausible, though usually overlooked, point of view is that confidence in government is something that government has to earn. The optimal amount of trust in government depends on how well government performs. A well-functioning democratic government deserves more trust than an inefficient, despotic one. That we can increase public trust in government by improving its performance is so obvious that it is amazing that that proposition receives so little attention compared to the view that we can improve government's performance by increasing the citizenry's confidence in it. One explanation for the emphasis on trust as prior to performance follows from public choice considerations. Narrowly focused interest groups can secure private gains at public expense more easily when there is a high level of trust in government. The greater is the trust in government, the greater is the political power organized interests can capture and use to expand and divert government into activities that harm the public by undermining economic efficiency.

So while the case is strong for a healthy skepticism about government, well-organized interests decry that skepticism, arguing for more trust in government in the name of achieving as much good as possible through the political process. Despite the special-interest pressure for what we see as too much trust in government, we do not deny that it is also possible to have too little trust in government. Any reasonable discussion of the appropriate level of trust in government must recognize the tension between improvements in government performance that can result, up to some point, from more trust in government and the greater discretion additional trust gives government to expand beyond efficiency limits.

The precise nature of the tradeoffs between public trust and governmental performance depends upon the particular political institutions in place, with constitutionally limited democracy surely providing the greatest scope for beneficial trust in government. But one attribute of voting severely limits the benefits of trust in such a government. Interestingly, that attribute is highlighted by Brennan and Buchanan (1984) in a work that implies that their later concern that public choice might undermine trust in government (Brennan and Buchanan 1988) is surely overstated, if not completely misplaced. Brennan and Buchanan (1984) begin with a stylized fact often emphasized in public choice analyses, namely that an individual's vote is highly unlikely to be decisive. They then examine an implication of this observation that has not been widely recognized even by public choice scholars. They argue that since an individual's vote is almost sure to have no influence on the outcome of an election, it costs the individual voter effectively nothing to make electoral choices for 'expressive' rather than 'instrumental' reasons. The voter who receives satisfaction from expressing support for a particular political proposal – helping the poor, for example – will not be deterred from doing so even though the high cost of the proposal, if passed, would have prevented him from voting for it if his vote were decisive. An important, but overlooked implication of 'expressive voting' is that the less decisive is an individual's vote, the more quickly trust in government will translate into voter support for a host of government activities that will be subverted by special-interest politics.

In the next section, we shall consider expressive voting in detail and show how, typically with the aid of politicians and special interests, this motive for voting puts voters in a prisoner's dilemma.[6] The greater is the trust in government, the more easily political interests can take advantage of this dilemma. In Section 3, we examine the difference between the political decisiveness of voters and organized interest groups to explain in more detail how trust in government is exploited and subverted by the latter. In Section 4, we shall consider some implications of our discussion. In particular we shall consider circumstances that call for more or less trust in government, and the possibility of an interaction between expressive voting, trust in government, and government performance leading to a long-run cycle between too much and too little trust. Concluding comments are offered in a final section.

2   Inexpensive expression

The tenuous connection between a voter's choice at the polls and the outcome of the election has been recognized by economists at least since the 1950s and the work of Anthony Downs (1957, chs 11–14). Downs elaborated on this connection to explain two widely observed features of voting behavior: widespread ignorance of the issues and candidates on the ballot, and relatively low levels of voter turnout. Until Downs, this voter behavior was subject to a lot of measuring and moralizing, but not very much explanation. Downs explained voter ignorance and apathy as rational behavior in response to the fact that no individual's vote is likely to determine an election's outcome. Voters quite rationally devote little time to becoming informed on political issues and realize little private advantage from voting at all, at least in terms of affecting the probability that their preferences will prevail. By contrast, there is a private payoff to becoming informed on, and actively involved in, decisions that one has decisive control over, even if they are far less important to one's welfare than the political decisions on the ballot. For example, decisions on Middle Eastern foreign policy are much more important to the price of gasoline than the filling station one chooses to patronize. But it is more sensible to spend time finding out which local station is selling gas a nickel a gallon cheaper than to spend time becoming informed on Middle Eastern foreign policy. Information can be used to 'vote' decisively in the former case, but not in the latter.

While 'rational ignorance' and 'rational apathy' provide useful insights into much observed political behavior, in one important sense they explain too much. In particular, rational apathy does such a good job of explaining low voter turnout that we are left wondering why turnout is not even lower. Why does voter participation ever exceed some extremely low level beyond which the decisiveness of an individual's vote becomes vanishingly small? We are aware of only one explanation for observed voter participation rates consistent with voter indecisiveness, and that is what has become known as 'expressive voting'.[7] People gain satisfaction from going to the polls and expressing themselves in favor of candidates and issues they deem deserving, and in opposition to those they deem not. Indeed, the very lack of decisiveness increases the net private benefit realized from expressive voting because it lowers the cost of political expression. Unfortunately, expressive voting is based on a disconnect between the choices and the consequences that often put voters in a prisoner's dilemma: the choices that are individually rational are collectively irrational. As we shall explain later, politically influential groups can capture private advantages by increasing the number of issues which put voters in this prisoner's dilemma, and by exacerbating this dilemma with pronouncements and promises that increase public trust in government. But first we consider expressive voting in more detail.

In situations typically examined by economists, when an individual chooses one option there is a clear opportunity cost in the sacrifice of another option. This opportunity cost is greatly reduced, if not eliminated, when one is voting. Because of the low probability that an individual's vote will decide the outcome of an election, when faced with a choice at the polls between options A and B, the voter is unlikely to sacrifice the value of B *because* he voted for A. This divergence between choice and cost can produce election outcomes significantly at variance with those voters would choose if their votes were decisive when, as is often the case, there is a difference between the option voters feel they should favor and the one that actually promotes their private advantage.[8]

For example, consider an individual who feels that protecting the environment is the right thing to do. Assume that he is considering a vote on a government proposal to reduce pollution,[9] which, if passed, will increase his taxes by $1100 while providing him with $100 worth of pollution reduction, for a net cost of $1000. We assume that he would decline to make a private contribution of $1100 to support the proposal, even though he knew that the contribution (whether or not matched by others) would do as much to reduce pollution as would the $1100 increase in his taxes. Will he vote against the proposal? Not necessarily. Voting for the proposal is far less costly than making a private contribution because the vote is almost guaranteed not to be decisive, while the decision to contribute privately is completely decisive. If, for example, the probability is 1/10 000 that his vote will break what would otherwise be a tie (an unreasonably high probability in most state or national elections), the expected net cost of voting for the proposal is only 10 cents. So if the voter receives more than a dime's worth of satisfaction from expressing support at the polls for protecting the environment, then a 'yes' vote is a bargain. In general, the less decisive his individual vote (the less electoral choice is connected to electoral consequence), the more likely a voter is to vote for a policy for expressive rather than instrumental reasons.

The prisoner's dilemma characteristics of this example can be illustrated with a standard two-dimensional payoff matrix. To have enough information to complete the matrix, we assume that the voter in the above example realizes $1.00 worth of expressive benefit if he votes for the environmental proposal, and suffers $1.00 worth of expressive cost if he votes against it. Ignoring for the moment the possibility of a decisive vote (that is, that all other voters are evenly divided) we have the traditional prisoner's dilemma represented in Table 23.1.

Table 23.1   Payoffs in an electoral prisoner's dilemma game

	All other voters	
Voter's strategies	Majority for P	Majority against P
Vote for P	−$999	$1
Vote against P	−$1001	−$1

In the table's second column, the majority supports the environmental proposal, and so the proposal will pass and our voter will suffer a $1000 loss from the proposal regardless of how he votes. But if he votes for the proposal, he will offset the $1000 loss by the $1 in expressive satisfaction, and reduce his loss to $999. A vote against the proposal will add another $1 loss from the dissatisfaction of expressing himself against what he considers to be a noble proposal, and his total loss will be $1001. Obviously, his largest payoff comes from voting for the proposal. If, on the other hand, a majority votes against the proposal, our voter will lose nothing from the proposal itself no matter how he votes. But, as before, a vote for the proposal provides him with $1 in expressive satisfaction, while a vote against costs him $1 in expressive dissatisfaction. So regardless of how everyone else will vote, as long as he believes that his vote will not affect the outcome, he will vote for the proposal.

If a majority of the voters receives enough expressive satisfaction from voting for the proposal, and it does not take much, the proposal will pass and everyone (assuming that they, like our voter, are harmed by the proposal) is made worse off. Because of the prisoner's dilemma they were placed in by the vote, their individually rational choices result in a collectively irrational outcome – the approved proposal imposes costs far in excess of its benefits. In the highly unlikely case that the voter knows his choice is decisive (without his vote, the election would be a tie), he will clearly vote against the proposal since the $1 expressive loss is far less than the instrumental loss of $1000 ($999 when the expressive satisfaction is included) from voting for it. In this case, there is a high cost to indulging expressive urges. But in the typical case, where voters realize that the probability that their vote will be decisive is close to zero, the private cost of expression is extremely low. Unfortunately, the social cost of expressive voting can be extremely high.

As indicated earlier, expressive voting is a factor in electoral choice only when there is a difference between what is in voters' private interests and what they feel good supporting expressively. Plenty of such differences exist. For example, most people under the age of 45 are affected adversely by the social security program, yet, at least until recently, even young voters supported the program electorally (and much of this support continues). The main reason is surely that most people feel that supporting Social Security is the right thing to do. Similar arguments can be made for welfare programs, agricultural price support programs, minimum wage legislation, mandated benefits for workers, protecting public schools against competition, import restrictions, and many others. Most people are harmed by such government policies, but large numbers of voters have been led to believe that these programs promote noble social objectives and they feel virtuous expressing support for them. And the cheapest way of expressing this support, with the possible exception of casual conversation, is in the voting booth.

The satisfaction people realize from expressing support for policies that reduce their welfare is not exogenous to the political process. Politicians and organized interest groups have strong incentives to persuade voters to support public policies that benefit the organized interests at the expense of the general voter. Hence, all attempts to secure private advantage through political influence are masqueraded behind the rhetoric of public advantage. This public-interest rhetoric does not necessarily attempt to convince voters that the recommended policy will be good for them, only that it will be good for the country. Public choice economists often argue that political interest groups take advantage of rational ignorance to fool voters into believing that special-interest legislation improves their welfare. Certainly this happens. Lobbyists for import protection for their industry clothe their case in arguments suggesting that foreign imports threaten all American jobs. Those pushing for agricultural price supports try to convince people that without these supports, farmers will be driven into bankruptcy, and food prices will increase. But much special-interest lobbying attempts to win over those who are clearly harmed, at least to some degree, by the policy being advocated. We are encouraged to support welfare programs that will cost most of us money because we should help the poor, or minimum wage legislation that will increase some prices we pay because all workers deserve a living wage. Such lobbying is explained, at least in part, by the calculus of expressive voting. Even if such appeals to voters' senses of duty result in their realizing just a little satisfaction from supporting a policy, voters are put in a prisoner's dilemma that dramatically increases electoral support for it.

We acknowledge that many policies which voters feel good about supporting, even though they work against their own private interests, are not ones upon which they vote directly. There are three responses to this criticism. First, a large and growing number of referenda on issues ranging from school choice to welfare eligibility for illegal aliens provide voters with many opportunities for expressive voting. Second, in a representative democracy a vote for a political candidate is a reasonable proxy for voting directly on issues. In fact, as reported by Kau and Rubin (1993), fairly close ideological agreement with constituents is a necessary condition for electoral success. Political markets do a good job controlling ideological shirking by legislators, which is strongly and quickly punished. Third, while political representatives may respond to public concerns, how those concerns are actually addressed depends far more on the influence of organized interests than on voter preferences. We elaborate on this point later in our discussion.

For our purpose, it is important to recognize that the greater is public trust in government, the more satisfaction voters will realize from expressive voting and the more vulnerable they will be to the threat of being led into an expressive-voting prisoner's dilemma by the public-interest rhetoric of pressure-group politics. People might be convinced that the poor should be helped, that American jobs should be saved, or that the environment should be protected. But if they have little confidence in government's ability to accomplish these worthy objectives, they are less likely to achieve any expressive satisfaction from voting for government attempts to do so. So those whose interests are tied to expanding government programs wish to promote public trust in government whether or not that trust is warranted. Indeed, their motivation to promote such trust is surely greater the less that trust is warranted, since their ability to benefit politically at public expense is inversely related to the trustworthiness of government in promoting the public interest.

Unfortunately, people often trust government independently of how trustworthy government is. Since most people quite accurately feel rather powerless to change government policies, they take some comfort in believing that those policies are accomplishing the good things their proponents claim they are. Where's the advantage for most taxpayers in finding out that the tax dollars they are paying supposedly to help the poor are mostly going to the non-poor, or that they are paying higher prices for products because import restrictions are saving less-efficient American jobs by destroying more-efficient American jobs? Such knowledge would simply create aggravation over policies that cannot be changed. Of course, if enough people took the trouble to become informed, and aggravated, the policies could be changed. But the prisoner's dilemma here is obvious. Relatedly, trusting government allows people to experience the low-cost sense of virtue that comes from expressive voting. People, convinced of the virtue of their support for minimum wages, for example, simply do not want to be told that the minimum wage fails to accomplish the good they believe it does. They could be better off if everyone sacrificed their feel-good virtue in favor of adopting a more informed perspective on government policy, but this just raises another prisoner's dilemma. Questioning trust in government could move people out of the prisoner's dilemma of expressive voting, but doing so would require overcoming other prisoner's dilemmas.

3   Subverting the public trust

One can agree with our discussion of expressive voting as a prisoner's dilemma aggravated by trust in government, but argue that more trust in government is good precisely because it does help put voters in a prisoner's dilemma. It is well known that the provision of public goods such as environmental quality or poverty reduction is plagued with a prisoner's dilemma of its own when left to the private sector.[10] And, the argument continues, government realizes an important advantage in providing public goods when the prisoner's dilemma of expressive voting helps overcome voters' reluctance to contribute to the financing of public goods arising from the prisoner's dilemma of public goods themselves. To be sure, expressive voting results in people voting for more government spending than they would if their votes were decisive, but as a result they receive public goods they would otherwise do without. And these public goods can easily be worth more than they cost, despite the biased example above of the environmental proposal that cost the voter $1100 but provided him with $100 in benefits. And so, if more trust in government encourages expressive voting, all the better.

This argument cannot be dismissed out of hand. Expressive voting can conceivably close the gap between the demands voters communicate for public goods and the socially optimal quantities of those goods. But serious problems remain even so. First, truthful revelation of demands for public goods does not ensure their efficient provision, or even their provision at all. Voting empowers government, but not necessarily to do what voters want. Voters may point government toward general objectives, but the power granted to achieve those objectives is invariably influenced by interest groups that help work out the details of what is done. Also, these interest groups influence the agendas that get voted on, agendas which commonly have nothing to do with providing genuine public goods. And, as indicated in the last section, the more trust the public places in government, the more power organized interest groups have compared to voters in general.

Consider that once voters have indicated majority support for a government program – relief for the needy, for example – they have taken only the first step toward that goal. Taking the necessary next steps requires designing an effective program and then implementing it properly so that it actually performs as intended. Public input, in the form of informed citizens monitoring their political agents, is crucial to ensuring that these steps are taken. But while voting for helping the poor costs an individual almost nothing, this is not true of becoming informed on the problems inherent in any attempt to help the poor, monitoring politicians and bureaucrats to see if they are avoiding these problems, and then attempting to correct them when they arise. Engaging in these activities is personally quite costly. Not surprisingly, once a person walks out of the voting booth feeling virtuous for voting to help the poor, he will spend more time watching TV commercials than working to improve the chances that his 'compassionate' vote translates into real help for the poor.

We do not mean to imply that there will be little interest in the design and implementation of government poverty programs. Numerous groups stand to gain or lose, depending on how those programs work. Obviously the poor have an interest, but so do farm groups (which benefit from food stamps); physicians and pharmaceutical companies (which benefit from Medicaid); the construction industry (which benefits from public housing); the self-proclaimed advocates of the poor; and the employees of the agencies that administer these programs. Except for the poor themselves, members of all of these groups can capture private benefits from policies that do less than is possible to help the poor for the money spent. And again, except for the poor, all of these groups can exert considerable political influence because they are well organized professionally, expert on the relevant programs, and vitally concerned with those programs.

Of course, members of these special-interest groups are no less concerned with behaving virtuously and doing the right thing by the poor than is the typical voter. So can we expect them, like the voters, to largely ignore their private interests and exert their influence on behalf of the needy? No. Not because they are less virtuous than voters, but because exercising that virtue costs them much more since their influence makes their 'votes' far more decisive. If public housing contractors knew that their support for housing vouchers which the poor could use to rent private apartments would not reduce the probability of massive government funding for public housing construction, it would cost them nothing, in terms of the political outcome, to provide that support. But since they can affect the outcome of housing policy, supporting housing vouchers requires that they sacrifice a very valuable alternative. As is true for all other goods, the demand curve for behaving virtuously is downward sloping. Virtue costs little in the voting booth, but it is expensive in the corridors of political influence. Public-interest considerations can control voter choices, but private interest is the dominant concern of special-interest groups.

So voters are seldom instrumental in achieving the noble objectives they vote for. They are in fact duped by the rhetoric of public concern and civic virtue into granting power to government that will be captured and corrupted by politically powerful private interests. This is true even when expressive voting communicates a public desire for something close to the efficient quantity of a genuine public good. It is even more true when, as is commonly the case, the temptations of expressive voting lead to public support for government actions that, despite the rhetoric, have nothing to do with public goods. The greater the public trust in the social good that government can do, the more easily that trust is subverted by the organized few into socially destructive policies.

4   Some additional implications

We have acknowledged that some minimum level of public trust may be necessary for government to function properly. But we have emphasized the negative influences of trust resulting from the indecisiveness of individual votes and the corresponding lack of any meaningful sense of voter responsibility for the consequences of electoral choices. We now consider some additional implications of expressive voting for the appropriate level of trust in government. An immediate implication of our discussion is that the more decisively the general citizen can influence political decisions, the more trust there can be in government before the benefit from that trust is offset by special-interest influence. This suggests that citizens can safely trust governments the more local they are, and there is evidence that they do. According to a recent survey of American opinion,

While just one-third of all Americans have 'a great deal' or 'quite a lot' of 'confidence in the federal government', only a slightly greater number (39 percent) has the same level of confidence in state government. Yet as one moves to the local community, the sentiment of disaffection begins to change appreciably. ... Fifty-seven percent of those surveyed say that they are at least content, if not pleased with their local government. (Hunter and Bowman 1996, p. 21)

According to a 1998 study by the Pew Research Center for the People and the Press, in 1997 every category (sex, race, age, education, and party affiliation) of respondents trusted (distrusted) the federal government less (more) than their state government to handle problems (Pew Research Center 1998, pp. 5–6). The message should be clear to those who want to restore trust in government: they should advocate more devolution of responsibilities from the federal level to the state and, better yet, local levels.

Voter decisiveness varies not only between levels of government, but also between different electoral decisions at each level. The probability of a decisive vote can vary significantly for a given number of voters, depending on how evenly the electorate is split.[11] Since trust in government can vary over issues, our model suggests that people should have less trust in government on issues for which there is large majority support than on those over which the public is evenly divided. Of course, overwhelming support for an issue may reflect the fact that the government can, with good reason, be trusted to handle it competently. But surely, people often trust government to perform particular tasks because of the expressive considerations discussed above. They believe some things are important to do, and they can feel better about themselves by first trusting in, and then voting for, government to do them. Consistent with this view are recent survey data showing that even when people have little trust in the general performance of government, they seem to trust government's ability to perform specific and emotionally appealing tasks. For example, the Pew Research Center study just cited found that 72 percent of those surveyed favored government's ensuring that no one goes without food, clothing, or shelter, and 74 percent thought it was government's responsibility to eliminate poverty. But in the same survey, 64 percent agreed that government controls too much of our daily lives, and 57 percent agreed that government regulation does more harm than good (ibid., p. 16). So the temptation to trust government on specific issues is obviously strong enough for significant majorities to do so, and this is precisely why the trust is misplaced. The more overwhelming is the majority coalition, particularly when votes are based primarily on expressive rather than instrumental considerations, the greater is the power transferred to government, and the less accountable are those who will end up controlling that power.

Similarly, the greater the emotional appeal of an issue, or the more charismatic a favored political candidate, the smaller is the desirable level of trust for a given degree of voter decisiveness. The lower level of trust is needed to counteract the temptation voters feel to make decisions on emotional grounds with little regard for the collective consequences.

Let us consider again proposals to protect the environment which, because they are packaged in emotionally appealing ways, tend to command overwhelming public support regardless of their benefit–cost implications. When expressive rather than instrumental considerations dominate voter choice, voters will favor pollution-control proposals that, even if implemented efficiently, cost more than they are worth, and empower organized groups to benefit from inefficient pollution-control programs. For example, the one-size-fits-all requirements typical of the command-and-control approach to pollution abatement allow well-established incumbent firms to restrict the entry of competitors and impose disadvantages on smaller, less-established competitors.[12] Also, government agencies enforcing environmental laws can justify larger budgets under command-and-control policies because more detailed involvement in pollution-control decisions is thereby required.[13] Unfortunately, these special-interest benefits come at an enormous cost. The uniform requirements of command-and-control regulation can cost 22 times more than the least-cost approach for the same amount of pollution reduction.[14] The inefficiencies in pollution policy would be reduced, though never eliminated, if the emotional appeal of environmental protection were countered with more skepticism about government's ability to protect the environment.

Nothing in our discussion suggests any natural tendencies toward the desirable level of trust in government. We could emphasize that people trust local governments more than the federal government as an indication of such tendencies, but in 1972 exactly the opposite was true (Pew Research Center 1998, pp. 6–7). As should be clear by now, we see strong and unrelenting pressures toward too much trust in government, although most discussions of trust in government we have read see a destructive dynamic leading to not enough trust. For example, according to Nye (1997, p. 4), 'if government can't perform [because of the lack of public trust], then people will become more dissatisfied and distrustful of it. Such a cumulative downward spiral could erode support for democracy as a form of governance'.

We do not dismiss Nye's concern out of hand, but we see it as less of a worry and more of a reassurance. We believe that the level of trust in government is subject to negative feedback. Trust is also subject to long cycles around some central, though unlikely most desirable, level, and the departures from that optimum are significant. Unlike Nye and others who worry about the erosion of trust in government, we have emphasized the power of organized interest groups to promote trust in government and then exploit that trust to secure private advantage at public expense. This power to exploit the public's trust, however, can eventually sow the seeds of its own destruction by creating mistrust in government. These seeds can take a long time to germinate and grow given the resistance of rational voter ignorance and apathy, the temptations of expressive voting, and a growing number of influential interest groups. But eventually, as government expands too far and its failures dominate its successes, public trust will reverse and begin declining.[15] During the decline phase, trust can fall too far, with the arguments of those who are worried about the erosion of trust in government becoming relevant. But, with a lag, declining trust can cause reductions in the size of government and the power of interest groups, with improved government performance over a more limited range of activities. The result can be a reversal in the declining trust in government, and the beginning of a new cycle as trust once again begins to build.[16]

Information on public trust in government going back to the early twentieth century is sketchy, but what does exist, along with more recent data, is consistent with the existence of long cycles. Robert Lane detected an increased trust in government in the 1930s,[18] which he attributed to the expectation that the federal government could bring the economy out of depression.[18] We add that the relatively limited economic role of the federal government prior to the 1930s, along with the perceived success of many of the progressive measures enacted at the century's turn, was also important in fostering the increased trust in government, an increase that probably began before the New Deal. As discussed at the outset, data from University of Michigan opinion polls that began being collected in 1958 indicate that trust in government continued to increase into the 1960s, peaking around 1964. Since that time trust has declined significantly (although not monotonically), reaching about 25 percent in 1994 (Orren 1997, p. 81). This decline in trust coincides with the expansion in the federal government's economic role, and corresponding increase in federal spending, beginning with President Johnson's 'Great Society' initiatives in the mid-1960s, which have been largely subverted by organized interest groups and seldom generated the public benefits promised. Whether this decline in trust results in a significant reduction in government spending and influence, with an eventual turnaround in public trust, remains to be seen.

5   Conclusion: is 'trust' incompatible with 'trustworthy'?

Addressing the issue of trust in government requires considering how well government does its job as an agent for the general interest of the public. The better agent government is (the more control the general public has over it), the more trust it can safely be granted. The more trustworthy the government, the more it can be trusted. While this point seems obvious, it is often ignored by those who plead for greater trust in government. But we agree with those concerned with the erosion of trust that the connection between trust and trustworthiness is more complicated than putting trustworthiness before trust. Surely, without some minimum level of trust, a government cannot be trustworthy. But we believe that this minimum level of trust is very minimal, with trust in government easily increased into the range in which it destroys trustworthy government.

Certainly when trust has reached the point where government action is recommended for solving almost every imaginable social problem, it is inconsistent with government performing in a manner that justifies that trust. Such a level of trust will open the door for politically compelling demands for government to do things it cannot do, or do only poorly, at costs that exceed the benefits. Public skepticism is necessary if government is to be limited to activities in which it can add to social value. Such skepticism is needed to overcome the temptation of voters to feel good by supporting government programs that will invariably be corrupted by organized interests. What do we mean by a healthy dose of skepticism in government? A level that would find a majority of voters feeling noble about voting against government proposals, *no* matter how noble the objectives of those proposals are claimed to be.

Notes

*   The authors gratefully acknowledge the financial support provided by the Earhart Foundation.
1.   See Figure 3-1 in Orren (1997, p. 81). There is some evidence that hostility toward government has declined somewhat since 1994, but the long-run trend in the public attitude toward government remains decidedly downward.
2.   Not everyone sees declining trust in government as a problem, but many do.
3.   See Hunter and Bowman (1996), Nye et al. (1997) and the Pew Research Center for the People and the Press (1998). The opinion poll data referred to herein are taken from Tables 6, 7, and 26 of the last-cited work (Pew Research Center 1998, pp. 5, 6 and 16).
4.   Quoted in Arthur M. Schlesinger, Jr, 'Government isn't the root of all evil', *Wall Street Journal*, 30 January 1998, p. A14.
5.   Quoted in Samuelson (1995, p. 187).
6.   This section draws heavily on the work of Brennan and Lomasky (1993).
7.   However, see Nelson (1994), who presents a theory that relies on ideology to motivate voting. In particular, he suggests that 'political positions are ... chosen not because these positions are the desired outcome for voters, but rather because one wants to associate with certain people and they have certain positions. People imitate others in choosing political positions' (p. 92).
8.   Tullock (1971a) was the first public choice scholar we are aware of to consider the role played by the low cost of voting against one's private advantage in explaining the political popularity of transfer programs. Brennan and Lomasky (1993) provide the most complete economic analysis of the implications of the low cost of voting expressively.
9.   Or is considering a vote on a candidate who promises to support such a proposal.
10.   One might question whether poverty reduction qualifies as a public good, but it does encounter a free-rider problem, or prisoner's dilemma, as famously articulated by Milton Friedman (1962, p. 191).
11.   One might be tempted to argue that the probability of a tied election is so small, no matter how evenly the voters are split, that any relevant difference in this probability can have no

noticeable effect on voter behavior. But this is not true, particularly for local elections, where the number of voters can be relatively small. For example, if the number of voters is 2001 and the voters are evenly split, that is, the probability is 1/2 that a randomly chosen voter will vote for A or B, then the probability that the total vote will end up 1000 to 1001, in which case each voter is decisive, is 1/56. In this case the individual considering a vote for an environmental proposal that, if passed, will cost him $1000, would have to receive at least $17.86 worth of expressive satisfaction to motivate him to vote yes. One can expect a lot less expressive voting when the cost is $17.86 than when the cost is $0.10, as in our example in Section 2. Even when the number of voters is 10 million, the probability of a tie vote is only 1/4000 when the voters are evenly split probabilistically. However, as the probability that a randomly chosen voter will vote for A and B diverges even slightly from 1/2, the probability of a tied election quickly becomes indistinguishable from zero, with the decline more dramatic the larger the number of voters. See Brennan and Lomasky (1993, pp. 55–9) for more detail on the relevant calculations.

12. The literature on this subject includes work by Ackerman and Hassler (1981), Buchanan and Tullock (1975), Maloney and McCormick (1982) and Pashigian (1984).

13. As observed by *The Economist*, 'the EPA exists to regulate things, not to see the market do the job for it'. See 'William Reilly's green precision weapons', 30 March 1991, p. 28.

14. See Table 15.2 and the accompanying discussion in Tietenberg (1992, pp. 402–5).

15. Samuelson (1995, pp. 200–201) discusses this phase of the cycle in trust in similar terms when he says:

> There is a vicious circle. Government that grows must do more of its work in obscurity; otherwise, it could not function at all and would inevitably fail in many of its missions. But government that works in obscurity will become increasingly dominated by narrow groups, which will bend it to their own purposes and make government seem even more removed from popular will.

16. Arthur Schlesinger (1986, p. 245) considers this stage in the cycle when he comments, 'The fewer responsibilities loaded on the national authority, the better it will be able to discharge those it cannot escape'. And three sentences later, he points to the beginning of the next stage in the cycle: 'Sometimes government intervenes too much. Its regulations become pointlessly intrusive. Its programs fail. After a time exasperations accumulate and produce indictments'.

17. One could argue that the polls from which our information on trust in government is drawn are also flawed because of 'expressive voting' considerations. When polls are taken, no individual attaches any instrumental or outcome significance to his or her response and, therefore, expressive motivations dominate the responses they give. However, there is no reason to believe that any bias resulting from this phenomenon has changed over time. So while the magnitude of the trust or distrust may not be accurately measured by the polls, the directions of change should be.

18. Lane's observations are discussed in Nye (1997, p. 10).

PART V

THE PUBLIC CHOICE
REVOLUTION

24 Public choice as an experimental science

Lisa R. Anderson

1 Introduction

This chapter reviews experimental studies in the field of public choice, including tests of foundational theories and potential remedies for problems of collective decision making. Economists conducted experiments as early as the 1930s, but laboratory research has only gained widespread acceptance in the profession in recent decades.[1] Experiments have proven to be extremely useful for testing theories in so far as they permit the experimenter to control assumptions about key variables such as incentives and information flows. Since many public choice theories pose interesting questions susceptible to laboratory methods, it is a popular area for experimental research. In addition, the laboratory provides a safe environment for testing and fine tuning policies that cannot easily be tested with naturally occurring data.

Section 2 examines laboratory studies of individual decision making with externalities. Positive and negative externalities are considered in the context of public goods provision and the overuse of common pool resources, respectively. In addition, some tests of the Coase theorem are discussed. Section 3 examines rent-seeking behavior in the laboratory and Section 4 reports results from voting experiments. Section 5 concludes.

2 Individual decision making with externalities

The assumption that humans are rational, utility-maximizing actors generates clean behavioral predictions. Generally, self-interest and market forces lead to an efficient allocation of resources. However, observed market failures prompt us to reconsider some aspects of human interaction. Many issues that interest social scientists arise because individual decisions are not made in a vacuum. Spillover effects, which have been termed externalities, can be positive or negative. Although they are two sides of the same coin, distinct laboratory mechanisms have evolved to examine behavior with positive versus negative externalities.

When an individual contributes to the provision of a public good, others may benefit from the good without compensating the donor. Hence, a positive externality is generated. Among the most commonly cited examples of public goods are national defense and clean air. With self-interested agents, economic theory predicts that these goods will be underprovided. This prediction has been tested using a voluntary contributions mechanism. The mechanism generally applies to pure public goods (that is, goods that are both non-excludable and non-rival in consumption). When a good is non-excludable, but rival in consumption, a different inefficiency arises, since one individual's consumption of the good diminishes its usefulness for other potential consumers. Hence, one person's consumption exerts a negative externality on other users of the resource. A classic example of a public good that is rival in consumption is a fishery. Negative externalities of this type are analysed in the laboratory using a common pool resource mechanism. These mechanisms, in addition to possible remedies for inefficiencies, are discussed in the sections that follow.

2.1   Public goods provision and the voluntary contributions mechanism

One of the first economics experiments was conducted in the early 1950s at the RAND Corporation. Melvin Dresher and Merrill Flood (1952) designed an asymmetric and repeated version of the now familiar prisoner's dilemma game. Because this story so convincingly characterizes the conflicting forces of private incentives and social good, a show of hands in any undergraduate economics course reveals that most students know of the game. Behavior in early prisoner's dilemma experiments was generally inconsistent with the theoretical prediction of complete defection, and this generated a lively debate among economists. The most voluminous body of laboratory research relating to public choice relies on a variation of this game known as the voluntary contributions mechanism (VCM). The VCM is used to investigate the degree to which people free ride on public goods.

The mechanism works as follows. Each person in a group of size N is given an endowment of tokens and offered the opportunity to contribute to a group account. Tokens kept for private consumption are transformed by some factor, v, and converted to cash earnings (for example, 1 token = 1 cent). The sum of all tokens allocated to the group account, G, is transformed by some factor, w, and each member of the group gets the amount Gw. Importantly, every member of the group receives Gw from the group account, regardless of whether or not they contribute to it. Hence, the group account is a pure public good. In the standard public goods experiment $w < v$, so the dominant strategy Nash equilibrium is for everyone to free ride on others' contributions. This decision problem is a dilemma (specifically, the prisoner's dilemma) when the social benefit of a token donated to the group account outweighs the value of a token kept for private consumption (that is, $Nw > v$).

Sociologists Gerald Marwell and Ruth Ames (1981) conducted one of the first public goods experiments. Unlike the VCM that has come to be the standard in experimental economics, Marwell and Ames administered many of their sessions via mail surveys of high school students. In some cases they were deceptive about the number of people involved, and most students participated only once in the game. Despite these procedural differences, the behavioral pattern observed by Marwell and Ames has held up to many replications. Namely, initial contributions to the group account are near the 50 percent level. Perhaps what drew economists so heavily into this line of research was one discovery that Marwell and Ames chose to emphasize. They concluded that free riding was not as pervasive as theoretical models might suggest, with one notable exception. The only significant free riding they found was in a group of economics graduate students at the University of Wisconsin. Hence their title became 'Economists free ride: does anyone else?'.

Hundreds of public goods (VCM) experiments have been conducted in the past 20 years. Initial baseline experiments confirmed the finding that people do not free ride to the extent predicted by economic theory. The first significant addition to our understanding of this anomaly was the discovery that free riding increases with repetition. Isaac et al. (1984) had the same group of subjects make contribution decisions for ten periods. At the end of each decision-making period, the total number of tokens allocated to the group account (but not individual contributions) was announced out loud, and subjects privately recorded their earnings for the period. In the first period, contributions ranged from 40 to 60 percent of the total token endowment. By the tenth period, contributions fell to the 20 to 40 percent range, which is still well above the Nash prediction of complete free riding. With this discovery, the focus of experimental research turned to isolating variables that influence contribution levels in VCM-based experiments.

Table 24.1 lists treatment variables, relevant studies, and findings for some factors of interest. One of the less intuitive findings from VCM experiments is that increases in the size of the group increase contributions to the group account. A number of prominent theoretical models demonstrate that relatively small groups foster more cooperation than large groups.[2] However, if altruism is the motivating factor for contributions to the group account, the positive relationship between group size and contributions should be expected, since the marginal benefit of each token allocated to the group account increases as the group grows.

Many of the other effects listed in the table are quite intuitive. For example, contributions to the group account are positively related to the conversion factor (w) for tokens placed in the group account. This simply means that people are more willing to give to the group account as it gets cheaper to do so (that is, as $v - w$ gets smaller). Given the evidence on repetition, it is also not surprising that contributions to the public account are lower in groups that have previously participated in a VCM experiment. This suggests that subjects merely need time to figure out the dominant strategy. Experienced subjects start at lower initial contribution rates and those rates decline faster

Table 24.1   Treatment variables in voluntary contributions experiments

Variable	Study	Effect on contribution rates
Repetition	Isaac, Walker and Thomas (1984)	Negative
Size of group	Isaac, Walker, and Williams (1994)	Positive
Conversion factor for tokens in public account	Isaac, Walker and Thomas (1984)	Positive
Experience	Isaac, Walker and Thomas (1984)	Negative
Framing as a public bad	Andreoni (1995b)	Negative
Anonymity	Laury, Walker and Williams (1995)	None
Provision point	Isaac, Schmidtz and Walker (1989)	Positive
Communication	Isaac and Walker (1988)	Positive
Heterogeneous agents	Chan, Mestelman, Moir and Muller (1998)	Positive

than is the case with inexperienced subjects. A number of innovations have been introduced to the VCM in attempts to separate learning from other possible hypotheses, like signaling or altruism.

For example, Andreoni (1988b) investigated whether the decrease in contributions was the result of learning or strategic signaling. Andreoni used a 2-person partners–strangers version of the VCM in which one subset of the subjects was paired with the same 'partner' for each repetition of the game and the other subset rotated through a group of people, meeting a 'stranger' for each new repetition.[3] All other parameters of the experiment were the same for both treatments. Surprisingly, the strangers were consistently more cooperative, but contribution rates fell over time in both groups. This suggests that the increase in free riding resulted more from learning than strategic play.[4]

Based on a lack of evidence that strategy was a motivating factor for contributions, Andreoni (1995a) introduced another design to separate the giving motive into learning and altruism components. In one treatment, subjects were ranked by token accumulations and paid based on their rank in the group. Another group of subjects played the standard VCM game with all other parameters identical to the rank treatment. Hence, in the rank treatment, private gains were emphasized over social gains. Andreoni concluded that about half of the contributions to the public good were the result of kindness and the other half were due to confusion about the game.

A common characteristic of the above studies is that deviations from the Nash prediction were only possible in the direction of overcontributing to the group account, since negative contributions were not possible. Saijo and

Nakamure (1995) and Palfrey and Prisbrey (1996) varied the value of the private good across subjects and across periods. In some cases, full free riding was the dominant strategy and, in other cases, contributing all tokens to the public account was optimal for an individual. Both studies found no systematic tendency to give too much to the public account. In fact, subjects sometimes kept tokens for private consumption when the tokens would have been worth more to them personally in the public account (that is, when $v <$ w). Saijo and Nakamura termed this a 'spite motive', since it appeared that subjects were willing to forgo earnings to deny public access to their tokens.

In a follow-up study, Palfrey and Prisbrey (1997) attempted to separate 'warm-glow giving' from altruism. When individuals get utility from the act of giving, independent of the benefit to the recipient, it is termed warm-glow giving. Altruism is defined as giving to the public account with the intent of increasing the earnings of others in the group. In this study, the marginal value of the private good varied across both subjects and periods and the (common) value of the public good varied across sessions. This facilitated a comparison of behavior with different relative values and costs for contributions to the private versus group account. Palfrey and Prisbrey found that 'warm glow' played a small but statistically significant role in decision making, but that altruism was not a factor. Using a logistic error model to analyse decisions, it was also concluded that random error played a non-trivial role in decisions.

Despite the fact that undergiving was possible in the two studies described above, the possible equilibria (complete free riding or fully contributing) were still on the boundaries of the choice set. Evidence that undergiving may also be a problem prompted a new line of research with interior equilibria. Interior equilibria are generated by having either a non-linear return from the group account or from tokens kept for private consumption. These studies are reviewed in Laury and Holt (2000).

Most notable from this group, Isaac and Walker (1996) designed three treatments that differed with respect to the Nash prediction for contributions to the group account. Predicted contributions to the group account were 'low', 'medium', or 'high' relative to a subject's token endowment.[5] Not inconsistent with the two boundary cases discussed above, Isaac and Walker found that contributions were still above the Nash prediction in the low case, close to predicted behavior in the medium case, and lower than the Nash prediction in the high case. Overall, the upward bias in contribution rates was greater than the downward bias.

Another interesting variation of the VCM explored the degree to which negative versus positive framing affected contributions to the public account. In the negatively framed version, all tokens were initially in the public account, and subjects were allowed to transfer a certain number to their private accounts. Andreoni (1995b) termed the positive effect of giving a 'warm glow' and the negative effect of taking the 'cold prickle'. Much more free riding was observed in the negatively framed VCM experiments. By the tenth period, almost all of the tokens were withdrawn from the group account.[6]

There is also evidence that individual-specific characteristics, like gender and nationality, affect behavior in the VCM.[7] This is consistent with Palfrey and Prisbrey's (1997) finding that errors and altruistic behavior vary widely across individuals. The challenge for economic theorists is to define new models that incorporate individual-specific rates of learning and other-regarding preferences. Holt and Laury (2000) review some new models that were designed to organize what we have learned from this plethora of public goods experiments into a useful predictive tool.

For policy makers, the pertinent question is 'what can experiments teach us about alleviating the free-riding problem?'. Two variants of the VCM have resulted in near efficient levels of contributions to the public account. One of these adds a 'provision point'. In the simplest case, if a predetermined number of tokens is allocated to the group account, each member of the group receives a benefit. If the provision point (that is, minimum level) is not reached, no one receives a benefit from the group account. Isaac et al. (1989) found that provision points were effective at increasing contributions to the group account as long as tokens allocated to the group account were returned if the threshold was not met. Marks and Croson (1998) reported that contribution rates were also sensitive to the way residual tokens were used when the provision point was exceeded.

The other treatment variable that increases contributions to the group account is the ability of subjects to engage in face-to-face communication. Isaac and Walker (1988) allowed subjects to communicate under a variety of experimental conditions. Interestingly, the effect of communication did not depend on the ability to enforce agreements. In general, however, infrequent opportunities to communicate and impersonal channels for communication diminish its effectiveness at increasing contribution rates. Agreements made during communication periods are often short-lived. In addition, communication by notes or computer terminals has little effect.

While communication and provision points can alleviate the free-riding problem, more formal methods have been developed to assist in the provision of public goods. Many of the laboratory studies in this area are tests of incentive-compatible mechanisms (ICMs). These mechanisms are designed to elicit private values for a public good. Further, some ICMs have a fully funding tax scheme in which individuals pay for the public good in proportion to the benefit they receive from it. These studies do not directly address the free-rider problem, rather they focus on providing an efficient level of a public good. Also unlike the VCM experiments discussed above, most experimental tests of ICMs induce heterogeneous individual preferences for the public good. Since symmetric outcomes (that is, subjects evenly split the cost of the public good) are not efficient, this setup actually provides a more stringent test of ICMs.[8] Chen (2000) provides a comprehensive survey of these mechanisms, including many theoretical issues that will not be discussed here.

One of the first theoretical studies to motivate experimental tests of ICMs was done by Groves and Ledyard (1977). They devised a quadratic tax rule to fund a public good. Each person has a private value schedule for the public good. Based on that schedule, the person proposes an amount of the public good to be provided. All of the proposals are collected and the cost for each participant depends on that person's proposal, the cost to produce the public good, the number of people in the group, and the sum of proposals by other people. The scheme has the desirable property that honest revelation of one's preferences is a dominant strategy.

Given the complicated nature of the tax mechanism, the dominance of true revelation is far from apparent. Hence, experimental tests of the mechanism were conducted in an iterative fashion. Subjects were first told their values for the public good, then asked to submit proposals in rounds. The process ended when all subjects submitted the same proposal twice in a row or after some designated number of rounds passed, in which case everyone earned $0. Iterating in this manner changed the equilibrium, but allowed subjects more time to figure out how the scheme works and to develop a strategy.

Initial experimental tests of the Groves–Ledyard mechanism were encouraging. Vernon Smith (1979) found that groups ranging in size from four to eight reached an efficient level of production. However, follow-up experiments by Smith (1980) and Harstad and Marrese (1981) were less encouraging. Specifically, with more complex revisions to the design, like full funding of the public good, individual bids were not demand revealing. Curiously, the quantity of the public good provided was generally close to the efficient level despite individual deviations from the optimal strategy. In another set of experiments, Chen and Plott (1996) introduced a punishment parameter to the Groves–Ledyard mechanism to fine a subject based on the deviation of her proposal from the mean of other proposals. They found that for a high enough punishment parameter, proposals converged to efficient levels. This result was replicated by Chen and Tang (1998).

In related work, Smith (1979) designed an alternative auction mechanism to reveal individual demands for a public good. In the Smith auction, each person reports how much of the public good she wants provided and how much she is willing to contribute. Each person is informed of the average quantity proposal and a proposed cost to them, which is the cost of the average quantity proposal minus the contributions proposed by all other participants. Subjects can agree to this scheme or veto it. Unanimous approval of a scheme ends the process. The Smith auction is not theoretically demand revealing. However, experimental results suggest that it is at least as effective as the Groves–Ledyard mechanism at achieving an efficient outcome.[9]

As noted above, the VCM and the tax schemes discussed thus far are appropriate to analyse pure public goods. Another class of public goods is impure in the sense that they are non-excludable, but rival in consumption. We generally think of individual maximization as imposing a negative externality in this case, since no one takes into account the fact that by using the resource they diminish its value to others. The section that follows includes a discussion of two different lines of laboratory research related to this class of goods. The first subsection reviews common pool resource experiments.

2.2   Negative externalities

Common pool resources   Gardner et al. (1990) introduced the experimental design that has been used extensively to study common pool resources. Similar to the voluntary contributions mechanism, the common pool resource mechanism (CPRM) has subjects divide tokens between two accounts. One account represents a private good and has a fixed rate of return. The other account represents the common pool resource, and has a potentially higher payoff that is a quadratic function of the total group investment in the account. Unlike the VCM, individual earnings from the common pool resource vary depending on the number of tokens invested in the resource. For example, an individual who invests nothing in the common resource earns nothing from it. The common pool resource is rivalrous in the sense that a token invested in the resource earns a lower return as other people invest more in it. The non-linear payoff function for the common pool resource makes both underinvestment and overinvestment possible. In the experiments reviewed here, the Nash prediction is between the socially optimal level of investment and complete depletion of the resource (that is, with zero or negative individual earnings from the account).

Gardner et al. (ibid.) present results from baseline CPRM experiments. Players were identical with respect to token endowments and marginal returns from the private account and the common pool resource. They found that aggregate investment in the common resource was close to the Nash prediction with a 'low' token endowment. However, individual behavior was not consistent with a symmetric Nash outcome. The most common individual strategy was to invest all tokens into the common account as long as its return was greater than the (fixed) return from the private account. If the return from the common account fell below the return from the private account, in the subsequent period all tokens were invested in the private account. Hence, behavior in these experiments was erratic with no discernible trends. When subjects were given a relatively high token endowment (25 versus 10), holding all other parameters constant, there was significantly more overinvestment in the common pool resource.

Walker and Gardner (1992) introduced the possibility that the common resource will be destroyed into the CPRM setup. The probability of destruction increased with the number of tokens invested in the common pool resource. In one treatment there was a 'safe option' where the probability of destruction was zero as long as the investment in the common account was below some threshold. With the possibility of destruction, behavior was close to theoretical predictions. In all cases, the resource was destroyed, normally within a few decision-making periods.

As with the VCM, communication helped to remedy the overuse of the common pool resource. Ostrom and Walker (1991) investigated the use of communication as a potential remedy for overinvestment in the common pool resource. With a costless, one-shot opportunity to communicate, there was an immediate improvement in efficiency. However, subjects subsequently defected on agreements about 25 percent of the time. With repeated opportunities to communicate, efficiency gains were more persistent. When subjects were offered the opportunity to purchase a discussion period, they did so, even though it required coordinating to pay for the privilege. This costly discussion also improved efficiency in the use of the common pool resource. In addition, Ostrom et al. (1992) found that subjects were willing to incur a cost to punish people who overinvested in the common pool resource.

In a related study, Casari and Plott (1999) altered the CPRM so that one subject was an inspector who could monitor and punish subjects who overinvested in the common resource. They found excessive monitoring, despite the fact that it was costly for the inspector. Further, their results suggested that a good model of behavior in this environment incorporates heterogeneous preferences for altruism and spite.

The Coase theorem   As noted above, while generally effective, agreements reached during communication periods were not binding in the experiments discussed thus far, since there was no designated enforcement agency. Hoffman and Spitzer (1982) designed an experiment with the opportunity for discussion and a mechanism for enforcing agreements. Their experiment was a direct test of the Coase (1960) theorem. Subjects were paired and had to jointly choose an activity level. The activity was a good for one of the people (person A) and imposed a negative externality on the other person (person B). Hence, person A preferred a high activity level and person B preferred a low activity level. One person in the dyad was designated 'controller' by flipping

a coin, meeting Coase's property rights requirement. The controller ultimately chose the activity level, but could be offered side payments to
compensate her for deviating from her individually optimal choice (the higher
activity level).

Hoffman and Spitzer found that subjects frequently reached an efficient
outcome, but controllers rarely exploited their power by demanding side
payments that were large enough to fully compensate them. In follow-up
experiments, Hoffman and Spitzer (1985) had subjects earn the right to be the
controller in a game of skill. Their basic finding was the same, but controllers
were more aggressive in demanding side payments when they perceived their
positions as having been earned.

McKelvey and Page (1998) stress-tested the Coase theorem by relaxing the
full information condition. In a variation of the Hoffman and Spitzer (1982)
experiment, subjects communicated via computer terminals and, in one treatment, were only given private information about payoffs. The controller role
was randomly assigned. Results from their full information treatment were
consistent with Hoffman and Spitzer's, but they found that the Coase theorem
failed to predict behavior in the private information treatment.

A huge body of literature related to Coase's work explores market-based
solutions for negative externalities in the context of tradable pollution permits.
Though beyond the scope of this review, permit experiments are especially
interesting from a public choice perspective because much of the early work in
this area was influential in the design of actual permit trading schemes. Some
initial experiments (for example, Plott 1983) demonstrated that permit trading
dominates traditional command and control on efficiency grounds. Much of the
current experimental work was motivated by policy proposals and initial implementation problems. An indication of the popularity of this topic is that the
most recent volume of *Research in Experimental Economics* (Isaac and Holt
1999) is devoted entirely to permit-related studies.

3   Rent seeking

One of the contentious issues in administering a decentralized or market-
based corrective policy is choosing winners and losers. Someone must decide
who is designated controller or how pollution permits are distributed. These
decisions give rise to another inefficiency that has come to be known as 'rent
seeking'. Rent seeking refers to the wasteful use of resources in pursuit of
some 'prize'. Early theoretical papers focused on competition for the right to
be the monopolist or to receive favorable trade status through tariffs as the
prizes that spawned rent-seeking behavior.

Tullock's (1980a) groundbreaking theory of 'efficient' rent seeking
explored the relationship between rent-seeking expenditures and the
mechanism that translates expenditures into probabilities of winning the prize.

Specifically, with two competitors, the probability of winning the prize is calculated as $P_A = A^r/(A^r + B^r)$, where A and B are lottery tickets purchased by players A and B, respectively. The parameter r determines the impact of differences in expenditures on probabilities of winning.

Millner and Pratt (1989) designed the first laboratory test of Tullock's model. In the experiment, two people were offered the opportunity to buy lottery tickets for a prize of known value. Students were told that the probability of winning was based on the function above, and this probability was calculated for them and displayed on their computer screens as purchasing decisions were made. In one treatment, the probability of winning was equal to a person's share of the total expenditure on lottery tickets (that is, $r = 1$). In another treatment a larger exponent ($r = 3$) was used to calculate probabilities. Each purchasing period lasted two and a half minutes and subjects could purchase tickets at any point during the period. In addition, all purchasing information was public information and was updated on computer screens throughout the period.

Millner and Pratt found that subjects spent more than the Cournot–Nash prediction on lottery tickets in the $r = 1$ treatment and less than the Cournot–Nash prediction in the $r = 3$ condition. Overall, the amount spent on lottery tickets was lower in the $r = 1$ treatment than in the $r = 3$ treatment. Shogren and Baik (1991) replicated Millner and Pratt's $r = 1$ treatment, but had a one-shot investment decision without information about others' purchasing decisions. They found that individual expenditures were consistent with the Cournot–Nash prediction. Millner and Pratt (1991) replicated their own 1989 study but added a pre-test to group people by risk preferences. In their 'less risk averse' group, expenditures were higher than the Cournot–Nash prediction. In the 'more risk averse' group, expenditures and rent dissipation were not significantly different from theoretical predictions.

Davis and Reilly (1998a) tested a variation of Tullock's model with two main changes. First, they compared results using the lottery ticket competition described above with a 'perfectly discriminative auction', in which the highest bidder wins the prize. Second, they added a strategic buyer who engaged in rent defending. This buyer was meant to represent consumer groups who might oppose the awarding of monopoly rights. The authors demonstrated that the value of being a monopoly seller might be lower than the value of blocking the monopoly to potential buyers. Hence, the rent defender was operationalized by adding a buyer with a higher value for the prize than other bidders in the auction. In all cases, five bidders participated. The role of the rent defender rotated among the subjects and was randomly determined by the throw of a die. In each auction, subjects submitted sealed bids and the results were announced aloud. This sequence was repeated 15 times for each group of subjects.

Davis and Reilly found that expenditures were higher in the discriminative auction than in the lottery-based auction. They also found that the presence of a strategic buyer reduced expenditures. However, expenditures were consistently higher than predicted by theory. In a follow-up study, Davis and Reilly (1998b) added additional rent defenders and concluded that expenditures increased relative to having only one rent defender.

In another extension of Tullock's (1980a) theory, Onculer and Croson (1998) examined rent-seeking behavior when the value of the prize was uncertain. They also varied the initial endowment and the size of the group from two to four people. Subjects participated in only one decision-making sequence. They found that subjects spent more on average than the Nash prediction and expenditures increased with group size and endowments.

4 Voting

When inefficiencies, such as the ones discussed above, cannot be corrected with decentralized or market-based methods, collective action is often required. As early as the 1940s, economists were analysing the majority voting rule and possible problems with it.[10] Fiorina and Plott (1978) conducted the first committee voting experiments. Subjects were given payoffs in a two-dimensional decision space. They were told that outcomes were decided by majority rule and very little additional structure was imposed on the situation. The authors were surprised to find recurring behavioral patterns.[11]

A major concern with pair-wise voting on a number of alternative proposals is the possibility of agenda manipulation. Consider the following example from Holt and Anderson (1999). A community is considering a school project and a highway project. One project, both projects, or neither project may be funded. Each voter pays a tax of $200 per approved project. If a voter uses a project, its value to her is $400. Otherwise, it has no value to her. There are seven members on the community board, two of whom prefer to fund both projects, two prefer to fund only the highway, and three prefer to fund only the school. Pair-wise voting over the alternatives can result in many different outcomes. For example, a voter with a preference for both projects can guarantee that outcome with the following three-vote agenda: Vote 1: School versus Highway, Vote 2: Winner of Vote 1 versus No Project, Vote 3: Winner of Vote 2 versus Both Projects. Furthermore, the agenda can be designed so that any outcome is possible.

In a more complicated laboratory environment, Plott and Levine (1978) designed a scenario with five possible outcomes. By manipulating the agenda, they were able to force three of the outcomes in only four sessions of the experiment. This result suggests that models assuming forward-looking individuals are inappropriate because, armed with information about the order of votes, subjects could vote strategically in early votes and ultimately avoid undesirable outcomes. Specifically, strategic voting in this context is voting against one's preferred outcome in early rounds when that makes it more likely that a desirable outcome will be reached in later rounds.

Eckel and Holt (1989) had subjects vote on pairs of options in sequence with full information about the upcoming agenda. Subjects voted naively initially, but experience increased the incidence of strategic voting. Holt and Anderson (1999) replicated this finding in a less-controlled classroom setting.[12]

The focus of some recent voting experiments has shifted to alternatives to majority rule. Forsythe et al. (1996) compared results in three-candidate elections using plurality rule, approval voting and Borda rule. In these experiments, Condorcet losers won more often under plurality than either of the alternatives. As in Eckel and Holt (1989), subjects voted more strategically as they gained experience.

McKelvey and Palfrey (1998) examined voting behavior of juries when a conviction required unanimity. In their clever design, subjects were given imperfect private information about the innocence or guilt of the defendant without using voting-related terminology. A red jar and a blue jar represented innocence and guilt, respectively. At the beginning of the experiment, subjects saw these jars and their contents. The red jar contained seven red balls and three blue balls. Symmetrically, the blue jar contained seven blue balls and three red balls. Subjects were told that one jar (that is, innocence or guilt) was to be randomly chosen by the roll of a die. Then each subject saw a private draw of a ball (but not the jar used for the draw), and was asked to predict which jar was used for the draw.

Payoffs depended on the group decision. In one treatment, subjects were rewarded if a majority of the decisions were correct. In another treatment, red (guilty) was the group decision only if all of the subjects predicted red. Otherwise, blue was the group decision, and subjects were rewarded only if the blue jar was actually used for the draws. In addition to varying the voting rule, there were two different jury sizes (three people or six people), and in some cases a straw poll was conducted prior to the actual prediction round.

McKelvey and Palfrey found that votes (that is, predictions) revealed a person's private signal 94 percent of the time with the majority voting rule. With the unanimous voting rule, most people voted guilty (that is, predicted red) when their draw indicated guilty, but with an innocent (blue) draw, mixed strategies were commonly used. In three-person juries, 36 percent of the people voted guilty when they saw an innocent signal. In six-person juries, this number increased to 44 percent. With the straw poll, more than 90 percent of the votes revealed private signals in the polling round. In the actual voting round, 80 percent of the people voted in favor of the option chosen most frequently in the straw poll. Overall, fewer innocent people were convicted under majority rule than under a rule of unanimity. In addition, larger juries convicted fewer innocent people when unanimity was required.

5   Summary and conclusion

Laboratory studies in the public choice arena provide mixed results when externalities arise from individual decisions. The evidence on public goods provision suggests that conventional theories are not good at predicting behavior. Further, theoretically irrelevant variables often influence decisions. In a sense, this failure is encouraging from a policy perspective, because we have learned that people do not free ride on public goods to the degree predicted by theory. Further, provision points and the ability to communicate can alleviate the problem. Experiments with common pool resources show that overuse is a problem, and in some cases, even more so than predicted by theory. However, communication also improves efficiency in this setup and subjects are willing to incur a cost to punish overuse of the resource.

Experiments also suggest that people engage in inefficient rent seeking, even with a prize of unknown value. Adding one rent defender decreases the amount spent by others, but expenditures are higher with multiple rent defenders than with none at all. Little experimental work has been done in this area relative to the number of theoretical studies. Hence, this is a fertile area for laboratory research in public choice.

Laboratory studies of voting behavior confirm the finding from VCM experiments that behavior is not always consistent with theory, especially when subjects have little experience with a particular design. A common theme throughout the studies reviewed here is that theories that assume homogeneous agents fail to predict behavior in the laboratory. Many person-specific characteristics such as learning, risk preferences, altruism and spite are significant factors in predicting the decisions people make. This heterogeneity complicates the job of policy makers and mandates that theorists and experimentalists continue to work together on more general models of behavior.

Notes

1. See Chapter 1 of *The Handbook of Experimental Economics* (Kagel and Roth 1995) for a thorough history of experimental economics.
2. See, for example, Coase (1960), Buchanan (1965b) and Olson (1965).
3. Subjects were told either that they would meet the same person each period or that they would meet a different person each period, depending on the treatment.
4. Some replications of the partner–stranger design have been inconsistent with this initial finding. See, for example, Croson (1996), Keser (1996), Keser and van Winden (1996), and Weimann (1994). These results are reviewed in Andreoni and Croson (2000).
5. In the 'low' treatment, the Nash prediction was for 19.4 percent of each person's tokens to be allocated to the group account. In the 'medium' and 'high' treatments, predicted contributions were 50 percent and 80.6 percent of the endowment, respectively.
6. Sonnemans et al. (1998) found similar results in a slightly different environment. Burlando

and Hey (1997) only used the negative version and their results fell between Andreoni's (1995b) positively framed and negatively framed results.

7. See, for example, Brown-Kruse and Hummels (1993) for an analysis of gender differences in the VCM. Burlando and Hey (1997) compare contribution rates across several countries.

8. There is mixed evidence regarding the effect of variable and asymmetric marginal values for the public good on free riding (see, for example, Chan et al. 1998).

9. See Smith (1979) and Banks et al. (1988) for results from laboratory tests of the Smith auction.

10. See, for example, Black (1948b).

11. McKelvey and Ordeshook (1990) discuss this experiment and survey the literature on voting experiments done prior to this decade.

12. The Holt and Anderson (1999) setup was used to demonstrate the possibility for agenda manipulation and strategic voting at a conference on classroom experiments held at the University of Virginia in the Spring of 1997. Conference participants, who were mostly college professors from Virginia and nearby states, also failed to vote strategically initially.

25 The public choice approach to economic history

Robert B. Ekelund, Jr and Audrey B. Davidson

1 Introduction

History is the supreme laboratory for economists and other social scientists. Public choice theory, viewed especially as interest-group theory undergirded by rent-seeking activities, has much to add to historical analysis. However, historical–institutional analysis includes many other features of modern economic theory. This chapter therefore has two interrelated purposes.

First, we seek to establish some of the links between public choice and a broader theory of institutional change. A simplified modern theory of institutional change premised on rational choice assumptions and neoclassical theorizing will be tentatively sketched. The discussion relates public choice principles to property rights assignments, transaction costs and economizing behavior to analyse the forces that shape institutions over time. In other words, the issues raised by public choice and interest groups are inextricably bound up with a richer theory of institutional change and it is a misconception to argue that public choice is somehow divorced from modern neoclassical theory. In order to approach an examination of the contributions of public choice to historical research, in other words, at least the suggestion or hint of how a *theory* of institutional change might be devised is necessary. Such a theory must contain elements relevant to market efficiency as well as to interest-group dynamics. It also should be noted that while many modern economists dealing with institutions seek explanations that impose some kind of order on history, they do so at greater or lesser distances from the assumptions of neoclassical rational economizing behavior.[1]

Our second aim is to survey some of the work that has been done so far relating public choice–institutional analysis to the explanation of economic history. While not pretending to be exhaustive, we present, in the second part of the chapter, a 'reader's guide' to a few of the historical episodes that have been illuminated by the public choice and the more-inclusive institutional economics paradigms. Our focus is, almost exclusively, directed to developments in England and the United States. These episodes are arranged, as far as possible, chronologically.

2   Public choice and its role in institutional change

The primary concern of economics, since its origins in Adam Smith and before, was with wealth generation and with the factors that frame, encourage or discourage economic growth. While that concern is no less pressing today, the methodologies by which these ends are studied have expanded greatly since Smith's day. An enormous body of largely deterministic economic theory was constructed around these fundamental questions in the classical and neoclassical ages and much of it survives in the foundations of the economic literature. This body of work has been mightily embellished in the latter half of the twentieth century. For example, the theories of property rights, externalities, transaction and information costs, voting, and business organization have emerged to alter and expand standard economic analysis. Closely related is the field of law and economics that has put forward, as one principal object, the description of how notions of economic efficiency and social welfare are related to legal change. Most apt, however, is the contemporary scholarship leading to the development of some conceptions of how institutions emerge, why they may or may not have 'staying power', and why they decline or disappear, only (perhaps) to re-emerge in some new form and context. This project is the ongoing activity of many economists, principally those dubbed 'neoinstitutionalists' (Olson 1965, 1982; North and Thomas 1973; North 1981, 1990; Ekelund and Tollison 1981, 1984, 1997b). These writers are not to be confused with a group of 'new institutionalists' who are modern-day followers of Veblenian strains of social science (Magnusson 1993; Rutherford 1994).[2]

The entire corpus of modern economic theory is relevant to historical study, a fact that is conceptually apparent perhaps but incredibly complex in any particular application.[3] In addition, the interrelationships between some political sector and the functioning of private markets must be integrated into a positive theory of institutional change. This is, of course, where public choice – broadly conceived as the economic analysis of political decision making, politics, and the democratic process – comes in. The form of constitutions, voting rules and, most particularly, the influence of interest groups are keys to understanding how institutional change comes about.

The all-encompassing nature of any well-specified *theory* of institutional change is, and for the present must remain, daunting to the analyst. Clearly, some desiderata must be stated at the outset in any historical study of institutions. Toward what range of phenomena is the theory directed? Does it seek to analyse change in the larger, macro sense (evolution of states or growth of nations), or does it home in on changes in particular markets or firms? Will the theory be applied to explicit economic markets (such as railway deregulation) or is the evolution of implicit markets (such as that for religion, marriage or sex) to be the subject of inquiry? Will the theoretical emphasis differ between these two types of studies? Critically, what does one want to do with the theory? Is the theory 'forward looking' (predictive)? Or, with some set of relevant tools of the trade, does the analyst wish to visit, frame and analyse particular historical episodes in the development of nations and the evolution of particular institutions?[4] As with any theory, moreover, some variables must be identified as exogenous and others as endogenous. No theory can treat all factors as being determined within the model.

Finally, and most importantly, what are the regularizing behavioral characteristics that will motivate a theory of institutional or historical change? Of what, in other words, does economizing behavior consist? Utility maximization – the pursuit of self-interest under given constraints – has been and remains the guiding star of economic explanation from Adam Smith to the present day. Is this assumption sufficient to form the basis for explaining institutional change in either predictive or historical contexts, or does chaos and the uncertainty of 'path dependence' inflict the study of institutions?[5]

We cannot, in the space of one chapter, address any or all of these questions in detail. Before turning to the outlines of a theory of institutional change, however, it is important for us to state our beliefs at the outset. Any theory of institutional change worth its salt must satisfy four criteria. First, it must apply to the whole range of social phenomena – from the origins of cuisine, marriage or forms of religious belief – as well as to the so-called purely economic concerns of markets where prices are largely explicit in nature. Second, it must of necessity be of mainly historical character, but must not exclude components of predictability and rational explanation. Third, it must rely in a fundamental manner on the assumption that individuals behave in ways consistent with rational economizing or weighing of costs and benefits under given constraints, such as positive transaction costs and particular property rights assignments. And, fourth, it must recognize some conception of dynamic or intertemporal efficiency with respect to the objectives of output, utility or wealth maximization.[6]

2.1   A tentative theory

The construction of any analysis relating public choice to historical episodes requires at least a tentative exploration of theory. At bottom, the processes of institutional development – which constitute 'history' – can only be understood in the context of some *initial* set of institutions, along with some regularized behavioral motivations of economic agents. With absolute simplicity, it is not too much to argue that institutional change may be described as follows: economizing individuals and groups interacting in the shadow of a given set of political and market processes establishing property rights, ultimately alter existing institutions. Manifestly, no particular historical episode or process may adequately be described without clearly specifying the context of the analysis. Wealth distribution, property rights assignments, the status of cultural and religious norms must be given in some compendium of *ceteris paribus*. Most particularly a system of polity and governance forms must be assumed. (This is where public choice comes in.) In so far as the forms of constitutions, political systems and related institutions affect the actions of self-interested economic actors (or sets of actors), the latter specification is crucial to the *explanation* of emerging institutional change. While this view may appear simple, it is in fact exceedingly complex. Two fundamental reasons may be noted.

As all know, political structures – constitutions, voting rules, bodies of law and legislation, means and methods of representation, and so on – are also institutions, some of which are in fact undergoing constant (if sometimes imperceptible) change. The neoinstitutional accounts of constitutional change over the late sixteenth, seventeenth and early eighteenth centuries (Ekelund and Tollison 1981, 1997b; North and Weingast 1989; Wells and Wills 1998) reveal quite clearly the directions in which such institutions might evolve and the course implied for subsequent economic growth and development in England. The point is that the particular historical account – using the tools of public choice and modern economic theory – must be clearly circumscribed by focusing on an episode and invoking a particular *ceteris paribus*. Studies of the economically driven evolution of medieval marriage institutions would not deal extensively with transportation costs within the countries of Western Europe, for example, although some parts of these institutional facts would be relevant. In this sense, no analysis is (or at the present state of technology can be) 'complete'.

Another critical problem is the matter of identifying the exogenous factors within some particular study. The complexity of even elementary forms of institutional change requires that unexpected 'shocks' be identified. Some parts of the *ceteris paribus* may be well understood and their interrelations with the markets at hand taken into account. Other elements of models of institutional change are less tractable. Thus, we have the exogenous effects of such factors as wars, famines, plagues, and rapid changes in climate, technology or 'ideas', which are only another form of technology. For example, in North and Thomas's (1973) account of economic growth in Western Europe – one essentially focusing upon the impact of property rights changes on wealth generation – we find the plagues of 1347 and 1351 as having unanticipated impacts on labor and product markets.[7] Changes in the relative prices of capital and labor, it is argued, spurred property rights changes and, ultimately, a technological revolution that propelled the 'rise of the Western world'.

These two factors – creation of an appropriate analysis where some institutional conditions are *known* but left outside the model and others are treated as exogenous surprises ('shock shifters' as in modern macroeconomic theory)

– pose powerful problems in developing a general theory of institutions and institutional change. Clearly, only partial analyses are feasible, and selection problems beset even the cleverest and best-executed analyses. Economists, however, have a particular advantage over many other social scientists in one day arriving at more general theories of institutional change. Regularities of self-interest, competition and economizing behavior on the part of all agents are the guideposts that must be followed in order to achieve generality of explanation. These neoclassical methods – raw neoclassicism embellished with modern theories of property rights, law and economics, information, and transaction costs – have routinely bested proffered alternatives where 'mistakes', irrationality, and path dependence take starring roles in explaining what appears to some analysts to be intractable chaos. The latter inevitably take refuge in the methods of purely historical analyses where history 'just happens'. While historical material and data are vital in any study, we reject these post-modern approaches to institutional economics as inferior alternatives to those which use self-interest as well as rational economizing behavior as the rudiments of analysis. While certainly not above criticism, an embellished Marshallian model (applied, in studying particular historical episodes, to explain *actual results*) has not been supplanted by any of the post-modern theorizing of other schools of thought, including elements of the so-called transaction-cost school (for example, Medema 1997).

Fortunately, a modified model, which captures some elements of institutional change, is there for the economist's taking. It is the economist's best friend – a generalized model of supply and demand (with full transaction costs taken into account). This theory, understood in all essentials for more than 150 years, encapsulates and summarizes but only adumbrates the factors affecting particular markets. (In order to operationalize the theory, an empirical apparatus including some particular institutional details must be attached.) The important point is that supply and demand summarize exchange conditions – full-cost conditions – in particular markets, given some *ceteris paribus* assumptions. Supply and demand are but organizing principles of shifts in market forces wherein exogenous shifters must be identified. Wealth (utility) is generated in the act of exchange so that the familiar welfare triangle measuring producers' and consumers' surpluses will be created and available for distribution. Appropriately summed across all markets, implicit as well as explicit, the total of those net gains from exchange provides an estimate of the wealth of a nation.

For expository purposes, as the foundation for virtually every basic course in economics, this familiar model has no equal. We argue that it may profitably be conceptualized in intertemporal terms as well. Clearly both demand and supply curves are drawn under many assumptions, such as a given assignment of formal or informal property rights, a level of science and technology, a state of transaction and information costs, an endowment of resources and given tastes or preferences. These factors, appropriately neglected over the short run, become the primary focus of analysis in understanding institutional change and the growth or decline of the volume of exchange and, therefore, wealth.

2.2   Change, history and path dependence: a digression

Against the rationalist and embellished supply and demand theory as a basis for studying history, some contemporary economists are searching for a new theoretical basis to analyse institutions. Some (for example, Williamson et al. 1975) claim that rational choice cannot apply to instances where transaction costs and bounded rationality lead to the emergence of non-market institutions (hierarchical organizations) to overcome problems of contracting. Allegedly, these problems, together with the 'path dependence' and 'rule following' associated with institutional change, have led observers to call for the sacking of large portions of traditional microeconomics and for replacing it with some kind of 'new' theory. We acknowledge these in-progress concerns with the theory of institutional change, but believe that the neoinstitutionalist paradigm based on modern neoclassical economics is more than sufficient for particular pre-classical analyses. None of these alternative approaches – those asserting informational problems or bounded rationality – have yet produced comparative analyses of historical institutional change, let alone ones superior to neoclassical-oriented neoinstitutional economics.[8]

Many of these approaches are difficult to assess since they reject the use of empiricism and utilitarian-based economics entirely (Samuels and Medema 1997).[9] Much of such work is actually sociological in nature, rejecting economics as a study that must use scientific methods. Unfortunately there is neither a new theory of any substance nor, to the best of our knowledge, has anyone produced a cogent and testable theory of historical or institutional change that includes non-rational elements as central to the analysis.[10]

An analysis of these non-rational elements in proposals for historical research is not attempted here. However, one so-called theory is so inimical to the use of rational elements, including public choice, in the study of history that it cannot be ignored. North (1990) argues for a modification of static neoclassical theory to accommodate the problem of path dependence. According to him,

> path dependence is the key to an analytical understanding of long-run economic change. The promise of this approach is that it extends the most constructive building blocks of neoclassical theory – both the scarcity/competition postulate and incentives as the driving force – but modifies that theory by incorporating incomplete information and subjective models of *reality* and the increasing returns characteristic of institutions. (p. 112; emphasis in original)

Formal analytical results – there are none yet produced within this paradigm, as North (p. 115) admits – would ostensibly attempt to bridge the gap between strict determinism and randomness, producing a *variety* of possible solutions. But would logical construction of such a theory be possible or useful in the context of economic history?

First, the issue of path dependence is clouded by a peculiar definition of the role and aim of the historical study of institutions. Perfect information – in terms of full knowledge of all possible future occurrences – does not and indeed can never exist. Is the study of economics and history forward or backward looking? If it is forward looking, all-too-fallible individuals make probabilistic decisions on the basis of the best information available to them. Could another agency (government? bureaucrats?) do better? As history unfolds with new and better information in hand, that may be the case but it is not obvious that there is not fallacious circularity in such an argument. Further, it is quite obvious and tautological that, from one perspective, current institutions are affected by the past. However, no methodological framework that we know of can even proximately analyse change without holding past institutions in abeyance. (That is, of course, the scientific manner of studying biology, meteorology or economics.) Many contemporary writers, like their heterodox forebears, latch on to such arguments because they contain the false promise of discovering new market failures that justify more government intervention. We find these approaches, like Keynesianism, to contain little substance or logic.

More critically, there is growing evidence that path dependence – a critical aspect of the so-called new economics – is a theoretically empty concept and an empirical unicorn. In an important series of papers, Liebowitz and Margolis (1990, 1994, 1995a, b) convincingly debunk the most common examples of alleged path dependence and note that (what they call) third-degree path dependence is the only kind that might conflict with the neoclassical model of rational behavior and efficient outcomes. In their words,

> *third-degree path dependence* occurs if an action is ex ante path inefficient, which means that at some time t_0 there is an alternative action $a_1 \in A_0$ such that the discounted present value of the total social benefit of selecting a_1 instead of a_0 is known to be greater than the discounted present value of costs, yet the action a_0 is taken nonetheless. (Leibowitz and Margolis 1995b, pp. 211–12; emphasis in original).

Such path dependence implies market failure in the form of 'lock-in' to past history that was or is (presumably by government action) *remediable*. An event (even a seemingly insignificant event), a choice of technology, or an institution *could* be subject to increasing returns. But, as Liebowitz and Margolis show, third-degree path dependence requires restrictive informational assumptions plus highly implausible and constrained market responses. There are *no* real-world examples of path dependence.[11]

More importantly for the current study, Liebowitz and Margolis address the problems raised for historical investigation. Rising to the allegations that under increasing returns many historical outcomes are possible, including those which are inefficient from a neoclassical (optimizing/behavioral) perspective (Arthur 1989), Liebowitz and Margolis provide a convincing argument that path dependence is demonstrably empty of empirical content. We are in full agreement with the conclusion that such a view is entirely baseless in so far as it avoids the key observation that important and frequent shocks do in fact take place over time so that 'a knowledge of some initial endowment alone could never tell us very much about the eventual path of real economies over time' (Liebowitz and Margolis 1995b, p. 223). Further, they cleverly separate two views of history – one based on neoclassical purposive behavior and the other on path dependence:

> One [the neoclassical] holds that efficiency explanations are important and that economic history, at least, is the search for purpose in past actions. We find, where we can, explanations of events that are based on purposeful behavior: technology responds to scarcities, technique responds to price, and so on. The other [the 'new economics' of path dependence] holds that history is important only to the extent that, for one reason or another, agents do not successfully optimize. History then is the tool to understand what rationality and efficiency do not explain – that is, the random sequence of insignificant events that are not addressable by economic theory. (ibid.)

The latter conception of history, in our view at least, would not be very interesting or informative in explaining the growth or evolution of nations or institutions even if a theory of the 'new economics' could be developed.

Claims of path dependence, therefore, are extremely conjectural, much like the entire body of criticisms that comprise the new institutional economics. Indeed, criticism rises above substance in the approach to history taken by such writers. As Leibowitz and Margolis (1994) argue, it is difficult to take seriously some of the claims made in this literature (for example, Arthur 1989) concerning the alleged superiority of processes or technology at some point in time. Science demands proof or at least demonstration that network effects, which are ubiquitous in the economy, actually constitute some kind of market failure. In short, mistakes are possible in retrospect, but it is difficult to analyse them prospectively. The only reasonable approach at present is to use the scientific method in analysing history and institutional change.

2.3 *Public choice, history and* ceteris paribus *assumptions*

The existence of government, in addition to other fundamental determinants of economic evolution, is critical to the entire process of change. At a fundamental level, alterations in constitutions or voting rules will obviously affect net wealth generated in exchange. However, modern research, such as that embodied in the writings of George Stigler (1971) and Sam Peltzman (1976) has focused more specifically (narrowly?) on how self-interested groups affect wealth in interactions between political and economic markets. They show that utility is generated or dissipated in political exchange.

Since constitutions and voting rules change slowly, interest groups may use their powers to redistribute rents through the political process. Naturally many factors affect the sizes of the surpluses available for transfer in markets so that the Stigler–Peltzman approach is only one aspect of explaining institutional change focusing, as it does, on rent distribution through regulations. It is not a self-contained theory of institutional change or even of government generally since, as we have noted, many factors affect the value of wealth creation in regulated markets over time. Peltzman (1989) has of course admitted as much. But this model does in fact provide an important and suitable basis for a good deal of historical analysis. It also suggests, we believe, how institutional change may come about over time.

Consider, for example, the institution of regulation. Leaving aside the clear possibilities that *some* of the *ceteris paribus* assumptions (new technology, altered transaction costs, property rights, and so forth) may (will) change over time, events will occur that alter the institution. Changes in tastes and technology will, over the long run, shift demand and supply. The ability to capture rents through the political process will also evolve over time. In particular, legal decisions, a new set of politicians or changes in enforcement or transaction costs may (will) create new political alignments and reconfigure potential access to rents.[12] Factors affecting the *size* of rents will ultimately be in evidence. The institutions that result from economizing responses to these events will either be fast moving – high rates of technological change, for example, recently triggered deregulation and freer markets in telecommunications – or slow moving – civil and religious laws respecting marriage have changed very slowly over the past thousand years. Economists must learn to identify when and where the economizing process reaches a critical mass that spurs new rates of institutional change, exchange and growth (Olson 1996).[13]

We return to our previous discussion and reiterate that any argument relating the institutions of public choice (or interest groups) to history must contain certain principles. Among them are that:

1. the domain of the prospective historical examination must be stated clearly in the form of a theory;

2. the theory must clearly separate those forces which are endogenous and those which are exogenous to the analysis, but include as much historical perspective as possible;
3. the role of politicians and interest groups must be carefully identified; and
4. the theory must be stated in a positive and, if at all possible, testable form so that alternative models may be set against it.

As such, all explorations of history using public choice or other modern tools of analysis must be partial in nature. The analytical domain of the analysis must of necessity be limited.

In a very real sense, the study of history or particular institutions using public choice is bound by the clearly stated limits (*ceteris paribus*) of the analysis.[14] It also involves an understanding, often implicit, of the longer-term factors that affect the size of the rent pie (that is, those affecting supply and demand) as well as those affecting the supply and demand for legislation (which includes all political institutions). In practice, of course, many of these factors are held constant in some implicit *ceteris paribus*. This is unavoidable, but some analysts may bring in factors (endogenous or, most often, exogenous) that act as a *deus ex machina* for an analysis of change.[15] Our point is simply that, absent a fully explicated theory of institutional change wherein public choice takes a central place, the reach or attempted reach of any historical study should be grounded in standard and traditional neoclassical economic theory, as currently received. To some degree or another, all of the studies discussed below possess this characteristic.

At bottom, the study of public choice and history – alone or as part of a more general theory of institutional change – demands a combination of scientific methods. There is of course no substitute for learning, through intense and careful historical study, a particular subject area (be it institutional change at a macroeconomic or a microeconomic level). For most researchers, however, modesty and humility are indicated when a *model* of historical change is attempted. Decisions about exogenous and endogenous factors or variables, while often made with good reasons, mean that of necessity the model must be piecemeal (and incomplete). Just as the Cubist masters Picasso and Braque attempted, in part, to achieve multidimensional apprehension of objects in two-dimensional space, the researcher of institutional change must attempt to place tiles into a mosaic that will hopefully be ever clearer but never complete. Alternative configurations of causal factors are always possible. But scientific methods and neoclassical economic theory, including the introduction of public choice reasoning, is the mortar that will hold the tiles in place.

3   History and public choice: a survey

No brief survey, including this one, could possibly summarize the growing body of literature dealing with history in the context of the public choice–neoclassical paradigm of institutional change. Further, and critical for any survey, is the fact that the neoclassical paradigm, as we have described it, includes modern neoclassicism – an approach that combines modern theories of property rights, legal change and transaction costs with public choice principles. All are interrelated. We therefore recognize that the following survey is, of necessity, highly selective and incomplete in nature. All of the studies discussed below mix these elements, although we have attempted to feature most prominently, although not exclusively, those works dealing most directly with the public choice aspects of historical evolution.

3.1   The ancient and medieval world

Strictly speaking, cultural and social anthropology, including the origin of species and the descent of man, is the appropriate starting point for applications of public choice principles to historical development. Few works deal directly with institutional change in early anthropological time, however. A superb exception (Smith 1975) reaches back to the Pleistocene Epoch, using property rights (or, more pointedly, the absence of property rights) to explain institutional change. Smith shows that extinction events and changes in the earliest economic organizations, such as shifts between nomadic and sedentary lifestyles, were in all likelihood driven by the common pool resource problem. Posner (1980a, b) is also an important exception. He contends that several factors are critical to analysing primitive economic and familial organizations. A key element is the availability of market insurance. Family size and organization are dependent on that availability. Becker's (1981) theory of marriage and the family is also relevant in analysing the structures of early kinship units.

Most writers pass over the ancient world in silence, but specialized studies, ultimately of a sociological nature, exist on particular topics. One example is a recent study of Roman tax institutions featuring, along with some neoinstitutional principles, sociological categories of power, ideology and extra-rational considerations (Levi 1988, pp. 21–2 and 26–7).[16] Levi attempts to explain the *forms* of revenue collection over critical episodes of Roman history. In particular, she argues that 'tax farming' and other methods of collecting revenue under the Empire were a function of constraints on emperors' relative bargaining power, their discount rates, and transaction costs (p. 5). Her intentional neglect of public choice, however, leaves the half-neoinstitutional, half-sociological analysis unable to explain certain important questions about 'rule and revenue'.[17] For example, the revenue requirements of the Roman government are bluntly taken as given. Constraints on the imperial government clearly mattered in explaining institutions and change, but Levi disdains the very forces that imposed such constraints. These forces included the self-interested nature and economic and political clout of particular interest groups and their *relative* power through time. Opportunistic political and economic behavior on the part of government bureaucrats in Rome and in the provinces – one of a host of transaction costs – are as relevant to the analysis as were Rome's 'tax farming' practices. While there are interesting aspects to her story, as in many such studies the failure to consider the public choice–rent-seeking process is a critical weakness.[18]

3.2 The feudal–medieval period

The fall of the Roman Empire led to two developments having enormous importance for the future of Western civilization and economic growth. The first of these was the rise of feudal estates, which exemplified new relations between land, labor and capital. The second was the rise of Christianity – first as a fledgling competitor in religious belief against late Greek and Roman varieties of gnosticism and later, after the tenth century, as a kind of supranational government with implications for economic growth in Western Europe. Both of these developments have received attention in the emerging neoinstitutionalist literature.

The property rights and transaction costs literature of the 1960s and 1970s (Alchian 1965a, b; Alchian and Demsetz 1972), based on the seminal contributions of Ronald Coase (1937, 1960), spawned interest in feudal land-tenure arrangements and more modern problems of a similar nature (Cheung 1973). One of the main features of this literature is how new property rights emerged and modifications in basic feudal institutions came about, altering the efficiency properties of the feudal contract and laying the groundwork for economic development.

One well-known study in the Coasian tradition is North and Thomas's *Rise of the Western World* (1973). Their story stresses changes in property rights assignments as, ultimately, increasing the volume of trade and providing the basis for economic growth in the modern world. While the model is not fully specified (with respect to exogenous and endogenous variables), it focuses on forces impacting the availabilities of productive resources. Population decline, especially that brought about by such catastrophic events as the Black Death of the mid-fourteenth century, is treated as the exogenous factor propelling institutional change. High ratios of land to labor after the Black Death triggered rising wages, falling land prices, and the emergence of new institutions with more secure property rights assignments. The increased economic efficiency and greater reliance on markets facilitated by new institutions ultimately cleared the road to economic development.[19]

One problem with institutional analysis of such broad historical scope is that variables ordinarily held constant in studies of particular events cannot be treated as such in studies of economic development spanning centuries. As an example, North and Thomas (1973) are forced into some *ad hoc* reasoning when, as they describe, population recovered and factor proportions reversed again in the last half of the fifteenth century. High manorial feudalism did not return, they argue, owing to an immigration safety valve, to longer leases (increased land tenancy), to the rise of a middle class, to the emergence of towns, and to other factors. Of greater import, however, is the neglect of other forces affecting the rise of the Western world, namely those attending inter-est-group activities operating through some political sector.[20]

3.3   Religion as a factor in medieval economic history

Neglect of implicit markets may also have deleterious consequences in long-period explanations of economic development. The waning of secular governments after the collapse of Rome was accompanied by the waxing of an institution that was as rationally worldly as it was otherworldly – the Roman Catholic Church. 'Markets' for assurances of eternal salvation have existed at all times, primitive, ancient and modern, but the medieval Roman Catholic Church elevated venality to new heights. This organization sought to extract wealth from secular society and to dominate civil authority in multi-form ways – suppressing heresy through violence and intimidation, regulating credit markets to its own benefit and striving to monopolize medieval religious dogma. All of the forces leading to historical change identified by North and Thomas (1973) and others were played out in an environment of interest-group competition and rent seeking between religious and secular interests over the period.

It is difficult to gauge the net effect of the Church and its policies on economic growth. Costs were raised in certain implicit markets, for example, the marriage market (Davidson and Ekelund 1997). The costs imposed on science (if not new technology) when discoveries about the natural world perceptibly threatened the supernatural basis of Church teachings were high and punitive (for example, the case of Galileo). Weighed against these and similar negative factors were others mitigating the impact of the dominant religion on capitalist institutions. The Church was a residual claimant that benefited from economic growth and secularization of society. Usury was overlooked, as was the doctrine of 'just price', especially when Church interests were at stake.[21] The Church was even a sponsor of pedestrian agricultural technology (especially in the medieval Cistercian monasteries).[22] Much work remains to be done before an adequate assessment of the effect of medieval religion on economic growth may be made. The critical point to remember, however, is that a public choice component must accompany neoinstitutional theorizing. The Church, as a kind of supranational government, undoubtedly clashed with the rent-seeking proclivities of secular authorities, including feudal aristocrats, town governments, and other nascent civil interests. These clashes clearly impacted upon economic growth and development in particular parts of Western Europe.[23]

3.4   Mercantilism and the rise of nation-states

One period that has clearly been of interest to neoinstitutional scholars is the so-called mercantile era, variously defined by the periods 1500–1650 or 1500–1776 (the later date marking the publication of the *Wealth of Nations*). There are no shortages of rationales for mercantilism, such as gold or specie acquisition, foreign trade regulation, suppression of the poor, and so on. The most famous explanation, originating in the work of Gustav Schmoller (1897), continuing in the writings of Heckscher (1934), and lingering in a mountain of less adequate treatments (for example, Coats, 1973, 1985; Magnusson 1994), is the so-called historical approach to mercantilism.[24] This approach emphasizes 'state power' as *the* central value. The public choice–neoinstitutional paradigm has been used to argue that such explanations fall to pieces when asked to answer a single question, namely who or what is 'the State'? External and internal mercantile policies, or the policies of any era for that matter, do not emerge full-blown as Athena from the head of Zeus. They are, at any moment, a pastiche and a product of particular rent-seeking interest groups within the context of a particular set of institutions.

In their 1981 study (*Mercantilism as a Rent-Seeking Society*), Ekelund and Tollison described how rational economic actors operating under a given set of constraints ultimately spawned new political and economic institutions, exemplified by a transfer of powers from the British monarchy to Parliament.[25] They described in some detail the political rent-seeking process through which property rights transfers were accomplished. The neoinstitutional reorientation of mercantilism was chiefly accomplished by describing (i) how jurisdictional disputes, of a largely self-interested nature, between the royal court system and the common law courts created shifts in the locus of political power and economic authority between the monarch and nascent democratic institutions, and (ii) how conflicts between the monarchy and its local enforcement agents (the sheriffs) led to de facto internal deregulation. The sequence was that rent-seeking activity altered property rights assignments; changes in property rights created new incentives that in turn redirected economic activities in ways that had important implications for growth and the nature of the economic and political system. The analysis broke new ground in treating rent seeking and property rights as part and parcel of the process through which competitive institutions emerged within the changing political and economic environment of the mercantile era.

This approach, with significant nuances and extensions, has been pursued by a number of analysts. North and Weingast (1989) utilize the central elements of the argument and press on to explain the stability of new institutions following the Glorious Revolution (1688).[26] They focus on the role of Crown–Parliament competition to extract taxes and to create monopoly rights and on the role of the independent judiciary in providing credible commitments as key elements in institutional change over the course of the seventeenth century. Their emphasis, however, is on the latter parts of the period and chiefly on fiscal developments after the Civil War, the Restoration and the Glorious Revolution. The initial argument, upon which they build, was that the foundation for institutional change was laid somewhat earlier (ibid., pp. 817–18). In particular, the competition between the king's courts and common law courts (such as Coke's Court of Common Pleas) over legal and monarchical jurisdiction was a late Tudor development which was finally resolved at the seventeenth century's close. Ekelund and Tollison (1981) also argued that the inability of the Crown to extract rents and wealth transfers through a system of *internal* regulation, and the economic activity that the attempt generated, was another factor in the demise of mercantilism and the economic ascendance of England at the time. North and Weingast (1989) extend this argument by providing a test of the new institutional structure of 'the King in Parliament' together with an independent judiciary. They present analyses of the post-1688 stock market and interest rates on long-term government loans as evidence of the stability of commitments made by the Crown. They make the important point that economic growth was fostered under the new institutions as investors gained confidence that monarchs could not change the rules capriciously.

Significant extensions amending, embellishing and enlarging on these arguments have been contributed to the literature. Wells and Wills (1998) show that the institutional changes in England spawned by all these developments were not inevitable at the time of the Glorious Revolution, as suggested by North and Weingast. That is, the modern world may not have arrived as described by Ekelund and Tollison and North and Weingast had other conditions not obtained. For twenty or more years after the Revolution of 1688, there were both domestic and foreign demands for the return of the Catholic monarchs in the line of Stuart succession, namely, the 'Jacobites' supporting James II (and later the 'Pretender', James III). Focusing on the effects that these dramatic developments had in the capital markets, Wells and Wills develop an econometric model to analyse threats to the institutional structures described in the two earlier contributions. In particular, they analyse the impact of events such as the Treaty of Ryswick (1697), French recognition of the Pretender (1701), the Pretender's invasion of Scotland (1708) and rumors of Queen Anne's death (1712) on stock-market data over the period. They conclude that, embryonic though the stock market was, investor reactions were clear harbingers of the credible commitments that were required of the new institutions leading to modern capitalism.

The institutional evolution of other nations has also been described. While English institutions developed in such a manner as to provide stability and growth, France and especially Spain languished by comparison over the ensuing centuries. Some of the reasons for this have been described in the terms of public choice and neoinstitutional economics (Ekelund and Tollison 1997a, b; Ekelund et al. 1997). Fundamentally, these nations did not experience political change creating the stable environment necessary for markets to develop, at least to the extent that England had achieved by 1720. Far more work is necessary on particular economies and particular institutions before a clear picture might be had of the forces in these and other Western nations that paved the way to the modern era.[27]

3.5   The emergence of the modern world
In the English case, however, it is fairly obvious that the conditions for growth were settled by 1720. Purely historical studies of the ensuing developments in Britain and the United States have provided an enormous amount of material. Studies using the methods of public choice and neoinstitutional analysis, however, are fragmentary, focusing generally on events in those two nations.

3.6   The eighteenth and nineteenth centuries
Broad and sweeping changes occurred over the period between the solidification of modern institutions over the first half of the eighteenth century and the opening of the nineteenth century and, in this brief survey, we can only touch upon a few of them. Clear areas of interest range from institutional interrelationships in agriculture to taxation and the interplay of interest groups pushing particular income legislative and regulatory (re)distribution schemes. Issues relating to urbanization in both Britain and the United States and the responses to perceived 'externalities' and forms of market failure (real and trumped up) also demand attention.

Interest-group activity did not magically disappear after the institutional conflicts and events of the late mercantile era settled the relations between the monarch, Parliament and the courts. Monarchs retained 'regalian' rights to customs duties, colonization of the New World proceeded apace and Parliament remained an engine for rent seeking, albeit at far lower levels than previously. Historical changes of a microanalytic character, such as fundamental evolution in the nature of firms as producing units directed by entrepreneurs, occurred within these larger institutional developments.[28] Changes also took place against a backdrop of wars and international conflicts over trade and colonization.

3.7   Agriculture, tariffs, and taxation

The role of agriculture as an interest group between the close of the Glorious Revolution and the end of the nineteenth century, along with the closely related issues of land tenure and the enclosures, has received only piecemeal treatment. The tariffs imposed on grains during the Napoleonic Wars marked a watershed in the structure of agricultural duties. Commerce and trade, however, has received more attention.

Tight international controls on trade with the colonies continued. A series of Navigation Acts (such as those passed in 1660, 1663, 1673, and 1696) were oriented to the business and merchant interests in England. This trend continued into the eighteenth century as rules (for example, all colonial imports had to move *through* England) and 'enumeration' (colonial exports could only be shipped *to* England) were imposed.[29] Rent-seeking interests in England and those of colonial governors and favored merchants explain this sort of mercantile regulation. For example, a Hat Act was passed by Parliament in 1732 under political pressures of London felt makers. Already under pressure from French competition, the London felt makers were fearful of competition from the colonists. The act prohibited the exportation of hats from one colony to another, required colonists to serve a seven-year apprenticeship before entering the trade, with the number of apprentices limited to two per shop, and barred the employment of Negroes in hat making altogether. A Molasses Act, passed in 1733, was of the same character (Morris 1961). These and other regulatory enactments, later helping to create profound institutional change, have not yet received full coverage from a public choice–neoinstitutional perspective.

A fine example of that perspective applied to early commercial restrictions in the fledgling American republic is Pincus's (1975, 1977) work on the 'Tariff of Abominations' (1824). In formal econometric tests of the sources of the tariff, Pincus provides evidence that the typical historical explanation, namely that it was based solely on regional interests, is not generally supportable. He argues that the ability to secure protectionist legislation was a function of the anticipated effects of the tariffs, the efforts motivated by these effects to have the restriction imposed, and the reactions of members of Congress to such efforts. It was a complex process wherein the distribution of firm sizes and market shares within particular jurisdictions was not as important as the national political clout of particular industries. That clout was most easily translated into protective legislation when pressure was brought to bear by groups 'speak[ing] for many establishments with output spread fairly evenly across states' (Pincus 1975, p. 757). Pincus's methodology could well be applied to numerous regulatory historical changes, tariffs being only one of them, over the eighteenth and nineteenth centuries.[30]

The tools of public choice and neoinstitutional analysis, formal or informal, are also applicable to tax structures in England and in the colonial and post-national periods of US history.[31] Regalian duties, such as customs and certain excises, were a key source of revenue, but property taxes on the aristocracy (vestiges of feudal land duties) were also a factor. But, to the best of our knowledge, few formal studies of this character exist.

3.8 Poverty and the distribution of income

Eighteenth- and nineteenth-century patterns of taxation in England helped produce an income distribution that followed along the lines cast by feudal relations. In general, the tax burden fell heaviest on the poor and working classes. Regressive taxation, urbanization (see below), labor immobility, and the rigidity of class structure all contributed to a highly skewed income distribution. Capitalism and the institutions it spawned had yet to radically disturb patterns established under feudal and mercantile institutions.

Once more, little has been done of a public choice–neoinstitutionalist nature on these particular problems. Many studies describe the contributions of classical economists to the ideological debates on the Poor Laws surrounding the reform movements of the 1830s. None (that we know of) deal, either formally or informally, with the problem from an interest-group perspective.

Other areas relating to particular institutions or institutional change in the area of income distribution are of interest. Rent seeking into the income distribution by well-organized interest groups certainly harks back to feudal times. The medieval guild system, codified by the Statute of Artificers in 1563, continued under various guises into the eighteenth and nineteenth centuries. Statutes formally tying individuals to their place of birth – the so-called 'settlement arrangements' – were in place over much of this period. The poor, in short, had to stay put. Such barriers to labor mobility undoubtedly had important implications for income distribution and economic efficiency. Later, the formal demands for unionization – and in particular the Chartist agitation circa 1838–48 – are important and neglected subjects for public choice–neoinstitutional analysis.

3.9 Legislation and internal regulation

Understandably perhaps, particular pieces of legislation over the eighteenth and nineteenth centuries relating to institutional change have proved more amenable to analysis than have broader and far more complex aspects of history such as sweeps of changes in income distribution. Such, for example, has been the case with early factory legislation. Agitation to bar children, and later women, from the textile factories was given a clear public-interest rationalization by historians and economic historians. The Acts of 1814 started the process, but the Factory Act of 1833 (Althrorp's Bill) was the first such law with enforcement provisions (children nine years old and younger were banned from the factories altogether and the number of hours worked by those between the ages of nine and 18 were restricted).

The tools of public choice as interest-group analysis have exploded the myth. Rather than protection for the 'exploited', Marvel (1977) argued, with evidence, that the owners of steam-driven mills increased their wealth by restricting competition from water-driven mills (which employed more children). But, in addition to capital interests, labor interests joined in supporting the bill. Corollary provisions relating to health and education meant that physicians and teachers benefited from the regulation of child labor (Anderson and Tollison 1984). Male operatives, especially the spinners, also acted as an interest group opposing the employment of youngsters who posed viable competition for their jobs (Anderson et al. 1987). These labor interests were buttressed by an effective voting franchise given to male operatives in the Reform Act of 1832. This new power in Parliament (which of course also demands explanation) made them an effective interest group. The group was so effective in fact that, in 1844, it was an important factor in legislation restricting the employment of women in factories.

Other important examples of legislation, regulation and institutional change have been subjected to public choice analysis. Indeed the most effective thrust of public choice analysis directed to historical episodes has been in the areas of antitrust and regulation. The new energy and transportation technologies that spurred the development of large-scale manufacturing and metallurgy brought many issues to the fore. The very concept of 'competition' was, in consequence, moving quickly away from what Adam Smith had in mind when he described England as a 'nation of shopkeepers'. In particular, the emergence of railway transportation (underway in both the United States and Britain by the 1830s) altered Smith's central notion of 'atomism'.[32] The result, for railroads and large manufacturing industries, was a focus on income distribution problems created by so-called monopolies.

Interest groups coalesced around these capital-intensive industries with the predictable results that, conditions apropos, legislation redistributing wealth and income could be expected. In the United States these interests were first felt at the state levels where interest-group analysis has been used to describe antitrust *before* the Sherman Act (Libecap 1992; Boudreaux et al. 1995) and its relation to the law's passage. Public choice methodology and empirical evidence is used by the latter to show that the impetus for antitrust law came from state agricultural lobbies of the American Midwest, particularly rural cattlemen. The Sherman Act itself has been scrutinized from a public choice perspective (Stigler 1985; DiLorenzo 1985), the latter revealing clear evidence that the very industries accused of being monopolized in the mid-1880s were in fact expanding output and lowering prices.[33] That self-interested politicians and very self-interested groups of businesses and laborers were involved is now indisputable. The political and interest-group underpinning of the Clayton Act of 1914 has also been suggested (Ekelund et al. 1995).

3.10 Urbanization

Developments at lower levels of government within the US and British economies have also attracted the interest of public choice–neoinstitutional economists. The rise of urban population centers over the period – a product of both demand-pull and supply-push pressures – triggered massive changes in the size and scope of government. Housing, water supply, sanitation and sewage systems, police powers, fire protection and the provision of highways, dams and bridges posed virtually all of the same resource-allocation problems treated under the modern rubrics of 'externalities' and 'public goods'. Rent seeking shaped all of these developments and, while some studies have clearly advanced our knowledge of the efficiency characteristics of the institutional responses of the eighteenth and nineteenth centuries, explanations of these developments remain far from complete.

A few studies are highly relevant, however. It is at the lower levels of government, apart from the matter of national defense, that the interface between private markets and public goods plays out. Problems associated with urban congestion, such as the provision of funerals, burial services and cemeteries, created at least perceived sources of market failure along with clear interest-group alliances (Ekelund and Ford 1997). The development of urban transportation networks is even more interesting from an institutional perspective. These goods, clearly regarded as 'public' at other times and in other places, were not treated as such in the eighteenth and nineteenth centuries. In France, but especially in England, bridges and some roads were basically financed during the nineteenth century by privately generated funds and tolls.

Economist Ralph Turvey (1996a, b, 1997), in an interesting and informative series of papers, has documented the institutional arrangements surrounding road and bridge provision in London. Turvey found evidence that London bridges, with three exceptions up to 1864 (London, Blackfriars and Westminister bridges), all charged tolls. These bridges were privately financed and operated subject to legislative authority, which set the maximum tolls to be charged. Competition between rival contractors led to different tolls based on elasticity considerations. An act of 1877 abolished the tolls and required the sale of these bridges to the state. The London Metropolitan Board bought out the seven companies (only some of which were profitable), but such forced nationalization undoubtedly was inspired by interest-group activity.[34]

The burgeoning US economy experienced similar urban problems in the nineteenth century. Evidence of some kind of market failure was not always necessary to establish the 'need' for institutional and regulatory change. Fred McChesney (1986) provides some keen insights into interest-group dynamics in his study of government prohibitions on volunteer fire fighting in nineteenth-century America. From colonial times, fire fighting was privately provided in the United States. Suddenly, between 1853 and 1871, public enterprise took over. 'Why?', asks McChesney. He finds the likely answer in a careful analysis of the interest groups which benefited from institutional change, in particular, firemen (obtaining rents for formerly 'free' work), insurance companies (eliminating costs to themselves), and municipalities (garnering more patronage to bestow). The public interest – cheaper and more effective protection – was circumvented by governments who failed to assign and enforce property rights and who encouraged violence between rival fire-fighting organizations to speed up the shift to public control. While relatively few studies deal with local governments in a historical context, the public choice, neoinstitutionalist paradigm evidently has much to contribute in this area of historical analysis.

3.11   *Into the twentieth century*

The range and applicability of public choice as an integral part of historical analysis continue into the twentieth century. As the theory expressed at the beginning of this chapter suggests, the processes of institutional development – which are embedded in and constitute history – can be understood best in Marshallian terms. Some initial set of institutions must be presupposed and a set of variables exogenous to the model must be identified to lay the foundation for discussing institutional change. This modeling process is highly complex and, once again, can only be undertaken piecemeal.

Historical trends in institutions, only some of which we have touched upon here, were being altered dramatically as Western economies confronted the rise of modern capitalism in the late nineteenth and early twentieth centuries. All of the developments considered above were a prologue to modern institutions. In particular, tax structures, reflecting changing transaction costs and interest-group pressure, were profoundly affected in England by the mid-nineteenth century and in America in the second decade of the twentieth.[35] Actual or perceived disparities in the distribution of income helped trigger opposition to unfettered capitalism from diverse quarters. Progressives and socialists, along with those supporting voting rights for women and, later, minorities, assembled powerful coalitions to push their reform agendas through democratic political processes. These coalitions, with both economic and social goals, helped fuel the institutional change that created the modern world. It would be naive, not to say impossible, to catalogue these changes even briefly. We satisfy ourselves with a nod to a few general subjects – leaving out whole areas of study – and with citations to some works in the public choice tradition. Much, but certainly not all, of this analysis involves rent-seeking models wherein special interests interact at some level of government.

3.12   Agriculture, tariffs, and taxation revisited

Institutional change relating to agriculture and tariffs continued apace from previous centuries. The twentieth-century twist, of course, is the relative increase in urbanization and industrialization that diluted the political impact of agricultural interests. For example, Ellison and Mullin (1995) examine sugar tariff legislation, revealing the variety of interests standing either to benefit or lose from sugar tariff reform in 1912. Political outcomes, they argue, were shaped by the interests of consumers as well as those of competing producers. Ellison and Mullin (p. 336) employ a model wherein politicians are 'single-minded seekers of reelection' and find that tariff reform was consistent with the desires of two larger, less-concentrated groups, namely beet interests and sugar-cane farmers. This result, in harmony with Pincus's argument concerning the Tariff of 1824, meant that sugar-cane-refining interests carried less weight in the political process.[36]

Other studies employing interest-group analysis deal with larger issues of tariffs and the types of taxation that have fueled the growth of government in the twentieth century. The importance of tariff policy at the turn of the century is not surprising given that tariffs were the primary revenue source – and election issue – of the day. Typically, Democrats were anti-tariff while Republicans supported protectionist legislation. The reverse was true with respect to the adoption of the income tax as a replacement for tariffs (Hall et al., pp. 321–2; Baack and Ray 1985, pp. 608–9). Hence, the industrial North, primarily Republican, voted in favor of tariffs to protect its manufacturing base while the agrarian South and much of the West favored the income tax.

One clear exception to the South's stance on tariffs is evident in the sugar industry's success in securing favorable tariff treatment. Here, the Democrats typically opted either to abstain from the tariff vote or to vote in favor of the tariff as a means of protecting the major industrial interests in their states at the time. This was the case in the voting on sugar tariff reform in 1912. While the voting was almost strictly along party lines,[37] both of Louisiana's senators crossed over and voted 'aye' in favor of tariffs while Colorado's Democratic senator abstained (Ellison and Mullin 1995, p. 359).[38]

As the century progressed, the electoral importance of tariffs began to wane. There are a few alternative explanations of the rise of the income tax and the decline of tariffs as tools of public finance. Hall et al. (1998) attribute the change in large part to the enfranchisement of women. They maintain that women were primarily interested in consumption goods in the early twentieth century since their labor force participation rate was low and it was thought that the women did much of the household purchasing. Hence, as women gained the right to vote, their interest in lower prices for consumption goods invigorated political opposition to high tariffs. The politicians responded to this new voting bloc and, combined with the impact of the Depression on international trade and the new strength of the Democratic party in the New Deal era, the importance of tariffs as a source of revenue was reduced and, to a large extent replaced, by the income tax (ibid., pp. 324–8).

Baack and Ray (1985) offer a different explanation for the income tax's adoption. They point out that the votes in favor of an income tax law in 1894 were cast almost exclusively by the Democrats in the House (p. 609). However, the Supreme Court ruled on the matter in 1895, declaring the income tax unconstitutional owing to its direct nature. Congress voted in 1909 to propose a constitutional amendment that authorized the taxation of income. By this time, support for an income tax was nearly unanimous. It was the financing of a military buildup between 1895 and 1909 as well as growth in a variety of income-transfer programs (veterans' pensions, subsidies to the merchant marine, and federal funding for naval construction in states traditionally opposed to the tax) that supplied the necessary conditions for adoption of the income tax (ibid., pp. 613–16). With the constitutional authority in place, the income tax was to provide government with the wherewithal to expand its role considerably, particularly in the New Deal era. These developments had, as it turned out, cataclysmic implications for the size and scope of government for the remainder of the century and beyond.[39]

3.13   Social legislation
More than any other area, perhaps, the hallmark of twentieth-century institutional–economic change has been in the realm of social legislation, including regulations affecting health and safety. Many social scientists trace the sources of such change to egalitarian motives, ideological shifts, market failures of various kinds, the costs of discrimination and so on. Whatever truth there may be in these explanations, it is clear that public choice–interest-group economics has much to say about such historical episodes.

3.14   Child labor legislation
The Progressive movement in American politics of the latter part of the nineteenth century and the first decades of the twentieth century was a product of the drive for new social policies (in addition, of course, to the 'trust-busting' legislation directed at American business). A number of the reforms did not come to fruition until the New Deal era or after. Two of the Progressives' goals – important for their subsequent impact on market institutions – included the passage of the Nineteenth Amendment to the Constitution (ratified in 1920), providing for the popular election of US senators, and the

development of child labor legislation (finally passed in 1938) and associated restrictions on children in the workforce. The tools of public choice have been applied to some of this legislation.

The Factory Acts suppressing child labor in the textile factories of nineteenth-century England have, as we have seen, been subjected to public choice analysis. Their American counterparts were also a feature of nineteenth-century policy, but only at the state level. High on the agenda of Progressives, national legislation and constitutional amendments were tried a number of times (in 1916, 1919 and 1924). Included in the National Industrial Recovery Act (in 1933), the legislative centerpiece of Franklin Roosevelt's First New Deal, restrictions on child labor were declared unconstitutional two years later along with the rest of the act (in *Schecter Poultry Co.* v. *United States*). Thrown in with the Fair Labor Standards Act (FLSA) of 1938, the child labor laws were finally passed. The FLSA banned the employment of children under 16 years of age in interstate commerce, regulated the hours of work and wages of 16- to 18-year-olds and prohibited their assignment to hazardous jobs. Was the act motivated by public-interest or private-interest concerns?

Davidson et al. (1995) provide evidence that this so-called social legislation had private-interest components. In econometric analyses of the Senate vote, they found that a constellation of interests combined to inspire passage of the FLSA. Business interests (in particular, small firms and firms in interstate commerce), labor interests (non-unionized) and regional interests (Southern states) opposed child labor regulation whereas their counterparts supported it. Senators representing agricultural interests were free to vote for the act since the farm sector was exempt. In short, private interests and not the public interest were shown to be decisive in passing child labor legislation.

Special interests act on many margins. The suppression of input competition for adult labor was further solidified by compulsory school attendance laws. In a 1978 study, Edwards (1978) stresses the importance of taking account of the endogenous nature of such legislation. In particular, she models the joint determination of school attendance laws and the enrollment rates of 16- and 17-year-olds, the children most likely to be affected by minimum working age provisions (pp. 205–6). Edwards argues that the groups most likely to benefit from compulsory school attendance legislation are those employed in the education industry, especially teachers, as well as individuals who compete with teenagers in the labor market (p. 216). The losers from such legislation will be the families of teenagers not currently enrolled who would be forced to return to school and, to a lesser extent, taxpayers in general, who will have to fund more school facilities (p. 216). As with the Factory Acts of nineteenth-century England, adult substitutes for teen labor benefit as well.

3.15   Sex and race discrimination

Sex and race discrimination have also been brought within the ambit of the public choice, interest-group paradigm. Fishback (1989) examined lax enforcement of both the property rights and civil rights of blacks, particularly with respect to unequal opportunities for schooling. The interaction of coal companies and segregated schools in early twentieth-century West Virginia is analysed to test the hypothesis that coal companies marshaled their political influence to reduce funding disparities between black and white schools. The various interests at hand include local school boards (charged with distributing state and local tax dollars to the schools), white constituents, and the coal companies (faced with a tight labor market).

Funding for education was determined, at least in part, by locally elected school boards whose members Fishback modeled as seeking the support of the median voter. In most cases, the median voter in West Virginia's school districts circa 1910 was white. That implies that little or nothing was spent on black schools and, hence, that black-paid property taxes and blacks' pro rata share of state education funds were used largely to fund white schools (ibid., p. 313).

Coal companies were likely to favor funding equalization for several reasons. They typically owned much of the property located in the vicinities of their mines and hired in a competitive regional labor market. Improving public education would help the coal companies attract greater numbers of productive workers to their towns. Moreover, given the tight labor markets in the early twentieth century, discrimination was a costly indulgence. Blacks accounted for 20 percent of the mine workforce in West Virginia throughout the boom period (ibid., p. 314). Hence, benefits would be gained by increasing spending on black education, which, since expenditures per pupil in the white schools already far exceeded those in the black schools, would attract more black workers at the margin. Fishback compared spending per pupil for black and white schools in West Virginia with Virginia, Alabama, and North Carolina – the primary areas where the coal companies recruited. He found that West Virginia actually spent slightly more per pupil on black students than on white students, while Virginia, Alabama, and North Carolina spent 3.4, 5.7, and 2.6 times more per white student, respectively (p. 317). The only other state showing results similar to West Virginia was Kentucky, where blacks also comprised roughly 20 percent of the workforce.

Interest-group theory suggests that although they seldom represented more than 10 percent of the population, blacks could organize as an interest group and trade their support on other issues for increased educational funding. Moreover, the coal companies, as the predominant employers in coal-producing counties, were well placed to influence local school board decisions. Fishback maintains that labor market competition, which reduced discrimination within the coal companies, also influenced local policy toward educational funding and mitigated governmental discrimination in public school funding.

Hunt and Rubin (1980) analyse legislative votes on the Equal Rights Amendment (ERA), which passed Congress in 1972, but ultimately failed to be ratified by the states, to explore the political economy of discrimination in the hiring and pay of women. The authors maintain that absent the legislation, married women would gain in the form of higher salaries for their husbands, which would compensate for the women's lower earnings. Single women, however, would have no such compensation. This observation leads to the conclusion that legislation prohibiting labor market discrimination against women should affect marriage rates more than female labor force participation rates. Single women have higher labor force participation rates as well as longer work-life expectancies than men, who in turn rank higher on these characteristics than married women do. The potential labor force advantages of single women, however, are discounted by the likelihood that they will marry, thereby making men the employees of choice (pp. 289–90). This becomes an even more likely scenario when the employer intends to invest in the employee's human capital. Many employers will be hesitant to invest in women if they are not expected to remain in the labor force long enough to recoup those investments. Hence, single women who plan to continue to work stand to gain the most by lobbying for anti-discrimination laws (ibid., p. 291). The authors test this hypothesis by relating the extent of female political activity by state to the percentage of votes favoring the ERA (p. 291).

3.16   *The New Deal and twentieth-century economic legislation*
The policies of the New Deal, which laid the foundation for the rapid growth of government experienced in ensuing administrations (notably Lyndon Johnson's), were as interest-group oriented as the theory predicts, according to contemporary public choice research. The transition from the minimal state of turn-of-the-century America to the era of 'big government' launched during the 1930s is the subject of a number of inquiries. This transition was of course facilitated by new taxing powers granted to the federal government by the sixteenth Amendment. Anderson and Tollison (1991a) analyse the beginnings of the transfer state in interest-group terms. The conventional explanation is that Franklin Roosevelt's New Deal saved capitalism by responding to its disastrous collapse with massive increases in social spending. Spending increased, to be sure, but as Anderson and Tollison show, state-by-state allocations of federal emergency relief funds were not based on economic 'need' but on political considerations. They find that the Roosevelt administration used federal spending – including spending on such non-social programs as highway construction – to reward electoral support and to penalize non-

support. As they put it, 'New Deal spending went partly to the needy and partly to those with political clout' (ibid., p. 175).

More recently, Couch and Shughart (1998) examine New Deal policies, dissagregating the data by program and by year. Further, they extend consideration of political influence to a greater number of congressional committees (Anderson and Tollison focused on the House Ways and Means and Senate Finance committees). Among a number of issues, Couch and Shughart test and refute the hypothesis that states that were hit less hard by the depression received more money from the federal government because of programmatic matching requirements. Harder-hit states were in fact required to contribute greater shares of the programs' costs. These and other related studies remind us that the politicization of governmental policy processes is not of modern origin.

In addition to the movement to write antitrust legislation in the late nineteenth and early twentieth centuries, the legislative delegation of business regulation to bureaucratic agencies was a hallmark of both the Progressive and New Deal eras. Despite protests from a few leading thinkers, the Act to Regulate Commerce, creating the Interstate Commerce Commission (ICC), was passed in 1887 to regulate railway rates, particularly with an eye toward prohibiting price discrimination. Though its success in controlling rates, even in the early period, is debatable (Spann and Erickson 1970; Zerbe 1980), the ICC's regulatory reach was extended in ensuing decades to include interstate trucking (1935), inland water carriers (1940), interstate pipelines (1906–77), and interstate telephony (1910–34). The New Deal triggered an explosion of regulation at all levels of government to encompass telecommunications and many industries and occupations that were (allegedly) 'affected with a public interest'. Federal regulation continued to expand through the 1960s and 1970s, abating only with the deregulation movement of the 1980s and 1990s. In reality, such regulation was inspired more by narrow self-interests than it was by consumers and the public interest. A positive theory of regulation (and deregulation) is thus the product of interest-group activity.[40]

These and many other developments have received in-depth treatment elsewhere (Peltzman 1989; Tollison 1991; Ekelund and Tollison, Chapter 17 this volume) and we eschew detailed consideration of them here.[41] Whether economic legislation and the institutional changes it creates are or are not in the public interest is an empirical matter, however. A growing body of evidence suggests that much regulatory activity over the twentieth century can only be understood as rent-seeking redistributions of income and wealth.

3.17   *Externalities, history, and public choice*
The myth that the public choice–neoinstitutionalist approach focuses only on 'government failure' (Levi 1988) is completely unfounded. Indeed, where

genuine market failures exist, for example, in flood control or the provision of streetlights, all parties to exchange stand to benefit. We therefore expect a greater demand for collective action in such areas. Conversely, policies that carry large net social costs are not expected to survive for long (Becker 1983, 1985; Wittman 1995).

A number of interesting studies may be cited in this regard. Giertz (1974) provides an interesting application of public choice in his analysis of the measures implemented in Ohio in response to flooding along the Miami River in 1913. A system of taxation grounded in the benefit principle was fashioned along the lines suggested by standard welfare theory to enable those who gained from the policy change to compensate those who were made worse off by it. Because flood control can be classified as a public good (exclusion is not possible once the protection is provided), private provision of flood protection through voluntary collective action was likely to encounter a free-rider problem (ibid., pp. 64–5). Ultimately, benefit taxation combined with compensation was critical in winning support for the quasi-governmental Miami Conservancy District (MCD). By forming the MCD, the costs and benefits of flood protection on the local level were internalized, a factor Giertz (p. 67) maintains contributed to the successful solution to the flooding problems.

A reservoir system was built that lowered the probability of flooding downstream while raising it upstream. The most significant problem was estimating associated changes in land values. The MCD created a measure, called the 'flooding factor', to rate a property's need for flood protection (ibid., p. 71). The benefit from flood protection was calculated as a multiple of the property's appraised value prior to the 1913 flood, the flooding factor, and the degree of protection provided. Taxes were then assessed based on the level of benefit conferred (pp. 71–2). To compensate losers – those residents and taxpayers upstream where flooding was made more likely – fees were levied on downstream municipalities, which paid the MCD from general tax revenues (p. 72). It was estimated that the overall benefits of the program were in excess of $100 million while the cost was under $25 million (administrative costs excluded). While the benefit estimates might have been inflated, the benefit–cost cushion was sufficient to absorb any such discrepancies, making the project a Pareto-superior move in Giertz's opinion.

Naturally, even if externalities – actual or perceived – are internalized by particular programs or policies, rent seeking by benefiting interest groups still shapes political outcomes. While it might by argued, for instance, that some of the activities of the Occupational Safety and Health Administration and the Environmental Protection Agency address market failure in a positive manner, that does not mean that their activities are free from political influence. Bartel and Thomas (1987) describe how firms may take advantage of regulatory processes to raise rivals' costs. The point is simple: interests within industries (and sometimes even within firms) are not homogeneous. Bartel and Thomas's key insight is that when the costs of regulatory compliance differ across firms, regulation will be supported by those members of the industry whose costs will rise the least. Heterogeneous firms within an industry and the frequently asymmetric effects of regulations can produce these kinds of wealth redistribution. The authors then examine the effects of environmental and safety regulations on 'Sun Belt' industries and other firms to adduce empirical support for their theory.

3.18   Property rights, interest groups, and public choice

As the Coasian tradition teaches, where formal property rights do not exist, informal bargains to prevent rent dissipations are often struck by the private parties to an exchange. Cheung's (1973) famous study of private contractual agreements between beekeepers and apple growers is one example and there are many others.[42] The establishment of property rights will in all cases supply the framework underlying a particular distribution of wealth, present or future. The property rights assignment, furthermore, will produce changes in that distribution. But since legal or political processes are most often the means for defining or redefining property rights, rent-seeking coalitions (interest groups) naturally coalesce around anticipated changes in wealth. One can, therefore, only fully understand the evolution of property rights assignments within the context of an interest-group model.

In an excellent 1986 survey article, Libecap (1986) analyses the interaction between property rights and economic and political behavior in a variety of times and places. These include property rights to natural resources in the American West, the enclosure movement in eighteenth-century England, land-tenure arrangements in the American South, and crude oil production in the United States (ibid., p. 229).

We have already examined some of these applications, but a series of articles addressing the development of property rights to natural resources in the Old (American) West is worth noting. Informal agreements, such as livestock associations, were a hallmark of the era. But where land-use rights were insecure, overgrazing resulted which led to a deterioration of both land values and incomes (ibid., p. 238). The point is that even loosely assigned rights establish a configuration of costs and benefits that differentially affect various groups.

Opposition to reforms allowing for larger, more efficient land claims is analysed by Libecap (1981a, b). Interest groups were clearly involved. The departments of Agriculture and the Interior both opposed the reform proposals. Libecap maintains that the former's opposition was based on budget considerations. The existing piecemeal allocation system justified more departmental oversight. Many ranchers nevertheless fenced the land illegally to more easily mark their claims and control access (Libecap 1986, pp. 238–9). The Department of the Interior opposed fencing because it created a barrier to homesteaders. The removal of fences and the open range regime that ultimately emerged led to higher costs and widespread overgrazing, thereby diminishing the value of the land.

Anderson and Hill (1975) analyse the evolution of property rights on the American Great Plains, particularly with respect to the use of land, water, and cattle. The authors focus on the costs and benefits of establishing and enforcing rights, maintaining that such a focus sheds light on institutional change. Anderson and Hill find in all cases that when benefits increase (or costs decline), additional resources are devoted to property rights definition and enforcement. The converse holds as well (ibid., pp. 178–9).

In an analysis of ownership rights to land in the American West, Libecap (1986, p. 236) explains that, as deposits of gold, silver and other minerals were discovered, land values increased. But because in most cases property rights were yet not assigned, establishing them produced few if any redistributional effects. This alleviated much of the political costs of allocating rights. Indeed, several of the studies surveyed by Libecap suggest that property rights were adopted quickly and relatively smoothly.[43]

Interest-group dynamics are evident in several studies of 'primitive' property rights assignments. Johnsen (1986), for example, examines the system of reciprocal exchange – called potlatching – used by the Southern Kwakiutl Indians (a group consisting of 28 autonomous tribal units) along the Pacific coast of North America.[44] Johnsen (ibid., pp. 41–2) maintains that potlatching was a means of maintaining exclusive territories and preventing overfishing of salmon, the primary source of wealth at the time. Exclusive territories were allocated to the tribe that either had captured it during war or claimed it as its place of ancestral origin (p. 47). Potlatching created a system of insurance whereby those tribes experiencing a poor fishing season were subsidized by those with successful seasons. This diminished the incentive to encroach on another tribe's territory and thereby helped avoid violent conflict. The system also incorporated mechanisms for discouraging free riding. Those tribes that continually had poor seasons would have their potlatch ranking reduced. This meant that the value of the transfers (or gifts) received from other groups would decline in value (p. 42). Since each tribe was likely to have a poor fishing season at some point, potlatching became a means of reciprocal exchange to enforce property rights and to smooth out variations in the opportunity cost of encroaching on another tribe's territory (pp. 62–3).

McChesney (1990) also analysed the assignment of property rights on Indian lands, but from a different perspective. From 1887 to 1934, the US government defined Indian rights to reservation land. But the property rights assignment was incomplete: the government continued as a trustee for 25 years, rationalizing its presence as being needed to preserve the Indian way of life (ibid., p. 299). The result of the incomplete assignment of property rights was to diminish the social gain of the privatization program. Prior to McChesney's analysis, the conventional explanation of the government's policy was that it was well intentioned but mistaken. The 'mistake' was corrected by prohibiting further privatization of Indian lands (ibid.). McChesney offers an alternative explanation. Using a Peltzman-type model of regulation, McChesney posits that the privatization of Indian land and the subsequent prohibition of new private ownership arrangements were complementary parts of an overall political policy that increased bureaucratic budgets, particularly for the Bureau of Indian Affairs (BIA), and also served the aims of well-organized non-Indian interest groups (ibid., pp. 299–306).

The BIA's problem was that budget growth could not continue unless privatization ended. The political decision to halt privatization was made easier by declining support from private interests, namely the interests of whites, politicians, and bureaucrats. All had initially favored privatization as all three groups stood to gain from the policy, but as time passed the whites lost interest, the bureaucrats had shifted from favoring to opposing privatization, and Congress sided with the bureaucratic interests (ibid., pp. 317 and 335). Hence, McChesney maintains that the interest-group hypothesis of the growth of BIA budgets is the only one consistent with all phases of Indian land privatization.

4   Conclusion

The contributions surveyed herein are but a sample of the growing literature relating property rights to institutional change. They reveal, however, the potential rewards of applying economic analysis, including interest-group analysis, to historical episodes. Without doubt, property rights are a key to understanding economic exchange and economic growth. But economically efficient property rights are not handed down by a benevolent state. They emerge from a very complex process of competing interest groups, positive transaction costs and system 'shocks' that constitute the real world. Public choice reasoning is, almost always, critical to the understanding of historical and institutional change.

It must be admitted that, despite decades of work, a unified theory of institutional change does not exist. Different writers emphasize alternative levels of rationality, information requirements, transaction costs and the impact of property rights imbedded in any particular system. Different roles are assigned to ideas, ideology, culture, norms and path dependence. While we adhere to a public choice, neoinstitutional view of change, the ongoing debate is sure to produce a clearer understanding of the forces that generate

change. The transmission mechanism of politics into property rights alterations and redistribution of wealth is and will always be a central element in
the discussion.

Reconstructing the past and the evolution of economic entities (including
social and political change) is vital to understanding processes that are constantly under way. Institutions and policies matter and are central to answering
the most important economic question of all. As the late Mancur Olson
(1996) put it, 'Why are some nations rich and some nations poor?'. Institutional processes determine a set of property rights which determine the volume
and quality of exchanges, the level of welfare generated and, ultimately, the
direction of economic growth and development. Public choice economics,
along with all of modern neoclassical economic analysis, has a pivotal role to
play in the explanation of that crucial process.

Notes

1. See, for example, Furubotn and Richter (1997) and Pejovich (1995). Both very ably
   summarize the theoretical underpinnings of the new institutional economics.
2. Again, terminology may get in the way of understanding. Furubotn and Richter (1997)
   call their study the 'new institutional economics' but they are clearly not writing in the
   Veblenian tradition.
3. Economists have known for quite some time that static theory is absolutely required as the
   basis for a theory of institutional change. For example, Friedrich von Wieser ([1914]
   1967, p. 457) argued that 'the theorist must always start from the static assumption. It
   yields most readily to his idealizing method. Dynamic relationships cannot be clearly
   defined in his thinking until after the static conditions have been fully apprehended'.
4. In a very real sense, all studies are 'historical' in nature. Ordinary empirical tests of
   particular hypotheses partake of the nature of such studies. A test, for example, of the
   impact of some aspect of a legal-regulatory change, such as that wrought by the Telecommunications Act of 1996, must take a specific historical period as the subject of the
   analysis.
5. Ekelund and Tollison (1997a, b) argue that rational economizing – a modern neoclassical
   approach containing these elements – is vastly superior to alternative explanations that
   deny the rationality postulate or deny that economic analysis extends to implicit as well as
   explicit markets. Non-economists – those at least innocent of modern economic analysis –
   argue, for example, that economics cannot reach such matters as religion (see Campbell
   1997).
6. The all-too-facile argument that Pareto optimality is inapplicable in intertemporal situations will simply not do. While it is obvious that intertemporal welfare maximization
   based on Paretian principles is inapplicable over long periods, and while measurement
   problems abound in intertemporal situations, as they do in all economic analyses, some
   components of an intertemporal maximand must be selected in order to make any sense of
   the direction of change. No wind is the right wind when a port has not been chosen. Chaos
   is the result of so much of the theoretical prognostications of 'new institutionalists' for the
   very reason that any parts of economics smacking of 'science' are rejected out of hand
   (for example, see Samuels and Mercuro 1984). Problems relating to Coasian developments and gross exaggerations of the difficulties posed by theoretical transaction costs are
   other examples of *ad hoc* reasoning marshaled to attack the modern neoclassical paradigm
   as applied to institutional economics (see Medema 1997).
7. An economic theory of institutional change carries numerous analogies to biology and
   anthropology. In many studies of biological and behavioral change, models of human life
   at some particular point in time are premised. Changes are then motivated by Darwinian

natural selection and bio-genetics. The great debate, of course, is whether humankind evolved gradually or discontinuously in response to particular exogenous forces such as climatic changes brought on by comets or other celestial events. Much is being learned from sociobiology – a field that closely parallels neoinstitutional economics. Accounts of early *Homo sapiens* are valuable, for example, in describing painful struggles to survive, the catastrophes wrought by common pool resource problems, the victory over the high transaction costs in transitions from nomadic to sedentary lifestyles, and so on.

8. There are those who believe that a neoinstitutional theory of institutional change is 'excessively schematic', presumably meaning that *no* theory of institutional change is possible (Rothbard 1995, p. 516).

9. For a counterpoint, at least on the matter of the value of empiricism, see McCloskey (1997).

10. Our opinion on this matter is not shaken given recent non-rationalist research into institutions and change. Young (1998), for example, positing a model with limited information, perverse behavior and generally non-rational activities on the part of participants, concludes that predictable patterns of institutional equilibrium occur nonetheless. Ostensibly, expectations 'shaping' (through game theory) is the *modus operandi* of Young's theory, although he also leaves room for the impact of 'great people', 'idiosyncratic shocks', and 'lock-in' in tentative explanations of institutions. Neoclassical theories of demand and relative prices (not mentioned by Young), however, are demonstrably useful in explaining actual institutions and change. *Ad hoc* coordination models have not been so useful. It is not that such models are uninteresting. It is, however, the case that non-rationalist approaches have yet to be given a fair comparative test.

11. Liebowitz and Margolis have summarily exploded the most commonly advanced examples, including the QWERTY typewriter (1990), the adoption of the VHS video-tape format (1995a), and the existence of so-called 'network externalities' (1994).

12. An elaborated analysis must also consider such factors as the transitional gains gap and the fact that rent capitalizations at one point in time may engender the demand for *new* regulations and policies to supply *new* profits to rent-seeking participants.

13. An interesting and important analysis, very much of this character, was presented by Higgs (1987).

14. This is of course no different in principle from the kinds of *ceteris paribus* assumptions invoked in studies which focus primarily on the development of property rights, such as those of the old West (Umbeck 1977) or the contractual rights to water in the twentieth-century West (Kanazawa 1998). All of these studies abstract from factors distant from primary areas of interest.

15. North and Thomas (1973) and North (1981) have, for example, used plagues and the cost and technology of warfare as shock variables in explaining change. We have been as guilty of inadequately specifying the factors exogenous to models of change (for example, see Davidson and Ekelund 1997).

16. One problem with elevating such concepts as 'power', 'ideas', and 'ideology' to the status of economizing behavior is that, unlike the latter, they have no clear empirical analogs (that is, they do not correspond to *particular* individuals or groups acting on self-interested grounds through processes which alter or amend institutions). Economists, in the main, do not accept 'moments of madness' (Levi 1988, p. 22) as explanations for events. History does not just happen. Some rational economizing behavior is at work whether a veil of ignorance covers it or not.

17. Levi (1988) criticizes the concept of 'rent seeking' on the dubious grounds (a) that it is too 'mathematical' and (b) that it makes proponents blind to the waste created in markets (that is, it is anti-government). In terms of public choice applications to economic history we are unaware of any such mathematical models – quite the contrary, the literature may well be overly discursive. On the second point, Levi is simply incorrect. One very plausible reason why the political process may be petitioned is the existence of externalities. Indeed, we might well expect law and legislation to be most likely when many parties, represented by interest groups, benefit from the internalization of externalities (see Becker 1983, 1985).

18. The same failure can be seen in Levi's (1988) explanation of the advent of the income tax in England, circa 1799–1816, to finance the Napoleonic Wars. Tax choice was, as Mill so clearly outlined in discussing the reinstitution of the income tax later in the century, a function of particular interest groups in British society (Ekelund and Walker 1996).

19. Naturally this process evolved slowly and varied across time and place. The 'enclosure movements', extending even to the nineteenth century in England, are examples.

20. North (1978, 1979, 1981, 1991) later added a governmental component to his analysis.

21. The role of usury doctrine in promoting the Church's financial interests is detailed in Ekelund et al. (1989). Other research (for example, Glaeser and Scheinkman 1998), while not denying this interpretation, argues that usury proscriptions were also a primitive form of social insurance.

22. The Weber–Tauney–Sombart thesis of the Protestant work ethic, when viewed from a micro-institutional perspective, appears to ignore much that is important in illustrating and motivating historical events over this critical period. See Ekelund et al. (1996).

23. Ekelund et al. (1996). In general, town interests combined with monarchical interests and heretics against feudal interests, the latter generally supported by the Church. One important example is the suppression of heretics by armed aggressions as in the Albigensian Crusade.

24. The lack of appreciation for economic theory in general and public choice ideas in particular is the hallmark of a certain historical literature that has created little of substance beyond the works of Heckscher. The establishment of facts – any facts – is to be encouraged. But facts without theory are worthless, particularly those overlain and suffused with normative notions of ideology and socialist method. Such is the sum and substance of most 'modern' work on mercantilism (Magnusson 1994). While ideas or 'doctrines' might be important, they are akin to a new science or technology that must be 'sold' to become part of history (see Stigler 1992). The failure to appreciate the interrelation between ideals, technology and rent seeking is only symptomatic of a general refusal to understand the forward-looking and explanatory nature of positive economics. Institutions that facilitate exchange and growth will never be understood by focusing on deconstruction of language and 'meaning' in mercantile or any other time. The posturing of those engaged in ideological historical research notwithstanding (Magnusson 1994), the only progress made in the development of institutional change over the past quarter century has starred an embellished neoclassical economics.

25. These ideas, with neoinstitutional embellishments, were revisited in *Politicized Economies* (Ekelund and Tollison 1997b).

26. Other writers focus on institutional aspects of this period. See Root (1994) and Levi (1988). These arguments may, of course, be used in other contexts (see Ades and Glaser 1995).

27. See North (1981) and DeSoto (1989) for attempts in this regard.

28. The microanalytics of firm organization and managerial efficiency as functions of opportunistic behavior and moral hazard are treated in a number of interesting works. See, in particular, Anderson and Tollison (1983a, b, 1993) and Anderson et al. (1983).

29. Naturally these restrictions had to be enforced and there is plentiful evidence of piracy, formal and informal smuggling and opportunistic enforcement by distant agents of monarchical and other British interests. Walker (1993) advances a convincing case that seventeenth-century enforcement of protectionist arrangements in the Virginia tobacco market were relatively unsuccessful. Walker notes that the Stuarts James I and Charles I both were unable, through their enforcement mechanisms, to get colonists to restrict production and to eliminate illegal and contraband trade with other nations. In short, high transaction and enforcement costs dissipated rents as cheating occurred. The same sorts of problems, where attempts at rent seeking were not always successful *ex post*, could be expected in the eighteenth century as well.

30. Pincus (1977) offers an important caveat when comparing results using his methodology with more recent, twentieth-century changes in tariffs and quotas. Over the earlier periods, the United States was a net importer of manufactured goods, so that the interest of the manufacturing sector in the institutions of regulation was clear. In twentieth-century

contexts, these interests are Balkanized. Within a single industry, for example, the imposition or elimination of tariffs will have diverse economic effects. For example, US textile producers have different interests than textile retailers in the elimination of import tariffs on foreign-made textiles or finished textile goods.

31.   Institutional change may be influenced by governments in ways more subtle than taxation. For example, Anderson and Tollison (1991b) relate, with evidence, how the pattern of mortality rates during the Civil War was influenced by politics. In particular, they find that electoral votes per capita provided a strong explanation of casualty rates across the states remaining loyal to the Union cause, holding a number of variables constant. As the authors note, 'Who faces what risk of death, wounds, and even disease, is (like the tax burden) subject to political control. Wartime military casualties are simply another form of government taxation' (p. 231).

32.   For a discussion of aspects of this development, see DiLorenzo and High (1988) and Ekelund and Hébert (1990).

33.   The high degree of complexity of institutional changes wrought by legislation and interests is also revealed in DiLorenzo's (1985) paper. He suggests that the Sherman Act of 1890 was in part a political smokescreen for the McKinley Tariff that was passed only three months later (with Senator Sherman as the sponsor).

34.   See, for example, Pashigian (1976), who discusses the political and economic forces motivating the shift from private to public ownership of urban mass transit systems in the United States.

35.   A recent calculation of income distribution and tax system changes in nineteenth-century England is very revealing. Estimates of the distribution of income in 1842 and 1867, a period of major tax changes, produces patterns that would today be typical only of less-developed nations. The British tax code tended to reflect the redistributional demands of newly enfranchised groups (see Ekelund and Walker 1996).

36.   Ellison and Mullin (1995) argue, correctly, that the larger, less-concentrated interest groups ultimately decisive in 1912 may have been animated by prior legislation, making them both exogenous and endogenous to the process of institutional change.

37.   Almost exclusively, Republicans voted in support of reform while Democrats opposed it. In this case, however, tariff 'reform' was the pro-tariff position (Ellison and Mullin 1995, p. 359).

38.   Colorado was a major beet-producing state (Ellison and Mullin 1995, p. 359).

39.   Explanations for government growth in other countries may be made on grounds of public choice and interest groups. Fratianni and Spinelli (1982), for example, adopt such an approach to analyse the growth of the Italian public sector from 1861 to 1979 in both absolute terms and relative to the rest of the economy.

40.   For example, see Urban and Mancke (1972), Haas-Wilson (1986), Barnett et al. (1993) and a host of other contributions. For an account and a collection of some of these contributions, see Ekelund (1998).

41.   Likewise, we neglect an entire literature on the sources and impact of voting, including those relating to congressional dominance, legislator shirking and the role of ideology. For only a small sample of this literature, see Weingast and Moran (1983), Kalt and Zupan (1984), Moe (1987a), Lott and Bronars (1993), Coates and Munger (1995), and Stratmann (1998). Also see Rubin (Chapter 15 this volume). Insights into the transmission of interests into political action are one of the chief contributions of this literature.

42.   See, for example, the comparison between private arrangements and government solutions to prevent rent dissipations in crude oil production (Libecap and Wiggins 1984) and in the Gulf of Mexico fishery (Johnson and Libecap 1982). Also see Bell (1986).

43.   See, for example, Dennen (1976), Hallagan (1978), Libecap (1978a, b, 1979), McCurdy (1976), and Umbeck (1977). Or, for a brief summary of these papers, see Libecap (1986, pp. 236–8).

44.   Also see Libecap and Johnson (1980).

26 Law and economics

Bruce L. Benson*

1 Introduction

David Friedman (1987, p. 173) explains that 'the economic analysis of law involves three distinct but related enterprises': (i) prediction of the effects of legal rules, (ii) determination of the efficiency of legal rules, usually in order to recommend what the rules ought to be, and (iii) prediction of what the legal rules will be. He suggests further that 'the first is primarily an application of price theory, the second of welfare economics and the third of public choice' (ibid.). This appears to be an accurate characterization of most of the law and economics literature, but all three areas of research actually require public choice analysis if predictions are going to be accurate and recommendations based on efficiency objectives have any chance of conforming with reality. For instance, one effect of rules that constrain behavior or impose costs on individuals is that those individuals have incentives either to change the rules or to break them. Efforts to change the rules obviously can involve public choice processes, and incentives to violate them mean that they will have to be enforced, perhaps by some bureaucratic agency, another focus of public choice analysis. Similarly, consideration of the efficiency implications of rules clearly should include recognition of the opportunity costs that arise in attempting to enforce them as well as the costs that people incur as they try to change the rules, prevent such changes, or both. In this regard, Lon Fuller (1964, p. 106) defines law as 'the enterprise of subjecting human conduct to the governance of rules'. That is, law is not simply a set of rules. For rules to be relevant (for example, to be part of a legal system) they generally must be accompanied by institutions of governance that induce individuals to recognize the rules (and, perhaps, to clarify them when disputes over their application arise and to change them as circumstances change). Thus, in contrast to the law-and-economics literature's focus on rules, an economic analysis of law should include the study of the institutions and processes of governance.

Richard Wagner (1993, p. 204) contends that public choice analysis is (or should be) changing into 'a general study of law as represented by Lon Fuller's formulation of law'. Combining Wagner's perceptions with the point made above suggests that both law and economics and public choice really should focus much more attention on analysing the 'enterprise of subjecting human conduct to the governance of rules'. The purpose of this chapter is to outline and illustrate some of the key components of such a focus. First,

Section 2 indicates why economic analysis is essential for understanding the enterprise of law, and why that analysis must incorporate public choice reasoning. The next three sections discuss key characteristics of Wagner's view of public choice as a study of the enterprise of subjecting human conduct to the governance of rules. In particular, Section 3 explains that this enterprise is being conducted by a polycentric system of interrelated institutions rather than by hierarchically structured, goal-directed organizations with identifiable geographic jurisdictions (nation-states, or governments in the popular sense) (Wagner 1993, p. 208). Section 4 then emphasizes that, theoretically, this polycentric system should be considered as a spontaneously evolving process (ibid., p. 204). Section 5 illustrates Wagner's (p. 207) point that the application of public choice (or law and economics) should 'focus on historical or evolutionary movement through time' by contrasting briefly the evolving rules and institutions of customary law, common law through its first several centuries, and modern common law's expanding role in the rent-seeking process. Concluding comments appear in Section 6.

2   Scarcity, transaction costs, rules, and governing institutions

'Rules' refer to behavioral patterns that individuals expect others to adopt and follow in the context of various interdependent activities and actions. Thus, the rules one individual is expected to follow influence the choices made by other individuals: like prices, rules coordinate and motivate interdependent behavior. Furthermore, rules are generally not necessary if there are no conflicts to resolve and, as David Hume ([1740] 1985) emphasized more than two and a half centuries ago, the primary source of conflict between individuals is scarcity. Thus, the incentives created by scarcity lead to the rationing processes that economists study, and they also underlie the evolution of many (all?) rules and institutions. Rules to coordinate competition (for example, to create incentives to compete through markets or through political institutions rather than through violence) establish the obligations that underlie the property rights to scarce resources and goods, as well as the procedures through which those property rights can be established, modified and transferred.

2.1   Transaction costs

Scarcity is not the only reason for creating rules. Ronald Coase (1960) shows that in the absence of transaction costs, rules and institutions do not matter from an efficiency perspective. Individuals will always bargain to achieve the most efficient allocation of resources. Of course, when transaction costs stand in the way of bargaining, the efficient allocation of resources need not arise, and since transaction costs are always positive, rules and institutions can influence allocative efficiency if they lower (or raise) transaction costs. For example, when a resource becomes scarce so that there are competing demands for its use, the resulting competition creates incentives to define property rights in order to internalize the costs (Demsetz 1967). Of course, more than one individual is likely to attempt to claim such a valuable resource or asset, and each may invest in efforts to exclude the others. The successful individual will probably have to continue investing in exclusion in order to maintain control of the resource as other individuals attempt to take it; that is, in order to motivate others to respect the claim. Thus, such unilateral efforts to define and enforce property rights involve considerable transaction costs, and individuals have incentives to create organizations or institutions that will lower or reallocate these costs. When such institutions can evolve, mutually recognized rules of obligation to respect each other's property rights can emerge without resorting to unilateral investments in exclusion (Benson 1994b, 1997b, 1998a). Transaction costs associated with delineating and securing property rights never fall to zero, however, so property rights are never fully defined or protected (Barzel 1989, p. 1; North 1990, p. 33). The desire to accumulate wealth in the face of scarcity means that incentives to discover and implement new rules and institutions to improve on the delineation and protection of property rights always exist, however. It is this drive to discover efficiency-enhancing rules and institutions that underlies the efficiency-of-common-law hypothesis.

As Friedman (1987, p. 180) indicates, efforts to use economic analysis to explain and predict what laws will arise have taken two different forms. First, Richard Posner and others associated with the Chicago school of law and economics contend that the common law tends to produce efficient rules (for example, Posner 1998, pp. 33–291, 1980a; Landes and Posner 1979; also see Hayek 1973; Priest 1977; and Rubin 1977). These scholars essentially combine Friedman's (1987, p. 180) points (ii) and (iii) listed above: 'The analysis of what legal rules are efficient thus provides an explanation of what legal rules exist – and the observation of what legal rules exist provides a test of theories about what rules are efficient'.[1] If the only motivations for creating rules were to eliminate externalities and facilitate voluntary interaction, the argument that law in general and common law in particular is a process of searching for efficient rules and efficient institutions of governance would appear to be unchallengeable.[2] However, Coase's (1960) analysis actually suggests that rules and institutions influence something besides efficiency, since even when bargaining is possible, rules can determine the distribution of bargaining power and therefore the distribution of wealth that results from the efficient use of resources. Public choice recognizes that these distributional consequences also create incentives to make and alter rules, and provides an alternative approach to explaining what rules exist: it sees laws as the outcomes of a political market dominated by narrowly focused interest groups seeking wealth transfers or rents. In such a setting, 'inefficient laws – laws which injure the losers by more than they benefit the gainers – may well pass, and efficient laws may well fail' (Friedman 1987, p. 180).[3] With few exceptions (for example, Rowley 1989), public choice analysis has focused on legislation and on bureaucratic activities rather than on common law, but as explained below, the approach to public choice suggested by Wagner (1993) provides a clear explanation of why the Chicago school's 'common-law-is-efficient' argument is not valid today (even though it may have some historical validity).[4]

More than 90 years ago, Franz Oppenheimer pointed out that an understanding of the formation and development of the state requires recognition of the fact that

> there are two fundamentally opposed means whereby man, requiring sustenance, is impelled to obtain the necessary means for satisfying his desires. These are work and robbery, one's own labor and the forceful appropriation of the labor of others. ... [T]he warriors' trade ... is only organized mass robbery. ... Both because of this, and also on account of the need for having, in the further development of this study, terse, clear, sharply opposing terms for these very important contrasts, I propose in the following discussion to call one's own labor and the equivalent exchange of one's own labor for the labor of others, the 'economic means' for the satisfaction of needs, while the unrequited appropriation of the labor of others will be called the 'political means'. (Oppenheimer [1908] 1914, pp. 24–5)

Rules can be institutionalized to facilitate the pursuit of either the economic or the political means of personal wealth enhancement. One way of distinguishing between Chicago-school law-and-economics and public choice might be to suggest that the former has focused on the role of rules that facilitate the economic means while the latter has focused on rules and institutions that facilitate the political means, but the fact is that 'law' involves both, and for the most part, the two cannot be separated. The existence of the political process raises the transaction costs of the economic process, and the economic process is necessary for the survival of the political process (wealth must be created to be transferred), so a study of the enterprise of subjecting human behavior to the governance of rules must recognize the resulting conflict between economics and politics (Benson 1998a).

2.2   Governing institutions and endogenous transaction costs[5]
Individuals must be motivated to recognize rules and adopt appropriate behavioral responses, of course, so many behavioral rules are supported by various institutions of governance. Property rights are always susceptible to involuntary transfer (for example, theft), for instance, and so potential victims have incentives to develop policing and other enforcement institutions that encourage people to respect property rules and reduce the probability of

such transfers. Furthermore, even if individuals within a community prefer to recognize and follow rules that facilitate cooperation and wealth creation (for example, rules such as fulfilling contractual promises), some governance institutions may still be required in order to resolve disagreements over interpretations of the rules and to facilitate changes in rules as conditions change. Not all policing, rulemaking, and rule-clarifying institutions are intended to secure property rights and facilitate wealth creation, however. Given enough power, the threat of violence alone may suffice to induce involuntary transfers, and rules to facilitate such extortion can be institutionalized (Levi 1988; Benson 1997a, 1998a). Incentives to resist extortion are strong, and so this 'political' environment, to use Oppenheimer's term, will have to involve coercive policing institutions in order to motivate compliance, as well as institutions to resolve disputes over interpretation of the rules and to change them as circumstances dictate.

Different institutional environments (for example, institutions facilitating voluntary interaction and wealth creation versus institutions facilitating involuntary transfers) involve different forms of transaction costs and therefore different incentives. Consider the implications of a process of wealth transfers for rules created through legislation, for instance, whether by kings, dictators, 'representative' parliaments, or courts. Conditions which lead to the demand for and supply of such political transfer rules have been examined at length in the rent-seeking literature, so only some of the relevant transaction costs will be mentioned here for illustrative purposes. In particular, note that such transfers involve the involuntary attenuation or reassignment of property rights (Benson 1984). After all, property rights 'convey the right to benefit or harm oneself or others' (Demsetz 1967, p. 348) and so they dictate the distribution of wealth and changes in property rights transfer wealth (Coase 1960; Benson 1984). But unlike voluntary exchange, which tends to improve allocative efficiency and increase wealth, rules that mandate involuntary transfers tend to reduce allocative efficiency and wealth for at least three reasons. First, comparative static analysis of a transfer (for example, through a tax, a subsidy, or the granting of a monopoly franchise) points to an associated deadweight welfare loss. Second, Tullock (1967b) explains that the resources consumed in the rent-seeking competition also have opportunity costs. But adding these 'Tullock costs' to the deadweight loss still underestimates the full opportunity cost of an ongoing transfer process. Faced with the prospect of involuntary transfers, productive individuals' property rights to their resources, wealth, and income flow are perceived to be relatively insecure, so their incentives to invest in and maintain their assets, and their incentives to earn income and produce new wealth that might be appropriated, are relatively weak. Indeed, if transfers are expected to be large, frequent, and arbitrary, most wealth production may have to be motivated by threats (for example, as under slavery). Such threats are imperfect, however, so production will be low compared to a situation wherein property rights are relatively secure. Victims of the transfer process have incentives to defend their property rights, of course, and part of these political defense costs are recognized as a component of the Tullock costs. Defensive efforts go beyond investing in political information and influence, however. Exit is another option that can be exercised by relocating to an alternative political jurisdiction or by hiding economic activity and wealth (for example, moving transactions 'underground' into black markets) in order to reduce its vulnerability to expropriation. Hence, in order to induce compliance with discriminatory transfer rules, the rulemakers will generally have to rely on an enforcement bureau, both to prevent exit and to execute the rules. Policing to prevent theft is likely to be required in any institutional environment, but policing to induce compliance in a political transfer process will have to be much more extensive.

In this light, efforts to legitimize political activities and deflect opposition should arise, of course. The legitimization effort can take many forms (Benson 1998a), but a significant component of this activity involves actions that raise transaction costs for potential political opponents. For instance, as Levi (1988, p. 67) explains, 'rulers are most successful at [legitimization] ... when there is uncertainty'. Therefore, tactics of misrepresentation and falsification of information are common in political institutions (Breton and Wintrobe 1982, p. 39), as they raise the transaction costs for those who might be tempted to oppose the rules if their actual effects were known. Uncertainty does not necessarily require outright falsification, of course: it can be increased by making laws very complex and difficult for most people to understand, for instance. Given the low payoff to individuals from trying to interpret the laws, rational ignorance suggests that such a tactic may effectively disguise the underlying redistributional process. Levi (1988) also suggests that quasi-voluntary compliance may increase if people believe that everyone is sharing the burdens imposed on them. Therefore, one tactic may be to establish complex rules that appear to apply to everyone, but then to selectively enforce them.

The development of specialists in regulating, policing and collecting transfers also creates transaction costs. These individuals are essentially acting as agents of those with rulemaking power or influence, but severe principal–agent problems arise as the specialists will be in a position to skim relatively large shares of the wealth being transferred or accept bribes to enforce the rules selectively. This creates incentives to limit the power of individuals and subgroups within the bureaucratic organization, and a number of monitoring and control processes are inevitably introduced. Control is incomplete, however, so bureaucrats are generally in a position to manipulate the process in order to capture some of the wealth in the form of discretionary budgets, bribes, or other perquisites (Niskanen 1975; Breton and Wintrobe 1982; Benson 1995b). This manipulation includes efforts to raise transaction costs for those outside the bureau (both legislators and interest groups) who may want to monitor and/or control the bureau's activities. After all, individuals who depend for their livelihoods on a particular institutional arrangement have incentives to increase transaction costs associated with either eliminating the arrangement or finding alternative (competitive) arrangements that might more effectively achieve the same objectives (for instance, see Breton and Wintrobe 1982; Gambetta 1993; Benson et al. 1995; Benson 1995b). Competitors in any environment have incentives to raise their rivals' costs, of course, but those operating within institutions that have coercive powers are in particularly strong positions to influence the level and distribution of transaction costs (Twight 1988; Crew and Twight 1990). In other words, transaction costs are, at least to a degree, endogenous: transaction costs influence the evolution of rules and institutions, but the rules and institutions also determine at least some of the transaction costs, and the distribution of those costs. Thus, the argument that any rule that survives must be efficient – in the sense that the costs of changing it are greater than the benefits of doing so (for example, see Stigler 1992) – only applies within a given institutional setting. An alternative institutional setting may involve a very different set of transaction costs, and in that setting such a rule may not survive, but those who benefit from the current institution may intentionally raise the costs of switching to the alternative. This point may not seem relevant in a comparative statics framework, but the fact is that the rules and institutions in place at a particular point in time are products of a path-dependent, evolutionary process. Before turning to this issue, however, let us consider the potential sources of rules and their accompanying institutions of governance.

3   Polycentric governance

Wagner (1993, p. 208) explains that 'government now is commonly construed in hierarchical fashion, as some consciously directed organization'. Indeed, many scholars believe that there must be a single centralized legal system within a geographic jurisdiction. Landes and Posner (1979, p. 239) put the case as clearly as any:

> there would appear to be tremendous economies of standardization in [law], akin to those that have given us standard dimensions for electrical sockets and railroad gauges. While many industries have achieved standardization without monopoly, it is unclear how the requisite standardization of commonality could be achieved in the [law] without a single source for [law] – without, that is to say, a monopoly.

But a monopoly in rulemaking power can only be achieved through coercion (if it can be achieved at all: see the following discussion), and such a coercive monopoly is likely to create rules that benefit the rulemakers and their supporters. Furthermore, even if an all-inclusive legal system is not used to redistribute wealth, it can have undesirable results in a dynamically uncertain world, in part because it eliminates the potential for competition, emulation, and migration. For instance, given the potential for 'bad' (biased, inefficient) rules to be produced and maintained no matter the legal system's extent – a potential that can increase dramatically as the size of the decision-making group falls relative to the size of the community affected by the decision, as suggested below – the effects of bad laws are less severe in a decentralized polycentric legal system. First of all, the effects of the bad law are confined to a relatively small community rather than being imposed on a much larger group. But more significantly, the possibility of secession and migration (perhaps geographic migration, but not necessarily if, as suggested below, there are numerous sources of rules and institutions within the same geographic area) means that individuals do not have to act unilaterally in an effort to *change* the law, an unlikely occurrence (Vanberg 1986, p. 93). *Nor* do they have to act deliberately as an organized group – the only alternative considered by Vanberg (ibid.) in arguing the merits of a relatively extensive legal jurisdiction. The existence of parallel groups with better rules means that migration may be possible, and even if no group has a better set of rules but some individuals believe that a better set can be developed, those individuals can secede and form a new contractual group. In the case of a good rule, as Osterfield (1989, p. 152) notes, it often does not matter how extensive the legal system is, as good rules tend to be emulated because of the competition for group members. In the case of a bad rule, the extent of the legal system clearly matters, however. Indeed, there is an even more fundamental issue involved. In the absence of alternatives, it may not be possible to evaluate the 'goodness' or 'badness' of a particular rule. A rule imposed in an overarching legal system, even by a benevolent ruler, may produce undesirable unintended consequences that another rule would not produce, but this may not be recognized if the other rule cannot be experimented with elsewhere so that its consequences can be observed. On the other hand, as individuals in parallel legal systems experiment with alternatives, the relative impacts of different rules can be observed and more effectively evaluated. In law, as in markets, competition is an important determinant of the 'efficiency' of the outcome (ibid., p. 162).

Whether law should be monopolized or not is moot since, in reality, every individual is subject to many sources of rules, and each source has different institutions of governance. Therefore, as Wagner (1993, p. 208) concludes, 'the very concept of government will [should?] change. It will come increasingly to be recognized that the myriad activities we ascribe to government are themselves the product of a polyarchy and not of some goal-directed organization'. Consider a few examples of the types of rules and governance institutions that an individual faces.

3.1 Conventions
Some rules, referred to as habits or conventions, may be self-created and self-enforced. They often arise as one individual strives to economize on the time and effort required to weigh the alternatives under similar sets of circumstances (for instance Hayek 1973). Such an individual may choose to use a fixed 'rule-of-thumb' for a particular type of recurring decision. Many of these habits or conventions are repeatedly observed by others who begin to anticipate the same behavioral pattern under like conditions, and take these expectations into account in making their own decisions. Thus, the convention serves to coordinate and motivate. If this is the case, the convention has become a 'rule' as defined above (behavioral patterns that an individual is expected to follow), but only for the individual who voluntarily adopted the behavior. Such rules are generally self-enforced since they are adopted to achieve some particular desired end (for example, reduce decision-making costs). An unexpected change in an individual's conventional behavior may disappoint other people's expectations, of course, creating uncertainty and reducing their incentives to interact with the individual, so there may also be some negative consequences to violating such a rule imposed by others. These consequences are not likely to be institutionalized, however (unless the convention has been emulated and become a widespread custom, as discussed below).

3.2 Contracts
Other rules are explicitly and voluntarily agreed to in the context of specific relationships. Like the prices of scarce resources and goods, after all, rules can be created by negotiation. However, because rules refer to expected (that is, future) behavior, the implication is that rules only arise through negotiations if the resulting bargain produces an explicit or implicit contract (for example, the bargain does not simply lead to an immediate exchange with no future obligations). The resulting contractual rules only apply for the negotiating parties and for the term of the contract. Others may voluntarily emulate the behavior by adopting the same contract, of course, but the scope of these rules is limited by the terms of the contracts.

If a contract is entered into voluntarily it must be the case that all of the parties expect to be better off as a consequence, suggesting that the incentives to follow the agreed-upon rules are largely positive. Institutions to resolve disputes over interpretation of the contract or to change its terms may be required, of course, since contracts involve commitments to act in the uncertain future where unanticipated contingencies may arise. Some institutionalized ability to create a credible threat of punishment for non-compliance may also be relevant at times if circumstances can change in ways that create incentives for one party unilaterally to withdraw from the contract, thereby imposing costs on the other. These institutions of governance may also arise through contract, however. For instance, many commercial agreements are governed by rules and institutions developed within contractually established trade associations and other private organizations (Bernstein 1992; Benson 1989, 1992a, 1995a, 1998b, d, e, 2000). These organizations virtually always include institutions to mediate or arbitrate disputes, as well as mechanisms to ostracize noncomplying members or to impose other sanctions, such as formal or informal means of rapidly dispersing information about parties who are not in compliance so others can avoid dealing with them.

3.3   Customs

Still other rules appear to have a 'community' basis in so far as everyone within a particular group is expected to behave in a certain way in a particular circumstance. Some of these rules may be explicitly agreed upon by all members of a community and, therefore, be determined contractually, but many are not. Rules can evolve spontaneously and be voluntarily accepted even though there never has been an explicit statement declaring that they are in force. That is, rules can arise like prices in competitive markets do: numerous individuals interact and observe each other's behavioral patterns (some of which begin as conventions, others as contractual obligations, and so on), emulating those that appear desirable so that the behavior spreads (Mises [1957] 1985, p. 192). Adopting such rules creates expectations and accompanying obligations for everyone in the relevant community (Hayek 1973, pp. 96–7). These 'shared values' might be labeled as norms or customs and, like explicit contractual agreements, they are also voluntarily adopted by individuals within the relevant community in recognition of the positive benefits arising from compliance. After all, conforming to widely shared values can be a low-cost means of influencing the allocation of scarce resources (for example, relative to violence), as the coordination of behavior through the group's multidimensional, multisided web of interactions creates opportunities to trade and to share jointly produced products. The outcome can be characterized in the same way Mises (1949, p. 283) describes the interdependence arising in a free market: 'the individual is not bound to obey and to serve the overlord. ... [Yet] he is certainly not independent. He depends on the other members of society. But this dependence is mutual'.

Individuals generally do not have to be forced to cooperate through market exchange, and similarly, they generally do not have to be forced to comply with shared norms and customs. Customary rules are, therefore, a primary source of 'social order' (Fuller 1964, 1981; Ellickson 1991; Benson 1989, 1991). Indeed, Fuller (1981, p. 213) suggests that customary rules might best be described as a 'language of interaction' since they coordinate the interdependent actions of those individuals who have adopted them. Still, some governance institutions are likely to arise in support of customs. After all, in an uncertain world some individuals inevitably face circumstances in which incentives to violate such rules are strong. Social pressures or ostracism threats may be important in some situations, for instance, if conditions arise that create non-compliance incentives for someone who has voluntarily complied in the past. Similarly, an individual who is suddenly made destitute, perhaps by a natural disaster, may feel compelled to violate customs (for example, steal from others in the relevant community) in order to feed his family. Ostracism threats may not be sufficient under these circumstances, so other institutions may evolve to counteract such incentives: many customary law communities develop mutual insurance arrangements, for instance, in which everyone accepts an obligation to aid those who are in distress (Benson 1997a, 1998a). Mechanisms may also be needed to clarify or change the rules if new circumstances arise that are not obviously covered by the existing norms. Such circumstances can lead to a dispute, and non-violent dispute resolution procedures, whether through negotiation or some third-party mechanism of mediation or arbitration, may be desirable. Violence is one means for resolving a dispute, of course, but it can be a costly one. Like a contract, an arbitrated or mediated dispute settlement applies only to the parties in the dispute, but the arbitrator's decision can also establish a new rule for others if the resulting behavior is emulated and spreads through the community.

3.4   Command

Another source of rules is 'legislation', promulgated intentionally by a governing authority using its coercive powers to command compliance. When that authority is the state, such rules are generally called codes or precedents (or laws), of course. But rules can also be imposed by a private authority – the Mafia (Gambetta 1993) or a religious sect (Berman 1983) – if the organization has sufficient power credibly to threaten punishment for non-compliance. At least some individuals will follow such rules voluntarily because they expect to be made better off as a result. Indeed, a benevolent authority might attempt to impose rules that are generally beneficial, but there clearly is no guarantee that this will be the case. In fact, as suggested above, imposed rules can be (and often are) discriminatory. They allocate, reallocate, or attenuate property rights in ways that make those individuals with power to influence the legislative or the enforcement process better off while making others worse off. Therefore, individuals who lose in the process will not voluntarily comply, and such rules must be backed by coercive institutions of governance.

A legal system that is performing significant wealth redistribution functions must also support wealth creation, of course. After all, wealth must be produced for it to be transferred, and private property rights create the strongest possible incentives for long-term wealth accumulation. Therefore, rulemakers face a tradeoff and legal evolution is shaped by this conflict. Large levels of transfers in the short term reduce productivity, wealth creation, and the potential for transfers over the long run. The actual level of transfers in any period, therefore, depends in part on the rulemaker's time horizon (Levi 1988, pp. 13, 32–3; Holcombe 1994, p. 112). If rulemakers are relatively short-sighted, perhaps because there is significant political competition, property rights become very insecure as high levels of transfers can be expected. The result is an economy in stagnation or decline (for example, Haiti). However, a long time horizon implies that the present value of potential future transfers is higher, so property rights will be relatively secure in order to stimulate wealth production. The rulemakers also should recognize that selectively supporting rules that originated within customary communities provides a low-cost mechanism for facilitating cooperation in wealth creation that can then be expropriated. Thus, legislation is likely explicitly to codify many of the customary norms that have evolved to support voluntary interaction. In this kind of situation, an economy may grow and prosper as rules tend to improve over time (for example, England under several centuries of common law, as indicated below). But even in such an environment, 'law' simultaneously serves many functions, some of which are widely seen as legitimate, and some of which are widely despised. The law protects some private interests and destroys others, it serves to integrate 'society' through force while disintegrating many of the groups that make up civil society, it fosters the production of wealth by some and the taking of wealth by others, it defines crimes and is used to commit crimes (involuntary takings). Law (in a positive sense) and justice (in a normative sense) are clearly not synonymous. And if conditions change (that is, rulemakers' time horizons shorten), so that the transfer function of law becomes too disruptive of property rights, an economy that was growing steadily can move into a period of economic stagnation or decline, at least relative to what could have been achieved with more secure property rights (for example, England and the United States for much of the twentieth century).

3.5   Polycentric governance

Every individual is likely to be constrained by a complex web of rules emanating from a variety of institutional environments. A person may simultaneously belong to many groups that have well-established customs, be a party to several contracts, and be subject to the commands of several rulemaking authorities (for example, as in a formal federalist system of government). Furthermore, the various types of rules clearly do not signify mutually exclusive jurisdictions. A contract may involve an explicit agreement to adopt standard practices or customs of a group, for example, or to behave in a way that differs from what would be expected under existing rules, whether those rules arose through custom, contract, or command (Benson 1998c). Similarly, many rules that first evolve as customs within a community can become codified, but codes can also explicitly contradict custom (Benson 1989, 1992b, 1998d, e). Codification of custom may simply be an effort to clarify unarticulated rules in order to facilitate better coordination within a group, so codes need not be discriminatory. However, even codified custom can be discriminatory if the norms from one group are imposed upon individuals who are not members of the original community. Coercively imposed discriminatory laws also drive many activities underground, and the resulting 'informal' sector often evolves into communities whose customs include rules encouraging the violation of formal rules mandated by the coercive legal institutions (de Soto 1989).

3.6 Polycentric law and the market economy

An almost universal belief among even strongly market-oriented economists is that the state must provide the law that is necessary for a market economy to function efficiently (for example, obligations to respect private property and live up to contractual promises). Recognition of the potential for (reality of!) polycentric governance suggests that this need not be the case, however, and history illustrates that the rules underlying a market economy need not be handed down by the state. For instance, private property rights evolved long before states did, as Ellickson (1993, p. 1366) notes:

> There is abundant evidence that a ... group need not make a conscious decision to establish private property rights in land [and other resources]. People who repeatedly interact can generate institutions through communication, monitoring, and sanctioning. ... Contrary to Hobbes and Locke, a property system can get going without an initial conclave.

And as Ridley (1996, p. 114) explains, 'the origin of the market, with all its capacity to exchange goods of different kinds, exploit the division of labor and provide a hedge against dependence on one good, may lie in the reciprocal food-sharing arrangements [and customary law] of a hunter-gatherer band'. In fact, an examination of relationships in modern international commerce (Benson 1992a, 1998e) and within domestic trade associations (Bernstein 1992; Benson 1995a) reveals that they are ruled by modern versions of the same kinds of institutions that develop in primitive customary law. Indeed, recognition of the transfer function of politics suggests that the state is actually a threat to market economies rather than a necessary precursor to them.

Resistance to efforts to transfer wealth is likely to be most effective where the benefits generated through voluntary interaction are very large (so the costs of submission are high) or the representative group member's wealth is mobile, so that interaction takes place across the jurisdictions of different authorities and interjurisdictional competition to attract that wealth occurs. The international merchant communities of early medieval Western Europe are examples of such groups (Benson 1989, 1998e). Commercial law, *lex mercatoria* or the 'Law Merchant', consisted of evolving customary norms and contractual forms, and disputes were resolved in the merchants' own courts. Strong incentives to cooperate through exchange, to live up to promises, to respect one another's property rights, and to support an unbiased and fair dispute resolution system arose because of the positive benefits associated with repeated-dealing reciprocities and reputation effects (including the potential for ostracism). Similarly, modern international commercial law, which evolved from this medieval legal system (with some interruptions, such as those arising under mercantilism in the late medieval period), remains a largely voluntarily produced and enforced system of spontaneously evolving custom, despite many attempts by various coercive states (some supported by politically powerful merchants seeking special privileges) to subjugate it over the centuries (Benson 1989, 1992a, 1998e). Much of US domestic commercial law has similar origins (Bernstein 1992; Benson 1995a); it too has fended off a great deal of political interference (Benson 1995a). Indeed, as Hayek (1973, pp. 81–2) explains,

> the growth of the purpose-independent rules of conduct which can produce a spontaneous order will ... often have taken place in conflict with the aims of the rulers who tended to try to turn their domain into an organization proper. It is in the *ius gentium*, the law merchant, and the practices of the ports and fairs that we must chiefly seek the steps in the evolution of law which ultimately made an open society possible.

The state is frequently called upon to establish and enforce rules having to do with economic activity, of course, and often by the same merchants who are able to enforce their own rules in international trade and within their trade associations. This is not surprising, since members of the merchant community are also susceptible to the incentives to seek wealth transfers. As Adam Smith observed,

> people of the same trade seldom meet together, even for merriment and diversion, but the conversation ends in a conspiracy against the public, or in some contriv-

ance to raise prices. It is impossible indeed to prevent such meetings, by any law which either could be executed, or would be consistent with liberty and justice. But though the law cannot hinder people of the same trade from sometimes assembling together, it ought to do nothing to facilitate such assemblies; much less to render them necessary. (Smith [1776] 1976, p. 144)

The first sentence in this passage is often quoted, of course, but the last two rarely are. Since the transfer process requires that wealth be created before it can be transferred, and capital is relatively mobile (able to exit), political rulemakers have strong incentives to establish mechanisms through which various business communities' political interests can be determined and facilitated. By granting merchants special privileges (that is, transferring wealth to the merchants) in exchange for their willingness to invest within the political jurisdiction, more wealth production occurs by relatively immobile resources that are inputs to (or complements of) the merchants' enterprises – and that wealth can therefore be appropriated more easily. Not surprisingly, merchants have actively sought and willingly accepted wealth transfers within political jurisdictions. Medieval mercantilism was a system dominated by merchants dealing with kings to restrict competition in favor of domestic monopolies and guilds, and that system has a firm hold within many twentieth-century economies (de Soto 1989). In fact, in every 'market economy' with a significant political sector, economic regulations limit competition and generate rents for business interests (Stigler 1971).

Today, individuals also must turn to the state in order to secure their property rights, of course, but it is not because states must be the source of those rights (Ellickson 1993; Benson 1991). Rather, the state with its coercive power is the primary threat to property rights, and the rise of the state tends to undermine the potential for non-state governance arrangements that can define and enforce rights (Benson 1998a). Indeed, this must be the case if the state is to be successful as a wealth-transfer institution. A rule that favors a particular minority cannot be imposed if individuals who do not benefit from the rule can either: (i) turn to a customary legal system like the medieval Law Merchant (Benson 1989, 1998e) or modern trade associations (Benson 1995a), where a different rule is applied; or (ii) find another claimant to authority who applies a different rule (Berman 1983; Benson 1994b, 1998a). As Taylor (1982, p. 57; emphasis in original) notes, the ability to impose laws through the state's institutions is increased 'by weakening or destroying *community*, which is … a necessary condition for the maintenance of social order without the state'. To the degree that coercion and legitimization efforts are incomplete, however, compliance will be incomplete and communities will remain.

Numerous examples of centralized coercive systems can be cited where 'parallel', predominantly cooperative systems of norms and institutions actually govern many (and at times even most) interactions, including even those taking place outside 'legally' recognized groups like trade associations (for example, de Soto 1989; Ellickson 1991; Benson 1998g). De Soto's (1989) detailed analysis of the 'informal' sector in Peru is particularly revealing in this regard, as he explains that the 'squatter communities' are very well organized, that members respect each other's property claims, cooperate to enforce rules of behavior, and so on. Nonetheless, the existence of a coercive ruler raises transaction costs for such groups. For instance, while these informal groups may still be able to enforce some of their own norms, doing so may require taking actions which violate the state's 'law'. After all, property rights are relatively insecure since the state can take them if they become sufficiently valuable, making time horizons short and reputations less valuable. Ostracism is less effective when property rights are tenuous. If ostracism is an ineffective threat, potential victims may opt for retribution. Cooperative clusters may still aid an actual victim in the vigilante exaction of retribution, of course. Under such circumstances, a considerable amount of 'crime' may be 'undertaken to exercise social control' (Ellickson 1991, p. 213; also see Benson 1998g and de Soto 1989).

If members of informal groups are successful in coalescing and establishing rules and institutions that allow them to accumulate wealth in the underground economy, they can also gain political influence (de Soto 1989). When they are seen as a threat to the stability of the political system, for instance, rulemakers may be willing to negotiate with them, and agree to recognize property rights to some of their wealth. As property rights become more secure, the group's economic performance improves. As such groups are recognized and some members improve their political skills, their political power can also grow. The point is that when a strong coercive power exists, economic success requires that property rights be recognized and supported by that power – that is the essence of a protection racket whether it is run by the Mafia or by the state. State recognition of property rights is required to achieve the most efficient use of resources that is possible within the institutional environment, but only because the state poses a threat to those rights.

4   Spontaneous evolution of rules and institutions

The concept of spontaneous order refers to the harmony that evolves from the interactions of separate choices made by individuals in the pursuit of their own subjective ends, wherein the behavior of each individual reflects independent responses to immediate environmental circumstances in light of some general rules of behavior. The emergence of spontaneous order has been widely recognized in the analysis of markets, of course, assuming general rules such as obligations to respect private property. However, Carl

Menger ([1883] 1963) emphasized that the origin, formation, and ultimate process of many social institutions, including systems of rules and supporting institutions, are essentially the same as the spontaneous order for markets. Similarly, Hayek (1973, p. 98) discusses the 'order of actions' which emerges from the spontaneous process governed by an 'order of rules', but he also argues that the order of rules can emerge spontaneously, just as an order of action does.[6] Building on Hayek and others (for example, Fuller 1964, 1981; Ellickson 1991, 1993; Taylor 1982), it can be demonstrated that many rules (for example, customs) and institutions (for example, mediation and arbitration, information systems to support ostracism sanctions, mutual insurance) evolve as the unintended consequences of individuals separately pursuing their own goals, just as markets do (Benson 1989, 1994b, 1997b, 1998a). But Wagner (1993, p. 204) suggests that 'the very conceptualization of government will [should?] change, away from that of a mind or a goal-directed organization and toward that of a catalaxy or spontaneous order'. This holds for both rules and institutions that appear to be created intentionally and for those, such as customs, which obviously arise spontaneously.

To be sure, some systems of rules and institutions clearly do involve deliberate 'human design'. And significantly, designed rules can disrupt spontaneous orders, as Hayek explains, if those rules are imposed on people (contractual rules can be 'designed' too, but they only apply to those agreeing to the contract, and only spread if others adopt them voluntarily). In particular,

> it is impossible, not only to replace the spontaneous order by organization and at the same time to utilize as much of the dispersed knowledge of all its members as possible, but also to improve or correct this order by interfering in it by direct commands. ... It can never be advantageous to supplement the rules governing a spontaneous order by isolated and subsidiary commands concerning those activities where the actions are guided by the general rules of conduct. ... The reason why such isolated commands requiring specific actions by members of the spontaneous order can never improve but must disrupt that order is that they will refer to a part of a system of interdependent actions determined by information and guided by purposes known only to the several acting persons but not to the directing authority. The spontaneous order arises from each element balancing all the various factors operating on it and by adjusting all its various actions to each other, a balance which will be destroyed if some of the actions are determined by another agency on the basis of different knowledge and in the service of different ends. (Hayek 1973, p. 51)

While the balance created by a spontaneous order does tend to be destroyed by deliberate efforts to implement 'isolated and subsidiary commands', however, consciously designed rules do not replace a spontaneous order with a designed order. Even when effectively implemented, deliberately designed rules are rarely able to completely dictate the targeted behavior, both because knowledge is incomplete for the rulemaker (Hayek 1973) and because policing is imperfect. There are too many uncontrolled margins and unanticipated responses for a rule designer to anticipate. Thus, deliberate efforts to impose rules create incentives to find and exploit the uncontrolled margins in order to avoid the full consequences of the rules (Benson 1998a, f; for example, see Cheung's 1974 and Barzel's 1989 discussions of the consequences of price controls). They set off a chain of spontaneous reactions. As ways around such rules are discovered, the rulemakers are likely to respond with new institutions intended to enforce them or with new rules intended to block such maneuvers, but those subject to the new institutions or rules react again, leading to more blocking efforts, and so on. Therefore, deliberately designed rules and institutions also evolve as rulemakers and their subjects attempt to discover ways to achieve their subjective and often conflicting ends. In other words, the evolution of intentionally created rules also tends to be 'path dependent', as such rules are influenced by what has gone before and they in turn influence the path of the spontaneous evolution that follows, but the result is clearly not a designed order. The perception that deliberate design is an alternative to spontaneous order is, therefore, incorrect.

5   Customary law, common law, and judge-made law

Wagner (1993, p. 207) also predicts that in future developments of scholarship focusing on the enterprise of law, 'equilibrium theorizing driven by a logic of relationships among abstract categories will give way to a focus on historical or evolutionary movements through time'. Let us consider from this historical–evolutionary perspective a customary law system, such as the international Law Merchant, which evolved over the centuries from the medieval Law Merchant (Trakman 1983; Benson 1989, 1998e) and the law of the Anglo-Saxon communities (Benson 1992b, 1994a, 1998g), and then compare customary law with both historical and modern variants of the common law.

5.1   Customary law

A key distinguishing characteristic of customary law is that a rule of obligation is initiated by an individual's decision to behave in particular ways under particular circumstances; the voluntarily adopted convention, custom, or contractual promise then spreads through observation and voluntary imitation by other individuals, creating expectations and accompanying obligations. But an obligation that achieves the status of a 'customary law' must be widely recognized and accepted by the individuals in the affected group. The result is analogous to a unanimous (or consensus) collective decision-making rule. If some individuals choose not to adopt the rule, for instance, then the rule cannot be imposed on them (if it is, it is legislation rather than custom).

A rule of unanimity implies that rules expected to be 'bad' (biased or inefficient) are not adopted. Indeed, customary law tends to be quite conservative in the sense that, in deferring to precedent, it guards against mistakes. Of course, unanimity could also mean that many 'good' rules (that is, unbiased rules that promise to enhance allocative efficiency) are not adopted. The view of custom frequently traced to Sir Henry Maine (1864, p. 74), but shared by many others (for example, Hart 1961; Landes and Posner 1979; Brunet 1987), is that it is static, or at least very slow to change, making it an 'inefficient' process for developing new rules in a dynamic environment. The fact of the matter is, however, that flexibility and change often characterize customary law systems (Trakman 1983; Mitchell 1904; Berman 1983; Pospisil 1971, 1978; Benson 1988, 1989, 1998d, e).

The perception that customary law is slow to change may arise from the belief that there is only one mechanism for initiating change, namely that an individual must begin behaving in a particular way under certain circumstances, others must observe the behavior, come to expect it, and then adopt similar behavior under similar circumstances, creating similar obligations for everyone in the community.[7] Certainly, this process can be a very important mechanism for changing custom (it has characterized the transmission of commercial customs among expanding networks of traders; see, for instance, Trakman 1983, p. 11; Mitchell 1904, pp. 7–9; Bewes 1923, p. 138; Benson 1989, 1998d, e). However, when that process proves to be too slow, there are other mechanisms for initiating change in customary law as well.

As conditions change, for example, the inadequacy of existing customary rules can be revealed when a dispute arises. Negotiation is probably the primary means of dispute resolution for members of a close-knit community, but if direct negotiation (perhaps facilitated by a mediator) fails, the parties to a dispute within a customary enterprise of law generally turn to a third party for arbitration. This is clearly the case for primitive societies (Pospisil 1971, 1978; Benson 1988, 1991), but even within modern commercial communities, arbitration is chosen in the vast majority of cases rather than adjudication in public courts (for example, see Lew 1978; Berman and Dasser 1990; Benson 1992a, 1995a, 1998b, d, e, 2000; reasons for choosing arbitration and accepting arbitration rulings are explored in Benson 1998b, 2000), and these arbitrators generally base their decisions on business custom (Berman and Dasser 1990; Lew 1978, pp. 584–5; Benson 1998b, 2000). Since the emergence of a dispute suggests that existing rules are unclear or insufficient, new customary rules can be and often are initiated as individuals resolve their conflicts (Fuller 1981, pp. 90, 110–11; Lew 1978, pp. 584–9; Wooldridge 1970, p. 104; Benson 1988, 1989, 1998b, d).

Contesting the claim that private arbitration can be an important source of new rules of behavior, Landes and Posner (1979, pp. 238–9, 245) argue that arbitrators seeking to maximize profits actually have incentives not to clarify rules because doing so will reduce the number of disputes to be resolved, and they conclude that arbitration in the commercial area is 'not a source of rules or precedents'. Similarly, Brunet (1987, p. 19) contends that precedents established by common law judges have the character of a 'public good' which will not be supplied at efficient levels by private arbitrators. He emphasizes that arbitration decisions are 'internal' to the parties involved and that the secrecy that surrounds much of the modern arbitration process means that others will not be able to learn about the resolution of any particular dispute anyway (pp. 14–15). Such arguments fail to recognize that when external benefits (for example, producing new customary law) are significant, strong incentives exist to develop institutions that can internalize them (Benson 1998b, d, 2000). This can be an important source of incentives underlying the formation of trade associations and other commercial groups, for instance (Benson 1995a, 1998d, 2000), and within such organizations, institutional arrangements easily can create incentives to minimize disputes by making clear rulings (as Landes and Posner 1979 recognize). Thus, Fuller (1981, pp. 110–11) contends that arbitrators' incentives are exactly the opposite of those suggested by Landes and Posner (1979) and Brunet (1987): when an arbitrator must be concerned with the acceptability of his decisions to more than just the parties directly involved there are strong incentives to get the facts and relevant law (custom) right and to justify the ruling in the context of those facts and customs. This clearly appears to be the case in customary law communities where public acceptance of an arbitrator's ruling is important. In many primitive societies, for instance, third-party dispute resolution is a highly ritualized public event wherein the arbitrator loudly explains the evidence and the reasons for his decision (Pospisil 1971; Benson 1988, 1991). But what of modern commercial arbitration and its emphasis on privacy or secrecy?

Consider Bernstein's (1992) examination of the systematic rejection of state-created law by the diamond industry in favor of its own internal rules and institutions (including both mediation and arbitration institutions and privately produced sanctions, as described in Benson 1995a, 1998b, 2000). She explains that the diamond merchants' Boards of Arbitrators resolve disputes on the basis of industry 'trade custom and usage'. But she also finds that within some trading clubs in the diamond industry arbitration decisions are 'officially kept secret' as long as the ruling is complied with (Bernstein 1992, p. 124), perhaps supporting the view that precedents are not 'produced'. Such 'official' secrecy does not mean that new rules are not created or spread, however, or even that too few customary rules exist. There are at least four reasons for this (Benson 2000). First, the parties to the dispute will consider the outcome in future dealings and contracts under similar circumstances even with different trading partners (Benson 1998b, 2000). Second, there is a tremendous 'unofficial' flow of information through word of mouth within and between diamond trading clubs (Bernstein 1992, p. 121). Arbitration results consequently do 'become known through gossip' (ibid., p. 126). Third, as indicated below, there are import mechanisms for initiating new customary rules in addition to dispute resolution (Benson 1998b, d). Fourth, arbitration mechanisms are very flexible so that if external benefits become attractive, a group can change its dispute resolution procedures to capture them (Benson 1998b, 2000). In regard to this last point, for instance, Bernstein (1992, p. 150) notes that diamond dealers have begun to recognize that their secrecy practices create uncertainty, and many trading clubs have begun to change their institutions. Within some trading clubs, arbitrators now publish written statements of the principles used to decide novel cases even though the names of the parties involved and other identifying facts are not disclosed.

The lawmaking consequences of commercial arbitration led Wooldridge (1970, p. 104) to suggest that its substantial growth in the United States is a 'silent displacement of not only the judiciary but even the legislature'. But even when a particular arbitration process does not appear to clarify existing customary rules or produce new ones, it may just be that dispute resolution is a relatively unimportant source of legal change for the relevant group. After all, new customary rules can be introduced by means other than dispute resolution. A very important source of new rules in customary law is bilateral negotiation and contracting. If conditions change, for example, and a set of individuals decide that, for their purposes, behavior that was acceptable in the past has ceased to be useful, they can voluntarily devise a new contract stipulating any behavior they wish. That is, old custom can be replaced quickly by a new rule of obligation toward certain other individuals without the prior consent of or simultaneous recognition by everyone in the group (or by some legal authority). Individuals entering into contracts with these parties are informed of the contractual innovation (or others outside the contract observe the results of a new contractual stipulation), so if it provides a more desirable behavioral rule than older custom, it can rapidly be emulated. Many contracts spread quickly as 'standard forms' throughout the relevant community, serving as 'powerful norms' with obvious 'legal character' (Rubin 1995, p. 115).[8] Indeed, many of commercial law's innovations have been initiated through contracts and dispersed quickly through the relevant merchant community (for example, see Mitchell 1904, p. 12; Berman 1983, pp. 349–55; Benson 1989, 1998b, d, e; Draetta et al. 1992).

Even if customary law is not inefficiently static, the unanimity rule may imply another source of inefficiency. Some scholars who recognize the potential for the spontaneous evolution of customary law argue that the resulting legal system is likely to be inefficiently narrow in scope. For example, Vanberg (1986, p. 96; emphasis in original) maintains that,

> in large groups of highly mobile individuals ... *organized enforcement* will be required in order to make cooperative behavioral regularities viable, whether such organized enforcement is based on some deliberate social contract entered into by the relevant group, or whether it is imposed by some sufficiently powerful (internal or external) party.

Similarly, Hayek (1973, p. 47) contends that an extensive spontaneous order will not be self-regulating and that it will have to be supplemented by 'an organization' which is typically called a government.

In fact, however, it took the privately produced and adjudicated medieval Law Merchant to *overcome* the limitations of political boundaries and localized protectionism, thus paving the way for the commercial revolution and development of international trade (Benson 1989, 1998e). Modern international commerce still relies on private customary law and arbitration to adjudicate disputes, as noted above. In other words, where the 'tremendous economies of standardization in law' that Landes and Posner (1979, p. 239) claim exist, a customary system is likely to be better able to take advantage of them. Government typically cannot because of the artificial constraints of geographic boundaries (a customary legal system's jurisdiction may reflect a functional rather than a geographical boundary, after all). Indeed, there is absolutely no reason to believe that any particular national government is of the ideal size to take full advantage of the economies of standardization in law. In some areas of law (for example, commerce) these economies appear to be greater than any existing nation can encompass. In other areas of law, such economies may be considerably more limited, so that existing political entities are too large (this is true for many aspects of criminal law: see Benson 1998g; Rasmussen and Benson 1994, pp. 177–206). After all, political boundaries are not drawn for the purpose of establishing optimally sized legal jurisdictions. Therefore, a customary system of polycentric law would probably generate efficient 'market areas' (jurisdictions) for the various legal communities involved – many perhaps smaller than most nations and others encompassing many existing political jurisdictions. The existence of *economies of standardization* really *provides an argument against state provision of adjudication and law*, in order to break away from the inefficient artificial political restrictions that exist. Thus, Bernstein (1992, p. 117) concludes that, in contrast to those who see customary law dominated by private dispute resolution (and sanctions) as being relatively inefficient, 'the private regime must be Pareto superior to the established legal regime in order to survive'.

Of course, even if a customary law system is inefficiently small relative to what might be produced by an idealized benevolent government with coercive powers, the costs of expanding the legal system and counting on such benevolence may be far greater than the anticipated benefits of doing so. Any legal system that is larger than what would evolve spontaneously through individual interaction will, by definition, require some concentration of coercive power in a centralized authority. Such power might be used simply to broaden the scope of basic customary rules, but it is much more likely to be used to alter those rules, thereby offsetting the gains from an expanded legal system.[9]

5.2 Common law

Following his successful invasion of England in 1066, William the Conqueror claimed all English land as property of the Crown. Several centuries later, England was the center of the Industrial Revolution, in part because of the incentives created by its legal system's support of private property. Posner's claim that the common law produces efficient rules would appear to have some historical validity. In order to see why this might be the case even though the public choice arguments about inefficient rules being generated through courts is also valid today, let us consider selected parts of this history. The central point is that the institutions of the common law process itself matter and that these institutions have been changing over time.

English kings and their councils were clearly in the business of lawmaking by the thirteenth century. However, it is generally thought that the busiest lawmakers during Henry III's reign were judges (Lyon 1980, p. 433). Henry apparently gave his judges free rein in devising new rules and writs, and they were as yet unconstrained by an active lawmaking parliament. He professionalized the judiciary, making those who performed the judicial function separate from those who did other government business. But was the resulting law judge-made?

The term 'common law' was not yet in wide use among practitioners of royal law during this period, although it was a concept of relevance to the canonists who distinguished it from statute law (Pollock and Maitland [1898] 1959, vol. 1, p. 176). And while the idea of an evolutionary law discovered through dispute resolution seems to have been recognized, judges were not 'making' much of this law. Rather than consciously attempting to devise rules, judges were generally facilitating the application and extension of local custom (much of which was shared across many local communities, of course, as a consequence of centuries of interaction, observation, and emulation). Indeed, as Hogue ([1906] 1985, p. 6) points out, one definition of common law is that it is 'a body of law based on custom alone', and at least some of the common-law-is-efficient arguments involve a dynamic evolutionary story not unlike the one suggested above about the discovery of new customary rules through dispute resolution (for example, Rubin 1977). Hogue ([1906]

1985, pp. 188–215) correctly rejects this definition of common law, emphasizing that while custom was the 'principal source' of common law before Parliament was firmly established as a lawmaking institution, medieval common law judges who assumed the authority to decide what 'good custom' was did refuse occasionally to validate local customary practices. They also recognized various royal 'enactments' as a source of law that could alter or negate custom. In fact, Edward I did not appreciate the directions in which the common law evolved, so he began, through statutes, 'to rigidify many points of law which judges and lawyers, however clever, cannot circumvent or modify' (Lyon 1980, p. 436). Custom has probably been losing ground relative to statute as a determinant of common law from Edward's reign on (although nothing that occurred during its early history can compare to the level of legislation we see today in Britain or the United States).[10]

Statute was not the only source of law other than local custom. Pollock and Maitland ([1898] 1959, p. 183) wrote of legal thinking during the thirteenth century that 'the unenacted part – and this is the great bulk – of the law seems to be conceived as custom (*consuetudo*). The most important of all customs is the custom of the kings court' (for example, feudal law, royal codifications of custom with various additions and emendations that benefited the king or his supporters). In addition, an increasingly 'heavy burden of proof is cast upon those who would apply other rules [local custom that might not have been explicitly recognized as part of the king's custom]; they must be prepared to show not merely that local tradition is in their favor, but that this tradition has borne fruit in actual practice and governed the decisions of local courts' (pp. 184–5). As a result, changes in the common law may have been slowed relative to a pure customary system.

There are at least three reasons for expecting that this substitution of royal procedures, statutes, and the 'king's custom' for evolving local customary law was relatively unimportant for several centuries, however, suggesting that common law was, for a substantial portion of its history, based largely on the customary law of English communities (Benson 1998c). First, virtually all decisions were actually made by knowledgeable juries chosen from local communities having discretion to make decisions on both matters of fact and of law, rather than by judges (or by juries tightly constrained by judicial instructions on the law and judicial rulings regarding the admissibility of evidence). Second, there was considerable competition for dispute resolution business. And third, people often could contract around common law decisions that they did not want to be binding. All three of these conditions have changed, however, and, as a result, the importance of custom in common law is decreasing and the courts are increasingly being used for political purposes (that is, for wealth redistribution). Let us consider each condition in turn in order to see their collective impact and the underlying reason for it.

5.3 Juries and the common law

The Constitution of Clarendon (1166) explicitly recognized the potential for turning to a panel of twelve men from the local community to decide questions of property (Levy 1968, p. 12), a customary practice that apparently traces back to the Anglo-Saxon hundreds. Henry II's royal courts replaced the hundred courts, however (Benson 1992b, 1994a, 1998g), and gradually introduced what would become the standard trial jury. Most civil cases were jury trials by the reign of Edward I. The original concept for juries was that they would be self-informing: that they would either be aware of the relevant evidence or gather it. These juries consisted of men of the community who presumably witnessed or had knowledge of the facts relevant to the case (the preferred group of men from which to draw all types of juries consisted of substantial landholders, the knights, but apparently many wealthy individuals purchased or secured exemption from jury duty, either legally or through bribery, and so juries almost inevitably included freemen of lower social and economic status as well). They were empaneled by the sheriff to hear the pleading and render a verdict. By the time of Magna Carta, civil trials of all kinds could be submitted to juries empaneled by the royal circuit courts if both parties agreed. They 'proved to be so popular that chapter eighteen of Magna Carta guaranteed that the circuit court would sit several times a year in each county for the purpose of getting verdicts on disputes that they settled' (Levy 1968, p. 13).

Trial by ordeal effectively ended for criminal cases in 1215, and 'neither the law nor the lawyer knew what to do about the indicted men overflowing the inadequate jails' (Lyon 1980, p. 450). Various inquisitional juries from the hundreds, townships and counties were always present at a session of a royal court. 'Surrounded by the various juries, the judge in a criminal case could take the obvious course of seeking the sense of the community' (Levy 1968, p 15). Writs had also developed for obtaining jury trials in a few criminal cases. For instance, an accused could obtain a writ to have a jury determine whether the accuser had lodged his complaint out of malice. This same type of writ could be used to determine whether an inquisitional jury had acted maliciously. These trial juries were called petty (*petit*) juries to distinguish them from the grand or inquisitional juries, and they set the stage for criminal jury trials. The development of universal use of trial by jury in criminal cases was not immediate, however (Benson 1992b, 1998c, g). The full history of jury trials cannot be told here, but to appreciate some of its implications, consider that in 1730 London it was common to empanel two twelve-man juries to try all of the roughly 150 felony cases heard in a typical court session (royal assizes outside the urban centers typically empaneled a single jury to hear all pending cases) (Langbein 1978, p. 276).[11] A single court session would last several days. The juries' sittings were staggered so that one could be hearing evidence on a series of cases while the other was out deliberating on other cases just presented. Furthermore, most jurors were experienced at the job, having served previously (ibid., p. 277). One procedural rule clearly followed from the use of experienced jurors. Judicial instructions to the jury were perfunctory (Beattie 1986, p. 376). Little time was needed to instruct jurors who already knew what was going on. Jurors themselves participated in the trial, questioning the accused and witnesses and making observations about facts, the characters of witnesses and so on. Rules of evidence apparently did not begin to develop until the fourth decade of the eighteenth century, primarily in an effort to control public prosecutors who were beginning to bargain with accused criminals, exchanging an agreement not to prosecute for testimony against other criminals (Langbein 1978; Benson 1992b, 1998g). Indeed, in general 'judges took the path of least resistance by accepting verdicts rather than making their own inquiries' (Levy 1968, p. 41) (the incentives to do so are discussed below). Therefore, in both civil and criminal trials, juries had a great deal of power to determine what the relevant law was, and to weigh all of the evidence that might be brought to bear.[12]

Whether juries actually tended to consistently apply local custom rather than statute or judge-made precedent cannot be said with certainty, but there is at least some evidence that they did. For one thing, most civil cases had to do with disputes over the possession and title to land (ibid., p.12), and since most jurors were themselves landholders, they presumably had incentives to rule in ways that would be consistent with their own expectations and desires to secure their own titles. Furthermore, since both parties had to agree to a civil jury trial, the fact that they were extremely popular methods for dispute resolution (ibid.) suggests that they tended to produce unbiased verdicts that were consistent with the expectations of the parties and community involved. More direct evidence comes from the criminal law. Note that kings, particularly after the Norman conquest, began shifting many offenses that had previously been treated as torts punishable by restitution to victims into crimes punishable by fines and forfeitures to the king or physical punishment (Benson 1992b, 1994a, 1998g). Restitution had been effective in promoting social order because it tended to restore the victim and eliminate his desire for violent revenge, and it benefited the offender in that he bought back the 'peace' and his place in society. Indeed, the creation of criminal law appears to have generated greater social *disorder* precisely because victims were no longer 'restored' to their original level of satisfaction, and thus became more likely to demand expulsion or severe physical punishment for offenders.

With the demise of restitution to victims, the punishment mandated by the Crown (and later by Parliament), following the collection of fines and forfeitures, became increasingly harsh. Well into the eighteenth century, statutes were extending the scope of existing offenses and creating new ones that were punishable by execution. But 'it is clear from the way the courts put these statutory changes into effect, however, that few men thought that all these laws needed to be rigidly enforced. ... The courts showed little inclination to execute men for relatively trivial offenses they mainly dealt with' (Beattie 1986, p. 420). Even before trial, facts in capital cases that had involved restitution in pre-Norman times, such as unpremeditated homicide (manslaughter) and non-violent thefts, were frequently manipulated by grand juries to forestall capital punishment, thus substituting local opinion (tradition, custom) for statutory criminal law (Green 1985). Mitigation of penalties by trial juries was also a widely practiced means for reducing the severity of punishment in such cases. Indeed, jury mitigation became so widespread that Parliament ultimately was forced to develop alternatives to capital punishment, including transportation and, later, imprisonment (ibid.; Benson 1992b, 1998g).

Legislators did not appreciate the law-judging power of juries, of course. Green (1985, p. 105) explains that 'the stronger central institutions became, the less they required of juries, either as substitute bureaucrats or as political mediators. Indeed, the stronger the position of central government, the more it was bound to regard the jury as part of the problem rather than the solution'. Thus, the power of the jury began to change in the eighteenth and nineteenth centuries. Rules of evidence evolved into the complex instructions to the juries that we see today. Juries no longer consist of people with considerable experience or knowledge about the process or the law. The expanding population base for jury pools means that juries are also much less likely to be composed of individuals who have strong interests in developing an understanding of customary rules of property and contract, let alone applying them. They are told what the law is, prevented from seeing evidence that might 'bias' their judgment, and instructed as to what they should conclude given the evidence that they are permitted to consider. Thus, the likelihood that juries are generally applying community standards rather than rules mandated by statute or dictated by judges is clearly much less today than it was through much of the evolution of the common law.

5.4   *Interjurisdictional competition and the common law*

The early development of common law also occurred during a period of intense competition for legal jurisdiction (Berman 1983; Levy 1968; Baker 1971; Rowley 1989). As royal law in England (including common law) was emerging as a recognized legal system, it had to contend with the canon law of the Roman Catholic Church, the evolving Law Merchant (and subsequently, the law of the urban centers), the manor law of the barons, and the local customary law of the hundreds. Furthermore, competition was intense even within the evolving system of royal law. By the middle of the thirteenth century the king's high courts were quickly moving toward the institutional structure that would last into the late nineteenth century. The Court of the King's Bench, the Court of Common Pleas and the Court of the Exchequer became identifiable entities with identifiable jurisdictions. The Court of Common Pleas supposedly had exclusive jurisdiction over all cases between private citizens unless a crime had occurred, in which case the King's Bench and Court of Common Pleas had concurrent jurisdictions. However,

> through fictitious legal means the king's bench stole much legal business from the court of common pleas. This is principally explained by the desire of the justices of the bench for more legal business; each case meant fees, from which the justices derived much of their living. Competition between the courts for legal business became very bitter with the result that jurisdictions became much less definite. The judges resorted to any subterfuge to attract cases into their courts. (Lyon 1980, p. 443)

Competition between the three common law courts was intense, and perhaps as a consequence, by the fourteenth century the king's power over these courts had been reduced substantially. In reaction to their increasing independence of the crown, various specialty courts also began evolving from the King's Council. These 'conciliar courts' or 'prerogative courts' included the Court of the Admiralty, the Court of Chivalry, the Court of the Chancery (or equity), the Star Chamber, and the Court of Requests.

The existence of alternative legal jurisdictions for dispute resolution processes tends to push all judges toward unbiased decisions. If a forum is expected to favor one party, and the other party can demand the use of an alternative venue, they will tend to compromise on the forum that will be least biased and therefore most fair. Thus, as Rowley (1989, p. 371) explains,

> the competitive nature of early common law evolution provided a powerful impulse for the law to reflect the interests of litigants and, in this sense, to be efficient. ... The royal courts succeeded by providing the best available justice, reflecting not least the preferences of merchants and money lenders attracted to England by the development of foreign trade. The law of property and the early law of contract undoubtedly benefited from the efficiency impulses thus provided.

Indeed, the benefits of competition went beyond such efficiency implications, as Berman (1983, p. 10) observes:

> it is this plurality of jurisdictions and legal systems that makes the supremacy of law both necessary and possible. ... The very complexity of a common legal *order* containing diverse legal *systems* contributes to legal sophistication. Which court has jurisdiction? Which law is applicable? How are legal differences to be reconciled? Behind the technical questions lay important political and economic

considerations. ... The pluralism of ... law ... has been, or once was, a source of development, or growth – legal growth as well as political and economic growth. It also has been, or once was, a source of freedom. (Emphasis in original)

Berman includes the 'or once was' phrase in recognition of the fact that diverse legal systems are increasingly being subjugated and centralized under the authority of coercive state governments. The common law courts triumphed over most of their competition in England (Baker 1971) and, ultimately, the competing common law courts were also combined. The full story of this competition cannot be explored here, but some indication of its implications can be seen by briefly discussing part of the competitive process.

The strength of competition varies across legal issues, and therefore, the ability of judges to legislate also varies. The government has claimed the exclusive right to try criminal cases for centuries (see additional discussion below), for instance, and criminal law appears to be very inefficient (Benson 1998g; Rasmussen and Benson 1994). In the area of commercial contract law, on the other hand, the availability of alternative forums (for example, arbitration) has tended to limit judicial discretion. Merchants actually had several forums to choose from during the formative period of the common law, including their own courts of the markets and fairs (Trakman 1983; Berman 1983; Benson 1989, 1998e). Merchants also could and did take disputes to ecclesiastical courts. After all, the Church was a major trader (Bewes 1923, p. 9) and, in addition, many of the major fairs were held at important priories and abbeys. It was therefore clearly in the interests of the Church's leaders to remain on good terms with the merchant community by offering them a source of dispute resolution that would recognize their customs and practices, at least when they did not conflict with canon law. Similarly, merchants naturally used the developing urban courts which evolved from the earlier market courts, and which merchants continued to dominate. And the Court of the Admiralty was an active and aggressive competitor for merchant disputes (Mitchell 1904). The availability of numerous alternative dispute resolution forums, including the courts of the fairs and markets, meant that the customary commercial law, the Law Merchant, remained a source of protection against the growing centralized power of kings (Berman 1983, p. 343). During the fifteenth century, common law courts began to attract more and more commercial cases of all kinds. Merchant courts remained available for commercial disputes until the early 1600s, however, and since the merchants remained relatively free to choose between their own courts, several other courts, and the common law courts throughout the fifteenth and sixteenth centuries, the fact that merchants were willing to choose the royal courts in increasing numbers implies that those courts must have been doing a good job of applying the Law Merchant. Thus, the customary laws of the

Law Merchant provided the foundation from which the common law's commercial rules would evolve (Bewes 1923, p. 19). The competition was not to remain intense, however.

The functional separation of the organs of government toward the end of the fourteenth century intensified the competition between the powers represented in Parliament, the king with his prerogative courts, and the common law courts. Some common law judges felt that the common law courts should be the supreme source of law rather than either the king or Parliament, but they clearly did not have sufficient power to achieve this goal. Most common law judges recognized that they had to pick sides, and over time their interests tended to become more aligned with Parliament (Ekelund and Tollison 1980, p. 584), in part because many common law lawyers and judges were members of that body (Holdsworth [1903] 1924, pp. 210–11). Common law judges therefore began characterizing Parliament as simply a common law court, supreme in that it could overturn other common law court decisions, legislate jurisdictional boundaries, and dictate other characteristics of the courts, but also dependent on the other common law courts to facilitate the implementation of the law. In light of the common law courts' alignment with Parliament, Henry VIII supported the prerogative courts in their expansionist moves and encouraged application of continental civil law rather than English common law. However, the common law courts had gained superiority over their 'weaker' competitors (for example, ecclesiastical, manorial, and hundred courts) by the later part of Elizabeth I's reign, so they also attacked the jurisdiction of the prerogative courts (ibid., p. 414).

Those asserting that the law emanating from Parliament and other common law courts was supreme also attacked any remaining non-royal sources of law. For instance, the great common law jurist and parliamentarian, Sir Edward Coke, who was intimately involved in the struggle between parliamentary and royal authority, ruled in *Vynior's Case*, 4 Eng. Rep. 302 (1609), that decisions of merchant courts could be reversed by common law judges, claiming that the merchant courts' purpose was to find a suitable compromise while judges ruled on the legal merits. In essence, Coke asserted that the Law Merchant was not a separate identifiable system of law, but rather that it was 'part of the law of this realm' (Trakman 1983, p. 26). Following Coke's ruling, the use of merchant courts in England declined dramatically, and they continue to function only in a few places (Gross 1974, p. xix). Furthermore and significantly, contracts binding the parties to submit to arbitration were declared to be revocable. The doctrine of revocability was justified and reinforced in *Kill* v. *Hollister*, 1 Wilson 129 (1746), when contracts to arbitrate were declared revocable because they 'oust courts of their jurisdiction'. Thus, the earliest judicial defenders of the revocability doctrine spoke of the courts' interests, suggesting that England's common law judges saw arbitration as an undesirable threat to their control of dispute resolution.

By the time the common law courts could be secure in their victory over competitors, 'much of the common law was already hardened and set' (Rowley 1989, p. 371). This was particularly true of contract law (as well as the law of property, but the common law of torts was a relatively late development and therefore not as firmly established). Common law judges refused to recognize the Law Merchant as a distinct branch of law, however, in contrast to other European countries, and they rejected some of its important principles. But sufficient similarity remained between England's common law of commerce and the law applied in France's commercial courts to imply that the customary Law Merchant was still an underlying source of much of England's commercial law (Bewes 1923, p. 14). After all, the three common law courts were still in competition. The competition between the common law courts probably reduced the impact of the Law Merchant's subjugation somewhat as each tried to attract merchant business. As long as competition for dispute resolution survived, some implicit recognition of custom was likely as no single court could fully monopolize business disputes and decide them exclusively as the court saw fit. Nonetheless, Trakman argues that

> by restricting the dynamic use of trade custom in various ways, the English common law courts precluded resort to the pliable framework of the Law Merchant. Either they refused to admit custom into the legal system in any form whatever, or custom was required to satisfy onerous tests of admissibility before it was received into English law. ... Custom had to comply with the rules of positive law. It had to be truly 'ancient' in its origins in order to be admitted in law, and it had to be consistently practiced, notwithstanding the changing environment of business itself. ... In this way, the Law Merchant became rigid as post-medieval English judges sought to integrate the Law Merchant into the established confines of a centralized common law. (Trakman 1983, p. 27)

It appears that with the demise of the prerogative and merchant courts, the intensity of competition was significantly reduced, and the subsequent evolution of contract law was clearly altered in England from what it might have been (ibid., p. 30).[13] Furthermore, demands for a unified court system increased in England, particularly during the nineteenth century, and ultimately (in 1875) the three common law courts were merged under a single Supreme Court. Competition from commercial arbitration re-emerged in England at the same time as pressure was mounting to centralize the common law (Benson 1989, 1998e), however (and it emerged even earlier in the United States; see Benson 1995a). But by then the evolutionary path of contract law had clearly been diverted, as numerous differences between English common law and the international Law Merchant developed (Draetta et al. 1992).[14]

5.5   *Contracting around 'bad' common law rulings*

Complete displacement of custom by judicial or parliamentary legislation requires limits on the use of contracting as well as on competition for dispute resolution and constraints on juries. De Alessi and Staaf (1991) emphasize that the historic ability to contract around the rules laid down by common law decisions has been an important safeguard against judicial legislation and judicial error that could lead to the creation of inefficient common law rules.[15] During much of its history, the application of many potential common law precedents was determined voluntarily, just as in customary law. 'The *right to contract around the rule* indirectly yields unanimity: all those parties who do not wish to be bound by a particular rule ... generally have the opportunity to adopt any other rule that is mutually satisfactory' (ibid., p. 112; emphasis in original).

The opportunity to contract around bad rules clearly varies considerably, of course. For commercial activities it is relatively easy, as contracting partners can specify their own rules and then designate an arbitration forum to handle their disputes under those rules. As long as the arbitrator focuses on the contract and on trade practice and usage (custom), rather than on common law precedent (as they typically do; see Benson 1998b, d, e, 2000), the combination of contracting and arbitration can nullify a potential precedent. Pre-dispute contracting is much less likely to arise when the dispute is over liability in accidents involving strangers, of course, so court precedent, whether good or bad, may be relatively durable. Mutual insurance arrangements may establish liability rules contractually for members of a close-knit group, but not for strangers (insurance markets provide contractual protection against tort liability but they probably do little to nullify potential tort precedents). After-the-accident bargains and contracts are also possible if the rules are 'bad' enough, as parties can settle out of court. But both parties must agree to do so since one of them can be forced into court by the other if the coercive institutions of the state are brought to bear. Thus, pre-trial settlements may imply that both parties expect to be better off by avoiding litigation costs, or that both parties believe that the common law rule is a bad one. Consider certain developments in the history of criminal law, for instance.

English monarchs claimed jurisdiction over criminal law centuries ago, largely in order to impose fines and to seize assets from criminals (Benson 1992b, 1994a, 1998g). Before this occurred, criminal offenses were treated as intentional torts with compensation paid to victims, however, as noted above, and many victims clearly preferred to get compensation rather than see fines and forfeitures go to the king (even considering the physical punishment that followed). As a consequence, negotiations between victims and criminals were common, with criminals agreeing to return property or compensate victims if they were caught, in exchange for not being prosecuted under the king's law (victims were under royal mandate to prosecute criminals in England for much of its history, so such a bargain could be made; see Benson 1992b, 1994a, 1998g). In an effort to generate prosecutions and collect their profits from criminal justice, kings were therefore forced to institute a series of rules against such negotiations (private contracting). The victim was declared to be a criminal if he obtained restitution prior to bringing the offender before a king's justice where the king could get his profits, for instance. The crime of 'theftbote' was created, making it a misdemeanor for a victim to accept the return of stolen property or to make other arrangements with a felon in exchange for an agreement not to prosecute. The earliest development of misdemeanor offenses only involved 'crimes' of this type. Similarly, civil remedies to a criminal offense could not be achieved until after criminal prosecution was complete; the owner of stolen goods could not get his goods back until after he had given evidence in a criminal prosecution, and fines were imposed on advertisers or printers who announced a reward for the return of stolen property, no questions asked. Coercive efforts to induce victims and communities to pursue and prosecute criminals were not successful, however, and state institutions gradually took over the supply of these services. Today, such negotiations between victims and criminals are rare in the common law world (although they are very common in some places, such as Japan; see Benson 1998g) and the resulting inefficiencies in criminal law are considerable (ibid.; Rasmussen and Benson 1994).

Since victims and criminals willingly contracted around criminal law prior to coercive efforts to prevent it, negligent parties and their victims should be able to contract around tort law too. And, in fact, there are examples of attempts to do so. Contracts with many hospitals and health maintenance organizations contain arbitration clauses, for instance, in an effort to move medical malpractice disputes out of the common law courts. This alternative has not been very successful in preventing litigation, however. Victims and criminals in England could agree to avoid the courts and royal justice because both expected to be better off as a consequence (victims got some compensation and did not have to bear the cost of prosecution, while criminals avoided the forfeitures and harsh physical punishments that resulted from a criminal conviction). However, when a coercively backed dispute resolution forum is expected to favor a particular category of litigants by transferring wealth to them, those litigants will not agree to avoid that forum or negate its biased rules (unless the costs of obtaining such biased results are high, as they could be in a repeated-dealing arrangement or a close-knit community such as a trade association), and there is a widespread perception that American courts tend to be biased in favor of patients in medical malpractice suits (the reasons for this are similar to those discussed below for changes in product liability rules). Growing empirical evidence supports the validity of this perception

(Benson and Fournier 1998), while also suggesting that there is a trend toward increasing awards to patients in medical malpractice tort actions. Clearly, other patients are not likely to take action against someone who sues his doctor since they also may be able to benefit from future malpractice litigation (collective action problems are also significant for consumer groups that might recognize unintended consequences such as reduced availability of some medical services and rising medical costs), and if doctors or hospitals attempt to boycott a litigious patient, the political fallout would be tremendous. Thus, in the current legal–political environment, medical malpractice tort law is not likely to be avoided through contract and arbitration. But even a contractual stipulation of arbitration is irrelevant if the coercive and biased court does not enforce it or if the arbitration ruling must be 'approved' by the court.

Historically, tort law has provided the default rules governing interpersonal disputes when the parties had not specified alternative rules or procedures in advance (that is, contractually), thereby providing a mechanism to encourage individual responsibility by forcing people to pay for the harms they inflict on others intentionally or negligently.[16] However, tort law has increasingly become a mechanism to provide 'social insurance' by imposing liability on the party best able to afford it (for example, a manufacturer) or by spreading the risk of injury across all members of society regardless of fault (for example, strict liability forces firms to buy more insurance and raise their prices to everyone in order to pay for that insurance). Tort law is therefore becoming a mechanism for redistributing wealth rather than a mechanism for compensating victims by imposing responsibility on tortfeasors. And furthermore, rather than being a default mechanism when contracting is not possible, 'the revolution in the law of tort ... began and ended with widespread repudiation of contract law' (Rowley 1989, p. 379).

Consider product liability, which used to be a contract issue at common law. Manufacturers owed a duty of care only to those who contracted directly with them, and damages could be specified by contract (for example, limited warranties), particularly if harms were likely or if courts made inefficiently large or small damage awards. However, beginning in 1916 with *MacPherson* v. *Buick Motor Co.*, 217 N.Y. 382, 111 N.E. 1050, this duty has gradually expanded. By 1960, manufacturers' duty had clearly been extended well beyond explicit contractual linkages to include anyone likely to use or be exposed to a product as part of a string of 'fictional contracts' (Rowley 1989, p. 380). Then, in *Henningsen* v. *Bloomfield Motors, Inc.*, 32 N.J. 358, 161 A.2d 69 (1960), a manufacturer was declared to be liable under an 'implied warranty principle', despite the lack of convincing evidence of any negligence by the manufacturer, of any product defect, or of any expressed contractual warranty covering the claimed failure of the product. This implied warranty principle contributed to the movement away from a negligence standard of tort liability itself toward strict liability as subsequently established in *Greenman* v. *Yuba Power Products*, 59 Cal. 2d 57, 27 Cal. Rptr. 697, 377 P. 2d 897 (1963). Under strict liability, the product liability issue no longer had to be rationalized in 'contractual' terms like 'implied warranty'. The doctrine serves as a transfer mechanism intended to aid those who are injured by imposing the costs on those with deep pockets or by shifting the costs onto others through higher prices, regardless of fault. A short time later, a contractual limitation of a warranty was explicitly rejected in *Vandermark* v. *Ford Motor Co.*, 61 Cal. 2d 256, 37 Cal. Rptr. 896, 391 P. 2d 168 (1964): the obligations assumed by contract were declared to be immaterial, as the seller was subject to strict liability. Thus, the potential for contracting around inefficient statutes and court rulings regarding product liability has been significantly limited, if not eliminated.

Product liability was shifted from contract law to tort law through a process that Richard Epstein (1982, p. 46) characterizes as 'unsystematic and unthinking judicial activism'. Some economists have argued that strict liability is desirable because classes of economic agents (manufacturers) now know for sure what they are liable for. Thus, administration costs should fall. In reality, though, the increasing application of strict liability (along with growing damage awards for intangible harms and for purposes of punishment, and reduced requirements of proof of causation) makes the property rights to producers' income increasingly insecure. These rights are 'up for grabs' for anyone who can establish a claim, and this has led to a rent-seeking race for property rights accompanied by tremendous dissipation of wealth (Benson 1996). Since 1960, product-liability tort litigation has exploded and whole domestic industries are threatened with extinction (ibid.). Consider American manufacturers of small airplanes who once dominated the world market: the number of small planes manufactured in the United States has fallen from over 17 000 in 1978 to under 600 in 1993, and 100 000 jobs have been lost, primarily because of product-liability tort costs (ibid.). Between 1989 and 1992, for instance, 203 crashes of Beech aircraft were caused by weather, faulty maintenance, pilot error, or air-control mishaps, according to National Transportation Safety Board investigations, but every one of these crashes resulted in product-liability lawsuits. Beech spent an average of $530 000 defending itself in these cases. Even those dismissed cost the company an average of $200 000. The other firms in this industry face similar litigation exposure. And this is only one example of the 'tortification of contract' (Olsen 1992), which has been

> driven by attorneys in search of high expected rents from increased litigation, supported by legal scholars of interventionist predilections and by judges and

> juries whose social consciences too frequently led to changes in precedents con-
> ducive to a flood-tide of litigation and to the widespread shift from consent to
> coercion in the law of accidents and personal injury. (Rowley 1989, p. 379)

Not surprisingly, manufacturers are exploring many options in an effort to
re-establish property rights to their income. In addition to vigorous litigation
in an effort to introduce new defenses against strict liability (for example,
assumption of risk defenses, unforeseen misuse defenses), huge liability
insurance premiums, and massive disinvestment in some industries, business
interests have lobbied hard for legislation by Congress and state legislatures
to overturn judicial precedents. Some relief has been gained (for example, a
1993 federal statute bars suits against small plane manufacturers after a plane
and its parts have been in service for 18 years), despite strong opposition
from the Association of Trial Lawyers of America. But trial lawyers are the
largest benefactors of the growing tort law wealth-transfer process (of the
over $12 billion that changed hands through 1992 as a result of asbestos tort
actions, for instance, $9 billion went to lawyers). Because they are also a very
powerful and effective lobby group (perhaps the most powerful in the country),
they have generally been successful in countering demands made by business
groups for tort reform.[17]

5.6   Interest-group politics and the courts

'Rent-seeking lawyers' (Rowley 1989, p. 383) are not the only private interests attempting to manipulate law through the modern common law courts.
Indeed, the courts have 'become a terrifying political force to a host of vested
interests' (Neely 1982, p. 26). Courts can be influenced by interest groups in
a number of ways. One of the most obvious channels of influence is in the
recruitment and appointment of judges. Justice-sector bureaucrats (police,
prosecutors, to name two), trial lawyers, bar associations, and many other
organized interest groups (for example, civil rights, labor, business, and
financial groups) all actively seek to influence judicial appointments at *all*
levels of government (Eisenstein 1973, pp. 66–7; Schmidhauser and Berg
1972, pp. 81–99; Peltason 1955; Blumberg 1970). The circuses surrounding
the nominations of Robert Bork in 1987 and Clarence Thomas in 1991 to the
Supreme Court were actually unusual only in the degree to which the activities of special-interest groups surfaced and attracted so much press attention.
The purpose of interest-group efforts to influence judicial appointments is
also obvious. In the legislative process, each pending bill can be lobbied for
or against, but lobbying on court decisions, which can both establish new law
and determine the bounds of enforcement of existing law, is much less
effective. Landes and Posner (1975) contend that the benefits gained through
legislative actions are insecure if the beneficiary group is unable to maintain

its position of influence with the courts and Crain and Tollison (1979a) find empirical support for this role of courts in interest-group competition. However, it is also more difficult for opposition groups to change rights assignments made by the courts, even if opposition groups become politically more potent in the future. Many judges do not face re-election or reappointment, for instance, and so the usual political tools of influence are relatively ineffective. Thus, the decision regarding who holds the office is a *relatively* more important avenue of political influence for judges than for legislators. Indeed, judgeships are often 'political rewards' for individuals who have demonstrated support for ('ideology' consistent with) powerful interest groups' desires. Other judges who do face re-election or reappointment, or who aspire to higher appointment, recognize that they will need the support of powerful groups in the future, and so they also tend to remain faithful to the interests of their political sponsors. As West Virginia Supreme Court Justice Richard Neely (also trained as an economist) explains, 'any concept of merit selection – that is, selection based exclusively on objective standards rather than politics – is chimerical. ... In the final analysis, interest groups are not looking for brilliant lawyers, they are looking for lawyers who will decide cases in their favor' (Neely 1982, p. 37).

Of course, even if an interest group plays a role in judicial selection, it typically must signal its wishes to the court in order to have significant influence over particular issues, and while groups that do not dominate the selection of judges may be at a disadvantage, they need not be destined to have their interests unrepresented (Peltason 1955, p. 43). The frequency of organized interest-group involvement in litigation is well documented. Several studies have focused on celebrated Supreme Court decisions and found interest-group support from the outset (Vose 1959; Manwarning 1962). Others have documented comprehensive patterns of group involvement by examining *amicus curiae* briefs filed in the Supreme Court (Kirslov 1963; Harper and Etherington 1953). Indeed, interest groups plan their litigation strategies just as meticulously as they do their legislative lobbying efforts. The factors affecting success include the makeup of the court bureaucracy, the status (or power) of the group, and the skill of the group's presentation (Murphy and Pritchett 1961, p. 275). A number of strategies have been employed by interest groups to present their views before the courts, including finding a person willing to break a law in order to initiate a test case to challenge the constitutionality or applicability of a law, arranging for a plaintiff and a defendant to have a friendly suit in which the group's lawyers prepare the arguments for both sides, having a member act as a plaintiff to enjoin administrative officials from enforcing a statute, filing class action suits, helping a non-member who is already involved in litigation that touches on the group's interests, and filing an *amicus curiae* brief (ibid., pp. 276–80).

Court time in the United States is increasingly being taken up by political issues or by disputes involving opposing interest groups, and these disputes are crowding out traditional private law disputes over property, contract and negligence. As Neely (1982, pp. 166–7) observes,

> there are certain classes of cases on the frontier of the law where there are real disputes, but these are political disputes between interest groups where the battle-ground is a lawsuit. Efforts to change existing laws can be characterized as 'disputes', but they are political disputes rather than the factual disputes that courts are theoretically in business to resolve.

There is no reason to expect that the resulting precedents are desirable in the sense that they enhance allocative efficiency. Benefits are likely to accrue to the interest group involved, but others can bear substantial costs. After all, 'the *easy* decision is the one that is politically inspired' (Blumberg 1970, p. 127; emphasis in original).

Common law clearly is no longer simply law based on custom. It is increasingly becoming part of the political process. According to Judge Neely,

> it is fair to say that courts are in the business of redistributing the wealth. ... The layperson usually envisages the court system as a neutral institution that applies preconceived, scientific rules. In fact, the courts are not neutral; the rules are not preconceived through a wide spectrum, and law is only partially a science. Much of law really reflects the political judgments and emotional passions of the judges. Consequently, political battles rage in the courts about the same issues that engage the executive and legislative branches. (Neely 1982, p. 10)

6   Conclusions

Superficial examinations of history suggest that systems of rules with significant elements of command and coercion tend to go through cycles, with some periods characterized by considerable order and others involving tremendous disorder (civil war, riots, and so on). The legal system of the United States has been evolving for over two centuries, for instance. That is a pretty long life as legal systems go, and while American society has probably been more orderly than many, its history has included periods of tremendous disorder (for example, the Civil War of the 1860s, the civil rights movement of the 1960s) as various groups' attempts to use the state to support wealth transfers have exploded into violent conflict. While much of the conflict in America is still being directed through the channels of formal state government, including the courts, even more dramatic disorder characterizes many societies around the world. Like the United States, Haiti has been a sovereign nation for over two centuries, for instance, but its history has been dominated by repeated cycles of violent conflicts, tremendous levels of corruption and criminal activity, arbitrary and gruesome uses of coercive power, a very large 'informal sector' (for example, relative to the portion of economic activity taking place in underground markets in the United States) attempting to operate without relying on (or more accurately, without being subject to) the formal legal system, and so on.

Very similar conditions often apply for long periods in societies with centralized coercive legal systems (for example, see de Soto 1989). Indeed, there are legal regimes in Africa, South and Central America, Asia, and Eastern Europe with levels of social disorder closer to that observed in Haiti than in the United States. Theorists and politicians who see order arising as more efficient rules and institutions are selected over time through the coercive powers of the state appear to have a very myopic view of history. The process of legal evolution inevitably seems to be interrupted by revolts, revolutions, *coups d'état*, and civil wars, even in societies that have managed to survive for long periods. An economic analysis of law that sees law as an exclusive product of the state and fails to consider the fact that law can be an instrument of wealth transfer, as stressed by public choice analysis, will therefore only be able to explain a portion of the rules that evolve even in relatively ordered societies, and probably will have little to say about the rules and institutions that influence most behavior in most of the world.

Notes

* This chapter is part of a larger project on 'The Evolution of Law', which has been supported by two Earhart Foundation Fellowships, grants from the Institute for Humane Studies and the Carthage Foundation, and a contract from the Independent Institute. Parts of it were motivated and strongly influenced by discussions with John Hasnas, Leonard Hochberg, and other participants in the Liberty Fund Colloquium on 'Government and Spontaneous Order in Hayek's *Law, Legislation, and Liberty*', organized by Eric Mack, with Mario Rizzo, Charles Rowley, Paul Rubin and other participants at George Mason University's Seminar in Austrian Economics on 'Law and Economics', and with Randy Holcombe.

1. Indeed, some writers in the Chicago-school tradition contend that the political marketplace is just as efficient as the economic market (Wittman 1989). See Rowley and Vachris (1993) for a public choice criticism of this view, however.

2. Certain components or implications of the argument may still be challenged, however. For instance, the contention that judges 'should' apply an efficiency norm (Posner 1980a), particularly on a case-by-case basis, can be challenged because judges are not likely to be able to anticipate the consequences of their rulings and because case-by-case rulings can create considerable uncertainty about what rules are going to apply in the future (Rizzo 1980a, b; Benson 1996). As explained below, uncertainty about what the rules are can have significant negative impacts on efficiency.

3. Many Chicago-school scholars recognize that law, particularly through legislation, can be used to generate wealth transfers, of course, and that such transfers can involve welfare costs, at least in the form of reduced consumer and producer surplus. Even these laws are expected to be 'efficient' in a different sense, however: either the deadweight losses from the transfer process are expected to be minimized (Becker 1983) or transaction costs are minimized. The evidence for this is survival of a transfer process, which demonstrates to Chicagoans that the transaction costs of resisting such transfers and changing the law must exceed the benefits of doing so (Stigler 1992). These arguments can also be rejected using the prospective proposed by Wagner (1993), however, as indicated below.

4. Note that Wagner's (1993) vision of the transformation of public choice involves adoption of the Austrian paradigm, as will be clear in the following presentation. In this regard, numerous criticisms of the Chicago approach to law and economics have been made from an Austrian perspective (for example, see Rizzo 1980a, b), although Hayek (1973) clearly saw the common law as an efficiency-enhancing process. There are many other ways to criticize this approach as well. For instance, see Kornhauser (1980), Tullock (1980b), Kimenyi et al. (1985), Aranson (1986), Rowley (1989), and Benson (1996, 1998c).

5. Note that the term 'institution' is used in a variety of ways. For instance, Vanberg and Kerber (1994) explain that it often means a 'configuration of interconnected rules' or, equivalently, the property rights arrangements established by these rules. In the presentation that follows, however, it is important to distinguish between different components of such an 'institution'. In particular, the primary rules of conduct will be distinguished from the procedural rules of governance. Procedural rules establish the mechanisms or processes that motivate individuals to recognize primary rules, as well as the means by which primary rules of conduct can be clarified (perhaps through dispute resolution) and changed. Thus, the procedural rules define the terms of any 'ongoing multi-party relationship' or 'joint enterprise' or 'collective action' which cannot be meaningfully decomposed into separate bilateral exchange contracts (Vanberg 1992, p. 241): they establish the institutions of multiparty governance. Therefore, in the following discussion, terms like 'rules' (as well as 'conventions', 'norms', 'customs', 'laws', and 'codes') will refer to primary rules, while the term 'institutions' usually will refer to the process constituted by the procedural rules of governance (that is, the configuration of constituted organizational rules), as in Benson (1994b). Finally, for clarity, the system of 'property rights' will not be referred to as an institution, even though it clearly can be (for example, as in North 1990), because it is useful to distinguish between a system's primary rules of obligation, their supporting governance institutions, and the system of property rights implied by the primary rules and supporting institutions.

6. Hayek's theory in this regard has attracted a good deal of criticism, however, in part because it is perceived to be based on a logically inconsistent mix of individual and 'group' selection processes rather than on individuals as the exclusive actors (for example, see Vanberg 1986). Whether such criticisms are valid or not, though, it can be demonstrated that Hayek is correct when the analysis is firmly based in methodological individualism (Benson 1997a, 1998a).

7. Another reason is that customary law is often confounded with primitive law, and anthropological studies of primitive societies often do not depict a dynamic changing law. However, as Pospisil (1971) explains, most anthropological studies of law look at a short period of time rather than at a long history, and most anthropologists have not been interested in the issue of legal change. The fact of the matter is that legal evolution occurs even in primitive societies and it can be detected if the researcher looks for it (Pospisil 1971; Benson 1988). However, legal change is not necessary when conditions are not changing, and since conditions that might demand new rules or extensions of old rules arise relatively slowly and infrequently in most primitive societies, the evolution of custom also appears to be slow. One must look to a dynamic changing environment ruled by customary law, such as modern international trade, to see rapid changes in that law.

8. While customary law and contract law are typically sharply differentiated, Fuller (1981, p. 176) argues that this distinction is inappropriate. He explains, for instance, that if contingencies arise which were not explicitly anticipated in a contract, they will generally be resolved by asking what 'standard practice' is with respect to similar issues. Are the parties bound by customary law or did they tacitly agree to incorporate standard practice into the terms of the contract? Actually, contract and customary law often are simply different terms for the source of a particular behavioral obligation. A contract may be implied entirely from the behavior of the parties, for instance, because they conducted themselves in such a way that a tacit exchange of promises occurred. Furthermore, while the roles of dispute resolution and contracting in the evolution of customary law are treated separately here, they are actually tightly intertwined. For instance, contracts can be used to expand voluntary interactions beyond a close-knit group bound by strong trust

relationships, but that means that disputes requiring third-party assistance may become more prevalent. Through contracts, parties can specify that arbitration will be employed rather than more adversarial adjudication processes (that is, public courts).

9.   Ellickson (1993, p. 1400) points out that while the consequences of spontaneously evolving law may well be efficient for members of the group, for instance, the relevant legal jurisdiction may still be inefficiently narrow in scope in the sense that there may be 'significant extraterritorial spillover effects that harm outsiders so much that the regime is undesirable from a broader social perspective. This suggests that in some instances a government might usefully act to overcome the selfish practices of subgroups within its control'. However, Ellickson goes on to suggest that the ideal against which such a system must be judged so as to draw conclusions that the system is inefficient is, in general, unobtainable. The fact is that such ideals generally are modeled by assuming zero enforcement costs, benevolent or tightly constrained lawmaking authorities, or both.

10.   During the period of intense confrontation between Henry and the barons, the barons tried to limit the judiciary's writ-making power, recognizing that new writs were actually new laws. The barons were particularly concerned when Henry dictated the nature of writs himself: 'In this fear the barons were joined by the common law judges, not because they feared new judicial writs, but because they wanted to have exclusive control over their invention and had strong feelings against outsiders' tampering with their law and its procedure' (Lyon 1980, p. 437). Thus, the Provisions of Oxford mandated that no new writs would be sealed without the consent of the council. Judges joined in this effort by deciding whether writs issued by the chancellor were innovations requiring council approval. They felt that the common law was virtually complete and would be harmed by further change, but

> the judges had abetted what became admitted principle under Edward I, that changes in the law could be made only with the consent of parliament. Henceforth any growth of common law was by the fiction and evasion of the judges, who preferred circumlocutions to law consciously and continuously changed by themselves. Thus confined, the common law lost jurisdiction and elasticity. (Lyon 1980, pp. 437–8)

11.   In 1219 the instructions of the *eyre* (a court of itinerant judges) indicated that the accused was treated as presumptively guilty. In 1221 some of the royal justices accepted the judgment of juries if an accused was willing to face a jury trial. However, the same men who took part in the inquisitional (or presentment) jury and accused the offender also made up the petty or trial jury, so there was considerable resistance to acceptance of a jury trial. Prevailing opinion of the day was that trial by jury meant a guilty verdict. The justices thus began searching for ways to force defendants to accept jury trials. Defendants were locked in prison for a year and a day with little food and water, for example, but many still refused. No uniform process developed until 1275 when the first statute of Westminster declared that those accused of a felony who refused to accept a jury inquest would be 'put in strong and hard imprisonment'. Thus, accused felons were loaded with heavy chains and stones, placed in the worst part of the prison, given a little water one day and a little bread the next, until they agreed to trial by jury or died. Many chose to die. The fact was that with a jury trial a guilty verdict was almost certain, followed by execution and forfeiture of all property to the Crown. Death under 'hard and severe pressure' meant that the accused was not convicted of a crime and therefore his property went to his family. The composition of the petty jury gradually began to change toward the end of the thirteenth century. Rather than the same men sitting both as an inquisitional and a petty jury, the grand jury was augmented by men chosen randomly from neighboring communities. Occasionally, such juries would reach verdicts of not guilty. The witness-bearing character still dominated, however, and throughout the thirteenth century, petty juries were not impartial groups receiving information, but groups sworn to tell what they knew about a case. The next phase of the evolution occurred at the beginning of the fourteenth century. A trial jury was typically selected from the relevant presentment jury and the presentment juries of various other communities. Nonetheless, the presentment jury and petty jury would not be completely distinct for another 50 years.

12. This does not mean that the judge had no control over the juries and the trial in general (Langbein 1978, p. 376). A judge often acted as an examiner, questioning the accused and the witnesses. He commented at will on the merits of a case. There was also a good deal of communication between the judge and jury. Furthermore, a judge could terminate a case prior to a verdict and remit the accused to jail if he felt that the jury was leaning toward an improper verdict, or if it was clear that relevant evidence was not being provided. Such actions were rare, however. Similarly, judges could also recommend that 'the jury ... find a special verdict' (ibid., p. 345), although this was also rare. The jury did not have to following the judge's recommendations, but when the judge had issued such a statement he opened up options to himself that he might not have otherwise. For instance, 'it was open to the judge to reject a proffered verdict, probe its basis, argue with the jury, give further instruction and require redeliberation' (ibid., p. 291). There are records of juries deliberating further and altering their verdicts, as well as of juries persisting in their original finding, so this judicial power did not imply that juries were forced to follow the judge's instructions. Rather, it meant that juries had a second chance if the judge disagreed with the verdict. Note that Langbein's discussion of judicial control of juries includes nothing about judicial instructions regarding the rules of evidence.

13. The development of royal influences in commercial law was not motivated just by those wishing to supply authoritarian law. Some members of the merchant 'community' also saw advantages in having royal authority established over commercial matters (Ogilvie 1984, p. 115; Benson 1989, 1998e). Indeed, parts of the business community have, for centuries, been very effective in the political arena. A merchant who wants to become wealthy in an unregulated competitive market must be concerned primarily with maintaining a reputation for fair dealings, because other merchants and consumers can always choose to buy from someone else. Similarly, a widely recognized, unbiased legal system is vital in order to create the incentives to cooperate in trade for everyone's mutual benefit. But the increasing power of some kings offered an alternative, particularly in nations with expanding colonial empires. In England, for instance, developing economic regulation involved domestic merchants trading support and money to kings in exchange for special privileges such as royal grants of monopoly rights within England or the colonies, the power to form exclusive guilds, and entry restrictions (Ekelund and Tollison 1980).

14. The rigidity of the common law, including economic regulations passed by Parliament, began to raise transaction costs for English businessmen. After all, England was faced with increasing resistance to its trade and navigation acts in parts of its colonial empire, and ultimately began to lose its hold on the colonies. Thus, facing the loss of captured markets and an increasingly competitive international environment, the business community demanded recognition of their evolving business practices as a source of law. In the late seventeenth century, particularly with Sir John Holt, and then in the eighteenth century with Lord Mansfield, common law decisions once again began to recognize the customs and practices of English merchants as a source of changes in English common law (Mitchell 1904, pp. 77–8). Mansfield used merchant juries to consider commercial disputes, for instance (Draetta et al. 1992, p. 11). While Mansfield's role in the revival of customary sources of legal change in common law was particularly important (there also were political motivations behind Mansfield's efforts; see Ogilvie 1984, p. 116), a significant impetus for once again recognizing merchants' evolving customs appears to have emerged as international trade became relatively more significant. Continental courts had been much more receptive to the Law Merchant than common law courts were, so common law courts were forced to compete with foreign courts and legal systems to regulate international commerce (Trakman 1983, p. 28). Still, substantial differences between civil law and common law in commercial matters remain, in part perhaps because of the influence the common law had over evolving business practices during the period when the civil law was more receptive to the Law Merchant. For instance, common law turns to money damages first when a breach of contract occurs, while the civil law relies much more heavily on specific performance (Ebke 1987, p. 612). As legal systems in Europe have become more centralized and less competitive, both civil law and common law courts have developed commercial contract law that departs from custom, however. Today, there

are many differences between contracts written under the modern international Law Merchant and those written under both common and civil law (Draetta et al. 1992).

15. Contractual nullification can even apply to legislation if the legal authority is not able to enforce its rules (see de Soto 1989 and Benson 1998g for examples of privately established property rights to supposedly 'publicly' owned lands).

16. This description of tort was suggested in recent correspondence with John Hasnas.

17. Because trial lawyers benefit so significantly from tort litigation, legislators themselves can also capture part of the insecure income, as suggested by McChesney (1987), by threatening to pass tort reform legislation. The mere threat of such legislation can lead trial lawyers to make large contributions to appropriate legislators in order to block such legislation and protect their lucrative source of income.

27 Public choice and the environment

Bruce Yandle

1 Introduction

From the beginning of the discipline, economists have focused on environmental issues. After all, the availability of land, rivers, and harbors is fundamental to the wealth of nations. In his review of North America's promising prosperity, Adam Smith ([1776] 1976, Bk II, ch. VII, p. 77) spoke glowingly of the availability of good harbors and 'plenty of good land' in the American colonies. Later, 'land', a catchall term that included all the commonplace gifts of nature, was regularly listed as one of the factors of production, and neoclassical economist Nassau Senior ([1836] 1938, p. 92) even went so far as to identify 'proprietors of natural resources' as a component of the economic order.

Generally speaking, the early concern of economists was with the supply of water, air, light, and land, not with the quality of these resources or what we today call environmental quality. But writing in the middle of the nineteenth century, John Stuart Mill ([1848] 1973, p. 7) suggested that 'if from any revolution in nature the atmosphere became too scanty for the consumption ... air might acquire a very high marketable value'.

The environmental revolution that began in the late 1960s for the developed world changed all of this. Air and water quality, pollution and related concepts of externalities and public goods captured the attention of economists (Cropper and Oates 1992). The count of articles on the environment published in economics journals is one important proxy that illustrates the attention the discipline has devoted to the subject. As seen in Figure 27.1, the number of all environmental articles published in economics journals rises from near zero in 1966 and reaches a peak of 81 in 1995. Clearly, the environment made its way into the economists' workshop.

While the number of articles on environmental economics rose sharply, those that took a public choice approach, also shown in Figure 27.1, were much fewer in number. The insights offered by these contributions to the literature were substantial nonetheless. After all, key policies affecting the allocation and management of environmental assets are in the hands of the public sector and involve collective decision making. In the absence of public choice thinking, it is impossible to explain important features of decisions taken by government in the apparent pursuit of environmental quality. Today, whether the topic is global warming, ozone depletion, hazardous waste, or

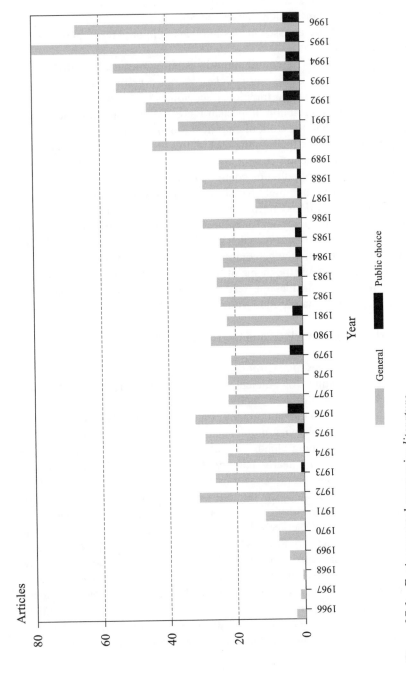

Figure 27.1   Environmental economics literature

emissions of sulfur and nitrogen oxides, economists and policy analysts know that political institutions have to be considered when explaining regulatory outcomes. Once an issue moves into the realm of politics, public choice logic is indispensable.

To appreciate fully the contributions of public choice analysis to the study of environmental programs and policies, one must first understand the linkages that connect it to the traditional economics of 'market failure'. Then, having made the connection, important theoretical contributions need to be identified. After that, the work of empirical economists needs to be surveyed.

Drawing on lessons from public choice, this chapter focuses on collective choice and environmental control. The chapter begins with a discussion of the simple analytics of pollution control and related policy prescriptions. Two paths are described that might be taken in dealing with environmental problems. Traditional notions of efficiency first reign supreme in this discussion. Later, the normative analysis that presumes a search for efficiency gives way to early notions of public choice that rescue traditional theory from its inability to explain actual policy outcomes. The theoretical contributions of public choice scholars provide the theme of Section 3. Then, armed with theory, the chapter moves to consider the results of empirical work based on public choice theory. The chapter ends with some final thoughts.

2   Environmental analysis and the rise of public choice

2.1   *Two approaches to the problem*
Economists searching for efficient solutions to environmental control take two fundamentally different approaches (Yandle 1997). A first approach, historically related to the work of A.C. Pigou (1920), introduces the problem of social cost. The Pigovian problem can be couched simply in terms of an industrial plant belching clouds of soot that fall on freshly washed clothes drying on the lines of a nearby laundry. Without explaining why the laundry would locate so close to the factory in the first place, or vice versa, or if the location decisions were based on appropriately adjusted land prices, Pigou describes how the factory's emissions impose costs on the laundry not accounted for by the factory's decision makers. The factory's management understandably reacts to all costs it must pay; these are the private costs of production. Management does not adjust its activities to account for the external or social costs imposed on neighbors. Focusing on these negative externalities, Pigou calls on government to close the gap between social and private costs: 'It is however, possible for the State, if it so chooses, to remove the divergence in any field by "extraordinary encouragements" or "extraordinary restraints" upon investment in that field' (ibid., p. 192). Pigou asserts further that

no 'invisible hand' can be relied on to produce a good arrangement of the whole from a combination of separate treatments of the parts. It is therefore necessary that an authority of wider reach should intervene to tackle the collective problems of beauty, of air and light, as those other collective problems of gas and water have been tackled. (p. 195)

Writing long before the advent of public choice, Pigou saw government as an environmental manager, a beneficent exogenous force, unaffected by special-interest demands for government favors. Always efficiency bound, the legislative body is asked to calculate external costs dispassionately and apply pollution taxes to internalize them. While Pigou later concluded that corrective taxes could never be applied effectively in the real world, his prescription nonetheless took hold and spawned government enterprises worldwide where public officials seized the opportunity to gain revenues through the use of effluent fees and other environmental taxes (Yandle 1998, pp. 127–8).

A vast literature followed on the heels of Pigou's analysis of externalities. Indeed, in the 1960s and 1970s, environmental economics was largely concerned with the development of analytical engines for the purpose of correcting perceived 'market failures', those Pigovian situations where private decision makers did not take account fully of social costs (Bator 1958). Baumol and Oates's major work, *The Theory of Environmental Policy* (1975), captures the essence of these explorations. All along, government was viewed implicitly as being beneficent at best or simply uninformed at worst in efforts to maximize welfare. In the eyes of many analysts, any unpleasant byproduct of the production process was viewed as an externality demanding to be internalized. The legal and political institutions that force economic agents to take account of the costs of their actions were largely overlooked or not fully understood.

Taking the Pigovian externalities model to task, Buchanan and Stubblebine (1962) stressed the difference between 'relevant externalities', where the cost of corrective action is less than the anticipated gains, and those they termed 'irrelevant', meaning that the costs imposed on third parties were less than the cost of government intervention. Their work supported Ronald Coase's (1960) seminal explanation of how market forces could deal effectively with Pigou's social cost problem, provided that property rights were defined and interested parties could transact at low cost.

The mention of Nobel laureate Coase introduces the second analytical approach for managing environmental use. An industrial plant discharging unwanted pollution is seen as evidence of a violated property right, if the right exists in the first place. Recognizing traditional common law rules that provide redress to those harmed by unwanted pollution, Coase called for a different solution. Instead of urging involvement by government in calculating and imposing complex taxes or managing pollution abatement technologies,

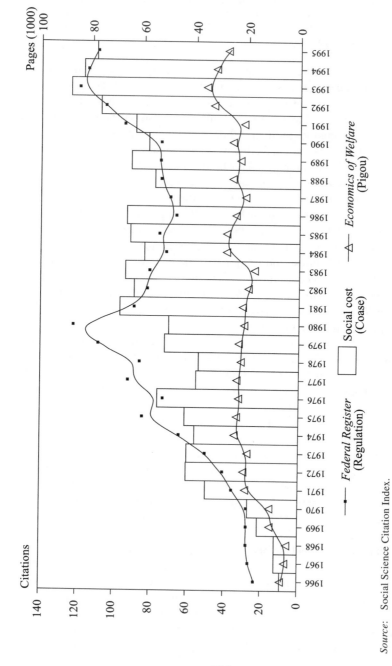

Pages (1000)

Citations

Source: Social Science Citation Index.

Figure 27.2   Coase, Pigou, and regulation

permits, and controls, Coase looked to contracting and reinforcement of property rights. Environmental problems could be seen as private matters that involve contracting between affected owners and occupiers of land. When it would be too costly for the parties involved to bargain separately with one another, market forces deliver environmental liability insurance, inspire the formation of river basin associations and environmental clubs, and promote the purchase of easements or the affected land by the polluter. Coase's prescription laid the foundation for free-market environmentalism, an approach to environmental management that minimizes government intervention and emphasizes the role played by property rights and markets (Anderson and Leal 1991).

The academic response to Pigou and Coase is shown in Figure 27.2, which graphs the citation count to Coase (1960) and Pigou (1920) superimposed on the count of pages of new and revised regulations in the US *Federal Register*, a daily government publication that reports all proposed and final regulations. Of course, not all of the regulations listed in the pages of the *Federal Register* pertain to environmental matters, though many do so.

The data in Figure 27.2 suggest that scholars responded systematically to Coase and to the rise of regulation. References to Pigou increased somewhat during the same period but reveal no particular correlation with the rising number of regulations. The chart suggests that Coase was far more influential than Pigou as economists reacted to the growth of regulation. While this may be the case, it is clearly not the case that property rights and markets dominated the regulatory solutions embraced by government. Indeed, Pigou seems to have won that battle.

2.2   Summary
Before turning to politics, two distinctly different approaches may be described for managing environmental use. Both are dedicated to the economist's efficiency standard. Both claim to seek outcomes that maximize net social benefits and wealth. One approach calls for government intervention and control. The other calls for well-defined and -enforced property rights and relies more on decentralized market forces. Government intervention can be based on taxes, technology mandates, or performance standards. The choice – public law and regulation or private law and markets – depends largely on the extent to which efficiency-enhancing forces survive when steps are taken to move from the world of theory to the world of practice. That is, we have to consider what happens when the legislature chooses.

3   Public choice enters the analysis
The discussion thus far has focused almost exclusively on economic efficiency with occasional reference to the body politic. To the extent that politics entered, the imaginary politicians were dedicated to finding efficient solu-

tions to environmental problems. Pigou innocently set the stage for a more complete analysis when he said that 'it is possible for the State, if it so chooses' (Pigou 1920, p. 192). But if we are to focus on choosing, the normative assumption of social welfare maximization must be replaced with a positive analysis of political choice.

Three major treatises, by Anthony Downs (1957), James M. Buchanan and Gordon Tullock (1962), and Mancur Olson (1965), lay the public choice foundation to assist in the investigation. Downs placed political decision making in an economics context and analysed some of the difficulties that emerge when votes replace dollars. Olson taught several fundamental public choice lessons. First, small, organized interest groups can sway politicians to transfer wealth to them while spreading costs across a large group of unorganized citizens. Second, public goods provision, whether by collective or private means, is fraught with problems. Pure public goods that provide non-excludable benefits to an open-ended number of people create opportunities for free riding. Because of this, Olson argued that public goods will tend to be underprovided.

Buchanan and Tullock apply the individualistic lessons of the market to collective decision making and provide fundamental public choice axioms that show how the rules of majoritarian politics can impose high costs on minorities. Their market-based explanation of political behavior assumes that self-interestedly motivated politicians dominate the political process. Their seminal work forms a major foundation stone that supports the later development of public choice, which goes on to suggest that, contrary to Olson's earlier conclusion, public goods can easily be overprovided.

Rejecting the notion that political behavior is best explained by a public-interest theory that presumes to find efficiency in politics, these contributors set in motion an analytical engine that would scrutinize political decisions as diverse as taxation and budget deficits, welfare reform, military casualties, antitrust action, and Federal Reserve monetary policy. In all cases, political agents are assumed to have the same incentives as other normal human beings. They are motivated to improve their own wellbeing, which generally means keeping their elected or appointed public-sector jobs while maximizing expected lifetime earnings. With the arrival of the environmental revolution that brought massive government intervention in markets, public choice economists used their new tools to explain political actions, predict outcomes, and analyse implications.

3.1   What public choice tells us

In an early examination of the pollution-control problem, Nobel laureate James M. Buchanan and Gordon Tullock (1975) – the two founders of the public choice school in economics – asked why command-and-control regulation seemed to win out over alternative environmental policies, such as performance standards that allow polluters to choose abatement technologies or emission fees and marketable pollution permits that induce cost-effective control. Their article had an insightful title: 'Polluters' profit and political response'. Arguing strictly in theoretical terms, and applying a heavy dose of public choice logic, Buchanan and Tullock argued that a competitive industry has something to gain from federally mandated pollution restrictions, which in practice meant command-and-control regulation, that can never be obtained by any other legal means. The industry can be cartelized.

Command-and-control regulation sets an emissions standard, and actually mandates methods and technologies for individual manufacturing facilities to meet the standard; the approach restricts plant capacity expansions and deters entry. There are no firm-level gains from discovering and applying lower-cost abatement technologies, since all producers must use the same government-approved technology. New entrants that might introduce lower-cost pollution-control methods are ushered away from the industry's door. In a growing economy, the output-constrained industry experiences demand increases and higher profits. Government regulators stop all producers who seek to expand their production capacities. In actual practice, more costly new-source performance standards make the restriction even more binding. Profitable stagnation follows.

As applied by the US Environmental Protection Agency (EPA), command-and-control technology-based standards are best suited to accomplish this result, since performance standards and emission fees do not limit expansions or deter entry. Playing to bureaucratic interests, the technology-based standards require no air- and water-quality monitoring. The bureaucrat must simply specify the engineering standard and then make certain the technology is installed and operated. The lower relative cost of command and control from the standpoint of the bureaucrat helps to explain the limited use of market-like incentives (Hahn 1989).

The Buchanan–Tullock story introduces a key industry group that logically supports a particular form of regulation at the national level. Industries with plants nationwide can cartelize, simplify the legal environment within which they operate, and obtain that much-sought-after 'level playing field' mentioned so often by industry spokesmen. On this basis, national regulation is much preferred to community, state and regional management of environmental quality. One suit that fits all economic agents seems better than struggling with 50 tailors for a different fit in each state.

Long before Buchanan and Tullock wrote about polluters' profit, Ralph Turvey (1963) explained what might happen when polluters are confronted by environmentalists seeking to reduce the cost imposed by unwanted pollution. Turvey's theoretical story focused on emission fees that might be imposed on polluters to reduce their discharges to some efficient level, that being the point where the marginal benefit to society of improved environmental quality is just equal to the marginal pollution-control cost. Turvey observed that fees or penalties imposed on polluters only address half the problem, thus setting the stage for possible overproduction of a public good. If those who value environmental quality for its own sake pay nothing for additional units of it, they will lobby for even higher pollution taxes or stricter controls. Turvey fortified Coase's point that efficiency requires that all demanders of environmental quality must face market-determined opportunity costs, a point that formed the basis of the work by Macaulay and Yandle (1977).

Turvey's analysis identifies another key interest group – 'greens' – that will favor rules that impose costs on polluters, but not on themselves. Command and control offers yet another attraction to environmentalists. The more dedicated environmentalists see pollution fees and taxes as a way for rich polluters to buy licenses to pollute, which in the extreme view was seen as being equivalent to selling permits to commit a felony (Nelson 1993).

Environmental organizations obviously played a crucial role in the regulatory saga. Armed with statutory provisions allowing them to bring suits against violators of the growing list of environmental rules and regulations, and thereby serving as 'policemen' in the Buchanan–Tullock cartel, environmentalists lifted the importance of their cause to religious heights (Nelson 1993). Indeed, R.C. Lowry (1998) analysed the determinants of membership in major environmental organizations and found strong empirical support for the notion that membership in those groups was indeed a substitute for membership in traditional religious organizations.

In his work on environmental policy, Paul Downing (1984) described how federal legislation supplies a national marketing opportunity for environmental organizations. From the standpoint of attracting new members and revenues, national programs and the accompanying publicity are far better than state or regional debates about environmental rules. Then, as the federal bureaucracy expands in size and its regulatory scope widens, opportunities surface for environmentalists to become entrenched in government. Niskanen's (1975) model of bureaucratic expansion, which explains how government bureaus become involved in all-or-nothing legislative trades when bargaining for budgets, has the bureaucracy producing more than the efficient level of output. Downing (1981) explains how, once entrenched in the bureaucracy, environmentalists work to provide grants and other taxpayer-financed support to assist environmental organizations in their lobbying efforts. Calling attention to bureaucratic incentives for expanding budgets and operations, Stroup and Baden (1983) explain how agencies involved in public land management engage in environmentally destructive practices as byproducts of timber harvesting and other revenue-generating activities.

Taking a later look at the connection between environmental groups and legislators, Farber (1992) documents how the high-profile organizations articulate a national demand for environmental quality improvements, serving as information brokers during the legislative debate and as law enforcers after laws are enacted. Like Downing, Farber then identifies the political payoff when politicians in turn provide the organizations standing to sue and tax-payer-financed resources for environmental litigators.

With industry, environmental organizations, and the bureaucracy connected by command-and-control regulation, the famous 'iron triangle' of politics is once again put in place. But the iron triangle is one that focuses on regulatory inputs, not policy effectiveness. Public choice explains why so little attention is devoted to monitoring and reporting environmental outcomes and so much effort is applied to writing detailed rules, limiting entry, and identifying new opportunities for imposing command-and-control regulation.

3.2   Lessons learned about political favor seeking

The foregoing brief outline of key public choice insights, while overlooking a vast number of significant contributions to the literature, sets the stage for discussing some watershed thinking that crystalized the public choice prob-lem encountered by efficiency-bound politicians. This crystalization came when James M. Buchanan, Robert D. Tollison and Gordon Tullock (1980) published a collection of articles under the title *Toward a Theory of the Rent-Seeking Society*, a book that coincided with the release of a companion volume by Terry L. Anderson and P.J. Hill, *The Birth of the Transfer Society* (1980). The former volume focuses on public choice theory, the latter on history and institutions. Both tell similar stories. In a political system where votes determine outcomes, special-interest groups have operational incen-tives to seek favors or rents in the resulting political economy. Political competition ensues, and efficiency loses out to restrictions that assist or protect successful special-interest groups.

An especially insightful piece by Gordon Tullock (1967b) reprinted in the Buchanan–Tollison–Tullock collection explains how the social cost of rent-seeking activities far exceeds the orthodox measure of deadweight loss. Tullock points out that resources consumed in seeking rents are specialized and non-productive, which is to say they produce output restrictions, not new goods and services. In the extreme, the expected special-interest gains from rent seeking can be exhausted in the struggle to gain the rents (Posner 1974; Shughart 1999).

Nobel laureate George J. Stigler (1971) and Sam Peltzman (1976) also explored the nature of competition in the political marketplace where regula-tions are devised and implemented. While Stigler portrayed the politician strictly as a broker auctioning off favors to the highest bidder, and never seeking efficiency for its own sake, Peltzman visualized a richer competition, where interest groups matter a lot, but the mass of consumers and unorganized voters also matter. Their combined stories tell us that tradeoffs will be made. After all, as Robert McCormick and Robert Tollison (1981) model the process, one group will bear the burden of financing the benefits obtained by another and politicians bear the burden of pleasing both. Efficiency is traded away partly for special-interest benefits and partly for operating the machinery of wealth redistribution. Neither group gets all that it wants.

Yet a third Nobel laureate in economics, Gary Becker (1983), added another component to the theory of regulation and public choice. Becker's model accepts existing constitutional constraints, voting rules, congressional committee assignments, and all of the other trappings of representative democracy, and asks the following question: if politicians could find a lower-cost, more effective approach to environmental or any other kind of regulation, would they not do so? In these restricted terms, what politicians do must be efficient. Responding systematically and balancing all meaningful pressures impinging on them, politicians design rules that, though compromising efficiency, in some more narrow sense of the word are indeed efficient when all political constraints are considered. Becker's argument suggests that if we desire more effective pollution control, we might best seek constitutional remedies.

3.3   Payoffs from protection from regulation

The focus on political decision making described thus far shines a bright light on the demand side of the political market. The politician–broker of wealth transfers plays a somewhat passive role. Interest groups that have something to gain, be they environmentalists, industrialists, or members of the bureaucracy, organize efforts to communicate their demands and bid for legislation. The unorganized and rationally ignorant suppliers of wealth play a minor role in all this (Downs 1957). Consumer–taxpayers end up bearing a substantial part of the cost of the special-interest benefits delivered by politicians, but the burden is spread thinly over a thick set of people. Until and unless the aggregate burden becomes large and onerous, the unorganized, by definition, have little incentive to make their voices heard.

But Fred S. McChesney (1991, 1997) adds another component to the public choice story, which places interest-group behavior in a different light. Politicians can orchestrate responses from groups that feel threatened by the prospect that burdensome regulation will be imposed on them. Instead of simply announcing a write-up on pending clean air legislation, for example, the politician can indicate that electric utilities are being targeted for dramatic reductions in sulfur dioxide emissions. Then, instead of the industry organizing to seek favors or rents conferred by regulation, the industry organizes and lobbies to deflect or soften the proposed rules. McChesney describes the politician's strategy as 'rent extraction', whereby the politician receives 'money for nothing', which is the title of McChesney's 1997 book on the topic.

Efforts to defend against extractions of wealth can be as socially costly as efforts to gain political favors outright, which were the initial focus of the rent-seeking literature. Consider the struggle over fuel economy standards that were first justified as a means of reducing dependence on imported crude oil and cutting harmful tailpipe emissions from automobiles (Crandall et al. 1986). In 1975, Congress announced a 1985 corporate average fuel economy goal and instructed the US Department of Transportation to promulgate a schedule of targets auto makers would be required to meet over the intervening years. From that point on, a struggle ensued with some firms seemingly using the regulation to their own advantage and others struggling to deflect it (Yandle 1980). As fuel prices rose and fell, auto producers took different positions. Some argued that they had followed the will of Congress and downsized their new car fleets (reducing vehicle weight was the least-cost method of improving fuel economy). They were in fact prepared to manufacture even more-fuel-efficient vehicles. Others argued the reverse. Consumers wanted larger vehicles, they said, and failing to meet this demand would lead to large worker layoffs. The two competing parties engaged in lobbying activities as they sought to shape the rules in their best interests.

The 1997 Kyoto Conference on global warming offers an unfolding episode worth watching. Representatives of the industrialized nations agreed to reduce carbon dioxide and other greenhouse gas emissions to 1990 levels by the year 2010 – a goal that would require the United States to cut its emissions by 40 percent below trend. If ratified by the US Senate, which was doubtful at the time, the agreement would then be translated into regulations. There are losers and winners to consider: coal producers will lose; the natural gas industry will win. Many Third-World countries that are exempt from the targets would also win. Production facilities that can reduce emissions at lower cost will sell permits to higher-cost operators. Each organized interest group will spend resources to influence the regulatory process. Some will seek to deflect costs and avoid rent extraction. Others will seek to impose costs on competitors in the hopes of gaining additional profits or rents.

3.4 Bootleggers and Baptists

Public choice theory tells us that addressing environmental or any other perceived social problem by political means is never simple. But as logical and sound as these theories may be, the matter of just how the political message is communicated needs to be addressed. How do messages get packaged and transferred from special interests to politicians? As Olasky (1987) tells us, packaging matters a lot in political markets.

Almost systematically it seems, groups representing otherwise divergent interests coalesce to lobby for the same outcome when the fine print in environmental rules is being written. Notice the focus on the construction of the rules, not the urge to write rules in the first place. These coalitions always include some economic interest groups, such as certain manufacturers, labor unions, or trade associations, joining forces with (normally anti-business) environmental organizations. One group takes the perceived high road calling for a cleaner world. The other is simply looking for improved profits and wealth. Both groups are seeking rents.

In struggles years ago over whether or not to allow the Sunday sale of alcoholic beverages in rural America, the local bootleggers saw opportunities to expand their markets if legal outlets were closed (Yandle 1983). The bootleggers could count on the Baptists, who officially opposed the consumption of alcoholic beverages at any time, to raise their voices in opposition to Sunday sales. The bootleggers and Baptists both worked the legislative corridors to gain passage of Sunday closing laws. It is worth noting that none of these laws limited the consumption of spirits on Sunday, just their legal purchase. Limits on consumption would lose bootlegger support.

As described by Yandle (1989a) and Greve and Smith (1992), a similar blending of apparently opposing interests is found in the demand for environmental regulation. Determined to prevent polluting activities, environmentalists oppose emission fees and market-based mechanisms for allocating environmental use by polluters. They favor command and control instead. Industries seeking cartelization join the chorus. Put in terms of the 1977 Clean Air Act, which mandated sulfur-reducing scrubbers for electric utilities even if low-sulfur coal was burned (Ackerman and Hassler 1981), producers of high-sulfur coal gained while environmentalists fought to suppress the use of sulfur-dioxide taxes. Members of Europe's Green Party support 'eco-labels' giving detailed information on the environmental consequences of specified consumer goods (Thomas 1997). Domestic producers who can use the labeling requirements to exclude imports support them as well. Organized labor in US manufacturing opposed the North American Free Trade Agreement for environmental reasons. Environmentalists welcomed the support.

We can see how the blending of disparate voices to form harmonious support for command-and-control regulation makes it easier for politicians to trade off efficiency for future political support. But what about the rank-and-file voters? Will they see through the rhetoric and penalize politicians who restrict output, raise costs, and thereby limit environmental protection?

Recent work by Geoffrey Brennan and Loren Lomasky (1993) explains why voters in general might support less than effective environmental programs. Their theory is based on the notion of 'expressive voting', the idea that voters with no financial interest in an outcome will choose to support what appear to be morally or socially important policies even though costs exceed benefits. If, for example, voters are asked to approve of measures with lofty titles like the Resource Conservation and Recovery Act or the Clean Air Act, they will more likely than not vote 'yes' because their votes will not be decisive. Burrowing beneath the concept of rational ignorance and apathetic citizens, Brennan and Lomasky argue that technically uninformed citizens still have a logical basis for pulling the voting booth lever. Otherwise disinterested voters will more likely support properly packaged command-and-control regulation, never knowing about outcomes or asking for a report card on past successes.

4   What does the evidence tell us?
A significant body of empirical work focuses on how politics affects environmental policy outcomes. Some of this work examines the incentives of politicians and bureaucrats to consider the long-run consequences and cost-effectiveness of regulatory intervention. In the private sphere, these considerations are generally reinforced by transferable property rights and well-functioning capital markets, but these institutions are not present in the political sphere.

4.1   Public choice and the bureaucracy
Looking at incentives, Congleton (1992) examines the horizon problem in political decisions involving the control of pollutants that could adversely affect the ozone layer. His analysis shows that democratic regimes, which have longer-term stability than autocratic ones, tend to be more active in regulating emissions. In related work, Schap (1988) examines the environmental record of the Soviet Union and explains how environmental protection declined and flourished with the rise and fall of communism. As shown by Congleton and Schap, public choice economists generally assume that bureaucrats will be less sensitive to economic incentives than their private-sector counterparts, since the reward prospects differ.

Using data on publicly owned treatment works (POTWs), Lyon (1990) tests this hypothesis both by observing actual data on pollution permit trading across a sample of POTWs and by conducting simulations. Lyon finds that public-sector managers are sensitive to the prospects of converting pollution-control cost savings to other activities they value, and are more inclined to sell than to purchase discharge rights. Their self-interest matters. His research indicates that POTWs are inclined to engage in 'too much' direct pollution control, a case of overproduction of a public good. Riggs and Yandle (1997) report related findings in their examination of decisions taken by POTW operators to join a cost-minimizing river basin management association; they indicate that incentives do matter to easily monitored local bureaucrats who face budget pressures. Close monitoring tends to yield more cost-effective behavior.

Public choice scholars have examined the bureaucracy to see if lobbying activities influence such things as EPA enforcement activities or US Forest Service management of public lands. Mixon (1995) searched to see if lobbyist influence could somehow seep into the EPA bureaucracy and affect the number of penalty citations issued in the struggle over global warming. Mixon examined data on urban area carbon emission violations in regions experiencing rising ambient temperatures. The results indicated that lobbyists per capita significantly reduced the magnitude of fines and the probability that the EPA would issue carbon violation citations.

Donald R. Leal (1993) examined state and federal government management of similar forest lands located in the northwestern United States. He found a key difference in underlying incentives. The net revenues from state-managed forest lands are dedicated to public education, which means that citizens in general and teachers in particular closely monitor the gains when cutting rights are sold and roads and other necessary forest management inputs are built and purchased. On federal land, the revenues from US Forest Service operations do not redound fully to the states, are not dedicated to highly visible functions, and are therefore not closely monitored. US Forest Service personnel are generally transferred from place to place and do not have generationally deep ties to the people in the communities where they reside.

On the basis of these incentives alone, public choice theory predicts different outcomes for otherwise similar forests. After examining data on operating costs, net revenues generated, and actions that reflect efforts to maximize net revenues, Leal found dramatic differences between state-operated and federally managed forests. Roads built for timber cutting on state land are crude, inexpensive, and less environmentally intrusive; similar roads on federal forest land are more numerous, wider, and more permanent. Transportation and other operating costs are higher in federal forests. Bureaucratic and other incentives evidently matter.

4.2   Politics and clean air

To support the broader public choice story, empirical studies must adduce evidence that environmental regulations provide identifiable benefits to special-interest groups, which include industrial firms, environmentalists, and others who can appropriate gains from government intervention. A study by Peter Pashigian (1985) examined congressional voting patterns on the 1977 amendments to the Clean Air Act. The specific amendment examined was known as Prevention of Significant Deterioration (PSD) and it required expanding plants in certain geographic areas to meet newly specified, technology-based standards that were stricter than those imposed on similar plants in industrialized regions with poorer air quality.

We might expect a vote based on human health and public interest to favor stricter standards in the more industrialized dirty-air regions where the marginal benefits of pollution control were the greatest. This was not the case. After adjusting for a number of other variables, such as income, population density and manufacturing concentration, Pashigian found that representatives from the older industrialized regions systematically supported tighter standards for competing regions that were beginning to attract new industrial plants.

Robert Crandall (1983) analysed votes cast by members of the US House of Representatives on major environmental statutes for each of the years from 1975 to 1980, as well as for three aggregated and pooled sets of votes by US senators over the same period. Crandall used the League of Conservation Voters (LCV) index as the dependent variable, entered either as the share of a state's House delegation voting 'favorably' in terms of the LCV ratings or, in the case of senators, the actual LCV index. To explain the voting pattern, Crandall included as independent variables four orthodox measures of environmental quality (for example, air and water pollution), income, income growth, and the share of state land owned by the public sector. Two indicator variables controlled for political party affiliation and identified legislators representing the older 'frost-belt' states. The model enabled Crandall to discriminate between environmental, economic, political, and regional forces that could influence the outcome.

Crandall's estimates confirmed Pashigian's earlier findings. Environmental factors were not associated with votes supporting environmental legislation. Income and, especially, income growth mattered a lot. Where income growth was lower, support for federal environmental legislation was higher. When income growth was removed from the model, the frost-belt dummy variable became significant and positive in its association with pro-environment votes. The fraction of politicians that were members of the Republican Party was negatively associated with votes favoring environmental regulation, as was the share of land owned by government, which is a strong proxy for the interests of western states.

Crandall concluded his analysis by noting that the results could not support an environmental quality theory of environmental legislation. The estimates did not reject the hypothesis that it was in the interest of older industrialized regions to restrict industrial development and income growth in the expanding sun-belt region. Having used the LCV index as the measure of voting outcomes, Crandall's findings imply that environmentalists joined forces with industrialists and other special interests in the frost-belt to limit competition from the sun-belt, which confirms a bootlegger and Baptist theory of regulation.

Yandle (1984) subsequently investigated the determinants of the LCV index in his research on congressional votes on an amendment that gave state governors veto power over certain aspects of federal sulfur-dioxide regulations. He regressed the LCV's ratings on the share of state population living in areas with SO_2 emissions that exceeded the national standard, the percentage of state workers employed in the five major polluting industries, and the percentage change in value added in manufacturing between 1972 and 1977. The coefficient on SO_2 emissions was not significant. Employment in polluting industries was not a significant variable. Industrial growth was the powerful variable, and it was negatively signed. The results implied that the environmental movement is more about reducing industrial development than reducing SO_2.

Following the prediction of Buchanan and Tullock (1975), Maloney and McCormick (1982) examined portfolios of stocks of US copper producers to see if their market values rose significantly following the EPA's announcement of strict emission guidelines for copper smelters. As noted at the time, the new standards would preclude the construction of additional US copper production capacity. The portfolios showed significant positive returns in association with the announcement.

Public choice analysis also suggests that a shift from state and local environmental control to federal control would bring different outcomes for identifiable interest groups. Quinn and Yandle (1986) examined air pollution control expenditures across the 50 US states both prior to and following the advent of federal regulation of air quality. They found a significant shift in the allocation of regulatory expenditures. In the pre-federal period, expenditures were positively correlated with private investment in real property and human exposure to air pollution. In the post-federal period, expenditures were explained by the presence of federally owned land and other national landmarks. Private investment in residential property and human exposure no longer seemed to matter.

Meyer and Yandle (1987) examined House and Senate votes on acid rain amendments to the Clean Air Act that ultimately required reductions in SO_2 emissions. Their models adjusted for population exposure to sulfur dioxide, tons of sulfur dioxide emitted by electric utilities, the presence of other industries that might be adversely affected by regulation, and whether or not the politician represented states in the eastern acid-rain-control region. The results showed that senators were less likely to vote in favor of controlling SO_2 emissions the greater the presence of forest products industries and federal lands. The lower a state's water quality, the more likely a senator would vote 'yes'. Population exposure to emissions did not seem to matter, nor did the amount of sulfur dioxide emitted by electric utilities. In other words, as Peltzman's (1976) theory of regulation predicts, the senators provided some environmental benefits and some industry protection.

While some empirical research provides evidence of special-interest influence and bootlegger and Baptist coalitions, only a few studies indicate that federal regulation may have actually harmed the environment. A study by Maloney and Brady (1988) falls into this category. Maloney and Brady examined capital turnover in electric utility generating capacity in conjunction with EPA regulations that set higher standards for new plants than for older ones. All else being equal, economists would predict that plant operators would delay rebuilding or replacing generating capacity if the regulatory penalty were significant. Using vintage data on electricity generators nationwide, Maloney and Brady determined a steady-state trend for capital replacement prior to the implementation of EPA new-source performance standards for utilities. As economic theory predicts, they found a significant slowdown in capital turnover. Going further, the two researchers estimated the amount of emissions that would be generated by older technologies versus newer ones. They found that stricter new-source standards increased the level of air pollution from the industry.

The Maloney–Brady study is the empirical counterpart of the Ackerman–Hassler (1981) episode described earlier that involved scrubbers and high-sulfur coal. The scrubber requirement emerged as a way to protect the interests of unionized coal workers and owners of eastern coal mines against the competition that was emerging from non-unionized producers of clean coal in the western states. The significant cost of scrubbers apparently was enough to encourage electric utility operators to postpone replacement of older-vintage – and dirtier – capital.

Investigations of the political economy of clean air do not always result in outcomes that neatly support public choice theories. For example, Joskow and Schmalensee (1998) probed almost endlessly the forces at work in congressional decisions that set the amount of tradable SO_2 emission permits provided to public utilities in conjunction with the 1990 Clean Air Act. Examination of the variation in the amounts of bonus allowances provided across states seemed to offer an ideal setting for revealing the power of interest-group politics. Would the number of potentially displaced coal workers explain the allocation? The conditions of air quality? Pending elections of state senators? Or what? The statistical modeling did not reveal a consistent pattern. Joskow and Schmalensee suggest that the analysis was complicated by the large number of contracts covered by the allocation process.

4.3   Public choice and hazardous waste

'Superfund', the US federal program designed to clean hazardous waste sites, has also been scrutinized by public choice scholars. Recognizing that Superfund seems to have much to do with administrative and litigation expenditures and less to do with cleaning up toxic wastes, J.A. Hird (1993) examined a series of congressional votes on the initial 1980 legislation and later (1986) amendments. Exploring the notion that Superfund was simply a pork-barrel program used by politicians to funnel more cleanup funds to their states and districts, Hird found no evidence to support that proposition. Instead, the evidence suggests that Superfund was an environmental icon; voting patterns favoring Superfund were strongly influenced by the concentration of membership in environmental groups in a politician's region, while negative influence came from the oil and chemical industries in those regions. The environmental pressure to continue the program was apparently so strong that politicians were unwilling to put their careers at risk by voting to oppose it.

Other work on Superfund (Barnett 1985; McNeil et al. 1988) probed EPA's internal Superfund decision making, looking to see if, among other things, the agency assigned key importance to the protection of groundwater when choosing to include a site on the agency's priority list. Barnett (1985) found that EPA decision making was strongly influenced by state regulatory efforts and surface water and air pollution issues, but that threats to groundwater were not significant in explaining agency choice.

McNeil et al. (1988) studied EPA data to see if the Superfund taxes paid by chemical-using industries were significantly related to Superfund expenditures in the states where the tax receipts originated. Superfund supporters sometimes argued that the program was about collecting revenues in contaminated regions and applying the funds for cleanups in those regions. The research showed just the opposite. Taxes were collected in one region, where chemical use was high, and spent in other regions. On the basis of these results, Superfund was a pork barrel (also see Yandle 1989b).

Dalton et al. (1997) examined the legislative process that produced the first Superfund statute, focusing on competing bills considered in committee and on the legislative floor. Using portfolios of stocks for the oil, chemical, waste management, and insurance industries, the investigators sought to identify winners and losers in a rent-seeking struggle as various legislative packages were considered. As expected, the waste management portfolio gained significantly when bills were considered that expanded the size of the Superfund program. However, little in the way of significant effects was discovered for the other portfolios.

4.4   Summary

The empirical work on environmental control provides strong support for the basic public choice theory that has developed over the past three decades. More often than not, outcomes generated by the political process are conditioned by special-interest struggles best explained by rent-seeking and bureaucratic behavior. Environmental legislation and regulation can be better understood in the light of public choice principles. In the absence of public choice considerations, legislative actions and regulatory outcomes in the environmental arena would remain a puzzle.

5 Final thoughts

To a large extent, environmental economics is a study of regulation and policy. It is therefore a study of public choice. If property rights to environmental assets, such as clean air and water, were tradable, as are those to land and other features of nature, environmental economics would lose its distinctive flavor. Environmental use would be no different from other scarcity-driven problems that people face in their daily lives.

Public choice warns of the pitfalls encountered when decisions are made collectively. The theory suggests that we should not expect efficiency to be the driving force that determines political outcomes. The greater the political involvement in allocating and managing a given resource, the less efficient the outcomes will be.

This chapter has provided a three-part survey of public choice and the environment. The chapter's first component traced major lines of economic inquiry on environmental issues. A division of thought was presented on how communities of people might deal with the spillovers generated by otherwise productive activity. One approach called for government intervention and politics. The other called for markets, property rights, and contracts.

For the last three decades, US environmental policy has relied primarily on government intervention and politics. Such things as economic incentives and tradable pollution permits have occupied the basement of the regulatory apparatus. The major statutes that have been enacted and the host of specialized regulations spawned have provided almost endless opportunities for special-interest groups to seek political favors. The high emotional content of environmental issues has galvanized the interests of vast numbers of people nationwide. In short, environmental protection could be called a politician's paradise.

The second part of this chapter has reviewed contributions of public choice scholars who established a theoretical framework for understanding the behavior, actions taken, and results to be expected when politicians respond to environmental control opportunities. Rent seeking becomes a major force in the theories, and the massive wealth available for transfer through environmental controls is the plum that has generated so much command-and-control regulation.

With background and theory provided, the chapter's final section surveyed empirical work that has explored the public choice experience with environmental matters. As scholars examined various statutes, regulations, and the operations of government bureaus, many theory-based predictions were confirmed. Indeed, were it not for public choice theory, it would be impossible to understand the causes and consequences of environmental policy.

The rise of the global economy with its more intense levels of competition and rapidly evolving technologies sets the stage for yet another chapter in the environmental policy story and also another challenge for public choice scholars. When competition is global, it is much more difficult for one nation to provide effective protection to its domestic industries. When ordinary people can gain accurate, low-cost information on environmental outcomes, rational ignorance is reduced. Public choice suggests that new global environmental issues will replace those faced by smaller regions and nations. But for rent seekers to be successful on a global scale, a global government (or a global regulatory body) is required. Public choice predicts that new efforts will be made to create a governing process that will address environmental issues of global proportions. The intense lobbying at Kyoto to transfer wealth from the First World to the Third foreshadows things to come. On the other hand, the cost of governing a global environment will be so large that the rent seekers may be forced to retreat, and market forces will engage environmental protection.

28 Institutions, policy, and economic growth

Gerald W. Scully

1 Introduction

Capitalism and freedom, along with the Industrial Revolution, stand among the greatest achievements of Western civilization. After more than a millennium of stagnation (Maddison 1982, p. 6), innovation and mass production made possible by the application of new sources of power and the rise and spread of freer markets, protection of private property, rule of law, and representative government brought sustained economic growth – a thirteenfold increase in the real living standard between 1820 and 1980 (ibid.). Economic growth remains high in the West today.

After decades of neglect, the unrelieved impoverishment of the Third World renewed interest in the theory of economic growth. The classic paper on exogenous neoclassical economic growth is that of Solow (1956). In that model, with a constant savings rate, s, a constant population growth rate, n, and no technical progress, economies continue to accumulate capital per head, k, and to have economic progress ($y_t = f(k_t)$, $dy_t/dt > 0$), until capital per head reaches its steady-state level, k^0, which is the solution to the differential equation $sf(k) - nk = 0$. At that point, economic progress ceases. Mature nations naturally have high capital–labor ratios and hence lower rates of economic growth than do immature nations. Hence, given the assumptions and the logic of the model these poor nations will converge toward and eventually catch up to the per-capita incomes of the developed nations. The prospect of convergence inherent in the Solow model completely vanishes if one assumes neutral technical change, since the capital–labor ratio rises forever and there is no upper bound on per-capita income. Thus, per-capita incomes need never converge. The Solow model is entirely devoid of institutions.

Also, there was debate about the appropriate socio-political structure necessary to start these nations on a path of economic progress. Two models competed: the Western model of democratic capitalism and the statist model of centralized control (that is, ideally, benign authoritarian government and command allocation of resources). The statist model won out, although there were dire warnings that government control of property and markets was doomed to failure (Bauer and Yamey 1957).

Naturally, political scientists and economists focused on different issues. For the political scientists, it was, then as it is now, a question of whether the liberality of political institutions contributed to or retarded economic growth, and whether democratization was a precondition of economic progress or a luxury good that was affordable only after a certain per-capita income was reached. Since much of the early literature on these issues was by political scientists, who also took the trouble to measure political freedom, the natural tendency was to focus on political institutions as if these were the only ones that mattered. Institutions such as the legal system (more generally, the rule of law), freedom of markets, private property, and so on, generally were ignored. While the link between these institutions and economic growth is pretty straightforward, that between political liberality and economic growth is ambiguous. As is well known, majority rule brings with it income redistribution, larger and more intrusive government, special-interest rent seeking, and so on, all of which may lower economic growth. On the other hand, many institutions and groups and their representatives compete for power in democracies, which makes single-minded control of policy difficult, if not impossible. With a wide variety of competing institutions (power diffusion) affecting policy, as in portfolio theory, diversification may lead to less variance in growth and more sustainable growth paths.

Judged by the frequency of citation, the fundamental papers on the link between institutions and economic growth have been those of Kormendi and Meguire (1985), Scully (1988), Grier and Tullock (1989), Barro (1991), and Barro and Sala-i-Martin (1991). While all find a positive link between freer institutions (variously defined and measured) and economic growth, all except one (Scully 1988) conflate the issue of convergence in per-capita incomes with that of the link between institutions and economic progress. In general, regressions of the following sort are estimated:

$$g_y = \alpha + \beta y_0 + \sum_i \delta_i \mathbf{X}_i + \sum_j \lambda_j \mathbf{I}_j,$$

where g_y is the real growth rate (usually, per capita), y_0 is some initial level of per-capita income, $\mathbf{X}_i$ is a vector of other economic variables, and $\mathbf{I}_j$ is a vector of institutional variables. The trouble with this specification of linking the change in the variable on the left-hand side with the level of the same variable on the right-hand side is that it suffers from what is termed regression toward the mean (Friedman 1992; Quah 1993). Moreover, since growth rates have high variance compared to the level of per-capita income, and the institutional variables and the level of per-capita income are pretty highly correlated with the various institutional variables, the correlation of the institutional variables with the growth rate is necessarily weakened.

Since many studies on the link between freedom and growth undertaken today continue to employ this misspecification, it is worth the trouble of providing a proof of the problem.

Conventionally, let current per-capita income, y_t, be linearly related to last period's per-capita income as:

$$y_t = \alpha + \beta y_{t-1}. \tag{28.1}$$

The solution to this linear difference equation is:

$$y_t = \beta^t[y_0 - \alpha/(1-\beta)] + \alpha/(1-\beta), \tag{28.1'}$$

where y_0 is some initial value of per-capita income. Equation (28.1') has the neoclassical properties (with $\beta < 1$, the function is concave) and if $\beta < 1$ as $t \rightarrow \infty$, y_t converges to its maximum value (asymptote or upper bound) of $\alpha/(1-\beta)$.

The change in per-capita income over time is:

$$dy/dt = \beta^t \ln(\beta)[y_0 - \alpha/(1-\beta)], \tag{28.2}$$

which is positive if and only if $0 < \beta < 1$ and $y_0 < \alpha/(1-\beta)$. The inter-period change is negatively correlated with y_{t-1}:

$$\Delta y = y_t - y_{t-1} = \beta^{t-1}(\beta-1)[y_0 - \alpha/(1-\beta)] \\ = \alpha - (1-\beta)y_{t-1}. \tag{28.3}$$

Alternatively, change may be expressed as a growth rate. Dividing equation (28.3) by y_{t-1}, we get

$$g_t = [\alpha - (1-\beta)y_{t-1}]/y_{t-1}. \tag{28.4}$$

The term $-(1-\beta)y_{t-1}$ in equations (28.3) and (28.4) is the problem of regression toward the mean that has been criticized in the literature.

The implication of Galton's fallacy is that the negative correlation between Δy and y_{t-1} guarantees convergence. This implication is false and also is a fallacy. While the negative correlation is a necessary condition for convergence, it is not sufficient. Observe that the α-term is positive in equation (28.3). The necessary condition for the convergence of y_j to y_i is:

$$\alpha_j/(1-\beta_j) = \alpha_i/(1-\beta_i). \tag{28.5}$$

Numerous studies have investigated convergence in different contexts. In cross-section studies, such as those cited above, the standard technique for measuring convergence is to regress the inter-period change in per-capita income against the initially observed level. An inverse relationship is taken to mean that nations with low initial per-capita incomes are growing faster than nations with high initial levels, and, hence, are catching up. Generally, cross-section empirical studies reject the null hypothesis of no convergence. Beyond the intractable problem of regression toward the mean, cross-section models have been further criticized. They are not able to distinguish between nations which are converging or not, nor between absolute and relative convergence (Bernard and Durlauf 1996, pp. 167–8).

In time-series analyses, convergence is interpreted to mean that differences in per-capita income are not sustainable in the long run. Per-capita income differences between nations cannot contain unit roots or time trends, and per-capita income levels may be cointegrated. Generally, time-series tests have accepted the no convergence null (Quah 1992; Bernard 1992; Bernard and Durlauf 1996; Evans and Karras 1996). Criticisms of the time-series methodology are that the power of unit root tests is known to be very low against the alternative of trend stationarity, and that tests for cointegrating ranks are very sensitive to the nuisance parameter in finite samples (see Reimers 1992; Toda 1995). Hence, a certain caution needs to be exercised about conclusions on convergence based on tests the powers of which are known to be weak.

Leaving aside these methodological issues, Bernard and Durlauf (1996, p. 170) point out that cross-section and time-series tests applied to the same data necessarily may yield opposite conclusions because they impose different implications on the data (that is, first differences of cross-national per-capita income differences have a non-zero mean, while a time series of the differences has a zero mean). Having different conclusions about convergence based on different testing frameworks is not satisfying.

2   The rule space and economic growth

There are two legal ways of obtaining income. People employ their resources productively and earn a return. Alternatively, they withdraw resources from productive pursuits and employ them in the political market to redistribute income from someone else to themselves. Resources employed in rent-seeking activities have an opportunity cost equal to their highest return in the private sector (Tullock 1967b).

In a previous paper (Porter and Scully 1995), a general taxonomy of institutions or rules based on Pareto criteria was identified. Rules arise from many sources: custom, religious precept, law, constitutions, and so on. A large subset of these rules have wealth effects. Some rules are efficient (wealth increasing) and some are inefficient (wealth reducing). A rule (or a change in a rule) is said to be efficient if someone's wealth rises and no one else's falls (Pareto efficient) or, less restrictively, if the total wealth gain to society is greater than the total wealth loss (Hicks–Kaldor efficient). A rule is said to be inefficient if the total wealth gain is less than the total wealth loss (Hicks–Kaldor inefficient). Government policy can be treated to the same taxonomy.

Define the rule space of a society as Ω. Let Ω_t be the sum of all separate rules, ω_i, that have been adopted and exist at time t: $\Omega_t = \Sigma_i \omega_i$. Let each rule have a private wealth effect, θ_i, which is positive for an efficient rule and negative for an inefficient one: $\theta_i = g(\omega_i)$.[1] The monetary value of the rule space at time t, which is a measure of the efficiency of the rule space, then, is $\Theta_t = \Sigma_i \theta_i = \Sigma_i g(\omega_i)$. Θ_t may be treated as an index and normalized: $0 < \Theta_t \leq 1$.

The rule space is not time invariant, although it tends to change slowly, except during periods of revolution or crisis. Let the rule space grow according to $\Theta_t = \Theta_0 e^{rt}$, where Θ_0 is some initial value and r is the growth rate of the rule space. The change in the rule space (efficiency) is:

$$dΘ = Θ_0 e^{rt}(drt + rdt). \tag{28.6}$$

Thus, the change in the efficiency of the rule space is determined by time and by the change in the rate of growth of the rule space. The rate of growth of the rule space may be positive, zero, or negative. For $dr = 0$, the rule space becomes more efficient, is constant, or becomes less efficient over time depending on the sign of the growth rate, r. If the change in the rate of growth of the rule space is positive (negative), the efficiency of the rule space accelerates (decelerates) over time for $r > 0$. For $r < 0$, the inefficiency of the rule space accelerates for $dr < 0$ and decelerates for $dr > 0$.

Let national output be produced by a Cobb–Douglas production function in intensive form: $y_t = k_t^\beta$, with $y = Y/L$ and $k = K/L$. The simplest way of incorporating the rule space into the production function is as a scalar. Suppressing the time subscript this is:

$$y = Θ_0 e^{rt} k^\beta. \tag{28.7}$$

Then, the effect of a change in capital per head on the change in output per head is the partial differential:

$$d_k y = (Θ_0 e^{rt} \beta k^{\beta-1})dk. \tag{28.8}$$

The effect of time on the change in output per head is:

$$d_t y = (Θ_0 e^{rt} rk^\beta)dt. \tag{28.9}$$

And, the effect of a change in the rate of evolution of the rule space on the change in output per head is:

$$d_r y = (\Theta_0 e^{rt} t k^\beta) dr. \tag{28.10}$$

The change in per-capita output is the total differential:

$$dy = \Theta_0 e^{rt} (t k^\beta dr + r k^\beta dt + \beta k^{\beta-1} dk)$$
$$= \Theta_0 e^{rt} [(t dr + r dt) k^\beta + \beta k^{\beta-1} dk]. \tag{28.11}$$

Expressed as a growth rate, we have

$$g_y = t dr + r dt + (\beta/k) dk. \tag{28.12}$$

The result can be illustrated. For simplicity, in Figure 28.1, let the growth rate of the rule space be some initial value, let the rate of capital accumulation per head be constant at two rates (that is, $dk = 0$ and $dk > 0$), and let there be various values for dr. For values of $dr > 0$, the rule space is becoming more efficient over time and the rate of economic growth is positively affected despite a constant rate of capital formation. Where there is no increase in capital per head (not uncommon in parts of the Third World) and the rule

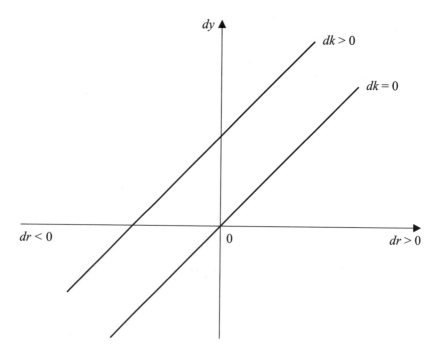

Figure 28.1   Rule space and economic growth

space is becoming less efficient over time ($dr < 0$), the rate of economic growth is negative. Even if there is positive growth in capital formation per capita, at some value of $dr < 0$ the rate of economic growth can turn negative.

3   Stylized facts on economic growth, institutions, and policy

Table 28.1 presents averaged data on economic growth, a measure of the institutional framework, a policy measure, and some other variables for regions of the world. Economic growth has remained high in the mature capitalist nations in the latter half of the twentieth century. For Europe/North America it has averaged 3.2 percent per year over the period 1951–92.[2] Aside from some Asian nations, with export-led growth policies, economic growth in the Third World has been low.[3] This is so despite roughly comparable rates of capital formation per head. Why do so many Third-World nations, particularly in Africa, have such poor rates of economic growth?

Table 28.1   Means of the variables

Area	1985 real GDP per capita ($)	Life expectancy (years)	g_y	g_k	Institutional framework	Policy measure
World	4 246	62.8	2.08	4.64	2.07	3.40
Advanced	12 776	76.3	2.83	3.38	1.01	2.39
Third World	2 705	60.3	1.94	4.86	2.26	3.61
Europe/N. America	11 076	75.9	3.20	3.89	1.06	2.43
Oceania	7 824	67.9	1.62	2.32	1.06	5.00
Asia	3 937	65.2	3.66	6.83	2.18	3.05
Latin/Caribbean	3 843	67.3	1.78	3.43	1.89	3.27
Africa	1 328	53.1	1.07	4.81	2.64	4.09

Notes: g_y = average rate of growth of real per-capita GDP; g_k = average rate of growth of real per-capita gross investment.

Capital formation (including human capital in modern treatments) and technical change are recognized as the main engines of economic growth. But, all nations are not equally adept at transforming increases in capital and technology into increases in output. Plainly, some are just economically inefficient. In this chapter I analyse the crucial roles of the rule space and policy as the main filters that affect economic efficiency.

Measures of the institutional framework and policy are also presented in Table 28.1. Both measures will be discussed in more detail in the next section. Briefly, the measure of the rule space is an average of four subindices: the type of political system, the degree of political and civil liberty, the type of economic system, and the degree of economic freedom. The scale is bound between 1.0 (most free) and 3.25 (least free). The policy measure is an average of three policy subindices: money growth and inflation, trade policy, and freedom of capital markets. It is scaled from 1.0 (best) to 5.0 (worst). As is seen in the table, Europe/North America and Oceania have the freest institutions; Africa the least free. Asia and Latin America/Caribbean are in between. Europe/North America has the best set of policies and Africa and Oceania the worst. Again, Asia and Latin America/Caribbean are in between.

4   Measures of the rule space and policy

Data are insufficient to measure the rule space comprehensively. But, important elements of the rule space can be approximated crudely with information on political institutions, political and civil freedoms, the economic system, and the degree of economic freedom.

Political regimes are classified as authoritarian or representative. Within that broad division some regimes are more constrained than others. Thus, I classify four types of political regimes that are coded as follows: freely democratic = 1, limitedly democratic = 2, limitedly autocratic = 3, and authoritarian = 4.

Freely democratic regimes are those with an elected government, universal (extensive) suffrage, credible political party competition, a credible legislative function, an independent judiciary, and extensive protection of political and civil liberties. Limited democracies have elections, but they may have dominant parties and other constraints on the electoral process, and they also have less protection of civil liberties. I have relied on the evidence of Freedom House's (Karatnycky 1994) and Banks's (1993) comparative political surveys in making these classifications. Where ambiguity existed, I read up on the post-Second World War histories of the nations for further evidence.

Many authoritarian governments are dictatorships or dominant one-party states with a powerful executive. It is transparent to make the classification. But, there are a number of nations with significant constraints on autocratic rule. As such, they were classified as limited autocracies.

Political regimes were classified over the period 1950–90. Some nations have been continuously democratic or authoritarian throughout the period. Others have had short bouts of one form of government, but long periods of another form. Where this is the case the classification is the modal form.

Africa has the highest incidence of dictatorship with 90 percent of the 50 nations in the sample classified as fully authoritarian. Only three African nations were classified as limited democracies. Asia had the next highest incidence of authoritarian rule. Of the 26 nations in the sample, nine were fully authoritarian and seven were limited autocracies. Three Asian nations were democratic and three were limited democracies. Among the 26 Latin and Caribbean nations roughly half were authoritarian and half were democratic, with about an equal division between full and limited. Europe/North America (22 countries) and Oceania (four nations) are democratic.

The political and civil freedom measure is based on data from Freedom House. It is coded as free = 1, partly free = 2, and not free = 3.

The measure of political rights basically is one of the degree to which citizens may choose their political leaders and get rid of them, if they do not care for the way they are running things. Obviously, in democratic systems there are elections, while in dictatorships the polity has no say. In democratic systems elections may be fair or not, political opposition may be strong or weak, the military may be under civilian control or not, power may be centralized or decentralized, and minorities may be included or excluded from the political process. In autocratic systems, dictatorship may be totalitarian or less malevolent. In some autocracies there may be some political freedom at the regional or local level.

The measure of civil liberty is based on considerations such as the degree of press freedom, the degrees of freedom of speech, assembly, and association, the degree of freedom from search and seizure of property, the degree of independence of the judiciary and the protection of the individual under the law, and so on.

The political and civil freedoms are combined into a single rating and are the modal values for the countries over the period commencing in 1973, when Freedom House began its survey, to 1990.

The highest incidence of a lack of political and civil freedom is in Africa. Some 29 nations were not free, 19 were partly free, and only two were free. In Asia six nations were not free, 12 were partly free, and four were free. In Latin America/Caribbean one nation was not free, 15 were partly free, and ten were free. Europe/North America and Oceania are overwhelmingly free.

Economies are classified as market-capitalist = 1, restricted market-capitalist = 2, and statist = 3, largely based on Freedom House's classifications. Among the African nations, 19 are market-capitalist, 13 are restricted market-capitalist, and 18 are statist. Africa has the highest incidence of statist economies. In Asia, seven nations are market-capitalist, 13 are restricted market-capitalist, and two are statist. In Latin America/Caribbean, five countries are market-capitalist, 20 are restricted market-capitalist, and one is statist. Europe/North America and Oceania are overwhelmingly market-capitalist.

The degree of economic freedom is coded as free = 1, partly free = 2, and not free = 3 and is based on the rank of economic freedom constructed from 15 attributes of economic liberty (Scully 1992).

Africa is mainly economically not free (15 nations) or partly free (30 nations). Only five African countries are economically free. In contrast, Asia is economically free (six countries) or partly free (13 nations), with only three countries not free. The situation is similar in Latin America/Caribbean, where ten countries are free, 13 are partly free, and three are not free.

In summary, Africa tends to be nearly uniformly authoritarian with restricted economic freedom. Asia and Latin America/Caribbean nations tend to have had fairly restricted political environments, but have a greater degree of economic liberty than does Africa. Obviously, Europe/North America and Oceania are mainly politically and economically free.

Measures of various aspects of the institutional framework tend to be rather highly intercorrelated (Scully 1988). This is true, also, for this set of measures.[4] As such, not a great deal of information is lost by combining them into one measure of the institutional framework. This was done by averaging them.

Apart from the rule space, governments make policy choices. Some measures of policy are available. Gwartney et al. (1993) have constructed measures on monetary growth and inflation, freedom of international trade, and freedom of capital markets for a large number of nations over the period 1970–90.

The measure of monetary growth and inflation is based on three components: the growth of the money supply less the real rate of economic growth, the standard deviation of the annual inflation rate, and restrictions on foreign currency holdings. The index is scaled from 0 (worst) to 10 (best) and is available for four five-year subperiods. I have averaged them to construct a long-term policy measure.

The second policy index is a measure of trade openness and is based on three subindices: trade taxes as a share of imports plus exports, exchange-rate controls, and a measure of the size of the trade sector. The data are available for 1975, 1980, 1985, and 1990 and I averaged them.

The capital-market index is composed of two subindices: the difference between the domestic and world real interest rate and direct foreign investment as a share of GNP. I dropped the 1975 observations, because of a paucity of observations, and averaged the 1980, 1985, and 1990 values.

Like the attributes of the institutional framework, the quality of policy is intercorrelated. The simple correlation of monetary policy with trade policy is 0.66 and of monetary and capital-market policy is 0.67. Hence, I averaged the three measures into an overall measure. The grade scaling is A = 1, B = 2, C = 3, D = 4, and F = 5.[5]

Africa has very poor policy with 30 of the 35 nations scoring a D or F and no nation scoring A. In Latin America/Caribbean 14 nations had a grade of B or C and eight had a grade of D or F. In Asia the nations were about evenly divided over the five grade intervals. In Europe/North America the modal grade was C (seven nations), but 11 countries had a grade of A or B and only three had a grade of D or F. Oceania had uniformly bad policy.

5   Empirical results

The aggregate neoclassical production function in intensive Cobb–Douglas form (suppressing the time subscript) is $y = k^{\beta}$. The total differential of the production function is $dy = \beta k^{\beta-1} dk$. Dividing through by y, we obtain $g_y = dy/y = \beta k^{\beta-1} dk/k^{\beta} = \beta dk/k = \beta g_k$. This specification of the determinants of economic growth entirely avoids the misspecification of regression toward the mean discussed earlier.

5.1   Economic growth

Estimation is by two methods: linear ordinary least squares (OLS) and nonlinear least squares (NLLS). The latter approach is justified on the basis of the theoretical existence of diminishing returns in the neoclassical growth model. The specific functional form for the NLLS estimation is:

$$g_y = [\alpha/(\beta + \delta e^{-\alpha g_k})]e^{(\gamma INST + \rho POLICY)}. \qquad (28.13)$$

The derivatives of g_y with respect to g_k are consistent with neoclassical growth theory.[6] The limits of the nonlinear function are:

$$\lim_{g_k \to 0} g_y = [\alpha/(\beta + \delta)]e^{(\gamma INST + \rho POLICY)} \qquad (28.14)$$

and

$$\lim_{g_k \to \infty} g_y = (\alpha/\beta)e^{(\gamma INST + \rho POLICY)}. \qquad (28.15)$$

Table 28.2 presents the linear OLS estimates for the world sample. The coefficient of the growth rate of real capital formation per head (g_k) exhibits only small variation as the institutional framework variable (*INST*) and policy variable (*POLICY*) are added as regressors. The institutional variable has a large coefficient value (−1.08). Multiplying the g_k coefficient times the mean value of g_k, adding it to the constant term and, then, subtracting −1.08 yields the mean growth rate of real per-capita GDP of 3.24 percent for nations with a free institutional rule space. At the other extreme, a representative nation with the least free institutional environment (*INST* = 3.25) has a mean growth rate of 0.80 percent for the same growth rate of real capital formation per head.

The policy variable is statistically significant when added as a regressor. The representative nation with the best policy (*POLICY* = 1) has a growth rate of 3.31 percent, while the representative nation with the worst policy (*POLICY* = 5) has a growth rate of 1.30 percent.

When both *INST* and *POLICY* are entered as covariates, the coefficient of *POLICY* on g_y is reduced in size by half, but remains significant. The repre-

Table 28.2   OLS estimates of economic growth rate
(dependent variable: g_y)

Variable	(1)	(2)	(3)	(4)
Constant	1.4652	3.7416	3.2166	4.2390
g_k	0.1317	0.1258	0.1289	0.1234
	(4.65)	(5.14)	(4.67)	(4.94)
INST		−1.0862		−0.9135
		(6.53)		(4.80)
POLICY			−0.5039	−0.2541
			(4.40)	(2.19)
adj. R^2	0.14	0.36	0.28	0.41
n	124	124	103	103

Note: Absolute values of *t*-statistics in parentheses.

sentative nation with the best rule and policy space has a growth rate of 3.64 percent, while the representative nation with the worst institutions and policies has a growth rate of 0.57 percent. Also, note that there is a tradeoff to be had between policy and institutional reform. Changing policy from a grade of F to B+ has the same effect on the growth rate as reforming the institutional framework one point (for example, from 3.0 to 2.0). Partly, this may help explain the above-average growth rates of some nations with rather poor rule spaces. Higher growth is being achieved through better policy.

The NLLS estimates in Table 28.3 are superior to the OLS estimates. Since $\beta > 0$, the function is concave, which is consistent with neoclassical assumptions.

Utilizing model (4) in Table 28.3, one can again compare the growth rate of the representative nation with the freest institutions and best policy with that of the representative nation with the least free institutions and worst policy. For the mean growth rate of investment per head $\alpha/(\beta + \delta e^{-\alpha g(k)}) = 7.45$ percent. For the free nation $e^{(\gamma INST + \rho POLICY)} = 0.563$. Thus, the growth rate is 4.2 percent. For the least free, worst policy nation $e^{(\cdot)} = 0.271$. Thus, the growth rate is 2 percent.

Another use of the parameters in model (4) in Table 28.3 is to answer the question of what gain in economic growth arises from increases in capital formation, improvements in the rule space, and amelioration of policy – and how is the gain distributed? The answer is obtained by taking the total differential of equation (28.13), which is $dg_y = w_{g_k} dg_k + w_{INST} dINST + w_{POLICY} dPOLICY$, where the weights (*w*) are the partial derivatives of the

Table 28.3 NLLS estimates of economic growth rate
(dependent variable: g_y)

Parameter	(1)	(2)	(3)	(4)
α	0.5333	0.4151	0.4547	0.4128
	(2.53)	(3.67)	(2.63)	(3.84)
β	0.1706	0.0368	0.0663	0.0295
	(2.11)	(2.55)	(2.00)	(2.50)
δ	0.7651	0.1962	0.3033	0.1758
	(0.96)	(1.58)	(1.13)	(1.64)
γ		−0.5420		−0.4882
		(6.98)		(5.84)
ρ			−0.2001	−0.0863
			(4.57)	(2.26)
adj. R^2	0.24	0.485	0.41	0.56
n	124	124	103	103

Note: Absolute values of *t*-statistics in parentheses.

variables with respect to the growth rate.[7] Assume that there is a 10 percent improvement in each of the independent variables around the mean. Then, using the parameters from model (4) in Table 28.3, we have $dg_y = 0.45 = 0.39(0.46) - 0.99(-0.21) - 0.175(-0.34)$. A 10 percent improvement in each factor (g_k from 4.64 to 5.1, *INST* from 2.07 to 1.863, and *POLICY* from 3.40 to 3.06) raises the rate of economic growth by 0.45 percent. Approximately 40 percent of the change in growth is due to the change in capital formation, 47 percent from improved institutional technology, and the remaining 13 percent from better policy.

In Table 28.4 the sample is subdivided into the advanced nations ($n = 19$) and the Third World ($n = 105$). Noteworthy is that the coefficient of g_k on g_y is four times as large in the advanced nations as in the Third World and this difference is more or less stable as the institutional and policy variables are added as regressors. The statistical results for the Third World are quite similar to those of the all-nations sample. This is satisfying, since it means that the statistical results in Tables 28.2 and 28.3 do not arise from lumping the advanced nations together with the less-advanced ones.

Table 28.5 contains the NLLS estimates. For facility of comparison, I calculated the path of g_y with respect to g_k for two representative nations: (1) less advanced with free institutions and good policy and (2) less advanced with institutions that are not free and poor policy. The predicted growth rate

*Table 28.4   OLS estimates of economic growth rate for advanced and
Third-World nations*

Variable	Advanced (1)	Third World (2)	Third World (3)	Third World (4)	Third World (5)
Constant	0.9590	1.2869	4.1430	3.3030	4.9192
g_k	0.5524	0.1343	0.1162	0.1263	0.1125
	(6.78)	(4.52)	(4.42)	(4.31)	(4.20)
INST			−1.2238		−1.0382
			(5.58)		(4.31)
POLICY				−0.5480	−0.3351
				(3.73)	(2.35)
adj. R^2	0.71	0.16	0.35	0.28	0.41
n	19	105	105	85	85

Note: Absolute values of t-statistics in parentheses.

*Table 28.5   NLLS estimates of economic growth rate for advanced and
Third-World nations*

Parameter	Advanced (1)	Third World (2)	Third World (3)	Third World (4)	Third World (5)
α	0.2500	0.5469	0.4340	0.5142	0.4277
	(1.62)	(2.43)	(3.05)	(2.48)	(3.09)
β	0.0250	0.1683	0.0386	0.0774	0.0276
	(0.067)	(1.97)	(2.15)	(1.90)	(2.00)
δ	0.1511	1.0656	0.2192	0.5349	0.1686
	(1.26)	(0.89)	(1.19)	(0.90)	(1.15)
γ			−0.5443		−0.5032
			(5.90)		(4.92)
ρ				−0.1968	−0.1141
				(3.71)	(2.40)
adj. R^2	0.70	0.26	0.455	0.41	0.54
n	19	105	105	85	85

Note: Absolute values of t-statistics in parentheses.

at the mean growth rate of capital accumulation is 4.74 percent and the
asymptotic growth rate $((\alpha/\beta)e^{(\cdot)})$ is 8.36 percent for the less-advanced nation
with free institutions and good policy. For the nation with institutions that are
not free and poor policy the predicted mean growth rate is 1.53 percent and
the asymptotic growth rate is 1.71 percent. While the less-advanced nations

with free institutions and good policy do not grow at quite the rate of the advanced nations for similar rates of capital formation, the performance differential is modest. The really poorly performing nations are those whose institutions are not free and who engage in poor policy.

5.2   Life expectancy

Economic growth is not the only welfare standard by which nations can be compared. Justifiably, life expectancy is an alternative standard on the argument that a longer life is preferred to a shorter one. Life expectancy is highly correlated with the living standard, and the relationship is nonlinear (the symbol y is used for the 1985 value of real GDP in the equation below). The question raised here is that given the living standard, does institutional freedom independently promote a longer life? The nonlinear function to be estimated parallels that in equation (28.6) and takes the form:

$$LE = [\alpha/(\beta + \delta e^{-\alpha y})]e^{(\gamma INST)}. \tag{28.16}$$

The NLLS estimates for all countries and for the Third-World countries appear in Table 28.6. The fitted function for all nations appears in Figure 28.2. The coefficient for the institutional framework is highly significant.

Focusing on the results for the Third World, consider two pairings of representative nations. One pair has a per-capita real GDP of $1000, the other pair has $5000. One of each pair is free (*INST* = 1.0), the other is not free

Table 28.6   NLLS estimates of life expectancy

Parameter	All countries (1)	All countries (2)	Third World (3)	Third World (4)
$\alpha*10^3$	0.5065	0.5852	0.5791	0.6244
	(9.09)	(7.39)	(6.05)	(5.46)
$\beta*10^3$	0.6687	0.7385	0.7834	0.7986
	(8.44)	(7.24)	(5.41)	(5.04)
$\delta*10^3$	0.4626	0.4358	0.5332	0.4724
	(6.21)	(5.18)	(4.52)	(3.93)
γ		−0.0418		−0.0398
		(3.02)		(2.59)
adj. R^2	0.80	0.81	0.72	0.74
n	121	121	102	102

Note: Absolute values of *t*-statistics in parentheses.

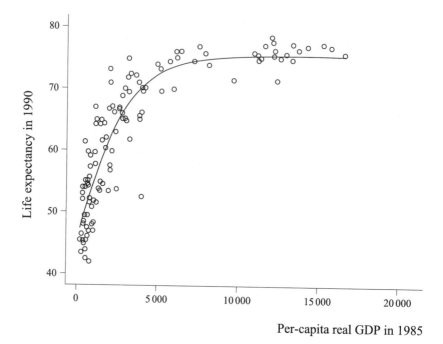

Figure 28.2   NLLS estimation of life expectancy

(*INST* = 3.25). The predicted life expectancies in the poor pair of nations are 57.1 and 52.2 years, respectively. The difference in life expectancies is 4.9 years. The predicted life expectancies in the moderate per-capita income pair are 73.2 and 67 years, respectively, a difference of 6.2 years.

6   Conclusions

I think it is now fairly well established that rules or the institutional framework matter a great deal for economic growth and, hence, for the achievable living standard. This chapter contributes to the measurement of the size of the effect of rules and policy on economic growth. The poor economic performance of many Third-World nations has less to do with capital accumulation and technology transfer, although they do matter, than with economic, legal, and political institutions and with policies which are anathema to development. One is tempted to conclude that a modern standard of living is quite impossible to achieve without free institutions.

Further insight into the importance of the rule space for economic growth will require finer measures of the attributes of the institutional framework. While the crude measures that have been utilized here capture the main differences across a wide sample of very heterogeneous nations, they are insufficient for distinguishing outcomes among more homogeneous blocs of nations (for example, Africa, Latin America).

Notes

1. The addition of a rule may make other rules more (less) efficient. For this reason one should think of the wealth effect of a new rule or a rule change as net of changes in other rules.
2. The data are the growth rates of real per-capita GDP from Summers and Heston (1991). The sample used throughout the chapter is all nations with at least ten years of data less the communist countries and the Middle East's oil-exporting nations.
3. The bloom is off the Asian 'miracle'. Owing to horribly weak financial institutions, a less than arm's distance between government and business, and conglomerate cross-ownership (for example, Korean chaebols) with less than transparent accounting procedures, many Asian nations are having trouble meeting their external foreign debt obligations and a number of large banks and firms are technically insolvent. The forecast is for many years of economic distress.
4. The correlation between the type of political system and the political–civil liberty measure, the type of economic system, and the degree of economic freedom is 0.87, 0.46, and 0.72, respectively. Other correlations among the variables are similarly high.
5. I followed the grading scheme in Gwartney et al. (1993, p. 22): 7.0 or greater = A, 6.0–6.9 = B, 5.0–5.9 = C, 4.0–4.9 = D, and less than 4.0 = F.
6. The first derivative of the first part of the expression is $\partial g_y/\partial g_k = \alpha^2 \delta e^{-\alpha g_k}/(\beta + \delta e^{-\alpha g_k})^2$; the second derivative is $\partial^2 g_y/\partial g_k^2 = -\alpha^3 \delta(-e^{\alpha g_k}\delta + e^{2\alpha g_k}\beta)/(\beta e^{\alpha g_k} + \delta)^3$.
7. $dg_y = [(\alpha^2 e^{\gamma INST + \rho POLICY}\delta e^{-\alpha g_k})/(\beta + \delta e^{-\alpha g_k})^2]dg_k + [(\alpha e^{\gamma INST + \rho POLICY}\gamma)/(\beta + \delta e^{-\alpha g_k})]dINST + [(\alpha e^{\gamma INST + \rho POLICY}\rho)/(\beta + \delta e^{-\alpha g_k})]dPOLICY = w_{g_k}dg_k + w_{INST}dINST + w_{POLICY}dPOLICY.$

29 Public choice and economic growth
Randall G. Holcombe

1 Introduction

Public choice offers fundamental insights into the process of economic growth, but only recently has the public choice approach been applied explicitly to growth issues. In large part, this is due to the longstanding view of much of the economics profession that an analysis of political institutions is largely irrelevant to economic growth. Indeed, as Krueger (1997) notes, economists often recommended central planning as the political foundation for growth, assuming that central planners would pursue optimal policies, with no analysis of political institutions or the political decision-making process. Economists such as Bauer (1972), who argued the virtues of markets, were the exception to the rule emphasizing central planning, but even then Bauer did not use a public choice framework in dissenting from the contemporary policy prescriptions of growth theorists.

Two recent developments have prompted public choice economists to become more interested in growth issues. First, the subject of economic growth has moved from being a minor subfield of economics into an area that is of much more interest to the profession's mainstream. Second, with the collapse of centrally planned economies around the world, it has become much more apparent that there is an intimate relationship between political institutions and economic prosperity. As a result, the public choice literature on growth has had a strong institutional orientation, and has focused more on the impact of fundamental institutional differences rather than on collective decision-making processes.

This emphasis on the relationship between institutions and economic growth stands in stark contrast to the direction of much of growth theory at the twentieth century's end. Modern growth theory takes a production function approach which focuses on inputs into the growth process, and (with some exceptions) neglects the impact that economic, legal, and political institutions have on growth. Whereas the production function approach focuses on the inputs into the production process – primarily human and physical capital and technological advances – the public choice approach views market institutions as the fundamental stimulus to growth. Of course, there is an element of truth in both approaches. More output can only be produced by using more inputs, or by making better use of existing inputs. It is also true that enhanced inputs will not by themselves produce growing output unless the institutional structure is conducive to growth. But the differences in these approaches are more fundamental than just looking at the problem from different vantage points. One might argue that both inputs into the production process and the institutional environment must be taken into account when considering growth issues. However, the right institutions are absolutely necessary for growth, and without an institutional structure conducive to growth, growth cannot occur. In other words, the public choice approach to growth is necessary for formulating public policy toward growth. On the other hand, if the institutional environment for growth is in place, the right institutions will attract the inputs that the production function approach emphasizes – human and physical capital, and advanced technology – so that policy makers do not need to worry about them. Thus, for policy purposes, the public choice approach is both necessary and sufficient for designing public policies conducive to economic growth.

If a nation's policy makers foster the 'right' institutional environment, they need not be concerned about procuring the inputs into the growth process, because market forces will make them available. Physical capital, human capital, and the most productive technologies will be drawn to an institutional environment conducive to growth. On the other hand, if economic policy makers assemble all of the right inputs into the production process but do not place those inputs into an institutional structure conducive to growth, growth will not occur. This is a strong claim for the public choice approach to economic growth, and the main purpose of this chapter is to review the literature on economic growth to substantiate that claim. The literature shows that the public choice approach to economic growth, which focuses on institutions, is crucial for formulating pro-growth policies, whereas the production function approach that has dominated mainstream growth theory not only is not essential for designing public policy, but has even misled policy makers into adopting counterproductive economic policies. To see what public choice has to contribute to the study of economic growth, the most appropriate place to begin is with a brief overview of the development of modern growth theory.

2   The growth of growth theory

Growth theory is, in one sense, the oldest area of inquiry in economics. As its title indicates, Adam Smith's *Inquiry into the Nature and Causes of the Wealth of Nations* ([1776] 1976) was about the causes and consequences of economic growth, and growth remained a central issue in political economy until the twentieth century. One of the most widely read economic treatises at the end of the nineteenth century was Henry George's *Progress and Poverty* (1889) which, again as the title indicates, focuses on issues related to economic growth. At the beginning of the twentieth century, as economics and political science split into separate areas of inquiry, interest in the topic of economic growth waned. Political scientists were more interested in studying the political process itself rather than its implications for economic growth, and economics became increasingly preoccupied with equilibrium conditions rather than growth.

The emphasis of economists on equilibrium rather than growth was a result of several factors. First, theoretical developments led in that direction as economics became increasingly quantitative, taking on the mathematical garb of physics, which characterized the equilibrium behavior of naturally occurring systems. The sheer elegance of mathematical general equilibrium models attracted economists to that more rigorous way of thinking about economic processes, but at the same time turned economists' attention from issues of growth toward a closer examination of the static equilibrium properties of markets. The Great Depression also contributed to the focus on the properties of economic equilibrium, as Keynes redefined much of economics with his argument that an economy could remain stuck in an underemployment equilibrium. By the 1950s, macroeconomics was focused on the problem of how to design policy to produce a full-employment equilibrium, and microeconomics was concerned with overcoming market failures so as to allocate resources Pareto optimally. In both macro- and microeconomics, the focus was on how to arrive at an optimal steady-state equilibrium allocation of resources rather than on how to create the conditions necessary for economic progress.

The issue of growth did not totally disappear from economics, but was relegated to the status of a minor area of inquiry by the mid-twentieth century. Schumpeter's *Theory of Economic Development* ([1912] 1934) remains an insightful treatise, but was regarded as outside the mainstream at least in part because Schumpeter depicted growth as a disequilibrating process, and therefore at odds with contemporary economic theory. Modern growth theory traces its origins to Solow (1956), who was able to bring the topic of growth into the economic mainstream by placing the growth process within the dominant equilibrium framework. Even then growth remained at the fringes of economic theory until the late 1980s, when Romer (1986) and Lucas (1988) tackled the issue, building on Solow's work. Following Lucas, economists such as Jones and Manuelli (1990) and Romer (1990) began developing a new macroeconomic theory of 'endogenous' growth, and at the end of the twentieth century the most visible strand of growth theory falls within the domain of macroeconomics rather than within the subdiscipline of economic growth and development.

These new general equilibrium growth models are substantially more sophisticated and complex than the model in Solow's seminal article, yet they share Solow's general approach and, more specifically, they still model increases in output either as being the result of increases in inputs or as the result of technological advances, without reference to the underlying institutional structure. Representing output as Q and capital and labor inputs as K and L, $Q = f(K, L)$. Growth means increasing Q, and the framework shows that Q can be increased only by using more K, more L, or both, or by changing the functional form f in order to get more Q from a given amount of K and L. This approach concludes that growth is produced by increasing the quantity (or quality) of inputs, and by using improved technology. While there is a sense in which this is true, this type of model tends to encourage policy makers to design growth policies that focus on creating more inputs, and on encouraging the development and use of more advanced technologies. This approach to analysing economic growth is seriously incomplete because it neglects the institutional framework within which growth occurs. The policy that tends to be produced by this type of model was critiqued long ago by Hayek (1945), who emphasized the importance of market institutions in the allocation of resources.

3   Institutions and economic growth

The idea that institutions can have a significant impact on economic growth has a long history in economics. Adam Smith ([1776] 1976) focused on institutional factors that increased the wealth of nations, and Schumpeter ([1912] 1934) focused on the entrepreneurial forces in the market system as the engine of growth. Similarly, Bauer (1972) sees market institutions as crucial for growth, and was openly critical of growth theory that ignored institutions, or that promoted central planning over market allocation of resources. More recently, North (1990) also emphasizes the impact of institutions on the performance of an economy. Yet despite the widespread recognition of the impact of institutions on growth, much of modern growth theory depicts the process of growth in a production function framework with no institutional foundations.

In contrast to the production function approach to growth, a literature focused on the relationship between institutions and growth, with strong public choice foundations, has been developing along with the general equilibrium growth models that take the production function approach. One of the early contributors to this literature, Scully (1988, 1992), has focused on the institutional structure by examining the relationship between freedom and growth empirically. Scully found that both economic and political freedoms were correlated with higher rates of economic growth. One of the challenges that has faced this literature is finding good empirical measures of institutions, and many studies, including Scully's, use data from Gastil (1982) to measure economic and political freedoms. Gastil's measures have been updated regularly and published by the Freedom House, and provide an ordinal ranking of freedoms on a number of dimensions. A substantial literature has developed using similar data to show a correlation between economic and political freedoms and economic growth (see Chapter 28, this volume).

Brunetti and Weder (1995) suggest that many studies trying to link institutional structures with economic growth have run into problems because available data do not adequately reflect the institutional differences that actually impact growth. Their article reviews a number of studies and discusses the problems involved. It is clear that when compared to measuring inputs into the production process, such as human and physical capital, the quantification of institutional differences is much less well developed. The notion that economic freedom, in the form of free markets, promotes economic growth dates back to Adam Smith ([1776] 1976), but quantifying the notion of free markets so that the relationship between free markets and growth can be subject to empirical investigation offers up a daunting challenge. In a very insightful study, economic historian David Landes (1998) presents the case that modern economic growth began in Britain with the Industrial Revolution and spread around the world as British institutions were adopted by other nations. Landes sees free trade, low taxes, and protection of property rights as key ingredients, but also points to social, religious, and cultural institutions as underlying factors. Landes makes a convincing case that institutions are the key, but at the same time he notes so many factors that it is hard to tell exactly what the contribution of any one of them is to the overall picture, or how the different institutional factors he cites might be interrelated.

Gastil's (1982) frequently used Freedom House indexes provide a good starting place for empirical analysis, but were not designed for studying economic issues. Gastil focuses heavily on political and civil liberties, and provides subjective ordinal rankings rather than rankings that are based on measurable economic data. With those issues in mind, several other indexes have been developed that focus specifically on economic freedom. Gwartney et al. (1996) have created an economic freedom index for the Fraser Institute, and Johnson et al. (1998) have created a similar index for the Heritage Foundation. Both measures focus on the degree to which property rights are protected and freedom of exchange is allowed, but deliberately leave out measures of political freedom and civil liberties. Johnson et al. rely to a degree on subjective ratings of various dimensions of economic freedom, whereas Gwartney et al. develop an index that is composed only of objectively measurable components. Their index has 17 different components divided into the four general categories: money and inflation, government operations and regulations, takings of property and discriminatory taxation, and restraints on international exchange. Their index is updated in Gwartney and Lawson (1997).

Hanke and Walters (1997) note that while the Fraser Institute and Heritage Foundation indexes are constructed differently, there is a high degree of correlation between them, suggesting that they are measuring much the same thing. These indexes were developed explicitly for the purpose of looking at the relationship between economic freedom and economic performance. This has the advantage of providing a more precise measurement of the idea Adam Smith had in mind when he argued the productivity merits of market institutions, but also raises the question of whether the indexes might be designed tautologically to define economic freedom as being those things that are correlated with economic growth.

Easton and Walker (1997) use the Gwartney et al. (1996) economic freedom index and find a strong correlation between that measure of economic freedom and economic growth. Similarly, using the updated Gwartney and Lawson (1997) index, Gwartney et al. (1999) also find that there is a strong correlation between economic freedom, as measured by the index, and economic growth. As previously noted, that economic freedom index has 17 components and, as a result, showing that it is correlated with economic growth leaves open a number of questions. First, there is the question about how the index's components should be weighted.[1] Second, there is the issue of how critical any one component is to economic growth. In such an index, some components may be irrelevant while others may be essential. As noted below, the literature addresses this issue to a degree, but many questions remain.

Both the Johnson et al. (1998) index and the Gwartney et al. (1996) index have the advantage that they are limited to economic institutions and ignore political freedom altogether. Because Gastil separately measures political freedom, this allows Gwartney et al. (1999) to compare the effects of economic institutions and political institutions on economic growth. They find that once economic institutions are controlled for, political variables have little measurable effect on economic growth. In contrast, controlling for political institutions, economic institutions have a significant effect. Thus, it appears that economic institutions are crucial for promoting economic growth, whereas political institutions are less relevant. However, the issue is not quite that simple, as will be discussed later.

Another issue dealt with by Gwartney et al. (ibid.) is causation. Regressing past measures of economic freedom on current growth rates indicates that more economic freedom leads to more economic growth, but might causation run the other way? It could well be that more growth fosters more freedom, yet when past economic growth is used to try to explain present levels of economic freedom, the results are not statistically significant. Thus, the direction of causality appears to go from economic freedom to economic growth, but not in the reverse.

Another question that arises in this literature is whether economic institutions affect the rate of growth, or just the level of income. This question emanates directly from the Solow (1956) model, which shows that (if the model's assumptions are met), long-run, steady-state, per-capita income growth rates will be the same across countries, although they can deviate from each other in the short run as nations move from one steady-state growth path to another. One troublesome aspect of this theoretical finding of 'convergence' is that, empirically, it appears that the actual income growth rates of nations do differ significantly from one another over long periods of time, as Quah (1996) notes. The theoretical literature has addressed this by developing models, using the production function approach, that show how economies can take advantage of increasing returns to have long-run growth rates that differ. The empirical public choice literature has not addressed this question directly, but rather has shown that different growth rates across countries are systematically correlated with institutional differences.[2] The question is potentially significant, however, because the impacts over time of differing institutions would be much greater if they permanently affected growth rates than if they just shifted economies to different growth paths exhibiting the same growth rates.

Most of the literature supporting the idea that institutions are important determinants of economic growth is empirical, but there is some theoretical support for the idea also. For example, Barro (1990) presents a formal model showing how government spending can have a negative impact on growth, and Schumpeter's ([1912] 1934) classic work suggests that growth is produced by entrepreneurship. Building on Kirzner (1973), Holcombe (1998a) relates the institutions that foster entrepreneurship to economic growth. Porter and Scully (1995) also pursue a theoretical approach to growth, relating constitutional rules to the process of innovation, and discuss the effects of constitutions on arriving at a steady-state equilibrium growth path.

All of the evidence strongly suggests that institutions have a significant effect on economic growth, but questions remain about exactly which institutions are important and how much of an impact they have. De Haan and Siermann (1998) note that while some measures of economic freedom are strongly correlated with economic growth, other measures exhibit a more fragile relationship. There may be the danger that in developing measures of economic freedom, economic freedom is defined tautologically to mean those things that are statistically correlated with economic growth. The recently developed economic freedom indexes focus on issues such as government regulation (less regulation means more growth), government ownership of resources (less government ownership means more growth), monetary freedom (less inflation, freedom to trade and maintain bank accounts in foreign currencies, and lack of exchange-rate controls mean more growth), and the size of taxes and transfers (lower taxes and transfers mean more growth). How much of an impact each of these institutional factors has, and how these different institutional factors might interact with each other, is still an open question. The next several sections deal with three specific areas in which institutions and growth rates interact: the protection of property rights, the size of government, and political freedom.

4 Property rights and economic growth

Knack and Keefer (1995) and Keefer and Knack (1997) present evidence that a legal system which protects property rights, enforces contracts, and establishes the rule of law enhances economic growth. One problem with estimating the relationship between property rights protection and economic growth is that the measurement of property rights protection is not straightforward. Keefer and Knack deal with this problem by using data from two different international investor services that rate countries on dimensions such as the risk of contract repudiation, the risk of expropriation of property or nationalization, and the degree to which a country adheres to an objective rule of law. While there is some subjectivity involved in such ratings, by choosing ratings done by companies that sell their ratings services to business, there is a market test suggesting that the ratings are worth something to the companies that pay for them. The ratings of various countries are subjective, but apparently the subjective ratings are accurate enough that they have a market value to companies that are evaluating the prospects for investing in various nations around the world.

Keefer and Knack find that there is a significant positive relationship between the protection of property rights and economic growth. In particular, they find that poor countries that do not protect property rights have low (or negative) economic growth rates, and that the lack of property rights protections keeps poor countries poor. Similarly, Torstensson (1994) finds that economic growth is higher in those countries that protect property rights more firmly. Knack (1996), examining the issue of convergence of growth rates, presents similar findings, concluding that convergence applies only to countries with secure property rights. The evidence shows a strong relationship between the degree to which property rights are protected and economic growth, but leaves open the question of how the protection of property rights interacts with other institutional variables. For example, is there a tradeoff between the protection of property rights and other measures of economic freedom, or is the protection of property rights a necessary prerequisite for economic growth? Olson (1996) and Landes (1998) suggest that the protection of property rights and rule of law are necessary for growth, but this question remains underexplored in the empirical public choice literature.

5 Size of government

The evidence suggests that institutional factors have a substantial impact on economic growth, and that institutions that protect property rights and facilitate market exchange enhance growth. Over the last half of the twentieth century, and even more over the century's last quarter, these institutions, as measured by Johnson et al. (1998) and Gwartney et al. (1996), have been increasingly oriented toward the promotion of market allocation of resources throughout most of the world. Property rights are better protected, monetary policy has been more conducive to exchange, and barriers to exchange in general have been lowered. In one notable area, however, nations have been moving away from the market allocation of resources, and that area is size of government. In most nations around the world, and especially in developed economies, government expenditures as a share of GDP have been rising. For example, for all OECD countries, government expenditures as a percentage of GDP averaged 27 percent in 1960, but had risen to 48 percent of GDP by 1996. If market allocation of resources is more conducive to economic growth than government allocation, then the growing public sector means more resources allocated through government, and less through the market. This could have an adverse impact on economic growth.

A substantial number of studies have looked at the issue, and consistently have found that higher government expenditures have a negative impact on economic growth, including Grossman (1988), Kormendi and Meguire (1985), Landau (1983, 1986), Peden (1991), Peden and Bradley (1989), Scully (1992, 1994), and Gwartney et al. (1998).[3] Gwartney et al. look at data for 23 OECD countries from 1960 to 1996, and at a larger data set of 60 countries from 1980 to 1995, and find a strong correlation between government size and economic growth. The data indicate that an increase in government spending as a share of GDP of 10 percentage points (for example, government spending rising from 40 to 50 percent of GDP) is associated with a one percentage point decline in the GDP growth rate. The study controlled for education levels, investment in physical capital, and used an index of property rights protection as in Keefer and Knack (1997) to control for government policy in that area. Not only is the relationship significant in a statistical sense, it is also significant in that the level of government expenditures appears to have a major negative impact on an economy's growth rate.

While the relationship appears to be strong, there are some unanswered questions about the mechanism by which additional government spending lowers growth. Government spending by itself is likely to have a negative effect because when more resources are allocated politically, there is an increased incentive for rent seeking. Tullock (1967b) first noted the possibility of rent seeking, and Krueger (1974) insightfully applied the concept to show how rent seeking stifles productive economic activity, stifling growth. Usher (1992) follows up on the idea by arguing that while some government is desirable to protect property from predation, government itself is predatory and excessive government has a negative effect on productivity because of the resource-wasting rent seeking it encourages. Thus, there are strong theoretical arguments to support the empirical finding that an increase in the size of government by itself results in a decrease in economic growth.

Some of the measured effect of the size of government on economic growth may come from other factors. For example, Easton and Rebelo (1993) find that higher marginal income tax rates lead to lower rates of economic growth. The excess burden of taxation discourages economic activity, as is well known. It might be that higher government expenditures hinder growth because of the costs of raising government revenues and, if this is a major factor, it may be possible to minimize the reduction in growth caused by government expenditures by adopting tax structures with smaller excess burdens, such as substituting a flat-rate income tax for a progressive one. Another factor that has been inadequately examined is the composition of government expenditures. Surely some expenditures, such as those on infrastructure and education, will not have as negative an impact on economic growth as transfer payments, for example, and the previous section argued that protection of property rights is an important institutional requirement for growth. Thus, expenditures on police protection and a legal system may have a positive impact on economic growth. In this area too, questions remain, and there is much room for work on the impact of the composition of government expenditures on economic growth.

If some government expenditures encourage economic growth, this suggests that there may be a growth-maximizing level of government expenditures, and that government expenditures that are below the growth-maximizing level might hinder growth. Along these lines, Peden (1991) estimates that for the United States, economic growth would be maximized if government expenditures at all levels were about 20 percent of GDP. Likewise, Scully (1994, p. 1) places the growth-maximizing level of government spending somewhere between 21.5 percent and 22.9 percent of US GDP. This would imply a reduction in total government expenditures of more than one-third to maximize economic growth. Estimates such as these require extrapolating beyond the recent US experience, a practice that is questionable from an empirical standpoint. Furthermore, these studies did not examine the composition of government expenditures, which must be critical to the question.

Using a different methodology, Gwartney et al. (1998) separate government expenditures into items that may have a positive impact on economic growth, including the legal and court systems, education, infrastructure, and national defense, and items that almost surely inhibit growth, such as transfers and subsidies. They find that those items which could have a positive impact on growth comprise less than 15 percent of GDP in industrialized economies at the end of the twentieth century. Based on that evidence, Gwartney et al. conclude that the growth-maximizing level of government expenditures is less than 15 percent of GDP. This would imply cutting total government expenditures from current levels by more than half to maximize economic growth.

6   Political institutions and growth

Studies that have looked at political institutions and growth have had mixed results. Some, such as Barro (1996), de Haan and Sierman (1995), Przeworski and Limongi (1993), and Gwartney et al. (1999), find that political institutions have little effect on economic growth. Gwartney et al. (1999) explicitly compare the effect of political freedom, as measured by the Freedom House index, with economic freedom, as measured by Gwartney and Lawson (1997), and find that once economic variables are accounted for, political freedom adds little if anything to economic growth. Similarly, Barro (1996) controls for differences in both political and economic institutions, and finds that once differences in economic institutions are held constant, political institutions have a minimal impact on economic growth.

Borner et al. (1995) find that political credibility, in contrast to freedom, is an important determinant of growth, and Brunetti (1997) reinforces this conclusion, finding that while democracy is unrelated to growth, political stability is an important factor in producing growth. Thus, while democratic political institutions by themselves seem to have little impact on economic growth, political institutions more generally are critical. Hong Kong and Singapore provide examples of economies that grew rapidly in the last half of the twentieth century without democratic institutions, but the political systems in both countries were stable, they protected property rights, and allowed freedom of exchange. Political stability and credibility appear to be key ingredients for economic growth, while democracy appears to be unimportant.

From a practical standpoint, the link between democracy and growth is a very important public policy issue. After the collapse of the Berlin Wall in 1989, followed by the demise of the Soviet Union in 1991, the former centrally planned economies enthusiastically undertook reforms to establish democratic governments, but were less enthusiastic about limiting the scope of government, securing property rights, and removing impediments to market exchange. These nations had hoped to attain levels of prosperity they observed in the West, but the result has been disappointment – with Russia being the most prominent example. The public choice literature indicates that democracy is largely irrelevant to the creation of economic prosperity, suggesting that Russia (and many other Eastern bloc countries) chose the wrong subset of Western institutions to adopt if their goal was economic growth. The public choice approach to economic growth has much practical policy advice to offer, especially to transition economies on the eve of the twenty-first century. The academic studies done to date leave some questions about the details unanswered, but the experience of former

Eastern bloc dictatorships is in line with the general findings of the academic literature.

Some ambiguities in the literature are the result of data availability. Because Gastil's (1982) measures of freedom were the first available, a number of studies have used his measures. Along with Scully (1988, 1992), Leblang (1996) and Nelson and Singh (1988) find a positive correlation between economic and political freedom and economic growth. Fedderke and Klitgaard (1998) find a positive correlation between social indicators, including political rights, and economic growth. Goldsmith (1995) also finds both economic and political freedoms to be correlated with growth. A review of the literature shows that some studies find that political freedoms enhance economic growth while others do not. One explanation is that democratic political institutions, as measured by Gastil, are closely correlated with protection of property rights and rule of law, and studies showing that political freedom enhances economic growth often rely on Gastil's index. Thus, in studies using Gastil's measure of political freedom, measures of democracy may actually be proxies for protection of economic freedoms, calling into question the conclusion that democracy fosters economic growth.

Two key institutional factors correlated with economic growth are the security of property rights and objective rule of law. These two components of economic freedom are a product of the political system, so if one accepts the evidence summarized above, then surely the political environment is important to economic growth. Part of the problem, from an empirical standpoint, is that it is hard to quantify the differences in political systems, so that it is not always clear what particular measures are actually measuring. From the results of studies done to date, it appears that the democratic political institutions have little if any effect on economic growth. Barro (1996) finds that the effect of democracy on growth may even be slightly negative, and de Haan and Siermann (1995) do not find a robust relationship between democracy and economic growth. The rule of law and protection of property rights have positive effects in all studies, however. Because protection of property rights often is correlated with the degree of democracy, the effects may be difficult to sort out, and the existing studies have not really attempted to do so. Appropriate legal and political institutions are critical to growth, but democracy does not appear to be one of the critical aspects. Again, however, this is an issue that would benefit from further research within a public choice framework.

7 An evaluation of approaches

This chapter has contrasted the production function approach to economic growth, which in its modern form is firmly grounded in general equilibrium analysis, with the institutional approach that has a solid public choice foundation. In one sense there are merits in both the production function approach to growth and the institutional approach. Economic growth requires both inputs into the production process and an institutional environment that is conducive to growth. However, from a policy standpoint, the institutional approach by itself provides both necessary and sufficient information to guide policy makers, whereas the production function approach to growth is inherently misleading from a policy perspective. Krueger (1993, 1997) has argued that policy advisers who have followed too narrowly the implications of theoretical models of economic growth have given bad advice to developing economies and stifled their growth as a result.

Taking the production function approach literally, output can be increased by increasing inputs, and by adopting more advanced technology so that a given amount of inputs can be transformed into more output. As the Solow model was originally interpreted, this implied that more investment, to produce more capital, and the adoption of more advanced technology, were strategies to generate economic growth. Subsequently, economists have emphasized the crucial role of human capital as well. Policy advisers from international organizations, such as the International Monetary Fund, the United Nations, and the World Bank, as well as from developed nations such as the United States (with predominantly market economies themselves) suggested that central planning is the best way to ensure that inputs are increased and the best technology is used. The reasoning was that rather than leave important economic policy decisions to the uncertainties of the market, economic planners can direct resources to ensure that investments in human and physical capital are made, and that production processes take advantage of state-of-the-art technology. Thus, following the recommendations of the overwhelming majority of policy advisers, developing economies employed government investment, government educational institutions, and government-directed technological innovations to try to enhance their economic growth.

These policies failed, as Krueger (1993, 1997) notes, because the institutional framework conducive to growth was not in place. While controlled experiments on actual economies are rare in economics, much of world development policy in the 1950s and 1960s comes close. Comparing the production function approach to growth with the institutional approach, policy makers supplied less-developed economies with human and physical capital and advanced technology, but deprived those economies of market institutions, and the economies did not grow. Meanwhile, in economies with market institutions, substantial economic growth occurred. In his comprehensive historical study, Landes (1998) argues that economic growth has occurred only in those nations that have adopted market institutions. Those nations that have embraced markets, protected property rights, and implemented a rule of law have grown, while those nations that have not have stagnated.

The lesson here is more than just that institutions are important. The evidence shows that even with all the 'right' inputs and technology, economic growth will not occur without market institutions. The former Soviet Union is a good example. The USSR emphasized investment, which was centrally planned, emphasized education and had a highly literate population, and made substantial efforts to adopt the latest technology. Yet despite having all the right ingredients according to the production function approach to growth, the failure of the Soviet economy eventually led to the dissolution of the empire. At the beginning of the twenty-first century, the importance of market institutions to growth is generally recognized in practice, if not in mainstream growth theory. However, the conventional wisdom was different only a few decades ago. For example, Paul Samuelson (1973, p. 883) stated in his best-selling introductory economics textbook that while the Soviet Union had a per-capita income only about half as large as that of the United States, its superior economic system gave it a higher growth rate, and as a result per-capita income in the Soviet Union would catch up to the United States, perhaps as soon as 1990 but almost surely by 2010. The production function approach to economic growth has advanced considerably in many ways since 1973, but it is unchanged in the crucial way that it continues to focus on the inputs into the production process rather on than the institutional environment conducive to growth.

Public policy that focuses only on inputs and technology is insufficient for growth. On the other hand, public policy that focuses solely on adopting institutions that are conducive to growth will create economic growth without any public policies that concern themselves with inputs and technology. A market economy provides incentives for productive activity, and with the proper incentives in place, people will invest in human and physical capital and will adopt the most productive technology because there is an economic reward for doing so. In other words, from a policy standpoint, growth policy will fail if it focuses only on inputs and technology, and ignores institutions. However, growth policy will succeed if it focuses only on creating an institutional structure conducive to growth and ignores inputs and technology. Inputs and technology will take care of themselves given the right institutional environment.

Readers might shy away from the arguments developed here because they seem to sound so ideological and (perhaps) anti-government, but the empirical evidence makes it clear that market institutions pave the road to economic growth. Olson (1996) makes the observation that profit opportunities do not lie in wait very long before an entrepreneur acts on them. Why, then, are some countries so slow to develop when they apparently have the resources that could produce more growth? Olson answers that the institutional structure has to be right for genuine profit opportunities to exist, and the literature on the subject is in substantial agreement that markets with secure property rights governed by the rule of law are the engine of economic growth.

8   Conclusion

This chapter makes some strong claims about the merits of the public choice approach to the study of economic growth, and especially about the merits of taking a public choice approach to public policy regarding economic growth. These claims are consistent with the application of public choice analysis to public policy issues more generally, however. Buchanan (1975b) argued that the main lesson of public choice from a policy perspective is that one must take account of the actual political decision-making process when analysing policy alternatives, rather than making policy based on how a benevolent and omniscient dictator would design policy so as to achieve Pareto optimality. Policy conclusions are often significantly at odds with the conventional wisdom once public choice factors are taken into account. Brennan and Buchanan (1985) note that the creation of a stable and predictable institutional structure is crucial to the establishment of a productive economy, and the empirical public choice literature on economic growth echoes the conclusions of Brennan and Buchanan. The right set of political institutions is essential for economic growth to occur.

When public choice analysis has been applied to public policy issues, conclusions often end up being quite different from an economic analysis that neglects public choice issues. Buchanan and Wagner (1977) argued that when the political decision-making framework is taken into account, the (then) conventional wisdom with regard to fiscal policy was exactly backwards, and discretionary fiscal policy was detrimental to the performance of the macro economy. The public choice approach had a substantial impact in revising the conventional wisdom toward fiscal policy. Brennan and Buchanan (1980) argued that when public choice considerations are taken into account, the excess burden of taxation is not reduced by broadening the tax base, in contrast to the conventional wisdom, and Holcombe (1998b) argues that when political costs are factored in, uniform tax rates rather than those conforming with the Ramsey rule may be optimal, again in contrast with the conventional wisdom. Economic growth is no different in this regard, and the apparently bold conclusion that the public choice analysis of growth is both necessary and sufficient for good economic growth policies is not so bold when compared with public choice applications in other policy areas.

At the beginning of the twenty-first century, growth theory is dominated by general equilibrium growth models that take a production function approach to increasing economic output. More output can be produced by increasing the inputs, or by more efficiently combining inputs by using improved technology. The models have advanced significantly since Solow's (1956) seminal article, but the general approach has remained the same, especially from a policy standpoint, with its focus on inputs and technology as the keys to economic growth. In contrast, the public choice approach to growth focuses on the role of setting economic and political institutions in establishing growth-friendly environments. The inputs and technology required for growth will be attracted to the right institutional setting, so policy makers need not concern themselves with inputs and technology. In contrast, even if all the required inputs and technology are combined, growth will not occur without the right institutions.

These general conclusions of the public choice literature on growth leave open a number of specific questions. In general, the economic institutions conducive to growth include a stable monetary policy, freedom to hold and trade in different currencies, free movement of money, goods, and capital across national borders, minimal regulation, and low taxes and government expenditures. Political institutions conducive to growth include a stable government with predictable policies, clear protection of property rights, and rule of law. With these institutions in place, the degree to which a nation is democratic appears irrelevant – or maybe even counterproductive – to growth. But unanswered questions include how much each of these components contributes to growth, and how they interact with each other. Also unanswered are the impacts of the productive activities of government on growth. Human capital is important to be sure, but what role should government play in education to maximize growth? This is a difficult question to answer empirically because government is so heavily involved in education in all nations. Similar questions about the government's role in infrastructure remain.

Public choice analysis provides both a powerful general critique of the bulk of growth theory that ignores public choice considerations, and solid general guidelines on policies that are conducive to economic growth. The many unanswered questions supply a broad agenda for a further public choice analysis of economic growth, however. It is not surprising that there are many loose ends in this literature. After all, public choice was not even recognized as a distinct subdiscipline when Solow published his pioneering article in 1956, and most of the public choice analysis of economic growth has been undertaken in the 1990s. Much progress has been made, but given the relative youth of this literature, there is every reason to believe that the most significant public choice analysis of economic growth is yet to come.

Notes

1. Gwartney et al. (1996) look at three different weighting schemes and find that the overall index is not substantially affected by the choice among them. Needless to say, the same would not be true of every possible weighting scheme.
2. Sala-i-Martin (1997) raises a question about the significance of these results, noting that

when lots of regressions are run with a poorly specified underlying theory, some of them are bound to be statistically significant even if the underlying data are random numbers. This raises the fundamental question of whether this literature has demonstrated anything more than which variables are correlated with each other.

3. Razzolini and Shughart (1997) find similar effects in cross-state comparisons of economic growth.

30 The international economy in public choice perspective

Charles K. Rowley

1 Introduction

One of the most important paradoxes in late twentieth-century economics concerns the marked discrepancy between theory and practice in the realm of international trade. Like the infamous guns of the French Maginot Line, the guns of economists point in one direction, in this case almost unequivocally defending the comparative advantage theory of international trade. In so doing, these guns, like those of France at the outbreak of the Second World War, apparently point in the wrong direction. The policies of all nations ignore the lessons of economics and endorse significant protection of domestic industries against the wealth-enhancing forces of free trade. The question addressed in this chapter is why democratic nations should impoverish the citizens they supposedly represent with policies that no economist of merit can or will endorse with reasoned analysis.

The explanation of this apparent paradox is not a pretty one. By this stage, readers of the *Companion* will already understand why public choice sometimes is referred to as the most dismal component of the dismal science of economics. This chapter does little or nothing to relieve the pessimistic view of Adam Smith that 'there is a great deal of *ruin* in a Nation'.[1] Rather it demonstrates that the political ruin even of once great nations (to say nothing about those nations that are not and probably never will be great) does not stop at the national borders, but rather intensifies as it reaches out into the international arena.

2 The institutional framework for individual exchange

Issues of international trade commonly are framed in terms of nations and not of individuals. For instance, this was the framework deployed by David Ricardo in formulating and presenting the law of comparative advantage. It is the way in which the theory of international trade typically is presented today. Yet, this use of language, while undoubtedly economical, has some problematic features. In reality, individuals trade, not nations, a fact of considerable importance for understanding international economic relations, yet one that is widely ignored.

Models that construe trade as between nations and not as between individuals stem from notions of economic nationalism that characterized the mercantilist era. Mercantilism was an economic doctrine that arose during the period of large European empires headed by autocratic kings, notably in England, France, Spain, Portugal and Holland. Economic policy was construed under this doctrine principally as a means of promoting the king's interest, notably by the acquisition of gold and other precious metals. The economic welfare of individual citizens was incidental to this objective, of significance only to the extent that it supported the selfish interest of the king.

It is very easy to deploy such nationalistic arguments to support modern-day mercantilism once the notion that international trade occurs between nation-states has infiltrated an unwary public. In essence, such arguments ignore the essential heterogeneity of individuals within any society and promote the fiction of some homogeneous national interest (equivalent to the king in the mercantilist era). For example, the terms of trade argument in favor of trade protection rests exclusively on this fiction, obscuring all the variations among individuals that are a central feature of the division of labor and knowledge in complex societies.

The problem of international economic policy is starkly different for a rights-based democracy than for an autocratic society. The autocratic society is composed of subjects who are simply inputs into the king's production function. They remain subjects even under the most enlightened despotism. The rights-based democracy, in contrast, is composed of citizens and not subjects and the problem of policy is no longer a matter of centralized administrative choice. The government in such a society is not the source of rights, but the protector of pre-existent rights. The presence of trade across national boundaries, in such an environment, differs not at all from, and requires the same measures of support and supervision that a minimal state ideally will provide for its citizens with respect to domestic trading.

In his 1996 monograph, *Before Resorting to Politics*, Anthony de Jasay attacks as unacceptable the current reliance of economists upon the Kaldor–Hicks potential compensation test as the basis for comparing the consequences of alternative economic policies. He observes that economists have known full well since the 1930s that utilities are neither measurable on a cardinal scale nor comparable among individuals. Yet, economists continue to deploy a potential compensation test that utilizes the measuring rod of money to circumvent this fundamental restriction on the policy reach of their discipline. There can be little doubt that the use of this technique is a fraud perpetrated on an unsuspecting public to claim policy significance where it does not exist (Rowley and Peacock 1975).

Despite much high-flown rhetoric, most individuals, according to Jasay (1996, p. 5–1), pursue the 'grand criterion' of political hedonism by which they approve of systems that mainly favor themselves and disapprove of systems that mainly favor others. Such a principle has no hope of generating basic agreement among individuals whose tastes and attributes differ. This judgment coincides with earlier skepticism about the scope for agreement in a heterogeneous society. 'It is difficult to see why a loser in a competitive struggle should support the market system when it encourages the development of character traits whose existence in others works to his disadvantage and which he himself does not possess' (Buchanan 1985, p. 51).

Before resorting to politics, individuals recognize that politics differs fundamentally from voluntary exchange. It involves the use of irresistible power, namely the monopoly of the legitimate use of force, to impose the will of some on all, including on those who would reject it if they could (Jasay 1996, pp. 5–9). In view of this threat, and given the failure of the utilitarian ethic to provide effective guidance for policy, the Hippocratic precept applies with particular stringency: *first, avoid doing harm*. This precept offers a basic presumption against the use of coercion by the state, requiring the state to, *when in doubt, abstain* (ibid.).

The *when in doubt, abstain* principle informs government that applying coercion is legitimate only when it is positively invited by those who wish to be coerced. Rational individuals may invite coercion when confronted by transaction costs – default temptations, free-rider temptations or hold-out temptations – that obstruct advantageous bargains.

It is important to note, however, that the state is bound by this principle to respond only to actual and not to hypothetical invitations from those who wish to be coerced. Hypothetical invitations have no higher standing than potential compensation in the perspective of the *when in doubt, abstain* principle.

Given the presumption against coercion, the basic rule for society is that an individual is presumed to be free to do what is feasible for him to do. This presumption is subject to two constraints. The first constraint relates an individual's proposed actions to his own obligations. The second constraint relates an individual's proposed actions to harm that such actions would impose on others. If neither of these two constraints binds, the individual confronts no burden of proof concerning the admissibility of feasible actions. The burden of proof rests with those who would challenge such actions.

If transaction costs are sufficiently high in the state of nature to persuade individuals to enter into civil society (Locke [1690] 1963), acceptance of Jasay's non-utilitarian principles has important implications for the nature of the institutional arrangements that ideally should govern trading between individuals. Specifically, it requires that the following legal rules should be applied.

1.   *The law of property*   The principle that should underpin the law of property may be summarized as: *let exclusion stand*. The legitimacy of what is variously called 'first possession' or 'first taking' is crucially important to this principle. If first possession is feasible and admissible, that is, if it is not a tort (trespass) and violates no right (true by definition), it is to be allowed. Taking exclusive possession is a liberty and only a contrary right can obstruct or oppose it.

In such an environment, two alternative acts constitute appropriation and vest ownership in the performer. The first such act can be labeled 'finding and keeping'; and the second can be labeled 'enclosure'. To the extent that taking possession by finding and keeping or by enclosure is feasible, it is also admissible, and hence a liberty, since the thing possessed, by definition, is previously unowned. Even though the act of first possession precludes the liberty of another person to assume that same first possession, a liberty cannot be countered by a rival liberty, only by a prior right (Jasay 1996, pp. 5–43).

Of course, countless arguments can be mounted by those who lack property, who are weak of will, who are short of talent or who are short of luck to justify the state in breaking down exclusion and in redistributing resources in their favor. They are all utilitarian in nature. They all breach the *when in doubt, abstain* precept.

When first possession rights are infringed, the appropriate remedy at law (be it the common law or the civil code) is injunction, at least when transaction costs are low. The use of such a property rule allows the parties concerned to seek gains through trade to the extent possible, given the initial distribution of rights. Following the logic of Ronald Coase (1960), where transaction costs are deemed to be obstructive to private bargaining, property may be defended by a liability rule. Since such a rule places the owners of property at the mercy of the courts, it should be applied only at the prior request of the property owner, not of those who wish to trespass on the liberties of such owners.

2.   *The law of contract*   Properly defined, property is not a right, or a bundle of rights, but a liberty to act upon owned objects. This liberty to act includes use and disposition. The most important liberty of disposition is freedom of contract, whereby an owner transforms some of his liberties to use into obligations for himself and rights for others. While the owner has a liberty to use, the non-owner requires a right to use, a right that he can obtain only through contract.

Contract, viewed from this perspective, is not a privilege conferred by the state. Non-interference with the liberty to contract follows directly from the *first, avoid doing harm* precept. Only if both parties request coercion to enforce a contract is this presumption legitimately displaced.

The law of contract that should prevail in such circumstances is the classical law of contract in which the necessary and sufficient conditions are offer, acceptance and consideration. Such contracts should be honored with respect to the precise wording of the bargain and should be void only in circumstances of fraud, coercion, mutual mistake or incapacity by reason of infancy or insanity. In particular, it is illegitimate for the state to void contracts on the grounds that they are unconscionable unless tortious harm is imposed on identifiable third parties.

The classical law of contract also has an answer to the question: what should be the remedy for breach of an enforceable promise? The promisee is entitled to the benefit that the bargain purported to provide, that is, to expectation damages.

3. *The law of tort* The liberty to act, whether with respect to property or to contract, is constrained by the rights of others not to have harms imposed upon them by such acts. In a legal system governed by the *first, avoid doing harm* precept, the law of tort will be narrowly defined, since a broad definition will jeopardize the liberty to exclude and to contract. The classical law of tort provides a basis for regulating third-party effects.

Three elements must be present for recovery by a plaintiff under this law. First, the plaintiff must actually have suffered harm; second, the defendant's act or failure to act must cause that harm; and third, the defendant's act or failure to act must constitute the breach of a duty owed to the plaintiff by the defendant.

These three conditions constitute the basis for a tightly constrained negligence-based system of tort law, supplemented by a contributory negligence constraint. In the case of tortious acts, compensatory damages is the appropriate remedy, save where the tort is of a continuous nature, making it feasible to apply the injunction remedy. Although strict liability rules offer a more comprehensive defense of property liberties than do negligence rules, they are too easily accessed as vehicles to invade contractual obligations. As such, they violate the precept of *first, avoid doing harm.*

Taken together, these legal rules constitute a consistent and coherent basis for the regulation of individual exchange. Where private acts are both feasible and admissible, state coercion is illegitimate; indeed it is tortious. It deforms the value of liberties and rights. Only by the explicit invitation of those who would be coerced by state intervention can this presumption be overruled.

Where private acts are feasible but inadmissible, as for example in the case of contract breaches and tortious harms, the presumption against state intervention is displaced. Even in such circumstances, the prudent state will delay in order to determine whether private resolutions to the problem can be devised.

3   The institutional limitations of political markets

Modern democracies are not characterized by the conditions of the minimal state, nor are they concerned to promote individual exchange even within their domestic markets. Even less are they concerned to promote such exchange across national boundaries. The deep-rooted instincts of mercantilism militate strongly against Jasay's (1996) conditions as outlined above. Rather the elected politicians of all parties are concerned to influence and to fetter exchange, whether domestic or international, primarily as a byproduct of self-serving programs of wealth redistribution. Viewed from this perspective, neither the voting nor the interest-group theory of government, or any hybrid of the two, offers an expectation that the ideal institutions for promoting individual exchange can long survive the emergence of democratic forms of government.

3.1   Indivisibilities in the electoral process
Economic markets are characterized by conditions of divisibility and continuity that enable all actors to participate effectively on an ongoing basis. Such is not the case with democratic political markets. Election campaigns typically bundle hundreds of issues into a single package, composed of complex mixes of social as well as economic policies. Individual voters are not allowed to decompose the bundle. They can exercise only one vote to express preferences over the few alternative bundles on offer.

Furthermore, voters can express such preferences only rarely over an election cycle. As Boudreaux (1996b, p. 117) has noted, each US voter, over each six-year span, has a maximum of nine ballots to cast in four national elections. These are the only windows of opportunity available for individuals to exert such vote power as they have politically on national issues. Even voters who are well informed and energized to vote in elections, therefore, have strictly limited opportunities to exert political influence. During the long intervals between elections, influences other than voting inevitably exert a significant role in political markets.

In the field of international economic relations, where policies are continuously brokered between national governments rather than determined by periodic elections or referenda, the problems posed by indivisibilities in the electoral process may be especially severe. These problems are compounded by other kinds of indivisibility associated with political markets.

3.2   Indivisibilities and the problem of information
In economic markets, individual consumers are assumed to be economically well informed, since they benefit or suffer directly from the consequences of

their decisions. Such is not the presumption in political markets (Downs 1957). In national elections, the probability that an individual's vote will determine the outcome of an election is vanishingly small. In such circumstances, even those who vote have little or no investment incentive to inform themselves about the details of the rival candidates' relative positions in policy dimension space. Many will effect their electoral responsibilities in a state of rational ignorance. Others will inform themselves at a minimum cost, by reference to party political labels, or by reference to favored (and quite possibly biased) media sources. Indivisibility, once again, raises its malevolent head in the democratic process, allowing elections to be determined on the basis more of the physical attractiveness of the competing candidates than of the good sense of their politics.

If individual voters are rationally ignorant in a market where advertising and campaign expenditures play a central role, they may be especially vulnerable to preference manipulation. In such circumstances, political outlays will not play an exclusively informative role, even under competitive conditions. The Chicagoan assertion that *de gustibus non est disputandum* (Stigler and Becker 1977), implying that changes in economic behavior are driven by changes in constraints and not by changes in preferences, then would not apply.

This problem of preference manipulation is more serious than one of simple persuasion. Even in countries like the United States, where free speech at least in principle is protected by the Constitution, irresolute individuals may be prepared to falsify their expressed political preferences where the social pressure to conform is high (Kuran 1995). On such politically correct issues as affirmative action, policy toward homosexuals, gun-control policy, policy towards tobacco and the debate over genetic versus environmental causes of performance differentials, political polls may express opinions widely at variance with the reality of majority opinion.

Yet, if such polls determine the positions taken by competing candidates for political office, the true preferences of the voters may not be reflected in policy outcomes:

> The pressure of public opinion may make minorities refrain from exercising their constitutional rights to dissent. Even without government coercion, majorities might submit to the wishes of vociferous minorities. Protections against government tyranny do not prevent societies from tyrannizing themselves through the force of public opinion. (ibid., p. 101)

If the media should involve themselves actively in support of this process of social pressure, as arguably is the case in the late twentieth-century United States, liberties may be severely eroded, not by trampling on the Constitution, but by suppressing open discourse on important issues of policy. The ensuing preference falsification will shape social action, bias knowledge and inhibit change, transforming once-free individuals into organized flocks of passive sheep, albeit without the formal trappings of dictatorship. In essence, this is the nature of much of media-induced 'expressive voting' under conditions of democracy.

3.3   Indivisibilities and the logic of collective action

Given that the vote motive is muted by problems of indivisibility, a vacuum potentially occurs in political markets. This vacuum is filled by the intervention of interest groups.

For a long period, political scientists took for granted the notion that groups of individuals with common interests acted collectively to further such interests through political markets. For the most part, such political activity was viewed as benign, serving to inform politicians of the relative intensity of demands for political action, especially in the lengthy intervals between elections. Since interest groups are free to form and to regroup in response to changing preferences and constraints, there seemed to be good reason to conjecture that collective action served to reinforce underlying voter preferences both by informing the electorate on issues under consideration and by ensuring that voters' preferences would be honored by incumbent governments. Interest-group pressures were rationalized as playing a role similar to that of informative advertising in competitive economic markets.

Such complacency was shattered in 1965 when Mancur Olson introduced the problem of indivisibility into the logic of collective action. If individuals contemplate organizing themselves into a group to pursue a common interest through the supply of political pressure, they face serious obstacles if they cannot exclude non-participants from the benefits of their effort. Non-excludability is a typical characteristic of political market outcomes. In such circumstances collective action is a public good, and individuals rationally will free ride in its supply. Free riding in the supply of political pressure results in underprovision, with important consequences for political market behavior.

The logic of collective action suggests that many interest groups that could achieve group gains from collective action will not organize and act to that end. The logic does not extend with equal effect to all interest groups, however, and herein lies a serious problem for political markets. Where interest groups have differential access to political markets, there is little likelihood that collective action will serve a neutral information-enhancing role helping politicians to discern underlying voter preferences.

There are three conditions, any one of which is sufficient to make collective action feasible, when associated with effective leadership. One condition is that the number of individuals that must act collectively to further the common interest is small and homogeneous. This condition substantially counters the free-rider problem. Many kinds of producer groups satisfy this condition. The second condition is that the leadership of the organization is able to force the supply of pressure, by legal or illegal mechanisms. Many professional associations and trade unions satisfy this condition, as does *La Cosa Nostra*.

The third condition is that the group, although large and heterogeneous, can bind itself to provide pressure for a common cause by the use of selective benefits made available only to participants. Although such selective benefits may be eroded by competition from outside the interest group (Stigler 1974), judicious abuse of non-profit status by the group may provide a margin for lobbying activities, even when the selective benefits must be provided at market prices.

The logic of collective action suggests that individuals with common interests will be differentially successful in achieving their goals through political markets. Those individuals who benefit from one or more of the conditions outlined above will do well in political markets even when they constitute a vote minority, whereas those individuals who do not will fail to achieve their goals even where they constitute a vote majority.

Rational ignorance will prevent median voters from penalizing politicians who indulge minority pressures as long as those politicians observe the golden rule of dispensing benefits to concentrated groups and dispersing costs widely across the voting public. To the extent that the successful interest groups can subvert the media and create bandwagon effects, preference falsification on the part of voters will further protect their special interests.

The impact of interest groups predictably will be greater with respect to international economic relations than with respect to domestic economic relations. The differential impact materializes both because voters tend to be less well informed about the former than the latter and because interest groups may be able to forge links across national boundaries whereas voters cannot do so. Inevitably, the influence achieved by interest groups depends on the structure of the political marketplace, which differs from country to country. This issue will be addressed later in this chapter.

3.4 Indivisibilities and the transaction costs of government

In economic markets, a system of well-defined property rights and contestable markets largely ensures that wealth-enhancing exchange proceeds at a minimal transaction cost (Coase 1960). Such is not the case with political markets. In political markets, property rights do not exist, or are so poorly defined and severely attenuated as to be devoid of efficiency incentives (Rowley and Vachris 1994; Rowley 1997; Chapter 2 of this volume).

The legislators who broker policies in political markets have strictly limited legal avenues available to appropriate personally any increase in the nation's wealth resulting from their interventions. They cannot easily transfer or bequeath such truncated rights as they temporarily hold. In such circumstances, resources do not flow easily to their most highly valued uses.

Even if a government desires to enter into credibly binding commitments with its electorate, it cannot do so. The sovereignty of each government implies that no government can impose its will upon its successors, or even indeed, upon itself (Stiglitz et al. 1989). The government itself is largely free to establish the conditions under which individual citizens may sue it for breach of contract, for tortious acts, or even for the taking of property. Even in the United States, the Constitution has provided little protection against the misuse of such powers, given the deference exhibited by the judicial to the legislative branch of government, certainly over the past half-century.

In the absence of a robust system of property rights, democratic political markets become focal points for wealth redistribution battles, battles in which middle-income voters predictably extract wealth transfers from both the rich and the poor (Tullock 1993). Such battles occur whether voters are rationally ignorant or rationally informed.

Politics fundamentally is about the exercise of public authority and the struggle to access that authority (Moe 1990, p. 221). When two poor individuals and one rich individual make up a polity governed by majority rule, the rich person is in trouble. He is not in trouble because of the instability of majority rule, or because a prisoner's dilemma prevents the three participants from realizing gains from trade. He is in trouble because the poor participants will take advantage of the public authority to invade his wealth.

In economic markets, wealth redistribution occurs on a voluntary basis and is utility enhancing. In political markets, wealth redistribution occurs coercively and takes the form of a negative-sum rent-seeking game (Rowley et al. 1988). In democratic political markets, wealth redistribution tends to be the primary focus of government once government itself expands beyond the functions of the minimal state (Rowley 1993). Since much of the redistribution occurs opaquely and carries high excess burdens, the transaction costs of the state tend to be high in terms of deadweight loss. In addition, rent-seeking and rent-protection outlays by interest groups engaged in the redistribution battle increase the overall cost of redistribution in the form of Tullock rectangles (Tullock 1993).

The transaction costs of government will vary with the institutional characteristics of particular political markets. Later sections of this chapter will explore alternatives from the perspective of international economic relations. In general, high rent-seeking costs will tend to limit the margins of redistribution as voters become rationally informed about the waste involved. Two alternative scenarios thus arise. In one, there is a great deal of wealth redistribution, with high associated excess burden costs. In the other, there is less wealth redistribution, with lower excess burden costs, but with high rent-seeking costs. Which of the two is the more costly cannot be determined *ex ante*. Both are clearly much more costly than the minimal state, which allows only for voluntary wealth redistribution. Coercive wealth redistribution policies are wealth reducing in nature.

3.5 Indivisibilities and bureaucratic behavior

Legislatures create and finance new public policies. They do not provide them. This is the function of bureaus located usually within the executive branch. Because public policies tend to be indivisible, it is rare for the legislature to provide for competitive provision of public policies. Bureaus thus tend to enjoy monopoly powers. It is also rare for legislatures to allow bureaus to sell their programs at market-clearing prices. Bureaus thus tend to be monopolists supplying goods and services at zero prices, relying upon the legislature for annual budget appropriations in exchange for a total output commitment. This indivisibility provides the bureau with the power, equivalent to that of a price-discriminating monopolist, to expropriate the entire producer and consumer surplus to its own budget.

Utilizing a bilateral bargaining model, in which the government bureau bargains with its legislative sponsor over the annual budget, with senior bureaucrats motivated to maximize the size of their budget, Niskanen (1971) demonstrated that bureaus would typically achieve output levels significantly in excess of those required for economic efficiency. Because of information asymmetries the bureau predictably would outmaneuver the government, securing excessively large budgets that would be dissipated in technically inefficient ways. In addition, bureaus predictably would secure policy discretion that enabled them to abuse the terms of their statutory goals.

More recently, there has been an attempt to recast the relationship between politicians and senior bureaucrats into a principal–agent format (Weingast and Moran 1983). Empirical analysis based on US data evaluating bureau behavior in a number of fields, including international trade, has demonstrated that principal–agent problems are ameliorated, at least to some extent, by the emergence of incentive-cost structures that induce bureaus to conform with the preferences of oversight committee members. Not all such studies, however, are favorable to this hypothesis (Rowley 1992). Moreover, the model is unlikely to predict behavior in political markets less specialized than that of the United States. Once again, indivisibilities in political markets militate against any easy resolution of the principal–agent problem (Rowley and Vachris 1994).

Economic markets ameliorate potential principal–agent problems through a proprietary setting in which individuals bear the consequences of their actions directly in terms of changes in their own net worth. The political setting, in contrast, is a non-proprietary environment in which individuals do not bear the full economic consequences of their decisions.

Behavioral differences in the two settings reflect these significant differences in institutional constraints. Even within the complex structure of US oversight and appropriations committees there is no equivalent of the capital market to revise the value of political portfolios in well-functioning and deviant markets. In such circumstances, agency problems will emerge and will not easily be removed (ibid.).

Because international bureaus operate in environments characterized by the existence of multiple, heterogeneous principals, opportunities for bureau deviancy are much greater. The implications of this circumstance for the international economy will be reviewed later in this chapter.

4   Protection for sale

With the general analytical framework now in place, it is time to review some of the most recent public scholarship dealing with issues of the international economy. A comprehensive survey is not possible in this chapter, but a number of significant contributions dealing with a number of important aspects of the international economy will be outlined and evaluated critically. The objective is to provide the reader with a flavor of the public choice contribution to understanding the nature of international political economy.

An excellent point of departure for this evaluation is the 1994 article by Grossman and Helpman that deals explicitly with the notion that trade protection is for sale in democratic political markets. This article is a first-class example of the application of the interest-group theory of politics to issues of trade policy. It is unfortunately also an archetypal example of a genre of theoretical contributions that attaches little significance to the importance of institutions.

Grossman and Helpman focus attention on a small competitive economy that faces exogenously given world prices. For such an economy free trade is efficient. Any policy interventions adverse to free trade can be ascribed to the political process. The economy produces a *numeraire* good with the use of labor alone. It also produces n additional products, each with the use of labor and an input specific to a particular sector of the economy. The ownership of many of the n sector-specific inputs is highly concentrated, and the various owners of some of these inputs band together to form lobby groups, surmounting the free-rider problems that prevent others from so doing.

Grossman and Helpman ignore the potential for competition between rival political parties and rival political candidates and focus attention exclusively on incumbent office holders. This enables them to analyse the behavior of lobby groups in offering political contributions to those office holders in a position to determine current trade policy. Each organized interest group representing one of the sector-specific factors confronts the government with a contribution schedule. The schedule maps every policy vector that the government might choose (where policies are import and export taxes and subsidies on the non-numeraire goods) into a campaign contribution level. Of course, some policies may evoke a zero campaign contribution from some lobbies.

Grossman and Helpman endow the government with preferences defined over campaign contributions and voter wellbeing. Because they are unaware of the insight of Black (1948b) and Downs (1957) concerning the dominance of the median in voter models, they incorrectly view the government as maximizing a weighted sum of aggregate social welfare and total contributions. Since their preoccupation is with the selling of protection, this flaw is not fatal to their analysis.

Political equilibrium in this model is the outcome of a two-stage non-cooperative game. Each lobby simultaneously chooses its political contribution schedules in the first stage, maximizing the joint welfare of its members given the schedules set by the other groups and the anticipated goals of the government. The government sets its policy in the second stage, taking the contribution schedules of the various lobbies as given. The interaction between the lobbies and the government, therefore, has the structure of a 'menu-auction' problem (Bernheim and Whinston 1986).

On this basis, the authors show that equilibrium trade policies obey a modified Ramsey rule. All else equal, industries with higher import demand or export supply elasticities will have smaller deviations from free trade. In equilibrium, however, the rates of protection will also reflect the relative political strengths of the various interest groups and parameters describing the country's political economy.

In their formal analysis, Grossman and Helpman limit the government's choice of policy instruments to trade taxes (tariffs) and subsidies. They recognize, however, that output subsidies transfer wealth to interest groups with lower excess burdens than tariffs and export subsidies. Where factor ownership is highly concentrated and the lobby groups account for only a small fraction of the total electorate, output subsidies would be favored. In equilibrium, such subsidies maximize the joint welfare of each lobby and the government, extracting the maximum available transfers from unorganized sectors of the economy.

Where the lobbies are at odds with each other, however, in competing for the favors of government their contributions tend to be higher and the net welfare of their members lower where the political regime deals in output subsidies. For this reason, competing lobbies prefer to tie the hands of government to the provision only of inefficient policies. In this manner, the authors explain the prevalence of such high excess burden instruments of trade protection as import quotas.

5   Trade wars and trade talks

In 1995, Grossman and Helpman (1995a) extended their public choice analysis to embrace trade relations between national governments. They discard the assumption that governments must take world prices as given. Accordingly, there is scope for interaction between governments and an opportunity for interest groups in one country to influence policy outcomes elsewhere.

The lobbies in each country are assumed to move first, setting contribution schedules that link their gifts to the various policy outcomes. The lobbies act simultaneously and non-cooperatively, each taking as given the schedules of all other lobbies in the same and in the other country. The governments then set their respective national trade policies either in a non-cooperative simultaneous-move game or through international negotiations. In both cases, it is assumed that the implicit contracts between the governments of each country and the interest groups are not observable to the other government.

In the case of the trade war, governments behave unilaterally, ignoring the impacts of their actions on political and economic agents in the other country. In this non-cooperative environment, the special interests restrict their lobbying activities to their respective national governments. Politically motivated governments tilt trade policies in favor of their organized special interests. The home tariff is higher and the foreign export tax is lower in political equilibrium than would be the case in the neoclassical model. If governments become more concerned with campaign finances and less with average-voter preferences, the new equilibrium entails a yet higher home tariff and a yet lower foreign export tax.

As viewed from the public choice perspective, government officials are willing to impose deadweight losses on their constituents as a means of amassing campaign contributions. By choosing their national policies non-cooperatively, however, they impose avoidable political costs on each other. Trade talks between politically motivated governments are viewed as an attempt to mitigate such costs. Successful trade talks pit the powerful lobbies in one country against those in the other, somewhat neutralizing the power of each. An efficient negotiation eliminates the terms-of-trade source of deadweight loss, while compensating the country that otherwise would have captured the benefit of this shift.

The Grossman and Helpman (1995a) model demonstrates that efficient trade talks remove the influence of foreign supply elasticities on each country's tariff rates. Tariff rates now reflect not only the political strength of domestic interest groups, but also the political strength of the interest group in the same industry abroad. Protection will be especially high where the domestic interest group is strong and the foreign interest group in the same industry is weak. When both interest groups are equally strong, their political influence will cancel out. In such circumstances, international prices under a trade agreement will reflect those that would prevail under free trade.

6   The politics of free trade agreements

In September 1995, Grossman and Helpman (1995b) further extended their model to evaluate the political viability of free trade negotiations between independent nations. They examined the likely nature of trade negotiations between two small countries that interact both with each other and with the rest of the world. As usual, they assume that the governments in question respond to political pressures from industry special interests, but also pay some attention to the preferences of the average voter.

If a free trade agreement (FTA) must liberalize completely trade among the partner nations, a particular government might endorse an agreement in two types of situations. The first is the situation in which the FTA generates substantial welfare gains for the average voter and in which the adversely affected interest groups fail to coordinate their efforts to defeat the accord. The second is the situation in which the agreement creates profit gains for exporters in excess of the combined losses imposed on import-competing industries and on the average voter.

A free trade agreement requires the assent of both governments. This outcome is most likely from the perspective of Grossman and Helpman (ibid.) when there is relative balance in the potential trade between the partner countries and when the agreement affords enhanced rather than reduced protection to most sectors. Thus the conditions that enhance the viability of a potential agreement also raise the expectation that the agreement will reduce aggregate social welfare.

If some industries can be excluded from an FTA, the prospects for an agreement improve. Each government seeks to exclude those sectors whose inclusion would impose the greatest political cost. Such cost reflects either the opposition of import-competing interests or the harm that would be suffered by the average voter as a consequence of inefficient trade diversion. By excluding such industries, a government diffuses opposition.

In a bargaining situation, the equilibrium agreement reflects the political pressures experienced by both negotiating governments. In the Nash solution, exclusions are granted to industries for which a weighted sum of the political benefit of market access, in the exporting country, and the political cost of more intense import competition, in the importing country, is most negative.

The weights on benefits in one country and costs in the other reflect the negotiating abilities of the two governments and the political implications for each of failure to reach an agreement. In suitable circumstances, treasury to treasury transfers may serve to cement otherwise infeasible agreements.

7   Foreign interests and voluntary export restraints

The public choice insights provided by Grossman and Helpman, both in 1994 and 1995 (a and b), relate to equilibrium rates of tariff protection under conditions of non-cooperation and international negotiation. Tariff protection now plays a diminished role in international markets, in large part owing to the success of a sequence of multilateral tariff-reduction rounds since the end of the Second World War. In its place, protection more frequently takes the form of bilaterally negotiated voluntary export restraints (VERs) negotiated between the governments of importing and exporting nations.

In 1988, Hillman and Ursprung developed a public choice model that incorporates foreign interests in the determination of a country's international trade policy. This model demonstrates the potential superiority of VERs over tariffs from the perspective of self-seeking candidates competing for elective office. The paper is important because the prevalence of VERs cannot be explained in terms of standard welfare economics.

If a VER is viewed as a substitute for an import quota, foreigners and not domestic interest groups secure the rents created by the restraint on trade. If a VER is viewed as a substitute for a tariff, revenue that would have accrued to the domestic government instead is transferred to foreigners. In neither case is it easy to explain the substitution by reference to standard theories of international trade.

Some theorists struggle to explain the phenomenon as a mechanism whereby powerful nations secure the acquiescence of foreign governments to policies that violate negotiated GATT (General Agreement on Tariffs and Trade) commitments. Others view it as a mechanism designed to pre-empt other more costly retaliations in export markets. Neither explanation is convincing from the perspective of powerful nation-states dealing with weaker nation-states in the absence of any binding rule of law.

Hillman and Ursprung evaluate the problem from a public choice perspective in which foreign interests exert an influence on domestic politics. They note that, under representative government, foreign participation in domestic politics takes the form of campaign contributions, or other transfers, legal or otherwise, directed at influencing the trade policy positions of political candidates. These foreign interests may be viewed as residual claimants in a foreign export industry.

These interests may be viewed as identical Cournot firms within the industry acting non-cooperatively unless directed by their government to restrain exports collectively on the basis of pre-allocated market shares. A similar Cournot portrayal of firms is adopted in the case of the domestic import-competing industry. Firms in the domestic industry, however, are constrained by antitrust laws and do not behave collusively.

In this model, firms choose campaign contributions to a favored candidate to maximize expected profits. These depend upon the rival candidates' prospects for election and upon the trade policy to which each candidate commits himself. Campaign contributions, though privately provided, have a public-good characteristic. Each firm's contributions help other firms that stand to gain or lose in the same way from a candidate's policy commitment. In this endogenous policy setting, the authors investigate the characteristics of protectionist proposals when the alternative forms of trade intervention are tariffs and VERs.

The outcome of political competition depends upon the instrument used by rival candidates to make trade policy pronouncements. The tariff equilibrium turns out to be politically divisive in that the protectionist candidate announces a prohibitive tariff whereas the liberal trade policy candidate announces for free trade. The policy platform of the protectionist maximizes domestic profits and minimizes foreign profits whereas the opposite is true for the free trader.

However, when candidates' policy proposals are formulated in terms of VERs, trade policy platforms converge to a Downsian equilibrium and there is a compromise between the conflicting economic interests of domestic and foreign producers. An interior equilibrium (which cannot occur under a tariff) is characterized by a level of export restraint more restrictive than foreigners require to maximize joint profits but less restrictive than is desired by domestic import-competing firms. Indeed, the political equilibrium associated with VERs is consistent with mutual economic gain to foreign and domestic producer interests.

Hillman and Ursprung define export restraints as voluntary only where both foreign and domestic industry rents increase as a consequence of foreigners' coordinated restriction of export sales. This definition avoids the hypocrisy implicit in the use made of the term by US trade policy bureaucrats as they coerce export restraints from foreign interests essentially by gunboat diplomacy. Whether or not an export restraint is voluntary in the sense of Hillman and Ursprung depends on the particular relationship that links domestic and foreign market structures and on the substitutability of foreign and domestic goods in domestic consumption.

The results of the model depend in part on two important assumptions. First, it is assumed that rival candidates place no value on revenues derived from a tariff. Such revenues accrue to the general fund to which the candidates have no claim. In contrast, there is a direct return to candidates, in the form of campaign contributions, from the creation of rents that can be transferred to private interests via export restraints. Second, it is assumed that consumers play no active role in the formulation of trade policy platforms. Consumers are viewed as being passively influenced in their voting behavior by campaign expenditures. In essence, they remain rationally ignorant on matters of trade policy.

An important determinant of the result that export restraints drive out tariffs in the domestic political contest is the assumed non-appropriability of tariff revenue by competing political candidates. Hillman and Ursprung may have overstated this aspect of rent seeking for tariff protection. Although the tariff revenues themselves may be lost in the general pool, rent seeking outlays by import-competing domestic interests will not. This explains why tariff protection and import quotas persist despite multilateral attempts to remove them even in countries like the United States where VER protection is widespread.

8   The role of antidumping procedures in reinforcing VERs

In a 1996 article, Rosendorff applies public choice analysis to explain the relationship between antidumping actions in both the United States and the European Community and voluntary export restraints negotiated between the industry determined to be in violation of domestic antidumping laws and the domestic government. Approximately one-third of all antidumping petitions are withdrawn in return for negotiated VERs. Rosendorff offers a rational choice explanation for this political phenomenon.

The antidumping administrative procedure allows the regulatory authorities to make a preliminary determination and to impose a preliminary remedy (usually a tariff) in favor of the affected domestic industry while an investigation is under way. This preliminary tariff acts as a signal of the willingness of the agency to impose an 'optimal' duty at the end of the investigation if a 'voluntary' undertaking is not forthcoming.

The sequence of moves in this game mirrors that of the administrative procedure. The game has three players, the agency of the domestic government, the domestic industry and the foreign firm or industry. The domestic industry moves first by filing an appeal with the agency of the domestic government for some relief under the antidumping statutes. The government responds by choosing a tariff level that it threatens to impose on the foreign interest. The foreign interest then offers an undertaking to cease dumping. If the offer is accepted, the game ends. If it is rejected, the preliminary determination becomes final and both domestic and foreign interests respond to the imposed tariff.

The paper assumes that the political sympathies of the domestic government agent are not fully known to the foreign interest at the commencement of the game. The equilibrium concept adopted is that of a perfect Bayesian equilibrium in an incomplete information environment. The first stage of the game resembles the standard signaling game in which the government agency chooses its actions optimally given the actions and beliefs of the foreign interest.

The agency at the first stage of the game chooses a preliminary tariff designed to signal to the foreign interest whether or not it is willing to accommodate a lower level of exports in return for a tariff reduction. Unwillingness to make this accommodation is signaled by a tariff that is optimal in the pure tariff game. Once the foreign interest is aware of the potential for a VER it negotiates with the government to determine whether a sharing of the surplus is feasible. If a VER is agreed to, the domestic firm or industry responds optimally to the reduced foreign exports into its market. In this way, the preliminary determination acts as a perfect signal about the type of regulator the foreign interest is facing.

Rosendorff's paper establishes two important results that conventional economic analysis cannot. First, it shows that a VER is preferred to a tariff by a government concerned about electoral returns when the weight on industry profits is large. Second, it shows that if the foreign interest is unsure of the exact nature of this political pressure, the antidumping code provides the opportunity for a complete transfer of the relevant information. Once again, the public choice perspective provides an understanding of an apparent paradox in trade protection practices.

9 Black hole tariffs

Without exception, the literature surveyed so far has focused on the deadweight losses associated with trade protection policies driven by the pressures of public choice. Such losses may well be only the tip of the iceberg. In their 1989 book, Magee et al. analyse the potential magnitudes of the social loss associated with rent seeking for trade protection in a special-interest model of government. They identify conditions under which there are no upper limits to redistributive lobbying. Under such conditions, the entire economy can disappear into an economic black hole as the output of the national economy approaches the limit of zero.

The analytical framework adopted by the authors differs from that of the preceding papers. Instead of industry-specific interest groups, the model focuses on the Cobb–Douglas version of the Heckscher–Ohlin–Samuelson trade model. From this perspective, two factor input lobbies, one representing labor and the other capital, contribute resources to politics. Each equates at the margin the returns to political and to economic activity.

Two political parties maximize their respective probabilities of election, trading off voter dissatisfaction with distortionary policies against votes gained from the lobbying resources that such policies elicit. Voters who remain rationally ignorant about trade policies select between the political parties on the basis of a *logit* probability of election function. Within this framework, the authors explore conditions sufficient to yield the black hole.

First, they assume the presence of countervailing power on the part of the two factors. Countervailing power is defined as equal probabilities of election for the pro-labor and the pro-capital political parties when the country's entire factor endowment is devoted to politics. The authors set up the problem symmetrically by assuming that both interest groups devote the same proportion of their respective factor inputs to lobbying. Second, they assume that both capital and labor exhibit constant relative risk aversion.

An important parameter of the black hole experiment is the elasticity of factor prices with respect to product prices. This elasticity is referred to as the *magnification elasticity* because it always exceeds unity in the general equilibrium Heckscher–Ohlin–Samuelson model. This implies that any given percentage change in product prices generates a larger percentage change in factor prices. The greater the magnification effect, the greater the payoff to the lobbies from increasing product prices through the political process.

What are the upper limits on the resources that the capital lobby will commit to the battle over relative prices? By the symmetry assumption the analysis concerning capital applies equally to that for labor. If the capital lobby devotes an additional unit of capital to the pro-capital party, its income is reduced because fewer units are employed in production. This is the 'negative units' effect. However, the additional unit of capital in the hands of the pro-capital party ultimately results in a higher export subsidy and a higher return to capital. This is the 'positive returns' effect. Because the authors model the political parties as Stackelberg leaders, the positive returns effect is not under the direct control of the capital lobby. Nevertheless, the larger the positive returns effect, the larger the fraction of capital that will be devoted to politics.

Consider next two possible ranges for the degree of relative risk aversion, p, by the two lobbies. If $p = 0$, the case of risk neutrality, no more than 50 percent of an economy's capital (and labor) will be devoted to rent seeking. If $p > 1$, the outer bound of rent seeking lies between one-third and one-half of the economy's resources. These upper limits are independent of other parameters in the model.

Consider now an economy whose factor inputs are risk averse and have degrees of relative risk aversion equal to 1. Let the factor intensities of production in the two industries move together. This implies that the capital–labor ratio in the labor-intensive import sector rises relative to the same sector in the export sector. When this occurs, product price changes have increasingly large effects on both wages and capital returns.

With high magnification, the transfer of capital (labor) into lobbying generates an arbitrarily large increase in capital (labor) returns. In such circumstances, it is rational for the capital (labor) lobby to throw nearly all its resources into the battle over redistribution. Such behavior takes the economy into a black hole in which political efficiency implies the absence of a functioning economy.

Black holes cannot exist for long periods of time without the collapse of the nation-state. Historically, they are rare or non-existent. 'Gray holes', in which non-trivial levels of resources are wasted in redistribution, are much more frequent and, according to the authors, have become more prevalent during the second half of the twentieth century. If they and other authors are correct, democracies are responding less and less efficiently to unambiguous economic arguments in favor of free trade. These failures are not the consequence of increasing systematic error but rather are rational responses to rising pressures in favor of protection within the political marketplace.

10   The cost of protection

The costs of protection manifest themselves in the form both of a loss of wealth and of personal liberty. Although neither cost is easy to enumerate, the former is more accessible than the latter. Indeed, Hufbauer and Elliott (1994) estimated for the year 1990 the potential consumer gains if the United States were to eliminate all tariffs and quantitative restrictions on their imports. This study is grounded on a simple, computable partial equilibrium analysis with four key assumptions:

1.   The domestic good and the imported good are imperfect substitutes.
2.   The supply schedule for the imported good is perfectly elastic.
3.   The supply schedule for the domestic good is less than perfectly elastic.
4.   All markets are perfectly competitive.

The effects of removing a trade barrier are illustrated in Figures 30.1 and 30.2. For example, the elimination of a tariff lowers the price of the import in the domestic market from P_m to P'_m in Figure 30.1. In Figure 30.2, the decrease in the price of the imported good causes an inward shift in the demand curve for the domestic commodity from D_d to D'_d. In equilibrium, the prices of both the imported and the domestic good are lower, the output of the domestic good is lower and the volume of imports is higher.

Using a methodology developed by Morkre and Tarr (1980), Hufbauer and Elliott (1994) estimated the economic effects of trade liberalization for the United States. Because imported and domestic goods are imperfect substitutes, the total gain to consumers must be calculated as the sum of the consumers' surplus in the two separate markets. In Figure 30.1, the consumers' surplus from liberalization in the import market is approximated by the area *aceg*, comprising the sum of the rectangle *acfg* and the triangle *cef*.

If protection takes the form of a tariff, the rectangle *acfg* represents a transfer from the government to consumers in the form of forgone tax rev-

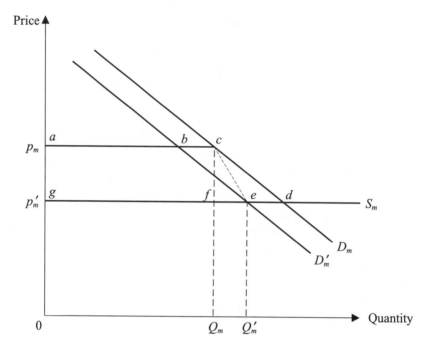

Figure 30.1   Effects in the import market of removing a trade barrier

enues while the triangle *cef* represents the recovery of the deadweight efficiency loss. In the case of quantitative restrictions, the area *acfg* represents a
transfer from foreign interests. In this latter case, the trapezoid *aceg* represents the net welfare gain.

In Figure 30.2, the domestic effects of trade liberalization are identified.
The consumer gains from lower domestic prices are approximated by the area
swyz. This gain is exactly offset by the loss of producers' surplus.

Hufbauer and Elliott focused particular attention on 21 US sectors protected by unusually high trade barriers, estimating in each case relevant
demand and supply functions and incorporating terms-of-trade effects into
their calculations. They estimated that the loss of consumers' surplus from
trade barriers in these sectors was in the neighborhood of $32 billion per
annum.

Using cruder measures, they added to these losses an estimated $38 billion
per annum in consumers' surplus losses from the imposition of all other
tariffs (averaging 3.5 percent in 1990). On this basis, they calculated that the
potential gain to US consumers from eliminating all tariffs and quotas on
imports was approximately $70 billion per annum.

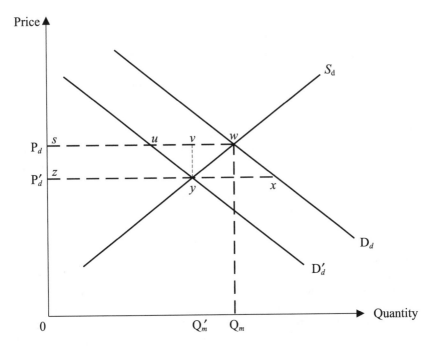

Figure 30.2 Effects in the domestic market of removing a trade barrier

This estimate significantly underestimates the true gains available from trade liberalization (Rowley et al. 1995). The error arises in treating perceived rents to US producers and to the US government as simple transfers in calculating the net gain to trade liberalization. Let us suppose that the efficient rent-seeking model applies and that the resources wasted in rent seeking for trade protection exactly equal the domestic rents created by trade protection. In such circumstances, the *Tullock rectangles* must be added to the *Harberger triangles* in calculating the full social cost.

For the 21 most protected sectors, Hufbauer and Elliott (1994) calculated that the producers' surplus based on trade protection was $15.8 billion in 1990 and that tariff revenues were $5.9 billion. In terms of the efficient rent-seeking model, the Tullock rectangles approximated $21.7 billion per annum in these sectors. Applying a pro-rata assessment to the rest of the US economy, Tullock rectangles amounted to an additional $25.6 billion per annum.

By adding all rent-seeking waste to consumers' surplus losses from trade protection, the net welfare loss to the US economy from trade protection in 1990 was in the neighborhood of $117 billion, or approximately 2 percent of GDP. These losses take no account of any longer-term costs associated with the diversion of entrepreneurial effort from productive to non-productive activities. Such losses may not come close to the black hole outer-bounds defined by Magee et al. (1989), but they represent a sizeable annual burden even for a prosperous nation.

It is often argued that trade protection preserves jobs in the United States (the so-called 'Perot effect'). If so, the cost to consumers of preserving such jobs is extremely high. In a quarter of the 21 sectors scrutinized by Hufbauer and Elliott (1994), the cost per job saved was in excess of $500 000 per annum even ignoring rent-seeking costs. Only in one of the 21 sectors (costume jewelry) was the cost per job saved less than $100 000 per annum. On average, the cost per job saved was $170 000 per annum. Thus, consumers expended more than six times the average annual compensation of manufacturing workers to preserve jobs through import restraints, even ignoring rent-seeking costs. Once rent-seeking costs are accounted for, consumers expended more than ten times the average wage earned by a worker in such a protected job.

Although the large majority of economists view the issue of free trade versus protection exclusively in utilitarian terms, the issue should also be viewed from a rights-based perspective. Free trade follows as an inevitable implication for any individual who endorses the philosophy of John Locke as it does for any individual who endorses Jasay's principles of *first, avoid doing harm* and *when in doubt, abstain.*

Protection violates the economic freedom of those who wish to engage in trade, encroaching as it does upon their property and contract rights. Any government that imposes trade restraints in the absence of the unanimous consent of those who are thus coerced commits a tort and should be exposed to potential civil suits to compensate those who suffer harm. Because governments typically use trade restrictions to pursue known traders in a discriminatory manner, they also breach the rule of law, without which individual liberty ultimately cannot survive. This is true especially in the case of quantitative restrictions that expose individual traders to the discretionary whims of bureaucratic agencies.

11   The constitutional perspective

The proposition that freedom of international trade is on the whole more beneficial than protection is one of the most fundamental propositions economic theory has to offer for the guidance of economic policy. This proposition has survived repeated scrutiny from economists from the time that Adam Smith made the case for free trade in the *Wealth of Nations* in 1776. It continues to enjoy overwhelming support (surveys indicate in excess of 88 percent) from professional economists in the late years of the twentieth century (Frey 1984).

The term 'free trade' has no unique definition (Sally 1998). In theoretical terms, free trade generally means that there exist no artificial impediments to the exchange of commodities across national markets; and that the prices confronted by domestic producers and consumers are the same as those determined by the world market, allowing for transportation and other transaction costs. In practical terms, free trade defines a policy of the nation-state toward international commerce in which trade barriers are absent, implying an absence of restrictions on the import of commodities from other countries and an absence of distortions impeding the flow of exports to other markets.

It is important to emphasize that, whereas the ideas underpinning the doctrine of free trade may be international in their reach, the process whereby that doctrine works its way into economic policy is grounded in the behavior of the citizens of the nation-state. The great scholars of the Scottish Enlightenment, most notably David Hume and Adam Smith, were unequivocal in their judgment that it is fundamentally a matter of appropriate domestic institutions and appropriate national policies as to whether an open international economy exists and prospers. Smith's famous 'sympathy' principle was not viewed as reaching out across national borders:

> We do not love our country merely as part of the great society of mankind: we love it for its own sake, and independently of any such consideration. ... [T]he interest of the great society of mankind would be best promoted by directing the principal attention of each individual to that particular portion of it, which was most within the sphere both of his abilities and of his understanding. (Smith [1759] 1982, p. 229)

Smith was a political realist. He did not believe that free trade would automatically lead to international peace. He was fully attentive to the permanent danger of interstate conflicts. Open commerce does engender greater contact and understanding between the citizens of different states; but it is an insufficiently powerful force to overcome permanently the inescapable problem of international anarchy. International order must rely on a pragmatic combination of open commerce and a network of alliances and treaties to maintain a balance of political power between states. International order cannot rest on a harmony of interests alone. Any realistic constitutional perspective on the issue of the international economy must reflect these important insights.

The nation-state, if it so chooses, can guarantee free trade for its own citizens, simply by eliminating all barriers to imports and all governmental support to exports. In essence, this was the route chosen by Great Britain in 1846 in the repeal of the Corn Laws. The public choice impediments to such a policy, despite its wealth-enhancing properties, are clear. In the end, the repeal of the Corn Laws turned on Prime Minister Robert Peel's intellectual conversion to the idea of free trade. This conversion led Peel to abandon the sectional landowning interests traditionally loyal to the Conservative Party. Despite his great service to the nation, Peel was charged by his rival Benjamin Disraeli with having betrayed the party for principles of political economy. Peel's political career was irreparably damaged (Bhagwati 1988).

All societies are founded on rules designed to regulate individual behavior and to facilitate social and economic exchange. These rules protect individuals from the threat of war of each against all and constitute the formal basis for a civil society. The rules that distinguish a constitutional from a parliamentary or legislative democracy, however, are more specific in nature. Such rules, designed to endure across successive governments, constrain the authority of the democratic political process in order to protect individuals from the transient temptations of in-period politics.

To the extent that such rules are sheltered from repeal by supramajority vote requirements, they must be viewed as obstructing the democratic political process as conventionally conceived (Rowley 1990). Inevitably, therefore, a tension exists between the constitutional parchment and the elected legislature, whenever the former threatens to constrain the discretionary authority of the latter. In the case of rules designed to secure unilateral free trade, this tension must be universally present.

Why then might unilateral free trade prove attractive from a constitutional perspective while remaining unattractive as a legislative option? The answer to this conundrum lies in the recognition that political markets fail to achieve economic efficiency in the absence of effective constitutional constraints.

Buchanan and Tullock (1962) confronted the market failure presumption of the new welfare economics by demonstrating that the problems associated with markets were ubiquitous, indeed entering into the calculus of political consent with much greater significance because of the indivisibility of collective choice. Politics is plagued by such problems as externalities, public goods, information and transaction costs. Recognition of this reality by individuals deliberating under conditions of uncertainty determines the constitutional range and extent of government as well as the voting rules to be applied over the constrained space of collective choice.

The emphasis placed on choosing among constraints rather than choosing subject to constraints distinguishes constitutional political economy from public choice (Buchanan 1990). Individuals make constitutional choices behind a veil of uncertainty, since rules, once established, are extremely difficult to adjust and are likely to be durable. In such circumstances, individuals find it difficult to identify their own special interests and instead fall back on generalized criteria, thus allowing gains from trade to dominate over redistributive considerations. At the constitutional level, a rule requiring unilateral free trade conceivably might achieve a supramajority vote even though a legislative vote on the same issue would surely fail.

The constitutional route to free trade can be accomplished only with respect to unilateralism. The multilateral route to free trade must traverse the anarchic jungle of international relations using a precarious network of international agreements, treaties and international agencies to obviate the protectionist impulses of public choice. In the absence of an effective international legal system, nation-states renege upon international agreements whenever it is advantageous so to do. The most powerful nation-states pursue multilateral free trade, to the extent that it suits their short-term interests, through the use of guns rather than parchment, as late twentieth-century US strategic trade policy clearly indicates. The less-powerful nations that do not rejoice in unilateral free trade are prey to such self-seeking predators.

The conventional wisdom of international economics is that free trade is preserved and protected by the GATT concluded in October 1947, initially between 23 nation-states and subsequently amended to create the World Trade Organization. This wisdom is misplaced. From the outset, the GATT was always an instrument of managed rather than of free trade. Although on balance its contributions have been trade liberalizing, its role as international policeman increasingly has been subverted by forces of protection (Rowley et al. 1995).

When giant traders such as the United States and the European Community determine, as they do, to play fast and loose with the GATT rules, there is a real danger that the entire GATT constitution will be destroyed. As the twentieth century draws to a close, the multilateral thrust of the GATT and its successor is gravely threatened by the misuse of non-tariff barriers, by the misuse of fair trade laws, by the misuse of regionalism loopholes and by resort to strategic trade policies. The principal transgressors of the GATT code are no longer the small developing nations. They are the rich and greedy nation-states of Western Europe and North America that have reactivated policies of mercantilism so wisely rejected by Great Britain in 1846.

The unilateral route is the only effective route to free trade in a world dominated by nation-states. For unilateral free trade to survive the predations of public choice it must be enshrined as a constitutional commitment. This is a formidable goal. In 1979, Friedman and Friedman contemplated a free trade amendment to the United States Constitution. This amendment would guarantee the right of the people to buy and sell legitimate goods and services at mutually acceptable terms and would eliminate the power of the US Congress to tax and to restrict foreign trade. Sheepishly, Friedman and Friedman (1979, p. 304) concluded that it was 'visionary to suppose that such an amendment could be enacted now'.

Good scholars should never falter at the hurdle of political impossibility when they know their case to be strong. If they do so, the case will rightly fail by default. The history of classical liberal political economy clearly demonstrates that there is no such thing as political impossibility. If a compelling case is forcefully argued and tested in the relevant political environment it may well succeed. The case for unilateral free trade is impeccably strong. It can be argued at the constitutional level in any country whose citizens desire to be wealthy and to be free. Of course, the case needs an effective advocate, prepared perhaps to sacrifice short-term power for immortal fame. Free trade awaits the next Robert Peel. Let us hope that it does not have long to wait and that some far-sighted electorate seizes the opportunity to show the mercantilist superpowers the error of their ways.

Note
1.   Smith was here replying to Sir John Sinclair of Ulster who, in lamenting the misfortunes of the Revolutionary War, exclaimed: 'if we go on at this rate, the nation *must be ruined*'. Quoted in Smith ([1977] 1987, p. 262; emphasis in original).

References

Abramowitz, Alan (1988), 'Explaining Senate election outcomes', *American Political Science Review*, **82**, 385–403.

Acheson, Keith and John F. Chant (1973) 'Bureaucratic theory and the choice of central bank goals', *Journal of Money, Credit and Banking*, **5**, 637–55.

Ackerman, Bruce A. and William T. Hassler (1981), *Clean Air/Dirty Air, or How the Clean Air Act Became a Multibillion Dollar Bailout to High-Sulfur Coal Producers and What Should Be Done about It*, New Haven, CT: Yale University Press.

Ades, A.F. and E.L. Glaser (1995), 'Trade and circuses: explaining urban giants', *Quarterly Journal of Economics*, **110**, 195–227.

Akerlof, George (1980), 'A theory of social custom of which unemployment may be one consequence', *Quarterly Journal of Economics*, **94**, 749–75.

Akerman, Johan (1947), 'Political economic cycles', *Kyklos*, **1**, 107–17.

Alchian, Armen A. (1965a), 'The basis of some recent advances in the theory of management of the firm', *Journal of Industrial Economics*, **14**, 30–41.

Alchian, Armen A. (1965b), 'Some economics of property rights', *Il Politico*, **30**, 816–29.

Alchian, Armen A. (1967), 'How should prices be set?', *Il Politico*, **32**, 369–82.

Alchian, Armen A. (1984), 'Specificity, specialization, and coalitions', *Journal of Institutional and Theoretical Economics*, **140**, 34–49.

Alchian, Armen A. and Harold Demsetz (1972), 'Production, information costs, and economic organization', *American Economic Review*, **62**, 777–95.

Aldrich, John (1993), 'Rational choice and turnout', *American Journal of Political Science*, **37**, 246–78.

Aldrich, John and David Rohde (1998), 'The transition to Republican rules in the House: implications for theories of congressional politics', *Political Science Quarterly*, **112**, 541–67.

Alesina, Alberto (1988), 'Macroeconomics and politics', in Stanley Fischer (ed.), *NBER Macroeconomics Annual*, Chicago: NBER, pp. 13–61.

Alesina, Alberto, Gerald D. Cohen and Nouriel Source Roubini (1993), 'Electoral business cycles in industrial democracies', *European Journal of Political Economy*, **9**, 1–23.

Alesina, Alberto and Dani Rodrik (1994), 'Distributive politics and economic growth', *Quarterly Journal of Economics*, **109**, 465–90.

Alesina, Alberto and Howard Rosenthal (1995), *Partisan Politics, Divided Government, and the Economy*, Cambridge: Cambridge University Press.

Alesina, Alberto and Nouriel Roubini with Gerald D. Cohen (1997), *Political Cycles and the Macroeconomy*, Cambridge, MA: MIT Press.

Alesina, Alberto and Guido Tabellini (1990), 'A positive theory of deficits and government debt', *Review of Economic Studies*, **57**, 403–14.

Ali, Abdiweli M. (1997), 'Economic freedom, democracy and growth', *Journal of Private Enterprise*, **13**, 1–18.

Allen, S., D. McCrickard, P. Cartwright and C. Delorme (1988), 'The use of inputs by the Federal Reserve System: an extended model', *Public Choice*, **59**, 205–14.

Alm, James (1985), 'The welfare cost of the underground economy', *Economic Inquiry*, **24**, 243–63.

Ambrose, Stephen E. (1997), *Citizen Soldiers*, New York: Simon & Schuster.

Anderson, Gary M. (1999), 'Electoral limits', in Donald P. Racheter and Richard E. Wagner (eds), *Limiting Leviathan*, Cheltenham, UK and Northampton, MA: Edward Elgar, pp. 176–202.

Anderson, Gary M., Robert B. Ekelund, Jr and Robert D. Tollison (1987), 'Nassau Senior as economic consultant: the factory acts reconsidered', *Economica*, **56**, 71–92.

Anderson, Gary M., Dennis Halcoussis and Robert D. Tollison (1996), 'Drafting the competition: labor unions and military conscription', *Defense and Peace Economics*, **7**, 189–202.

Anderson, Gary M., Delores T. Martin, William F. Shughart II and Robert D. Tollison (1990), 'Behind the veil: the political economy of constitutional change', in W. Mark Crain and Robert D. Tollison (eds), *Predicting Politics: Essays in Empirical Public Choice*, Ann Arbor: University of Michigan Press, pp. 89–100.

Anderson, Gary M., Robert E. McCormick, and Robert D. Tollison (1983), 'The economic organization of the East India Company', *Journal of Economic Behavior and Organization*, **4**, 221–38.

Anderson, Gary M., Charles K. Rowley and Robert D. Tollison (1988a), 'Rent seeking and the restriction of human exchange', *Journal of Legal Studies*, **17**, 83–100.

Anderson, Gary M., William F. Shughart II and Robert D. Tollison (1988b), 'A public choice theory of the great contraction', *Public Choice*, **59**, 3–23.

Anderson, Gary M., William F. Shughart II and Robert D. Tollison (1989), 'On the incentives of judges to enforce legislative wealth transfers', *Journal of Law and Economics*, **32**, 215–28.

Anderson, Gary M. and Robert D. Tollison (1983a), 'Apologiae for chartered monopolies in foreign trade, 1600–1800', *History of Political Economy*, **15**, 549–66.

Anderson, Gary M. and Robert D. Tollison (1983b), 'The myth of the corporation as a creation of the state', *International Review of Law and Economics*, **3**, 107–20.

Anderson, Gary M. and Robert D. Tollison (1984), 'A rent-seeking explanation of the British factory acts', in David C. Collander (ed.), *Neoclassical Political Economy: The Analysis of Rent-Seeking and DUP Activities*, Cambridge, MA: Ballinger, pp. 187–201.

Anderson, Gary M. and Robert D. Tollison (1991a), 'Congressional influence and patterns of New Deal spending, 1933–1939', *Journal of Law and Economics*, **34**, 161–76.

Anderson, Gary M. and Robert D. Tollison (1991b), 'Political influence on Civil War mortality rates: the Electoral College as a battlefield', *Defense Economics*, **2**, 219–33.

Anderson, Gary M. and Robert D. Tollison (1993), 'Barristers and barriers: Sir Edward Coke and the regulation of trade', *Cato Journal*, **13**, 49–67.

Anderson, Terry L. and P.J. Hill (1975), 'The evolution of property rights: a study of the American West', *Journal of Law and Economics*, **18**, 163–79.

Anderson, Terry L. and P.J. Hill (1980), *The Birth of the Transfer Society*, Stanford, CA: Hoover Institute Press.

Anderson, Terry L. and Donald R. Leal (1991), *Free Market Environmentalism*, San Francisco: Pacific Research Institute for Public Policy.

Andreoni, James (1988a), 'Privately provided public goods in a large economy: the limits of altruism', *Journal of Public Economics*, **35**, 57–73.

Andreoni, James (1988b), 'Why free ride? Strategies and learning in public good experiments', *Journal of Public Economics*, **37**, 291–304.

Andreoni, James (1995a), 'Cooperation in public goods experiments: kindness or confusion?', *American Economic Review*, **85**, 891–904.

Andreoni, James (1995b), 'Warm-glow versus cold-prickle: the effects of positive and negative framing on cooperation in experiments', *Quarterly Journal of Economics*, **110**, 1–21.

Andreoni, James and Rachel Croson (2000), 'Partners versus strangers: random rematching in public goods experiments', in Charles R. Plott and Vernon L. Smith (eds), *The Handbook of Experimental Economics Results*, Amsterdam: North-Holland, forthcoming.

Andres, G. (1985), 'Business involvement in campaign finance: factors influencing the decision to form a corporate PAC', *PS*, **18**, 156–81.

Aranson, Peter M. (1986), 'Economic efficiency and the common law: a critical survey', in J.-Mathais Graf von der Schulenberg and Goran Skogh (eds), *Law and Economics and the Economics of Legal Regulation*, Dordrecht: Kluwer Academic Publishers, pp. 51–84.

Aranson, Peter M. (1990), 'Theories of economic regulation: from clarity to confusion', *Journal of Law and Politics*, **6**, 247–86.

Aristotle ([c. 350 BCE] 1979), *Politics and Poetics*, trans. by Benjamin Jowett and S. H. Butcher, Norwalk, CT.: Easton Press.

Arrow, Kenneth J. ([1951] 1963), *Social Choice and Individual Values*, 2nd edn, New Haven, CT: Yale University Press.

Arrow, Kenneth J. ([1950] 1983), 'A difficulty in the concept of social welfare', in *The Collected Papers of Kenneth J. Arrow*, vol. 1: *Social Choice and Justice*, Cambridge, MA: Belknap Press of Harvard University Press, pp. 1–29.

Arrow, Kenneth J. ([1977] 1983), 'Extended sympathy and the possibility of social choice', in *The Collected Papers of Kenneth J. Arrow*, vol. 1: *Social Choice and Justice*, Cambridge, MA: Belknap Press of Harvard University Press, pp. 147–61.

Arrow, Kenneth J. ([1986] 1995), 'Kenneth J. Arrow', in William Breit and Roger W. Spencer (eds), *Lives of the Laureates: Thirteen Nobel Economists*, 3rd edn, Cambridge, MA: MIT Press, pp. 34–58.

Arthur, W. Brian (1989), 'Competing technologies, increasing returns, and lock-in by historical events', *Economic Journal*, **99**, 116–31.

Ashenfelter, Orley, T. Eisenberg and S.J. Schwab (1995), 'Politics and the judiciary: the influence of judicial background on case outcomes', *Journal of Legal Studies*, **24**, 257–81.

Atkinson, A.B. (1995), *Public Economics in Action: The Basic Income/Flat Tax Proposal*, Oxford: Clarendon Press.

Ault, Richard W. and Robert B. Ekelund, Jr (1988), 'Habits in economic analysis: Veblen and the neoclassicals', *History of Political Economy*, **20**, 431–45.

Austen-Smith, David (1992), 'Explaining the vote: constituency constraints on sophisticated voting', *American Journal of Political Science*, **36**, 68–96.

Axelrod, Robert (1984), *The Evolution of Cooperation*, New York: Basic Books.

Azfar, Omar (1998), 'Sufficient conditions for rapid convergence', unpublished manuscript, IRIS Center, University of Maryland.

Azzi, Corry and Ronald G. Ehrenberg (1975), 'Household allocation of time and church attendance', *Journal of Political Economy*, **83**, 27–56.

Baack, Bennett D. and Edward J. Ray (1985), 'Special interests and the adoption of the income tax in the United States', *Journal of Economic History*, **45**, 607–25.

Bailey, Michael A. and Kelly H. Chang (1999), 'Influencing the court: a formal and empirical analysis of Supreme Court appointments', unpublished manuscript.

Baker, George P., Michael C. Jensen and Kevin J. Murphy (1988), 'Compensation and incentives: practice versus theory', *Journal of Finance*, **43**, 593–616.

Baker, John H. (1971), *An Introduction to English Legal History*, London: Butterworths.

Banks, A.S. (ed.) (1993), *Political Handbook of the World 1993*, Binghamton, NY: CSA Publications.

Banks, Jeffrey S. (1989), 'Agency budgets, cost information and auditing', *American Journal of Political Science*, **33**, 670–99.

Banks, Jeffrey S., Charles R. Plott and David P. Porter (1988), 'An experimental analysis of unanimity in public goods provision mechanisms', *Review of Economic Studies*, **55**, 301–22.

Banks, Jeffrey S. and Rangarajan K. Sundaram (1998), 'Optimal retention in agency problems', *Journal of Economic Theory*, **82**, 293–310.

Banks, Jeffrey S. and Barry R. Weingast (1992), 'The political control of bureaucracies under asymmetric information', *American Journal of Political Science*, **36**, 509–24.

Barber, Benjamin (1984), *Strong Democracy: Participatory Politics for a New Age*, Berkeley: University of California Press.

Barlow, Robin (1970), 'Efficiency aspects of local school finance', *Journal of Political Economy*, **78**, 1028–40.

Barnett, A.H., T. Randolph Beard and David L. Kaserman (1993), 'Inefficient pricing can kill: the case of dialysis industry regulation', *Southern Economic Journal*, **60**, 393–404.

Barnett, Harold C. (1985), 'The allocation of Superfund, 1981–1983', *Land Economics*, **61**, 255–62.

Barr, J.L. and O.A. Davis (1966), 'An elementary political and economic theory of the expenditures of state and local governments', *Southern Economic Journal*, **33**, 149–65.

Barro, Robert J. (1973), 'The control of politicians: an economic model', *Public Choice*, **14**, 19–42.

Barro, Robert J. (1974), 'Are government bonds net wealth?', *Journal of Political Economy*, **82**, 1095–117.

Barro, Robert J. (1990), 'Government spending in a simple model of endogenous growth', *Journal of Political Economy*, **98**, S103–S125.

Barro, Robert J. (1991), 'Economic growth in a cross-section of countries', *Quarterly Journal of Economics*, **106**, 407–43.

Barro, Robert J. (1996), 'Democracy and growth', *Journal of Economic Growth*, **1**, 1–27.

Barro, Robert J. and Donald B. Gordon (1983), 'Rules, discretion, and reputation in a model of monetary policy', *Journal of Monetary Economics*, **12**, 101–21.

Barro, Robert J. and Xavier Sala-i-Martin (1991), 'Convergence across states and regions', *Brookings Papers on Economic Activity*, **1**, 107–82.

Barrow, Deborah J., Gary Zuk and Gerard S. Gryski (1996), *The Federal*

Judiciary and Institutional Change, Ann Arbor: University of Michigan Press.

Bartel, Ann P. and Lacy Glenn Thomas (1987), 'Predation through regulation: the wage and profit effects of the Occupational Safety and Health Administration and the Environmental Protection Agency', *Journal of Law and Economics*, **30**, 239–64.

Barzel, Yoram (1989), *Economic Analysis of Property Rights*, Cambridge: Cambridge University Press.

Barzel, Yoram (1997), 'Parliament as a wealth maximizing institution: the right to the residual and the right to vote', *International Review of Law and Economics*, **17**, 455–74.

Barzel, Yoram and Tim R. Sass (1990), 'The allocation of resources by voting', *Quarterly Journal of Economics*, **105**, 745–71.

Barzel, Yoram and Eugene Silberberg (1973), 'Is the act of voting rational?', *Public Choice*, **16**, 51–8.

Basuchoudhary, Atin, Paul Pecorino and William F. Shughart II (1999), 'Reversal of fortune: the politics and economics of the superconducting supercollider', *Public Choice*, **100**, 185–210.

Bator, Francis M. (1957), 'The simple analytics of welfare maximization', *American Economic Review*, **47**, 22–59.

Bator, Francis M. (1958), 'The anatomy of market failure', *Quarterly Journal of Economics*, **72**, 351–79.

Bauer, Peter T. (1972), *Dissent on Development: Studies and Debates on Development Economics*, Cambridge, MA: Harvard University Press.

Bauer, Peter T. and Basil S. Yamey (1957), *The Economics of Underdeveloped Countries*, Chicago: University of Chicago Press.

Baumol, William J. (1967), 'Macroeconomics of unbalanced growth: the anatomy of urban crisis', *American Economic Review*, **57**, 415–26.

Baumol, William J. and Wallace E. Oates (1975), *The Theory of Environmental Policy*, Englewood Cliffs, NJ: Prentice-Hall.

Bawn, Kathleen (1995), 'Political control versus expertise: congressional choices about administrative procedures', *American Political Science Review*, **89**, 62–73.

Beard, Charles A. ([1913] 1986), *An Economic Interpretation of the Constitution of the United States*, New York: Free Press.

Beattie, J.M. (1986), *Crime and the Courts in England, 1660–1800*, Oxford: Clarendon Press.

Beck, Nathaniel (1990a), 'Congress and the Fed: why the dog does not bark at night', in Thomas Mayer (ed.), *The Political Economy of American Monetary Policy*, Cambridge: Cambridge University Press, pp. 131–50.

Beck, Nathaniel (1990b), 'Political monetary cycles', in Thomas Mayer (ed.),

The Political Economy of American Monetary Policy, Cambridge: Cambridge University Press, pp. 115–30.

Beck, R., Colin Hoskins and J.M. Connolly (1992), 'Rent extraction through political extortion: an empirical examination', *Journal of Legal Studies*, **21**, 217–24.

Becker, Gary S. (1974), *Essays in the Economics of Crime and Punishment*, New York: Columbia University Press.

Becker, Gary S. (1976a), 'Comment', *Journal of Law and Economics*, **19**, 245–8.

Becker, Gary S. (1976b), *The Economic Approach to Human Behavior*, Chicago: University of Chicago Press.

Becker, Gary S. (1981), *A Treatise on the Family*, Cambridge, MA: Harvard University Press.

Becker, Gary S. (1983), 'A theory of competition among pressure groups for political influence', *Quarterly Journal of Economics*, **98**, 371–400.

Becker, Gary S. (1985), 'Public policies, pressure groups, and dead weight costs', *Journal of Public Economics*, **28**, 329–47.

Becker, Gary S. and George J. Stigler (1974), 'Law enforcement, malfeasance, and compensation of enforcers', *Journal of Legal Studies*, **3**, 1–18.

Bell, F.W. (1986), 'Mitigating the tragedy of the commons', *Southern Economic Journal*, **52**, 653–64.

Ben-Porath, Yoram (1975), 'The years of plenty and the years of famine – a political business cycle?', *Kyklos*, **28**, 400–403.

Bender, Bruce and John R. Lott, Jr (1996), 'Legislator voting and shirking: a critical review of the literature', *Public Choice*, **87**, 67–100.

Bendor, Jonathan (1999), 'Approving bad projects and rejecting good ones: adaptive versus optimal organizational reliability', unpublished manuscript, Stanford University.

Bendor, Jonathan and Terry M. Moe (1985), 'An adaptive model of bureaucratic politics', *American Political Science Review*, **79**, 755–74.

Bendor, Jonathan, Serge Taylor and Roland van Gaalen (1985), 'Bureaucratic expertise vs. legislative authority: a model of deception and monitoring in budgeting', *American Political Science Review*, **79**, 1041–60.

Bendor, Jonathan, Serge Taylor and Roland van Gaalen (1987), 'Politicians, bureaucrats, and asymmetric information', *American Journal of Political Science*, **31**, 796–828.

Benson, Bruce L. (1984), 'Rent seeking from a property rights perspective', *Southern Economic Journal*, **51**, 388–400.

Benson, Bruce L. (1988), 'Legal evolution in primitive societies', *Journal of Institutional and Theoretical Economics*, **144**, 772–88.

Benson, Bruce L. (1989), 'The spontaneous evolution of commercial law', *Southern Economic Journal*, **55**, 644–61.

Benson, Bruce L. (1991), 'An evolutionary contractarian view of primitive law: the institutions and incentives arising under customary American Indian law', *Review of Austrian Economics*, **5**, 65–89.

Benson, Bruce L. (1992a), 'Customary law as a social contract: international commercial law', *Constitutional Political Economy*, **2**, 1–27.

Benson, Bruce L. (1992b), 'The development of criminal law and its enforcement: public interest or political transfers?', *Journal des Economistes et des Etudes Humaines*, **3**, 79–108.

Benson, Bruce L. (1994a), 'Are public goods really common pools? Considerations of the evolution of policing and highways in England', *Economic Inquiry*, **32**, 249–71.

Benson, Bruce L. (1994b), 'Emerging from the Hobbesian jungle: might takes and makes rights', *Constitutional Political Economy*, **5**, 129–58.

Benson, Bruce L. (1995a), 'An exploration of the impact of modern arbitration statutes on the development of arbitration in the United States', *Journal of Law, Economics and Organization*, **11**, 479–501.

Benson, Bruce L. (1995b), 'Understanding bureaucratic behavior: implications from the public choice literature', *Journal of Public Finance and Public Choice*, **8**, 89–117.

Benson, Bruce L. (1996), 'Uncertainty, the race for property rights, and rent dissipation due to judicial changes in product liability tort law', *Cultural Dynamics*, **8**, 333–51.

Benson, Bruce L. (1997a), 'Endogenous morality', unpublished manuscript, Florida State University.

Benson, Bruce (1997b), 'Institutions and the spontaneous evolution of morality', in G. Radnitzky (ed.), *Values and the Social Order*, vol. 3: *Voluntary versus Coercive Orders*, Aldershot, UK: Avebury, pp. 245–82.

Benson, Bruce L. (1998a), 'An economic theory of the evolution of governance and the emergence of the state', unpublished manuscript, Florida State University.

Benson, Bruce L. (1998b), 'Arbitration in the shadow of the law', in Peter Newman (ed.), *The New Palgrave Dictionary of Economics and the Law*, vol. I, London: Macmillan and New York: Stockton Press, pp. 93–8.

Benson, Bruce L. (1998c), 'Common law versus judge-made law', unpublished manuscript, Florida State University.

Benson, Bruce L. (1998d), 'Evolution of commercial law', in Peter Newman (ed.), *The New Palgrave Dictionary of Economics and the Law*, vol. II, London: Macmillan and New York: Stockton Press, pp. 89–92.

Benson, Bruce L. (1998e), 'Law Merchant', in Peter Newman (ed.), *The New Palgrave Dictionary of Economics and the Law*, vol. II, London: Macmillan and New York: Stockton Press, pp. 500–508.

Benson, Bruce L. (1998f), 'Regulation, more regulation, deregulation, and reregulation: the dynamics of a rent-seeking society', unpublished manuscript, Florida State University.

Benson, Bruce L. (1998g), *To Serve and Protect: Privatization and Community in Criminal Justice*, New York: New York University Press.

Benson, Bruce L. (2000), 'Arbitration', in Boudewijn Bouckaert and Gerrit De Geest (eds), *Encyclopedia of Law and Economics*, vol. V, Cheltenham, UK and Northampton, MA: Edward Elgar, pp. 159–93.

Benson, Bruce L. and Gary Fournier (1998), 'Jury composition as a determinant of changes in civil damage awards', unpublished manuscript, Florida State University.

Benson, Bruce L., David W. Rasmussen and David L. Sollars (1995), 'Police bureaucrats, their incentives, and the war on drugs', *Public Choice*, **83**, 21–45.

Bentley, A.F. (1908), *The Process of Government*, Chicago: University of Chicago Press.

Berelson, Bernard R., Paul F. Lazarsfeld and William H. McPhee (1954), *Voting: A Study of Opinion Formation in a Presidential Election*, Chicago: University of Chicago Press.

Bergson, Abraham (1938), 'A reformulation of certain aspects of welfare economics', *Quarterly Journal of Economics*, **52**, 310–34.

Bergson, Abraham (1948), 'Socialist economics', in H.S. Ellis (ed.), *A Survey of Contemporary Economics*, vol. 1, Philadelphia: Blakiston, pp. 412–48.

Bergstrom, Theodore C., Lawrence Blume and Hal R. Varian (1986), 'On the private provision of public goods', *Journal of Public Economics*, **29**, 25–49.

Berman, Harold J. (1983), *Law and Revolution: The Formation of Western Legal Tradition*, Cambridge, MA: Harvard University Press.

Berman, Harold J. and Felix J. Dasser (1990), 'The "new" Law Merchant and the "old": sources, content, and legitimacy', in Thomas E. Carbonneau (ed.), *Lex Mercatoria and Arbitration: A Discussion of the New Law Merchant*, Dobbs Ferry, NY: Transnational Juris Publications, pp. 21–36.

Bernard, Andrew B. (1992), 'Empirical implications of the convergence hypothesis', unpublished manuscript, MIT.

Bernard, Andrew B. and Steven N. Durlauf (1996), 'Interpreting tests of the convergence hypothesis', *Journal of Econometrics*, **71**, 161–73.

Bernheim, B. Douglas and Michael D. Whinston (1986), 'Menu auctions, resource allocation, and economic influence', *Quarterly Journal of Economics*, **101**, 1–31.

Bernstein, Lisa (1992), 'Opting out of the legal system: extralegal contractual relations in the diamond industry', *Journal of Legal Studies*, **21**, 115–58.

Bernstein, Richard (1994), *Dictatorship of Virtue: Multiculturalism and the Battle for America's Future*, New York: Knopf.

Besley, Timothy and S. Coate (1997), 'An economic model of representative democracy', *Quarterly Journal of Economics*, **112**, 85–114.

Besley, Timothy and S. Coate (1998), 'Sources of inefficiency in a representative democracy: a dynamic analysis', *American Economic Review*, **88**, 139–56.

Bewes, W.A. (1923), *The Romance of the Law Merchant: Being an Introduction to the Study of International and Commercial Law with Some Account of the Commerce and Fairs of the Middle Ages*, London: Sweet & Maxwell.

Bhagwati, Jagdish (1988), *Protectionism*, Cambridge, MA: MIT Press.

Bianco, William (1994), *Trust: Representatives and Constituents*, Ann Arbor: University of Michigan Press.

Black, Duncan (1948a), 'On the rationale of group decision-making', *Journal of Political Economy*, **56**, 22–34.

Black, Duncan (1948b), 'The decisions of a committee using a special majority', *Econometrica*, **16**, 245–61.

Black, Duncan ([1958] 1987), *The Theory of Committees and Elections*, Boston and Dordrecht: Kluwer Academic Publishers.

Blin, Jean-Marie and Mark Satterthwaite (1978), 'Individual decisions and group decisions', *Journal of Public Economics*, **10**, 247–67.

Blumberg, Abraham (1970), *Criminal Justice*, Chicago: Quadrangle Books.

Boies, John (1989), 'Money, business and the state: material interests, Fortune 500 corporations and the size of political action committees', *American Sociological Review*, **54**, 821–33.

Bolton, John (1980), 'Constitutional limitations on restricting corporate and union political speech', *Arizona Law Review*, **22**, 373–421.

Booth, Alison L. (1984), 'A public choice model of trade union behavior and membership', *Economic Journal*, **94**, 883–98.

Booth, Alison L. (1985), 'The free rider problem and a social custom model of trade union membership', *Quarterly Journal of Economics*, **100**, 253–61.

Borcherding, Thomas E. (1985), 'The causes of government expenditure growth: a survey of the US evidence', *Journal of Public Economics*, **28**, 359–82.

Borda, Jean-Charles de (1781), 'Mémoire sur les élections au scrutin', *Histoire de l'Académie Royale des Sciences*, in Duncan Black ([1958] 1987), *The Theory of Committees and Elections*, Boston and Dordrecht: Kluwer Academic Publishers, pp. 156–9.

Border, Kim (1984), 'An impossibility theorem for spatial models', *Public Choice*, **43**, 293–306.

Borner, Silvio, Aymo Brunetti and Beatrice Weder (1995), *Political Credibility and Economic Development*, New York: St Martin's Press.

Boudreaux, Donald J. (1996a), 'The Coase theorem and strategic bargaining', *Advances in Austrian Economics*, **3**, 95–105.

Boudreaux, Donald J. (1996b), 'Was your high school civics teacher right after all? Donald Wittman's *The Myth of Democratic Failure*', *Independent Review*, **1**, 111–28.

Boudreaux, Donald J., Thomas J. DiLorenzo and Steven Parker (1995), 'Antitrust before the Sherman Act', in Fred S. McChesney and William F. Shughart II (eds), *The Causes and Consequences of Antitrust: The Public Choice Perspective*, Chicago: University of Chicago Press, pp. 255–70.

Boudreaux, Donald J. and Roger E. Meiners (1998), 'Existence values and others of life's ills', in P.J. Hill and Roger E. Meiners (eds), *Who Owns the Environment?*, Lanham, MD: Rowman & Littlefield, pp. 153–85.

Brams, Steven J. and Peter Fishburn (1984), *Approval Voting*, Boston: Birkhauser.

Brams, Steven J. and Jack H. Nagel (1991), 'Approval voting in practice', *Public Choice*, **71**, 1–18.

Brehm, John (1993), *The Phantom Respondents: Opinion Surveys and Political Representation*, Ann Arbor: University of Michigan Press.

Brennan, H. Geoffrey (1990), 'The tale of the slave-owner: reflections on the political economy of communist reform', Virginia Political Economy Lecture Series, Fairfax, VA: George Mason University.

Brennan, H. Geoffrey and James M. Buchanan (1980), *The Power to Tax: Analytical Foundations of a Fiscal Constitution*, Cambridge: Cambridge University Press.

Brennan, H. Geoffrey and James M. Buchanan (1984), 'Voter choice: evaluating political alternatives', *American Behavioral Scientist*, **28**, 185–201.

Brennan, H. Geoffrey and James M. Buchanan (1985), *The Reason of Rules*, Cambridge: Cambridge University Press.

Brennan, H. Geoffrey and James M. Buchanan (1988), 'Is public choice immoral? The case for the "Nobel" lie', *Virginia Law Review*, **74**, 179–89.

Brennan, H. Geoffrey and José Casas Pardo (1991), 'A reading of the Spanish Constitution', *Constitutional Political Economy*, **2**, 53–79.

Brennan, H. Geoffrey and Alan P. Hamlin (1995), 'Constitutional political economy: the political philosophy of *Homo economicus*', *Journal of Political Philosophy*, **3**, 280–303.

Brennan, H. Geoffrey and Alan P. Hamlin (1998a), 'Constitutional economics', in Peter Newman (ed.), *The New Palgrave Dictionary of Economics and the Law*, Vol. I, London: Macmillan and New York: Stockton Press, pp. 401–9.

Brennan, H. Geoffrey and Alan P. Hamlin (1998b), 'Expressive voting and electoral equilibrium', *Public Choice*, **95**, 149–75.

Brennan, H. Geoffrey and Alan P. Hamlin (1999), 'On political representation', *British Journal of Political Science*, **29**, 109–27.

Brennan, H. Geoffrey and Alan P. Hamlin (2000), *Democratic Devices and Desires*, Cambridge: Cambridge University Press.

Brennan, H. Geoffrey and Loren Lomasky (1993), *Democracy and Decision: The Pure Theory of Electoral Preference*, Cambridge: Cambridge University Press.

Brennan, H. Geoffrey and Gordon Tullock (1982), 'An economic theory of military tactics', *Journal of Economic Behavior and Organization*, **3**, 225–42.

Breton, Albert (1991), 'The organization of competition in congressional and parliamentary governments', in Albert Breton, Gianluigi Galeotti, Pierre Salmon and Ronald Wintrobe (eds), *The Competitive State: Villa Colombella Papers on Competitive Politics*, Dordrecht: Kluwer Academic Publishers, pp. 13–38.

Breton, Albert and Ronald Wintrobe (1975), 'The equilibrium size of a budget-maximizing bureau: a note on Niskanen's theory of bureaucracy', *Journal of Political Economy*, **82**, 195–207.

Breton, Albert and Ronald Wintrobe (1982), *The Logic of Bureaucratic Conduct*, Cambridge: Cambridge University Press.

Brown, Donald (1974), 'An approximate solution to Arrow's problem', *Journal of Economic Theory*, **9**, 375–83.

Brown-Kruse, Jamie and David Hummels (1993), 'Gender effects in laboratory public goods contribution: do individuals put their money where their mouth is?', *Journal of Economic Behavior and Organization*, **22**, 255–67.

Browning, Edgar K. (1976), 'The marginal cost of public funds', *Journal of Political Economy*, **84**, 283–98.

Broz, Lawrence (1997), *The International Origins of the Federal Reserve System*, Ithaca: Cornell University Press.

Brozen, Yale (1990), 'The economic impact of government policy', in K. Groenveld, J.A.H. Maks and J. Muysken (eds), *Economic Policy and the Market Process: Austrian and Mainstream Economics*, Amsterdam: North-Holland, pp. 65–106.

Brubaker, E. (1998), 'The common law and the environment: the Canadian experience', in P.J. Hill and Roger E. Meiners (eds), *Who Owns the Environment?*, Lanham, MD: Rowman & Littlefield, pp. 87–118.

Brunet, Edward (1987), 'Questioning the quality of alternative dispute resolution', *Tulane Law Review*, **62**, 1–56.

Brunetti, Aymo (1997), *Politics and Economic Growth: A Cross-Country Data Perspective*, Paris: OECD.

Brunetti, Aymo and Beatrice Weder (1995), 'Political sources of growth: a critical note on measurement', *Public Choice*, **82**, 125–34.

Bryce, James ([1873] 1904), *The Holy Roman Empire*, rev. edn, New York and London: Macmillan.

Buchanan, James M. (1954), 'Social choice, democracy, and free markets', *Journal of Political Economy*, **62**, 114–23.

Buchanan, James M. (1965a), 'An economic theory of clubs', *Economica*, **32**, 1–14.

Buchanan, James M. (1965b), 'Ethical rules, expected values, and large numbers', *Ethics*, **76**, 1–13.

Buchanan, James M. (1967), *Public Finance and Democratic Process*, Chapel Hill: University of North Carolina Press.

Buchanan, James M. (1968), *Demand and Supply of Public Goods*, Chicago: Rand-McNally.

Buchanan, James M. (1969), *Cost and Choice: An Inquiry in Economic Theory*, Chicago: University of Chicago Press.

Buchanan, James M. (1972), 'Toward analysis of closed behavioral systems', in James M. Buchanan and Robert D. Tollison (eds), *Theory of Public Choice*, Ann Arbor: University of Michigan Press, pp. 11–23.

Buchanan, James M. (1975a), *The Limits of Liberty: Between Anarchy and Leviathan*, Chicago: University of Chicago Press.

Buchanan, James M. (1975b), 'Public finance and public choice', *National Tax Journal*, **28**, 383–94.

Buchanan, James M. (1976), 'Taxation in fiscal exchange', *Journal of Public Economics*, **6**, 17–29.

Buchanan, James M. (1977), 'Good economics – bad law', in James M. Buchanan, *Freedom in Constitutional Contract*, College Station: Texas A&M University Press, pp. 40–49.

Buchanan, James M. (1979), 'Politics without romance: a sketch of positive public choice theory and its normative implications', *IHS Journal, Zeitschrift des Instituts für Hohere Studien*, **3**, B1–B11.

Buchanan, James M. (1985), *Ethics, Efficiency and the Market*, Oxford: Clarendon Press.

Buchanan, James M. (1987a), 'The constitution of economic policy', *American Economic Review*, **77**, 243–50.

Buchanan, James M. (1987b), 'Constitutional economics', in John Eatwell, Murray Milgate and Peter Newman (eds), *The New Palgrave Dictionary of Economics*, vol. 1, London: Macmillan, pp. 585–8.

Buchanan, James M. (1988), 'Market failure and political failure', *Cato Journal*, **8**, 1–13.

Buchanan, James M. (1990), 'The domain of constitutional economics', *Constitutional Political Economy*, **1**, 1–19.

Buchanan, James M. (1992), *Better than Plowing and Other Personal Essays*, Chicago: University of Chicago Press.

Buchanan, James M. (1999), *The Collected Works of James M. Buchanan*, vol. 1: *The Logical Foundations of Constitutional Liberty*, ed. by Geoffrey

Brennan, Hartmut Kliemt and Robert D. Tollison, Indianapolis: Liberty Fund.

Buchanan, James M. and Dwight R. Lee (1982), 'Tax rates and tax revenues in political equilibrium: some simple analytics', *Economic Inquiry*, **20**, 344–54.

Buchanan, James M. and W. Craig Stubblebine (1962), 'Externality', *Economica*, **29**, 371–84.

Buchanan, James M., Robert D. Tollison and Gordon Tullock (eds) (1980), *Toward a Theory of the Rent-Seeking Society*, College Station: Texas A&M University Press.

Buchanan, James M. and Gordon Tullock (1962), *The Calculus of Consent: Logical Foundations of Constitutional Democracy*, Ann Arbor: University of Michigan Press.

Buchanan, James M. and Gordon Tullock (1975), 'Polluters' profits and political response: direct controls versus taxes', *American Economic Review*, **65**, 139–47.

Buchanan, James M. and Viktor Vanberg (1989), 'Interests and theories in constitutional choice', *Journal of Theoretical Politics*, **1**, 49–62.

Buchanan, James M. and Richard E. Wagner (1977), *Democracy in Deficit: The Political Legacy of Lord Keynes*, San Diego, CA: Academic Press.

Burke, Edmund ([1756] 1982), *A Vindication of Natural Society. Or, a View of the Miseries and Evils Arising to Mankind from Every Species of Artificial Society. In a Letter to Lord **** by a Late Noble Writer*, ed. by Frank Pagano, Indianapolis, IN: Liberty Fund.

Burlando, Roberto and John D. Hey (1997), 'Do Anglo-Saxons free-ride more?', *Journal of Public Economics*, **64**, 41–60.

Burnham, Walter D. (1965), 'The changing shape of the American political universe', *American Political Science Review*, **59**, 7–28.

Butler, Henry N. and Larry E. Ribstein (1995), *The Corporation and the Constitution*, Washington, DC: AEI Press.

Byars, John, Robert E. McCormick, and Bruce Yandle (1999), *Economic Freedom Across America's Fifty States: A 1999 Analysis*, Indianapolis, IN: State Policy Network.

Calvert, Randall L., Mathew D. McCubbins and Barry R. Weingast (1989), 'A theory of political control and agency discretion', *American Journal of Political Science*, **33**, 588–611.

Cameron, Charles M., Albert D. Cover and Jeffrey A. Segal (1990), 'Senate voting on Supreme Court nominees: a neoinstitutional model', *American Political Science Review*, **84**, 525–35.

Campbell, Angus, Philip E. Converse, Warren E. Miller and Donald E. Stokes (1960), *The American Voter*, New York: John Wiley & Sons.

Campbell, William F. (1997), 'Review of *Sacred Trust: The Medieval Church as an Economic Firm'*, Association of Christian Economists *Bulletin*, 24–7.

Canzoneri, Matthew B. (1985), 'Monetary policy games and the role of private information', *American Economic Review*, **75**, 1056–70.

Carniero, Robert (1970), 'A theory of the origin of the state', *Science*, **169**, 207–11.

Carr, Jack and Frank Mathewson (1990), 'The economics of law firms: a study in the legal organization of the firm', *Journal of Law and Economics*, **33**, 307–30.

Carter, John R. and Michael D. Irons (1991), 'Are economists different, and if so, why?', *Journal of Economic Perspectives*, **5**, 171–8.

Casari, Marco and Charles R. Plott (1999), 'Agents monitoring each other in a common-pool resource environment', unpublished manuscript, California Institute of Technology.

Casella, Alessandra and Bruno S. Frey (1992), 'Federalism and clubs: towards an economic theory of overlapping political jurisdictions', *European Economic Review*, **36**, 639–46.

Chamberlain, John R. (1974), 'Provision of public goods as a function of group size', *American Political Science Review*, **68**, 707–16.

Chan, Kenneth S., Stuart Mestelman, Rob Moir and R. Andrew Muller (1998), 'Heterogeneity and the voluntary provision of public goods', unpublished manuscript, McMaster University.

Chandler, Alfred D., Jr (1977), *The Visible Hand: The Managerial Revolution in American Business*, Cambridge, MA: Belknap Press of Harvard University Press.

Chang, Kelly H. (1998), 'The president versus the Senate: appointments in the American system of separated powers and the Federal Reserve', unpublished manuscript, University of Wisconsin.

Chant, John F. and Keith Acheson (1972), 'The choice of monetary instruments and the theory of bureaucracy', *Public Choice*, **12**, 13–33.

Chappell, Henry W. (1982), 'Campaign contributions and congressional voting: a simultaneous Probit–Tobit model', *Review of Economics and Statistics*, **64**, 77–83.

Chappell, Henry W., Thomas Havrilesky and Rob Roy McGregor (1993), 'Partisan monetary policies: presidential impact through the power of appointment', *Quarterly Journal of Economics*, **108**, 185–218.

Chappell, Henry W., Thomas M. Havrilesky and Rob Roy McGregor (1995), 'Policymakers, institutions, and central bank decisions', *Journal of Economics and Business*, **47**, 113–36.

Chen, Yan (2000), 'Incentive-compatible mechanisms for pure public goods: a survey of experimental research', in Charles R. Plott and Vernon L.

Smith (eds), *The Handbook of Experimental Economics Results*, Amsterdam: North-Holland, forthcoming.

Chen, Yan and Charles R. Plott (1996), 'The Groves–Ledyard mechanism: An experimental study of institutional design', *Journal of Public Economics*, **59**, 335–64.

Chen, Yan and Fang-Fang Tang (1998), 'Learning and incentive compatible mechanisms for public goods provision: an experimental study', *Journal of Political Economy*, **106**, 633–62.

Cheung, Stephen N.S. (1973), 'The fable of the bees: an economic investigation', *Journal of Law and Economics*, **16**, 11–33.

Cheung, Steven N.S. (1974), 'A theory of price control', *Journal of Law and Economics*, **17**, 53–72.

Chicoine, David L., Norman Walzer and Steven C. Deller (1989), 'Representative versus direct democracy and government spending in a median voter model', *Public Finance*, **44**, 225–36.

Choi, Kwang (1983), 'A statistical test of Olson's model', in Dennis C. Mueller (ed.), *The Political Economy of Growth*, New Haven, CT: Yale University Press, pp. 57–78.

Clark, Derek and Jonathan Thomas (1995), 'Probabilistic voting, campaign contributions, and efficiency', *American Economic Review*, **85**, 254–9.

Clotfelter, Charles T. (1980), 'Tax incentives and charitable giving: evidence from a panel of taxpayers', *Journal of Public Economics*, **13**, 319–40.

Coase, Ronald H. (1937), 'The nature of the firm', *Economica*, **4**, 386–405.

Coase, Ronald H. (1960), 'The problem of social cost', *Journal of Law and Economics*, **3**, 1–44.

Coase, Ronald H. (1964), 'The regulated industries', *American Economic Review*, **54**, 194–7.

Coates, Dennis (1998), 'Additional incumbent spending really can harm (at least some) incumbents', *Public Choice*, **95**, 63–87.

Coates, Dennis and Michael C. Munger (1995), 'Win, lose, or withdraw: a categorical analysis of career patterns in the House of Representatives, 1948–1978', *Public Choice*, **83**, 95–111.

Coats, A.W. (1973), 'The interpretation of mercantilist economics: some historiographical problems', *History of Political Economy*, **5**, 449–84.

Coats, A.W. (1985), 'Mercantilism, yet again!', in P. Roggi (ed.), *Gli economisti e la politica economica*, Naples: Edizione Scientifiche Italiane, pp. 25–46.

Cohen, Mark A. (1989), 'The role of criminal sanctions in antitrust enforcement', *Contemporary Policy Issues*, **7**, 36–46.

Cohen, Mark A. (1991), 'Explaining judicial behavior or what's "unconstitutional" about the Sentencing Commission?', *Journal of Law, Economics and Organization*, **7**, 183–99.

Coleman, James S. (1966), 'The possibility of a social welfare function', *American Economic Review*, **56**, 1105–22.

Coleman, James S. (1990), *Foundations of Social Theory*, Cambridge, MA: Belknap Press of Harvard University Press.

Collander, David C. (ed.) (1984), *Neoclassical Political Economy: The Analysis of Rent-Seeking and DUP Activities*, Cambridge, MA: Ballinger.

Collie, Mellissa P. (1988), 'The legislature and distributive policy making in formal perspective', *Legislative Studies Quarterly*, **13**, 427–58.

Condorcet, Jean-Antoine-Nicolas de Caritat, Marquis de ([1785] 1994), 'Essai sur l'application de l'analyse à la probabilité des décisions rendues à la pluralité des voix' (selections), in Iain McLean and Fiona Hewitt (trans. and ed.), *Foundations of Social Choice and Political Theory*, Aldershot, UK and Brookfield, VT: Edward Elgar, pp. 131–8.

Congleton, Roger D (1991), 'Ideological conviction and persuasion in the rent-seeking society', *Journal of Public Economics*, **44**, 65–86.

Congleton, Roger D. (1992), 'Political institutions and pollution control', *Review of Economics and Statistics*, **74**, 413–21.

Congleton, Roger D. and William F. Shughart II (1990), 'The growth of social security: electoral push or political pull?', *Economic Inquiry*, **28**, 109–32.

Cornes, Richard and Todd Sandler ([1986] 1996), *The Theory of Externalities, Public Goods, and Club Goods*, 2nd edn, New York: Cambridge University Press.

Couch, Jim F. and William F. Shughart II (1998), *The Political Economy of the New Deal*, Cheltenham, UK and Northampton, MA: Edward Elgar.

Coughlin, Peter J. (1992), *Probabilistic Voting Theory*, Cambridge: Cambridge University Press.

Coughlin, Peter J. and Shmuel Nitzan (1981), 'Electoral outcomes with probabilistic voting and Nash social welfare maxima', *Journal of Public Economics*, **15**, 113–22.

Courant, Paul, Edward Gramlich and Daniel Rubinfeld (1979), 'The stimulative effects of intergovernmental grants: or why money sticks where it hits', in Peter Miezkowski and William Oakland (eds), *Fiscal Federalism and Grants in Aid*, Washington, DC: Urban Institute, pp. 5–21.

Cox, Gary W. (1984), 'Strategic electoral choice in multi-member districts: approval voting in practice?', *American Journal of Political Science*, **28**, 722–38.

Cox, Gary W. (1987), 'Electoral equilibrium under alternative voting institutions', *American Journal of Political Science*, **31**, 82–108.

Cox, Gary W. (1990), 'Centripetal and centrifugal incentives in electoral systems', *American Journal of Political Science*, **34**, 903–35.

Cox, Gary W. (1997), *Making Votes Count: Strategic Coordination in the World's Electoral Systems*, New York: Cambridge University Press.

Cox, Gary W. and Eric Magar (1999), 'How much is majority status in the U.S. Congress worth?', *American Political Science Review*, **93**, 299–309.

Cox, Gary W. and Mathew D. McCubbins (1993), *Legislative Leviathan: Party Government in the House*, Berkeley: University of California Press.

Cox, Gary W. and Michael C. Munger (1989), 'Contributions, expenditure, turnout: the 1982 US House elections', *American Political Science Review*, **83**, 217–31.

Cox, Gary W. and Michael C. Munger (1991), 'Putting last things last: a sequential barriers model of turnout and voter roll-off', unpublished manuscript, Department of Political Science, University of North Carolina, Chapel Hill.

Crain, W. Mark (1977), 'On the structure and stability of political markets', *Journal of Political Economy*, **85**, 829–42.

Crain, W. Mark (1979), 'Cost and output in the legislative firm', *Journal of Legal Studies*, **8**, 607–21.

Crain, W. Mark (1990), 'Legislative committees: a filtering theory', in W. Mark Crain and Robert D. Tollison (eds), *Predicting Politics: Essays in Empirical Public Choice*, Ann Arbor: University of Michigan Press, pp. 149–66.

Crain, W. Mark and Daniel C. Coker (1994), 'Legislative committees as loyalty-generating institutions', *Public Choice*, **81**, 195–221.

Crain, W. Mark and Nicole V. Crain (1998), 'Fiscal consequences of budget baselines', *Journal of Public Economics*, **67**, 421–36.

Crain, W. Mark, Donald R. Leavens and Robert D. Tollison (1986), 'Final voting in legislatures', *American Economic Review*, **76**, 833–41.

Crain, W. Mark and Robert E. McCormick (1984), 'Regulators as an interest group', in James M. Buchanan and Robert D. Tollison (eds), *The Theory of Public Choice II*, Ann Arbor: University of Michigan Press, pp. 287–304.

Crain, W. Mark and Timothy J. Muris (1995), 'Legislative organization of fiscal policy', *Journal of Law and Economics*, **38**, 311–33.

Crain, W. Mark and Lisa K. Oakley (1995), 'The politics of infrastructure', *Journal of Law and Economics*, **38**, 1–18.

Crain, W. Mark, William F. Shughart II and Robert D. Tollison (1988a), 'Legislative majorities as nonsalvageable assets', *Southern Economic Journal*, **55**, 303–14.

Crain, W. Mark, William F. Shughart II and Robert D. Tollison (1988b), 'Voters as investors: a rent-seeking resolution of the paradox of voting', in Charles K. Rowley, Robert D. Tollison and Gordon Tullock (eds), *The Political Economy of Rent Seeking*, Boston: Kluwer Academic Publishers, pp. 241–9.

Crain, W. Mark, William F. Shughart II and Robert D. Tollison (1991), 'Legislative majorities as nonsalvageable assets: Reply', *Southern Economic Journal*, **57**, 857–8.

Crain, W. Mark and Robert D. Tollison (1979a), 'Constitutional change in an interest-group perspective', *Journal of Legal Studies*, **8**, 165–75.

Crain, W. Mark and Robert D. Tollison (1979b), 'The executive branch in the interest-group theory of government', *Journal of Legal Studies*, **8**, 555–67.

Crain, W. Mark and Robert D. Tollison (1980), 'The sizes of majorities', *Southern Economic Journal*, **46**, 726–34.

Crain, W. Mark and Robert D. Tollison (eds) (1990), *Predicting Politics: Essays in Empirical Public Choice*, Ann Arbor: University of Michigan Press.

Crain, W. Mark and Robert D. Tollison (1991), 'The price of influence in an interest group economy', *Rationality and Society*, **15**, 437–49.

Crain, W. Mark and Robert D. Tollison (1993), 'Time inconsistency and fiscal policy: empirical analysis of US states, 1969–89', *Journal of Public Economics*, **51**, 153–9.

Crandall, Robert W. (1983), *Controlling Industrial Pollution: The Economics and Politics of Clean Air*, Washington, DC: Brookings Institution.

Crandall, Robert W., Howard K. Gruenspecht, Theodore E. Keller et al. (1986), *Regulating the Automobile*, Washington, DC: Brookings Institution.

Crew, Michael A. and Charlotte Twight (1990), 'On the efficiency of law: a public choice perspective', *Public Choice*, **66**, 15–36.

Crihfield, John B. and John H. Wood (1993), 'Bureaucracy, altruism, and monetary policy', *Public Choice*, **76**, 233–48.

Cropper, Maureen L. and Wallace E. Oates (1992), 'Environmental economics: a survey', *Journal of Economic Literature*, **30**, 675–740.

Croson, Rachel T.A. (1996), 'Partners and strangers revisited', *Economics Letters*, **53**, 25–32.

Cukierman, Alex (1992), *Central Bank Strategy, Credibility and Independence*, Cambridge, MA: MIT Press.

Dahl, Robert A. (1957), 'Decision-making in a democracy: the Supreme Court as a national policy-maker', *Journal of Public Law*, **6**, 279–95.

Dahl, Robert A. (1961), *Who Governs? Democracy and Power in an American City*, New Haven, CT: Yale University Press.

Dalton, Brett A., David W. Riggs and Bruce Yandle (1997), 'The political production of Superfund', *Eastern Economic Journal*, **30**, 110–21.

D'Arista, Jane W. (1994), *The Evolution of US Finance*, vol. 1, London: M.E. Sharpe.

d'Aspremont, Claude and Louis Gevers (1977), 'Equity and the informational basis of collective choice', *Review of Economic Studies*, **44**, 199–209.

Davidson, Audrey B., Eleanor Davis and Robert B. Ekelund, Jr (1995), 'Political choice and the child labor statute of 1938: public interest or interest group legislation?', *Public Choice*, **82**, 85–106.

Davidson, Audrey B. and Robert B. Ekelund, Jr (1997), 'The medieval Church and rents from marriage market regulations', *Journal of Economic Behavior and Organization*, **32**, 215–45.

Davis, Douglas D. and Robert J. Reilly (1998a), 'Do too many cooks always spoil the stew? An experimental analysis of rent-seeking and the role of a strategic buyer', *Public Choice*, **95**, 89–115.

Davis, Douglas D. and Robert J. Reilly (1998b), 'Multiple buyers, rent-defending and the observed social costs of monopoly', unpublished manuscript, Virginia Commonwealth University.

De Alessi, Louis (1980), 'The economics of property rights: a review of the evidence', *Research in Law and Economics*, **2**, 1–47.

De Alessi, Louis (1982), 'On the nature and consequences of private and public enterprises', *Minnesota Law Review*, **67**, 191–209.

De Alessi, Louis (1983), 'Property rights, transaction costs, and x-efficiency: an essay in economic theory', *American Economic Review*, **73**, 64–81.

De Alessi, Louis (1988), 'How markets alleviate scarcity', in V. Ostrom, D. Feeny and H. Picht (eds), *Rethinking Institutional Analysis and Development: Issues, Alternatives, and Choices*, San Francisco: International Center for Economic Growth, pp. 339–76.

De Alessi, Louis (1995), 'The public choice model of antitrust enforcement', in Fred S. McChesney and William F. Shughart II (eds), *The Causes and Consequences of Antitrust: The Public Choice Perspective*, Chicago: University of Chicago Press, pp. 189–200.

De Alessi Louis (1997), 'Value, efficiency, and rules: The limits of economics', in G. Radnitzky (ed.), *Values and the Social Order*, vol. 3: *Voluntary versus Coercive Orders*, Aldershot, UK: Avebury, pp. 289–304.

De Alessi, Louis (1998a), 'Reflections on Coase, cost, and efficiency', in B. Monissen and James M. Buchanan (eds), *The Economists' Vision*, Frankfurt, Germany: Campus Verlag Frankfurt, pp. 91–114.

De Alessi, Louis (1998b), 'Private property rights as the basis for free market environmentalism', in P.J. Hill and Roger E. Meiners (eds), *Who Owns the Environment?*, Lanham, MD: Rowman & Littlefield, pp. 1–35.

De Alessi, Louis and Raymond P.H. Fishe (1987), 'Why do corporations distribute assets? An analysis of dividends and capital structure', *Journal of Institutional and Theoretical Economics*, **143**, 34–51.

De Alessi, Louis and Robert J. Staaf (1991), 'The common law process: efficiency or order?', *Constitutional Political Economy*, **2**, 107–26.

De Alessi, Michael (1998), *Fishing for Solutions*, London: Institute of Economic Affairs.

de Figueiredo, John M. and Emerson H. Tiller (1996), 'Congressional control of the courts: a theoretical and empirical analysis of expansion of the federal judiciary', *Journal of Law and Economics*, **39**, 435–62.

de Figueiredo, Rui J.P., Jr (1998a), 'Electoral competition, political uncertainty and policy insulation', unpublished manuscript, University of California.

de Figueiredo, Rui J.P., Jr (1998b), 'A theory of the political firm: a multitask agency theory of bureaucratic jurisdictions', unpublished manuscript, University of California.

de Figueiredo, Rui J.P., Jr, Pablo T. Spiller and Santiago Urbiztondo (1999), 'An informational perspective on administrative procedures', *Journal of Law, Economics and Organization*, **15**, 283–305.

de Haan, Jacob and Clemens L. J. Siermann (1995), 'New evidence on the relationship between democracy and economic growth', *Public Choice*, **86**, 175–98.

de Haan, Jacob and Clemens L. J. Siermann (1998), 'Further evidence on the relationship between economic freedom and economic growth', *Public Choice*, **95**, 363–80.

Deller, Steven C. and David L. Chicoine (1988), 'Representative versus direct democracy: a Tiebout test of relative performance: comment', *Public Choice*, **56**, 69–72.

Deller, Steven C. and David L. Chicoine (1993), 'Representative versus direct democracy: a test of allocative efficiency in local government expenditures', *Public Finance Quarterly*, **21**, 100–114.

De Long, J. Bradford and Andrei Shleifer (1993), 'Princes and merchants: European city growth before the Industrial Revolution', *Journal of Law and Economics*, **36**, 671–702.

Demsetz, Harold (1964), 'The exchange and enforcement of property rights', *Journal of Law and Economics*, **7**, 11–26.

Demsetz, Harold (1967), 'Toward a theory of property rights', *American Economic Review*, **57**, 347–59.

Demsetz, Harold (1968), 'Why regulate utilities?', *Journal of Law and Economics*, **11**, 55–65.

Demsetz, Harold (1982), 'Barriers to entry', *American Economic Review*, **72**, 47–57.

Dennen, R. Taylor (1976), 'Cattlemen's associations and property rights in land in the American West', *Explorations in Economic History*, **13**, 423–36.

Denzau, Arthur and Robert J. Mackay (1981), 'Structure-induced equilibria and perfect foresight expectations', *American Journal of Political Science*, **25**, 762–79.

Denzau, Arthur and Robert J. Mackay (1983). 'Gatekeeping and monopoly

power of committees: an analysis of sincere and sophisticated behavior',
American Journal of Political Science, **27**, 740–61.

Denzau, Arthur and Michael C. Munger (1986), 'Legislators and interest
groups: how unorganized interests get represented', *American Political
Science Review*, **80**, 89–106.

Denzau, Arthur and Douglass C. North (1994), 'Shared mental models: ideologies and institutions', *Kyklos*, **47**, 3–32.

Denzau, Arthur, William H. Riker and Kenneth A. Shepsle (1985),
'Farquharson and Fenno: sophisticated voting and home style', *American
Political Science Review*, **79**, 1117–34.

Derthick, Martha (1990), *Agency under Stress: The Social Security Administration in American Government*, Washington, DC: Brookings Institution.

Deschamps, Richard and Louis Gevers (1978), 'Leximin and utilitarian rules:
a joint characterization', *Journal of Economic Theory*, **17**, 143–63.

De Soto, Hernando (1989), *The Other Path: The Invisible Revolution in the
Third World*, New York: Harper & Row.

De Vany, Arthur S. (1977), 'Land reform and agricultural efficiency in Mexico:
a general equilibrium analysis', *Journal of Monetary Economics*, Supple-
mentary Series, **6**, 123–47.

Dewatripont, Mathias, Ian Jewitt and Jean Tirole (1999), 'Application to
missions and accountability of government agencies', *Review of Economic
Studies*, **66**, 183–99.

DiLorenzo, Thomas J. (1985), 'The origins of antitrust: an interest-group
perspective', *International Review of Law and Economics*, **5**, 73–90.

DiLorenzo, Thomas J. and Jack C. High (1988), 'Antitrust and competition,
historically considered', *Economic Inquiry*, **26**, 423–35.

Dodd, Lawrence C. and Richard L. Schott (1979), *Congress and the Administrative State*, New York: John Wiley & Sons.

Doernberg, Richard L. and Fred S. McChesney (1987), 'On the accelerating
rate and decreasing durability of tax reform', *Minnesota Law Review*, **71**,
913–62.

Dougan, William R. (1984), 'Tariffs and the economic theory of regulation',
Research in Law and Economics, **6**, 187–210.

Dougan, William R. and Michael C. Munger (1989), 'The rationality of
ideology', *Journal of Law and Economics*, **32**, 119–42.

Downing, Paul. B. (1981), 'A political economy model of implementing
pollution laws', *Journal of Environmental Economics and Management*, **8**,
255–71.

Downing, Paul B. (1984), *Environmental Economics and Policy*, Boston:
Little, Brown.

Downs, Anthony (1957), *An Economic Theory of Democracy*, New York:
Harper & Row.

Downs, Anthony (1967), *Inside Bureaucracy*, Boston: Little, Brown.

Draetta, U., R.B. Lake and V.P. Nanda (1992), *Breach and Adaptation of International Contracts: An Introduction to Lex Mercatoria*, Salem, NH: Butterworth Legal Publishers.

Dresher, Melvin and Merrill M. Flood (1952), 'Some experimental games', Research memorandum RM-789, RAND Corporation.

Dudley, L.M. (1991), *The Word and the Sword: How Techniques of Information and Violence Have Shaped Our World*, Oxford: Blackwell.

Dugatkin, Lee (1999), *Cheating Monkeys and Citizen Bees: The Nature of Cooperation in Animals and Humans*, New York: Free Press.

Duncombe, William, Jerry Miner and John Ruggiero (1997), 'Empirical evaluation of bureaucratic models of inefficiency', *Public Choice*, **93**, 1–18.

Dupuit, Jules (1853), 'De l'utilité et de sa mesure: de l'utilité publique', *Journal des Économistes*, **36**, 1–27.

Dworkin, Ronald (1978), *Taking Rights Seriously*, Cambridge, MA: Harvard University Press.

Easton, Stephen T. and Sergio Rebelo (1993), 'Marginal income tax rates and economic growth in developing countries', *European Economic Review*, **37**, 409–17.

Easton, Stephen T. and Michael A. Walker (1997), 'Income, growth, and economic freedom', *American Economic Review*, **87**, 328–32.

Ebke, W.F. (1987), 'Review of *The Law Merchant: The Evolution of Commercial Law*, by Leon E. Trakman', *The International Lawyer*, **21**, 606–16.

Eckel, Catherine and Charles A. Holt (1989), 'Strategic voting in agenda-controlled committee experiments', *American Economic Review*, **79**, 763–73.

Eckert, Ross D. (1973), 'On the incentives of regulators: the case of taxicabs', *Public Choice*, **14**, 83–99.

Edwards, Linda N. (1978), 'An empirical analysis of compulsory schooling legislation, 1940–1960', *Journal of Law and Economics*, **21**, 203–22.

Eggertsson, Thráinn (1990), *Economic Behavior and Institutions*, Cambridge: Cambridge University Press.

Eisenstein, James (1973), *Politics and the Legal Process*, New York: Harper & Row.

Eismeier, Theodore J. and Philip H. Pollock III (1998), *Business, Money, and the Rise of Corporate PACs in American Elections*, New York: Quorum Books.

Ekelund, Robert B., Jr (ed.) (1998), *The Foundations of Regulatory Economics*, 3 vols, Cheltenham, UK and Northampton, MA: Edward Elgar.

Ekelund, Robert B., Jr and George S. Ford (1997), 'Nineteenth century urban market failure? Chadwick on funeral industry regulation', *Journal of Regulatory Economics*, **12**, 27–51.

Ekelund, Robert B., Jr and Robert F. Hébert (1990), 'E.H. Chamberlin and contemporary industrial organization theory', *Journal of Economic Studies*, **17**, 5–19.

Ekelund, Robert B., Jr, Robert F. Hébert and Robert D. Tollison (1989), 'An economic model of the medieval Church: usury as a form of rent-seeking', *Journal of Law, Economics and Organization*, **5**, 307–31.

Ekelund, Robert B., Jr, Robert F. Hébert, Robert D. Tollison, Gary M. Anderson and Audrey B. Davidson (1996), *Sacred Trust: The Medieval Church as an Economic Firm*, New York: Oxford University Press.

Ekelund, Robert B., Jr, Michael J. McDonald and Robert D. Tollison (1995), 'Business restraints and the Clayton Act of 1914: public- or private-interest legislation?', in Fred S. McChesney and William F. Shughart II (eds), *The Causes and Consequences of Antitrust: The Public Choice Perspective*, Chicago: University of Chicago Press, pp. 271–86.

Ekelund Robert B. Jr, Donald R. Street and Robert D. Tollison (1997), 'Rent seeking and property rights' assignments as a process: the Mesta cartel of medieval-mercantile Spain', *Journal of European Economic History*, **26**, 9–35.

Ekelund, Robert B., Jr and Robert D. Tollison (1980), 'Economic regulation in mercantile England: Hecksher revisited', *Economic Inquiry*, **18**, 565–72.

Ekelund, Robert B., Jr and Robert D. Tollison (1981), *Mercantilism as a Rent-Seeking Society*, College Station: Texas A&M University Press.

Ekelund, Robert B., Jr and Robert D. Tollison (1984), 'A rent-seeking theory of French mercantilism', in James M. Buchanan and Robert D. Tollison (eds), *Theory of Public Choice II*, Ann Arbor: University of Michigan Press, pp. 206–23.

Ekelund, Robert B., Jr and Robert D. Tollison (1997a), 'On neoinstitutional theory and preclassical economics: Mercantilism revisited', *European Journal of the History of Economic Thought*, **4**, 375–99.

Ekelund, Robert B., Jr and Robert D. Tollison (1997b), *Politicized Economies: Monarchy, Monopoly, and Mercantilism*, College Station: Texas A&M University Press.

Ekelund, Robert B., Jr and Douglas M. Walker (1996), 'J.S. Mill on the income tax exemption and inheritance taxes: the evidence reconsidered', *History of Political Economy*, **28**, 559–81.

Ellickson, Robert C. (1991), *Order Without Law: How Neighbors Settle Disputes*, Cambridge, MA: Harvard University Press.

Ellickson, Robert C. (1993), 'Property in land', *Yale Law Journal*, **102**, 1315–400.

Ellison, Sarah Fisher and Wallace P. Mullin (1995), 'Economics and politics: the case of the sugar tariff reform', *Journal of Law and Economics*, **38**, 335–66.

Elster, Jon (1983), *Sour Grapes*, Cambridge: Cambridge University Press.

Elster, Jon (1989), *The Cement of Society: A Study of Social Order*, Cambridge: Cambridge University Press.

Elster, Jon, Claus Offe and U. Preuss (1998), *Institutional Design in Post-Communist Societies*, Cambridge: Cambridge University Press.

Emerson, Niou and Peter C. Ordeshook (1985), 'Universalism in Congress', *American Journal of Political Science*, **29**, 246–54.

Enelow, James M. (1981), 'Saving amendments, killer amendments, and an expected utility theory of sophisticated voting', *Journal of Politics*, **43**, 1062–89.

Enelow, James M. and Melvin J. Hinich (1984), *The Spatial Theory of Voting*, Cambridge: Cambridge University Press.

Enelow, James M. and David Koehler (1980), 'The amendment in legislative strategy: sophisticated voting in the US Congress', *Journal of Politics*, **42**, 396–413.

Epstein, David L. and Sharyn O'Halloran (1999), *Delegating Powers: A Transaction Cost Politics Approach to Policy Making under Separate Powers*, Cambridge, MA: Harvard University Press.

Epstein, Richard A. (1982), 'Manville: the bankruptcy of product liability', *Regulation*, **6**, 14–19 & 43–6.

Epstein, Richard A. (1985), *Takings: Private Property and the Power of Eminent Domain*, Cambridge, MA: Harvard University Press.

Epstein, Richard A. (1995), *Simple Rules for a Complex World*, Cambridge, MA: Harvard University Press.

Erikson, Robert (1981), 'Why do people vote? Because they are registered', *American Politics Quarterly*, **9**, 259–76.

Eskridge, William and John Ferejohn (1992), 'Making the deal stick: enforcing the original constitutional structure of lawmaking in the modern regulatory state', *Journal of Law, Economics and Organization*, **8**, 165–89.

Esty, Daniel and Richard Caves (1983), 'Market structure and political influence', *Economic Inquiry*, **21**, 24–38.

Evans, Paul and Georgias Karras (1996), 'Do economies converge? Evidence from a panel of US states', *Review of Economics and Statistics*, **78**, 384–8.

Fahy, Colleen A. (1998), 'The choice of local government structure in Massachusetts: a historical public choice perspective', *Social Science Quarterly*, **79**, 433–44.

Fair, Ray C. (1978), 'The effect of economic events on votes for president', *Review of Economics and Statistics*, **60**, 159–73.

Farber, Daniel A. (1992), 'Politics and procedure in environmental law', *Journal of Law, Economics and Organization*, **8**, 59–89.

Farquharson, Robin (1969), *Theory of Voting*, New Haven, CT: Yale University Press.

Farr, James and Raymond Seidelman (1993), *Discipline and History*, Ann Arbor: University of Michigan Press.

Fedderke, J. and R. Klitgaard (1998), 'Economic growth and social indicators: an exploratory analysis', *Economic Development and Cultural Change*, **46**, 455–87.

Feddersen, Timothy J. and Wolfgang Pesendorfer (1996), 'The swing voter's curse', *American Economic Review*, **86**, 408–24.

Feiwel, George R. (1974), 'Reflection on Kalecki's theory of political business cycle', *Kyklos*, **27**, 21–48.

Feld, Lars P. and Gebhard Kirchgässner (1999), 'Public debt and budgetary expenditures: top down or bottom up? Evidence from Swiss municipalities', in James Porterba and Juergen von Hagen (eds), *Budgeting Institutions and Fiscal Performance*, Chicago: University of Chicago Press and National Bureau of Economic Research, pp. 151–79.

Feld, Lars P. and Marcel R. Savioz (1997), 'Direct democracy matters for economic performance: an empirical investigation', *Kyklos*, **50**, 507–38.

Feltham, Gerald A. and Jim Xie (1994), 'Performance measure congruity and diversity in multi-task principal/agent relations', *The Accounting Review*, **69**, 429–53.

Ferejohn, John and Morris P. Fiorina (1974), 'The paradox of not voting: a decision theoretic analysis', *American Political Science Review*, **68**, 525–36.

Ferejohn, John and David Grether (1977), 'Weak path independence', *Journal of Economic Theory*, **14**, 19–31.

Ferejohn, John and Charles Shipan (1990), 'Congressional influence on bureaucracy', *Journal of Law, Economics and Organization*, **6**, 1–43.

Ferguson, Thomas (1995), *The Golden Rule*, Chicago: University of Chicago Press.

Field, Barry C. (1985), 'The evolution of individual property rights in Massachusetts agriculture, 17th–19th centuries', *Northeastern Journal of Agricultural and Resource Economics*, **14**, 97–109.

Fields, Gary S. (1980), *Poverty, Inequality, and Development*, New York: Cambridge University Press.

Finer, Samuel E. (1997), *The History of Government*, vol. I: *Ancient Monarchies and Empires*, Oxford: Oxford University Press.

Fiorina, Morris P. (1976), 'The voting decision: instrumental and expressive aspects', *Journal of Politics*, **38**, 390–415.

Fiorina, Morris P. (1989), *Retrospective Voting in American National Elections*, 3rd edn, New Haven, CT: Yale University Press.

Fiorina, Morris P. and Charles R. Plott (1978), 'Committee decisions under majority rule: an experimental study', *American Political Science Review*, **72**, 575–98.

Fischer, Stanley (1980), 'Dynamic inconsistency, cooperation and the benevolent dissembling government', *Journal of Economic Dynamics and Control*, **2**, 93–107.

Fishback, Price V. (1989), 'Can competition among employers reduce governmental discrimination? Coal companies and segregated schools in West Virginia in the early 1900s', *Journal of Law and Economics*, **32**, 311–28.

Fishburn, Peter C. (1973), *The Theory of Social Choice*, Princeton, NJ: Princeton University Press.

Fishkin, James (1991), *Democracy and Deliberation*, New Haven, CT: Yale University Press.

Foldvary, Fred (1994), *Public Goods and Private Communities: The Market Provision of Social Services*, Aldershot, UK and Brookfield, VT: Edward Elgar.

Foner, Eric (1988), *Reconstruction, 1863–1877*, New York: Harper & Row.

Forsythe, Robert, Thomas Rietz, Roger Myerson and Robert Weber (1996), 'An experimental study of voting rules and polls in three-candidate elections', *International Journal of Game Theory*, **25**, 355–83.

Fort, Rodney (1995), 'A recursive treatment of the hurdles to voting', *Public Choice*, **85**, 45–69.

Fratianni, Michelle, Jurgen von Hagen and C. Waller (1997), 'Central banking as a political principal–agent problem', *Economic Inquiry*, **35**, 378–93.

Fratianni, Michelle and F. Spinelli (1982), 'The growth of government in Italy: evidence from 1861 to 1979', *Public Choice*, **39**, 221–43.

Frey, Bruno S. (1976), 'Theorie und Empirie politischer Konjunkturzyklen', *Zeitschrift für Nationalökonomie*, **36**, 95–120.

Frey, Bruno S. (1984), 'The public choice view of international political economy', *International Organization*, **38**, 199–223.

Frey, Bruno S. (1994), 'Direct democracy: politico-economic lessons from Swiss experience', *American Economic Review*, **84**, 338–42.

Frey, Bruno S. (1997), 'The public choice of international organizations', in Dennis C. Mueller (ed.), *Perspectives on Public Choice: A Handbook*, Cambridge: Cambridge University Press, pp. 106–23.

Frey, Bruno S. and Friedrich Schneider (1975), 'On the modeling of politico-economic interdependence', *European Journal of Political Research*, **3**, 339–60.

Frey, Bruno S. and Friedrich Schneider (1978), 'A politico-economic model of the United Kingdom', *Economic Journal*, **88**, 243–53.

Friedman, David (1987), 'Law and economics', in John Eatwell, Murray Milgate and Peter Newman (eds), *The New Palgrave: The Invisible Hand*, New York: Norton, pp. 173–82.

Friedman, Milton (1962), *Capitalism and Freedom*, Chicago: Phoenix Books.

Friedman, Milton (1968), 'Should there be an independent monetary authority?', in Milton Friedman (ed.), *Dollars and Deficits*, Englewood Cliffs, NJ: Prentice-Hall, pp. 173–94.

Friedman, Milton (1978), 'The limitations of tax limitations', *Policy Review*, **5**, 7–14.

Friedman, Milton (1982), 'Monetary policy: theory and practice', *Journal of Money, Credit and Banking*, **14**, 98–118.

Friedman, Milton (1992), 'Do old fallacies ever die?', *Journal of Economic Literature*, **95**, 427–43.

Friedman, Milton and Rose Friedman (1979), *Free to Choose: A Personal Statement*, New York: Harcourt, Brace, Jovanovich.

Friedman, Milton and Anna J. Schwartz (1963), *A Monetary History of the United States, 1867–1960*, Princeton, NJ: Princeton University Press.

Frohlich, Norman and Joe A. Oppenheimer (1992), *Choosing Justice: An Experimental Approach to Ethical Theory*, Berkeley: University of California Press.

Frohlich, Norman and Joe A. Oppenheimer (2000), 'Kenneth Arrow, Welfare aggregation and progress in political theory', in James Alt, Elinor Ostrom and Margaret Levi (eds), *Taking Economics Seriously: Conversations with Nobelists about Economics and Political Science*, New York: Russell Sage Foundation, pp. 4–33.

Fudenberg, Drew and Jean Tirole (1992), *Game Theory*, Cambridge, MA: MIT Press.

Fuller, Lon (1964), *The Morality of Law*, New Haven, CT: Yale University Press.

Fuller, Lon (1981), *The Principles of Social Order*, Durham, NC: Duke University Press.

Furubotn, Eirik G. and Rudolf Richter (1997), *Institutions and Economic Theory: The Contribution of the New Institutional Economics*, Ann Arbor: University of Michigan Press.

Galbraith, J. Kenneth (1958), *The Affluent Society*, Boston: Houghton Mifflin.

Gambetta, Diego (1993), *The Sicilian Mafia: The Business of Private Protection*, Cambridge, MA: Harvard University Press.

Gardner, Roy, Elinor Ostrom and James M. Walker (1990), 'The nature of common pool resource problems', *Rationality and Society*, **2**, 335–58.

Garman, Mark and Morton Kamien (1968), 'The paradox of voting: probability calculations', *Behavioral Science*, **13**, 306–16.

Garrett, Elizabeth (1996), 'Term limitations and the myth of the citizen-legislator', *Cornell Law Review*, **81**, 623–97.

Gastil, Raymond D. (1982), *Freedom in the World: Political Rights and Civil Liberties*, Westport, CT: Greenwood Press.

Gehrlein, William V. and Peter C. Fishburn (1976), 'The probability of the paradox of voting: a computable solution', *Journal of Economic Theory*, **13**, 14–25.

George, Henry (1889), *Progress and Poverty: An Inquiry into the Cause of Industrial Depressions, and of Increase of Want with Increase of Wealth – The Remedy*, London: K. Paul, Trench.

Gerber, Alan (1998), 'Estimating the effect of campaign spending on Senate election outcomes using instrumental variables', *American Political Science Review*, **92**, 401–11.

Gibbard, Allan (1969), 'Intransitive social indifference and the Arrow dilemma', unpublished manuscript.

Gibbard, Allan (1973), 'Manipulation of voting schemes: a general result', *Econometrica*, **41**, 587–602.

Giertz, J. Fred (1974), 'An experiment in public choice: the Miami Conservancy District, 1913–1922', *Public Choice*, **19**, 63–75.

Gilligan, Thomas W. and Keith Krehbiel (1987), 'Collective decision-making and standing committees: an informational rationale for restrictive amendment procedures', *Journal of Law, Economics and Organization*, **3**, 287–335.

Gilligan, Thomas W. and Keith Krehbiel (1989a), 'Asymmetric information and legislative rules with a heterogeneous committee', *American Journal of Political Science*, **33**, 459–90.

Gilligan, Thomas W. and Keith Krehbiel (1989b), 'Collective choice without procedural commitment', in Peter C. Ordeshook (ed.), *Models of Strategic Choice in Politics*, Ann Arbor: University of Michigan Press, pp. 295–314.

Gilligan, Thomas W. and Keith Krehbiel (1990), 'Organization of informative committees by a rational legislature', *American Journal of Political Science*, **34**, 351–64.

Glaeser, Edward L. and José Scheinkman (1998), 'Neither a borrower nor a lender be: an economic analysis of interest restrictions and usury laws', *Journal of Law and Economics*, **41**, 1–36.

Glantz, Stanton, Alan Abramowitz and Michael Burkhart (1976), 'Election outcomes: whose money matters?', *Journal of Politics*, **38**, 1033–8.

Glazer, Amihai (1989), 'Politics and the choice of durability', *American Economic Review*, **79**, 1207–13.

Goff, Brian L. and Mark Toma (1993), 'Optimal seigniorage, the gold standard, and central bank financing', *Journal of Money, Credit and Banking*, **25**, 79–95.

Goldman, Sheldon (1966), 'Voting behavior on the U.S. Courts of Appeals, 1961–1964', *American Political Science Review*, **60**, 373–83.

Goldsmith, Arthur A. (1995), 'Democracy, property rights, and economic growth', *Journal of Development Studies*, **32**, 157–74.

Gopoian, David (1984), 'What makes PACs tick? An analysis of the allocation patterns of economic interest groups', *American Journal of Political Science*, **28**, 259–81.

Gordon, Robert J. (1975), 'The demand for and supply of inflation', *Journal of Law and Economics*, **18**, 807–36.

Graaf, J. de V. (1957), *Theoretical Welfare Economics*, Cambridge: Cambridge University Press.

Green, Donald and Jonathan Krasno (1988), 'Salvation for the spendthrift incumbent: reestimating the effects of campaign spending in House elections', *American Journal of Political Science*, **32**, 884–907.

Green, Donald and Jonathan Krasno (1990), 'Rebuttal to Jacobson's "New evidence for old arguments"', *American Journal of Political Science*, **34**, 363–72.

Green, Thomas A. (1985), *Verdict According to Conscience: Perspectives on the English Criminal Trial Jury, 1200–1800*, Chicago: University of Chicago Press.

Greif, Avner (1997), 'Microtheory and recent developments in the study of economic institutions through economic history', in David M. Kreps and Kenneth F. Wallis (eds), *Advances in Economics and Econometrics: Theory and Applications*, Seventh World Congress, Cambridge: Cambridge University Press, pp. 79–113.

Grenzke, Janet (1989), 'PACs and the congressional supermarket: the currency is complex', *American Journal of Political Science*, **33**, 1–24.

Greve, Michael S. and Fred L. Smith, Jr (1992), *Environmental Politics: Public Costs, Private Rewards*, New York: Praeger.

Grier, Kevin B. (1987), 'Presidential elections and Federal Reserve policy', *Southern Economic Journal*, **54**, 475–86.

Grier, Kevin B. (1989a), 'Campaign spending and Senate election, 1978–1984', *Public Choice*, **63**, 201–19.

Grier, Kevin B. (1989b), 'On the existence of a political monetary cycle', *American Journal of Political Science*, **33**, 376–89.

Grier, Kevin B. (1991), 'Congressional influence on US monetary policy: an empirical test', *Journal of Monetary Economics*, **28**, 201–20.

Grier, Kevin B., Michael McDonald and Robert D. Tollison (1995), 'Electoral politics and the executive veto: a predictive theory', *Economic Inquiry*, **33**, 427–40.

Grier, Kevin B. and Michael C. Munger (1991), 'Committee assignments, constituent preferences, and campaign contributions to House incumbents', *Economic Inquiry*, **29**, 24–43.

Grier, Kevin B. and Michael C. Munger (1993), 'Corporate, labor, and trade association contributions to the U.S. House and Senate, 1978–1986', *Journal of Politics*, **55**, 614–43.

Grier, Kevin B., Michael C. Munger and Brian Roberts (1991), 'The industrial organization of corporate political participation', *Southern Economic Journal*, **57**, 727–38.

Grier, Kevin B., Michael C. Munger and Brian Roberts (1994), 'The determinants of industry political activity, 1978–1986', *American Political Science Review*, **88**, 911–26.

Grier, Kevin B. and Gordon Tullock (1989), 'An empirical analysis of cross-national economic growth, 1951–1980', *Journal of Monetary Economics*, **24**, 259–76.

Grofman, Bernard and Arend Lijphart (eds) (1992), *Parliamentary versus Presidential Government*, Oxford: Oxford University Press.

Groseclose, Tim, Steve Levitt and Jim Snyder (1999), 'Comparing interest group scores across time and chambers: adjusted ADA scores for the US Congress', *American Political Science Review*, **93**, 33–50.

Gross, C. (ed.) (1974), *Selected Cases Concerning the Law Merchant, A.D. 1270–1638*, London: Professional Books.

Grossman, Gene M. and E. Helpman (1994), 'Protection for sale', *American Economic Review*, **84**, 833–50.

Grossman, Gene M. and E. Helpman (1995a), 'Trade wars and trade talks', *Journal of Political Economy*, **103**, 675–708.

Grossman, Gene M. and E. Helpman (1995b), 'The politics of free-trade agreements', *American Economic Review*, **85**, 667–90.

Grossman, Philip J. (1988), 'Government and economic growth: a non-linear relationship', *Public Choice*, **56**, 193–200.

Groves, Theodore and John O. Ledyard (1977), 'Optimal allocation of public goods: a solution to the "free rider" problem', *Econometrica*, **45**, 783–809.

Gunning, J.P., Jr (1972), 'Towards a theory of the evolution of government', in Gordon Tullock (ed.), *Explorations in the Theory of Anarchy*, Blacksburg: Center for Study of Public Choice, Virginia Polytechnic Institute and State University, pp. 19–26.

Gwartney, James D., Walter E. Block and Robert A. Lawson (1993), 'Rating the economic freedom of 100 countries: 1975–1990', *Rating Economic Freedom VI*, Sonoma, CA: Liberty Fund/Fraser Institute.

Gwartney, James D., Randall G. Holcombe and Robert A. Lawson (1998), 'The scope of government and the wealth of nations', *Cato Journal*, **18**, 163–90.

Gwartney, James D. and Robert A. Lawson (1997), *Economic Freedom of the World 1997*, Annual Report, Vancouver: Fraser Institute.

Gwartney, James D., Robert A. Lawson and Walter E. Block (1996), *Economic Freedom of the World: 1975–1995*, Vancouver: Fraser Institute.

Gwartney, James D., Robert A. Lawson and Randall G. Holcombe (1999), 'Economic freedom and the environment for economic growth', *Journal of Institutional and Theoretical Economics*, **155**, 643–63.

Haddock, David D. (1994), 'Foreseeing confiscation by the sovereign: lessons from the American West', in Terry L. Anderson and P.J. Hill (eds), *The Political Economy of the American West*, Lanham, MD: Rowman & Littlefield, pp. 129–45.

Hahn, Robert W. (1989), 'Economic prescriptions for environmental protection: how the patient followed the doctor's orders', *Journal of Economic Perspectives*, **3**, 95–114.

Hall, H.K., C. Kao and D. Nelson (1998), 'Women and tariffs: Testing the gender gap hypothesis in a Downs–Mayer political economy model', *Economic Inquiry*, **36**, 320–32.

Hall, Richard and Frank Wayman (1990), 'Buying time: moneyed interests and the mobilization of bias in congressional committees', *American Political Science Review*, **84**, 797–820.

Hallagan, W.S. (1978), 'Share contracting for California gold', *Explorations in Economic History*, **15**, 196–210.

Hamilton, Alexander, James Madison and John Jay ([1787–88] 1996), *The Federalist*, Benjamin F. Wright (ed.), New York: Barnes and Noble Books.

Hamilton, James and Helen Ladd (1996), 'Biased ballots? The impact of ballot structure on North Carolina elections in 1992', *Public Choice*, **87**, 259–80.

Hammond, Peter J. (1976), 'Equity, Arrow's conditions and Rawls' difference principle', *Econometrica*, **44**, 793–804.

Hammond, Thomas H. (1986), 'Agenda control, organizational structure, and bureaucratic politics', *American Journal of Political Science*, **30**, 379–420.

Hammond, Thomas H. (1994), 'Structure, strategy, and the agenda of the firm', in Richard P. Rumelt, Dan E. Schendel and David J. Teece (eds), *Fundamental Issues in Strategy: A Research Agenda*, Boston: Harvard Business School Press, pp. 97–154.

Hammond, Thomas H. and Jeffrey S. Hill (1993), 'Deference or preference? Explaining Senate confirmation of presidential nominees to administrative agencies', *Journal of Theoretical Politics*, **5**, 23–59.

Hammond, Thomas H. and Jack H. Knott (1996), 'Who controls the bureaucracy? Presidential power, congressional dominance, legal constraints, and bureaucratic autonomy in a model of multi-institutional policymaking', *Journal of Law, Economics and Organization*, **12**, 119–66.

Handler, Edward and John R. Mulkern (1982), *Business in Politics: Campaign Strategies of Corporate Political Action Committees*, Lexington, MA: Lexington Books.

Hanke, Steve H. and Stephen J. K. Walters (1997), 'Economic freedom, prosperity, and equality: a survey', *Cato Journal*, **17**, 117–46.

Hansman, Henry (1996), *The Ownership of Enterprise*, Cambridge, MA: Harvard University Press.

Harberger, Arnold C. (1954), 'Monopoly and resource allocation', *American Economic Review*, **44**, 77–87.

Hardin, Russell (1982), *Collective Action*, Baltimore, MD: Johns Hopkins University Press.

Hardin, Russell (1988), 'Constitutional political economy: agreement on rules', *British Journal of Political Science*, **18**, 513–30.

Hardin, Russell (1997), 'Economic theories of the state', in Dennis C. Mueller (ed.), *Perspectives on Public Choice: A Handbook*, Cambridge: Cambridge University Press, pp. 21–34.

Harper, Fowler and Edwin Etherington (1953), 'Lobbyists before the court', *University of Pennsylvania Law Review*, **101**, 1172–7.

Harsanyi, John (1977), 'Morality and the theory of rational behavior', *Social Research*, **44**, 623–56.

Harstad, Ronald M. and Michael Marrese (1981), 'Implementation of mechanisms by processes: public good allocation experiments', *Journal of Economic Behavior and Organization*, **2**, 129–51.

Hart, H.L.A. (1961), *The Concept of Law*, Oxford: Clarendon Press.

Haas-Wilson, Deborah (1986), 'The effect of commercial practice restrictions: the case of optometry', *Journal of Law and Economics*, **29**, 165–86.

Havrilesky, Thomas (1995), *The Pressures on American Monetary Policy*, Boston: Kluwer Academic Publishers.

Havrilesky, Thomas and John A. Gildea (1992), 'Reliable and unreliable partisan appointees to the Board of Governors', *Public Choice*, **73**, 397–417.

Havrilesky, Thomas and Robert Schweitzer (1990), 'A theory of FOMC dissent voting with evidence from the time series', in Thomas Mayer (ed.), *The Political Economy of American Monetary Policy*, Cambridge: Cambridge University Press, pp. 197–210.

Hayek, Friedrich A. von (1945), 'The use of knowledge in society', *American Economic Review*, **35**, 519–30.

Hayek, Friedrich A. von (1960), *The Constitution of Liberty*, Chicago: University of Chicago Press.

Hayek, Friedrich A. von (1973), *Law, Legislation, and Liberty*, vol. 1, Chicago: University of Chicago Press.

Hayes, Kathy J., Laura Razzolini and Leola B. Ross (1998), 'Bureaucratic choice and nonoptimal provision of public goods: theory and evidence', *Public Choice*, **94**, 1–20.

Haynes, Stephen E. and Joe A. Stone (1990), 'Political models of the business cycle should be revived', *Economic Inquiry*, **28**, 442–65.

Heckman, James (1976), 'The common structure of statistical models of truncation, sample election, and limited dependent variables and a simple estimator for such models', *Annals of Economic and Social Measurement*, **5**, 475–92.

Heckman, James (1979), 'Sample selection bias as a specification error', *Econometrica*, **47**, 153–61.

Heckscher, Eli F. (1934), *Mercantilism*, trans. by M. Shapiro, 2 vols, London: Allen & Unwin.

Herodotus ([c. 450 BCE] 1987), *The History*, trans. by David Grene, Chicago: University of Chicago Press.

Hersch, Phillip L. and Gerald S. McDougall (1997), 'Direct legislation: determinants of legislator support for voter initiatives', *Public Finance Review*, **25**, 327–43.

Hettich, Walter and Stanley L. Winer (1988), 'Economic and political foundations of tax structure', *American Economic Review*, **78**, 701–12.

Hetzel, Robert L. (1990), 'The political economy of monetary policy', in Thomas Mayer (ed.), *The Political Economy of American Monetary Policy*, Cambridge: Cambridge University Press, pp. 99–114.

Heymann, Philip B. (1987), *The Politics of Public Management*, New Haven, CT: Yale University Press.

Hibbs, Douglas A., Jr (1987), *The American Political Economy: Macroeconomics and Electoral Politics*, Cambridge, MA: Harvard University Press.

Higgins, Richard S., William F. Shughart II and Robert D. Tollison (1985), 'Free entry and efficient rent seeking', *Public Choice*, **46**, 247–58.

Higgs, Robert (1987), *Crisis and Leviathan: Critical Episodes in the Growth of American Government*, Cambridge: Cambridge University Press.

Hillman, Arye L. and Heinrich W. Ursprung (1988), 'Domestic politics, foreign interests, and international trade policy', *American Economic Review*, **78**, 729–45.

Hinchman, James F. (1988), 'Letter to Congress from the acting comptroller general of the General Accounting Office', 31 March.

Hinich, Melvin J. (1981), 'Voting as an act of contribution', *Public Choice*, **36**, 135–40.

Hinich, Melvin J., John O. Ledyard and Peter C. Ordeshook (1972), 'Nonvoting and existence of equilibrium under majority rule', *Journal of Economic Theory*, **4**, 144–53.

Hinich, Melvin J. and Michael C. Munger (1994), *Ideology and the Theory of Political Choice*, Ann Arbor: University of Michigan Press.

Hinich, Melvin J. and Michael C. Munger (1997), *Analytical Politics*, Cambridge: Cambridge University Press.

Hinich, Melvin J. and Peter C. Ordeshook (1969), 'Abstentions and equilibrium in the electoral process', *Public Choice*, **7**, 81–106.

Hinich, Melvin J. and Peter C. Ordeshook (1970), 'Plurality maximization vs vote maximization: a spatial analysis with variable participation', *American Political Science Review*, **64**, 772–91.

Hird, J.A. (1993), 'Congressional voting on Superfund: self-interest or ideology?', *Public Choice*, **77**, 333–57.

Hirschman, Albert O. (1970), *Exit, Voice and Loyalty*, Cambridge, MA: Harvard University Press.

Hirshleifer, Jack (1976), 'Comment', *Journal of Law and Economics*, **19**, 241–4.

Hobbes, Thomas ([1651] 1991), *Leviathan*, ed. by Richard Tuck, New York: Cambridge University Press.

Hoffman, Elizabeth and Matthew L. Spitzer (1982), 'The Coase theorem: some experimental tests', *Journal of Law and Economics*, **25**, 73–98.

Hoffman, Elizabeth and Matthew L. Spitzer (1985), 'Entitlements, rights, and fairness: an experimental examination of subjects' concepts of distributive justice', *Journal of Legal Studies*, **14**, 259–97.

Hogue, Arthur R. ([1906] 1985), *Origins of the Common Law*, Indianapolis, IN: Liberty Press.

Holcombe, Randall G. (1978), 'Public choice and public spending', *National Tax Journal*, **31**, 373–83.

Holcombe, Randall G. (1980), 'An empirical test of the median voter model', *Economic Inquiry*, **18**, 260–74.

Holcombe, Randall G. (1985), *An Economic Analysis of Democracy*, Carbondale: Southern Illinois University Press.

Holcombe, Randall G. (1986), 'Non-optimal unanimous agreement', *Public Choice*, **48**, 229–44.

Holcombe, Randall G. (1992), 'The distributive model of government: evidence from the Confederate Constitution', *Southern Economic Journal*, **58**, 762–9.

Holcombe, Randall G. (1994), *The Economic Foundations of Government*, New York: New York University Press.

Holcombe, Randall G. (1997a), 'Selective excise taxation from an interest-group perspective', in William F. Shughart II (ed.), *Taxing Choice: The Predatory Politics of Fiscal Discrimination*, New Brunswick, NJ: Transaction Publishers, pp. 81–103.

Holcombe, Randall G. (1997b), 'A theory of the theory of public goods', *Review of Austrian Economics*, **10**, 1–22.

Holcombe, Randall G. (1998a), 'Entrepreneurship and economic growth', *Quarterly Journal of Austrian Economics*, **1**, 45–62.

Holcombe, Randall G. (1998b), 'Tax policy from a public choice perspective', *National Tax Journal*, **51**, 359–71.

Holcombe, Randall G. and James D. Gwartney (1989), 'Political parties and the legislative principal–agent relationship', *Journal of Institutional and Theoretical Economics*, **145**, 669–75.

Holcombe, Randall G. and Jeffrey A. Mills (1995), 'Politics and deficit finance', *Public Finance Quarterly*, **23**, 448–66.

Holdsworth, Sir William ([1903] 1924), *A History of English Law*, vol. I, London: Methuen & Co.

Holmstrom, Bengt (1982), 'Moral hazard in teams', *Bell Journal of Economics and Management Science*, **13**, 324–40.

Holmstrom, Bengt and Paul Milgrom (1991), 'Multitask principal–agent analysis: incentive contracts, asset ownership, and job design', *Journal of Law, Economics and Organization*, **7**, 24–52.

Holt, Charles A. and Lisa R. Anderson (1999), 'Agendas and strategic voting', *Southern Economic Journal*, **65**, 622–9.

Holt, Charles A. and Susan K. Laury (2000), 'Theoretical explanations of treatment effects in voluntary contributions mechanisms', in Charles R. Plott and Vernon L. Smith (eds), *The Handbook of Experimental Economics Results*, Amsterdam: North-Holland (forthcoming).

Hopenhayn, Hugo and Susanne Lohmann (1996), 'Fire-alarm signals and the political oversight of regulatory agencies', *Journal of Law, Economics and Organization*, **12**, 196–213.

Horn, Murray J. (1995), *The Political Economy of Public Administration*, Cambridge: Cambridge University Press.

Hotelling, Harold (1929), 'Stability in competition', *Economic Journal*, **39**, 41–57.

Huberman, D.A. (1990), 'An alternative to "A public choice theory of the Great Contraction"', *Public Choice*, **67**, 257–68.

Hufbauer, G.C. and K.A. Elliott (1994), *Measuring the Costs of Protection in the United States*, Washington, DC: Institute for International Economics.

Hume, David ([1740] 1985), *A Treatise of Human Nature*, 2nd edn, ed. by L.A. Selby-Bigge, Oxford: Clarendon Press.

Humphries, Craig (1991), 'Corporations, PACs and strategic link between contributions and lobbying activities', *Western Political Quarterly*, **44**, 353–72.

Hunt, Janet C. and Paul H. Rubin (1980), 'The economics of the women's movement', *Public Choice*, **35**, 287–95.

Hunter, James D. and Carl Bowman (1996), *The State of Disunion: 1996 Survey of American Political Culture*, vol. 1: *Summary Report*, The Post-Modernity Project, Charlottesville: University of Virginia.

Iannaccone, Laurence R. (1990), 'Religious participation: a human capital approach', *Journal of the Scientific Study of Religion*, **29**, 297–314.

Iannaccone, Laurence R. (1992), 'Sacrifice and stigma: reducing free-riding in cults, communes, and other collectives', *Journal of Political Economy*, **100**, 271–91.

Iannaccone, Laurence R. (1998), 'Introduction to economics of religion', *Journal of Economic Literature*, **36**, 1465–96.

Inman, Robert P. (1978), 'Testing political economy's "as if" assumption: is the median income voter really decisive?', *Public Choice*, **33**, 45–65.

Isaac, R. Mark and Charles A. Holt (eds) (1999), *Research in Experimental Economics*, vol. 7, Stamford, CT: JAI Press.

Isaac, R. Mark, Kenneth McCue and Charles R. Plott (1985), 'Public good provision in an experimental environment', *Journal of Public Economics*, **26**, 51–74.

Isaac, R. Mark, David Schmidtz and James M. Walker (1989), 'The assurance problem in a laboratory market', *Public Choice*, **62**, 217–36.

Isaac, R. Mark and James M. Walker (1988), 'Communication and free-riding behavior: the voluntary contributions mechanism', *Economic Inquiry*, **26**, 585–608.

Isaac, R. Mark and James M. Walker (1996), 'Nash as an organizing principle in the voluntary provision of public goods: experimental evidence', unpublished manuscript, University of Arizona.

Isaac, R. Mark, James M. Walker and Susan H. Thomas (1984), 'Divergent evidence on free riding: an experimental examination of possible explanations', *Public Choice*, **43**, 113–49.

Isaac, R. Mark, James M. Walker and Arlington W. Williams (1994), 'Group size and the voluntary provision of public goods', *Journal of Public Economics*, **54**, 1–36.

Isham, John and Satu Kähkönen (1997), 'Improving the delivery of water and sanitation: a model of co-production of infrastructure services', IRIS Working Paper No. 210, University of Maryland.

Isham, John and Satu Kähkönen (1998), 'What determines the performance and impact of community-based water and sanitation services? Evidence from Sri Lanka and India', unpublished manuscript, IRIS Center, University of Maryland.

Itoh, Hideshi (1993), 'Job design, delegation and cooperation: a principal–agent analysis', *European Economic Review*, **38**, 691–700.

Jackson, Brooks (1988), *Honest Graft: Big Money and the American Political Process*, New York: Knopf.

Jacobson, Gary (1978), 'The effects of campaign spending in congressional elections', *American Political Science Review*, **72**, 469–91.

Jacobson, Gary (1985), 'Money and votes reconsidered: congressional elections, 1972–1982', *Public Choice*, **47**, 7–62.

Jacobson, Gary (1990), 'The effects of campaign spending in House elections: new evidence for old arguments', *American Political Science Review*, **34**, 334–62.

Jasay, Anthony de (1996), *Before Resorting to Politics*, The Shaftesbury Papers, 5, Cheltenham, UK and Brookfield, VT: Edward Elgar.

Jensen, Michael C. and William H. Meckling (1976), 'Theory of the firm: managerial behavior, agency costs, and ownership structure', *Journal of Financial Economics*, **3**, 305–60.

Jensen, Michael C. and Kevin J. Murphy (1990a), 'CEO incentives: it's not how much you pay, but how', *Harvard Business Review*, **68**, 138–53.

Jensen, Michael C. and Kevin J. Murphy (1990b), 'Performance pay and top-management incentives', *Journal of Political Economy*, **98**, 225–84.

Johnsen, D. Bruce (1986), 'The formation and protection of property rights among the Southern Kwakiutl Indians', *Journal of Legal Studies*, **15**, 41–67.

Johnson, B.T., K.R. Holmes and M. Kirkpatrick (1998), *The Index of Economic Freedom*, Washington, DC: Heritage Foundation.

Johnson, Ronald N. and Gary D. Libecap (1982), 'Contracting problems and regulation: the case of the fishery', *American Economic Review*, **72**, 1005–22.

Johnson, Ronald N. and Gary D. Libecap (1989), 'Agency growth, salaries, and the protected bureaucrat', *Economic Inquiry*, **27**, 431–51.

Jones, L.E. and R. Manuelli (1990), 'A convex model of equilibrium growth: theory and policy implications', *Journal of Political Economy*, **98**, 1008–38.

Joskow, Paul L. (1988), 'Asset specificity and the structure of vertical relationships: empirical evidence', *Journal of Law, Economics and Organization*, **4**, 95–117.

Joskow, Paul L. and Richard Schmalensee (1998), 'The political economy of market-based environmental policy: the US acid rain program', *Journal of Law and Economics*, **41**, 37–83.

Kagel, John H. and Alvin E. Roth (1995), *The Handbook of Experimental Economics*, Princeton, NJ: Princeton University Press.

Kahneman, Daniel and Amos Tversky (1979), 'Prospect theory: an analysis of decision-making under risk', *Econometrica*, **47**, 263–91.

Kahneman, Daniel and Amos Tversky (1984), 'Choices, values, and frames', *American Psychologist*, **39**, 341–50.

Kalecki, Michael (1943), 'Political aspects of full employment', *Political Quarterly*, **14**, 322–31.

Kalt, James P. and Mark A. Zupan (1984), 'Capture and ideology in the economic theory of politics', *American Economic Review*, **74**, 279–300.

Kalt, Joseph P. and Mark A. Zupan (1990), 'The apparent ideological behavior of legislators: testing for principal–agent slack in political institutions', *Journal of Law and Economics*, **33**, 103–32.

Kanazawa, Mark T. (1998), 'Efficiency in western water law: the development of the California doctrine, 1850–1911', *Journal of Legal Studies*, **27**, 159–86.

Kane, Edward J. (1980), 'Politics and Fed policymaking', *Journal of Monetary Economics*, **6**, 199–211.

Karatnycky, A. (1994), *Freedom in the World: The Annual Survey of Political Rights and Civil Liberties 1993–1994*, New York: Freedom House.

Kau, James B., Donald Keenan and Paul H. Rubin (1982), 'A general equilibrium model of congressional voting', *Quarterly Journal of Economics*, **97**, 271–93.

Kau, James B. and Paul H. Rubin (1978), 'Voting on minimum wages: a time series analysis', *Journal of Political Economy*, **86**, 337–42.

Kau, James B. and Paul H. Rubin (1979), 'Self-interest, ideology and logrolling in congressional voting', *Journal of Law and Economics*, **22**, 365–84.

Kau, James B. and Paul H. Rubin (1982), *Congressmen, Constituents, and Contributors*, Boston: Martinus Nijhoff.

Kau, James B. and Paul H. Rubin (1993), 'Ideology, voting, and shirking', *Public Choice*, **76**, 151–72.

Kaufman, Herbert (1975), 'The natural history of human organizations', *Administration and Society*, **7**, 131–49.

Keech, William R. (1995), *Economic Politics*, Cambridge: Cambridge University Press.

Keech, William R. and Irwin L. Morris (1996), 'Appointments, presidential power, and the Federal Reserve', unpublished manuscript.

Keefer, Phil and Stephen Knack (1997), 'Why don't poor countries catch up? A cross-national test of an institutional explanation', *Economic Inquiry*, **35**, 590–602.

Kelley, S., R. Ayres and W. Bowen (1967), 'Registration and voting: putting first things first', *American Political Science Review*, **61**, 359–79.

Kelly, Jerry S. (1978), *Arrow's Impossibility Theorems*, New York: Academic Press.

Kelly, Jerry S. (1988), *Social Choice Theory: An Introduction*, Berlin: Springer-Verlag.

Kelman, Steven (1987), '"Public choice" and public spirit', *Public Interest*, **87**, 80–94.

Kennelly, Brendan and Peter Murrell (1991), 'Industry characteristics and interest group formation: an empirical study', *Public Choice*, **70**, 21–40.

Keser, Claudia (1996), 'Voluntary contributions to a public good when partial contribution is a dominant strategy', *Economics Letters*, **50**, 359–66.

Keser, Claudia and Frans van Winden (1996), 'Partners contribute more to public goods than strangers: conditional cooperation', unpublished manuscript, University of Karlsruhe.

Kessel, Reuben A. (1974), 'Transfused blood, serum hepatitis, and the Coase theorem', *Journal of Law and Economics*, **17**, 265–89.

Key, V.O. (1966), *The Responsible Electorate*, Cambridge, MA: Harvard University Press.

Kiefer, David (1997), *Macroeconomic Policy and Public Choice*, Berlin: Springer.

Kiewiet, D. Roderick (1991), 'Bureaucrats and budgetary outcomes: quantitative analysis', in André Blais and Stéphane Dion (eds), *The Budget-Maximizing Bureaucrat*, Pittsburgh: University of Pittsburgh Press, pp. 143–73.

Kiewiet, D. Roderick and Kristin Szakaly (1996), 'Constitutional limitations on borrowing: an analysis of state bonded indebtedness', *Journal of Law, Economics and Organization*, **12**, 62–97.

Kim, Oliver and Mark Walker (1984), 'The free rider problem: experimental evidence', *Public Choice*, **43**, 3–24.

Kimenyi, Mwangi S. (1989), 'Interest groups, transfer seeking, and democratization', *American Journal of Economics and Sociology*, **48**, 339–49.

Kimenyi, Mwangi S. and John M. Mbaku (1993), 'Rent-seeking and institutional stability in developing countries', *Public Choice*, **77**, 385–405.

Kimenyi, Mwangi S. and William F. Shughart II (1989), 'Political successions and the growth of government', *Public Choice*, **62**, 173–9.

Kimenyi, Mwangi S., William F. Shughart II and Robert D. Tollison (1985), 'What do judges maximize?', *Economia delle Scelte Pubbliche*, **3**, 181–8.

Kimenyi, Mwangi S., William F. Shughart II and Robert D. Tollison (1988), 'An interest-group theory of population growth', *Journal of Population Economics*, **1**, 131–9.

Kirchgässner, Gebhard (1994), 'The institutional foundations of democratic government: a comparison of presidential and parliamentary systems: comment', *Journal of Institutional and Theoretical Economics*, **150**, 196–202.

Kirslov, Samuel (1963), 'The *amicus curiae* brief', *Yale Law Journal*, **72**, 694–721.

Kirzner, Israel M. (1973), *Competition and Entrepreneurship*, Chicago: University of Chicago Press.

Kirzner, Israel M. (1997), 'Entrepreneurial discovery and the competitive market process: an Austrian approach', *Journal of Economic Literature*, **35**, 60–85.

Klein, Benjamin and Keith Leffler (1981), 'The role of market forces in assuring contractual performance', *Journal of Political Economy*, **89**, 615–41.

Knack, Stephen (1993), 'The voter participation effects of selecting jurors from registration lists', *Journal of Law and Economics*, **36**, 99–114.

Knack, Stephen (1994), 'Does rain help the Republicans? Theory and evidence on turnout and the vote', *Public Choice*, **79**, 187–209.

Knack, Stephen (1996), 'Institutions and the convergence hypothesis: the cross-national evidence', *Public Choice*, **87**, 207–28.

Knack, Stephen and Phil Keefer (1995), 'Institutions and economic performance: cross-country tests using alternative institutional measures', *Economics and Politics*, **7**, 207–27.

Kolm, Serge-Christophe (1996), *Modern Theories of Justice*, Cambridge, MA: MIT Press.

Kormendi, Roger C. and P.G. Meguire (1985), 'Macroeconomic determinants of growth: cross-country evidence', *Journal of Monetary Economics*, **16**, 141–63.

Kornhauser, Lewis A. (1980), 'A guide to the perplexed claims of efficiency in the law', *Hofstra Law Review*, **8**, 591–640.

Kramer, Gerald H. (1971), 'Short-term fluctuations in US voting behavior, 1896–1964', *American Political Science Review*, **65**, 131–43.

Krehbiel, Keith (1990), 'Are congressional committees composed of preference outliers?', *American Political Science Review*, **84**, 149–63.

Krehbiel, Keith (1993), 'Where's the party?', *British Journal of British Political Science*, **23**, 235–66.

Kreps, David M. (1990), *A Course in Microeconomic Theory*, Princeton, NJ: Princeton University Press.

Kroszner, Randall and Thomas Stratmann (1998), 'Interest group competition and the organization of Congress: theory and evidence from financial services' PACs', *American Economic Review*, **88**, 1163–87.

Krueger, Anne O. (1974), 'The political economy of the rent-seeking society', *American Economic Review*, **64**, 291–303.

Krueger, Anne O. (1993), *Political Economy of Policy Reform in Developing Countries*, Cambridge, MA: MIT Press.

Krueger, Anne O. (1997), 'Trade policy and economic development: how we learn', *American Economic Review*, **87**, 1–22.

Kuhn, Thomas S. (1970), *The Structure of Scientific Revolutions*, 2nd edn, Chicago: University of Chicago Press.

Kuran, Timur (1995), *Private Truths, Public Lies: The Social Consequences of Preference Falsification*, Cambridge, MA: Harvard University Press.

Kurrild-Klitgaard, Peter (2000), 'The constitutional economics of autocratic succession', *Public Choice*, **103**, 63–84.

Kydland, Finn E. and Edward C. Prescott (1977), 'Rules rather than discretion: the inconsistency of optimal plans', *Journal of Political Economy*, **3**, 473–92.

Laband, David N. and Richard O. Beil (1999), 'Are economists more selfish than other "social" scientists?', *Public Choice*, **100**, 85–101.

Landa, Janet T. (1994), *Trust, Ethnicity, and Identity: Beyond the New Institu-*

tional Economics of Ethnic Trading Networks, Contract Law, and Gift-Exchange, Ann Arbor: University of Michigan Press.

Landau, Daniel (1983), 'Government expenditures and economic growth: a cross-country study', *Southern Economic Journal*, **49**, 783–92.

Landau, Daniel (1986), 'Government and economic growth in the less developed countries: an empirical study for 1960–1980', *Economic Development and Cultural Change*, **35**, 35–75.

Landes, David S. (1998), *The Wealth and Poverty of Nations: Why Some are So Rich and Some So Poor*, New York: Norton.

Landes, William M. and Richard A. Posner (1975), 'The independent judiciary in an interest-group perspective', *Journal of Law and Economics*, **18**, 875–901.

Landes, William M. and Richard A. Posner (1979), 'Adjudication as a private good', *Journal of Legal Studies*, **8**, 235–84.

Langbein, John H. (1978), 'The criminal trial before the lawyers', *University of Chicago Law Review*, **45**, 262–316.

Lanyi, Anthony and Young Lee (1999), 'Governance aspects of the East Asian financial crisis', paper presented at the IRIS Conference on Market-Augmenting Government.

Laury, Susan K. and Charles A. Holt (2000), 'Voluntary provision of public goods: experimental results with interior Nash equilibria', in Charles R. Plott and Vernon L. Smith (eds), *The Handbook of Experimental Economics Results*, Amsterdam: North-Holland, forthcoming.

Laury, Susan K., James M. Walker and Arlington W. Williams (1995), 'Anonymity and the voluntary provision of public goods', *Journal of Economic Behavior and Organization*, **27**, 365–80.

Laver, Michael and Norman Schofield (1990), *Multiparty Governments: The Politics of Coalition in Europe*, Oxford: Oxford University Press.

Leal, Donald R. (1993), 'Turning a profit on public forests', PERC Policy Series, PS-4, Political Economy Research Center, Bozeman, MT.

Leblang, David A. (1996), 'Property rights, democracy and economic growth', *Political Research Quarterly*, **49**, 5–26.

Ledyard, John O. (1981), 'The paradox of voting and candidate competition: a general equilibrium analysis', in George Horwich and James P. Quirk (eds), *Essays in Contemporary Fields of Economics*, West Lafayette, IN: Purdue University Press, pp. 54–80.

Ledyard, John O. (1984), 'The pure theory of large two candidate elections', *Public Choice*, **44**, 7–41.

Leibowitz, Arleen A. and Robert D. Tollison (1978), 'Learning and earning in law firms', *Journal of Legal Studies*, **7**, 65–81.

Leibowitz, Arleen A. and Robert D. Tollison (1980), 'A theory of legislative organization: making the most of your majority', *Quarterly Journal of Economics*, **94**, 261–77.

Leidy, Michael P. and Bernhard M. Hoekman (1994), '"Cleaning up" while cleaning up? Pollution abatement, interest groups and contingent trade policies', *Public Choice*, **78**, 241–58.

Lemieux, Peter H. and Charles H. Stewart III (1990), 'Senate confirmation of Supreme Court nominations from Washington to Reagan', Working Papers in Political Science, P–90–3, Hoover Institution, Stanford University.

Levi, Margaret (1988), *Of Rule and Revenue*, Berkeley: University of California Press.

Levitt, Steven (1994), 'Using repeat challengers to estimate the effect of campaign spending on election outcomes in the U.S. House', *Journal of Political Economy*, **102**, 777–98.

Levitt, Steven (1998), 'Are PACs trying to influence politicians or voters?', *Economics and Politics*, **10**, 19–35.

Levy, Leonard W. (1968), *Origins of the Fifth Amendment: The Right Against Self-Incrimination*, New York: Oxford University Press.

Lew, J.D.M. (1978), *Applicable Law in International Commercial Arbitration: A Study in Commercial Arbitration Awards*, Dobbs Ferry, NY: Oceana Publications.

Lewis, David (1969), *Convention: A Philosophical Study*, Cambridge, MA: Harvard University Press.

Libecap, Gary D. (1978a), 'Economic variables and the development of the law: the case of western mineral rights', *Journal of Economic History*, **38**, 338–62.

Libecap, Gary D. (1978b), *The Evolution of Private Mineral Rights: Nevada's Comstock Lode*, New York: Arno Press.

Libecap, Gary D. (1979), 'Government support of private claims to public minerals: western mineral rights', *Business History Review*, **53**, 362–85.

Libecap, Gary D. (1981a), 'Bureaucratic opposition to the assignment of property rights: overgrazing on the western range', *Journal of Economic History*, **41**, 151–8.

Libecap, Gary D. (1981b), *Locking Up the Range, Federal Land Controls and Grazing*, Cambridge, MA: Ballinger.

Libecap, Gary D. (1986), 'Property rights in economic history: implications for research', *Explorations in Economic History*, **23**, 227–52.

Libecap, Gary D. (1992), 'The rise of the Chicago packers and the origins of meat inspection and antitrust', *Economic Inquiry*, **30**, 242–62.

Libecap, Gary D. and Ronald N. Johnson (1980), 'Legislating commons: the Navajo Tribal Council and the Navajo range', *Economic Inquiry*, **18**, 69–86.

Libecap, Gary D. and Steven N. Wiggins (1984), 'Contractual responses to the common pool: prorationing of crude oil production', *American Economic Review*, **74**, 87–98.

Liebowitz, Stan J. and Stephen E. Margolis (1990), 'The fable of the keys', *Journal of Law and Economics*, **33**, 1–26.

Liebowitz, Stan J. and Stephen E. Margolis (1994), 'Network externality: an uncommon tragedy', *Journal of Economic Perspectives*, **8**, 133–50.

Liebowitz, Stan J. and Stephen E. Margolis (1995a), 'Path dependence: from QWERTY to Windows 95', *Regulation*, **18**, 33–41.

Liebowitz, Stan J. and Stephen E. Margolis (1995b), 'Path dependence, lock-in, and history', *Journal of Law, Economics and Organization*, **11**, 205–26.

Lijphart, Arend (1992), *Parliamentary versus Presidential Government*, Oxford: Oxford University Press.

Lindahl, Eric ([1919] 1967), 'Just taxation – a positive solution', in Richard A. Musgrave and Alan T. Peacock (eds), *Classics in the Theory of Public Finance*, New York: St Martin's Press, pp. 168–76.

Lindbeck, Assar (1976), 'Stabilization policy in open economies with endogenous politicians', *American Economic Review Papers and Proceedings*, **66**, 1–19.

Lindblom, Charles E. (1959), 'The "science" of muddling through', *Public Administration*, **19**, 79–88.

Lindgren, J. (1993), 'Theory, history, and practice of the bribery–extortion distinction', *University of Pennsylvania Law Review*, **141**, 1695–740.

Lissowski, Grzegorz and Piotr Swistak (1995), 'Choosing the best social order: normative dimensions of choice', *American Political Science Review*, **89**, 74–96.

Little, I.M.D. (1952), 'Social choice and individual values', *Journal of Political Economy*, **60**, 422–32.

Locke, John ([1690] 1963), *Two Treatises of Government*, ed. by P. Laslett, Cambridge: Cambridge University Press.

Lohmann, Susanne (1992), 'Optimal commitment in monetary policy: credibility versus flexibility', *American Economic Review*, **82**, 273–86.

Lohmann, Susanne (1997), 'Partisan control of the money supply and decentralized appointment powers', *European Journal of Political Economy*, **13**, 225–46.

Lott, John R., Jr (1987), 'Political cheating', *Public Choice*, **52**, 169–87.

Lott, John R., Jr (1991), 'Does additional campaign spending really hurt incumbents?', *Public Choice*, **72**, 87–92.

Lott, John R., Jr (1997), 'Donald Wittman's *The Myth of Democratic Failure*', *Public Choice*, **92**, 1–13.

Lott, John R., Jr (1998), 'A simple explanation for why campaign expenditures are increasing: the government is getting bigger', Law & Economics Working Paper no. 52 (2nd series), University of Chicago Law School.

Lott, John R., Jr and Steven G. Bronars (1993), 'Time series evidence on shirking in the US House of Representatives', *Public Choice*, **76**, 125–50.

Lott, John R., Jr and Michael L. Davis (1992), 'A critical review and extension of the political shirking literature', *Public Choice*, **74**, 461–84.

Lowry, Robert C. (1998), 'Religion and the demand for membership in environmental citizen groups', *Public Choice*, **94**, 223–40.

Lucas, Robert E., Jr (1972), 'Expectations and the neutrality of money', *Journal of Economic Theory*, **4**, 103–24.

Lucas, Robert E., Jr (1988), 'On the mechanics of economic development', *Journal of Monetary Economics*, **22**, 3–42.

Luce, R. Duncan and Howard W. Raiffa (1957), *Games and Decisions*, New York: Wiley.

Lupia, Arthur (1994), 'Bounded rationality and "The Institutional Foundations of Democratic Government"', *Journal of Institutional and Theoretical Economics*, **150**, 203–10.

Lupia, Arthur and Mathew D. McCubbins (1994), 'Designing bureaucratic regulation', *Law and Contemporary Problems*, **57**, 91–126.

Lyon, Bruce (1980), *A Constitutional and Legal History of Medieval England*, 2nd edn, New York: Norton.

Lyon, Randolph M. (1990), 'Regulating bureaucratic polluters', *Public Finance Quarterly*, **18**, 198–220.

Macaulay, Hugh H. and Bruce Yandle (1977), *Environmental Use and the Market*, Lexington, MA: Lexington Books.

Machiavelli, Niccolò ([1513] 1981), *The Prince*, trans. and ed. by Daniel Donno, New York: Bantam Books.

MacRae, C. Duncan (1977), 'A political model of the business cycle', *Journal of Political Economy*, **85**, 239–63.

Macy, Jonathan R. (1986), 'Promoting public-regarding legislation through statutory agreements', *Columbia Law Review*, **86**, 227–49.

Maddison, A. (1982), *Phases of Capitalist Development*, Oxford: Oxford University Press.

Magee, Stephen P., William A. Brock and Leslie Young (1989), *Black Hole Tariffs and Endogenous Policy Theory: Political Economy in General Equilibrium*, Cambridge: Cambridge University Press.

Magnusson, L. (ed.) (1993), *Evolutionary and Neo-Schumpeterian Approaches to Economics*, Boston: Kluwer Academic Publishers.

Magnusson, L. (1994), *Mercantilism: The Shaping of an Economic Language*, London and New York: Routledge.

Maine, Sir Henry S. (1864), *Ancient Law*, 3rd American from 5th English edn, New York: Henry Holt.

Maloney, Michael T. and Gordon L. Brady (1988), 'Capital turnover and marketable pollution rights', *Journal of Law and Economics*, **31**, 203–26.

Maloney, Michael T. and Robert E. McCormick (1982), 'A positive theory of environmental quality regulation', *Journal of Law and Economics*, **25**, 99–124.

Maloney, Michael T., Robert E. McCormick and Robert D. Tollison (1984), 'Economic regulation, competitive governments, and specialized resources', *Journal of Law and Economics*, **27**, 329–38.

Mankiw, N. Gregory (1987), 'The optimal collection of seigniorage: theory and evidence', *Journal of Monetary Economics*, **20**, 327–41.

Mankiw, N. Gregory (1992), *Macroeconomics*, New York: Worth.

Mansbridge, Jane (1983), *Beyond Adversary Democracy*, Chicago: University of Chicago Press.

Manwarning, David (1962), *Render Unto Caesar*, Chicago: University of Chicago Press.

March, James G. (1978), 'Bounded rationality, ambiguity, and the engineering of choice', *Bell Journal of Economics and Management Science*, **9**, 587–608.

March, James G. and Herbert A. Simon (1958), *Organizations*, New York: John Wiley & Sons.

Marks, Melanie and Rachel Croson (1998), 'Alternative rebate rules in the provision of a threshold public good: an experimental investigation', *Journal of Public Economics*, **67**, 195–220.

Marshall, Alfred (1887), 'The old generation of economists and the new', *Quarterly Journal of Economics*, **11**, 115–35.

Marvel, Howard P. (1977), 'Factory regulation: a reinterpretation of early English experience', *Journal of Law and Economics*, **20**, 379–402.

Marwell, Gerald and Ruth E. Ames (1979), 'Experiments on the provision of public goods I: Resources, interest group size, and the free-rider problem', *American Journal of Sociology*, **84**, 1335–60.

Marwell, Gerald and Ruth E. Ames (1981), 'Economists free ride, does anyone else?', *Journal of Public Economics*, **15**, 295–310.

Mas-Colell, Andrew and Hugo Sonnenschein (1972), 'General possibility theorem for group decisions', *Review of Economic Studies*, **39**, 185–92.

Mas-Colell, Andrew, Michael D. Whinston and Jerry R. Green (1995), *Microeconomic Theory*, New York: Oxford University Press.

Maskin, Eric, Yingyi Qian and Chenggang Chu (1997), 'Incentives, information, and organizational form', unpublished manuscript, Harvard University.

Masters, Marick F. and Gerald Keim (1985), 'Determinants of PAC participation among large corporations', *Journal of Politics*, **47**, 1158–73.

Matsusaka, John G. (1992), 'The economic approach to democracy', in Mariano Tommasi and Kathryn Ierulli (eds), *The New Economics of Human Behavior*, Cambridge: Cambridge University Press, pp. 140–56.

Matsusaka, John G. (1995), 'Fiscal effects of the voter initiative: evidence from the last 30 years', *Journal of Political Economy*, **103**, 587–623.

Matsusaka, John G. (1998), 'Fiscal effects of the voter initiative in the first half of the twentieth century', unpublished manuscript, University of Southern California.

Matsusaka, John G. and Filip Palda (1993), 'The Downsian voter meets the ecological fallacy', *Public Choice*, **77**, 855–78.

May, Kenneth O. (1952), 'A set of independent, necessary, and sufficient conditions for simple majority decision', *Econometrica*, **20**, 680–84.

Mayhew, David (1974), *Congress: The Electoral Connection*, New Haven, CT: Yale University Press.

McCallum, Bennett T. (1995), 'Two fallacies concerning central bank independence', NBER Working Paper Series, no. 5075.

McCarty, Nolan and Rose Razaghian (1998), 'Hitting the ground running: the timing of presidential appointments in transition', unpublished manuscript, Columbia University.

McChesney, Fred S. (1986), 'Government prohibitions on volunteer fire fighting in nineteenth-century America: a property rights perspective', *Journal of Legal Studies*, **15**, 69–92.

McChesney, Fred S. (1987), 'Rent extraction and rent creation in the economic theory of regulation', *Journal of Legal Studies*, **16**, 101–18.

McChesney, Fred S. (1990), 'Government as definer of property rights: Indian lands, ethnic externalities, and bureaucratic budgets', *Journal of Legal Studies*, **19**, 297–335.

McChesney, Fred S. (1991), 'Rent extraction and interest-group organization in a Coasean model of regulation', *Journal of Legal Studies*, **20**, 73–90.

McChesney, Fred S. (1997), *Money for Nothing: Politicians, Rent Extraction, and Political Extortion*, Cambridge, MA: Harvard University Press.

McChesney, Fred S. (1999), 'Of stranded costs and stranded hopes: the difficulties of deregulation', *Independent Review*, **3**, 485–509.

McChesney, Fred S. and William F. Shughart II (eds) (1995), *The Causes and Consequences of Antitrust: The Public Choice Perspective*, Chicago: University of Chicago Press.

McCloskey, Deirdre N. (1997), 'The good old Coase theory and the good old Chicago school: a comment on Zerbe and Medema', in Steven G. Medema (ed.), *Coasean Economics: Law and Economics and the New Institutional Economics*, Boston: Kluwer Academic Publishers, pp. 239–48.

McCormick, Robert E. (1984), 'The strategic use of regulation: A review of the literature', in Robert A. Rogowsky and Bruce Yandle (eds), *The Political Economy of Regulation: Private Interests in the Regulatory Process*, Washington, DC: Federal Trade Commission, pp. 13–32.

McCormick, Robert E., William F. Shughart II and Robert D. Tollison (1984), 'The disinterest in deregulation', *American Economic Review*, **74**, 1075–9.

McCormick, Robert E. and Robert D. Tollison (1978), 'Legislatures as unions', *Journal of Political Economy*, **86**, 63–78.

McCormick, Robert E. and Robert D. Tollison (1981), *Politicians, Legislation, and the Economy: An Inquiry into the Interest-Group Theory of Government*, Boston: Martinus Nijhoff.

McCubbins, Mathew D., Roger G. Noll and Barry R. Weingast (1987), 'Administrative procedures as instruments of political control', *Journal of Law, Economics and Organization*, **3**, 243–77.

McCubbins, Mathew D., Roger G. Noll and Barry R. Weingast (1989), 'Structure and process; politics and policy: administrative arrangements and the political control of agencies', *Virginia Law Review*, **75**, 431–82.

McCubbins, Mathew D., Roger G. Noll and Barry R. Weingast (1994), 'Legislative intent: the use of positive political theory in statutory interpretation', *Law and Contemporary Problems*, **57**, 3–37.

McCubbins, Mathew D. and Thomas Schwartz (1984), 'Congressional oversight overlooked: police patrols versus fire alarms', *American Journal of Political Science*, **28**, 165–79.

McCurdy, C.W. (1976), 'Stephen J. Field and public land law development in California, 1850–1856: a case study of judicial resource allocation in nineteenth century America', *Law and Society Review*, **10**, 235–66.

McEachern, William A. (1978), 'Collective decision rules and local debt choice: a test of the median voter hypothesis', *National Tax Journal*, **31**, 129–36.

McGuire, Martin C. (1974), 'Group size, group homogeneity, and the aggregate provision of a pure public good under Cournot behavior', *Public Choice*, **18**, 107–26.

McGuire, Martin C. and Mancur Olson (1996), 'The economics of autocracy and majority rule: the invisible hand and the use of force', *Journal of Economic Literature*, **34**, 72–96.

McGuire, Robert A. (1988), 'Constitution making: a rational choice model of the Federal Convention of 1787', *American Journal of Political Science*, **32**, 483–522.

McGuire, Robert A. and Robert L. Ohsfeldt (1986), 'An economic model of voting behavior over specific issues at the Constitutional Convention of 1787', *Journal of Economic History*, **46**, 79–111.

McKelvey, Richard D. (1976a), 'General conditions for global intransitivities in formal voting models', *Econometrica*, **47**, 1085–111.

McKelvey, Richard D. (1976b), 'Intransitivities in multidimensional voting bodies and some implications for agenda control', *Journal of Economic Theory*, **12**, 472–82.

McKelvey, Richard D. (1986), 'Covering, dominance, and institution-free properties of social choice', *American Journal of Political Science*, **30**, 283–314.

McKelvey, Richard D. and Richard Niemi (1978), 'A multistage game representation of sophisticated voting for binary procedures', *Journal of Economic Theory*, **18**, 1–22.

McKelvey, Richard D. and Peter C. Ordeshook (1990), 'A decade of experimental research on spatial models of elections and committees', in James M. Enelow and Melvin J. Hinich (eds), *Advances in the Spatial Theory of Voting*, Cambridge: Cambridge University Press, pp. 99–144.

McKelvey, Richard D. and Talbot Page (1998), 'An experimental study of the effect of private information in the Coase theorem', Working Paper 1018, California Institute of Technology.

McKelvey, Richard D. and Thomas R. Palfrey (1998), 'An experimental study of jury decisions', unpublished manuscript, California Institute of Technology.

McKelvey, Richard D. and Norman Schofield (1986), 'Structural instability of the core', *Journal of Mathematical Economics*, **15**, 179–98.

McKenzie, Richard B. and Gordon Tullock (1989), *The Best of the New World of Economics*, Homewood, IL: Richard D. Irwin.

McKeown, Timothy (1994), 'Epidemiology of corporate PAC formation: 1974–1984', *Journal of Economic Behavior and Organization*, **24**, 153–68.

McLean, Iain and Arnold B. Urken (eds) (1993), *Classics of Social Choice*, Ann Arbor: University of Michigan Press.

McNeil, Douglas W., Andrew W. Foshee and Clark R. Burbee (1988), 'Superfund taxes and expenditures: regional redistribution', *Review of Regional Studies*, **18**, 4–9.

Medema, Steven G (ed.) (1997), *Coasean Economics: Law and Economics and the New Institutional Economics*, Boston: Kluwer Academic Publishers.

Medema, Steven G. (1998), 'The trial of Homo economicus: what law and economics tells us about the development of economic imperialism', in John B. Davis (ed.), *New Economics and Its History*, Durham, NC: Duke University Press, pp. 122–42.

Megdal, Sharon B. (1983), 'The determination of local public expenditures and the principal and agent relation: a case study', *Public Choice*, **40**, 71–87.

Meltzer, Allan H. (1991), 'The growth of government revisited', in S.G. Pendse (ed.), *Perspectives on an Economic Future: Forms, Reforms, and Evaluations*, New York: Greenwood Press, pp. 131–43.

Meltzer, Allan H. and Scott F. Richard (1981), 'A rational theory of the size of government', *Journal of Political Economy*, **89**, 914–27.

Meltzer, Allan H. and Marc Vellrath (1975), 'The effects of economic policies on votes for the presidency: some evidence from recent elections', *Journal of Law and Economics*, **18**, 781–98.

Mencken, Henry Louis (1926), *Notes on Democracy*, New York: Knopf.

Menger, Carl ([1883] 1963), *Problems of Economics and Sociology*, trans. by Francis J. Nook, ed. by Louis Schneider, Urbana, IL: University of Illinois Press.

Meone, K. (1986), 'Types of bureaucratic interaction', *Journal of Public Economics*, **29**, 333–45.

Mercuro, Nicholas and Steven G. Medema (1998), *Economics and the Law: From Posner to Post-Modernism*, Princeton, NJ: Princeton University Press.

Meyer, Richard and Bruce Yandle (1987), 'The political economy of acid rain', *Cato Journal*, **7**, 527–45.

Migué, Jean-Luc and Gerard Bélanger (1974), 'Toward a general theory of managerial discretion', *Public Choice*, **17**, 27–43.

Milgrom, Paul and John Roberts (1992), *Economics, Organization and Management*, Englewood Cliffs, NJ: Prentice-Hall.

Mill, John Stuart ([1848] 1973), *Principles of Political Economy, with Some of their Applications to Social Philosophy*, ed. by Sir William Ashley, Clifton, NJ: Augustus M. Kelley.

Miller, Gary J. and Terry M. Moe (1983), 'Bureaucrats, legislatures, and the size of government', *American Political Science Review*, **77**, 297–322.

Miller, Geoffrey (1998), 'An interest-group theory of central bank independence', *Journal of Legal Studies*, **27**, 433–55.

Miller, N.R. (1983), 'Pluralism and social choice', *American Political Science Review*, **77**, 734–47.

Millner, Edward L. and Michael D. Pratt (1989), 'An experimental investigation of efficient rent seeking', *Public Choice*, **62**, 139–51.

Millner, Edward L. and Michael D. Pratt (1991), 'Risk aversion and rent seeking: an extension and some experimental evidence', *Public Choice*, **69**, 91–2.

Milyo, Jeffrey (1997), 'Electoral and financial effects of changes in committee power', *Journal of Law and Economics*, **40**, 93–111.

Minasian, J.A. (1964), 'Television pricing and the theory of public goods', *Journal of Law and Economics*, **7**, 71–80.

Miron, Jeffrey A. (1986), 'Financial panics, the seasonality of the nominal interest rate, and the founding of the Fed', *American Economic Review*, **76**, 125–40.

Mirrlees, James A. (1971), 'An exploration in the theory of optimum income taxation', *Review of Economic Studies*, **38**, 175–208.

Mirrlees, JamesA. (1976), 'Optimal tax theory – a synthesis', *Journal of Public Economics*, **6**, 327–58.

Mises, Ludwig von (1944), *Bureaucracy*, New Haven, CT: Yale University Press.

Mises, Ludwig von (1949), *Human Action: A Treatise on Economics*, 3rd rev. edn, Chicago: Contemporary Books.

Mises, Ludwig von ([1957] 1985), *Theory and History: An Interpretation of Social and Economic Evolution*, Auburn, AL: Ludwig von Mises Institute.

Mitchell, Wesley C. (1904), *An Essay on the Early History of the Law Merchant*, Cambridge: Cambridge University Press.

Mitchell, William C. (1978), *The Anatomy of Public Failure*, Los Angeles: International Institute for Economic Research.

Mitchell, William C. (1988), 'Virginia, Rochester, and Bloomington: twenty-five years of public choice and political science', *Public Choice*, **56**, 101–19.

Mitchell, William C. and Michael C. Munger (1991), 'Economic models of interest groups: an introductory survey', *American Journal of Political Science*, **35**, 512–46.

Mixon, Franklin G., Jr (1995), 'Public choice and the EPA: empirical evidence on carbon emission violations', *Public Choice*, **83**, 127–37.

Mixon, Franklin G., Jr and J.B. Wilkinson (1988), 'Maintaining the status quo: federal government budget deficits and defensive rent-seeking', unpublished manuscript.

Moe, Terry M. (1980), *The Organization of Interests: Incentives and the Internal Dynamics of Political Interest Groups*, Chicago: University of Chicago Press.

Moe, Terry M. (1984), 'The new economics of organization', *American Journal of Political Science*, **28**, 739–77.

Moe, Terry M. (1985), 'Control and feedback in economic regulation: the case of the NLRB', *American Political Science Review*, **79**, 1094–116.

Moe, Terry M. (1987a), 'An assessment of the positive theory of "congressional dominance"', *Legislative Studies Quarterly*, **12**, 475–520.

Moe, Terry M. (1987b), 'Interests, institutions, and positive theory: the politics of the NLRB', *Studies in American Policy Development*, **2**, 236–99.

Moe, Terry M. (1989), 'The politics of bureaucratic structure', in John E. Chubb and Paul Peterson (eds), *Can the Government Govern?*, Washington, DC: Brookings Institution, pp. 267–329.

Moe, Terry M. (1990), 'Political institutions: the neglected side of the story', *Journal of Law, Economics and Organization*, **6**, 213–53.

Moe, Terry M. (1991), 'Politics and the theory of organization', *Journal of Law, Economics and Organization*, **7**, 106–29.

Moe, Terry M. (1997), 'The positive theory of public bureaucracy', in Dennis C. Mueller (ed.), *Perspectives on Public Choice: A Handbook*, Cambridge: Cambridge University Press, pp. 455–80.

Moe, Terry M. and Michael Caldwell (1994), 'The institutional foundations of democratic government: a comparison of presidential and parliamentary systems', *Journal of Institutional and Theoretical Economics*, **150**, 171–95.

Moe, Terry M. and William G. Howell (1998), 'The presidential power of unilateral action', *Journal of Law, Economics and Organization*, **15**, 132–79.

Moe, Terry M. and Scott A. Wilson (1994), 'Presidents and the politics of structure', *Law and Contemporary Problems*, **57**, 1–44.

Mokyr, Joel (2000), 'Innovation and its enemies: the economic and political roots of technological inertia', in Mancur Olson and Satu Kähkönen (eds), *A Not-So-Dismal Science*, New York: Oxford University Press, pp. 61–91.

Moraski, Bryon J. and Charles R. Shipan (1999), 'The politics of Supreme Court nominations: a theory of institutional constraints and choices', *American Journal of Political Science*, **43**, 1069–95.

Morkre, Morris and David G. Tarr (1980), *Effects of Restrictions on United States Imports: Five Case Studies and Theory*, Washington, DC: Federal Trade Commission.

Morris, Irwin L. (1994), 'Congress, the President, and the Federal Reserve: the politics of American monetary policy', unpublished PhD dissertation, University of North Carolina, Chapel Hill.

Morris, Irwin L. and Michael C. Munger (1996), 'First branch, or root? The Congress, the President, and the Federal Reserve', *Public Choice*, **96**, 363–80.

Morris, Richard B. (ed.) (1961), *Encyclopedia of American History*, New York: Harper & Brothers.

Morton, Rebecca (1991), 'Groups in rational turnout models', *American Journal of Political Science*, **35**, 758–76.

Moser, Peter (1997), 'Checks and balances, and the supply of central bank independence', unpublished manuscript, University of St Gallen, St Gallen, Switzerland.

Mounts, W. Stewart, Jr and Clifford Sowell (1986), 'The structure and use of inputs by the Federal Reserve reconsidered: the monetary constitution, human capital, and property rights', in Eugenia Froedge Toma and Mark Toma (eds), *Central Bankers, Bureaucratic Incentives, and Monetary Policy*, Dordrecht: Kluwer Academic Publishers, pp. 91–104.

Mounts, W. Stewart, Jr and Clifford Sowell (1990), 'Historical considerations, property rights, and budgets: a comment on the use of inputs by the Federal Reserve', *Public Choice*, **66**, 155–60.

Mounts, W. Stewart, Jr and Clifford Sowell (1996), 'Bureaucracy, altruism, and monetary policy: a note from a forecasting perspective', *Public Choice*, **89**, 27–34.

Mueller, Dennis C. (1985), 'The Virginia school and public choice', Virginia Political Economy Lecture Series, Fairfax, VA: George Mason University.

Mueller, Dennis C. (1987), 'The growth of government: a public choice perspective', *International Monetary Fund Staff Papers*, **34**, 115–47.

Mueller, Dennis C. (1989), *Public Choice II*, Cambridge: Cambridge University Press.

Mueller, Dennis C. (1997), 'Constitutional public choice', in Dennis C. Mueller (ed.), *Perspectives on Public Choice: A Handbook*, Cambridge: Cambridge University Press, pp. 124–46.

Mueller, Dennis C. and Peter Murrell (1986), 'Interest groups and the size of government', *Public Choice*, **48**, 125–45.

Mulvey, Jane (1994), 'Paying physicians under Medicare: an empirical application of the interest-group theory of government', unpublished PhD dissertation, George Mason University.

Munger, Michael C. and Brian E. Roberts (1990), 'The Federal Reserve and its institutional environment: a review', in Thomas Mayer (ed.), *The Political Economy of American Monetary Policy*, Cambridge: Cambridge University Press, pp. 83–98.

Murphy, Walter and C. Herman Pritchett (1961), *Courts, Judges, and Politics*, New York: Random House.

Murrell, Peter (1983), 'The comparative structure of growth in the West German and British manufacturing industries', in Dennis C. Mueller (ed.), *The Political Economy of Growth*, New Haven, CT: Yale University Press, pp. 109–31.

Myagkov, Mikhail and Charles R. Plott (1997), 'Exchange economies and loss exposure: experiments exploring prospect theory and competitive equilibria in market environments', *American Economic Review*, **87**, 801–28.

Nagler, Jonathan (1991), 'The effect of registration laws and education on US voter turnout', *American Political Science Review*, **85**, 1393–406.

Neely, Richard (1982), *Why Courts Don't Work*, New York: McGraw-Hill.

Nelson, Douglas and Eugene Silberberg (1987), 'Ideology and legislator shirking', *Economic Inquiry*, **25**, 15–25.

Nelson, M.A. and R.D. Singh (1998), 'Democracy, economic freedom, fiscal policy, and growth in LDCs', *Economic Development and Cultural Change*, **46**, 677–96.

Nelson, Philip (1994), 'Voting and imitative behavior', *Economic Inquiry*, **32**, 92–102.

Nelson, Richard R. and Sidney G. Winter (1982), *An Evolutionary Theory of Economic Change*, Cambridge, MA: Belknap Press of Harvard University Press.

Nelson, Robert H. (1993), 'Environmental Calvinism', in Roger E. Meiners and Bruce Yandle (eds), *Taking the Environmental Seriously*, Lanham, MD: Rowman & Littlefield, pp. 233–55.

Nicholson, Walter (1995), *Microeconomic Theory: Basic Principles and Extensions*, 5th edn, Chicago: Dryden Press.

Niemi, Richard G. and Herbert F. Weisberg (1968), 'A mathematical solution for the probability of the paradox of voting', *Behavioral Science*, **13**, 317–23.

Niskanen, William A. (1971), *Bureaucracy and Representative Government*, Chicago: Aldine-Atherton.

Niskanen, William A. (1975), 'Bureaucrats and politicians', *Journal of Law and Economics*, **18**, 617–44.

Niskanen, William A. (1979), 'Economic and fiscal effects on the popular vote for the president', in Douglas W. Rae and Theodore J. Eismeier (eds), *Public Policy and Public Choice*, Beverly Hills: Sage, pp. 93–120.

Niskanen, William A. (1991), 'A reflection on bureaucracy and representative government', in André Blais and Stéphane Dion (eds), *The Budget-Maximizing Bureaucrat*, Pittsburgh: University of Pittsburgh Press, pp. 13–32.

Niskanen, William A. (1994), 'A reassessment', in William A. Niskanen, *Bureaucracy and Public Economics*, Aldershot, UK and Brookfield, VT: Edward Elgar, pp. 269–83.

Nitzan, Shmuel and Jacob Paroush (1985), *Collective Decision Making: An Economic Outlook*, New York: Cambridge University Press.

Nokken, Timothy P. and Brian R. Sala (1996), 'A spatial interpretation of Senate confirmations', paper presented at the annual meetings of the American Political Science Association, San Francisco, CA.

Nordhaus, William D. (1975), 'The political business cycle', *Review of Economic Studies*, **42**, 169–90.

North, Douglass C. (1978), 'Structure and performance: the task of economic history', *Journal of Economic Literature*, **16**, 963–78.

North, Douglass C. (1979), 'A framework for analyzing the state in economic history', *Explorations in Economic History*, **16**, 249–59.

North, Douglass C. (1981), *Structure and Change in Economic History*, New York: Norton.

North, Douglass C. (1984), 'Three approaches to the study of institutions', in David C. Collander (ed.), *Neoclassical Political Economy: The Analysis of Rent-Seeking and DUP Activities*, Cambridge, MA: Ballinger, pp. 33–40.

North, Douglass C. (1990), *Institutions, Institutional Change and Economic Performance*, Cambridge: Cambridge University Press.

North, Douglass C. (1991), 'Institutions and economic growth: an historical introduction', *World Development*, **17**, 1319–32.

North, Douglass C. and Roger LeRoy Miller (1971), *The Economics of Public Issues*, New York: Harper & Row.

North, Douglass C. and Robert Paul Thomas (1973), *The Rise of the Western World*, Cambridge: Cambridge University Press.

North, Douglass C. and Barry R. Weingast (1989), 'Constitutions and commitment: the evolution of institutions governing public choice in seventeenth-century England', *Journal of Economic History*, **49**, 803–32.

Nozick, Robert (1975), *Anarchy, State, and Utopia*, New York: Basic Books.

Nye, Joseph S., Jr (1997), 'Introduction: The decline of confidence in government', in Joseph S. Nye, Jr, P.D. Zelikow and D.C. King (eds), *Why People Don't Trust Government*, Cambridge, MA: Harvard University Press, pp. 1–19.

Nye, Joseph S., Jr, P.D. Zelikow and D.C. King (eds) (1997), *Why People Don't Trust Government*, Cambridge, MA: Harvard University Press.

Ogilvie, M.H. (1984), 'Review of Leon Trakman's *The Law Merchant: The Evolution of Commercial Law*', *Canadian Bar Review*, **62**, 113–16.

Ogul, Morris (1976), *Congress Oversees the Bureaucracy*, Pittsburgh: University of Pittsburgh Press.

Olasky, Marvin N. (1987), *Corporate Public Relations*, Hillsdale, NJ: Lawrence Erlbaum Associates.

Oliver, J. Eric and Raymond E. Wolfinger (1999), 'Jury aversion and voter registration', *American Political Science Review*, **93**, 147–52.

Olmsted, George, Judith Roberts and Arthur Denzau (1988), 'We voted for this? Institutions and educational spending', Political Economy Working Paper 128, Washington University.

Olsen, W. (1992), 'Tortification of contract law: displacing consent and agreement', *Cornell Law Review*, **77**, 1043–8.

Olson, Mancur (1965), *The Logic of Collective Action: Public Goods and the Theory of Groups*, Cambridge, MA: Harvard University Press.

Olson, Mancur (1982), *The Rise and Decline of Nations: Economic Growth, Stagflation, and Social Rigidities*, New Haven, CT: Yale University Press.

Olson, Mancur (1992), 'Foreword', in Todd Sandler, *Collective Action: Theory and Applications*, Ann Arbor: University of Michigan Press, pp. vii–xvi.

Olson, Mancur (1993), 'Dictatorship, democracy, and development', *American Political Science Review*, **87**, 567–76.

Olson, Mancur (1996), 'Big bills left on the sidewalk: why some nations are rich and others poor', *Journal of Economic Perspectives*, **10**, 3–24.

Olson, Mancur (2000), *Power and Prosperity: Outgrowing Communist and Capitalist Dictatorships*, New York: Basic Books.

Olson, Mancur and Richard Zeckhauser (1966), 'An economic theory of alliances', *Review of Economics and Statistics*, **48**, 266–79.

Onculer, Ayse and Rachel Croson (1998), 'Rent-seeking for a risky rent: a model and experimental investigation', unpublished manuscript, University of Pennsylvania.

Oppenheimer, Franz ([1908] 1914), *The State: Its History and Development Viewed Sociologically*, trans. by John M. Gitterman, Indianapolis, IN: Bobbs-Merrill.

Ordeshook, Peter C. (1969), 'The theory of the electoral process', unpublished PhD dissertation, University of Rochester.

Ordeshook, Peter C. (1986), *Game Theory and Political Theory*, Cambridge: Cambridge University Press.

Orren, Gary (1997), 'Fall from grace: the public's loss of faith in government', in Joseph S. Nye, Jr, P.D. Zelikow and D.C. King (eds), *Why People Don't Trust Government*, Cambridge, MA: Harvard University Press, pp. 77–107.

Osterfield, David (1989), 'Anarchism and the public goods issue: law, courts, and police', *Journal of Libertarian Studies*, **9**, 47–67.

Ostrom, Elinor (1990), *Governing the Commons: The Evolution of Institutions for Collective Action*, Cambridge: Cambridge University Press.

Ostrom, Elinor and James M. Walker (1991), 'Communication in a commons: cooperation without external enforcement', in Thomas R. Palfrey (ed.), *Laboratory Research in Political Economy*, Ann Arbor: University of Michigan Press, pp. 287–322.

Ostrom, Elinor, James M. Walker and Raymond Gardner (1992), 'Covenants with and without a sword: self-governance is possible', *American Political Science Review*, **86**, 404–17.

Palfrey, Thomas R. and Jeffrey E. Prisbrey (1996), 'Altruism, reputation and noise in linear public goods experiments', *Journal of Public Economics*, **61**, 409–27.

Palfrey, Thomas R. and Jeffrey E. Prisbrey (1997), 'Anomalous behavior in public goods experiments: how much and why?', *American Economic Review*, **87**, 829–46.

Palfrey, Thomas R. and Howard Rosenthal (1983), 'A strategic calculus of voting', *Public Choice*, **41**, 7–53.

Palfrey, Thomas R. and Howard Rosenthal (1985), 'Voter participation and strategic uncertainty', *American Political Science Review*, **79**, 62–78.

Palmer, Matthew S. (1995), 'Toward an economics of comparative political organization: examining ministerial responsibility', *Journal of Law, Economics and Organization*, **11**, 164–88.

Parker, Glenn R. and Suzanne L. Parker (1998), 'The economic organization of legislatures and how it affects congressional voting', *Public Choice*, **95**, 117–29.

Parks, Robert (1976), 'Further results on path independence: quasi-transitivity and social choice', *Public Choice*, **26**, 75–87.

Pashigian, B. Peter (1976), 'Consequences and causes of public ownership of urban transit facilities', *Journal of Political Economy*, **84**, 1239–59.

Pashigian, B. Peter (1984), 'The effects of environmental regulation on optimal plant size and factor shares', *Journal of Law and Economics*, **27**, 1–28.

Pashigian, B. Peter (1985), 'Environmental regulation: whose interests are being protected?', *Economic Inquiry*, **23**, 551–84.

Peden, Edgar A. (1991), 'Productivity in the United States and its relationship to government activity: an analysis of 57 years, 1929–1986', *Public Choice*, **69**, 153–73.

Peden, Edgar A. and Michael D. Bradley (1989), 'Government size, productivity, and economic growth: the post-war experience', *Public Choice*, **61**, 229–45.

Pejovich, Svetozar (1995), *Economic Analysis of Institutions and Systems*, Dordrecht: Kluwer Academic Publishers.

Peltason, Jack (1955), *Federal Courts in the Political Process*, New York: Random House.

Peltzman, Sam (1976), 'Toward a more general theory of regulation', *Journal of Law and Economics*, **19**, 211–40.

Peltzman, Sam (1980), 'The growth of government', *Journal of Law and Economics*, **23**, 209–87.

Peltzman, Sam (1984), 'Constituent interest and congressional voting', *Journal of Law and Economics*, **27**, 181–210.

Peltzman, Sam (1985), 'An economic interpretation of congressional voting in the twentieth century', *American Economic Review*, **75**, 656–75.

Peltzman, Sam (1989), 'The economic theory of regulation after a decade of deregulation', in Martin Neal Baily and Clifford Winston (eds), *Brookings Papers on Economic Activity*, 1–41.

Peltzman, Sam (1990), 'How efficient is the voting market?', *Journal of Law and Economics*, **33**, 27–63.

Perrow, Charles (1986), *Complex Organizations: A Critical Essay*, 3rd edn, Glenview, IL: Scott, Foresman.

Perrson, Torsten (1988), 'Credibility of macroeconomic policy: an introduction and a broad survey', *European Economic Review*, **32**, 519–32.

Perrson, Torsten and Lars Svensson (1989), 'Why stubborn conservatives run deficits: policy with time-inconsistent preferences', *Quarterly Journal of Economics*, **104**, 325–45.

Pew Research Center for the People and the Press (1998), *Deconstructing Distrust: How Americans View Government*, Washington, DC: Pew Research Center for the People and the Press.

Pierce, James L. (1978), 'The myth of congressional supervision of monetary policy', *Journal of Monetary Economics*, **4**, 363–70.

Pigou, Arthur C. (1920), *The Economics of Welfare*, London: Macmillan.

Pincus, Jonathan J. (1975), 'Pressure groups and the pattern of tariffs', *Journal of Political Economy*, **83**, 757–78.

Pincus, Jonathan J. (1977), *Pressure Groups and Politics in Antebellum Tariffs*, New York: Columbia University Press.

Pinker, Steven (1997), *How the Mind Works*, New York: Norton.

Pipes, Richard (1999), *Property and Freedom*, New York: Knopf.

Pittman, Russell (1976), 'The effects of industry concentration and regulation on contributions in three 1972 U.S. Senate campaigns', *Public Choice*, **27**, 71–80.

Pittman, Russell (1977), 'Market structure and campaign contributions', *Public Choice*, **31**, 37–51.

Plott, Charles R. (1972), 'Ethics, social choice theory, and the theory of economic policy', *Journal of Mathematical Sociology*, **2**, 181–208.

Plott, Charles R. (1973), 'Path independence, rationality, and social choice', *Econometrica*, **41**, 1075–91.

Plott, Charles R. (1976), 'Axiomatic social choice theory: an overview and interpretation', *American Journal of Political Science*, **20**, 511–96.

Plott, Charles R. (1983), 'Externalities and corrective policies in experimental markets', *Economic Journal*, **93**, 106–27.

Plott, Charles R. and Michael E. Levine (1978), 'A model of agenda influence on committee decisions', *American Economic Review*, **68**, 146–60.

Plutarch ([1517] 1932), *The Lives of the Noble Grecians and Romans*, trans. by John Dryden, rev. and ed. by Arthur Hugh Clough, New York: Modern Library.

Pocock, J.G.A. (ed.) (1977), *The Political Works of James Harrington*, Cambridge: Cambridge University Press.

Pollock, Sir Frederick and Frederick W. Maitland ([1898] 1959), *The History of English Law*, Washington, DC: Lawyers' Literary Club.

Pommerehne, Werner W. (1978), 'Institutional approaches to public expenditure: empirical evidence from Swiss municipalities', *Journal of Public Economics*, **9**, 255–80.

Pommerehne, Werner W. (1983), 'Private versus Öffentliche Müllabfuhr – nochmals betrachtet', *Finanzarchiv*, **41**, 466–75.

Pommerehne, Werner W. and Bruno S. Frey (1978), 'Bureaucratic behavior in democracy: a case study', *Public Finance*, **33**, 98–111.

Pommerehne, Werner W. and Friedrich Schneider (1978), 'Fiscal illusion, political institutions, and local public spending', *Kyklos*, **31**, 381–408.

Pommerehne, Werner W. and Hannelore Weck-Hannemann (1996), 'Tax rates, tax administration and income tax evasion in Switzerland', *Public Choice*, **88**, 161–70.

Poole, Keith T. and Howard Rosenthal (1997), *Congress: A Political–Economic History of Roll Call Voting*, New York: Oxford University Press.

Poole, Keith T. and Thomas Romer (1985), 'Patterns of political action committee contributions to the 1980 campaigns for the United States House of Representatives', *Public Choice* (Carnegie Papers on Political Economy), **47**, 63–113.

Porter, Philip K. and Gerald W. Scully (1995), 'Institutional technology and economic growth', *Public Choice*, **82**, 17–36.

Posner, Richard A. (1974), 'Theories of economic regulation', *Bell Journal of Economics and Management Science*, **5**, 335–58.

Posner, Richard A. (1980a), 'The ethical and political basis of the efficiency norm in common law adjudication', *Hofstra Law Review*, **8**, 487–508.

Posner, Richard A. (1980b), 'A theory of primitive society, with special reference to law', *Journal of Law and Economics*, **23**, 1–53.

Posner, Richard A. (1993), 'Blackmail, privacy and freedom of contract', *University of Pennsylvania Law Review*, **141**, 1817–47.

Posner, Richard A. (1998), *Economic Analysis of Law*, 5th edn, New York: Aspen.

Pospisil, Leopold (1971), *Anthropology of Law: A Comparative Theory*, New York: Harper & Row.

Pospisil, Leopold (1978), *The Ethnology of Law*, 2nd edn, Menlo Park, CA: Cummings Publishing.

Poterba, J.M. (1996a), 'Budget institutions and fiscal policy in the US states', *American Economic Review*, **86**, 395–400.

Poterba, J.M. (1996b), 'Do budget rules work?', National Bureau of Economic Research Working Paper No. 5550.

Priest, George L. (1977), 'The common law process and the selection of efficient rules', *Journal of Legal Studies*, **6**, 65–82.

Przeworski, Adam and F. Limongi (1993), 'Political regimes and economic growth', *Journal of Economic Perspectives*, **7**, 51–69.

Quah, Danny T. (1992), 'International patterns of growth I: Persistence in cross-country disparities', unpublished manuscript, London School of Economics.

Quah, Danny T. (1993), 'Galton's fallacy and the tests of the convergence hypothesis', *Scandinavian Journal of Economics*, **95**, 427–43.

Quah, Danny T. (1996), 'Convergence empirics across economies with (some) capital mobility', *Journal of Economic Growth*, **1**, 95–124.

Quattrone, G.A. and Amos Tversky (1988), 'Contrasting rational and psychological analyses of political choice', *American Political Science Review*, **82**, 719–36.

Quinn, Robert and Bruce Yandle (1986), 'Expenditures on air pollution control under federal regulation', *Review of Regional Studies*, **16**, 11–16.

Raines, J. Patrick and Charles G. Leathers (1993), 'Evolving financial institutions in Veblen's business enterprise system', *Journal of the History of Economic Thought*, **15**, 249–64.

Ramsey, Frank P. (1927), 'A contribution to the theory of taxation', *Economic Journal*, **37**, 47–61.

Ramseyer, J. Mark and Eric B. Rasmusen (1997), 'Judicial independence in a civil law regime: the evidence from Japan', *Journal of Law, Economics and Organization*, **13**, 259–86.

Rasmusen, Eric B. (1987), 'Moral hazard in risk-averse teams', *RAND Journal of Economics*, **18**, 428–35.

Rasmussen, David W. and Bruce L. Benson (1994), *The Economic Anatomy of a Drug War: Criminal Justice in the Commons*, Lanham, MD: Rowman & Littlefield.

Rawls, John (1971), *A Theory of Justice*, Cambridge, MA: Harvard University Press.

Razzolini, Laura and William F. Shughart II, 'On the (relative) unimportance of a balanced budget', *Public Choice*, **90**, 215–33.

Reimers, Hans-Heggart (1992), 'Comparisons of tests for multivariate cointegration', *Statistical Papers*, **33**, 335–59.

Ridley, Matt (1996), *The Origins of Virtue: Human Instincts and the Evolution of Cooperation*, New York: Viking.

Riggs, David and Bruce Yandle (1997), 'Environmental quality, biological envelopes and river basin markets for water quality', in Terry L. Anderson and P.J. Hill (eds), *Water Marketing: The Next Generation*, Lanham, MD: Rowman & Littlefield, pp. 147–66.

Riker, William H. (1961), 'Voting and the summation of preferences', *American Political Science Review*, **55**, 900–911.

Riker, William H. (1962), *The Theory of Political Coalitions*, New Haven, CT: Yale University Press.

Riker, William H. (1965), 'Arrow's theorem and some examples of the paradox of voting', in John Claunch (ed.), *Mathematical Applications in Political Science*, vol. 1, Dallas: Arnold Foundation, Southern Methodist University, pp. 41–69.

Riker, William H. (1980), 'Implications from the disequilibrium of majority rule for the study of institutions', *American Political Science Review*, **74**, 432–46.

Riker, William H. (1982), *Liberalism against Populism: A Confrontation between the Theory of Democracy and the Theory of Social Choice*, San Francisco: Freeman.

Riker, William H. and Peter C. Ordeshook (1968), 'A theory of the calculus of voting', *American Political Science Review*, **62**, 25–42.

Rizzo, Mario J. (1980a), 'Law amid flux: the economics of negligence and strict liability in tort', *Journal of Legal Studies*, **9**, 291–318.

Rizzo, Mario J. (1980b), 'The mirage of efficiency', *Hofstra Law Review*, **8**, 641–58.

Robbins, Lionel (1935), *An Essay on the Nature and Significance of Economic Science*, 2nd edn, London: Macmillan.

Roberts, Brian (1990), 'A dead senator tells no lies: seniority and the distribution of federal benefits', *American Journal of Political Science*, **34**, 31–58.

Roberts, Kevin W.S. (1980a), 'Interpersonal comparability and social choice theory', *Review of Economics Studies*, **47**, 421–39.

Roberts, Kevin W.S. (1980b), 'Possibility theorems with interpersonal comparable welfare levels', *Review of Economics Studies*, **47**, 409–20.

Roberts, Kevin W.S. (1980c), "Social choice theory: the single-profile and multi-profile approaches', *Review of Economics Studies*, **47**, 441–51.

Rogoff, Kenneth (1985), 'The optimal degree of commitment to an intermediate monetary target', *Quarterly Journal of Economics*, **100**, 1169–90.

Rogoff, Kenneth (1990), 'Equilibrium political budget cycles', *American Economic Review*, **80**, 21–36.

Rohde, David W. (1991), *Parties and Leaders in the Postreform House*, Chicago: University of Chicago Press.

Romer, Paul M. (1986), 'Increasing returns and long-run growth', *Journal of Political Economy*, **94**, 1002–37.

Romer, Paul M. (1990), 'Endogenous technological change', *Journal of Political Economy*, **98**, S71–S102.

Romer, Thomas and Howard Rosenthal (1978a), 'The elusive median voter', *Journal of Public Economics*, **12**, 143–70.

Romer, Thomas and Howard Rosenthal (1978b), 'Political resource allocation, controlled agendas, and the status quo', *Public Choice*, **33**, 27–43.

Romer, Thomas and Howard Rosenthal (1979), 'Bureaucrats vs voters: on the political economy of resource allocation by direct democracy', *Quarterly Journal of Economics*, **93**, 563–87.

Romer, Thomas and Howard Rosenthal (1982), 'Median voters or budget maximizers: evidence from school expenditure referenda', *Economic Inquiry*, **20**, 556–78.

Romer, Thomas and James M. Snyder (1994), 'An empirical investigation of the dynamics of PAC contributions', *American Journal of Political Science*, **38**, 745–69.

Root, Hilton R. (1994), *The Fountain of Privilege: Political Foundations of Markets in Old Regime France and England*, Berkeley: University of California Press.

Rose-Ackerman, Susan (1978), *Corruption: A Study in Political Economy*, New York: Academic Press.

Rosendorff, B. Peter (1996), 'Voluntary export restraints, antidumping procedure, and domestic politics', *American Economic Review*, **86**, 544–61.

Rosenthal, Howard (1990), 'The setter model', in James M. Enelow and Melvin J. Hinich (eds), *Advances in the Spatial Theory of Voting*, Cambridge: Cambridge University Press, pp. 199–234.

Rothbard, Murray N. (1995), *Economic Thought before Adam Smith: An Austrian Perspective on the History of Economic Thought*, vol. I, Aldershot, UK and Brookfield, VT: Edward Elgar.

Rousseau, Jean-Jacques ([1761] 1964), *Discourse on the Origin and Foundation of Inequality among Men*, New York: St Martin's Press.

Rousseau, Jean-Jacques ([1762] 1973), *The Social Contract*, trans. by G.D.H. Cole, London: Dent.

Rowley, Charles K. (1989), 'The common law in public choice perspective: a theoretical and institutional critique', *Hamline Law Review*, **12**, 355–83.

Rowley, Charles K. (1990), 'The reason of rules: constitutional contract versus political market conflict', *Annual Review of Conflict Knowledge and Conflict Resolution*, **2**, 195–228.

Rowley, Charles K. (1992), *The Right to Justice: The Political Economy of Legal Services in the United States*, Aldershot, UK and Brookfield, VT: Edward Elgar.

Rowley, Charles K. (ed.) (1993), *Social Choice Theory*, 3 vols, Brookfield, VT: Edward Elgar.

Rowley, Charles K. (1997), 'Donald Wittman's *The Myth of Democratic Failure*', *Public Choice*, **92**, 15–26.

Rowley, Charles K. and Alan T. Peacock (1975), *Welfare Economics: A Liberal Restatement*, Oxford: Martin Robertson.

Rowley, Charles K., Willem Thorbecke and Richard E. Wagner (1995), *Trade Protection in the United States*, Aldershot, UK and Brookfield, VT: Edward Elgar.

Rowley, Charles K., Robert D. Tollison and Gordon Tullock (1988), *The Political Economy of Rent Seeking*, Boston and Dordrecht: Kluwer Academic Publishers.

Rowley, Charles K. and Michelle A. Vachris (1993), 'Snake oil economics versus public choice', in Charles K. Rowley (ed.), *Public Choice Theory*, vol. 3: *The Separation of Powers and Constitutional Political Economy*, Aldershot, UK and Brookfield, VT: Edward Elgar, pp. 573–84.

Rowley, Charles K. and Michelle A. Vachris (1994), 'Why democracy does not necessarily produce efficient results', *Journal of Public Finance and Public Choice*, **12**, 95–111.

Rubin, Edward L. (1995), 'The nonjudicial life of contract: beyond the shadow of the law', *Northwestern University Law Review*, **90**, 107–31.

Rubin, Paul H. (1977), 'Why is the common law efficient?', *Journal of Legal Studies*, **6**, 51–64.

Rutherford, M. (1994), *Institutions in Economics: The Old and the New Institutionalism*, Cambridge: Cambridge University Press.

Sachs, Jeffrey and Andrew Warner (1995), 'Economic reform and the process of global integration', *Brookings Papers on Economic Activity*, 1–118.

Sachs, Jeffrey and Andrew Warner (1997), 'Fundamental sources of long run growth', *American Economic Review*, **87**, 184–8.

Saijo, T. and H. Nakamura (1995), 'The "spite" dilemma in voluntary contributions mechanism experiments', *Journal of Conflict Resolution*, **39**, 535–60.

Sala-i-Martin, Xavier (1997), 'I just ran two million regressions', *American Economic Review*, **87**, 178–88.

Sally, Razeen (1998), *Classical Liberalism and International Economic Order*, New York: Routledge.

Samuels, Warren J. and Stephen G. Medema (1997), 'Ronald Coase on economic policy analysis: framework and implications', in Stephen G. Medema (ed.), *Coasean Economics: Law and Economics and the New Institutional Economics*, Boston: Kluwer Academic Publishers, pp. 161–84.

Samuels, Warren J. and Nicholas Mercuro (1984), 'A critique of rent-seeking theory', in David C. Collander (ed.), *Neoclassical Political Economy: The Analysis of Rent-Seeking and DUP Activities*, Cambridge, MA: Ballinger, pp. 161–84.

Samuelson, Paul A. (1947), *Foundations of Economic Analysis*, Cambridge, MA: Harvard University Press.

Samuelson, Paul A. (1954), 'The pure theory of public expenditures', *Review of Economics and Statistics*, **36**, 387–9.

Samuelson, Paul A. (1973), *Economics*, 9th edn, New York: McGraw-Hill.

Samuelson, Robert J. (1995), *The Good Life and Its Discontents: The American Dream in the Age of Entitlement, 1945–1995*, New York: Times Books.

Sandler, Todd (1982), 'A theory of intergenerational clubs', *Economic Inquiry*, **20**, 191–208.

Sandler, Todd (1992), *Collective Action: Theory and Applications*, Ann Arbor: University of Michigan Press.

Sandler, Todd, (1993), 'The economic theory of alliances: a survey', *Journal of Conflict Resolution*, **37**, 446–83.

Sandler, Todd (1997), *Global Challenges: An Approach to Environmental, Political, and Economic Problems*, Cambridge: Cambridge University Press.

Sandler, Todd and John F. Forbes (1980), 'Burden sharing, strategy, and the design of NATO', *Economic Inquiry*, **18**, 524–44.

Sandler, Todd and John Tschirhart (1980), 'The economic theory of clubs: an evaluative survey', *Journal of Economic Literature*, **18**, 1481–521.

Sandler, Todd and John Tschirhart (1997), 'Club theory: thirty years later', *Public Choice*, **93**, 335–55.

Santerre, Rexford E. (1986), 'Representative versus direct democracy: a Tiebout test of relative performance', *Public Choice*, **48**, 55–63.

Santerre, Rexford E. (1988), 'Representative versus direct democracy: a Tiebout test of relative performance: Reply', *Public Choice*, **56**, 73–6.

Santerre, Rexford E. (1989), 'Representative versus direct democracy: are there any expenditure differences?', *Public Choice*, **60**, 145–54.

Santerre, Rexford E. (1993), 'Representative versus direct democracy: the role of public bureaucrats', *Public Choice*, **76**, 189–98.

Santoni, Gary (1984), 'A private central bank: some olde English lessons', *Federal Reserve Bank of St Louis Review*, **66**, 12–22.

Santoni, Gary and T. Norman Van Cott (1990), 'The ruthless Fed: a critique of the AST hypothesis', *Public Choice*, **67**, 269–76.

Sargent, Thomas J. (1983), 'The end of four big inflations', in Robert Hall (ed.), *Inflation*, Chicago: Chicago University Press, pp. 41–98.

Sartori, Giovanni (1997), *Comparative Constitutional Engineering: An Inquiry into Structures, Incentives, and Outcomes*, Washington Square, NY: New York University Press.

Sass, Tim R. (1991), 'The choice of municipal government structure and public expenditures', *Public Choice*, **71**, 71–87.

Sass, Tim R. (1992), 'Constitutional choice in representative democracies', *Public Choice*, **74**, 405–24.

Sass, Tim R. and David S. Saurman (1991), 'Legislative majorities as nonsalvageable assets: Comment', *Southern Economic Journal*, **57**, 851–6.

Satterthwaite, Mark (1975), 'Strategy-proofness and Arrow's conditions: existence and correspondence theorems for voting procedures and social welfare functions', *Journal of Economic Theory*, **10**, 187–218.

Schap, David (1988), 'Property rights and decision making in the Soviet Union: interpreting Soviet environmental history', *Economic Inquiry*, **26**, 389–401.

Schattschneider, E.E. (1935), *Politics, Pressures and the Tariff*, New York: Prentice-Hall.

Schattschneider, E.E. (1960), *The Semisovereign People*, New York: Holt, Rinehart & Winston.

Schattschneider, E.E. (1969), *Two Hundred Million Americans in Search of a Government*, New York: Holt, Rinehart & Winston.

Schelling, Thomas (1960), *The Strategy of Conflict*, Cambridge, MA: Harvard University Press.

Schickler, Eric and Andrew Rich (1997a), 'Controlling the floor: parties as procedural coalitions in the House', *American Journal of Political Science*, **41**, 1340–75.

Schickler, Eric and Andrew Rich (1997b), 'Party government and the House reconsidered: a response to Cox and McCubbins', *American Journal of Political Science*, **41**, 1387–94.

Schlesinger, Arthur M., Jr (1986), *The Cycles of American History*, Boston: Houghton Mifflin.

Schmeidler, David and Hugo Sonnenschein (1978), 'Two proofs of the Gibbard–Satterthwaite theorem on the possibility of a strategy-proof social choice function', in H.W. Gottinger and W. Leinfeller (eds), *Decision Theory and Social Ethics*, New York: Reidel, pp. 227–34.

Schmidhauser, John and Larry Berg (1972), *The Supreme Court and Congress: Conflict and Interaction, 1945–1968*, New York: Free Press.

Schmoller, Gustav (1897), *The Mercantile System and Its Historical Significance*, New York: Macmillan.

Schneider, Friedrich and Bruno S. Frey (1988), 'Politico-economic models of macroeconomic policy: a review of the empirical evidence', in Thomas D. Willett (ed.), *Political Business Cycles: The Political Economy of Money, Inflation, and Unemployment*, Durham, NC: Duke University Press, pp. 239–75.

Schofield, Norman (1978), 'Instability of simple dynamic games', *Review of Economic Studies*, **45**, 575–94.

Schofield, Norman (1984), 'Social equilibrium and cycles on compact sets', *Journal of Economic Theory*, **33**, 59–71.

Schumpeter, Joseph A. ([1912] 1934), *The Theory of Economic Development*, Cambridge, MA: Harvard University Press.

Schumpeter, Joseph A. (1939), *Business Cycles*, New York: McGraw-Hill.

Schumpeter, Joseph A. (1950), *Capitalism, Socialism, and Democracy*, New York: Harper & Row.

Schwartz, Edward P., Pablo T. Spiller and Santiago Urbiztondo (1994), 'A positive theory of legislative intent', *Law and Contemporary Problems*, **57**, 51–74.

Schwartz, Thomas (1982), 'No minimally reasonable collective choice process can be strategy-proof', *Mathematical Social Sciences*, **3**, 57–72.

Schwartz, Thomas (1986), *The Logic of Collective Choice*, New York: Columbia University Press.

Schwartz, Thomas (1995), 'The paradox of representation', *Journal of Politics*, **57**, 309–23.

Scott, W. Richard (1992), *Organizations: Rational, Natural, and Open Systems*, 3rd edn, Englewood Cliffs, NJ: Prentice-Hall.

Scully, Gerald W. (1988), 'The institutional framework and economic development', *Journal of Political Economy*, **96**, 652–62.

Scully, Gerald W. (1992), *Constitutional Environments and Economic Growth*, Princeton, NJ: Princeton University Press.

Scully, Gerald W. (1994), *What is the Optimal Size of Government in the United States?*, Dallas, TX: National Center for Policy Analysis.

Seabright, Paul (1989), 'Social choice and social theories', *Philosophy and Public Affairs*, **18**, 365–87.

Segal, Jeffrey A., Charles M. Cameron and Albert D. Cover (1992), 'A spatial model of roll call voting: senators, constituents, presidents, and interest groups in Supreme Court confirmations', *American Journal of Political Science*, **36**, 96–122.

Seidman, Harold and Robert Gilmour (1986), *Politics, Position, and Power: From the Positive to the Regulatory State*, New York: Oxford University Press.

Selgin, George (1997), *Less than Zero: The Case for a Falling Price Level in a Growing Economy*, London: Institute of Economic Affairs.

Selten, Reinhard and Rolf Stoecker (1986), 'End behavior in sequences of finite prisoner's dilemma supergames: a learning theory approach', *Journal of Economic Behavior and Organization*, **7**, 47–70.

Selznick, Philip (1948), 'Foundations of the theory of organization', *American Sociological Review*, **13**, 25–35.

Sen, Amartya K. ([1970] 1984), *Collective Choice and Social Welfare*, 2nd edn, Amsterdam: North-Holland.

Sen, Amartya K. (1970), 'The impossibility of a Paretian liberal', *Journal of Political Economy*, **78**, 152–7.

Sen, Amartya K. (1977), 'Social choice theory: a re-examination', *Econometrica*, **45**, 53–89.

Sen, Amartya K. (1979), 'Personal utilities and public judgements: or what's wrong with welfare economics?', *Economic Journal*, **89**, 537–58.

Sen, Amartya K. (1982), *Choice, Welfare and Measurement*, Cambridge, MA: MIT Press.

Sen, Amartya K. (1987), *On Ethics and Economics*, Oxford: Basil Blackwell.

Sen, Amartya K. (1995), 'Rationality and social choice', *American Economic Review*, **85**, 1–24.

Senior, Nassau W. ([1836] 1938), *An Outline of the Science of Political Economy*, New York: Augustus M. Kelley.

Sethi, Rajiv and E. Somanathan (1996), 'The evolution of social norms in common property resource use', *American Economic Review*, **86**, 766–88.

Shachar, Ron and Barry Nalebuff (1999), 'Follow the leader: theory and evidence on political participation', *American Economic Review*, **89**, 525–47.

Shapiro, Martin (1964), *Law and Politics in the Supreme Court: New Approaches to Political Jurisprudence*, New York: Free Press.

Shepsle, Kenneth A. (1978), *The Giant Jigsaw Puzzle: Democratic Commit-*

tee Assignments in the Modern House, Chicago: University of Chicago Press.

Shepsle, Kenneth A. (1979), 'Institutional arrangements and equilibrium in multidimensional models', *American Journal of Political Science*, **23**, 27–59.

Shepsle, Kenneth A. (1982), 'Review of "The Politics of Regulation" by James Q. Wilson', *Journal of Political Economy*, **90**, 216–21.

Shepsle, Kenneth A. and M.S. Bonchek (1997), *Analyzing Politics: Rationality, Behavior, and Institutions*, New York: Norton.

Shepsle, Kenneth A. and Barry R. Weingast (1981), 'Structure induced equilibrium and legislative choice', *Public Choice*, **37**, 503–20.

Shepsle, Kenneth A. and Barry R. Weingast (1987a), 'The institutional foundations of committee power', *American Political Science Review*, **81**, 85–104.

Shepsle, Kenneth A. and Barry R. Weingast (1987b), 'Why are congressional committees powerful?', *American Political Science Review*, **81**, 935–45.

Shibata, Hirofumi (1998), 'The budget minimizing bureaucrat: working of the invisible hand in the public sector', unpublished manuscript, presented at the 1998 annual meeting of the Public Choice Society.

Shleifer, Andrei and Robert W. Vishny (1993), 'Corruption', *Quarterly Journal of Economics*, **108**, 599–617.

Shogren, Jason F. and Kyung H. Baik (1991), 'Reexamining efficient rent-seeking in laboratory markets', *Public Choice*, **69**, 69–97.

Shubik, Martin (1987), *Game Theory in the Social Sciences*, Cambridge, MA: MIT Press.

Shugart, Matthew S. and John M. Carey (1992), *Presidents and Assemblies: Constitutional Design and Electoral Dynamics*, Cambridge: Cambridge University Press.

Shughart, William F. II (1999), 'The reformer's dilemma', *Public Finance Review*, **27**, 561–5.

Shughart, William F. II and Robert D. Tollison (1983), 'Preliminary evidence on the use of inputs by the Federal Reserve System', *American Economic Review*, **73**, 291–304.

Shughart, William F. II and Robert D. Tollison (1985), 'Corporate chartering: an exploration in the economics of legal change', *Economic Inquiry*, **23**, 585–99.

Shughart, William F. II and Robert D. Tollison (1986), 'On the growth of government and the political economy of legislation', in Richard O. Zerbe, Jr (ed.), *Research in Law and Economics*, vol. 9, Greenwich, CT: JAI Press, pp. 111–27.

Shughart, William F. II and Robert D. Tollison (1998), 'Interest groups and the courts', *George Mason Law Review*, **6**, 953–69.

Sidak, J.G. (1998), 'The petty larceny of the police power', *California Law Review*, **86**, 655–70.

Sidgwick, Henry ([1901] 1962), *The Methods of Ethics*, 7th edn, Chicago: Chicago University Press.

Silberman, Jonathan and Garey Durden (1975), 'The rational behavior theory of voter participation: the evidence from congressional elections', *Public Choice*, **23**, 101–8.

Simon, Herbert A. ([1945] 1976), *Administrative Behavior*, 3rd edn, New York: Macmillan.

Skaggs, N. and C. Wasserkrug (1983), 'Banking sector influence on the relationship of Congress to the Federal Reserve System', *Public Choice*, **41**, 295–306.

Slemrod, Joel and N. Sorum (1984), 'The compliance cost of the US individual income tax system', *National Tax Journal*, **37**, 461–74.

Slutsky, Steven (1979), 'Equilibrium under α-majority voting', *Econometrica*, **47**, 113–25.

Smith, Adam ([1759] 1976), *The Theory of Moral Sentiments*, Glasgow Edition of the Works and Correspondence of Adam Smith, vol. I, ed. by D.D. Raphael and A.L. Macfie, Oxford: Oxford University Press.

Smith, Adam ([1776] 1976), *An Inquiry into the Nature and Causes of the Wealth of Nations*, ed. by Edwin Cannan, Chicago: University of Chicago Press.

Smith, Adam ([1977] 1987), *Correspondence of Adam Smith*, Glasgow Edition of the Works and Correspondence of Adam Smith, edited by E.C. Mossner and I.S. Ross, Indianapolis, IN: Liberty Press.

Smith, Vernon L. (1975), 'The primitive hunter culture, Pleistocene extinction, and the rise of agriculture', *Journal of Political Economy*, **83**, 727–56.

Smith, Vernon L. (1979), 'Incentive compatible experimental processes for the provision of public goods', in Vernon L. Smith (ed.), *Research in Experimental Economics*, vol. 1, Greenwich, CT: JAI Press, pp. 59–168.

Smith, Vernon L. (1980), 'Experiments with a decentralized mechanism for public good decisions', *American Economic Review*, **70**, 584–99.

Smith, Vernon L. (1998), 'Property rights as natural order: reciprocity, evolutionary and experimental considerations', in P.J. Hill and Roger E. Meiners (eds), *Who Owns the Environment?*, Lanham, MD: Rowman & Littlefield, pp. 55–85.

Snyder, James M. and Tim Groseclose (1999), 'Estimating party influence in congressional roll call voting', unpublished manuscript, MIT.

Snyder, Susan and Barry R. Weingast (1996), 'The American system of shared powers: the president, Congress, and the NLRB', unpublished manuscript, Stanford University.

Solow, Robert M. (1956), 'A contribution to the theory of economic growth', *Quarterly Journal of Economics*, **70**, 65–94.

Sonnemans, Joep, Arthur Schram and Theo Offerman (1998), 'Public good provision and public bad prevention: the effect of framing', *Journal of Economic Behavior and Organization*, **34**, 143–61.

Spann, Robert M. and Edward W. Erickson (1970), 'The economics of railroading: the beginning of cartelization and regulation', *Bell Journal of Economics and Management Science*, **1**, 227–44.

Spiller, Pablo T. and Rafael Gely (1992), 'Congressional control or judicial independence: the determinants of U.S. Supreme Court labor-relations decisions, 1949–1988', *RAND Journal of Economics*, **23**, 463–92.

Sproul, Curtis (1980), 'Corporations and unions in federal politics: a practical approach to federal election law compliance', *Arizona Law Review*, **22**, 465–505.

Stigler, George J. (1960), 'The influence of events and policies on economic theory', *American Economic Review*, **50**, 36–45.

Stigler, George J. (1970), 'Director's law of public income redistribution', *Journal of Law and Economics*, **13**, 1–10.

Stigler, George J. (1971), 'The theory of economic regulation', *Bell Journal of Economics and Management Science*, **2**, 3–21.

Stigler, George J. (1972), 'Economic competition and political competition', *Public Choice*, **13**, 91–106.

Stigler, George J. (1973), 'General economic conditions and national elections', *American Economic Review Papers and Proceedings*, **63**, 160–67.

Stigler, George J. (1974), 'Free riders and collective action: an appendix to theories of economic regulation', *Bell Journal of Economics and Management Science*, **5**, 359–65.

Stigler, George J. (1976a), 'Do economists matter?', *Southern Economic Journal*, **42**, 347–54.

Stigler, George J. (1976b), 'The sizes of legislatures', *Journal of Legal Studies*, **5**, 17–34.

Stigler, George J. (1985), 'The origins of the Sherman Act', *Journal of Legal Studies*, **14**, 1–10.

Stigler, George J. (1992), 'Law or economics', *Journal of Law and Economics*, **35**, 455–68.

Stigler, George J. and Gary S. Becker (1977), 'De gustibus non est disputandum', *American Economic Review*, **67**, 76–90.

Stiglitz, Joseph E. et al. (1989), *The Economic Role of the State*, ed. by Arnold Heertje, Oxford: Basil Blackwell.

Strasnick, Steven (1976), 'The problem of social choice: Arrow to Rawls', *Philosophy and Public Affairs*, **5**, 241–73.

Stratmann, Thomas (1992a), 'Are contributors rational? Untangling strategies of political action committees', *Journal of Political Economy*, **100**, 646–64.

Stratmann, Thomas (1992b), 'The effects of logrolling on congressional voting', *American Economic Review*, **82**, 1162–76.

Stratmann, Thomas (1998), 'The market for congressional votes: is timing of contributions everything?', *Journal of Law and Economics*, **41**, 85–113.

Stroup, Richard and John A. Baden (1983), *Natural Resources: Bureaucratic Myths and Environmental Management*, San Francisco: Pacific Institute for Public Policy Research.

Stubblebine, W. Craig (1985), 'On the political economy of tax reform', paper presented at the annual meeting of the Western Economic Association.

Sugden, Robert (1993), 'Welfare resources and capabilities: a review of "Inequality Reexamined" by Amartya Sen', *Journal of Economic Literature*, **31**, 1947–62.

Sullivan, John T. (1994), 'Deregulation and the political economy of institutional change', unpublished PhD dissertation, George Mason University, Fairfax, VA.

Summers, Robert and Alan Heston (1991), 'The Penn world table (mark 5): an expanded set of international comparisons, 1950–88', *Quarterly Journal of Economics*, **106**, 327–68.

Tabarrok, Alexander and Eric Helland (1999), 'Court politics: the political economy of tort awards', *Journal of Law and Economics*, **42**, 157–88.

Tate, C. Neal (1981), 'Personal attribute models of the voting behavior of U.S. Supreme Court justices: liberalism in civil liberties and economic decisions, 1946–1978', *American Political Science Review*, **75**, 355–67.

Taylor, Charles (1985), *Philosophy and the Human Sciences*, vol. 2, Cambridge: Cambridge University Press.

Taylor, Michael (1982), *Community, Anarchy and Liberty*, Cambridge: Cambridge University Press.

Thomas, Scott (1989), 'Do incumbent campaign expenditures matter?', *Journal of Politics*, **51**, 965–75.

Thomas, Stacie (1997), 'Eco-seals as market-based incentives for improving the environment: promises, pitfalls, opportunities, and risks', unpublished manuscript, Clemson University Center for Policy and Legal Studies.

Thompson, Earl A. (1973), 'Bureaucracy and Representative Government' (book review), *Journal of Economic Literature*, **11**, 950–53.

Tideman, Nicolaus T. and Gordon Tullock (1976), 'A new and superior process for making social choices', *Journal of Political Economy*, **84**, 1145–59.

Tiebout, Charles M. (1956), 'A pure theory of local expenditures', *Journal of Political Economy*, **64**, 416–24.

Tietenberg, Tom (1992), *Environmental and Natural Resource Economics*, 3rd edn, New York: HarperCollins.

Ting, Michael M. (1998), 'Pulling the trigger: on the resource-based control of bureaucracy', unpublished manuscript, Stanford University.

Ting, Michael M. (1999), 'A theory of bureaucratic policy learning', unpublished manuscript, Stanford University.

Tirole, Jean (1994), 'The internal organization of government', *Oxford Economic Papers*, **46**, 1–29.

Toda, Hiro Y. (1995), 'Finite sample performance of likelihood ratio tests for cointegrating ranks in vector autoregressions', *Econometric Theory*, **11**, 1015–32.

Tollison, Robert D. (1982), 'Rent seeking: A survey', *Kyklos*, **35**, 575–602.

Tollison, Robert D. (1988), *Clearing the Air*, Lexington, MA: D.C. Heath & Co.

Tollison, Robert D. (1991), 'Regulation and interest groups', in Jack C. High (ed.), *Regulation: Economic Theory and History*, Ann Arbor: University of Michigan Press, pp. 59–76.

Tollison, Robert D. (1997), 'Rent seeking', in Dennis C. Mueller (ed.), *Perspectives on Public Choice: A Handbook*, Cambridge: Cambridge University Press, pp. 506–25.

Tollison, Robert D., W. Mark Crain and Paul Paulter (1975), 'Information and voting: An empirical note', *Public Choice*, **24**, 39–43.

Tollison, Robert D. and Richard E. Wagner (1988), *Smoking and the State*, Lexington, MA: D.C. Heath & Co.

Tollison, Robert D. and Thomas D. Willett (1973), 'Some simple economics of voting and not voting', *Public Choice*, **16**, 59–71.

Tollison, Robert D. and Thomas D. Willett (1979), 'An economic theory of mutually advantageous issue linkages in international negotiations', *International Organization*, **33**, 425–49.

Toma, Eugenia F. (1991), 'Congressional influence and the Supreme Court: the budget as a signaling device', *Journal of Legal Studies*, **20**, 131–46.

Toma, Eugenia F. (1996), 'A contractual model of the voting behavior of the Supreme Court: the role of the chief justice', *International Review of Law and Economics*, **16**, 433–47.

Toma, Eugenia F. and Mark Toma (1985), 'Research activities and budget allocations among Federal Reserve Banks', *Public Choice*, **42**, 175–91.

Toma, Eugenia F. and Mark Toma (1992), 'Tax collection with agency costs: private contracting or government bureaucrats?', *Economica*, **59**, 107–20.

Toma, Eugenia F. and Mark Toma (eds) (1986), *Central Bankers, Bureaucratic Incentives and Monetary Policy*, Dordrecht: Kluwer Academic Publishers.

Toma, Mark (1982), 'Inflationary bias of the Federal Reserve System: a bureaucratic perspective', *Journal of Monetary Economics*, **10**, 163–90.

Toma, Mark (1997), *Competition and Monopoly in the Federal Reserve System, 1914–1951*, Cambridge: Cambridge University Press.

Torstensson, J. (1994), 'Property rights and economic growth: an empirical study', *Kyklos*, **47**, 231–47.

Trakman, Leon E. (1983), *The Law Merchant: The Evolution of Commercial Law*, Littleton, CO: Fred B. Rothman & Company.

Trivers, Robert (1971), 'The evolution of reciprocal altruism', *Quarterly Review of Biology*, **46**, 35–57.

Truman, David B. (1951), *The Governmental Process: Political Interests and Public Opinion*, New York: Knopf.

Tufte, Edward R. (1978), *Political Control of the Economy*, Princeton, NJ: Princeton University Press.

Tullock, Gordon (1959), 'Some problems of majority voting', *Journal of Political Economy*, **67**, 571–79.

Tullock, Gordon (1965), *The Politics of Bureaucracy*, Washington, DC: Public Affairs Press.

Tullock, Gordon (1967a), 'The general irrelevance of the general impossibility theorem', *Quarterly Journal of Economics*, **81**, 256–70.

Tullock, Gordon (1967b), 'The welfare costs of tariffs, monopolies and theft', *Western Economic Journal*, **5**, 224–32.

Tullock, Gordon (1967c), *Toward a Mathematics of Politics*, Ann Arbor: University of Michigan Press.

Tullock, Gordon (1970), *Private Wants, Public Means: An Economic Analysis of the Desirable Scope of Government*, New York: Basic Books.

Tullock, Gordon (1971a), 'The charity of the uncharitable', *Western Economic Journal*, **9**, 379–92.

Tullock, Gordon (1971b), 'The costs of transfers', *Kyklos*, **4**, 629–43.

Tullock, Gordon (1974), *Further Explorations in the Theory of Anarchy*, Blacksburg, VA: University Publications.

Tullock, Gordon (1975), 'The transitional gains trap', *Bell Journal of Economics and Management Science*, **6**, 671–8.

Tullock, Gordon (1980a), 'Efficient rent seeking', in James M. Buchanan, Robert D. Tollison and Gordon Tullock (eds), *Toward a Theory of the Rent-Seeking Society*, College Station: Texas A&M University Press, pp. 97–112.

Tullock, Gordon (1980b), 'Two kinds of legal efficiency', *Hofstra Law Review*, **8**, 659–70.

Tullock, Gordon (1982), 'Why so much stability?', *Public Choice*, **37**, 189–202.

Tullock, Gordon (1987), *Autocracy*, Boston: Kluwer Academic Publishers.

Tullock, Gordon (1993), *Rent Seeking*, The Shaftesbury Papers, no. 2, Aldershot, UK and Brookfield, VT: Edward Elgar.

Tullock, Gordon (1998), 'The growth of governments', unpublished manuscript, University of Arizona.

Turvey, Ralph (1963), 'On divergences between social cost and private cost', *Economica*, **30**, 309–13.

Turvey, Ralph (1996a), 'Road and bridge tolls in nineteenth century London', *Journal of Transport History*, **17**, 150–64.

Turvey, Ralph (1996b), 'Street mud, dust and noise', *London Journal*, **22**, 131–48.

Turvey, Ralph (1997), 'A note on the profitability of private enterprise metropolitan bridges', paper delivered at the Institute for Historical Research of London University, Conference on Metropolitan River Crossings, 1–8.

Tversky, Amos and Daniel Kahneman (1986), 'Rational choice and the framing of decisions', *Journal of Business*, **59**, 251–84.

Twight, Charlotte (1988), 'Government manipulation of constitutional-level transaction costs: a general theory of transaction-cost augmentation and the growth of government', *Public Choice*, **56**, 131–52.

Uhlaner, Carole (1989a), 'Rational turnout: the neglected role of groups', *American Journal of Political Science*, **33**, 390–422.

Uhlaner, Carole (1989b), '"Relational goods" and participation: incorporating sociability into a theory of rational action', *Public Choice*, **62**, 253–85.

Umbeck, John (1977), 'The California gold rush: a study of emerging property rights', *Explorations in Economic History*, **14**, 197–226.

United States Department of Commerce (1975), *Historical Statistics of the United States*, Washington, DC: USGPO.

United States Department of Commerce (1998), *Statistical Abstract of the United States 1997*, Washington, DC: USGPO.

Urban, R. and R. Mancke (1972), 'Federal whiskey labeling: from the repeal of prohibition to the present', *Journal of Law and Economics*, **15**, 411–26.

Usher, D. (1992), *The Welfare Economics of Markets, Voting, and Predation*, Ann Arbor: University of Michigan Press.

van Bastelaer, Thierry (1998), 'The political economy of food pricing: an extended empirical test of the interest group approach', *Public Choice*, **96**, 43–60.

Vanberg, Viktor J. (1986), 'Spontaneous market order and social rules: a critical examination of F.A. Hayek's theory of cultural evolution', *Economics and Philosophy*, **2**, 75–100.

Vanberg, Viktor J. (1992), 'Organizations as constitutional systems', *Constitutional Political Economy*, **3**, 223–53.

Vanberg, Viktor J. and Wolfgang Kerber (1994), 'Competition among institutions: evolution within constraints', *Constitutional Political Economy*, **5**, 193–219.

Varian, Hal R. (1995), *Microeconomic Analysis*, 4th edn, New York: Norton.

Veblen, Thorstein (1898), 'Why economics is not an evolutionary science', *Quarterly Journal of Economics*, **12**, 373–97.

Veblen, Thorstein (1899–1900), 'The preconceptions of economic science', *Quarterly Journal of Economics*, **13**, 121–50, 396–426; **14**, 240–69.

Veblen, Thorstein (1909), 'The limitations of marginal utility', *Journal of Political Economy*, **17**, 620–36.

Vedder, Richard and Lowell Gallaway (1986), 'Rent seeking, distributional coalitions, taxes, relative prices and growth', *Public Choice*, **51**, 93–100.

Vickrey, William S. (1960), 'Utility, strategy, and social decision rules', *Quarterly Journal of Economics*, **74**, 507–35.

Voigt, Stefan (1997), 'Positive constitutional economics: a survey', *Public Choice*, **90**, 11–53.

Vose, Clement (1959), *Caucasians Only: The Supreme Court, the NAACP and the Restrictive Covenant Cases*, Berkeley: University of California Press.

Wagner, Richard E. (1977), 'Economic manipulation for political profit: macroeconomic consequences and constitutional implications', *Kyklos*, **30**, 395–410.

Wagner, Richard E. (1993), 'The impending transformation of public choice scholarship', *Public Choice*, **77**, 203–12.

Wagner, Richard E. (1999), 'Austrian cycle theory: saving the wheat while discarding the chaff', *Review of Austrian Economics*, **12**, 65–80.

Walker, Donald A. (1993), 'Virginian tobacco during the reign of the early Stuarts: a case study of mercantilist theories, policies, and results', in L. Magnusson (ed.), *Mercantilist Economics*, Boston: Kluwer Academic Publishers, pp. 143–74.

Walker, James M. and Roy Gardner (1992), 'Probabilistic destruction of a common-pool resource: experimental evidence', *Economic Journal*, **102**, 1149–61.

Wallace, N. (1983), 'A legal restrictions theory of the demand for money and the role of monetary policy', *Federal Reserve Bank of Minneapolis Quarterly Review*, **7**, 1–7.

Waller, Christopher J (1992a), 'A bargaining model of partisan appointments to the central bank', *Journal of Monetary Economics*, **29**, 411–28.

Waller, Christopher J. (1992b), 'The choice of a conservative central banker in a multi-sector economy', *American Economic Review*, **82**, 1006–12.

Waller, Christopher J. and Carl E. Walsh (1996), 'Central-bank independence, economic behavior, and optimal term lengths', *American Economic Review*, **86**, 1139–53.

Walsh, C. (1995), 'Optimal contracts for central bankers', *American Economic Review*, **82**, 92–107.

Warr, Peter (1983), 'The private provision of a public good is independent of the distribution of income', *Economics Letters*, **13**, 207–11.

Weck-Hannemann, Hannelore (1990), 'Protectionism in direct democracy', *Journal of Institutional and Theoretical Economics*, **146**, 389–418.

Weimann, Joachim (1994), 'Individual behavior in a free riding experiment', *Journal of Public Economics*, **54**, 185–200.

Weingast, Barry R. (1979), 'A rational choice model perspective on congressional norms', *American Journal of Political Science*, **23**, 245–62.

Weingast, Barry R. (1984), 'The congressional-bureaucratic system: a principal agent perspective (with applications to the SEC)', *Public Choice*, **44**, 147–91.

Weingast, Barry R. and William J. Marshall (1988), 'The industrial organization of Congress; or, why legislatures, like firms, are not organized as markets', *Journal of Political Economy*, **96**, 132–63.

Weingast, Barry R. and Mark J. Moran (1983), 'Bureaucratic discretion or congressional control? Regulatory policy-making by the Federal Trade Commission', *Journal of Political Economy*, **91**, 765–800.

Weingast, Barry R., Kenneth A. Shepsle and Christopher Johnsen (1981), 'The political economy of benefits and costs: a neoclassical approach to distributive politics', *Journal of Political Economy*, **89**, 642–64.

Weintraub, Ronald (1978), 'Congressional supervision of monetary policy', *Journal of Monetary Policy*, **4**, 341–62.

Welch, William (1981), 'Money and votes: a simultaneous equation model', *Public Choice*, **36**, 209–34.

Wells, John and Douglas Wills (1998), 'Revolution, restoration, and debt repudiation: the Jacobite threat to England's institutions and economic growth', unpublished manuscript, Auburn University.

Wheeler, Harvey J. (1967), 'Alternative voting rules and local expenditure: the town meeting versus city', *Papers on Non-Market Decisionmaking*, **2**, 61–70.

Wicksell, Knut ([1896] 1967), 'A new principle of just taxation', trans. by James M. Buchanan, in Richard A. Musgrave and Alan T. Peacock (eds), *Classics in the Theory of Public Finance*, New York: St Martin's Press, pp. 72–118.

Wieser, Fredrich von ([1914] 1967), *Social Economics*, trans. by A.F. Hinrichs, New York: Augustus M. Kelley Reprint.

Williams, B.A.O. with J.J.C. Smart (1973), *Utilitarianism: For and Against*, Cambridge: Cambridge University Press.

Williamson, Oliver E. (1968), 'Wage rates as a barrier to entry: the Pennington case in perspective', *Quarterly Journal of Economics*, **82**, 85–116.

Williamson, Oliver E. (1975), *Markets and Hierarchies: Analysis and Antitrust Implications*, New York: Free Press.

Williamson, Oliver E. (1976), 'Franchise bidding for natural monopolies – in general and with respect to CATV', *Bell Journal of Economics and Management Science*, **7**, 73–104.

Williamson, Oliver E. (1985), *The Economic Institutions of Capitalism*, New York: Free Press.

Williamson, Oliver E. (1990), 'A comparison of alternative approaches to economic organization', *Journal of Institutional and Theoretical Economics*, **146**, 61–71.

Williamson, Oliver E. (1996), *The Mechanisms of Governance*, New York: Oxford University Press.

Williamson, Oliver E. (1999), 'Public and private bureaucracies: a transaction cost economics perspective', *Journal of Law, Economics and Organization*, **15**, 306–42.

Williamson, Oliver E., M. Wachter and J. Harris (1975), 'Understanding the employment relation: the analysis of idiosyncratic exchange', *Bell Journal of Economics and Management Science*, **6**, 250–78.

Wilson, James Q. (1980), *The Politics of Regulation*, New York: Basic Books.

Wilson, James Q. (1989), *Bureaucracy: What Government Agencies Do and Why They Do It*, New York: Basic Books.

Wintrobe, Ronald (1997), 'Modern bureaucratic theory', in Dennis C. Mueller (ed.), *Perspectives on Public Choice: A Handbook*, Cambridge: Cambridge University Press, pp. 429–54.

Wintrobe, Ronald (1998), *The Political Economy of Dictatorship*, Cambridge: Cambridge University Press.

Wittfogel, Karl (1991), *Oriental Despotism: A Comparative Study of Total Power*, New York: Vintage.

Wittman, Donald (1977), 'Candidates with policy preferences: a dynamic model', *Journal of Economic Theory*, **14**, 180–89.

Wittman, Donald (1983), 'Candidate motivation: a synthesis of alternative theories', *American Political Science Review*, **77**, 142–57.

Wittman, Donald (1989), 'Why democracies produce efficient results', *Journal of Political Economy*, **97**, 1395–424.

Wittman, Donald (1995), *The Myth of Democratic Failure: Why Political Institutions Are Efficient*, Chicago: University of Chicago Press.

Wolfinger, Raymond and Steven Rosenstone (1980), *Who Votes?*, New Haven, CT: Yale University Press.

Wood, B. Dan and Richard W. Waterman (1993), 'The dynamics of political–bureaucratic adaptation', *American Journal of Political Science*, **37**, 497–538.

Wood, B. Dan and Richard W. Waterman (1994), *Bureaucratic Dynamics: The Role of Bureaucracy in a Democracy*, Boulder, CO: Westview Press.

Wooldridge, W.C. (1970), *Uncle Sam, the Monopoly Man*, New Rochelle, NY: Arlington House.

Woolley, John (1984), *Monetary Politics: The Federal Reserve and the Politics of Monetary Policy*, Cambridge: Cambridge University Press.

World Bank (1994), *The World Development Report: Infrastructure for Development*, New York: World Bank.

Wright, C.W. (1949), *Economic History of the United States*, New York: McGraw-Hill.

Wright, Gavin (1974), 'The political economy of New Deal spending', *Review of Economics and Statistics*, **56**, 30–38.

Wright, John (1985), 'PACs, contributions, and roll calls: an organizational perspective', *American Political Science Review*, **79**, 400–414.

Wright, John (1990a), 'PAC contributions, lobbying, and representation', *Journal of Politics*, **51**, 713–29.

Wright, John (1990b), 'Contributions, lobbying, and committee voting in the U.S. House of Representatives', *American Political Science Review*, **84**, 417–38.

Wyckoff, Paul G. (1988), 'A bureaucratic theory of flypaper effects', *Journal of Urban Economics*, **23**, 115–29.

Wyckoff, Paul G. (1990), 'The simple analytics of slack-maximizing bureaucracy', *Public Choice*, **67**, 35–47.

Yandle, Bruce (1980), 'Fuel efficiency by government mandate: a cost–benefit analysis', *Policy Analysis*, **6**, 291–301.

Yandle, Bruce (1983), 'Bootleggers and Baptists: the education of a regulatory economist', *Regulation*, **7**, 12–16.

Yandle, Bruce (1984), 'Sulfur dioxide: state versus federal control', *Journal of Energy and Development*, **10**, 63–72.

Yandle, Bruce (1989a), *The Political Limits of Environmental Regulation*, Westport, CT: Quorum Books.

Yandle, Bruce (1989b), 'Taxation, political action, and Superfund', *Cato Journal*, **8**, 751–64.

Yandle, Bruce (1997), *Common Sense and Common Law for the Environment: Creating Wealth in Hummingbird Economies*, Lanham, MD: Rowman & Littlefield.

Yandle, Bruce (1998), 'Coase, Pigou, and environmental rights', in P.J. Hill and Roger E. Meiners (eds), *Who Owns the Environment?*, Lanham, MD: Rowman & Littlefield, pp. 119–52.

Young, H. Peyton (1998), *Individual Strategy and Social Structure: An Evolutionary Theory of Institutions*, Princeton, NJ: Princeton University Press.

Young, Robert A. (1991), 'Budget size and bureaucratic careers', in André

Blais and Stéphane Dion (eds), *The Budget-Maximizing Bureaucrat*, Pittsburgh: University of Pittsburgh Press, pp. 33–58.

Zardkoohi, Asghar (1985), 'On the political participation of the firm in the
electoral process', *Southern Economic Journal*, **51**, 804–17.

Zegart, Amy Beth (1996), 'In whose interest? The making of American
national security agencies', unpublished PhD dissertation, Stanford University.

Zerbe, Richard O., Jr (1980), 'The costs and benefits of early regulation of
the railroads', *Bell Journal of Economics and Management Science*, **11**,
343–50.

Index

Magee, S.P. 663, 668
Magna Carta 571
magnification elasticity 664
Magnusson, L. 371, 513, 525
Maine, Sir H. 565
Maitland, F.W. 569–70
majority rule xxxii, 229–31, 318–19,
    399–400, 508–10
  Chicago School versus Virginia
      School 8–9, 13–14
  collective action 104–8, 110–11
  institutions, policy and economic
      growth 612
  public finance 409, 411–13, 418, 419
  voting 211–13, 215, 218, 219–24,
      225, 235
Malaysia 78
Maloney, M.T. 361, 607, 660
manipulation 111, 467
Mankiw, N.G. 78, 450
Mansbridge, J. 102
Manuelli, R. 630
Manwarning, D. 583
Mao Tse-tung 145
March, J.G. 275–6
Marco Polo 154
Marcus Aurelius Antonius 149
Margolis, S.E. 518–19
market economy 559–62
market-capitalism 619
Marks, M. 502
Maros, F. 150
Marrese, M. 503
Marshall, A. 316–17, 370, 372, 516, 532
Marshall, W.J. 177, 286
Marvel, H.P. 361, 366–7, 530
Marwell, G. 68, 498–9
Marx, K. 144
Marxists 63, 374
Mas-Colell, A. 66
Masters, M.F. 312
Mathewson, F. 350
Matsusaka, J.G. 19, 167–8
Mayhew, D. 278, 318
Mbaku, J.M. 345
McCallum, B.T. 452
McCarty, N. 283
McChesney, F.S. xxxviii, xxxix, 10, 190,
    379–95, 532, 541–2, 600–601
  property rights 50, 51, 53, 54, 57

McCormick, R.E. xxvi, xxxvii, 10,
    240–57, 293, 298, 392, 401, 434,
    600, 660
  interest-group theory of government
      357, 359, 360, 361, 363, 369
McCubbins, M. 233, 272, 277, 278, 284,
    318, 445
McDougall, G.S. 160, 162
McEachern, W.A. 167, 400
McGuire, M.C. 66, 134, 150
McGuire, R.A. xxxiv
McKelvey, R. 109, 230, 233, 506, 509
McKenzie, R.B. 7
McKeown, T. 312
McNeil, D.W. 608
Meckling, W.H. 159
Medema, S.G. 374, 375, 516, 517
median voter xxv, 107–8, 163–5, 167,
    210, 221–3, 365–6, 400, 464–6
  institutional change 536
  politics of government growth 463,
      468, 473
  politics and macro economy 430–31,
      433
mediation 566
medieval period 524–5
Megdal, S.B. 167
Meguire, P.G. 612, 636
Meiners, R.E. 53
Meltzer, A.H. 24, 53, 411–12, 425–6
membership 340
  condition 339
Mencken, H.L. 201–2
Menger, C. 562–3
Meone, K. 442
mercantilism 525–7, 561, 646, 650
Mercuro, N. 373, 375
Merrill, M.F. 498
Mexico 38, 147, 149
Meyer, R. 606
Miami Conservancy District 539
Michigan, University of 491
micro politics 13–17, 24–32
Middle East 482
Migué, J.-L. 264
Milgrom, P. 290, 291
military 352
milker bills 385, 387, 392
Mill, J.S. 84, 590
Miller, G. 112, 188–9, 265, 278